D0075012

A PERILOUS PROGRESS

A PERILOUS PROGRESS

ECONOMISTS AND PUBLIC PURPOSE
IN TWENTIETH-CENTURY AMERICA

Michael A. Bernstein

PRINCETON UNIVERSITY PRESS   PRINCETON AND OXFORD

Copyright © 2001 by Princeton University Press
Published by Princeton University Press, 41 William Street,
Princeton, New Jersey 08540
In the United Kingdom: Princeton University Press,
3 Market Place, Woodstock, Oxfordshire OX20 1SY
All Rights Reserved

Library of Congress Cataloging-in-Publication Data

Bernstein, Michael A. (Michael Alan), 1954–
A perilous progress : economists and public purpose in twentieth-century
America / Michael A. Bernstein.
p. cm.
Includes bibliographical references and index.
ISBN 0-691-04292-6 (alk. paper)
1. United States—Economic policy—20th century. 2. Economists—
United States—History—20th century. 3. Economics—United States—
History—20th century. 4. Council of Economic Advisers (U.S.)—History.
I. Title.

HC103.B43 2001
338.973'009'04—dc21   2001036265

This book has been composed in Times Roman

Printed on acid-free paper. ∞

www.pup.princeton.edu

Printed in the United States of America

10 9 8 7 6 5 4 3 2 1

For Edward L. Bieber

CORPORAL, 7TH CAVALRY/1ST CAVALRY DIVISION, UNITED STATES ARMY

KILLED IN ACTION, QUANG TIN PROVINCE, VIETNAM

23 OCTOBER 1967

Contents

List of Illustrations   ix

A Note on the Notes   xi

Prologue. Being Ignored   1

Introduction. Professional Expertise as a Historical Problem   7

1. Shaping an Authoritative Community   15

2. Prospects, Puzzles, and Predicaments   40

3. The Mobilization of Resources and Vice Versa   73

4. On Behalf of the National Security State   91

5. Statecraft and Its Retainers   115

6. Statecraft and Its Discontents   148

Epilogue. Being Ignored (Reprise)   185

Notes   195

Bibliography and Reference Abbreviations   291

Acknowledgments   343

Index   347

List of Illustrations

Davis R. Dewey	65
Edwin F. Gay	66
Wesley C. Mitchell	67
Thorstein Veblen	68
Herbert Hoover	69
Simon Kuznets	70
Tjalling C. Koopmans	71
Charles Hitch	72
Edwin G. Nourse	141
Robert Taft	142
Arthur F. Burns	143
Walter Heller	144
James Tobin	145
Arthur M. Okun	146
Arthur Laffer	147

A Note on the Notes _____

IN ORDER to avoid cluttering the text with an exceedingly large number of superscripts, I have chosen in most cases to place a single general reference at the end of whole paragraphs or segments of text. In the corresponding note, I then cite specific documentation in reverse order; that is, the first citation in a given note refers to the last quotation or piece of evidence in the text in question, and so on, so that the last citation in a note refers to the first portion of the paragraph or text.

A PERILOUS PROGRESS

Prologue _____

Being Ignored

> What social science needs is less use of elaborate tech-
> niques and more courage to tackle, rather than dodge,
> the central issues. But to demand that is to ignore the so-
> cial reasons that have made social science what it is. To
> understand that we need first to look more deeply into
> its history.
>   —JOHN DESMOND BERNAL [1957][1]

ON A MUGGY, partly cloudy day in May 1930, a Swarthmore College professor took up the considerable task of writing the president of the United States. From an office not far from Philadelphia's Main Line, Clair Wilcox posted his letter along with a petition endorsed by over one thousand members of the American Economic Association (AEA); the memorial "urg[ed] that any measure which provide[d] for a general upward revision of tariff rates be denied passage by Congress, or if passed, be vetoed." Three days later a full copy of the entreaty thus sent to the White House appeared in the *New York Times*. Herbert Hoover neither privately nor publicly acknowledged receipt of Wilcox's communication, although he would, over the weeks and months that followed, sometimes reply to individuals who chose to write him about pending tariff legislation. Keeping his own counsel, the president stood silent when, a bit over a month later, the Congress passed a bill, one that implemented a huge across-the-board increase in import duties, crafted by Senator Reed Smoot (Republican of Utah) and Representative Willis Hawley (Republican of Oregon).[2]

To this day, the Smoot-Hawley Act remains the most restrictive and punitive international trade legislation of which Washington has ever conceived. It was (and is) widely regarded as one of the singularly disastrous moments in the history of national economic policy making, its impacts generally understood to have worsened the Great Depression that began just before Halloween in 1929. It stood· as a powerful example of the pitfalls of mercantilism; in the hands of free-trade advocates, its painful lessons have often been invoked in debates over the regulation of global commerce. Moreover, given the ultimate indifference with which the opinions of a remarkable cross-section of the membership of the AEA were treated in the weeks leading up to the vote (the signatories of Wilcox's petition alone had represented well over a third of the Association's membership at the time), the circumstances surrounding the implementation of the Smoot-Hawley tariff gave American economists at the time great cause for worry. Their views, their expertise, their measured assessments were completely and utterly ignored.

If this episode was taken to be an example of a profession's stature and influence, it was a tenuous, even perilous, progress indeed.[3]

When he signed the tariff bill into law, Herbert Hoover had far more on his mind than the sensibilities of professional economists. Indeed, that the president felt compelled to cleave to political pressures at odds with the prevailing wisdom of their discipline only made more obvious to Clair Wilcox and his colleagues that theirs was a guild not yet recognized as a reliable and worthy participant in public affairs. For close to a half century, American economists had struggled both to establish the rigor of the processes by which individuals were admitted to their ranks and to demonstrate the usefulness of the skills of which their credentials and institutional affiliations bespoke. Yet events in the early summer of 1930 were but part of a larger list of particulars concerning how meager were the returns to their earlier investments. It was thus for American economists in the interwar years of the twentieth century to wonder indeed if their expertise might ever claim an unambiguous mission on behalf of a public purpose.

Subsequent decades brought experiences that would do much to resolve the frustrations and anxieties of this earlier generation, but in ways far more complicated and ironic than anyone could anticipate. The very determination with which a community of professionals cultivated a visibility virtually unique among their peers in other academic fields would also in time subvert both the means with which they secured their influence and the political and bureaucratic contexts within which it could be most efficaciously displayed. Toward a retreat from the public realm and a scholastic introversion of their own research protocols and techniques, American economists would ultimately work by century's end. How that paradoxical outcome was fashioned, and why its elaboration had ramifications far beyond the cloistered realm of a cadre of experts, are the burden of the story that follows.[4]

A history of a social scientific community, in a particular national setting at a particular time, is no doubt an enterprise requiring some justification.[5] To be sure, the role of professions and experts in the United States has emerged as an important theme in the work of political, social, and intellectual historians. In the minds of these scholars, professionalization was a significant, perhaps even crucial, part of the process by which a national culture was forged and a new political elite sustained in modern America. During the Progressive Era at the turn of the century, an extremely volatile political climate nurtured, on the one side, certain anticapitalist and reactionary factions that found themselves rather quickly marginalized in ways such that they were easily repressed or swiftly co-opted. On the other, it encouraged burgeoning groups of reformers with closely held convictions concerning the virtues of meritocracy, individuals who sought to establish their ability and right to reorder social and political affairs for the benefit of all. Of these latter Progressives, professional communities were a striking example. Decades of inspired scholarship that has sought to understand the rise of these modern experts have also afforded great insight regarding that most peculiarly American political and social phenomenon—the ascent of an upper middle class.[6]

Yet even beyond the contexts and preoccupations of the academy, there would appear to be good reason to pursue once again a multifaceted historical investigation of the world of expertise in general and of economic experts in particular. Not the least remarkable aspect of the emergence of economics as a preeminent academic discipline in late-twentieth-century America has been the displacement of almost all other social scientists in significant and influential political and bureaucratic positions. Indeed, it has often been asserted that this development is symptomatic of a contemporary impatience with what have come to be regarded as the wasteful and inefficient practices of well-meaning yet poorly trained meliorists. The systematic, hardheaded, thrifty realism of economists has taken on a special appeal in this context and has animated much policy debate in the present day. Paralleling this peculiar constellation of attitudes has been the influence economists have enjoyed within academic life itself. As a discipline, the field has more and more tended to dominate the formulation of curricula and research agendas in all of the social and policy sciences and, in some cases, even in the humanities. In this specific sense, economists may have eclipsed other professionals—such as attorneys and physicians—who deploy substantial amounts of authority but have not been in a position to frame directly the schooling of entire generations. All the more reason to study this particular expert community, which occupies such a unique place in the social and political life of contemporary America.

It is also hardly surprising that the history of a discipline which over time evolved into the rigorous examination of rational decision making under the constraints of resource availability and uncertainty may also provide particular insights into some of the essential characteristics of modern American culture. Arguably the preeminent capitalist society in the world today, the United States finds itself predominantly peopled by those disposed toward calculation, acquisition, and accumulation in ways far more accepting than elsewhere. In a nation in which "the pursuit of wealth, stripped of its religious and ethical meaning, . . . become[s] associated with purely mundane passions, which often actually give it the character of sport," the agendas and methodologies of contemporary economists speak directly to the manner in which Americans go about their daily affairs, understand and order the world around them, and apprehend those different than themselves. Rethinking the history of the American economics profession is thus very much tied up with rethinking the history of modern American culture itself.[7]

Economic practitioners have also sought to have an enormous impact on political affairs and public debate in twentieth-century America. Indeed, the expertise they have displayed with increasing vigor since the turn of the century has brought the attention of government officials and elected representatives to rest increasingly on questions of policy means rather than ends. Similar to the movement of the profession itself, from what are today viewed as the politicized analytical conventions of the nineteenth century to a more "scientific" and "rigorous" orientation in the twentieth, contemporary policy debate, framed within the vocabulary and conceptual categories of mainstream economic theory, has assumed a decidedly desiccated aspect. Ends, objectives, goals fall from view; means, techniques, trade-offs become the sole object of discussion. Assessments of the historical processes that have shaped the American economics profession thus also hold the promise that they might unpack a vast array of unspoken and frequently unconscious beliefs, languages, and presumptions that have come to mold and define, and in certain contexts actually deform, contemporary public discourse. Reckoning with the history made by American economists and their discipline is clearly no esoteric venture.

Neither as well is a determination to focus that accounting within the context of the twentieth century. For it is, as the following pages will show, in the growing involvement of economists with the work of the federal government during that century that one finds one of the singularly most important sets of forces shaping the evolution of both the discipline and its community of practitioners. As the past eighty years have witnessed the rise of the United States to unprecedented levels of economic, military, and political power, reconsiderations of the sources and consequences of that dominion have captured the imagination of many scholars. Consequently, this narrative is as well part of an ongoing and wide-ranging conversation about the historical meanings and contemporary impacts of national power both at home and abroad. This is all to say that grappling with the recent history of American economics necessitates coming to terms with the history of the "American century"—an era not simply of national sway in world affairs but also of growing levels and complexities of state functions overall. While they often celebrate the virtues of market systems that function independently of statist intervention, American economists have themselves most ironically been the creatures of a history powerfully and dramatically configured by statism itself.[8]

Having made these points, it would be a mistake if I left the reader with the impression that what follows is part of an effort to exhort economists and their fellow travelers to "be aware." Far less is the narrative constructed as some kind of *j'accuse*. The objective here is not to reform economics nor to presume to tell a community of scholars how to conduct their business. While nine years of advanced study, a bachelor's degree, two master's degrees, and a doctorate in the discipline have left me with an enduring respect for and fascination with economics, my intentions in this work beckon me toward a much wider audience. It is moreover for this reason that I have been determined to avoid much technical discussion in preference for a narrative that I hope will engage a wide array of interests and sensibilities. In short, what follows is a *history*—one that seeks to contribute to a debate among scholars and interested readers that far transcends the specific confines of a particular field of study.

Needless to say, the historian's work is defined as much by the evidence and information included in the text as by that which is left out. Having made a variety of decisions concerning the use of evidence and the coverage of particular issues, I am obliged to explain my expository strategy.[9] I have confined discussion to a focus on economics and professional economists per se and their involvement in national policy making. Save for a few digressions, agricultural economics, business administration, industrial relations, and other applied domains of the field have not been the primary objects of concern. Even more to the point, it has been my essential goal to discuss prevailing trends in the discipline (and the profession) and to avoid much consideration of alternatives. Those readers anxious to learn about the history of schools of thought outside the mainstream of debate among professional American economists in the twentieth century—such as Marxian economics, Austrian economics, more recently feminist economics, cultural economics, and social economics, even monetarism in its most refined forms—will look in vain in these pages. Other than certain ancillary notes, I have privileged what I take to be the core of the discipline itself rather than its critics. While I intend no disrespect by this choice, at the same time I do not flinch from it. The field of economics may be no monolith, in some intellectual sense, but it is (as I hope this book will in part show) quite remarkable the extent to which a prevailing doctrine reigns among its most influential and visible practitioners.

Finally, there is the question of context. It will quickly become apparent that this is a study resolutely focused on *American* economics. Far from a chauvinistic reflex, this chosen perspective stems from both an effort to make the current study more tractable and a conviction that it is the evolution of the discipline within this country that has had a far greater influence on the professional trajectory of the field elsewhere than the other way around. Certain implications of this contention will be taken up in the pages that follow; others have been addressed elsewhere. Overall, they constitute a worthy agenda for future investigation of a more thorough and capacious sort.[10]

I should also confess that those readers and colleagues particularly wedded to the use of falsifiable propositions in analytical arguments may be aggrieved that the discussion that follows carries within it no testable hypotheses, no counterfactual arguments. Economists in particular may instinctively seek to render my core theses in "strong" formats that lend themselves to unambiguous assessments of "proof." Aside from differences of a methodological sort, the avoidance here of such inferential claims stems from the objectives of the work. Far from an effort to argue that the historical forces examined here constituted the *sole* agents of change under review, this narrative is assembled in the belief that it offers a particular frame of reference for understanding the modern history of the American economics profession that has heretofore been either ignored or underappreciated. That the result is a history written very much from the "top down," and configured in ways that defy the construction of simple mechanisms of causality, is not, I think, cause for regret. As for the contemporary disputes noted at the end of this book, I see no reason nor need to apologize for finding a historical interest within present-day controversies; the danger, rather, lies in the reverse, I think, by imposing presentist assumptions on the struggles of the past.

Retrospection is, of course, the very nature of the historical enterprise. Engagement in it always runs the risk of taking to be inevitable what is itself the product of a complicated array of contingencies, fortune, and choice. Whatever determina-

tion the historian may have to distill from the past evidence of forces and mechanisms that far transcend individual agency and the indeterminacy of events themselves must always be tempered with the realization that history is a process, not
a preordained script. If that awareness leaves one with an appreciation of the
fragility of historical outcomes, that is all to the better. Even more to the point,
and this is particularly poignant in any assessment, historical or otherwise, of
professional expertise, it renders the apprehension of "necessity" in an altogether
different light. Far from the inexorable product of nature, what seems "necessary"
in history, when closely examined, appears more social and political, more condi-
tioned than anything else. In their own efforts to understand society with reference
to mechanisms they sought to cast in ever-more "rigorous" ways, American economists themselves encountered that reality. Necessity may seem comprehensible
in ways that professional elites find straightforward, even comforting. Yet when
inadequately appreciated as itself a historically specified perception, it becomes
simply an excuse to avoid and ignore imagination and hope, a thoughtless justification of the idea that the world we know is neither changing nor changeable.

M.A.B.
University Heights
San Diego, California

Introduction

Professional Expertise as a Historical Problem

All professions are conspiracies against the laity.
—GEORGE BERNARD SHAW [1906][1]

IN HIS REMARKABLE farewell address to the nation in January 1961, during which he introduced the phrase "military-industrial complex" to the lexicon of American politics, President Dwight Eisenhower spoke also of his fear that, in the future, "public policy could itself become the captive of a scientific-technological elite." By this utterance, the president wished to draw attention to the increasingly prominent role and influence of experts in the policy-making activities of government, the undemocratic and antidemocratic implications of that development, and the peculiar array of political and social forces it could and would unleash in a parliamentary democracy. Engagement in the critical assessment of the history of public policy formulation, to which the thirty-fourth president of the United States once invited his fellow citizens, remains a significant and necessary challenge—for citizens and scholars alike—almost a half century later.[2]

Even so, attempting to understand professional expertise as a historical problem involves being as much concerned with the obverse of Eisenhower's speculation as with its initial premise. In other words, it is necessary to explore not only the extent to which policy formulation and implementation have been captivated by expertise but also the ways in which disciplinary knowledge and professional influence have themselves been molded by statist agendas. It may be understandable that a sitting president would be leery of indulging in the exploration of a dialectical premise. It is nonetheless precisely in the resonance between professions and the state to which Eisenhower gestured that historians may find much that beckons them toward a reconsideration of political and social developments in this century. By examining American economics and public policy in particular, such a reappraisal of twentieth-century politics, political culture, and economic and social history may quite readily be attempted.

A comprehensive examination of public policy, embedded within any particular historical episode, would obviously benefit from an approach that allowed for the interaction of material interests, economic circumstances, and political agency. Yet, in this strategy, the scholar quickly encounters a quandary. The historical literature on the rise of interventionist economic policy in the twentieth century is quite fragmentary. Understood primarily in terms of the Keynesian revolution in economic thought, the course of the "mixed economy" of the postwar United States, for example, has been discussed in most cases in surprisingly inelaborate terms by both economists and historians alike.

On the one side, economists have often referred to the rise and fall of particular "policy regimes," as they call them, in their effort to explain some of the most dramatic transformations in modern political economic history—the demise of the gold standard in the interwar era, for example, or the articulation of countercyclical fiscal policy in the post–World War II years. But the precise mechanisms of so-called regime change have been either ignored or explained in ways too wooden to bear up under closer scrutiny. Historians, on the other hand, have tended to leave economic policy aside, either in the hope that economists might fully explain it or on the assumption that changes in policy practice are most usefully understood in terms of the succession of governmental administrations (and of individuals within those bureaucracies) responsible for their execution. Ironically enough, both economists and historians have frequently embraced a rather positivist, even Whiggish, view of the subject: policy is understood to have become more sophisticated and effective over time as the professional knowledge that undergirds it has itself matured.

John Maynard Keynes, arguably the greatest historical figure in the evolution of modern macroeconomic policy, embraced just this sort of perspective. He asserted in his 1936 masterwork, *The General Theory of Employment, Interest, and Money*, that "the ideas of economists and political philosophers, both when they are right and when they are wrong, are more powerful than is commonly understood. Indeed the world is ruled by little else." While he welcomed a general readership of his effort to revise deeply ingrained ways of thinking about economic matters, he nonetheless believed the "general public" to be, as he put it, "only eavesdroppers at an attempt . . . to bring to an issue the deep divergences of opinion . . . which have for the time being almost destroyed the practical influence of economic theory." The success of his effort at reestablishing the usefulness of economic theory in public policy practice would, he believed, allow economic problems to become tractable in the hands of a specialized cadre of experts.[3]

The wonderful naïveté in that thought of Keynes's has an especially poignant quality for recent generations who have witnessed the virtual collapse of Keynesianism in modern economic affairs. Yet it also conveys an unalloyed optimism, characteristic of earlier generations of scholars in both the social and the natural sciences, that their work could be utilized for the public good. This sanguinity left aside tremendously complicated questions about the goals, as distinct from the means, of public policy, and most of all it ignored the ways in which involvement in the affairs of state would affect disciplinary knowledge itself; this despite the authority and influence such visibility would allow, at times even require, professionals to wield in public life.

To be sure, Keynes also took for granted the very notion of professional expertise, troubling himself not at all with questions regarding the historical, political, and social foundations of what has become an ever more prominent feature of contemporary policy debate. In what fashion one might understand the origins of professional authority, and to what extent one might regard its manifestations as either the welcome representation of a higher learning or, in more cynical terms, as the tocsin of a set of "conspiracies against the laity," have of course never been questions of concern to professionals themselves.

On the one side, those who have celebrated professionalism as the functional expression of intellectual progress have, whether self-consciously or not, embraced the view of one of this century's most eminent sociologists, who, over four decades ago, noted that the scientific knowledge on which expertise subsists rests upon four central principles: "universalism"—accepting or rejecting truth claims independent of personal or political considerations; "communism"—taking scientific knowledge to be the common property of all; "disinterestedness"—insisting upon neutrality in the evaluation of evidence and arguments; and "organized skepticism"—testing and scrutinizing all analytic claims. On the other, social and cultural historians have tended to assess professionalism in a more critical way, noting that while "[s]cience as a source for professional authority transcend[s] the favoritism of politics, the corruption of personality, and the exclusiveness of partisanship," its mobilization in the hands of professionals often involves the explicit pursuit of class privilege and antidemocratic authority.[4]

Whatever the relative virtues of a positivist or critical approach to an understanding of professional expertise, clearly both the institutional setting within which scientific authority is both nurtured and judged and the social contexts within which professionals organize and utilize their skills powerfully determine the actual impacts of expert knowledge in a particular time and place. Here, too, of course, a conflict or consensus approach will yield dramatically different conclusions, but it is perhaps the focus on process that a sociohistorical perspective necessitates which in this case rightfully takes center stage. Both the university and the professional society may be assessed as either domains of objectivity and rigor or venues of corruption within which "disinterested and dispassionate" learning is sacrificed to the goal of " 'practical' efficiency" and "the needs of earning and spending."[5] Yet, either way, far too many investigations have rested upon the examination of final results, however construed, rather than a close perusal of the particular paths—political, intellectual, social—by which they were reached.[6]

Decades of debate among historians and sociologists of science, concerning "internalist" and "externalist" notions of the evolution of learning, have served to place the points at issue in any study of professionalism and expert knowledge in sharp relief. Mid-twentieth-century notions of science, fashioned at the hands of mainstream social theorists, emphasized the functionalist attributes of expert practice and of the institutional forms within which it subsisted. Closely identified with the work of Robert Merton and Talcott Parsons, this literature focused on the behavioral norms by which scientists pursued their work. Early in the 1960s, this approach came under powerful attack by Thomas Kuhn. Rather than invoking a set of general rules by which science and scientists pursued progress, Kuhn argued that the community of scientists actually constituted a plurality of groups, each committed to contesting paradigms in particular disciplines. Discriminating among these approaches involved assessing the extent to which particular paradigms were more or less capable of solving particular problems. Transformations in prevailing wisdom, upheld by a majority of practitioners in a given field, represented themselves as a series of "revolutions" in science itself. For Kuhn and his followers, expert knowledge and communities of expertise were thus revealed to have foundations more in conflict and debate than functional consensus.[7]

Situating scientific controversy within its social and historical contexts has become the preoccupation of scholars ever since Kuhn's intervention in the literature. During the 1970s, the elaboration of a new understanding of scientific progress focused on the circumstances—social, cultural, and political—that allowed for the rise and fall of competing "belief systems" in a given scholarly community. This new approach, some versions of which examined the rhetorical and analogical strategies used in the creation of scientific belief, others of which more resolutely emphasized the social practices and ideological interests of participants in scholarly debate, served to beckon investigators not simply to adopt novel interpretations of "scientific revolutions" but also to undertake altogether innovative studies of research practice itself. Recognizing particular groups of scientists as "interest groups" competing as much for prestige and influence as over a given set of ideas inspired several scholars, while others looked to ethnographic examinations of "laboratory life" as a means to understand more fully the modern evolution of science itself. Yet another sociological strategy used the insights of "network theory" to explicate the ways in which groups of scientists elicited the support of others by the judicious use of incentives (rhetorical, institutional, and material) offered in exchange. Overall, these more recent techniques in the study of the creation of scientific knowledge privileged the social examination of epistemological conflicts over the textual appreciation of canonical outcomes.[8]

Yet above and beyond the substantive content of expert knowledge, and the complicated processes by which it evolves, scholars have always appreciated the fact that expertise is most often deployed by credentialed elites. Professions and professionalization have thus necessarily commanded the attention of investigators as well. In a classic interwar period study of the history of some two dozen British professions, Alexander Carr-Saunders and Paul Wilson firmly established a functionalist approach to the phenomenon of professionalization. With this positivistic outlook on professional authority and influence, which emphasized the service provided by expertise to society as a whole, an emphasis on the rise of specialized techniques, formal training and licensing practices, and codes of ethics was a logical research protocol. At the same time, the very findings of the functionalist "school" offered both empirical support and conceptual inspiration to the arguments of others who saw, in professionalizing processes in modern life, a self-interested pursuit of monopoly power. Needless to say, drawing attention to the exclusionary nature of professions—and its attendant denigration of amateurs, "cranks," and "quacks"—emboldened the claims of both those who viewed its impacts as desirable and welcome and those who took a more critical, even condemnatory, stance. As with studies of the sociology and the history of scientific doctrines, research on professions and professionalization tended to yield an array of ambivalent conclusions.[9]

More recent scholars have drawn attention to the system of professions as a whole, and to its complex patterns of both interlocking skills and competing jurisdictional claims to authority. Not surprisingly, this more aggregative assessment of professionalization, one that consciously avoids a focus on the nature and history of one profession at a time, draws inspiration from and affords support to both functionalist and monopolistic notions of professionalism. An integral part of this "systems" approach is its close identification of work practices and skills with professional identity itself. In this regard, the practical impacts and problem-solving capabilities of experts become the essential foundation of any understanding of professional evolution and differentiation. At the same time, the "work" of professionals may also be analyzed in terms of the rhetoric and discursive strategies used to legitimate it; the "power" of an expert vernacular, in this case, "lies not in the language itself, but in the group which authorizes it and invests it with authority."[10]

To the rather sprawling domain of the sociology of science and professionalization, the contributions of historical scholarship seek to bring both empirical precision and a catholic analytical stance. Far from an abdication of responsibility for claiming a particular theory as their own, the unwillingness of historians of professionalization to endorse exclusively a given approach to the phenomenon they study is grounded, in large measure, in their concern to remain faithful to the evidence they survey. In point of fact, most historical examples of professionalization yield narratives consistent with a variety of theories, the applicability of which usually depends on the time frame of the investigation under way. The earliest stages of a profession's development often conform more to structuralist views than later evolutionary trends that often portray struggles for authority more consistent with conflict assessments. Moreover, to the extent historians focus on the attitudes of experts themselves, an understanding of professional ideology and rhetoric must grapple with the self-deception frequently characteristic of the group as a whole. In short, the inherently broad purchase of historical inquiry militates in favor of a multivalent view of professionalization as a social (and political) process.[11]

Instinctively oriented toward the documentation of agency and contingency in the past, historians find it only logical to assume that the construction of reason and "objectivity" is itself a socially grounded outcome. "[N]o abstract force pushing inexorably toward greater freedom," expert knowledge, in both its formal manifestations and its applications, is understood by historians to be "determined by the narrower purposes of men and women; their interests and ideals shape even what counts as knowledge." It is in this way that the evolution of professional authority has "cast up a new world of power" that captivates the attention of historians and draws them to analyze, as well, "the vast institutions that have arisen to manage and finance the rationalized forms of human labor." Not only expert knowledge itself but also the institutional and social frameworks within which it is both culti-vated and utilized necessarily capture the historical imagination.[12]

For historians of the American experience, scrutinizing the links between pro-fessional authority, expert knowledge, and social and political institutions inevita-bly gravitates toward a reconsideration of Progressivism, one of the most potent and maddeningly complicated components of the nation's political life since the late nineteenth century. It had been, of course, the Progressives of the late nine-teenth and early twentieth centuries who had embraced the emergence of bureau-cracy and, as they understood it, a meritocratic order—a network of new social relationships premised on educational achievement, professional accomplish-ment, and adherence to ethical codes of conduct. This "modernized" and increas-ingly urbanized social setting stood in sharp contrast to the small, isolated, self-sufficient settlements of rural America, the "island communities" of which Robert Wiebe has written so cogently and evocatively in more recent decades. In their determination to widen the arena within which professional expertise might shape public policy and choice, in their powerfully held conviction that "progressivist" doctrines would serve to shatter all distinctions and judgments based on consider-ations other than those of objective quality and virtuosity, these activists worked to transform a social and political world that had, for well over a century, grounded its decisions in considerations of region, race, class, gender, and na-tional origin.[13]

Yet in the determination to reform their world, the Progressives did not create a new order that was inherently tolerant and inclusive. Theirs was a wholly self-confident vision that reduced every question about the power of large corporations (and of the credentialed elites that served them), every anxiety about the loss of kinship networks and the rise of impersonal market ties, every approving gesture toward the communal values of the preindustrial farm to the frantic demonstra-tions of a reactionary, paranoid, and sentimental constituency—one quite often identifiable not simply by its aversion to modernity and progress but also by its flirtation with racist and nativist ideologies. What is more, to the inward-looking and often atavistic sentiments of their opponents, the Progressives often count-erposed a celebration of ambition and individual (not to mention individualized) achievement. Regulating and stabilizing the terms under which individuals could thus rise within a competitive meritocracy necessarily preoccupied these reform-ers on the make and turned their attention toward matters of professionalization themselves.[14]

Routinization and impartiality in training and advancement, an insistence on objectivity and probity in the pursuit of knowledge, the employment of learning for beneficent ends—these all constituted, in the minds of Progressives, not only universally desirable goals but also the logical outcome of professionalizing strat-egies. Government "by science, not by people" was a creed, not a contradiction. Whatever antidemocratic tendencies might be inherent in the ideal theory of Pro-gressivism, its practice—exemplified by the highly skilled and honest expert, a knowledgeable and discriminating public, and efficient and judicious bureaucra-cies—would and could guard against any objectionable eventuality. Just as a merchant class in the seventeenth century had facilitated the demise of feudalism, a modern middle class would, in the twentieth century, remove the last vestiges of unprincipled and thoughtless passion from politics and replace them with the cool reason of logic and tested performance.[15]

It is therefore not too much of an exaggeration to claim that the history of Progressivism is indeed the history of the middle class and, in turn, that the history of the middle class, in its American variants, is bound up with the history of professionalization itself. The great mass of the American people, who throughout the twentieth century have identified themselves as either of the middle class or aspiring to be part of that class, have embraced a particular veneration for the authority and influence that credentialed expertise nurtures. Indeed, throughout this century, the enhancement of American authority in the wider world has been closely linked with the utilization of professional skills that have been represented as both the source of and justification for the nation's superiority in world affairs, a hegemony observable along any dimension one wishes to examine—cultural, diplomatic, economic, intellectual, military, and political. This "American century" of power and influence has been, first and foremost, an era of professional accomplishment and perquisites.[16]

The significance and importance of a century-long perspective on matters of professional authority in American society should not be overlooked. It may be quite plausible to argue, as many scholars have done, that the emergence of expert knowledge and credentialed elites has, at certain points in history, followed an "internalist" pattern. Even so, the twentieth century has left a record that seriously challenges any resort to such an inward-looking method. Modern state institutions have so powerfully molded every facet of social life that even the seemingly obscure realms of disciplinary knowledge have revealed themselves to be far more complicated historical products than many earlier treatments have allowed. In this regard, the salience of national mobilization and war as motifs within which scientific change may be understood has now become almost universally accepted as an appropriate starting point for contemporary intellectual histories. This is all to say that coupled with any appreciation of the doctrinal evolution of a discipline, tied to any chronicling of the social and political forces wielded by elites in an effort to cultivate their own authority and influence in particular areas of endeavor, there is now a broad recognition of the dramatic role played by collective (and collectivizing) events such as war, natural catastrophes, economic transformations, and political upheavals. For this understanding, the historical models afforded by twentieth-century experience have been especially important for reasons that are as obvious as they are disturbing.[17]

To understand the particular evolution of an expert discipline, one must no doubt utilize an array of methodologies and research techniques. In the case of American economics, the field's close connection with matters of public policy and governmental operations makes the historian's task all the more difficult.[18] Separating the mechanisms, internal and external, responsible for the elaboration of a professional economic sensibility as well as for the articulation of an expert community of economists themselves becomes, in this context, a particularly

daunting task. Even so, the objectives of the enterprise, unlike those of philosophers and sociologists who study science, have far less to do with the testing of
specific propositions or the evaluation of certain cognitive and analytical models
than they have to do with making sense of a complicated and, at times, quite
ambivalent historical record. The goal, then, is not to provide grist for the mills
of those determined to test specific hypotheses regarding scientific evolution and
professionalization. Rather, the end in view is to provide a narrative that both
justifies and animates a particular approach to the study of twentieth-century
American history, one that by its focus upon the unique experience of a remarkable professional community (and of the powerful discipline it practiced) is en-
lightening and persuasive. Even more to the point, as with all of historical argument, the proof of the propositions it advances must be found in the telling.

1

Shaping an Authoritative Community

[E]conomists have altogether too little influence; they
are too silent on public questions, and when they do
speak their opinion commands less respect than it
deserves.
　—IRVING FISHER (1902)[1]

THE EMERGENCE of an American economics profession was not uncomplicated,
nor was it, in its particular features, uncontroversial. The founding of the American Economic Association (AEA) itself stimulated an array of debates concerning
the society's objectives, practices, and public image.[2] With a cadre of original
leaders like Richard T. Ely, a social activist and intellectual who had taken up his
first academic appointment at Johns Hopkins, the AEA was, as its most eminent
historian has argued, originally an "offspring of mixed parentage—European
scholarship and Yankee social reform." The "Young Turks" who, like Ely, saw in
a new economics an opportunity for social scientific research to be more relevant
and more apposite to the resolution of vexing political questions enjoyed a brief
but heady period of influence. Eager to see the AEA "play an active part in dis-
seminating 'sound' economic ideas and [in] shaping public policy," they were
also determined "to enlist the support of a wide variety of non-academic persons"
in the realization of their goals.[3]

Yet by 1905, in the wake of what had been a two-decade struggle over the roles
of "advocacy and objectivity" in modern social science, the AEA (not unlike
several other social science societies) set course toward the realization of a more
"scientistic" and seemingly dispassionate set of professional ideals. Nurtured in
"the belief that the objective methods of the natural sciences should be used in
the study of human affairs; and that such methods [we]re the only fruitful ones
in the pursuit of knowledge," a new breed of American economist rejected the
notions of Ely and his protagonists. These "militants" would ultimately use professionalization as a tool to gain access to the academy, the media, and the councils of government; moreover, "[w]ith professionalization, objectivity grew more
important as a scientific ideal and also as a practical necessity."[4]

By the first decade of the twentieth century, therefore, American economists
were ready to initiate a project of professional fulfillment that stood at the end of
centuries of intellectual evolution in their discipline. At the same time, having
already weathered strenuous disputes over the nature of their founding professional society, they were particularly sensitive to questions of objectivity and
scientific rigor in their work. Indeed, both in the example of the physical sciences

and in an ideology of American exceptionalism, these "neoclassical" theorists detected worthy and inspiring guides to the advancement of economics itself.[5] Precision in method would secure the field respectability, influence, and self-enforced boundaries; a conviction that modern America was devoid of the atavistic conflicts and retrograde traditions of the Old World would allow for the widespread acceptance of the need for an ostensibly value-free social science, one that would place in the hands of experts the means with which to secure the common good—a common good about which all reasonable (and well-educated) men and women could agree.[6]

In shaping an authoritative community, American economists could, by the early 1900s, look with satisfaction on the intellectual and institutional processes that had, in both the long and the short run, set the terms of their task. What they could not anticipate, of course, were the particular historical circumstances within which they would have to work toward its completion. Making a virtue of the necessities those situations would impose came, to be sure, as second nature to many. Yet the ironies and ramifications of that history would remain and have remained hidden to most.[7]

Under its charter of incorporation, the AEA committed itself to "the encouragement of economic research, especially the historical study of the actual conditions of industrial life," as well as to "the encouragement of perfect freedom of economic discussion." In particular, "the Association as such [took] no partisan attitude, nor commit[ed] its members to any position on practical economic questions." While the formal organization was thus made distinct from the individual activities and convictions of its members, nevertheless the stresses and strains attendant upon the struggles over its initial establishment were, in its earliest years, never far from the surface. These anxieties in turn framed the process by which major decisions were ultimately made concerning AEA membership criteria, annual meetings, publications, and operational procedures; what is more, they made the Association's leadership particularly eager to seize upon whatever opportunities and circumstances within the public arena might enhance the prestige and sway of their field.[8] The implications and ramifications of those choices, while in many cases obscure for some time, had a profound impact on the twentieth-century evolution of the profession and its discipline.

Of immediate concern to the fledgling community of experts that was the AEA itself was the building of a substantial, not to mention impressive, membership. During the first decade of its existence, their new professional association committed itself to the attraction of both scholars and businesspeople to its ranks. The instinct for a catholicity in recruitment was no doubt an outgrowth of an effort to overcome the divisive arguments that had taken place leading up to the chartering of the AEA at Saratoga. Yet it was also born of an increasingly confident vision of an objective and scientific organization. By the first decade of the new century, that image had assumed a coherence that allowed AEA president (and distin-

guished professor at the University of Pennsylvania) Simon N. Patten to put earlier controversies in perspective. Patten told none other than Richard Ely, in the
fall of 1909, that even if the Association "was a protest not only against the narrow
English economists but also against . . . current political and social ideas[,]" nonetheless it "ha[d] narrowed its functions since the Political Science Association
and the Sociologists ha[d] split off from it."[9]

A few weeks later, Thomas N. Carver, professor of economics at Harvard and
then secretary of the AEA, went further than Patten in describing the "character"
of the Association to an official of the American Historical Association. Noting
that in its earliest days, the Association was split between two groups, one of
which "desired to make [it] a propagandist party leading a reaction against . . .
laissez faire doctrines," and another of which "opposed any form of propagan-
dism," he made clear that it was the latter faction that prevailed. "It was the desire
of this party," he wrote, "that the Association . . . be kept a purely scientific body,
with perfect freedom of discussion, and [with] room for every possible difference
of individual opinion."[10]

How precisely to define the nature and contours of a "purely scientific body"
was a not uncomplicated task, especially when it was counterposed to the obvious
need to expand the new Association's membership. AEA leaders like Carver thus
often found themselves forced to mediate between the conflicting claims and
interests of academic economists and members of the business and wider professional community. When, for example, an attorney from Portsmouth, Ohio, complained that the AEA needed more "young, active and aggressive business men
to balance the Colleg [sic] and University professors . . . to give it a composite
tone, largely influenced by the business element," diplomacy rather than scholarly
self-assurance was the ticket. Eager to avoid alienating a nonacademic member
of the Association, Carver sought to mollify him, arguing in reply that "it [wa]s
the general opinion of economists that [they] have much to learn from lawyers
and business men"; indeed, it was the desire of the AEA secretariat "to increase
[its] membership from among that class." He thus asked his correspondent to feel
free to submit nominations of new members drawn from outside the academy.[11]

In 1910, when Carver wrote Evans, the membership of the AEA stood at 1,360.
Four years later, in a report to his superiors, the new secretary, Allyn Young (of
Cornell University), could note with satisfaction that this figure had almost doubled. Even so, there was the obvious challenge that expanding the membership
further would require extending the reach and appeal of the AEA beyond the
professoriate per se. To the extent that the field of economics, in academic institutions nationwide, remained of modest dimensions, it seemed clear that growth
would necessarily be premised upon an expanding domain of interested participants. On the one side, a rising number of academic economics programs, and of
faculty and students within them, would provide an obvious stimulus. On the
other, maintaining a presence in the nonacademic community would also be necessary. Efforts along these lines would, of course, require energy and application;
they would, as well, create rather than simply resolve problems.[12]

By the winter of 1914, Secretary Young had resolved to undertake a major initiative to increase the size of the AEA rank and file. Compiling a mailing list on the basis of suggestions garnered from his colleagues in the Association leadership, and from others primarily within the academic arena (such as department chairs and tenured faculty members), he began a direct solicitation campaign that ultimately reached out to some fifty-three hundred addressees. In this project he had taken to heart the suggestion of one distinguished colleague who had urged him to target specifically "junior [academic] staff" because it might then be "possible to develop a sense of professional loyalty, such as is to be found in other professions, particularly the engineering and scientific [ones]." Moreover, Young solicited rosters of graduate students, making them a recruitment target as well.[13]

Despite his remarkably energetic foray, however, Young had to admit to a former AEA president and current editor of the recently established *American Economic Review*, just before the Thanksgiving holiday in 1914, that the returns to his mailing blitz were "disappointingly small." His frustration, in this regard, was actually the result of two tendencies that, when taken together, conspired to keep the net growth of Association membership at relatively low levels. For graduate students and junior faculty, Association dues were not trivial, and it appears that many of this younger generation found the "price of admission" literally too high. Professor H. J. Davenport of the University of Missouri had warned Young of this mundane yet telling fact some six months earlier. Graduate matriculants at Missouri, he noted, were "so poor financially" that it would be best if the membership drive "not waste ammunition on them." Even some older members found AEA dues a burden. "I know of no one not already a member," a history teacher at Mechanic Arts High School in Boston told Young, "who is interested [in AEA membership] to the extent of $5 a year. I doubt if I am."[14]

Beyond the difficulty of persuading newcomers to join, Young and his colleagues in the AEA secretariat had the additional challenge of convincing current members to stay on. This test was especially acute with respect to the nonacademic affiliates whose numbers were believed to be so essential to the Association's well-being. Davis Dewey, in fact, had warned Young that past April that membership "withdrawals [were] almost uniformly [occurring] among the nonprofessional class." To the extent that "teachers or experts rarely resign[ed]," it seemed obvious to Dewey that "[i]t would add greatly to [the Association's] strength if [its] membership could be more largely confined to those whose interest [wa]s permanent." Dewey, Young, and the AEA leadership as a whole had more than good reason to be concerned; 59 members had left the Association in 1910, although some 400 new recruits had joined. The net balance between arrivals and departures remained positive for two more years; but in 1913 a truly bad patch had been encountered. In a twelve-month period, close to 500 members had resigned while only 270 new participants had been added. At that rate, the Association would simply fade away in about a decade.[15]

Yet in urging the confinement of AEA membership "to those whose interest [wa]s permanent," Dewey had engaged in a curious choice of words. The issue, for those members who took the time to inform the Association of their decision to withdraw, was not the transience of their engagement with economic matters, but rather the uncertainty that their particular interests could be accommodated to suit. When Horace Hoadley, the president and treasurer of the Waterbury (Connecticut) Tool Company, wrote to resign his membership, he explained that he was not "a thoroughly educated economist." He thus felt compelled to "devote [his] efforts to ... other organizations rather than in one that [wa]s primarily scientific." The chief of the Bureau of Foreign and Domestic Commerce at the Department of Commerce in Washington, D.C., was by contrast quite blunt. "[T]here seems to be so little of interest in your periodical and so little of real vital interest in your meetings," he wrote Young, that he wished to leave the Association. Further, he complained, the lack of any individuals in the AEA leadership drawn from the business community was most unfortunate. In reply, Young reiterated that the Association wanted members drawn "from all walks of life who [we]re interested in any way in practical economic problems." Yet the organization, he wrote, was reluctant "to try to extend [its] membership among business men except insofar as they thoroughly underst[oo]d [its] purposes and work."[16]

In his rejoinder to a disgruntled colleague at the Department of Commerce, however, Young had been, if not disingenuous, then certainly oblique. Just months before he had told a business manager from Albany that, in his view, "the Association ha[d] gone too fare [*sic*] in catering to the interests of business men and to the outside public generally." To be sure, Young may have felt more freedom to unburden himself of his true feelings in this case given that he was communicating with a member who had argued for either stringent membership standards for the AEA or a separate scientific branch. Even so, Young (ostensibly representing the interests of the AEA leadership as a whole) believed that what he referred to as a *general* organization could not have the exacting standards of recruitment that the upstate New York administrator had described. Delicately treading the line between several conflicting points of view, Young's seeming prevarication epitomized the conundrums that faced an organization determined to build its ranks yet also equally convinced of the need to police them.[17]

Their insecurities and misgivings notwithstanding, Young and Dewey and their colleagues pushed ahead with their membership efforts. By the end of 1915, they were determined to pursue the expansion of AEA membership so long as "that c[ould] be secured without any sacrifice of [thei]r position as an organization of persons interested in the scientific study of economic problems." Even some anxiety that they might "be liable at some time to charges of dominance by an 'inner ring' such as [George] Bancroft and others ha[d] raised against the Historical Association" did not deter these men from their task. If, at times, it was necessary to humor the occasional eccentric or adventurer, all for the sake of nurturing an open and democratic face for the new Association, nevertheless its self-identity was clear. "[I]nterested in the scientific study of economic problems," the roughly twenty-three hundred members of the AEA were, by 1916, mostly academic and professional economists, businesspeople, and government officials. Clearly, then, as Young put it to an Atlantic City physician who inquired about membership in the spring of that year, "The American Economic Association [wa]s the professional organization of the political economists of the country and occupie[d] in that field the same position that the American Chemical Society, the American Historical Association and the American Medical Association d[id] in theirs."[18]

With a clearer and more self-conscious notion of what their Association was about, AEA leaders like Young believed their membership problems to be well on the way toward resolution. Growth in the rank and file that outstripped losses due to resignation became the norm by the time of the nation's entry into World War I. At war's end, the Association initiated one more recruitment effort, the success of which was deeply gratifying to its architects. Improvement in the membership profile, at that point, was linked with the increasing number of academic economists now interested in the work of the organization; it was also tied to the larger and larger number of economists working in "government agencies, and independent research institutions." After the early years of the 1920s, AEA officials evinced little concern with respect to the size of their organization. The Association, in their view, had clearly weathered at least some of its earliest growing pains.[19]

Fretting over the size of their professional society was, for the AEA leadership, one thing; firmly articulating the Association's raison d'être was something else. Declarations of purpose, no matter how frequently or even stridently made, served only to a point. It was in actual practice, and in the decisions that animated it, wherein the professional community of the AEA truly explained and revealed itself. No amount of enforcement of particular boundaries of expertise could substitute for the rigorous refinement of colleagues that would result from the inculcation of specific ways of doing the community's business. Whether self-consciously or not, Association members and officials were, from the earliest years of the century, concerned to frame the interests, activities, and procedures of their group in ways that would, more powerfully and vividly than any set of membership standards might, decisively create and preserve the profession that it was their goal to foster.

Nowhere were the convictions, values, and goals of the early-twentieth-century AEA leadership more apparent than in their efforts to hold annual meetings and in their decision to establish a professional journal. When Yale's Irving Fisher wrote AEA president Edwin Seligman (of Columbia University) in the winter of 1902 to complain "that economists ha[d] altogether too little influence," he placed his finger on a central anxiety that greatly preoccupied his colleagues. For Fisher it seemed obvious that a rectification of this sorry state of affairs could be achieved through the judicious pursuit of two objectives—the holding of annual meetings that would "discuss topics of the day from a more practical point of view" and "the establishment, if possible, of an economic journal in [the United States] which [w]ould be so authoritative as to place it at the head of economic journals in the world." The trick, of course, would be to balance the desire for relevance (even notoriety) of the work of the Association and its members with the determination to retain the scientific and professional status of the enterprise as a whole. If expertise was to have influence, it should not at the same time forfeit its claim to objectivity and impartiality.[20]

Fisher's prescriptions were not, however, simple or straightforward in their fulfillment; what is more, their implications and consequences were neither obvious nor uncontroversial. Precisely what a serial would publish, not to mention how annual meetings would be organized, became matters of some debate and discussion among AEA officials and members. In large measure this was due to the fact that there was indeed general agreement that conventions and journals would lend respectability and authority to those participating in their production. Articulating standards of publication for an AEA publication and setting procedures to determine who would participate in annual meetings (and what would be discussed at those gatherings) thus became significant concerns for all involved. Added to these challenges was the generally recognized need to compete effectively not simply with other professional organizations in allied fields but also with other professional publications, which, in many cases, had provided venues for the reporting of economics and ancillary research since the 1890s. Chief among the former were the American Sociological Association and the American Political Science Association; prominent among the latter were the *Quarterly Journal of Economics*, the *Political Science Quarterly*, the *Journal of Political Economy*, the *Yale Review*, and the *Annals of the American Academy of Political and Social Science*. On the one hand, the need to maintain the open contours of a "general association" was clear enough, and this militated against, for example, issuing a narrow editorial policy statement for a new journal. On the other, striving for catholicity in the discipline could not translate into a complete lack of standards.[21]

It seemed prudent, therefore, to canvass the members of the AEA Executive Council on the matter of a new professional journal. Secretary-Treasurer Frank Fetter (of Princeton) wrote his council colleagues early in 1902 soliciting their suggestions with regard to such a project, noting "[t]he peculiarly favorable quality of the present moment, with its larger recognition of economic opinion in Washington and elsewhere, for extending the influence and increasing the usefulness of the Association." Responses to this inquiry were swift, thoughtful, and direct. They represented the aspirations of a new generation of professional social scientists eager to establish firmly the reputation of a relatively new discipline. Further, they bespoke the particular ways in which these scholars conceived of their unseasoned profession, its role in both public life and social research, and the workings of the academic world itself.[22]

Virtually all of the respondents to Fetter's inquiry expressed enthusiasm for the establishment of a new, flagship journal in their field, even allowing, as some of them did, for the proliferation of scholarly publications that had already taken place. As one prominent authority put it, "Journals ha[d] multiplied until it [wa]s scarcely possible even to read the titles of articles. Many of the articles ha[d] little value; and, if an article of excellence d[id] appear, it r[an] great danger of being overlooked." Nevertheless, he could not "think of anything which, at the present juncture, would do more for economics in th[e] country" than the creation of the *American Economic Review*. In this perception, Richard Ely well represented the attitude of the vast majority of the Executive Council.[23]

What seemed obvious to the Executive Council was the fact that a full realization of a new journal's potential required clarity as to its purpose and high standards as to its quality. It would not do simply to add to the published material on economic ideas and matters; there lay the path to further adulteration of the product in question. Indeed, it was arguable that "[a] great deal too much [wa]s written in th[e] country on the subject of Economics but the censorship [wa]s not stern enough and too much [wa]s published with the result that the wheat [wa]s often buried in the chaff." There was thus "no proof that the difficulty [lay] in the low standard or the bad judgment of those in charge of [other economics] publications. The difficulty [lay] in the fact that not enough good things [we]re written to fill all [of the] publications [already] issued." Put another way, the challenge of starting a new journal derived from the fact "not that the articles [in other serials] [we]re generally so poor, but that they [we]re occasionally so good." What was clearly the core issue, then, was quality. The success of the venture was thus "entirely dependent upon the character of [those] who [we]re to run the journal and the amount of time and energy they [we]re willing to put into it."[24]

That a new economics review should pursue excellence in its authors seemed both obvious and unassailable in principle. The advantages to be won in the process could not be denied. "[I]f the proposed quarterly [c]ould establish a standard and the value of a writer could thus be estimated in some degree by ascertaining whether he [or she] was accepted as a contributor to it, much good [could] be accomplished." Carl Plehn, an economics professor at the University of California–Berkeley, put it in even more personalized terms. "There is no one," he wrote, "who would not be glad of the opportunity to have [their] results carefully criticized before put into print." A rigorously refereed journal would therefore be most welcome indeed. Needless to say, Plehn obviously had in mind a particular kind of individual who would be "glad of the opportunity" to submit to an exacting and time-consuming referee process—a research scholar whom the journal "would stimulate . . . to more careful work." The conclusion was inescapable: "Let urgent articles and any which [we]re not worthy of [referee] treatment go to other journals. True scholarship kn[ew] nothing of the element of time."[25]

Plehn's faith in the merits of disciplinary rigor notwithstanding, reflection upon the substantive meaning of "standards" provoked anxiety and concern among some Executive Council members. The measurement of distinction would necessarily rest in the hands of particular individuals. How, then, could the risk of the deployment of narrow-minded agendas be avoided? Was it not essential that the new journal represent all points of view "and not merely the thought of this or that University[?]" As Henry Carter Adams of the University of Michigan, the

AEA's president in 1896, put it to Jacob Hollander, one "should regard it as a misfortune if the review [were] given up to theory or if anything of the character of a school of thought [were to] give it color." Academic virtue no doubt lay in the eye of the beholder.[26]

When subjected to close scrutiny, the question of publication standards threatened to destabilize the general consensus about the desirability of creating the *American Economic Review* in the first place. Argument over the implementation of standards not only raised questions of intellectual freedom and openness but also drew attention back to the general and often delicate matter of the journal's purpose. Utilizing an analogy drawn from one of the most conspicuous developments in American industrial life at the time, Davis Kinley made no bones of his opposition to a serial that might become hidebound. "[I]f there is any department of our life," he declared, "in which we should keep free from the trust movement and in a regime of entirely open and free competition, it is in that of our professional literature." Another critic put it in even more pointed terms, having noted his support for the publication of a new journal as a device to provide "additional facility for free expression of opinion." What he did not favor was the notion that a new quarterly should be started "as a corrective of any evils associated with [other] publications." To his mind, "schemes for quality sifting [we]re [apt] to paralyze rather than foster the scientific spirit." Indeed, maintaining the breadth and accessibility of the serial would ostensibly help to make it "of use to those who direct[ed] political affairs. To this end generally accepted economic principles could be stated [in the journal] as they affect[ed] problems under consideration by . . . officers and representatives in state and nation."[27]

If the goal of cultivating influence with public officials, by means of the issuance of a new journal, conflicted with the desire of instituting the highest professional standards in its production, resolution of that paradox would provide little if any useful insight regarding the cultivation of intellectual diversity. More to the point, an overweening application of "standards," if not self-consciously undertaken, could yield a highly undesirable result—scholarly inbreeding and the suppression of emergent yet not prestigious ideas. This was obviously an affront to the principles of academic freedom and scientific objectivity that laid the foundation for the issuance of a serial in the first place. If "the standard set by a professional journal which h[eld] a sole authoritative position, [wa]s [to]o exacting," worried future *American Economic Review* editor Davis Dewey, "writers . . . just struggling to an expression of their ideas [would] not have sufficient encouragement." How could the profession and discipline benefit from that? An editor in the offices of a potential competitor for the *Review* hoisted the AEA Executive Council by its own petard when, reflecting on the issue, he said to them:

> I am opposed to the idea of publishing the best "and only the best." I believe in publication of the *second best* as well. I find much helpful information in articles that are only mediocre from the scholarly point of view, and I doubt whether the ten *best* articles of the year are the ones that I find most helpful. I am more interested in second class essays on some topics than in first class ones on other topics.[28]

Not simply value as to method and technique, but significance and appropriateness as to subject figured prominently in the deliberations of the AEA Executive Council respecting the new journal and the Association's annual meetings. These discussions continued for years and ultimately decades to come. They were, in fact, often intertwined, touching upon related concerns about professional status and prestige, scientific conduct and codes, and the boundaries (topical and methodological) of economics itself. Stoutly defining what economics was involved being clear-minded about what it was not. Prominent AEA members, at the very moment they were wrestling with the nature of a new publication for the Association, vigorously protested to President Seligman that sociologists be kept at bay from the annual meeting and even the quarterly itself. "We have heard [the sociologists] so many times," Henry Carter Adams wrote Seligman in the spring of 1902, "that we know absolutely what each one of the[m] will say upon any subject." When gathered in an annual convention, Thomas Carver argued, "Economists would prefer to stick to the subject of Economists. [One] should especially doubt whether the members of [the] association would easily find a common ground of discussion with Miss [Jane] Addams or Mr. Felix Adler, admirable as these persons are and valuable as their work is. [One] should be afraid that there would be difficulty in trying to think in the same language." The same, Carver believed, was true for the *Review*. He doubted very much if "it would be wise to include much sociology, except such as has a distinctly economic coloring."[29]

Enforcing disciplinary boundaries, in both publication strategies and convention planning, also involved making precise decisions about the relationship between scholarly research and contemporary policy debate. With apparently little discussion or debate, the AEA Executive Committee formally chose to exclude from the pages of the *American Economic Review* a "department of current economic events." Even if contemporary policy concerns found their way into the submissions to the Association's quarterly, the editors were determined "that current economic questions . . . be treated by scholarly men and not left to the sensational magazine writer." In some respects this was a curious position for the leadership to assume given the additional concern that the work of economists be made visible and influential in the world of public affairs. The notion that the *Review* should be "a craftsman's tool" had, after all, animated a great deal of the effort of the editorial office from the earliest days. Maintaining a dispassionate, scholarly tone while encouraging a wide and even diverse readership was neither a simple nor an obvious task. Editor Davis Dewey put it well to the distinguished English theorist Francis Edgeworth in January 1911 when he wrote, "We are trying to appeal to a somewhat varied membership who are interested in current questions. We do not, however, wish to be popular in a commonplace way, but shall endeavor to have our articles prepared by men of scholarly standards." The problem of attracting "a somewhat varied membership" while adhering to "scholarly standards" that would guard against being "popular in a commonplace way" was truly vexing.[30]

AEA annual meetings also constituted an arena within which varying conceptions of professional expertise, scholarly deportment, and disciplinary authority could be counterposed. Making a convention a controlled venue for scientific discussion necessarily raised a host of questions about exclusivity and access that troubled some members. For nonacademics, it was not an infrequent experience at a meeting session "that if [one] were not a professor your time for discussion was almost nil." Sensing that these events were "the professors' party," these outsiders usually concluded that "it was good policy to stay out of the discussions." Viewed, however, from the opposite perspective, the suppression of participation by those lacking appropriate credentials seemed a justified and necessary strategy. That "[i]t [might] be necessary to require every one who sp[oke] from the floor [at a session] to give his credentials, i.e., what if anything he represent[ed]" struck one distinguished academic member of the AEA as a necessary deterrent against "cranks" who, if not aggressively controlled, could "talk half of the sessions to death." Lashing out at those "who masquerade[d] as an economist" at the annual meetings, Royal Meeker sarcastically concluded that such impostors "should be summarily shot without waiting for sunrise; fined $500.00; expelled from the Association in disgrace; [and] exiled on Robinson Crusoe's far famed islet."[31]

Structuring the annual conventions also engaged AEA officials and members in efforts to distinguish their work from that of other elite professionals. At times their convictions in this regard militated against involvement with other scientific societies. Even allowing for the prospect of sharing in the prestige of other experts, the need to sustain the distinctive identity of a social science discipline won out. Fearing that holding a formal Association meeting with the American Association for the Advancement of Science (AAAS) would jeopardize the "unity and strength of the social science societies," former AEA president Frank Fetter argued forcefully to the Executive Council that "economics [could] never be anything but an excrescence [sic]" at the annual convention of "the stronghold of the natural sciences." His view represented a climate of opinion that served to persuade the current Association president, John Gray of the University of Minnesota, to avoid joining the AAAS for the time being. It was not, however, a decision that sat well with others "interested in getting the scientific stamp upon economics and in getting economists to assume the scientific point of view prevailing in the older sciences." For those with such a professionalizing vision, like Irving Fisher at Yale, membership in the AAAS was a worthy end.[32]

Utilizing the annual meeting as a device to facilitate the intergenerational reproduction of the profession also commended itself to AEA officials as a valuable enterprise. As plans moved forward for the 1916 convention, scheduled at Columbus, AEA secretary-treasurer Allyn Young made Executive Council views on this matter clear to the local arrangements committee chair, C. E. Parry of Ohio State University. Urging Parry to schedule a reception where younger Association members could meet older colleagues, Young further informed him that the council felt that such a "smoker" should ideally facilitate interaction among established members and new professional recruits. Toward that end, "some 'circulation' should be encouraged and . . . groups of old cronies should not be allowed to hold down a particular table or corner for the whole evening." Council members "also felt very distinctly," Young noted, "that . . . certain tables should be especially reserved for our women members, many of whom fe[lt] 'out of it' when they [we]re not allowed to be present at such functions."[33]

Even so, the solicitousness of the Executive Council toward the sensibilities and needs of "women members" at the AEA annual meeting was, if not insincere, certainly deceptive. For some years, in fact, the pursuit of a wholly professional-ized image for the field of economics had taken on, in the hands of the AEA secretariat and other prominent members, a decidedly gendered aspect—one that worked resolutely toward the exclusion of feminist concerns and ideas in the discipline as a whole. Ironically enough, in a discipline the very name of which was derived from the Greek word for household management—*Oikonomika*—the study of what had for so long been regarded as a "women's sphere" of home and hearth remained, more often than not, beyond its ken. It was a strange quaran-tine, this, especially given the earliest foundations of economic analysis in the investigation of subsistence and demographic viability. For professional Ameri-can economists early in this century, welcoming women colleagues to social events was one thing; admitting a "women's sphere" of analytical concerns to the science was something else entirely.[34]

With no debate among AEA secretariat colleagues, the founding editor of the *American Economic Review*, Davis Dewey, had rejected a suggestion from Theo-dora B. Cunningham that the journal include "a Women's Department of house-hold economics, which would [have been] to the busy intelligent wife what the Economic Review [wa]s to her thinking husband." Dewey's decision in this re-gard was thoroughly consistent with not one but two strategies of professionaliza-tion in early-twentieth-century America. On the one hand, it furthered the con-scious effort of AEA founders to secure a distinctive place for economics as a scientifically grounded enterprise that avoided the lesser prestige of feminized occupations like "home economics." On the other, it actually dovetailed with efforts dating from 1900 to constitute home economics as a separate discipline in its own right. Women professionals eager to find in the home economics field the same authority and influence that their male counterparts struggled for in an array of other disciplines had worked assiduously to establish collegiate degree pro-grams, journals, and a national association—the American Home Economics As-sociation (AHEA). Their very success made the "defeminization" of economics, at the hands of professional communities like the AEA, rather easy.[35]

In large measure, avoiding the study of household management and activities within the economics discipline seemed conceptually justified on two grounds. To the extent housework was unremunerated, within the contexts of a traditional marriage, it was more than plausible to argue that it fell outside the domain of economic analysis given this separation from the marketplace. Viewed as "role-playing, . . . a hobby, a vocation, a proof of love, a character trait, in brief anything and everything except work," domestic labor was thus of no concern to practicing economists. Insofar as domestic relations and decision making were understood to involve affective expectations, rituals, and beliefs, they, too, sat beyond the investigative tools of a field that privileged rational choice and decision making as the focus of its inquiries. In all these respects, early-twentieth-century American economists sought to define their work in ways that would enhance their prestige and expertise. Most of all, they strove to avoid the difficulties encountered by their female colleagues who studied household matters; it was quite obvious that "[h]ome economics lacked . . . one essential professional criterion: exclusivity."[36]

Precision, impartiality, rectitude, these were the traits, expected of all economists, that would garner the profession the authority, influence, and resources essential not simply to its survival but also to its enduring success. Vetting them, thereby ensuring the selectness and particularity of the expert company being formed, was thus an overriding concern for AEA executives and for the editorship of the *Review*. It was the journal, in fact, that constituted the central locus within which this interest was worked through—for it was on matters of article and topic selection, book review strategies, and expository modes that definitive choices affecting it had to be made. When Davis Dewey complained that certain prospective journal authors "when it c[ame] to a pinch, sacrifice[d] their economics in favor of some temporary policy," when he reflected upon the competition for published space between scholarship and "popularization," between theory and "useful" investigations, he simply gave voice to the tensions inherent in any project of professionalization.[37]

Of immediate concern to the founding editor of the *AER* was the problem of handling "polemical" articles. Though such screeds, in his view, might be lively in style, they carried the risk of damaging the reputation of economics as a discipline and of economists as an expert community. "Lord knows economists ha[d] had enough hard sledding," Dewey believed; it was "their merits rather than their defects [that] should be emphasized" in a venue like the *Review*. As he gained more confidence in his work in the offices of the journal, Dewey became more and more optimistic about the accomplishments of his fellow economists. By 1922, a decade into his editorship, he could declare that "economics ha[d] abandoned the controversial stages and begun to work under the cooperati[on] of investigation and analysis." While "there [might] be, here and there, a cantankerous controversialist left who [would] insist upon defending his own point of view regardless of facts," Dewey felt increasingly justified in "leaving them by the wayside whenever [he] detect[ed] this quality" in submissions.[38]

Needless to say, it was neither Dewey's responsibility nor indeed his authority alone to make the qualitative judgments that ultimately framed the nature and practice of the *Review* and thereby of one of the profession's leading platforms. An array of colleagues, acting as formal judges, joined him in serving as gatekeepers of the journal. That access to its pages was a sure sign of professional distinction and merit made the assessments of *AER* referees singularly important; it also not infrequently made those decisions difficult, even contentious. Be that as it may, editors and readers both struggled toward measured and balanced decisions, usually quite aware of the charged and sometimes political contexts within which they were framed. If they were self-consciously aware of the professional goals they sought to achieve, and they usually were, these scholars nonetheless took great pains to pursue those objectives in ways consistent with deeply held convictions about academic probity, honesty, and decency. What problems might be inherent in the exercise had less to do with intentions than with consequences.

As soon as they began their work, *AER* officials reckoned with a variety of controversial and unresolved questions in their fields of interest—and they did so with open eyes. Assessing the quality of an essay submitted on the theory of interest, Harvard's Thomas Carver was entirely forthcoming on the charged nature of the subject. "In view of the rapid growth of socialistic sentiment and opinion," he wrote the editor, "it is of the very highest importance that this question 'Is Interest Earned?' be threshed out fully and completely. Upon the answer . . . will turn the whole question of socialistic policy." That the piece in question answered that question in the affirmative met with Carver's enthusiastic approval. "If it [wa]s answered in the negative," he declared, "we [would all have] to become socialists sooner or later. There [wa]s, therefore, no economic question . . . of greater importance." Carver recommended that the article be condensed and run.[39]

Frank Fetter of Princeton (and AEA president at the time) found the paper "Capital and Profits" unacceptable not so much because its conclusions were wrong but rather because its style of argumentation was potentially inflammatory. By favoring corporations excessively in his discussion, the author, in Fetter's opinion, provided dangerous grist for "trade unionists and radical agitators." His approach to "so great and so difficult a subject" was not, therefore the "basis of a satisfactory scientific treatment." Dewey himself could fret over the broader implications of a prospective author's work—making his misgivings clear to a referee even before an evaluation had been made. When calling upon Fetter to evaluate "The Economic Significance of Degeneracy among the Negroes," an essay by James Bardin (of the University of Virginia), the *AER* editor specifically asked his referee "whether [he] th[ought] any of the phraseology should be changed, as this [essay] was written from the Southern standpoint. Would it not be well to change the word 'degeneracy' in the title?" Fetter avoided Dewey's questions, perhaps finding them too pointed. Recommending against publication of the piece in its submitted form, he adroitly linked what he hoped was a rigorous consideration of the paper with a clear but equitable indication of his own distaste for Bardin's point of view. "I think I am entirely free from any northern prejudice in this matter," he wrote Dewey, "and [I] have not the slightest desire to champion the negro or to minimize any facts that are unfavorable to the race." Nevertheless, in his estimation, it was "evident that the author ha[d] a strong southern anti-negro prejudice, of which he [wa]s unconscious and which serve[d] him in place of facts."[40]

In addition to broad questions of political import and social practice, a decision to publish or reject a submission could also turn upon certain notions regarding appropriate expository techniques as well as proper scientific discourse. In the fall of 1919, the chief economist for the Southern Wholesale Grocers' Association rejected an article because of its use of mathematical techniques, all the while neglecting to discuss any of the author's ideas. "[A]s is usually the case with mathematical economists," the referee noted, "[the author] assumes several things, attaches a letter to each of his several assumptions, shakes them up a little bit, and comes out with his assumptions intact." With equanimity and tact, yet similarly concerned about a writer's style of reasoning, Willard Hotchkiss (the director of the National Industrial Federation of Clothing Manufacturers) discarded John Bennett's "Wage Disputes and Profiteering" because the author "[wa]s one of those men with rather limited scientific training, who ha[d] thought much of [the nation's] industrial ills, and ha[d] probably felt somewhat more deeply than he ha[d] thought." Nevertheless, "[f]rom the standpoint of citizenship, it [wa]s so wholesome to have men of this sort thinking seriously upon industrial subjects that [Hotchkiss] always fe[lt] a certain regret at discouraging them."[41]

Ever cognizant of the impact *AER* publication policy had on the professional group of which he was a part, Davis Dewey sometimes gave consideration to an author's background when facing a difficult decision on a submitted piece. Concluding that a particularly abstract essay would best be published elsewhere (specifically the *Quarterly Journal of Economics*), the editor made clear that it was not the exceedingly theoretical nature of the work that prompted his choice. Rather, it was his belief that "it [wa]s just as well not to appropriate much space in this field to a foreigner. If the article [had been] written by an American student [Dewey would have been] inclined to consider it favorably." Time and again, Dewey would canvass his editorial board for suggestions regarding article topics and prospective authors—all with a view both to stimulate interest in the journal as a whole and to cultivate an American network of contributors. Even the iconoclast Thorstein Veblen was directly solicited. "As I understand it," Dewey wrote him in March 1915, "you do not write or publish until the spirit moves [*sic*] and are impregnable to all appeals. I write to inquire, however, if the spirit is not moving you at about this time; and if it is, if you can not let it quicken the pages of the *American Economic Review*."[42]

It was, interestingly enough, in the book review function of the *AER* that authors, editors, and referees alike found the source of much uncertainty and controversy regarding publications strategies and professional standards. In large measure this may have been due to the fact that, unlike the evaluation of article manuscripts, book reviews were signed; the identities of both a book's author and its reviewer were matters of public record. The potential for disputes was therefore magnified, and the opportunity for communication, whether composed or shrill, between authors and *AER* editors enhanced. Put another way, published book reviews could (and did) invite replies—more often than not from aggrieved authors—whereas published articles, precisely because they had already passed muster with referees, did not. Perhaps for this reason, the *Review* leadership early on exhibited great concern for fairness and equanimity in book reviews as distinct from their oft-repeated concern that articles be held to a high professional accounting. "[I]n the case of some controverted questions where the economic fraternity is divided in opinion," Frank Fetter told Davis Dewey in the spring of 1911, "it would be desirable to have both wings represented in the review of important books." Executive Council member Horace Taylor, of Columbia University, put it in even more direct terms when he fashioned a general statement on book review policy for the journal. "If a book, for example, is written by a socialist," he declared, "it should be judged as to its merits from the point of view of socialistic philosophy; this, however, does not prevent an appraisal of its value judged by what the reviewer considers to be the canons of universal truth." In this fashion, Taylor believed, "intelligent and acute discussion" could be encouraged. "[I]f frankly and courteously given, [such commentary] w[ould] do much to stimulate sound reasoning and accurate research."[43]

AEA president Henry Farnam, of Yale University, had in fact written Dewey a month before Fetter to make a similar suggestion regarding book review practice. He asked the editor if it "would . . . do in the case of books on controverted subjects like Socialism, to occasionally have a doubled [sic] barreled review, one by a sympathizer, one by an outsider[?]" Dewey appears never to have taken up this specific proposal—in some respects, concern with space limitations and printing costs may have been an issue. Yet there is no doubt that it was a "live," genuine issue, one with which Dewey struggled for years. The puzzle was obvious enough: book reviewing invited the very kind of debate and struggle over professional norms that the article-referee process was meant to avoid. At the same time, the public nature of signed book reviews not only encouraged dissension and argument but also necessitated close attention to rubrics of impartiality and openness.[44]

Ultimately, over the years, Dewey found himself forced to rely on his own instincts and goodwill, not to mention that of his colleagues, in seeing to it that the integrity of the journal was not subverted by the book review task. When, for example, he asked Frank Fetter to review a new work by Frank Taussig, the renowned Harvard economist and past president of the AEA, he was refused. Of Taussig, Fetter wrote Dewey: "I regard him personally so highly but differ so hopelessly with his fundamental economic analysis. He represents in theory so extremely the *right wing*, that it is not fair to him to have his reviewer come from the left wing." Sometimes it was for Dewey to enforce a code of professional courtesy and evenhandedness—before or after the fact. When asking Paul H. Douglas, then of Amherst College, later of the University of Chicago (and the future Democratic senator from Illinois), to review Carl D. Thompson's new work, *Public Ownership*, he bemoaned the difficulty of finding unprejudiced evaluators for that particular volume. "The ordinary reviewer who is opposed to government ownership," he wrote Douglas, "will simply ransack the book for possible errors [while] an advocate who has already committed himself to government ownership will glorify the book." If a reviewer overstepped the boundaries of proper deportment, Dewey similarly could be the final arbiter of professional conduct. In rejecting a review of a new work by Ralph G. Hawtrey on imperialism, he told A. W. Calhoun (of Limestone College, South Carolina) that even if "Hawtrey's analysis of present-day imperialism [was] 'incredibly naive,' [nevertheless] that [wa]s hardly a proper characterization for a scientific journal." At the same time, he could accept a particularly tough review from Gardiner C. Means (then of Columbia University Law School) given its sagaciousness and respect for the castigated author. With its founding editor, the *American Economic Review* enjoyed the services of a tactful yet firm umpire.[45]

Yet no matter how skillful Dewey was in piloting his *Review* through sometimes choppy waters, the enforcement of professional standards could prompt some, prospective *AER* authors and AEA members alike, to wonder if the passage had a welcome destination and if its various captains were not like Cerberus. "Make your publications worth the money," one angered *AER* subscriber wrote to Secretary-Treasurer Young. A consulting engineer from Brooklyn, "led to believe that [he] was to unite with a body of men engaged in advanced, constructive thought," was less than impressed with some issues of the "Quarterly" that he had received upon joining the AEA. Dismayed to find "nothing at all progressive or worthy of serious attention," he resigned his membership. Mount Holyoke College professor Bertha Haven Putnam was particularly chagrined "that neither the *Review* nor [the AEA] annual program contain[ed] any thing on economic history." She thus found herself avoiding AEA events and focusing her energies on attendance at the annual gatherings of the American Historical Association.[46]

Particularly disturbing to Dewey were suggestions that the *Review* was dominated by an "inner circle." Like a controversy that had swirled around the American Historical Association in the early twentieth century, a tempest that had even found its way into the pages of the *Nation*, charges that the American Economic Association had become a clique were hard to refute. Simply responding to them, by conveying perhaps an excessively defensive style, was to run risks. For the editor of the *AER* the notion "that certain names [we]re appearing perhaps too often in the list of [the journal's] contributors" was particularly galling. "If these commentators only knew how I sweat over this phase of the work," Dewey declared to David Kinley in the fall of 1913, "there probably would be no criticism." Specifically, Dewey believed that his critics were unaware of "how many declinations there were, all in good will, because of lack of time and other engagements"—all from prospective authors whose presence would have vastly diversified the pages of the *Review* as a whole. So stung was Dewey by what became a nagging question for his editorship that he sometimes distributed free copies of the journal to seemingly peculiar recipients believing that even "radicals [we]re worth cultivating" in his effort to portray the *AER* as an open and fair-minded scholarly publication. Sad to say, for Dewey and his colleagues, what might appear to be a generous and disinterested spirit to some could manifest itself to others as at best a disingenuous waste of time, at worst rank condescension.[47]

Standing accused of partisanship or worse, the leadership of most professional societies, rather than self-consciously addressing questions of privilege, bias, and unexamined assumptions, would instead extol and pursue the observance of an ideal neutrality. In this regard, the AEA secretariat was no exception. But in the practice the Association's leaders only served to make more pointed the contradiction between the goal of objectivity and the desire for influence and authority. It might, on the one hand, be easy to refuse to offer an official AEA endorsement of the work of the National One Cent Letter Postage Association in the belief that a professional body could not give "any concerted opinion upon any matter of public policy." Further, it seemed obvious the annual meeting of the AEA had to be planned with adherence "to a policy of strict neutrality" on public questions while, at the same time, the *AER* had to avoid "declaration[s] of opinion" on policy matters "in order to ward off the cranks . . . clamoring for an opportunity to use the Review." It could even be straightforward, years later, to turn down a request from the United States Department of Commerce to help in efforts to "eliminat[e] those economic wastes caused by over-diversification." But it was altogether something else if the notion "that the American Economic Association as a purely scientific body [was] inhibited by its constitution from taking any attitude on matters of practical politics" eventually prevented economists from achieving the esteem and sway they desired. It was just possible that the distinction between the public posture of the AEA and the political choices and commitments of its individual members was too fine consistently to sustain.[48]

Certain challenges served to place the difficulties associated with maintaining the separation between professional image and individual values in sharp relief. One of these involved continuing struggles over academic freedom issues, involving economists at certain educational institutions across the nation. The most celebrated of these, although by no means the only ones, were the cases of Richard Ely at the University of Wisconsin, Edward Bemis at the University of Chicago, and Edward Ross at Stanford. All three scholars had been accused in the 1890s, in different contexts and in various ways, of poisoning the minds of their students with ideas and beliefs inimical to corporate interests and private wealth. Two of them, Ely and Ross, managed to bring their careers back from the brink of the abyss; Bemis was not as fortunate and, in the end, was condemned to oblivion. Whether in success or failure, however, the defense of colleagues placed in jeopardy for their political convictions and beliefs relied more on the *individual* support of powerful champions within the profession rather than on the *collective* imprimatur of the AEA.[49]

This is not to say that the Association was indifferent to the question of academic freedom and intellectual comity. Quite the contrary. Academic freedom could be and was defended by the AEA leadership, and arguably by the vast majority of the Association's membership, as an essential part of the unfettered pursuit of knowledge and learning. Indeed, the AEA charter had explicitly made "the encouragement of perfect freedom of economic discussion" a singular part of the Association's mission. Yet, by the earliest decades of the twentieth century, the issue of specific academic freedom cases was sharply distinguished from the general principle. In the winter of 1913 the Association joined with representatives of the American Political Science Association (APSA) and the American Sociological Association (ASA) to see to the creation of the Joint Committee to assess "liberty of thought, freedom of speech, and security of tenure" for scholars in their respective fields. Substantively little came of this group's work, save for the declaration of broad commitments of an ideal sort. Mention of specific cases, let alone involvement in the details of those contests, was studiously avoided. In this, the Joint Committee simply repeated behaviors embraced by the AEA and its leadership for some time. During the high tide of the Ross case at Stanford in 1900, AEA officials had quietly charged a special committee to look into the circumstances surrounding Ross's "enforced resignation." So delicate was the entire affair that the committee's creation was neither officially nor publicly acknowledged, and the group itself failed to issue a formal report.[50]

Far from a covert conspiracy of repression and silence, the separation of the AEA, as a professional society, from the particulars of academic freedom quarrels was but the outward representation of the powerfully held, and often declared, convictions of some of its most influential members. Secretary-Treasurer Allyn Young told Edwin Seligman, the Association's representative on the Joint Committee, that "the facts of specific cases which [we]re springing up in all parts of the country [we]re so difficult of ascertaining and frequently complicated with personal views that [there was] no good in even [AEA] attempts of investigation." In the case of a failed reappointment or promotion, Young believed, the aggrieved party might believe it all the result "of his [or her] opinions on controverted questions of public policy. On the other hand those in authority m[ight] insist that the professor . . . [wa]s a persona non grata or that [their] want of tact impair[ed] [their] usefulness." The puzzle, for Young, was "[h]ow . . . to judge between such contentions." Better to remain aloof. Young's immediate predecessor had similarly tried to navigate between rough shores. When Willard Fisher, in the spring of 1913, had been fired by Wesleyan College for lectures and remarks taken to be antichurch, then AEA secretary-treasurer Thomas Carver saw to it that letters on the matter, from individual Association members, were printed in the *American Economic Review*; they were, however, published with no comment by *Review* editors or Association officials.[51]

In more pointed style, former AEA president Henry Adams made clear his suspicion that academic freedom cases were often spurious; it was, as a consequence, his strong belief that the Association should steer clear of them. On the occasion of a dismissal from a faculty appointment, he argued, "Nine times out of ten, it [wa]s the fault of the [individual] rather than of the institution." If Adams's declaration further implied that there was a 10 percent rate of unjustified separation from academic positions, nevertheless Secretary-Treasurer Young agreed "that what abuse of academic freedom there [wa]s c[ame] largely from professors rather than from administrative officials." But two months later, Young refused to involve the AEA in a questionable firing that had taken place at Dartmouth College. Similarly, when Scott Nearing was fired at the University of Pennsylvania, and charges of political perfidy surrounding that decision were made, AEA officials, like Davis Dewey and Frank Fetter, were content "to make a brief and colorless mention of the fact [in the *AER*] but not to enter into any details." Fetter felt such agnosticism on the case was most prudent, "confess[ing] to some prejudice against Nearing as an economist because he seem[ed] to be weak on the most elementary principles." A professional organization could, in the abstract, forcefully advocate for freedom of inquiry and ideas; its individual members, on the other hand, were on their own.[52]

Another test of the early-twentieth-century attitudes and aspirations of what had become an increasingly professionalized community of American economists was posed by changes in the needs and functions of government—none more important than those attendant upon the coming of the Great War. While not in all cases solely linked with the war, and in some cases even predating the nation's entry into the conflict, these transformations in governmental expectations, needs, and practice had a decisive impact on the professional attitudes and self-image of American economists—not to mention on a broad array of other professions, disciplines, and scholarly institutions. They also contributed to the acceleration of those processes that had, since the late nineteenth century, prompted a pursuit of "scientism" in the social and policy sciences as a whole. As the leading authority on the history of this intellectual development in the United States has noted, "[World War I] suggested to social scientists, as the Progressive period had earlier, the possibilities of power and usefulness inherent in technical expertise." Yoked to "objective version[s] of empiricism and social intervention," an increasingly scientistic approach to social investigations, spurred by the wartime experience, privileged quantitative and behavioristic work that "eschew[ed] ethical judgments." By the time of the assassination of Austria's Archduke Ferdinand at Sarajevo, American economists had become as much a part of this reformation of American social sciences as any other disciplinary cadre.[53]

In point of fact, prior to American participation in the world war, the leadership of the AEA sought to involve itself, and its membership, in the work of the federal government. It tried to do so in ways that spoke directly to the new sense of professionalism and purpose that had animated the Association since its earliest days. To be sure, the goals and objectives of government policy were always at the core of any interaction between professionals and the state; yet the emphasis in this case was more on *how* rather than *what* governmental work was done. Through their most prominent representatives, American economists were eager to use the new tools of their discipline to improve the practice of statecraft, whatever its purposes or goals. On the question of means, professional social scientists could speak with an authority and influence that debates over ends would neither allow nor sustain.

In the spring of 1914, the AEA secretariat fashioned a special opportunity to bring the potential benefits of professional economics expertise to the attention of federal officials. Not surprisingly, it involved concerns with the ways in which the United States Department of Agriculture (DOA) calculated and reported statistical data on the performance of the nation's farms. Allyn Young contacted the secretary of agriculture, David F. Houston, to express the fear of the AEA leadership that "much of the statistical work . . . issu[ed] from government offices [wa]s of disgracefully poor quality." He noted that the failures of the DOA in this regard were by no means unique. Clearly, "many of the activities of [federal] government bureaus furnish[ed] statistical by-products that [c]ould be of the greatest usefulness." There was a clear need, in Young's opinion, that these data be "properly tabulated and published."[54]

Secretary Houston was much impressed with Young's arguments. A week after having heard from the AEA secretary-treasurer, he concluded that the Association should establish a committee to "investigate the statistical work of the government" with a view toward improving its reliability and enhancing its usefulness. Seeing that this suggestion also provided a framework for interdisciplinary cooperation, Young contacted President John Koren of the American Statistical Association (AStA) shortly thereafter to pursue strategies to make this work "a joint affair" of the two professional societies. Koren and Young initiated plans to make "the statistical work of the government" the theme for several sessions at upcoming annual meetings of both the AEA and the AStA. Even before those meetings were held, AEA president John Gray expressed his eagerness to have Association members (along with colleagues from the AStA) "memorialize Congress for some action [to] give better recognition to the opinion of scientific or academic statisticians" regarding quantitative work in government. On matters of technique, experts should have their say.[55]

Both President Gray and Secretary-Treasurer Thomas Carver (who would become president in two more years) were particularly aggressive in seeking for economists the privilege of speaking with authority on civic operations and projects. In January 1914 they established the joint Committee on Practical Training for Public Service with the American Political Science Association—believing that involvement with statecraft raised an assortment of issues in the fields of economics and political science concerning training curricula, methodologies, and standards of conduct. A month later, Gray contacted the United States Department of State to inform that agency of an AEA resolution—approved at the annual meeting in December 1913—calling on the federal government to "take such administrative and legislative action as w[ould] assure the proper representation of the United States . . . at important international congresses . . . relating to economic, sociological, political, or statistical subjects." He believed it was imperative that Washington develop an "appropriate procedure" to select "the most suitable persons to act as delegates" at these events. Furthermore, Gray concluded, the government had to stand ready to fund these representatives with public resources because a failure to help with travel expenses would no doubt involve the risk that "the United States [wa]s represented . . . by persons not most competent or most prominent with respect to the subject matter of [a] meeting." The State Department deflected Gray's proposal with the suggestion that he take it up with members of Congress. While there is no evidence that Gray did so, his instinct to raise these issues with Washington says volumes about the degree of professional self-confidence already nurtured within the AEA itself.[56]

An interest in the undertakings of the state may have been exciting and stimulating. Yet it was the need to mobilize for America's first participation in an international wartime alliance that truly braced AEA leaders and their professional colleagues. Now the roles were reversed: it was no longer the government that was a target for the deployment of economic expertise; rather, it was economic expertise that became the lure for the state.

John Perrin, the chair of the Federal Reserve Bank of San Francisco, anticipated an impending change in the relationship between the AEA and the federal bureaucracy when, six months after the sinking of the *Lusitania* off Kinsale Head (Ireland), he wrote to Allyn Young about the upcoming annual meeting of the Association in Washington. Noting the complete absence in the convention program of any sessions or papers dealing with the conflict, Perrin complained that his academic colleagues were a "rather impractical lot. Here [wa]s a world crisis, the greatest in half a thousand years, or more," and economists did not even deign to discuss it. James LeRossignol, of the University of Nebraska, was more direct. "[T]he Economic Association should take action," he declared but two weeks before Woodrow Wilson's war message to the Congress, "to mobilize all the economists of the country for special war service."[57]

Whatever the apparent hesitation of AEA officials (not to mention members) to involve themselves directly in contemporary issues surrounding the world war, the United States Civil Service Commission brought matters to a head shortly after the nation declared war on Germany early in April 1917. The response of the Association secretariat was swift. At the request of the commission, Secretary-Treasurer Young saw to it that the entire AEA membership was circularized to prepare a composite list of individuals ready, willing, and able to engage in national service during the wartime emergency. By the fall, commission president John McIlhenny could contemplate with satisfaction the thorough canvass Young had devised. It was, at that point, necessary to engage the Association executives in a more refined exercise of judgment. McIlhenny asked that the roster be purged of "the names of persons who d[id] not properly come within the classification of economic expert," that the remaining individuals be grouped under appropriate specialty headings, and that "such comment in individual cases" be made as AEA authorities deemed "advisable." Here, within the context of national mobilization for war, was an unprecedented and official stimulant for the professionalizing efforts and pursuit of influence that had characterized the Association's work since its founding. It was an opportunity seized upon with alacrity and spirit.[58]

Three eminent members and one official of the AEA took up the task posed by the Civil Service Commission. George Barnett (of Johns Hopkins and a future AEA president), John Bates Clark (of Columbia and the Carnegie Endowment for International Peace, and a former AEA president), Frank Taussig (of Harvard and the United States Tariff Commission, as well as a former AEA president), and Allyn Young evaluated over nine hundred cards returned pursuant to the Civil Service survey. By June 1918, their work was complete. In the interim, their engagement with the needs of state had galvanized others within the AEA to additional war-related action. Then AEA president John Commons (of the University of Wisconsin) garnered Executive Committee approval to form an array of committees to assist "national agencies" in the war effort.[59] At the same time, twenty-five senior Association members took up administrative service duties in just over a dozen federal war agencies. Compared with the involvement of colleagues in the American Political Science Association and the American Socio-logical Association, the average participation rate of AEA members in govern-ment war-related work was the highest on record. American economists and the state had found one another; their mutual interaction and interdependence would continue and flourish long after the Armistice.[60]

It was new AEA president Irving Fisher who, not long before the Second Battle of the Marne that would start the war's endgame, became one of the most inspired and determined of AEA notables in striving to use the national emergency as a springboard for growing and longer-term involvement of economists with public affairs. Using clerical staff at Yale, he sought to create a national clearinghouse of information on war-related research by economists, writing AEA members directly to gather the necessary data. He was convinced that the effort could be extended to work on the problems of demobilization and reconstruction come war's end. Fisher endeavored to bring both academic and business-world mem-bers into the work of the special war committees, and on several occasions he would use this as an example of the broad appeal of the AEA—all in the effort to expand the society's ranks. He saw to it that the general theme of the Associa-tion's annual meeting at the end of 1918 would be "War and Reconstruction." As the war drew to a close, Fisher also took the lead in responding to an inquiry from the Department of the Interior. Officials at the Bureau of the Census wished to create an advisory committee to assist them in their operations. Fisher was deter-mined that the members of such a group be those "who [we]re experienced in some of the more advanced statistical methods" of the time. In all these initiatives, he took up the challenge of another distinguished friend and colleague, Walton Hamilton (of Amherst College), who had advised him that "any suggestion for making the work of economists more effective deserve[d] consideration."[61]

As with so much else in the nation's life and culture, World War I transformed the context within which economics, both as a discipline and as a professional occupation, would evolve. Perhaps Wesley Mitchell, who had served on the War Industries Board, put it best when he observed that "[t]he grave problems of the war and of reconstruction w[ould] restore to economic theory the vitality it had after the Napoleonic wars." Fisher himself noted this fact in his presidential ad-dress to the AEA annual meeting in December 1918. "War work," he believed, had at last given the profession a sense of what it could achieve when and if it involved itself with "feeling the pulse of real events." Fully realizing all of the potential to be enjoyed in sustained engagement with public purposes would re-quire, in his view, that economists not simply reorient their scholarly efforts; it would also necessitate that colleagues undertake the responsibility to keep the public (and its elected representatives) aware of the "fundamental principles" of the discipline. Only in this way could the profession achieve the authority and influence it sought and deserved.[62]

Yet "war work" itself, not to mention participation in the formulation of public policy, was a not uncomplicated thing. If, before the Great War, "[t]he social status of the newly professionalized professoriate was uncertain, reflecting the ambivalence of American society to the life of the mind," the experience of wartime mobilization nonetheless "brought into sharp focus questions concerning the uses of knowledge and the uses of the university." Engagement with a public purpose, especially one framed within the extraordinary circumstances of war, could obviously give scholars a sense of mission, not to mention prestige and authority, altogether unprecedented. Indeed, it was this sort of prospect that so animated specialists in economics like Fisher. Yet "service to the state" ran the risk of tempting intellectuals to assume "that knowledge [wa]s effective chiefly in association with power," encouraging them "to serve the interests of power rather than the interests of truth."[63]

That the war could coax many American scholars across the boundary between open inquiry and propaganda was demonstrated by the fact that it clearly contributed to the creation of an environment in which, cloaked in the rhetoric of loyalty and security, several academic nonconformists were purged from their respective professions. Even Richard Ely, an iconoclast among economists if there ever was one, was provoked by the struggle with Germany to lash out at colleagues who, in his view, hindered the war effort. He argued that they should be summarily fired from their college and university positions. In a public address, in the last months of the war, Ely's anti-German agenda "clearly compromised the standards of [his] profession." Yet his career did not suffer. Rather, it was those who, like the radical economist Scott Nearing at the University of Pennsylvania, presumed to question the nation's involvement in the world war who were stigmatized as traitors, hounded and harassed.[64]

In the three decades since the founding of their professional society, mainstream American economists had achieved a great deal. With eminent satisfaction they could contemplate the successful creation of a visible national organization, a flagship scholarly journal, and an increasingly refined and credentialed cadre of experts. Amid such accomplishment there was little room for second thoughts or regrets about some of the potentially undemocratic and exclusionary tendencies of their professionalizing strategies. Even the conundrums of involvement with the government in wartime, as epitomized by various struggles over intellectual freedom of inquiry and speech, did little to dampen the enthusiasm and confidence that more and more surrounded this self-conscious enterprise of expertise.

In the minds of its chief architects, the shaping of an authoritative community of American economists was a self-contained process dependent upon cultivating and deploying disciplinary rigor, professional standards, and scholarly deportment. Historical circumstances, especially yet not solely those surrounding the Great War itself, placed new opportunities and challenges in the path of that evolution. Yet turning those situations to best effect served only to make more apparent not how far economists had come in their pursuit of influence but rather how far they still had to go. Indeed, when Irving Fisher had complained in 1902 that the opinion of economists on public matters "command[ed] less respect than it deserve[d]," he merely anticipated a rueful observation of Allyn Young made almost two decades later. A bit over a year before the United States entered World War I, Young unburdened himself to John Perrin of the Federal Reserve Bank of San Francisco. "[W]e economists failed in securing the influence that we might have had," Young argued, "largely because we have neglected to attempt to secure a concert of opinion among us on important questions." It was necessary, in Young's opinion, to find "effective ways of bringing [economic] opinion to a focus, and expressing it in a way to secure attention."[65]

As with so many other aspirations stoked by the nation's participation in "the most terrible and disastrous of all wars," the high hopes of Fisher and Young were unfulfilled when hostilities ceased in November 1918.[66] The interwar decades provided ever more promising, as well as complicated, terrain across which those goals could be further pursued. Constructing what Young had called a "concert of opinion" among economists was daunting enough; utilizing it "to secure attention" would put a premium on the profession's ability to garner respect for the objectivity of its practitioners and elicit appreciation for the scientific character of its discourse. To be sure, the articulation and acceptance of ideas played a singularly important role in this story. Yet it was events and institutions that powerfully framed the outcomes. American economists made their own history, but not wholly under circumstances of their own choosing.

2

Prospects, Puzzles, and Predicaments

[I]t is not the business of economists to teach woollen
manufacturers how to make and sell wool, or brewers
how to make and sell beer, or any other business
[people] how to do their job.
　—ARTHUR C. PIGOU (1922)[1]

A BIT OVER a month after the Armistice, the American Economic Association and
the American Statistical Association held a joint meeting on the benefits social
scientific knowledge and practice could offer the public sector. The conference
was, in particular, focused upon "[c]redentialed economic inquiry [that] a number
of prominent government and business figures . . . believe[d] could greatly enhance a society's capacity for planning and purposeful management." In arousing
this conviction among social scientists, the wartime experience had played an
important part. In fact, the pressures and challenges of national mobilization had
created an unprecedented demand for the skills of economists. While "hundreds"
of specialists ultimately took up responsibilities in a wide array of federal agencies, many of them were pooled into the Central Bureau of Planning and Statistics.
As one eminent authority on the history of this unique period in the formation of
the modern American state has concluded, the success of this first generation of
governmental economists who, in offices like that of the Central Bureau, gathered
and summarized data on national economic performance, "helped to change attitudes about the value and practical utility of the economist's product."[2]

Yet far from a full consignment of economic expertise, the war period actually
offered more in the way of a promissory note. To be sure, the administrative
and managerial achievements of 1917–18 "greatly increased the appreciation of
economics in the public service." Indeed, perhaps it was true, as one particularly
influential member of the founding cadre of AEA leaders claimed, that "[n]o other
academic discipline gained more in popular esteem." Nevertheless, like the Army
and Navy Departments, the nation's administrative agencies very quickly diminished in size and scope after 1918; for the last time in the twentieth century,
demobilization of both civilian and military activities within a wartime American
government was thorough and swift. Given the reality of a shrinking public sector,
American economists thus tended to look upon the experiences of the Great War
as less a compendium of impressive accomplishments than a set of tantalizing
prospects of what might have been.[3]

Whatever the inspirations (and frustrations) of the war episode, American economists—and their counterparts in many other fields—faced a novel challenge in

the interwar decades. On the one hand, they were resolutely committed to the pursuit of a professional agenda that would secure the benefits of a recognized and respected expertise. So essential to the success of that project were the cultivation and elaboration of rigorous theory coupled with powerful statistical tools that even a flirtation with the risks of esotericism might, at times, have to be endured. On the other hand, these same scholars sought a privileged and powerful access to public policy debate, formulation, and implementation. If, as the masterful Arthur Pigou had claimed in 1922, "it [wa]s not the business of economists to teach woollen manufacturers how to make and sell wool, or brewers how to make and sell beer," if a professionalized discourse necessarily removed economic analysis from the practical demands of day-to-day decision making, what plausible claims could be made for the distinctive place of the discipline in statecraft? Moreover, could these stipulations be successfully made without jeopardizing the status of economics as an objective and scientific field? The alluring possibilities for a young and vibrant profession thus also revealed themselves, in the interwar years, to be a series of puzzles.[4]

Circumscribing these prospects and puzzles were, as well, the peculiar characteristics of American political culture in the early decades of this century. In a nation in which a constitutional charter was most commonly interpreted to delimit federal power, in which the distinctions between individual rights and corporate license were always blurred, in which a tense standoff between the technocratic faith of Progressivism and the democratic instincts of populism (not to mention socialism) was neither acknowledged nor resolved, and in which international isolationism was at least a widespread and appealing aspiration if not a genuine material reality, any statist impulses of a professionalizing elite were problematic at best.[5]

If it was toward a managerial bureaucracy that many economists looked for a domain within which the usefulness and significance of their skills could be proved, the paucity of appropriate venues in Washington suitable for such a display and the associated underdevelopment of federal agencies (relative, for example, to their counterparts in western Europe) fit for the task constituted the central predicaments facing American economists in the 1920s and 1930s.[6] How could an ostensibly and increasingly technical, scientific, and objective expertise demonstrate its claims to recognition if the dimensions—both ideological and institutional—within which it could do so were so meager? Here were the features, the contours of a professionalizing project—the prospects, puzzles, and predicaments—that American economists faced during the time between the world wars.

––––––––––

Faced with the particular constraints within which their pursuit of public purpose and influence had to be pressed, some interwar American economists were captivated by opportunities they perceived in nonprofit-sector activities. Indeed, one possible goad to their efforts was the continuing success of agricultural economists in carving out special niches for their work within the comparatively sophisticated governmental apparatus of the United States Department of Agriculture.[7] In a series of adroit maneuvers, leading scholars such as Edwin Gay and Wesley Mitchell, among others, succeeded in garnering support from private foundations for policy-oriented economics investigation. At the same time, they tried to link the research establishments thus created to public-sector needs and thereby sought to cloak their work in the trappings of governmental authority and influence. In this regard, the examples of the Brookings Institution, the National Bureau of Economic Research, and the unprecedented statistical projects of Herbert Hoover's Commerce Secretariat were most telling. Latent in all these strategies, not surprisingly, were as well a series of increasingly strident debates about the future evolution of economic theory and its applicability to immediate policy concerns.

One of the first attempts to provide a venue for elite economic research in the private, nonprofit sector was actually made during World War I. The Institute for Government Research (IGR) was established in 1916 "for the purpose of promoting efficiency and effectiveness in government through the scientific study of administration." While the Rockefeller Foundation was involved in the institute's founding, it did not commit funds to the venture. Private donations provided initial support, and a founding board of trustees was composed of academics, nonprofit management professionals, and corporate leaders. By the early 1920s, Robert S. Brookings (a successful businessman from St. Louis) became the key figure in the work of the IGR. Believing that more research focused on economic issues per se would be a welcome addition to the institute's labors, Brookings created a companion institution in 1922, the Institute of Economics (IE). With the resources afforded by a ten-year Carnegie Corporation grant of $1.65 million, IE quickly eclipsed IGR in visibility and prestige. By 1927, the two institutes merged to form the Brookings Institution.[8]

Motivated by a similar desire to establish an economics research facility viewed to be free of special interests and partisan cranks, Edwin Gay and Wesley Mitchell started the National Bureau of Economic Research (NBER) in the winter of 1920. Administered by a board composed of government officials, leading academicians, and corporate managers, the Bureau received the bulk of its initial funding from the Carnegie Corporation and the Commonwealth Fund.[9] Since 1914, Gay and Mitchell had been much inspired, in their goal of founding an independent economics research institute, by the example of the Rockefeller Institute for Medical Research. Within two years they had developed an organizational plan and began to raise funds for its realization. By 1920, "in the context of the managerial visions and professional aspirations flowing from the war experience, [they were] successful in securing the funding, staff, directors, and endorsements to put the design into operation." The NBER became an immensely successful operation. While the Brookings Institution certainly achieved an enviable reputation for the professional quality of its staff, its engagement with specific policy issues and its increasing identification with leading figures in the Democratic Party soon earned it a partisan notoriety. By contrast, the NBER, not least because of its studious avoidance of policy recommendations, maintained a widely acknowledged image of disinterested and objective scholarship.[10]

Focusing the early work of the Bureau on national income accounting techniques, Gay (as NBER president) and Mitchell (as research director) were strategically well placed, for at the same time they served on a committee to assist in the creation of what ultimately became one of the most successful periodic publications of the United States Department of Commerce—the *Survey of Current Business*.[11] Along with its work on national economic statistics, the NBER also took up a major project on business cycles and economic fluctuations. Here, too, the fledgling organization was poised to reap the benefits of its close links with the central government, for Secretary of Commerce Hoover was also eager to establish a presidential conference on unemployment in the wake of the severe recession of 1920–21. Gay and Mitchell persuaded Hoover to engage the NBER as the empirical arm of the conference's inquiry, thereby securing the support of arguably the most influential presidential cabinet secretary in modern American history in winning foundation grants and awards for the Bureau's work. At the same time they had, whether consciously or not, provided an example of how a private research organization could combine forces with government in novel ways that "create[d] an American alternative to European statism" in the execution of economic policy analysis and implementation.[12]

Representing perhaps an "exceptionally American" approach to the problems of intellectual and political leadership in modern societies, the NBER exemplified an important strategy for professionalizing elites in the interwar period. As a professional research organization, the NBER offered a platform for the mobilization and promotion of a social science elite precisely at a time when, in comparison with other cases, especially in Europe, the proliferation of national funding mechanisms in the United States was still several years in the future. As a nonprofit entity, it served as a crucial link between academic economists and professional administrators and foundation executives in the philanthropic community—a bridge between individuals "who shared . . . postwar hopes for a new social science geared to managerial uses." Finally, as a technical and empirically oriented research enterprise, the Bureau served as an exemplar to many, in government, in the academy, and in the wider community, of the deployment of professional expertise in the solution of public problems. In all these respects, it is not surprising that individuals like Edwin Gay and Wesley Mitchell were thus well situated to sway continuing debates about the role and authority of economists.[13]

An economic history specialist who had also served as founding dean of the Harvard University Business School, Edwin F. Gay had been, for a short time, the editor of the *New York Evening Post*. An untiring activist, he "devoted his whole life to mobilizing social science in the service of society." In addition to the NBER, Gay had participated in the establishment of both the Council on Foreign Relations and the Social Science Research Council. A few years before the Great War, he had worked on behalf of the Massachusetts Citizens' Committee, along with the American Association for Labor Legislation, the Women's Educational and Industrial Union, and the Boston Chamber of Commerce, to secure the passage of new factory regulations. During the war, Gay became an effective and influential government economist—taking up duties as director of the Division of Planning and Statistics of the United States Shipping Board. In addition to his specific task of formulating trade regulations that would provide the largest possible merchant tonnage for Allied military needs, Gay also played a central part in various ad hoc groups working on federal statistics and plans. It was thus no surprise that in the postwar era he would focus his energies on projects like the NBER. Seeking "to influence policy through . . . private scholarly research agencies," the NBER "was but one agency in which Gay meant to use his training."[14]

Unlike his colleague Gay, Wesley Clair Mitchell was more the theoretician—although as an undergraduate student of Thorstein Veblen's at the University of Chicago he had, in the early 1890s, developed a taste for an economics that was "useful." Having completed a doctoral dissertation on the inflation caused by the American Civil War, Mitchell took up his first faculty appointment at the University of California in 1903. Ten years later, when he moved to Columbia, Mitchell began publishing research on what would remain the dominant focus of his studies for the rest of his life—business cycles. In addition to other public service assignments, he served as chief of the Price Section of the War Industries Board and went on to chair the Research Committee on Social Trends that was convened by President Hoover a decade later. In 1919, Mitchell briefly left the Columbia faculty to help create the New School for Social Research—an institution that, in no small measure, sought to become a haven for scholars whose opposition to American participation in the Great War had threatened their careers elsewhere.[15]

Surely not alone in their endeavors, Gay and Mitchell were perhaps the most visible and energetic representatives of what was fast becoming a distinctive breed of American economists—the "institutionalists." While John R. Commons of the University of Wisconsin and Veblen himself were often regarded as two of the most significant founders of an "American school of institutional economics," it was Mitchell most of all, with the crucial support and commitment of Gay, who set much of the methodological agenda for which the school would long be known.[16] In his emphasis on the singular importance of gathering data as extensively as possible, Mitchell marshaled an inductive approach to the study of society that, in his view, would help the discipline avoid errors that had ill served an earlier generation of scholars.

Private, nonprofit organizations like the National Bureau of Economic Research thus afforded American economists a special venue within which they could demonstrate the usefulness of their knowledge. Situated between a private sector somewhat suspicious of what academic economists had to offer and a public sector both small in size and ideologically predisposed to resist statist applications of social theory, the NBER was a crucial (and quite conspicuous) stage upon which a still relatively new expertise could be arrayed. At the same time, precisely because of its rather distinct intellectual pedigree (and the associated analytical proclivities of its guiding lights), the Bureau's cachet lent credibility and authority to those who, like Mitchell, wished to challenge prevailing disciplinary orthodoxy. In an ironic twist, the very success of professionalizers such as Mitchell brought to full boil debates over the theoretical trajectory of economics. Seeking greater visibility and influence, American economists of the interwar period found themselves forced back to the parsing of first principles.

Although not always understood or admitted by its most prominent protagonists, institutionalist economics found its intellectual roots in the work of Thorstein Veblen. It was the philosopher turned economist who had, in large measure, issued the clarion call of institutionalism in the late 1890s and early 1900s when he attacked neoclassical theory for what he took to be its excessive abstraction.[17] The inability and unwillingness of orthodox investigators to attend "to a consideration of the living items" of economic life was a direct consequence, Veblen believed, of a dysfunctional fascination with deductive modes of thinking. Orthodox economic theory, in his view, rested on a presumption of rationality that ignored the social and cultural factors that modulated behavior. The resulting separation of economic argument from factual detail left the discipline, as far as Veblen was concerned, "helplessly behind the times . . . unable to handle its subject-matter in a way to entitle it to standing as a modern science." A solution to this sorry state of affairs, he concluded, could only be found in close attention to empirical data and to the "laws of developmental continuity, genesis and proliferation" of an economy as a whole. Fighting words were these, for they challenged almost every claim held dear by Veblen's mainstream colleagues.[18]

Similarly, when Wesley Mitchell, or one of his colleagues or disciples, argued that a phenomenon like business cycles was "systematically generated by economic organization itself," neoclassical notions of market equilibrium—premised upon postulates concerning human instincts and cognition—were put at grave risk. The belief (and the determination) of orthodox theorists that economics could be a truly objective science of society rested on a commitment to the legitimacy of understanding the whole by studying its parts; a focus on individual transactions behavior thus served as an appropriate (and defensible) starting point for the science. If, however, this methodological posture were destabilized, if the parts were understood to be dependent on the whole, the need to address a diverse array of historical, sociological, and descriptive issues would leave economics bereft of a strong case for its disciplinary birthright. To be sure, the struggle between the institutionalists and the neoclassical theorists was a contest over the nature of economics itself; more than this, it was a confrontation over the professionalizing project that had virtually defined the field since the 1880s.[19]

Into the lists of the institutionalist debate came those determined to preserve for economics a pride of place, grounded in rigorous theory, among the social sciences. For these scholars it was clear that, in the words of the eminent Alfred Marshall, "the raison d'être of economics as a separate science [wa]s that it deal[t] chiefly with the part of [people's] action which [wa]s most under the control of measurable motives." It was necessarily the case, therefore, that economists had to employ "selective principles" in order to understand human behavior. Utilizing "a series of deductions from the fundamental concept of scarcity," the discipline's practitioners were thus in a position to engage in truly "analytical" studies that were, given a "correspondence [between] original assumptions and the facts," realistic approximations of social conduct. While history, institutions, law, and ideology could provide more detailed and nuanced explanations of actual economic events, the core analytical principles of economic explanation remained distinct.[20]

By contrast, the institutionalists conceived of economics as a far more catholic field in which any claims to realism rested perforce on broadly construed disciplinary boundaries. Indeed, both Mitchell and Veblen themselves had aggressively attacked the manner in which neoclassical investigators ignored human activity that could not be understood simply as the "rational" and calculating response of individuals to the constraints of the market. To their minds "such institutions as the market, trade, contract, property, and competition" were themselves the product of political, cultural, and historical circumstances all of which were worthy of the economist's attention. If such broad delineations of the "economic" were not embraced by scholars, if the discipline did not study "historical-cultural problems" and the institutions that at a given time and place mapped them, economics itself would simply substitute scholasticism for authentic social science. In their disputes over the very domains of their field, institutionalist and neoclassical economists alike made vividly clear their methodological and epistemological convictions.[21]

That neoclassical theorists would emphasize the superiority of their approach to economic analysis because of its focus on "measurable motives" in human life was both revealing and, in an important sense, specious. Revealing because, by their insistence on the need to utilize particular analytical propositions concerning economic behavior, neoclassical researchers exhibited a self-conscious determination to make their work conceptually distinct from that of other social scientists and statisticians; specious because, though the principle of an individual's rational and calculated pursuit of utility maximization seemed an intuitively clear and plausible foundation on which to construct an economic science, there was obviously no clear and unambiguous way in which to identify (and thereby quantify) individuals' preferences and motivations.[22] Abstract reasoning aside, any *empirical* economics necessarily rested on the manipulation of price and quantity data, the source of which was to be found in day-to-day market transactions rather than some ethereal gradient of individual satisfaction. In the absence of running controlled experiments, economists were faced with the choice of either arguing by deduction from certain axiomatic starting points or indulging in a simple (some said naïve) empiricism. In point of fact, it was this conceptual dichotomy that framed one of the most celebrated, and arguably one of the last, substantive confrontations between institutionalism and neoclassicism.

From the moment that Wesley Mitchell and his colleagues at the NBER began their voluminous publishing on the measurement and understanding of business cycles, their studies invited the critical reception of neoclassical theorists worried about its empiricist bias. By the late 1920s, a series of attacks on the work of the

NBER began, both in published forums and at conferences. Although the finest published expression of the neoclassical anxiety over institutionalism came to light only after World War II, its sentiments well summarized the series of debates that had transpired throughout the interwar period. In a 1947 review of one of the most visible products of the NBER research program, Tjalling C. Koopmans, writing in the prestigious *Review of Economics and Statistics*, excoriated the institutionalist paradigms that informed the work of the NBER and complained that the book in question was solely "concerned with the character of [business cycles] rather than with the underlying economic behavior of [individuals]." In provocatively titling his essay "Measurement without Theory," Koopmans sought to emphasize his conviction that an institutional economics that occupied itself with the compilation of data alone, even on such a dramatic and significant economic phenomenon as the business cycle, was intellectually suspect and scientifically immature. He concluded his assessment of this latest volume from the NBER enterprise by noting its "unbendingly empiricist . . . outlook" and "its decision not to use theories of man's [*sic*] economic behavior." These qualities of the publication "limit[ed] the value to economic science and to the maker of policies, of the results obtained or obtainable by the methods developed." Representing an entire generation of neoclassical theorists, Koopmans linked the "lack of guidance from theoretical considerations" with "[t]he pedestrian character of the statistical devices employed" in the institutionalist research paradigm. A scientific economics, one that would command the respect of the learned community while at the same time influencing "the maker of policies," had necessarily to be made of sterner stuff.[23]

If the outcome of a theoretical confrontation with the institutionalists seemed, in the minds of neoclassical economists, a foregone conclusion, a resolution of the challenges institutionalism posed regarding the practicality and influence of the discipline was not. Wheresoever the twists and turns of academic debate might have led, the force of circumstances could not be denied. An increasingly complicated array of policy questions imposed themselves on the consciousness of economists; answering them in unambiguous fashion was the goal of analysts of all theoretical persuasions. Institutionalists like Wesley Mitchell might attack the neoclassical paradigm for its normative agnosticism, fearing the development of "an academic discipline, cultivated by professors and neglected by [people] of action, modest in its pretensions to practical usefulness, more conspicuous for consistency and erudition than for insight." Neoclassical investigators, like Frank Knight of the University of Chicago, could reject an institutionalist strategy that minimized the importance of positive analysis for the successful prosecution of any scientific research protocol, insisting that "the exercise of informed judgment," while useful for policy making, was nevertheless not a substitute "for reasoning according to the canons of science." Yet all were united in the conviction that economics was a uniquely valuable discipline, one that could powerfully inform the realization of a public purpose. Struggles over the relative merits (and indeed prestige) of theoretical and applied research aside, professional authority was the common ground about which contending "schools" of economic thought could instinctively agree. It was only necessary to locate the venues within which that expertise might be most efficaciously displayed.[24]

As the cases of the Brookings Institution and the National Bureau of Economic Research demonstrate, American economists in the early twentieth century were in no position simply to choose the institutional formats through which they could demonstrate their skill at meeting particular public policy needs. Often they had to invent them; sometimes they had to suffer them. In every respect they found themselves at the mercy of the relatively undeveloped state bureaucracy in Washington. As with so much else of the federal bureaucracy, the coming of the Great War had only served to reveal the undeveloped nature of those structures within which and by which professional economic expertise could be brought to the attention of and utilized by government officials. Secretary of the Treasury William Gibbs McAdoo put it well, four months after the nation's formal entry into World War I, when he wrote President Wilson to complain that the conflict "ha[d] brought to [his] Department a large number of new problems for which there [wa]s little precedent in the history of the country." Resolving those questions necessitated, he believed, the use of "a number of special reports by experts." Be that as it may, the secretary found himself "handicapped because of the lack of any available fund for th[at] purpose."[25]

In mentioning the constraints imposed by a lean ministerial budget upon the commissioning of professional consultants to assist the government, McAdoo had placed his finger on but a small part of the difficulty. Even in the progressivist atmosphere that Woodrow Wilson brought to Washington, the identification and employment of expertise in pursuit of various administration objectives was an extremely informal process, one utterly dependent upon personalized networks of deference and authority, not to mention political calculation. But a few weeks after his first inauguration, the president made this circumstance clear to his Treasury secretary (and other cabinet officials) when he directed that all proposals for executive branch appointment be accompanied "with a memorandum showing, if possible, the political affiliations of the person suggested, stating by whom [the] name was recommended, and as many other particulars as might assist . . . in determining just what [their] temper and attitude in affairs would be." Substantive Civil Service reform may have been a feature of Chester Arthur's presidency (and the passage of the Pendleton Act) in the early 1880s; some three decades later, clearly the highest echelons of the executive service would be peopled still by those with appropriate imprimaturs, the retainers of high political privilege.[26]

Having the ear of the president and thus influencing the promulgation of national policy on a wide assortment of significant issues taken up at the time was thus a not uncomplicated matter for a generation of professionalizing economists. Whether it was the creation of a national banking system, the revision of tariff schedules, or indeed the effective management of the unique resource problems occasioned by mobilization for world war, the activism (and circumstances) of the Wilson presidency proffered a tantalizing set of policy questions that experts could address. Doing so, however, was in large measure an unsystematic affair premised, on the one side, upon patronage and, on the other, upon sheer luck. No matter how elite their institutional affiliations, in seeking to persuade the president of the probity of a particular policy strategy, most economists, in direct correspondence, had to compete with the entreaties of political leaders, party functionaries, prominent citizens, and of course the occasional "unsound" expositor.[27]

Professional economists were, in fact, infrequently consulted and thus became only a small voice in the momentous debate over the creation of a Federal Reserve System, the single most important economic policy achievement of the Wilson administration.[28] If Yale's Arthur Hadley felt possessed to communicate with the president in July 1913 to express his opposition to what he believed were the inflationary tendencies of the Owen-Glass Bill that would create a Federal Reserve, nevertheless he was also moved to apologize for writing directly. Feeling no such compunction, Edwin Seligman of Columbia implored Wilson to "to use [his] influence to turn the bill in the right direction." Somewhat defensively, he allowed that "[e]conomists differ on pretty much everything"; indeed "there [we]re cranks even among economists," but "really important men" in the field were agreed that Owen-Glass had dangerous implications for the national cost of living. Seligman was particularly upset that Member of Congress Carter Glass, rather than soliciting the input of professionals, had apparently consulted with individuals who "would get very few votes from [their] compeers as . . . expert[s] of the first magnitude." Noting "the political difficulties involved," the professor nonetheless urged President Wilson "to remain in harmony with the important teachings of experience elsewhere and with the best thought on the subject" of financial regulation and monetary control. Hadley's timidity and Seligman's pique spoke volumes about the liminal status professional economists held both on Capitol Hill and at 1600 Pennsylvania Avenue, N.W.[29]

Operating the new Federal Reserve network, managing an internal revenue system empowered by the Sixteenth Amendment to tax incomes, and dealing with the always vexing questions of tariff policy were obvious and no doubt enticing arenas within which economic expertise could be deployed. Yet again, the special opportunities afforded by Wilson's progressive politics notwithstanding, American economists more often than not found themselves on the outside looking in. During the first summer of his administration, Wilson was content, for example, to leave to the Treasury Department alone the task of dividing up the nation into internal revenue districts. The "scientific rearrangement" of those precincts was a task that McAdoo took up on his own. Similarly, commencing operation of the Federal Reserve System was a time more for consideration of patronage appointments to the Board of Governors itself than for close attention to the opinions of academicians, nonprofit organization analysts, or eminent authorities.[30]

Most likely because of its disproportionate significance in national politics at the time, the question of tariff scheduling did admit of some degree of expert advising in high governmental circles. President Wilson, at the urging of both

Treasury secretary McAdoo and Federal Trade Commission chairman Edward N. Hurley, saw to it that coveted Tariff Commission appointments were tendered to the likes of Irving Fisher, Ida Tarbell, and Frank Taussig. Indeed, the president thought it further prudent to ask for Taussig's advice on subsequent appointments. At the same time, the considerations of party politics always intruded. McAdoo could note with satisfaction that the commission was "well balanced," with, among others, "practical shipping men," "one admiralty lawyer," "one electrical engineer," and a lumber producer. The president appointed a "Judge Wallace of Missouri" to the commission on the suggestion of McAdoo, who, in a letter of recommendation on the jurist, noted that "[h]e [wa]s a delightful man, and . . . would make an excellent member of the [commission], although . . . not an economist in the professional sense of the term." Needless to say, the avowedly political nature of the commission and its work was stipulated to by statute; enabling legislation specified that "not more than three of the members of the Commission [could] be of the same political party." What's more, as the fiasco of the Smoot-Hawley Tariff would show during the Hoover presidency, the opinions of professional economists on tariff matters, no matter how strenuously put, held no special power over the conduct of lawmakers.[31]

It was, however, the extraordinary exigencies imposed by the nation's participation in global war that made most vivid both the potential need for professional economics advising in governmental affairs and the limitations that contemporary practice imposed on its realization. Before the nation's overt entry into the conflict, the economy succumbed to the pressures of World War I. The disruption of maritime trade caused by the strategic offensive of Germany's Imperial Navy immediately depressed tariff receipts and, combined with the attendant decline in traffic on the Panama Canal, by its deleterious impact on the volume of tolls, siphoned off some $60 million in federal revenues. McAdoo believed it essential that internal taxation be adjusted to make up the difference—yet his proposals in this regard, not to mention his quantitative estimates, were not informed by expert assessments. Allocative distortions within the domestic economy itself, made worse by American entry into the war in the spring of 1917, made the gap between administrative decision making and professional expertise only more obvious.[32]

Of most immediate concern after Congress declared war on Germany and its allies was the management of inflation. Incipient food shortages and bottlenecks in the supply of strategic materials militated in favor of price controls. At the same time, the need to provide for the optimal utilization of an array of resources, both for the national war effort and for the needs of Allied governments, prompted the creation of a wartime administrative apparatus that, at long last, provided unique opportunities for the employment of professional economists. In addition, "[t]he responsibility of lending $3,000,000,000 to foreign governments making war upon the enemies of the United States" imposed novel claims upon the workings of both the State Department and the Treasury. While in ever-increasing numbers economists left their civilian pursuits to toil at the execution of these remarkable federal tasks, a general economic strategy for the making of war remained the result of a sometimes chaotic interaction between the president, his cabinet, and prominent citizens. Wilson had no reluctance, for example, in encouraging his Treasury secretary to consider the imposition of a land-value tax to help finance the war—all because a Jersey City attorney, "of somewhat erratic temper but of very clear grasp of some fundamental things," had captured his attention by invoking their previous acquaintance.[33]

Above all it was on matters of resource allocation that the economic pressures of the Great War made themselves most dramatically felt. It was in the effort to alleviate those burdens that professionals had the most, albeit an attenuated, influence. The distortions attendant upon price controls, whereby efforts to keep the costs of crucial materials down generated scarcity by affording the manufacturer an insufficient profit margin and thereby an inadequate incentive to increase supply, were quickly noted. Their rectification was the direct result of the intervention of such distinguished economic authorities as Benjamin Strong, governor of the Federal Reserve Bank of New York. It was on Strong's advice that McAdoo persuaded the president, in the winter of 1918, to see to "increasing the reward in some way to those who produce [essential] articles and when a price [wa]s fixed . . . too low, consumption of th[o]se articles for purposes not necessary to the war . . . restricted."[34]

Transportation problems were one of the most significant preoccupations of the wartime administration. The head of the Food Administration, Herbert Hoover, forcefully pointed out to the president that inefficient utilization of rolling stock jeopardized Allied food shipments and, at the same time, even limited supplies for domestic consumption. Cross-country troop movements further hampered the timely shipment of agricultural and industrial supplies. McAdoo even challenged War Secretary Newton Baker to shift the transportation of doughboys from inland routes to the coastal waterways. Yet in his capacity as director general of the railroads for the wartime Railroad Administration, Treasury Secretary McAdoo troubled himself little with the cultivation and employment of economics advisers. Instead, he strove to solve the many problems with which he was faced on his own, at times reaching out to other civilian appointees to such special units as the War Industries Board, most prominent among them Bernard Baruch. Amid allocative problems "without precedent alike in kind and in scope," the nation's highest leadership remained attuned to instincts honed in the time-honored traditions of party loyalties and bureaucratic choreographies.[35]

On problems with war finance, professional expertise was also unsystematically applied. Having heard that the administration was considering the use of income taxation rather than debt accumulation as the primary means of paying for the war, AEA president John Commons wrote President Wilson on the eve of the chief executive's submission of a war message to the Congress. He encouraged Wilson to note the work of O.M.W. Sprague, Converse Professor of Banking and Finance at the Harvard University Business School, a well-known authority on the issue of public spending. "[A]ny one who has read Professor Sprague's scholarly and scientific analysis of th[is] subject," Commons informed the president, "will at once agree that if the administration follows [an income taxation] plan it will not only meet the popular demand of the country but will be scientifically correct." In what was singular testimony to the rather modest stature of professional economists in political circles, it was in a somewhat plaintive note that the elected executive of the nation's leading professional economics organization could only suggest a course of action to the nation's president in time of war. Clearly this was a frail reed on which to premise the hopes and aspirations of a social scientific elite. If the nation's first involvement in a world war did little to enhance the visibility of professional economists, what would peacetime bring?[36]

The Armistice brought a rapid demobilization not simply of the nation's armed forces but also of the relatively large governmental apparatus that had emerged to prosecute the war in the first instance. While, on the one side, this transition to "normalcy" severely circumscribed what limited opportunities might have existed for the deployment of social scientific expertise in government, it also, on the other side, set the stage for the Republican ascendancy of the interwar decades. Ironically enough, three successive presidents drawn from the ranks of the Grand Old Party arguably did more in the way of facilitating what would ultimately become the increasing engagement of professional economists with statist objectives than their immediate predecessor, who had proudly carried the banner of the Progressive Democracy. If Woodrow Wilson's "New Freedom" signaled the beginnings of a federalism that would become a defining characteristic of twentieth-century American political history, it was nevertheless the administrations of Warren Harding, Calvin Coolidge, and Herbert Hoover that gave professional social scientists, in particular economists, the first genuine sense of the role they could play in national affairs. Perhaps it is safe to say that whatever irony seems apparent in this generalization is more an artifact of perceptions born of subsequent experience rather than what were at the time contemporary views. After all, from the time of its founding on the eve of the Civil War, the Republican Party had always paid far more attention to political economic issues than its more regionally focused and ideologically diverse counterpart. An Alexander Hamilton could have richly appreciated the fact that it was Lincoln's party, not Jefferson's, that oversaw the first stirrings of a centralized, "associative" state in the interwar decades of this century. As retainers of that process, economists stood to benefit.[37]

It is, of course, worth emphasizing that individual practitioners, in particular those with special standing in the economics profession, had long believed their input on public policy questions was useful and constructive. That conviction in fact had been an animating principle for some of the founders of the American Economic Association itself. As AEA secretary-treasurer, Thomas Carver had had no hesitancy in writing President William Howard Taft on Christmas Eve in 1912 to urge him to approve a pending immigration restriction bill before the Congress. Skirting the edges of the AEA's strictures regarding partisanship, Carver invoked the sentiments of his colleagues when he declared on that occasion "that the economists of the country [we]re more and more coming to the opinion that some sort of restriction of immigration [wa]s of paramount importance." Without benefit of data, in fact, he went on to note "that a proper restriction of immigration w[ould] make unnecessary a great deal of the social legislation which [had been] placed upon the statute books of so many states and municipalities." Indeed, Carver's intrepid communication with the president merely represented the public service aspirations of the vast majority of economists; an AEA Committee on Practical Training for Public Service was in fact created shortly thereafter.[38]

The sporadic intervention of an AEA official in a public debate was, to be sure, no substitute for the genuine article of privileged access to the minds of policy makers. Perhaps it was this uncompromising observation that Carver's successor, Allyn Young, had had in mind when he told the distinguished Edwin Cannan of his disappointment with the relative isolation of economists from the pressing controversies attendant upon the coming of World War I. "[T]he world still seems to be ruled by economic notions born in the days when national policies were framed in terms of dynastic advantage," he wrote a month before President Wilson delivered his ultimatum to Berlin regarding the practice of unrestricted submarine warfare on the high seas. Clearly "[t]his [wa]s something about which the economists of the world [should] have something to say." Yet Young feared "that in [the United States] many of [his colleagues] ha[d] lost the courage of [thei]r convictions and [we]re content to be mere critics and expounders." If the Great War did not serve to embolden social science professionals, what would?[39]

Modest attempts to link the work of the Association with wartime concerns had in fact gone forward. Henry Adams of the University of Michigan planned a special session of the 1916 annual meeting focused on the economics of "national preparedness." Carver saw to the creation of the Committee on Teaching Economics in Secondary Schools, believing that the world conflict offered a unique opportunity to attract youngsters' interest in the discipline. Special task forces on economic issues related to mobilization and war had also been formed. Yet none of these initiatives garnered much public attention, and the energy surrounding them quickly dissipated with the war's end. Even the Armistice did little to stimulate organized interest in matters pertaining to demobilization and postwar reconstruction.[40]

It was peace, not war, that brought American economists into closer proximity with statist designs; it was Republican administrations concerned with the needs of a burgeoning economy, not a Democratic government overwhelmed by world war and the negotiation of the Treaty of Versailles, that provided the opportunity. Of singular importance to this development was the unique visionary and tireless advocate of a "rationalized" capitalism, Secretary of Commerce Herbert Hoover. Born of a hardscrabble background in eastern Iowa, Hoover trained as a geologist at Stanford University, worked as a miner in Nevada, and then moved on to an engineering position with a San Francisco corporation. The "Great Engineer" accumulated wealth and stature quite rapidly, moving through a variety of executive positions in corporate life and traveling worldwide in the deployment of his skills. By 1914 he was in London, a venue from which he organized food relief for the beleaguered people of Belgium, who, by dint of geography, had suffered some of the worst of what the kaiser's "Schlieffen Plan" had had to offer. So successful was Hoover in this widely admired (and publicized) activity that President Wilson charged him with responsibility to organize the nation's agricultural sectors for war mobilization in the spring of 1917. Actively courted by the Democrats to run for the presidency, Hoover remained nonetheless a loyal Republican. When Warren Harding took office in March 1921, Hoover assumed the Commerce portfolio; in the words of one of his less ardent admirers, he became "secretary of Commerce and assistant secretary of everything else."[41]

Within months of his move to Washington, Hoover began the transformation of the Department of Commerce for which he is arguably best known. Determined to estimate and gather data that would allow for precise measurements of national economic performance, particularly with a view toward developing the means to anticipate cyclical instability, Hoover found himself drawn to the work of leading economists generally and, to be sure, of the institutionalists at the Institute for Government Research and the National Bureau of Economic Research. Unlike Woodrow Wilson, not to mention William Gibbs McAdoo, Hoover enjoyed close personal and professional ties with some of the leading economists of his day. Frank Taussig thought of the commerce secretary as his "much beloved friend," and Wesley Mitchell was as intimately involved as anyone with a variety of projects spawned under Hoover's department leadership. Hoover aggressively cultivated ties with the professoriate; when he desired the services of particular academics, he made very clear, both to them and to their institutions, that public service was both a duty and a beneficence. When, for example, he wished to extend the term of service for Julius Klein as director of the Foreign and Domestic Commerce Bureau (of the Department of Commerce), Hoover appealed directly to the president of Harvard University. "Dr. Klein has secured the confidence of Congress and the commercial community," Hoover wrote A. Lawrence Lowell in the winter of 1922. "[I]t is vital . . . that [he] should stay[.] Another year for Dr. Klein in this position will give him a reputation throughout the United States preeminently as a most constructive economist in international economic questions." It seemed obvious to Hoover that Harvard stood to gain from this arrangement because "it add[ed] strongly to a university when [government service] add[ed] strongly to the reputation of its men." Lowell agreed, and he renewed Klein's leave of absence.[42]

That he could so deftly characterize the mutual aggrandizement that stood at the center of any interaction between government officials and professional academics was eloquent testimony to the power of Hoover's grasp of the vast potential of an associative state whose construction he envisioned. His contemporaries among economists similarly appreciated the point. During his first summer in Washington, Hoover commenced the work on revision and elaboration of national economic and social statistics that stands to this day not simply as one of the crowning achievements of his public career but also as a standard of excellence in data gathering toward which most foreign governments and international agencies still aspire. Given his special perception of the possibilities inherent in the utilization of professional expertise on behalf of a public purpose, it was only natural for Hoover to turn to academicians, rather than bureaucrats or politicians, in what was then a novel statistical enterprise. Economists were only too eager to return the compliment.

His experience as both an engineer and a uniquely accomplished business executive had convinced Hoover that "certain types of statistical publicity" would serve "to mitigate booms and crises." By providing investors and managers the requisite information to anticipate fluctuations in trade, he believed, centrally reported data would alleviate the worst consequences of forecasting error. That such information would be provided by the executive branch of the federal government would overcome any anxieties within the business community concerning its veracity and reliability.[43] A close reading of contemporary literature on business cycle theory led Hoover to the conclusion that an essential starting point was to be found in the collection and distribution of periodic information on nationwide plant construction and orders for materials. He turned to Taussig for advice. The Harvard economist was delighted to assist; he encouraged Hoover to expand the effort to include the collection of "statistics of security issues and flotations" and of "statistics of stocks of goods in dealers' hands, both wholesale and retail." While he also encouraged the secretary to consult "bankers and business men," he felt it essential that Hoover secure the guidance of "the two best experts on the subject"—Wesley Mitchell and Warren Persons (the distinguished Harvard econometrician). Taussig's suggestions were taken up with alacrity; his input became a crucial ingredient in the development of the celebrated (and continuing) Commerce Department publication, the *Survey of Current Business*.[44]

Emboldened by the immediate success of the *Survey*, Hoover worked, in succeeding years, to expand its coverage. Beyond that specific task, he also commissioned a general investigation that would formulate a strategy to expand "the statistical gathering and reporting functions of government" as a whole. He contracted with the Institute for Government Research to lead the study, and he created an oversight committee composed of representatives from the national Chamber of Commerce, the Federated Farm Bureau, the American Bankers Association, the American Federation of Labor, the American Statistical Association, the National Bureau of Economic Research, and the American Economic Association to provide guidance. Even if the relative prominence of institutionalists (from both the IGR and the NBER) in Hoover's Commerce secretariat discomfited some more theoretically (and neoclassically) oriented colleagues, the opportunities thus afforded the profession as a whole were undeniably welcome. Here, after all, was a seemingly objective undertaking about which all economists— irrespective of methodological, let alone ideological, stripe—could agree: the development of ever-more-rigorous and thorough statistics and related data. The deployment of expert skills and the realization of professionalizing strategies, both bearing the exceedingly valuable warrant of governmental requisition, had rarely been more successfully linked.[45]

Born of his faith that accurate statistical reporting might serve well to attenuate the business cycle, Secretary Hoover moved on to launch an investigation of what he took to be the worst representation of economic instability itself—unemployment. By mid-fall of 1921, he had helped create the President's Conference on Unemployment, for which he leased the services of the National Bureau of Economic Research, charged to elucidate "the causes and remedies of periodic business depressions." It was of course in this context that Wesley Mitchell and Edwin Gay had triumphed in yoking the fortunes of their still-fledgling nonprofit research organization both to the federal government and to the likes of the Carnegie Corporation and the Commonwealth Fund, all of which participated in funding the NBER commission. Through the Bureau's board of directors, leading economists such as John Commons and Allyn Young also figured significantly in the work of the conference. Conference secretary Edward Eyre Hunt, a special deputy of Hoover's at Commerce, was filled with enthusiasm regarding the participation of the economists at the NBER. He put it well to Henry Pritchett, president of the Carnegie Corporation, when he noted that "[t]he great quality of such investigations . . . wa]s that they [c]ould be carried out under auspices as guarantee[d] not only the soundness of its conclusions, but w[ould] carry weight with the entire community." It was thus essential that the study "be technically first-class, and that it be presented to the business public under the auspices of a disinterested group." Hunt was, moreover, quite optimistic that systematic control of the cycle was well within reach. The clear success of the Federal Reserve Board in "prevent[ing] the crisis of 1920 from degenerating into panic" had been, in his view, a harbinger of great things to come. The ultimate outcome of the conference's labors was the 1923 NBER volume *Business Cycles and Unemployment*.[46]

Along with the Conference on Unemployment, a Commerce Department "Study of Business Cycles" provided another venue within which professional economists could flourish. Several investigators, drawn from the NBER, the Wharton School at the University of Pennsylvania, the Harvard Business School, and the statistical departments of certain major banks, trade associations, and the national Chamber of Commerce were drafted for the project. When, in the spring of 1923, the working group issued its "Report of the Business Cycle Committee," the response was quite positive and, for all involved, quite gratifying. William Berridge, an economics professor at Brown University, saw to the distribution of literally hundreds of copies of the report throughout New England, so impressed was he with its quality. Hoover himself, never reluctant to seize an opportunity to garner attention for his department, its work, and its retainers (both inside and outside of Washington), sought a powerful endorsement for the report. Given that the document provided genuine insight "on the forces that affect[ed] the ebb and flow of business," it was obvious to the secretary that "[i]t would certainly give the subject attention and wider consideration if the Federal Reserve Board [w]ould call authoritative attention to it in their bulletin and commend its consideration and economic solidity." Fed governor Adolph C. Miller did Hoover's bidding. Perhaps the greatest accolade the report could receive came in the form of the eagerness of the Carnegie Corporation, four years later, to commit funds for a second business cycle study. Carnegie managers had obviously tolerated the hyperbole of Edward Hunt when he had declared that the first cycle study had been "one of the most important in [American] economic history." More to the point, they had been persuaded by his assessment that the report had "served to carry over into [American] business thought and practice, matters which economists had known for some time, but which business [people] with a few exceptions had ignored." For the interwar community of American economists, Hunt's words spoke of a triumph long awaited.[47]

It is therefore hardly surprising that the publication of the first business cycle report evoked a great deal of interest among economics researchers far afield of Washington. Once the report was released, Mitchell was detailed to attend a variety of meetings across the country announcing its findings. Leading academicians, such as Frank Dixon of Princeton's Department of Economics, sought permission to employ the data that the business cycle study team had amassed in order to pursue their own research agendas. Such authorization was freely given. Indeed, during the execution of the study itself, Hunt and Mitchell had frequently consulted about the current scholarly literature, establishing in the process a network of correspondents to be kept informed of the latest and most high quality analysis being done, across the entire spectrum of academic research institutions, on economic fluctuations and their consequences. Here again, government needs, public service work, and the professionalizing structures and qualitative screens afforded by prestigious journals and publishing houses smoothly dovetailed in the pursuit of common objectives.[48]

Worthy and successful outcomes aside, the culmination of the endeavors of both the Conference on Unemployment and the Business Cycle Committee also served to resurrect precisely those questions regarding the links between social scientific research and public policy advocacy that had preoccupied American economists since the late nineteenth century. Wesley Mitchell had been particularly concerned that the Commerce Department appreciate that the goal of the business cycles study did not include formulating "recommendations concerning policy." To Edward Hunt he made clear that "the Bureau [wa]s by its constitution limited to the accurate and impartial determination of facts." It was thus imperative that the published findings of the commissioned investigations the NBER oversaw "be fact-finding reports alone." Hunt took the point, but he (and Hoover) were always eager to explore what possibilities might exist for the practical application of professional practice.[49]

If Mitchell and his colleagues in New York insisted on refining their manuscripts on behalf of a policy agnosticism, so be it. Officials at the Department of Commerce were nevertheless far from reluctant to question the policy relevance of what was being done. Members of the Conference on Unemployment, for example, were asked if their work might not provide "a constructive national program" to mediate wage and hours disputes between capital and labor. Mitchell worked to table the request; when pressed, he enlisted the support of conference participant Owen Young, a lawyer then serving as the board chair of General Electric (who would be mentioned in both 1928 and 1932 as a possible Democratic Party nominee for president), in deflecting the issue. At the same time, and with Commerce Department urging, Mitchell did not hesitate to encourage conference colleagues to write their senators in support of a pending public works bill that, he believed, could mitigate unemployment. A concern with professional detachment and the cultivation of an image of disinterested scholarship prevailed over any temptation to become part of public policy debates that, while furnishing exposure and even fame for some economists, could always threaten to get out of hand. Even so, professional expertise could still serve to animate one's own political commitments.[50]

Through the balance of the twenties, Herbert Hoover's Commerce Department continued to provide an important venue within which professional economists could engage in research infused with a public purpose (and notoriety) yet seemingly unsullied by normative agendas. An effort to spearhead an economy-wide program of "waste elimination" and the standardization of production practices, so characteristic of the interventionist strategies that Hoover brought to his duties as a cabinet officer, utilized the same mix of public-sector and nonprofit-sector resources that had made possible the unemployment and business cycle studies. The Bureau of Business Research at Harvard University was employed for consultative purposes in this project; its participation was made possible by crucial funding provided by the Carnegie Foundation. Concerned that the competitive proliferation of products, coupled with the linked multiplication of production methods and techniques, generated costly and profligate duplications of effort, Hoover and his colleagues were eager to promulgate "standardized" regimens of production, distribution, and inventory control. Hardly a successful initiative (indeed, the goal of "simplified practice" clashed directly with significant changes in corporate strategies for the interwar era), the "waste elimination" studies of Commerce nonetheless exhibited the special combination of statist agendas, nonprofit sector activities, and professional expertise that was the signature of Hoover's distinctive leadership.[51]

Closely linked to Hoover's progressivist endeavors to "rationalize" economic practice in the 1920s were the reformist activities of Secretary of State Charles Evans Hughes. Concerned to place the vetting and recruitment of personnel for the Foreign Service on a more meritocratic basis, thereby building upon the "good government" achievements he had overseen as governor of New York prior to World War I, Hughes succeeded in provoking a wholesale reconsideration of civil service procedures generally and of the utilization of experts in federal agencies in particular. While the Rogers (Foreign Service) Act of 1924 established the first specific requirements for employment in the nation's diplomatic corps, it was the Classification Act of 1923 that looked toward a far broader reorganization of the national civil service as a whole. Such changes in federal workforce operations necessarily had an impact on professional groups; in this regard, American economists were no exception.

Passed by the Sixty-seventh Congress, the Classification Act provided for the categorization and grading of technical and professional employees in the civilian branches of the federal government. Like their counterparts in many other fields, the leaders of the American Economic Association succeeded in linking this particular federal effort to their own continuing pursuit of professional cultivation. An early 1924 resolution of the AEA Executive Committee began steps to "secure the classification of the technical economists in the professional and scientific services" of the federal government. The findings of a committee tasked to collate the results of this survey were reported to the Personnel Classification Board (of the U.S. Civil Service Commission), the Committees on the Civil Service of the two houses of the Congress, and to the Executive Office of the President. In many respects the classification survey powerfully resonated with what had begun a decade earlier as part of the effort to support national mobilization for war. Yet here, in peacetime, it extended beyond the confines of an emergency canvass and became instead the basis of a continuing and ever-more-specific detailing of economics subspecialties. Indeed, for some older members of the profession, the steps taken to stipulate as precisely as possible the expertise of individual practitioners could at times appear to narrow, and thereby adulterate, what the discipline as a whole had to offer. For most colleagues, however, that governmental needs could jibe so well with professionalizing strategies was cause for satisfaction rather than regret.[52]

Statist concerns during the interwar period further broadened the opportunities and public engagement of American economists in the realms of international finance, world trade policy, and macroeconomic management at home. Even so, the record of accomplishment in this regard was mixed. As Commerce secretary, Hoover was, for example, particularly eager to send a "technical assistant" drawn from an economics faculty in the United States to assist the U.S. delegation at the 1924 conference on German war reparations and continuing postwar reconstruction—a gathering that would, among other things, result ultimately in the formulation of the Dawes Plan. Joseph Davis of Stanford University, a future AEA president, was specifically proposed for the task. Yet bureaucratic politics prevailed, and Walter Tower, the commercial attaché at the London embassy, was selected for the purpose. Similarly, Hoover believed it essential that "experts" rather than "public personages" be part of the national delegation poised to attend the 1927 International Economic Conference. But there was an inadequate budget to provide for "the expenses and salaries" of such individuals. In the end, Henry M. Robinson, president of the First National Bank of Los Angeles and a member of the Dawes Commission, participated as an "expert," paying a substantial part of his own costs.[53] While the instinct to see to the deployment of expertise in economic matters of state intensified throughout the 1920s, the mechanisms and the resources to secure that arrangement remained incomplete and most often ineffective.

Interwar trade protectionism afforded another context within which an emergent professionalism clashed with prevailing political prejudices and with traditional institutional arrangements. When agricultural interests sought to preserve a relatively high domestic price structure—that had emerged as a result of World War I—while seeking to "dump" farm surpluses overseas at very low values, the opinion of professional economists was, at least at the legislative level, uniformly ignored. The congressional debate that eventuated in passage of the McNary-Haugen Act provoked both Hoover and his allies in the professoriate to attempt a public relations campaign against the proposal. Alonzo Taylor, the director of

Stanford's Food Research Institute, led the foray, arguing that "McNary-Haugen-ism" would merely serve to raise domestic prices to unwarranted levels, impose regulatory costs without justification or merit, and create widespread market distortions and "maladjustments." Members of Congress, more solicitous of the concerns of constituents rather than of a fledgling professional elite, passed McNary-Haugen nonetheless. President Coolidge, whether inspired by the traditional anti–farm belt proclivities of his party or the arguments emanating from within his administration from people like Hoover, refused to sign the bill. If there was, for experts like Taylor, some grim satisfaction to be taken from Coolidge's veto, the catastrophe of the Smoot-Hawley Tariff but a few years later, ironically enough due in no small degree to the timidity and complicity of Herbert Hoover himself, would make it a dim memory.[54]

Finally, on matters of macroeconomic structure and control, the commissioning of an investigation of recent economic changes in the United States was the last opportunity, prior to the Great Depression, Hoover provided economists to harness the prestige and resources of the Commerce Department to a focused research agenda.[55] Thoroughly grounded in empirical detail, providing a rich overview of the national economy that remains impressive to this day, *Recent Economic Changes* portrayed a vibrant commercial system that had, since World War I, experienced sustained growth combined with general price stability. High rates of technological innovation were vividly documented along with their most direct and beneficial consequence—economy-wide productivity enhancement. While the "leading business men and economists" Hoover had tapped "to supervise [this] far reaching inquiry into the changes in economic currents in the country" thus found much to be pleased about, they also voiced concerns about trends toward the increasing concentration of capital in major sectors and the apparent inability of the agricultural regions to participate fully in the nation's general prosperity. Even more prophetically (and ominously), they noted that "[u]ntil comparatively recent times, the problem of industry [had been] to produce a sufficient quantity to supply the demand. [By contrast, in the interwar American economy,] the problem of industry [wa]s largely that of disposing of its products." Here, but months before the crash on Wall Street, a presidential commission had succeeded in identifying the central dilemma of several advanced capitalist states—the puzzle of underconsumption. A clinical diagnosis, however, was one thing; recommending a successful therapeutic course was entirely something else.[56]

A month after the Committee on Recent Economic Changes completed its research, Herbert Hoover took the oath of office as the thirty-first president of the United States. It is entirely plausible that "[n]o American president ha[d] come into office with a more detailed conception of what he wanted to accomplish in economic policy and of the way to go about it than [he]." Yet it was the cruel irony of history that Hoover, who as commerce secretary had done more than any other cabinet officer to utilize the skills of professional economists in the work of government, would be so ill served by the very experts whom he had cultivated with such zeal. No economist forewarned him of the devastating collapse in financial markets that would occur a half year after his inauguration; only a few would provide him with compelling and practical ideas to attempt a resolution of the crisis once it took hold. One of a very few Republican presidents to have been denied reelection when they have sought it, Hoover experienced the utter collapse of his political fortunes because of the impact of the very kind of disaster he had worked so hard to prevent in his years at Commerce. Assisting the professionalization of economics like few government officials in modern American history, Hoover won little credit for the policy initiatives of his administration. Even the Reconstruction Finance Corporation, an inspired institutional invention that the Hoover White House used to combat the slump, was absorbed in the activism of the New Deal—and indeed was most often wrongly remembered as the invention of his successor. A cadre of American economists had been the relatively fortunate beneficiaries of Hoover's grand designs for an associative state; in the final analysis, when the harsh circumstances of the Great Depression obtained, they were neither valiant nor capable lieges of their patron.[57]

Late in January 1931, Edwin Brown, the pastor of the Broadway Methodist Church of Cleveland, wrote President Hoover to suggest the establishment of a presidential commission to study the great slump that had begun two and a half years earlier. He was "convinced that a conference of business men w[ould] not solve the problem." The unprecedented severity of the crisis had impressed upon Brown the fact that "[f]undamental economic laws [we]re involved." Clearly then, the pastor argued, "[i]t would be a good strategy to have at [the president's] disposal . . . the candid impartial judgement of the best minds" in the nation; he recommended in particular "[s]uch men as Irving Fisher, Prof. Paul Douglas of the University of Chicago, Prof. Harry F. Ward of New York, [and] Roger Babson [of Boston]" for the task. When the president replied a few days later, he stated blithely that such work was "already in progress, being carried on by various agencies of importance." Only hindsight illuminates the seemingly cavalier attitude of a man whose lengthy and distinguished public career would, in the end, be ruined by a calamity that contravened "fundamental economic laws" and so chastened "the best minds" in the discipline.[58]

Perhaps it is safe to say that during his years at Commerce, Herbert Hoover had developed an unhealthy confidence in the capabilities of professional social scientists. Upon taking office in March 1929, as the economy stumbled toward the free fall that would begin in the autumn, it was predictable that the new president would once again enlist the services of those economic experts with whom he had become familiar throughout the twenties.[59] His initial instinct, one no doubt born of years of experience as commerce secretary and one shared by the professionals to whom he turned, was to embark on an empirical examination of just what was happening in the economy at large. With the strong support of Irving Fisher, Hoover called upon the Department of Commerce to take steps to estimate unemployment data for the upcoming 1930 census. The ultimate goal was to make the reporting of monthly unemployment statistics a permanent feature of the work being done at Commerce. Once again, analysts retained through the good offices of the NBER led the effort.[60]

Precisely characterizing the employment problems of the American economy of the late interwar era was, to be sure, an important first step toward their resolution. Indeed, the statistical initiative that President Hoover started became, in the long run, the foundation of one of the most sophisticated and continuous governmental measurements of labor market performance in the world. But empirical precision was no substitute for policy decisions. More to the point, whatever the fascination quantitative precision held for professionals, the challenges of political leadership that impinged upon the Hoover administration militated against scholarly detachment and in favor of an engaged activism. To the extent that distinction went unappreciated, especially in a representative democracy within which networks of communication (as epitomized by the radio, not to mention motion-picture newsreels) were becoming increasingly rapid and widespread, enhanced data gathering by government would only serve to make more apparent the severity of the problems at hand and the inexplicable paralysis of the national leadership in solving them. One of the greatest ironies of the professionalization of the federal bureaucracy to which Hoover was a major contributor lay in this contradiction.

All the energy and flair for organization the Hoover White House could bring to the task of, say, revising governmental statistics was notably absent from the consideration and formulation of economic policies to combat the Great Depression. Enjoying an intellectual vitality that few occupants of the Oval Office have ever displayed, President Hoover could, for example, solicit suggestions from a cabinet officer of professional standing about highly regarded publications on the economics of business cycles. But securing advice from economists on the greatest crisis of his presidency was strikingly informal and episodic.[61]

Policy suggestions from eminent theorists occasionally received relatively more extensive replies from President Hoover's staff, suggesting that the specific matters raised had been closely assessed. Certain figures, moreover, Irving Fisher most prominent among them, enjoyed the president's confidence, sometimes even being invited to Washington to meet with Hoover privately. There is, therefore, evidence to suggest that with the advice of such professionals, the president recognized the serious problems that had emerged in the nation's financial markets, the difficulty of stimulating investment in a recessionary environment that encouraged the hoarding of funds, and even the need for certain forms of compensatory aggregate demand management. An innovation like the Reconstruction Finance Corporation, with its unique "off-budget financing" of industrial expansion, was also part of Hoover's bag of policy tricks. Yet there remained a striking rigidity in the overall approach of the executive branch, especially on matters of banking and monetary control, that expert advising was both unable and in some ways unwilling to overcome.[62]

To be sure, Hoover's reluctance to pursue certain heterodox solutions to the crisis derived more from his own analytical limitations than from those of his economic advisers. If the president had a blind spot, it was due to the glare from gold ingots. Despite repeated suggestions to the contrary, Hoover refused to abrogate or modify the nation's adherence to the gold standard in ways that would have allowed for rapid reflation. He only timidly embraced the notion of public works spending to alleviate unemployment; the idea of federal deficit spending held no appeal whatsoever. To the specific suggestion that he directly intervene in the setting of interest and discount rates, as a means to stimulate spending by both consumers and investors and preserve the liquidity of the banking network, he turned a blind eye. Indeed, when in October 1931 a professor of finance at the University of Chicago implored Hoover by telegram to declare an emergency suspension of Federal Reserve System regulations that limited the rediscounting of commercial paper by individual banks, and that prevented such rediscounted paper from being used as security for federal reserve notes themselves, the president was chagrined.[63] He understood, and in fact agreed with, a substantial part of the scholar's reasoning; the problems were to his mind constitutional. "[I]f you will consult with your legal friends," Hoover wrote Stuart Putnam Meech, "they would inform you that any such a proclamation from the President as you suggest would at once be upset by the Courts." Yet it was this very kind of iconoclastic and intrepid manipulation of the banking system, epitomized by the passage of the Emergency Banking Act in March 1933 (and its associated bank moratorium or holiday), that made Franklin Delano Roosevelt a hero to much of the nation in the worst hour of the Great Depression. Herbert Hoover, by sad contrast, was the goat.[64]

As the unprecedented economic crisis of the interwar years worsened, it became possible for some experts to find common ground with respect to emergency policy measures. In the fall of 1931, the University of Chicago sponsored an economics conference "attended by almost every prominent student of the subject in the United States." A general resolution, passed at that gathering, called upon the federal government to avoid any reduction in annual spending targets—all this with a view toward maintaining what little stimulus for demand existed in the nation's markets. It was a vain enterprise; indeed, in the electoral contest that followed a year later, both President Hoover and his Democratic challenger made the *reduction* of fiscal spending—to be undertaken with the goal of balancing the federal budget when tax receipts, from a labor force a vast proportion of which were idle or on short time, had of course been significantly reduced—a central campaign theme. Having been defeated at the polls, Herbert Hoover could regard the economic ruin that had sabotaged his presidency with vexation and pessimism; a month before Roosevelt's inauguration, the "Great Engineer" could only vent his spleen, so unlucky had been his efforts to bring a dispassionate expertise to the service of government. "[Our] economic system cannot survive," he wrote longtime colleague and ally Arch Shaw, "unless there are real restraints upon unbridled greed or dishonest reach for power." Grasping at some unarticulated notion that the Great Depression was, at its root, the result of a betrayal of capitalism by some of its most fortunate beneficiaries, Hoover believed it obvious that the future of an American "production and distribution system" rested necessarily on "effective restraints o[f] manipulation, greed and dishonesty." While history had proved that the nation had the "ability to put its unruly [economic] occupants under control," the instinct to do so only obtained after the fact when "their conduct ha[d] been a public scandal and a stench." The "forgotten Progressive," the engineer, the wonderfully effective administrator and manager, the resolute advocate of professional expertise in the public service, Herbert Hoover left the White House indulging in the kind of impassioned rhetoric that could only make professionalizing social scientists cringe.[65]

Like a physician or surgeon whose reputation is besmirched by the egregious loss of a patient, American economists hardly found themselves celebrated for their practice during the nation's worst depression. For all its enshrinement in the public memory as a strikingly effective response to unique economic troubles, the New Deal of the 1930s was not remotely as successful in fomenting recovery as so many believed. More to the point, the flurry of efforts to secure the "relief, recovery, and reform" of the nation's economy that defined the Roosevelt presidency were far more the creatures of political calculation and electoral manipulation than the products of social scientific reasoning.[66] After all, Roosevelt's brain trust and the progeny it begot throughout the executive branch of the government principally created more opportunities for attorneys in the federal service than almost all other professional and academic fields combined. Having approached the interwar years with an almost boundless optimism about the usefulness and the stature of their science, American economists had little of which to boast during the Great Depression; not one prominent figure in the discipline had, in fact, come close to predicting the collapse of the last quarter of 1929, let alone formulated a compelling and persuasive policy response to the crisis itself.

In the final analysis, the best-laid plans of theoreticians along with those of a professional leadership aside, events and contingencies in the mid–twentieth century would do more to shape the evolution of American economics than any set of ideas alone. Whatever analytical rigor and disciplinary self-confidence had been won in the course of its theoretical maturation, it was in the application that a science proved its genuine mettle. For economists, the policy accomplishments to which they might have beckoned after the Great War must have indeed seemed sparse. The unrequited prospects for greater influence and visibility during the interwar years must have been another spur as well. Yet, ironically enough, the Great Depression, rather than demonstrating the efficacy of a new learning in a time of unparalleled hardship, simply served to demonstrate how weak and ineffective had been the profession's learning. Attendance to the analytics of resource allocation may have succeeded in grounding a relatively new social science in the abstractions of the lecture hall, the seminar room, and the refereed journal. What it could not provide was the kind of practical performance that so enhanced the reputations of colleagues in the natural, life, and engineering sciences. For such fame and privilege, American economists continued to look necessarily to the public arena. Like the architects of the New Deal, however, they would find success not in the attempted remediation of failed markets but rather in meeting the peculiar and altogether extraordinary demands of national mobilization.

Davis R. Dewey

The founding editor of the *American Economic Review*, Davis Dewey did more than almost any other member of the economics profession to establish the prestige of what ultimately became the nation's flagship journal in the field. As he took up his task in 1911, he declared, "We are trying to appeal to a somewhat varied membership who are interested in current questions. We do not, however, wish to be popular in a commonplace way, but shall endeavor to have our articles prepared by men of scholarly standards." Dewey soon discovered that the problem of attracting "a somewhat varied membership" while adhering to "scholarly standards" that would guard against being "popular in a commonplace way" was truly vexing. (The MIT Museum)

Edwin F. Gay

Economic historian and founding dean of the Harvard Business School, Edwin F. Gay wholeheartedly embraced a vision of disinterested and objective scholarship in economics. He was determined to facilitate the deployment of professional expertise in the solution of public problems. Gay's participation in the creation of the National Bureau of Economic Research and the Social Science Research Council set a powerful example for the promotion of a social science elite at a time when the expansion of national funding for such groups still lay several years in the future. (Baker Library, Harvard Business School)

Wesley C. Mitchell

Committed to the development of a "useful" social science, Wesley Mitchell forged crucial links between academic economists and foundation executives in the philanthropic community, all in an effort to create disciplinary knowledge "geared to managerial uses." The nonprofit organizations to which he devoted himself were situated between a private sector somewhat suspicious of what academics had to offer and a public sector both small in size and ideologically predisposed to resist statist applications of social theory. (The Columbia University Archives and Columbiana Library)

Thorstein Veblen

A philosopher-turned-economist, Thorstein Veblen condemned what he took to be the inability and unwillingness of orthodox investigators to attend "to a consideration of the living items" of economic life. The resulting separation of economic argument from factual detail left the discipline, as far as he was concerned, "helplessly behind the times [and] unable to handle its subject-matter in a way to entitle it to standing as a modern science." Fighting words were these, for they challenged almost every claim held dear by Veblen's mainstream colleagues. Once regarded as the most original economic thinker the United States ever produced, Veblen today nevertheless enjoys little regard among students in the field, the vast majority of whom complete undergraduate (not to mention graduate) programs without hearing his name mentioned once. (Carleton College Archives, Gould Library)

Herbert Hoover

As secretary of commerce, Herbert Hoover constructed a venue within which economists could engage in research infused with a public purpose yet seemingly unsullied by normative agendas. In this respect, he assisted in the professionalization of economics like few government officials in modern American history. Yet it was a cruel irony that Hoover was so ill served by the very experts whom he had cultivated with such zeal. No economist warned him of the coming of the Great Depression that began a half year after his inauguration as president; only a few provided him with compelling and practical ideas to attempt a resolution of the crisis once it took hold. Hoover experienced the utter collapse of his political fortunes because of the impact of the very kind of national disaster he had looked to a professional economics to prevent. (Herbert Hoover Library)

Simon Kuznets

Simon Kuznets played a crucial part in the development of a modern system of national income accounting in the United States. The most obvious and immediate impact of his work in this regard was to provision academics and policy makers alike with the kind of empirical information and precision that made their work all the more authoritative and persuasive. Kuznets's contributions, along with those of his colleague Robert R. Nathan, were thus an essential ingredient for the elaboration of a professionalized economics in America. Even so, it was the coming of war in East Asia and Europe in the late 1930s that truly fostered the application of new economic accounting methods to the needs of government. As one astute observer put it years later, "If the war gave the medical profession antibiotics, it gave economists new tools and techniques and comparable optimism about what their future rôle would be." (The American Economic Association)

Tjalling C. Koopmans

Having fled to the United States as Germany invaded the Low Countries in the spring of 1940, Tjalling Koopmans served on the Combined Shipping Adjustment Board in Washington, D.C., a joint Anglo-American effort to utilize the merchant fleets of the Allied nations in the most efficient ways possible. His work for the board exemplified the ways in which the needs of government decisively influenced the articulation of a wide array of new techniques and applications in modern social science. It was during their military work that investigators like Koopmans demonstrated the paramount usefulness of economic analysis in solving problems of planning, allocation, and choice. Not surprisingly, their activities encouraged the emergence of an unprecedented degree of engagement with public policy issues throughout their profession's ranks. In this very important respect, the entire wartime experience of American economists profoundly affected the postwar evolution of the discipline as a whole. (The American Economic Association)

Charles Hitch

A leading authority on the economic analysis of defense problems, Charles Hitch was one of the central participants in a dramatic effort to overhaul budgetary processes in the United States Department of Defense after World War II. Ultimate policy choices on matters of national security understandably reflected the outcomes of interactions (and confrontations) between political constituencies, bureaucratic cliques, and the general staffs of the various branches of the armed forces. But it was nevertheless striking how involved professional economists became in the cold war debate over military matters. "[W]hat they had," one historian wrote, "was something very general, a way of approaching issues, that went right to the heart of [a] strategic problem," which cultivated interest, respect, and support within the federal government. Such official esteem and backing was one of the single most important factors in framing the modern history of the economics discipline. (Tom F. Walters)

3

The Mobilization of Resources and Vice Versa

> [T]he last war was the chemist's war ... this one is the
> physicist's. It might equally be said that this is the
> economist's war.
> —PAUL A. SAMUELSON (1944)[1]

IN 1933, THE WORST YEAR of the Great Depression, American economists had little about which to be pleased. The nation's physical output of goods and services had, from the onset of the New York stock market collapse in the fall of 1929, contracted by almost a third. A quarter of the labor force stood idle. Capital accumulation came to a standstill. The heady optimism of the twenties, inspired by a general expansion the likes of which had been virtually unknown to earlier generations, gave way to despair and fear. Many experts wondered if capitalism itself could survive such an unprecedented crisis. Yet at this very moment of economic calamity, the opinions of professionals were regarded with a powerful indifference, if not an outright contempt. When, for example, in November 1933, over two score academic economists petitioned President Roosevelt to return the nation's financial markets to the gold standard, the press barely took notice. The signatories found themselves "completely at sea as to why [their] letter [had] not attain[ed] more publicity." Like the embarrassment of the Smoot-Hawley Tariff memorial, these scholars had been given an object lesson on the all too obvious limitations of intellectual argument in a highly charged political environment.[2]

If economists craved respect, especially at a time of national need, almost a half century of self-conscious professionalization had created as many obstacles to, as accommodations for, the task. Having "occupied themselves mostly with refinements of economic theory and economic minutia at times when the fundamental principles were rocking under the most terrific bombardments they ha[d] ever taken," perhaps it was the case that academic specialists had done themselves tremendous harm. J. Russell Smith, a professor of economic geography in the Columbia University School of Business, put the issue to his colleagues in the American Economic Association in the baldest possible terms. "If [we] cannot render service in [this] emergency," he asked Secretary-Treasurer Frederick Deibler just before Christmas in 1932, "would it not be a wise economy for the universities to dispense with departments of economics, and await the arrival of a new generation?" Invoking the example of another professional elite, Smith wondered what would be done with engineering specialists "if most of the structures and machines approved by them or designed by them collapsed, and the appropriate faculties had nothing much to say or could not agree as to how they should be repaired?" From self-doubt and regret, the move to self-condemnation was a short one indeed.[3]

Smith's analogy to engineering was most apposite; like an inoperative contraption that had betrayed its inventor, the interwar American economy challenged specialists to engage in a kind of troubleshooting for which they were singularly unprepared. Generations of received wisdom apparently could not solve the greatest puzzle in American economic history—the persistent failure of investment activity during the 1930s to generate a full recovery from the slump. Low demand for the products of industry limited the incentive for enterprise to invest; the absence of large investment expenditures, sufficient to increase productive capacity, create new jobs, and expand output, enervated consumption spending itself. Caught in a vicious circle of idle plant and equipment linked with feeble levels of demand, the economy as a whole was frozen in place, captivated by a paralysis from which there was seemingly no escape.

If America's interwar economic stagnation necessarily evoked, from theoreticians and policy makers alike, a soul-searching pessimism concerning the effectiveness of their practice, it also encouraged among them a determination to address the nation's difficulties from a collective point of reference. It was in fact this willingness to experiment, to rethink the manner in which markets functioned and by which government could manipulate the outcome, that in large measure animated the New Deal itself. A unique set of historical circumstances thus framed the contexts within which a host of economic theorists, John Maynard Keynes most famously and most prominently among them, attacked the prevailing convictions of neoclassical doctrine. But the salience of that critique ultimately depended less on its analytical power than on events and contingencies that made it both useful and plausible; its enduring impact derived primarily from the aggregative point of view it legitimated, not from specific policy prescriptions that were eagerly embraced and indisputably effective.

In point of fact, America's greatest depression was not brought to an end by inspired policy choices. Far from it. World War II achieved what the New Deal could not. National unemployment fell to only 7 percent by the time of the Japanese naval offensive in the Hawaiian and Aleutian Islands. America's formal entry into the conflict brought almost instantaneous resolution of the nation's persistent economic difficulties. A wholly collectivized and centralized approach—through rationing, price controls, and federal allocative planning—provided for the kind of reflation and economic recovery that had seemed so unattainable during the worst years of the depression itself. When unemployment fell to just over 1 percent in the last year of the war, it was clear that, while hardly inspired by specific economic concerns, President Roosevelt's "arsenal of democracy" nevertheless contained rather vivid policy lessons for economists, politicians, government officials, and the public at large. In all these respects, what Paul Samuelson called "the economist's war" stimulated a mobilization of resources that in its relative efficiency and speed was altogether unprecedented in the nation's history. By creating an arena within which the demand for professional skills could be enhanced and the expediency of their application unambiguously demonstrated, war against the Axis powers provided American economists with their best chance to date to prove themselves. At the same time, because of the mobilization of resources that a national emergency demanded, these social science professionals could also marshal the means, the opportunities, the will and cohesion, indeed the very "resources," to mobilize their discipline like never before.

———————

Whatever occasion the Great Depression afforded for the battering of economists' self-confidence, it also stimulated just the sorts of professional introspection, intellectual controversy, and institutional experimentation that could help set the stage for the disciplinary triumphs of the 1940s and later years. The worldwide specter of moribund capital markets and hoards of unemployed revitalized the analytical heterodoxy of the American institutionalist school, provoked novel interpretations of the slow growth tendencies of so-called mature economies, and of course emboldened the iconoclastic speculations of Keynes himself. A continual proliferation of New Deal programs, initiatives, and agendas created an ever-increasing number of new positions within a burgeoning federal bureaucracy to be filled by appropriately credentialed specialists—and, along with that, the need to expand doctoral training programs to see to the continuing supply of those experts. Their anxieties and pessimism notwithstanding, most economists were thus eventually tempted to reconsider their role in the work of the government.[4]

To be sure, for the leadership of the American Economic Association, old habits of avoiding partisanship and specific engagement with governmental policy agendas died hard. In the spring of 1933 the AEA Executive Committee rejected a proposal to establish a special Association commission to collate the "recommendation[s] of properly qualified persons for scientific positions in governmental service." But a year and a half later, the committee substantively reversed itself, joining in a nationwide effort to link professional societies in encouraging their memberships to undertake government work. Perhaps the difference lay in the fact that the latter effort had been suggested by a federal agency itself—the Commission of Inquiry on Public Service Personnel. This was not solely a matter of government pressure overcoming fastidious attention to notions of professional impartiality; more and more economists had become impatient with what they took to be the disengaged scholasticism and intellectual ambivalence of their peers. With all due respect for the freedom of ideas, several colleagues fast came to the conclusion that it was nonetheless "high time to state some of the things to which 'most economists' agree[d]" and to apply that consensus of opinion to pressing affairs of state.[5]

Needless to say, one person's like-mindedness could easily be and often was, in the case of the Roosevelt administration, another's dissension. For all of their activism and esprit de corps, New Deal officials in general and economists in particular were neither unified in their diagnosis of the causes of the Great Depression nor of one mind concerning the best curative policies to pursue. While the resultant debates allowed for the kind of conceptual wrangling out of which the "bold, persistent experimentation" the president sensed the nation demanded could emerge, and presumably to which many academics were accustomed in their scholarly endeavors, they could not of course generate consistent and determinate conclusions. It is therefore hardly surprising that New Deal recovery policy was beset by a fundamental contradiction between two strategies. That dissonance was epitomized by the conflict within Roosevelt's inner circle between the advocates of economic planning, who celebrated the efficiency and rationality of large-scale enterprise, and those committed to "trust-busting," who maintained that excessive concentrations of market power in major sectors of the economy had caused the interwar crisis. The consequences of this disagreement were the strange brew of New Deal economic policy, the bewildering movement of the president from a planning initiative to a reform agenda, and the generally poor record of Roosevelt's first two terms with respect to recovery itself.[6]

To be sure, an extraordinary collection of economics talent was recruited to New Deal government agencies. Eminent senior scholars, such as Princeton's Jacob Viner, who served as a special assistant to Treasury Secretary Henry Morgenthau, joined younger specialists, Lauchlin Currie (recently denied tenure at Harvard because of his early devotion to Keynesian ideas) one of the most prominent among them, in Washington. Adolph Berle, Mordecai Ezekiel, John Kenneth Galbraith, Richard Gilbert, Isador Lubin, Gardiner Means, Robert Nathan, Walter Salant, Alan Sweezy, to name but a few, "[a]ll of them formed an informal president's council of economic advisers before there was such an institution." Entire executive branch offices, such as the National Resources Board, which numbered among its members the economists John Maurice Clark, Arthur Gayer, Alvin Hansen, Albert Gaylord Hart, and Beardsley Ruml, were transformed into virtual economics research institutes. In size and scope, the activities of economists in New Deal Washington far transcended the comparatively meager achievements of colleagues who had, in previous decades and under far different circumstances, labored in the nation's service.[7]

Visibility and numbers, however, did not necessarily translate into influence and authority. Economists, both in Washington and elsewhere, often found themselves competing for the president's attention in ways they must have found both frustrating and confusing. Ever the consummate strategist, Roosevelt evaluated economic policy proposals primarily with reference to electoral and political impacts, far less with convictions concerning the logical coherence or intellectual (not to mention professional) pedigree of the argument. As a result, his economic decisions tended to be skittish, sometimes timid, often unpredictable. Federal government vacillation between the imposition of a centralized blueprint for recovery, as exemplified by the Industrial Codes of the National Recovery Administration, and the prosecution of antitrust tactics to foster a competitive revival never ceased. Fiscal spending targets were more often than not simply too low to do the job, and their allotment was driven as much by hardheaded projections of their influence in the electoral college as by closely measured multiplier effects on consumption and investment. When, for example, the president made the crucial decision in the summer of 1933 to take the nation off the gold standard, seeking the kind of monetary flexibility he believed was essential for reflation, the news came as much of a shock to his economic advisers as to the nation's major trading partners. Customary historical perceptions aside, when it came to economic policy, the New Deal had more the appearance of a storm-tossed vessel struggling at the helm than of a close-hauled ship of the line stoutly tacking on high seas.[8]

Given his political goals and his misgivings about economic theory, it is hardly surprising that President Roosevelt kept the profession's elite at arm's length. Indeed, this was no isolated prejudice but rather part of a general mistrust and impatience he had with intellectuals as a whole. The tendency of academics to get bogged down in debates and finely honed arguments could simply not be tolerated in the face of the wrenching depression hardship of the nation's farm belt and industrial centers. Surely academic style and intellectual precision had to be sacrificed in the face of widespread hunger and squalor, not to mention imminent violence. To the extent professional scholars could not submit to the demands of political pragmatism and public order, they would remain very much on the fringes of power.[9]

At the same time, interwar American economists, determined to participate in actual policy making, were sooner or later forced to make excruciating choices between intellectual probity and political influence. Having the power of one's convictions more often than not left an expert speaking to an audience of one; forfeiting what one took to be scientific precision, on the other hand, risked one's reputation, if not self-respect. For Yale's Irving Fisher, for example, who in fact enjoyed a special friendship with the president, it was the former circumstance that prevailed. Convinced that a "sound money" policy offered the only true depression remedy, Fisher often wrote Roosevelt to try to persuade him to rely on monetary stimulants rather than industrial regulations in federal economic intervention. A strident opponent of the National Recovery Administration, Fisher flattered himself in thinking he was an adviser of some influence with the president, an "emeritus" member of the vaunted brain trust. In point of fact, while ever polite and solicitous in his replies to Fisher's arguments, Roosevelt had more or less ignored the great theoretician's views since he had taken high office. Professional rectitude and reputation notwithstanding, political savvy and effectiveness necessarily held sway in the corridors of power, and the wherewithal to deploy those skills was not necessarily conferred with a doctoral degree. Far from it.[10]

If instincts to mobilize economics expertise on behalf of a nation in the throes of depression necessarily required conceptual flexibility and open-mindedness, they also took advantage of, and subsisted within, the institutional changes in governmental operations that had emerged during the 1920s. Arguably the most significant and enduring of these legacies was the expansion of the data-gathering activities of the Department of Commerce initiated during Herbert Hoover's watch as secretary. The trauma of the depression only made more obvious the need for reliable and timely statistical calculations that could serve as the foundation for effective statecraft. That the federal government should and would assume responsibility for the dissemination of economic knowledge, the accuracy of which was essential to the development of a rigorously grounded set of policy choices, was widely acknowledged. It was, moreover, testimony to the fine reputation so rapidly and adroitly cultivated by Wesley Mitchell that, having been tasked in the summer of 1932 by the United States Senate to report national income estimates for the period 1929–31, Secretary of Commerce Robert P. Lamont immediately turned to the National Bureau of Economic Research for help. In yet another demonstration of the special conduit a nonprofit organization like the NBER could provide for the interaction of academic specialists with the federal bureaucracy, Mitchell turned the national income accounting project over to a University of Pennsylvania professor of statistics (and future Nobel Memorial Prize laureate)— Simon Kuznets.[11]

The development of a modern system of national income accounting provided a crucial ingredient for the elaboration of a professionalized economics in interwar America. Its most obvious and immediate impact was to provision academics and policy makers alike with the kind of empirical detail and precision that made their work all the more authoritative and persuasive. At the same time, it afforded specialists a unique and fairly visible venue within which to deploy their skills; Kuznets's remarkable career, and the prominence he achieved as one of the profession's most accomplished quantitative experts, is only the most prominent case in point. Even more striking was the connection such an exercise in applied statistics forged between intellectual developments in the economics discipline and alterations in government practice. Indeed, it was that historical juxtaposition that decisively facilitated the transition, in the analytical preoccupations of an entire generation of economists, from a focus on ending a depression to a concentration on waging war.

Hardly the first to approach the analysis of economic performance from an aggregate perspective, John Maynard Keynes nevertheless provided, in the 1936 publication of his *General Theory*, a theoretical apparatus by which to array the constituent parts of a macroeconomic system in a discrete framework that aided the compilation of data. While others, most notably the eminent British economist John R. Hicks, would devise the specific accounting identities ultimately and universally used in national product estimates, Keynes's focus on consumption, investment, and government spending parameters as the core determinants of total economic output supplied the conceptual map so necessary to the completion of their task. If the New Deal years did not witness the genuine application of the aggressive compensatory fiscal spending that Keynes himself advocated as a depression remedy, they nonetheless allowed for the creation of a national income accounting system that would be one of the most essential parts of the later revolution in economic policy making that would bear his name.[12]

Income accounting techniques were as well an important (and tractable) mechanism in the shift, in the Washington of the late 1930s, from a concern with the economics of revival to a focus on the economics of conflict.[13] The persistent depression era problems of excess capacity and unemployed resources were, by the time of British prime minister Neville Chamberlain's fateful 1938 meeting with Adolph Hitler at Munich, quickly forgotten. Of concern now, to a government predominantly convinced of the inevitability of war with Germany and Japan, was the need to rearm, expand capacity, improve technology, and forestall price inflation. Management of a slack economy, victimized by gluts in almost every one of its major markets, gave way to the need to regulate an economy that would, in short order, be pushed to its limits. Measurement of the weaknesses in the nation's capacity to consume, a central objective of the Commerce Department statistical effort, was deftly transformed into an urgent calculation of the limits to the nation's capacity to produce. What had been viewed as therapeutic during the worst years of the slump, output restriction and price reflation, became in war outcomes to be avoided at all costs.

Like a proverbial hothouse, the coming of war in East Asia and Europe accelerated the application of the new macroeconomic accounting methods to the needs of the state. Indeed, it is hard to imagine, in the absence of the forced stimulant of militarization, a more rapid elaboration of what is, to this day, the national accounts system. On behalf of the United States War Production Board, Kuznets and his colleague Robert R. Nathan embarked on a rushed project to estimate both the speed with which the national economy could convert to a wartime footing and the levels of output that could be achieved. In what a chronicler has called "one of the great technical triumphs in the history of the economics discipline," they succeeded not simply in generating reliable projections but also in detailing the precise steps to be taken to realize military procurement targets. Their achievement was magnified by the fact that President Roosevelt had unilaterally increased the output levels they had originally calculated to be feasible. Its accomplishment crucially depended upon the utilization of the national accounts system that had been developed throughout the interwar period.[14]

Perhaps even more significant than the sheer computational virtuosity that Kuznets and Nathan deployed on behalf of the state was the "demonstration effect" their work had for government and military officials. For the year 1942, Kuznets and Nathan provided a blueprint for the achievement of a $17 billion expansion in the national product that nonetheless avoided inflationary distortions. By the more intensive use of existing plant and resources (for example, the imposition of longer hours and workweeks and the disbursement of less overtime wages), the reallocation of $7 billion of resources from civilian to military use, the utilization of existing inventories valued at $4.5 billion, and the reduction of $7 billion worth of consumer demand by rationing and excise taxation, the first steps in the making of the tremendous economic success story of World War II were taken. That military planning and procurement could be made a "science" was thus an idea much impressed upon the minds of the executive branch, not to mention those in the offices of the army chief of staff and of the chief of naval operations. The tools and experience developed by Kuznets and Nathan would not simply be used throughout World War II; they would continue to frame military thinking in subsequent decades as well.[15]

That contemporary economic expertise could so ably assist the central government in the computation of wartime production possibilities was indeed impressive; but the special usefulness of the discipline to the nation's mobilization was even more dramatically demonstrated in two broad areas—the allocation of resources and the simulation of strategic decision making.[16] It was for this reason that economists quickly became integral parts of many government agencies established to meet the various needs and challenges thrown up by American entry into World War II. These included the Board (later Office) of Economic Warfare, the Combined Production and Resources Board, the Defense Plant Corporation, the Foreign Economic Administration, the Office of Merchant Ship Control, the Office for Coordination of National Defense Purchases, the Office of Defense Transportation, the Office of Price Administration, the Petroleum Administration for War, the War Manpower Commission, the War Production Board, and the War Resources Board, to name only a few.[17]

A great deal of economics talent was also marshaled in the Research and Analysis Branch of the Office of Strategic Services (OSS), a brainchild of President Roosevelt's, created to oversee military intelligence operations and ultimately the institutional forerunner of the Central Intelligence Agency. Edward S. Mason, a distinguished Harvard University specialist in industrial organization economics, spearheaded the OSS recruitment of many immensely capable and accomplished individuals for the purpose of studying enemy economic capabilities, examining strategies of economic warfare, and assessing the impact of military (especially Army Air Force bombing) operations against military-industrial targets. Mason signed on such eminent (and promising) scholars as Emile Despres (of the Federal Reserve Board), Chandler Morse (also of the Fed), Calvin Bryce Hoover (dean of the Duke University Graduate School), and Harvard instructors and graduate students Moses Abramowitz, Abram Bergson, Carl Kaysen, Charles Kindleberger, and Wassily Leontief. Even the (subsequently renowned) Marxist theorists Paul Baran and Paul Sweezy were made part of the effort. In all, Mason assembled a stunning array of some of the nation's leading economic authorities, including "five future AEA presidents and a [future] Nobel Laureate."[18]

Even before the attack on the American Pacific Fleet at Pearl Harbor, conversion to defense production had created virtually intractable problems of resource scarcity and waste for government officials. How to choose efficiently the timing and distribution of various productive activities necessary for the war effort became a major concern. With the nation's declaration of war on the Axis powers, allocation problems became even more intense. The "growing scarcity of resources" made vivid the fact that "a broad economic strategy" to settle "questions of [production] priority" would be necessary. If the nation's economic capacity was in principle large and growing, it nevertheless would never be sufficient "to meet all needs." Perhaps most vexing of all, the difficulties faced by government planners and military leaders were not simply derived from budgetary and resource constraints per se. They were uniquely linked as well to the problem of scheduling and sequencing. This is to say that the cost of every productive decision was much more than direct; building a particular piece of military hardware, for example, also meant *not* constructing, at least for the time being, something else. Every economic action in the war, therefore, involved absorbing the straightforward debits for materials, equipment, and labor along with the implicit, and perhaps even more significant, costs of failing to utilize those resources for another purpose. In short, allocative choice (and, attendant upon that, strategic and tactical choice) necessarily depended upon accurate calculations of both the direct costs and the *opportunity costs* of each decision.[19]

Reckoning not simply the absolute but also the *relative* burdens of particular actions was precisely the challenge of wartime administration for which neoclassical economics was singularly well prepared. A choice-theoretic calculus, deployed to describe individual behavior in competitive market transactions and the conditions under which "equilibrium" could be achieved, was directly applicable to the puzzles facing government and military leaders with respect to defense procurement, production, and mobilization. Substituting the state for the individual, pursuing the maximization of "utility" in the guise of a series of output targets, for example, was an obvious and most useful application of neoclassical price theory to the exceptional challenges faced by a nation at war. Precisely because of their focus on optimality scenarios in which no improvements in "utility" could be achieved by the reallocation of resources, mainstream economic concepts served to link assessments of the costs of particular output goals with an awareness of the implicit expenses associated with the foregone opportunities inherent in every economic decision. "[T]errific waste in [the] conversion" of productive capacity to wartime needs could thus be avoided. Decades of professional evolution, years spent cultivating the rise of both an elite scholarly community and a privileged expertise, the intellectual virtuosity of neoclassical theory itself, all would now find their epiphany in the century's greatest armed conflict.[20]

Not surprisingly, American military and allied government agencies were particularly eager to develop allocative techniques for the production and distribution of essential matériel. These procedures had to minimize costs and waste and, as a corollary, maximize some objective such as output, frequency, or endurance. Tjalling C. Koopmans, a Dutch physicist-turned-economist who came to the United States as Germany launched its invasion of the Low Countries in 1940, played a significant role in relevant research that, in the short run, stimulated a wide variety of research on related programming problems and, in the long run, had a tremendous impact on the future course of research in mathematical economics in particular, and in economic theory in general. Serving on the Combined Shipping Adjustment Board in Washington, a joint Anglo-American effort to utilize most efficiently the merchant fleets of the Allied nations, Koopmans developed a mathematical model of transportation routes that aided decision makers in the establishment of transport routes, schedules, and tonnage objectives in both Asian and European theaters of military operations. His work dealt with the central issues posed in the neoclassical perception of rational choice problems: the need to maximize a particular outcome (in this case the amount of cargo to be moved among ports separated by vast distances), the minimization of the direct costs (in fuel, shipping capacity, and personnel) of achieving that outcome, and (perhaps most important) the measurement and attenuation of the opportunity costs incurred (by sending merchant fleets along certain routes rather than others) by the ultimate strategy deployed. His work became a linchpin, especially when he moved in 1944 from the Shipping Adjustment Board to the Cowles Foundation for Research in Economics in Chicago (and later at Yale University), in the articulation of a wide array of applications that would provide the foundation for major developments in economic theory and analysis in the 1950s and 1960s.[21]

Indeed, the entire wartime experience of American economists would profoundly affect the postwar evolution of the discipline. The work of Simon Kuznets and Robert Nathan on national income accounting and that of Tjalling Koopmans on the most efficient routing of shipping convoys were but two examples of the ways in which the 1940s were an extremely innovative decade in the field's history. Of course, these intellectual developments, the demonstration of the paramount usefulness of the neoclassical approach to problems of planning, allocation, and choice, all took place within the context of a grand crusade against fascism and totalitarianism. In this sense, World War II "imparted to a community of humanist and social scientific scholars a concrete sense of the embeddedness of their ideas—and themselves—in history, which they brought back with them to their universities" and, it should be added, that they sought to communicate to their respective colleagues and students.[22]

If wartime exigencies uniquely animated the efforts of individual investigators to make modern economic analysis useful in the realization of national objectives, they also facilitated the emergence of an unprecedented degree of engagement and activism on behalf of the profession as a whole. On the one side, the pressures of mobilization and combat afforded precisely the kind of circumstances, not to mention the venues and operational support, within which the wisdom and effectiveness of neoclassical techniques could be demonstrated. On the other, the needs of the state coupled with the engagé sensibilities that armed conflict fostered in the citizenry at large elicited a renewed sense of purpose within the leadership of the American economics profession, not to mention their allies and retainers. In a fashion thoroughly unanticipated, history now brought the intellectual agendas of neoclassical theory into a special harmony with the twentieth-century aspirations of a professionalizing community. This rare opportunity, an uncommon alignment of circumstances, was not squandered.[23]

Not surprisingly, the most immediate concerns around which the activities of a nation preparing for war and the self-conscious efforts of a profession determined to demonstrate its capabilities as well as its patriotism could coalesce were those pertaining to the classification and utilization of personnel. No doubt recalling mobilization efforts during the Great War, not to mention the experience of the 1920s with respect to such governmental initiatives as the Classification Act, the Executive Committee of the American Economic Association held a special session in the winter of 1940 to discuss the organization of AEA personnel for national needs. A mere two months before Germany would launch the offensive across the frontiers of Belgium, Luxembourg, and the Netherlands that would culminate in the Battle of France, Executive Committee members began the process of differentiating economics talent by fields, all in anticipation of the call to "professional arms" that the federal government would no doubt soon issue. Their work would span the summer months; by the fall they would be in close contact with officials in Washington regarding the fruits of their labors.[24]

Actually, carrying on work begun almost three decades earlier, in the spring of 1940 a special Executive Committee of the AEA took up the matter of professional subfield classification. Fourteen major fields were identified at that time: economic theory, economic history, quantitative economics, natural resource economics, labor, industrial organization, public utilities, commerce, public finance, private finance, social problems, population, business cycles, and government-business relations. By the fall of that year, however, the Association leadership was approached by the National Resources Planning Board regarding the creation of a National Roster of Scientific and Specialized Personnel. The classification of economists in the roster had proved especially difficult. Two methods had been employed. One involved distinguishing specialists by particular commodities or services, the production of which they studied. The other utilized field group distinctions upon which the AEA itself had been working.[25]

Continuing with its work on field groupings, but nonetheless now aware of new and special needs attendant on the effort, the special AEA committee added six new fields to its classification list: money and banking, international trade, economic geography, insurance, national income and its distribution, and national defense. Thus began a multiyear association with the Resources Planning Board and ultimately other war agencies whose objective was the effective utilization of economic talent for the war effort.[26]

In the fall of 1941, the National Resources Planning Board sought the aid of the Association not only in classifying its membership by field but also in judging the credentials of economists of military age so that their skills and capabilities could be most effectively employed should war arise. The board was particularly anxious that the AEA nominate for such a task individuals from "different fields of specialization within economics." Clyde Holmes of the National Office of Production Management approached the Association two months before the outbreak of war, "recruiting personnel for [that] defense agency." One day after the attack in Hawaii, yet another official from the Office of Production Management contacted Sumner Slichter (of Harvard University and then AEA president), urging the passage of a proposal made at a recent Association meeting in New Orleans that "standards of minimum competence for economists" be promulgated as soon as possible. Slichter agreed and, two weeks later, asked the Association's Executive Committee to take up a rather large agenda of matters posed by "the emergency." In particular, he wished that ways be sought to provide for the effective allocation of personnel to government and military jobs and for the continued and expanded "training of as many graduate students as conditions permit." The memories and experience of the Great War would now be brought to bear on a much larger and demanding effort.[27]

As America's participation in World War II expanded, so too did the interaction of the AEA with the federal government and the armed services. In this the Association was fortunate but not unique. Most professional societies were caught up in the war effort. Early in 1942 the presidents and secretaries of all such groups were contacted directly by Steuart Henderson Britt, an official of the National Roster of Scientific and Specialized Personnel. Britt informed these men and women that it was now necessary to compile as systematically as possible information on the classification of professional personnel, where such personnel could be best recruited, and (by so doing) to coordinate these data with a determination of the needs of the military, industry, and civilian government agencies for professional skills. The War Labor Board directly sought to recruit Association members. Much as the National Roster had done, the War Manpower Commission also sought AEA help in classifying and properly tasking economists.[28]

Recruitment and utilization of personnel in wartime was one thing. The effective nurturing and, what's more, the proper accrediting of talent was quite another. American economists, under the pressures of the war emergency, quickly turned their attention to the matter of training students—most important, graduate students. Not surprisingly, while receiving repeated inquiries from the federal government regarding field classification and recruitment, the profession became aware of the need to maintain the supply of experts at an appropriate level. Indeed, once the question of standards of competence for government service was raised, it was a logical next step to begin examining curricula at both the collegiate and the graduate level.[29]

Concern with curricula, and in fact with the topics examined both at annual meetings and in the *American Economic Review* (*AER*), dated back to the period prior to direct American involvement in the war. Late in 1940, AEA officials began communicating about the possible revision of courses "in the direction of problems of preparedness." At the same time, efforts commenced at the editorial offices of the *AER* to bring into its pages more material dealing with the economics of preparedness, mobilization, and war-making. Along with essays on the perennial theoretical problem of what one colleague called "butter and bullets," it was hoped that work could be solicited, even commissioned, on such matters as the financing of a preparedness program and on the "problems of industrial mobilization for preparedness (and possibly war) in the United States." Unfortunately, several of the potential authors *Review* editors had in mind were already doing defense-related work "and consequently [were] not free to publish." Whatever surprises may have been in store at the navy's fleet anchorage in Honolulu in December 1941, American economists had moved toward a war footing as early as the climax of the Battle of Britain.[30]

Concerns both with the training of economics students during the crisis and with bringing professional opinion to bear on major issues led the Association, in the early years of America's war involvement, to establish committees to investigate such matters. In the summer of 1943 a special AEA committee issued the formal "Report on Wartime Changes in Economics Curriculum." It had been widely agreed that "the impact of the war ha[d] caused such an upheaval that [the Association wished to] take advantage of th[e] occasion to make a thorough appraisal not only of the subject matter and the place of economics in [the] educational system and the function which it perform[ed] in society but also a reexamination of . . . teaching methods and techniques." While it was clear that "because of the insistence of the Department of War and of the Navy there [had to] be modifications . . . for courses that [would be] immediately applicable to the two services," there was still strong feeling "for maintaining the fundamental, the eternal values even during these times of emergency."[31]

Just what those "fundamental, eternal values" might be was a subject ripe for controversy and debate. While there was some consensus that the "applied" revisions of the economics curriculum would touch upon such matters as war aims, how the United States became involved in the conflict, economic organization for war, and postwar economic adjustment, there was genuine difference of opinion on how to teach theory. John Maurice Clark of Columbia University (and a former AEA president) rejected, on the one side, the idea that everything taught should be linked with "the immediate conflict." But he also felt that simply teaching orthodox price theory would be mistaken as well. American economists had spent "too many decades cultivating the attitude that everything . . . outside [traditional] system-theory [was] a problem[.] [P]ut the Keynesian elements in front," Clark told his colleagues, "as having a more direct and active relevance." War could aid the triumph of the Keynesian revolution as much on earnest classroom blackboards as in driving up the budget ledgers of government and military agencies.[32]

Curriculum revision and reform was a project that lasted throughout the war years, indeed well into the 1950s. Two months before the opening of the second front in western Europe the Association Executive Committee asked that the new Committee on Undergraduate Teaching and the Training of Economists concern itself with "the long-run postwar period." Ultimately, of particular interest to this committee with regard to the matter of undergraduate instruction were "problems of indoctrination [of students] as to social consciousness and professional responsibility." Four months after the surrender of Japan, 160 college and university economics departments around the country received questionnaires from the AEA soliciting information on undergraduate instruction. By the autumn of 1950 the AEA secretariat initiated plans for a conference on social science teaching at the precollegiate and collegiate levels. At the same time, the Committee on Graduate Training in Economics began its work, seeking to formalize in detail the professional requirements for the Ph.D. degree. To this effort, the Rockefeller Foundation donated $16,000. When the committee transmitted its findings to university deans and presidents, return correspondence was grateful and enthusiastic. War-related agendas thus carried over into long-standing peacetime activities.[33]

Hand in hand with the curriculum project went an increased concern with the "focusing of informed opinion" among economists. Actually, insofar as a desire to distill professional opinion dated back to the early years of the Association's founding, it is not surprising to find that renewed interest along these lines emerged as economists turned their attention to planning for the postwar period and anticipating the role of economists in government during peacetime. During World War II the AEA leadership asked Harry Gideonse, Charles Noyes, and Frank Graham to begin deliberations "to [consider ways of] making the informed opinion of our membership more effective in matters of public policy." Because the Association, by the terms of its charter, could take no partisan positions, the trio nevertheless believed that the "technical competence" of members could be expressed on "matters of public importance." This would require of course that "all academically respectable views on any posed controversial question be repre-sented" on committees formed to pronounce on policy matters. Moreover, Gi-deonse, Graham, and Noyes thought it additionally appropriate to "include some members not committed to any particular position on the matter at hand."[34]

Another device utilized to increase the influence of the profession was that of the "Consensus Report." As the war came to a close, and as attention turned to postwar economic policy needs, an Association task force investigated the "desirability and workability" of formulating concerted opinions on major issues. There was some concern with violating the body's charter once again. "A learned society c[an] not long remain one," the committee declared, "if it passe[s] resolu-tions and promote[s] special interests and causes." Given that the AEA "record [wa]s . . . clean in this regard," the group concluded that the Association "must keep it so." Nevertheless, they agreed that "the professional economist ha[d] a formal background of preparation and special training which . . . g[a]ve him com-petence to pass on the economics aspects of [policy] questions." Thus, "as a scholar, he [wa]s relatively free from the influences of special interests and [wa]s qualified to view controversial questions objectively and from a broader social point of view than [wa]s the layman or the advocate."[35]

Consensus reports not only could educate the public but also would certainly bolster the reputation of the profession. By December 1945, AEA officials worked to centralize Association members' opinions with regard to the government's postwar economic role, the continuation of agricultural price supports, monetary policy, and the future of the Webb-Pomerene Act. Rather than stake out a particu-lar position on these issues, they hoped that "something [could] be done to help the public distinguish between important and unimportant issues, recognize clap-trap arguments, and become aware of economic considerations which members of the profession [thought] significant." All in all, in the opinion of the AEA secretariat, the "experiment" of consensus reports would "throw more evidence on the wisecrack '[p]lace all of the economists in the country end to end and they will arrive at no conclusion' a reference which might be true when applied to quacks but which [was] of doubtful validity when referring to professional econo-mists." It is not surprising, therefore, that the Association at this time also became "involved in publicity connected with the Bretton Woods proposals."[36]

War's end also brought attention back to the matter of defining and classifying economic expertise. Officials at the War Manpower Commission, continuing their work on the National Roster of Scientific and Specialized Personnel, contacted Association leaders repeatedly for information about the profession to be distributed to returning veterans. The roster, as well as the Federal Security Agency, also had other reasons to make such inquiries. It was now hoped to maintain data on file regarding professional personnel in the United States. As government concerns shifted from making war to maintaining national security, continued interaction by government agencies with professional associations similarly evolved.[37]

Postwar reconstruction also brought the Association into the business of aiding professionals in devastated areas overseas. It was, however, a far more sophisticated effort than a brief one that had been undertaken after the Great War. For now, in addition to contributing free books and copies of the *American Economic Review* along with cash donations to scholarly libraries in Europe and East Asia, the AEA became involved in the revision of curricula and the rehabilitation and vetting of foreign faculties. American economists going overseas, on either official or personal tours, were asked by government authorities to check up on colleagues who had perhaps been imprisoned, wounded, or otherwise victimized by German national socialism or Japanese imperialism. Letters to Association members from economists abroad often contained information regarding colleagues who either had or had not collaborated with the enemy. Efforts were made to raise money for the relief of those who had opposed fascism and militarism. A note from a German colleague to former AEA president Paul Douglas was forwarded to the Association offices because in it there was "a very valuable list of economists who either opposed Hitler or kept their honor clean." American economists were now in a position not only to secure greater influence and prestige at home but also to reconstitute virtually from scratch the European and Asian branches of the guild.[38]

The reconstruction of foreign scholarly libraries prompted the American Library Association to ask professional societies to provide book lists in their fields to guide rebuilding efforts. AEA officials canvassed the membership for suggestions and ultimately provided such lists, with regard to economics, to the ALA. With such recommended titles as *Stalin, A Critical Survey of Bolshevism* and *Marxism: An Autopsy*, the ideological content of the library aid effort seems clear. This is of course hardly surprising. The point here is not that American economists would generally be loath to suggest books that extolled Marxism or Stalin, but that Allied victory had the added impact of giving them a great deal of influence on the future course of foreign scholarship in the field. If postwar reconstruction served to recast Europe and Asia in America's image, as some scholars have suggested, the representations of that process in the academic and intellectual world should not be overlooked.[39]

Participation of the American economics profession in the emergent Pax Americana of the 1950s also expressed itself in a continuation and evolution of links between economists and the military-industrial establishment that had necessarily arisen in the forties. Economists of course participated both in the private sector and at the government level in the mobilization and allocation of resources for war. In addition, the profession became increasingly involved in establishing curricula at the nation's armed service academies on the economics of national security and defense. Defense-related research and support of basic economics investigations by armed forces agencies became more and more common. Moreover, the emergence of wholly new aspects of the discipline—such as "linear programming" and "input-output analysis"—was inherent in the association of professional economics with the national security state. The AEA even helped the U.S. Information Agency in securing prominent and competent personnel to do radio broadcasts on economic subjects for the Voice of America. From the end of the Great War to the advent of the cold war, the American economics profession had come of age.[40]

If the nation's culture, economy, polity, and society were enduringly transformed by World War II, it is also clear that its professional communities were hardly immune from the process. Yet the wartime emergency was far less the igniter than the accelerant of change. For over a half century the values, the self-perceptions, the aspirations, and the practices of American economists had evolved with reference to an overarching set of goals—objectives having to do with the pursuit of authority, influence, and practicality for the discipline. Neither the Great War, nor the Great Depression, nor World War II had set these challenges before the profession; rather, they reframed the circumstances within which they were met. Moreover, as was especially the case with the world conflict of the 1940s, they facilitated the emergence of economics as a rigorous, accomplished, and capable body of learning, one from which its experts could draw legitimacy, prestige, and sway in both academic and public-policy environments.

What enhancements of the discipline's prospects the historical contingency of mobilization and war provided American economists were both subjective and objective. In its demonstration of the unique efficacy of choice-theoretic analysis, and of the tractability and usefulness of quantitative rigor, the wartime work of economists served to privilege the more fundamental aspects of neoclassical theory at the expense of alternatives such as institutionalism.[41] If not vanquished entirely, the criticisms of those who, throughout the interwar period, had viewed with despair and regret the elaboration of an increasingly formalistic and mathematical discourse in the discipline were certainly (and decisively) weakened. After all, had not the work of a Koopmans, a Kuznets, a Nathan, to mention a few, not demonstrated the power and importance of quantitative reasoning in economics? Had not the success of economists in government service, along with the ever-increasing interest of the state in the applicability of their methodology to an array of policy and operational problems, proved the worth of a rigorous methodology devoid of ideological, historical, and social assumptions? In the face of their intellectual critics, neoclassical economists now had, in addition to whatever logical arguments they cared to marshal, a remarkable reference with which to make their professional claims—the impressive achievements of national and international mobilization in the victory over the Axis powers.[42]

A bit over a decade before V-J Day, when J. Russell Smith of Columbia University had complained to Davis Dewey that economics lacked the influence and prestige of a genuinely accomplished science, the *AER* editor had instinctively defended the discipline from the charge. "[I]t seems to me that you expect too much of [us]," he wrote Smith. To the extent that "[t]he economic structure was not designed by [economists]," Dewey declared, "they [we]re not necessarily responsible for the errors . . . nor for the confusion [of contemporary policy making]." He reminded his correspondent that "[s]ocial institutions, and much more democratic institutions, [we]re the product of a great many factors, many of which long antedate[d] the birth of economic science." If social and institutional change exceeded the grasp of the discipline, the useful application of the principles of economic analysis to problems set within a particular social and political context clearly did not. In this sense, "economists [we]re rendering some service . . . to society."[43]

In an act of historical anticipation of which he could not have been aware, Dewey thus explained what was arguably the most significant aspect of the success of "the economist's war" during the 1940s. Under the novel and unrelenting demands posed by national mobilization, modern economic theory had proved its worth. Born of an intellectual legacy tied to the investigations of scholars predisposed to privilege individualism and democratic ideals in the systematic study of social life, neoclassical analysis was requited in the historical accident of a command economy. Not individualism but rather statism provided the special circumstances within which the high hopes and great expectations of generations of professionalizers could be realized. Under a wartime emergency, economists did not face the vexing and ideologically charged questions about political and social institutions that bedeviled any effort to constitute a rigorous social science. Given the reality of a nation at arms, these scholars could devote their energies to a comparative (and measurable) assessment of means rather than an absolute (and divisive) argumentation over ends. It is one of the great ironies of this history that a discipline renowned for its systematic portrayals of the benefits of unfettered, competitive markets would first demonstrate its unique operability in the completely regulated and controlled economy of total war.[44]

To these tremendously important advancements in the reputation of American economics at midcentury, the war also brought welcome expedients of a more material sort. Government and armed service work brought with it not simply the imprimatur of national interest but also the resources, both human and material, to get the job done. The discipline was most fortunate in this outcome, for the years of the Great Depression had withered the funding available—from both private and public sources—for advanced study and research. Indeed, during the 1930s universities throughout the nation began to cultivate federal patronage of their scholarly activities on an altogether greater scale than ever before. It seemed clear to administrators and faculty members alike that the economic deprivations of the slump coupled with the increasingly complex and expensive nature of scientific and artistic endeavor militated in favor of a "federalism" in higher education previously unimagined. The tribulations of the independent sector only encouraged the elaboration of this new funding strategy; foundation support of research in the social sciences, for example, fell by almost half during the depression decade, while such funding for research in the natural sciences, social sciences, and health sciences combined shrank by a quarter. World War II provided the first systematic demonstration of the beneficence to be won from the largesse of the central government. It was, therefore, also a lesson that only reinforced the convictions of an academic community, seared by the harsh experiences of the Great Depression, that a new partnership with the state was essential to their success.[45]

Wartime challenges had also of course provoked an unprecedented degree of activism in the leadership of the American economics profession. With government demands for the classification and ultimate mobilization of talent in the war effort, the AEA secretariat had found both the necessity of and the will for a far more sustained intervention in the work and engagements of its members than ever before. As a matter of course, there emerged a determination to evaluate and reconfigure educational programs in the field, more rigorously stipulate its varieties of expertise and methodologies, and pursue consensus about its central principles and policy orientations. This is to say that out of the crucible of national mobilization came the beginnings of a professional identity and self-confidence that, while resolutely sought after since the late nineteenth century, had, up to that point, been elusive and fleeting.

Peace and its consequences would bring an array of new opportunities and pressures to bear upon the profession. None would be more remarkable than the proposal that the expertise of economists become formally institutionalized within the Executive Office of the President of the United States. In the passage of the Full Employment and Stabilization Act of 1946, all the yearnings and hopes of those who, like Irving Fisher, had labored to enhance the influence and visibility of social scientific learning in the public realm would seemingly be fulfilled. With that accomplishment, and with the heady optimism it would instill in a new generation of scholars, the prestige of what remained a very new discipline in the human sciences was preeminently secured. Only time would tell if that distinction could endure, and if the history that had fostered it would either enrich or impair its destiny.

4

On Behalf of the National Security State

> There is, of course, no exclusive connection between
> defense or war and the systematic study of allocation
> and programming problems. . . . If the apparent promi-
> nence of military application at this stage is more than a
> historical accident, the reasons are sociological rather
> than logical.
> —TJALLING C. KOOPMANS (1951)[1]

WHILE the material exigencies of war in the 1940s provided both a solution to the economic puzzles of the 1930s and an unprecedented set of opportunities for economists to deploy and legitimate their expertise, the imperatives of the immediate postwar era, in ways that both surprised and inspired contemporaries, afforded still more of the same. Even though many economists and businesspeople had worried about the possibility of a dramatic peacetime drop in the levels of prosperity and employment achieved during World War II, their apprehensions proved unwarranted. A bit over a year after the defeat of the Axis powers, aggregate spending (the sum of domestic consumption, investment, and government disbursements) had not fallen; unemployment had not even reached 4 percent. If robust economic performance was hardly surprising in wartime—especially when conflict was global and, with few exceptions, kept outside national boundaries— then the enduring growth and prosperity of the postwar years in the United States were extraordinary. Part and parcel of that beneficence was the ever-increasing visibility, influence, and respectability of the economics discipline itself.[2]

Consumption and investment behavior played a major part in the construction of the great American affluence of the late forties and fifties. On the domestic side, reconversion was itself an investment stimulus. Modernization and deferred replacement projects required renewed and large allocations of funds. Profound scarcities of consumer goods, the production of which had been long postponed by mobilization needs, necessitated dramatic retooling and expansion efforts. Even fear of potentially high inflation, emerging in the wake of the dismantling of the price and wage controls of the war years, prompted many firms to move forward the date of ambitious and long-term investment projects. On the foreign side, both individuals and governments were eager to find a refuge for capital that had been in virtual hiding during the war itself. Along with a jump in domestic investment, a large capital inflow began in the United States in late 1945 and early 1946.

Domestic consumption was the second key component of immediate postwar growth. Bridled demand and high household savings due to wartime shortages, rationing, and controls, coupled with the generous wage rates of the high-capacity war economy all contributed to a dramatic growth in consumer spending once hostilities ceased. A jump in disposable income was further bolstered by the rapid reduction in the surtaxes and excises that had been a central part of the federal government's strategy of war finance. The celebrated baby boom of the wartime generation expressed itself economically in high levels of demand for significant items like appliances, automobiles, and housing. The Servicemen's Readjustment Act of 1944 (or so-called GI Bill) granted benefits to veterans that additionally served to increase the demand for housing and such things as educational services, with associated impacts on construction and other bellwether sectors.

Foreign demand for the nation's exports also grew rapidly after the summer of 1945. In part the needs of devastated areas could only be met by the one major agricultural and industrial base in the world that had been nearly untouched by combat-related destruction. Explicit policy commitments to the rebuilding of Allied and occupied territories, such as the Marshall Plan in Europe, also increased the overseas market for the output of American industry. These factors notwithstanding, one of the most powerful influences on the impressive postwar expansion of the American economy was the unique and special set of arrangements developed for international trade at the Monetary and Financial Conference of the United Nations in 1944.

When the Allied nations' financial ministers gathered at Bretton Woods in New Hampshire, just before the war's end, they were concerned to reconfigure world trade and financial flows such that the disputes so characteristic of the interwar years could be avoided and stability maintained. Along with the creation of the International Bank for Reconstruction and Development (known today as the World Bank) and the International Monetary Fund, the conference also decided to establish fixed exchange rates between the U.S. dollar and all other traded currencies. The value of the dollar was itself set in terms of gold at thirty-five dollars per ounce. Thus was installed a benchmark against which the value of all other currencies was measured. Because the American economy was, by far, the most powerful at the time, it seemed prudent and indeed necessary that the dollar play such a central international role. Perhaps even more to the point, the other industrialized nations of the day were powerless to stop the United States from assuming this central position in world finance.[3]

American postwar prosperity and the benefits the country derived from world economic leadership continued throughout most of the 1950s. The added fiscal stimulus of the Korean War also served to maintain the high levels of growth and employment characteristic of the decade. In the midst of halcyon circumstances, American economists could, in contradistinction to their experience during the 1930s, contemplate postwar national economic performance with satisfaction and pride. That composure was only heightened by the evident success of the Council of Economic Advisers that, since August 1946, served both the Congress and the president as a seemingly final authority on matters of policy. What went hand in hand with such stunning success in the highest echelons of public leadership in Washington was a corresponding improvement in the discipline's reputation and status within the academy.

Public regard and academic deference mutually subsisted upon a corpus of ideas, and the articulation of methodologies, ever more rigorous and purportedly devoid of value-laden assumptions. Abstruseness and intricacy could make economic argument all the more the domain of the professionally trained specialist; impartiality and detachment in matters of political faith were essential to achieve for the scholar the renown with which to speak and act commandingly. It was therefore in the elaboration of a science of rational choice that American economists had secured both rank and privilege. The exemplary achievements of the 1940s, when experts had strikingly proved the effectiveness of a new wisdom by which the nation's productive capacity could be accurately measured, configured, and utilized for military purposes, had successfully cast intellectual evolution and professional aspirations within an unyielding mold of events and circumstances. In this regard, an "exclusive connection between defense or war and the systematic study of allocation and programming problems . . . [had been] a historical accident." Like the extrusion of a multiton press, moreover, the resulting shape had varying degrees of both ductility and brittleness.

Yet beyond the vagaries of happenstance and adventure, "the apparent prominence of military application" in mid-twentieth-century American economics had equally compelling causes more "sociological . . . than logical." Mobilizing a nation for world war, coupled with the unique circumstances of the peace forged in the last months of 1945, caused transformations in both the role of government and the expectations of Americans that had lasting effects far transcending particular events. From the impacts (and implications) of a now vast defense apparatus, of a large and growing domain of federal activism and largesse, of an array of international commitments diplomatic, financial, and military, and of a population now sensitized to a panoply of economic, political, and social aspirations unimagined by the overwhelming majority of its ancestors, American scholars in general and economists in particular were hardly immune.[4]

Amid the constellation of forces that shaped the postwar United States, none was more significant nor as pervasive as the cold war itself. By the confrontation of the superpowers that emerged from the war with Germany and Japan, every facet of the nation's life, even the rather esoteric and specific feature of a profession's discourse and practice, was affected. Faced now with a struggle for global influence and supremacy that only in its most immediate manifestations involved the counterposition of armed forces on land, in the air, and at sea, the United States also joined the contest with the Soviet Union and the People's Republic of China (as well as their "communist bloc" allies) along dimensions economic, political, social, and cultural. The geopolitical confrontation of the superpowers, in the latter half of the twentieth century, thus had as much to do with foreign affairs and military posture per se as with intellectual and cultural life as a whole.

On behalf of the national security state, the most significant and spectacular appurtenance of that conflict, American economists accordingly entered upon a period in their history that, while easily one of the most exciting and successful, was at the same time uniquely exacting and consequential.[5]

In its theoretical and methodological trajectory, the American economics profession was decisively affected by the pressures, constraints, and opportunities afforded by the cold war preoccupations of the federal government, colleges and universities, and private foundations and think tanks. It had been, of course, during the 1940s that the needs of the War Department and related government agencies for guidance in resource allocation had led to the stimulation of economics research on "activity analysis" and "linear programming" that ultimately had a decisive impact on the nature of the discipline through the rest of the twentieth century. Activity analysis and linear programming made possible the precise understanding of what specialists called maximization and minimization problems. If, for example, a particular event—such as the distance traveled by a vehicle in a given time period—could be described in mathematical form, analysts discovered that it would then be possible to determine maximum and minimum values for that equation if certain variables, such as time and velocity, were known. Further research demonstrated that the calculation of such maximum or minimum values could be refined by inserting certain constraints into the picture—for example, limits on fuel availability, attainable speeds, and the feasibility (not to mention safety) of particular routes—thus allowing for more useful approximations of real-life scenarios. These "programming problems" had indeed been found characteristic of a vast array of events, operations, and decisions facing government during wartime.[6]

From such work, schemes of calculation (or "algorithms") to discover the constrained maximums or minimums of particular activities were developed. These techniques were used to aid the navy, for example, in the most rapid scheduling and most efficient sequencing of supply shipments (given limits of fuel, shipping capacity, seagoing speeds, and the like) throughout its various theaters of operations. These advances in decision-making science, prompted by the wartime needs of the state, ultimately affected the course of research and teaching in microeconomics at colleges and universities across the country. Moreover, during the ensuing cold war, the continuing needs of government for assistance in the direction of military buildups and overseas troop and matériel deployment called forth further research efforts in such areas as strategic defense economics, economic intelligence analysis, and development economics. In a variety of ways, state-inspired activities profoundly affected research protocols and pedagogical agendas in the economics discipline as a whole.

Where the cold war had, however, an enduring impact on American economics was in the impetus it gave to the refinement of game theory and mathematical approaches to the problem of simulating competitive behavior. The formal approximation of contests between two or more actors, undertaken by mathematical economists with the support of the Department of Defense, the Office of Naval Research, and other federal agencies, linked up directly with strategic concerns, during the 1950s, about the bipolar nuclear rivalry (or, if you will, "duopoly") of the Soviet Union and the United States, and the potential for bilateral and/or multilateral conflict in the postwar world. Economists, therefore, not only had a key role to play in the articulation of American cold war military and diplomatic strategies but also were themselves especially privileged and influenced by the growing interest of the federal government in their strategically important work. The ultimate impacts of this mutual interaction between economists and the national security state suggest an array of ironic and ambiguous outcomes in the domestic history of the cold war.

When Tjalling Koopmans, during his wartime service with the Combined Shipping Adjustment Board, had developed a mathematical model of transportation routes to aid decision makers in the establishment of global transport routes, schedules, and tonnage, coupled with the cost-benefit estimation of the optimal sizes of shipping convoys, he was already aware of the potential his work might have in a much broader array of applications. Indeed, his board research eventually became a linchpin for the future evolution of economic theory in the 1950s and 1960s. By 1949, Koopmans's work and that of many investigators in mathematics and economic theory had reached sufficient maturity for a more aggressive collaborative effort. At a June conference jointly supported by the Cowles Commission for Research in Economics (then still in Chicago) and the RAND Corporation, that cooperative instinct was put to the test. To say the gathering was a tremendous success, generating information and publications quite dramatic in their impact and significance, would be a tremendous understatement.[7]

The Cowles conference was Koopmans's brainchild, born of the conviction that there was a connection between much of the allocation and operations research studies done during World War II and economic theory more generally. As one eminent participant at the meeting remembered, Koopmans was "like a man on fire," and the visibility that the conference garnered for its organizers brought "instant respectability to the field" of linear programming and operations research in the eyes of many economic theorists. By "mechanizing" the problem of maximization (or minimization) subject to constraints, the work of the conference participants served to unify, at least in the formal constructs of mathematics, a large and diverse set of problems in economics having to do with such things as the maximization of output, the maximization of utility, and the minimization of costs.[8]

Even more striking was the manner in which the proceedings of the Chicago gathering resonated with what had, by that time, become long-standing efforts to redefine the economics discipline itself. No longer the study of "the nature and causes of the wealth of nations" (as Adam Smith had claimed), or "a critical analysis of capitalist production" (as Karl Marx suggested), economics had become the formal study of "the adaptation of scarce means to given ends." The development of linear programming and operations research served to legitimize this transformation in the object of economics research in ways that seemed entirely scientific, objective, and formal.[9]

The authority and legitimacy of the new work in economic theory that had been, in large measure, an outgrowth of the war years carried over to the postwar era and the years of the cold war. Economic analysis came to play a significant role in many activities related to the defense establishment and to the new global involvements and responsibilities of the United States. From cost minimization, to budgeting objectives, to the scheduling of transportation and logistical support activities, to estimations of the amounts of materials needed for military-industrial production and deployment, the research of the World War II years began to pay off. Indeed, in the wake of the interservice rivalries sparked by the creation of a unified Department of Defense (DOD) in 1947, formal economic analysis had played a central part in the work of the Weapons Systems Evaluation Group, an advisory agency established to mediate between the competing claims advanced by the different services. Even in the private corporate economy, not to mention in the civilian activities of government, operationally useful techniques developed by economists bore fruit. With these successes, the prestige of those engaged in such research, along with the governmental and private support for such research activity, were powerfully enhanced.[10]

It was within the development of game theory, however, where the intellectual evolution of American economics and the concerns of a burgeoning national security state truly melded. On a strictly mathematical level, the development of both linear programming and game theory depended on advances in the understanding of linear inequalities in constrained maximization or minimization problems. In this sense, the mathematical techniques used in both areas were the same. But game theory had an even more powerful appeal for strategic analysis because of its focus on *conflict* and decision making. In other words, game theorists moved the analysis of calculating constrained maximums or minimums in a particular activity away from the simple reckoning with resource limits toward an awareness of the fact that one's objectives were often also framed by the behavior of competitors. The ability to "make a move" in a particular activity, to choose specific operational targets given particular resource limits, was obviously further delimited by what one's adversaries might be doing. A decision by one party could reduce resource availability to another. Game theory became a powerful tool to understand this further (and obviously more realistic) wrinkle to human decision making—all the more so because such conflictive choices were most often made in an atmosphere of uncertainty about precisely what one's opponents might choose to do.[11]

Not surprisingly, the theory of games was also a field greatly stimulated by the World War II years, but in certain ways it did not actually achieve the prestige to which it was destined until the coming of the cold war. The 1940s work of John von Neumann and Oskar Morgenstern signaled the entrance of game theory as an important part of economic analysis.[12] Their demonstration that it was possible to derive definite results from mathematical simulations of complicated scenarios of conflict and uncertainty was revolutionary. They showed that under certain conditions and assumptions, game participants could implement strategies that would secure at least certain minimum gains (or their corollary, sustain at most certain maximum losses). It was immediately clear that their findings would be useful in resolving certain puzzles in advanced microeconomic theory.[13] It also rather quickly became obvious that their work would be applicable to strategic choice problems and national defense planning.[14]

Albert Wohlstetter of the RAND Corporation was also a major figure in the application of game theory to defense concerns. His work, in the late 1950s, focused on nuclear deterrence and what had come to be called the "balance of terror."[15] Game-theoretic approximations and simulations of two-person conflicts seemed appropriate scenarios in which to investigate the implications of the nuclear duopoly of the cold war years. It was no idle exercise for Wohlstetter and his colleagues at RAND to relax over games of "Kriegspiel" and "liar's poker" while taking a break from their investigations of strategic choice and conflictive outcomes.[16]

The dramatic intellectual impact of the work of von Neumann and Morgenstern among academic economists was paralleled by the willingness of the state to support the continued evolution of this particular line of inquiry. Research funding, distributed by the Department of Defense and affiliated agencies—such as the Office of Naval Research and subordinate service arms—was rapidly made available to those economic theorists, in particular mathematical economists, whose work in game theory and linear programming seemed to have potential value for the realization of the missions of the national defense and security establishment.[17]

Interestingly enough, the navy and the air force proved most eager to lend support to the work of game theorists and operations research specialists. The navy, in particular, supported much of the work in mathematical economics—in large part done by Kenneth Arrow and Gerard Debreu (both future Nobel Memorial Prize laureates)—through its Office of Naval Research. In a retrospective survey of the office's work, the Arrow-Debreu project was noted for its "modelling of conflict and cooperation . . . whether it be [for] combat or procurement contracts or exchange of information among dispersed decision nodes." "Military operations research," the report went on to note, "is founded on the basic concepts of scientific calculation of optimal, stable equilibria and analysis of processes and behaviors that achieve or fail to reach those goals." As for game theory, military planners and foreign policy analysts were similarly impressed—the "rationality" of strategic decisions could now be evaluated by means of the calculus of utility maximization.[18]

Crucial support, both financial and logistic, was also given to these activities by the RAND Corporation. During the 1950s, what had been Project RAND (an acronym for Research and Development) under air force supervision, and later devolved as the nonprofit RAND Corporation of today, underwrote much of the work on linear and dynamic programming that had been so decisively stimulated

by the Cowles Conference at Chicago. It was at RAND that Dantzig further refined his crucial contributions of the late forties (with the enormously important
contributions of applied mathematician Richard Bellman). RAND scientists also
began the application of game-theoretic principles to war gaming and simulation.
Such work was viewed to have "important uses as a training device for government officials to help them understand what kinds of behavior to be prepared for
in various crisis situations." In future years, it would be the presidential administration of John F. Kennedy that would be most engaged by and committed to this
sort of experience for its officials.[19]

As one of RAND's historians has noted, economists played an increasingly
important part in the work of the corporation. In contrast to the experience of
World War II, where government (and associated nonprofit research institutes)
deployed the expertise of physical scientists in large numbers, the cold war years
saw an increasing emphasis on the work of social scientists. In large measure, it
appears that this was the case because "economists could act as the generalists and
integrators in analyses of general war." The major challenges facing government
officials in times of conflict—such as the "allocation of resources among expensive competing weapons systems . . . [and] bargaining with a single opponent in
a two-sided [gaming] matrix, and so on—were well-suited to treatment by traditional economic concepts."[20]

Not surprisingly, it was RAND economists (and their colleagues drawn, in
some cases, from other institutions) who, at the behest of leading government
officials, also grappled with the seemingly insurmountable budgetary problems
of the national security state. Once again, it was Robert McNamara who assumed
overall command of the effort; Charles Hitch took point. A leading national authority on the economic analysis of defense problems, Hitch had also spent a great
deal of time during his tenure at RAND examining military budgeting techniques.
Charged by the defense secretary, just after John Kennedy's inauguration, to undertake a systematic review of the department's programs and resource requirements, the Missouri native fashioned what came to be known as the Planning-
Programming-Budgeting System (PPBS).[21]

While the results of Hitch's overhaul of the Pentagon's budgetary process had
their critics (among some it was fashionable to say that, in PPBS, one needed
more "PP" and less "BS"), the fact remains that the system was a prime feature
of DOD economic practice until the first term of the Nixon presidency.[22] As two
of its primary architects retrospectively explained, "The purpose of PPBS was to
develop explicit criteria, openly and thoroughly debated by all interested parties,
that could be used by the Secretary of Defense, the President, and the Congress
as measures of the need for and adequacy of defense programs." In other words,
PPBS sought to ground managerial choice in the relative assessment of competing
defense (and attendant resource) objectives "as opposed to decision making by
compromise among various institutional, parochial, or other vested interests in the
Defense Department." PPBS economists wished to replace the traditional "horse

trading" of legislative and bureaucratic settlements with closely measured *relative judgments* made with reference to clearly articulated goals.[23]

To the complicated and demanding claims of defense budgeting, the professional economists who devised PPBS worked to apply the central principles of neoclassical analysis. In keeping with the essential methodology of their training, they eschewed absolute policy commitments in favor of the comparative appraisal of competing ways in which to meet those obligations. Executing that task involved answering "questions [that] [we]re not, '[w]hat [wa]s good?' but, '[w]hich [wa]s better,' not whether more [wa]s better than less, but whether it [wa]s enough better to be acquired at the expense of something else." Relative valuation and the close metering of opportunity cost, those two notions so paradigmatic of neoclassical doctrine as a whole, whose functionality had been so impressively demonstrated during World War II, understandably became the lodestars of an even more pervasive and expensive task of national mobilization during the cold war.[24]

Under the auspices of RAND, research in game theory and linear and dynamic programming continued during the late 1950s and 1960s. The corporation funded "Defense Policy Seminars" at UCLA, the University of Chicago, Columbia, Dartmouth, Johns Hopkins, MIT, Ohio State, Princeton, and Wisconsin. By 1965, RAND had created a graduate fellowship program to support training in a wide variety of fields in the physical sciences but also including economics and international relations. In that year, eight such fellowships were distributed among Berkeley, Chicago, Columbia, Harvard, Princeton, Stanford, and Yale.[25] Not infrequently, talented graduate students and young postdoctoral investigators received major support from RAND for their work in economics that touched upon matters of strategic decision making. One such individual for whom this was true, whose career as a cold war analyst would take many twists and turns, was Daniel Ellsberg. His research at Harvard University and at RAND dealt primarily with strategic choice under risk and uncertainty—and in this regard his work was quite representative of the new trends in economic theory that so expediently dovetailed with the concerns of the American government during the cold war.[26]

A conjunction of historical processes—in this case, the professionalization of American economics and the emergence of the national security state—had obvious correlative yet more subtle causative features. While the needs of the state, in the altogether new geopolitical environment of the latter half of the twentieth century, had a profound effect on the thinking (and the access to funding) of an entire generation of American economists, the extent to which new theories of risk, conflict, and decision making decisively shaped American strategic thought is less apparent. Ultimate policy choice on matters of defense and diplomatic posture understandably reflected the outcomes of interactions (and confrontations) between political constituencies, bureaucratic cliques, and the general staffs of the various branches of the armed forces. It is nevertheless striking the degree to which "economists, and people heavily influenced by their style of thinking, were for a variety of reasons drawn into [the debate over national security matters]." As one of the leading historians of American strategic thought has argued,

"What they had was something very general, a way of approaching issues, rather than anything that in itself suggested substantive answers that went right to the heart of [a] strategic problem" that cultivated interest, respect, and support from the federal government. Such official esteem and backing was one of the single most important factors in framing the modern history of the discipline.[27]

It would be misleading, of course, to suggest that state support for new trends in economics research only took the form of the largesse distributed by defense-related agencies. On the contrary, the experience of the war years, and of the immediate postwar period, suggested to both federal officials and academic economists the need for continued research support on civilian levels as well. Federal research expenditures had increased more than tenfold between 1938 and 1944, from $68 million to $706 million per year. While the War and Navy Departments and the wartime Office of Scientific Research and Development (OSRD) had accounted for the lion's share of the increase, major "civilian" agencies, such as the Departments of Agriculture, Commerce, and Interior, had also held title to significant portions of the rise. Private foundations had also played no small role, although the difficulties occasioned by the Great Depression had weighed heavily upon them with the coming of World War II. Perhaps even more telling was the fact that, while in 1930 the country's universities combined had spent a bit more than $20 million on research, during the 1940s the OSRD alone had distributed $90 million to campuses nationwide. Overall, especially in light of the unique importance of the contributions of scientific and engineering research to the success of the American war effort, that research funding in the postwar era required a continuing governmental presence—a socialization of its cost—seemed clear to most lawmakers irrespective of political stripe.[28]

Even so, when the Congress, in May 1950, created the National Science Foundation (NSF) as a direct offshoot of the activities of the Office of Naval Research, a debate immediately ensued as to whether it should support social science investigations along with those of scholars in the physical and life sciences. The original NSF proposal, brought forward by Senator Harley M. Kilgore (Democrat of West Virginia), had been animated "by a belief in the efficacy of science and technology, properly directed, to solve national social and economic problems." Yet for many business leaders such rhetoric heralded "the [frightening] prospect of a revived New Deal." More challenging was the criticism of Thomas C. Hart, the Republican senator from Connecticut, who sought a formal exclusion of social scientific research from the charter of NSF because "no agreement [could be] reached with reference to what social science really mean[t]. It [could] include philosophy, anthropology, all the racial questions, all kinds of economics, including political economics, literature, perhaps religion, and various kinds of ideology." The conclusion, in his view, was inescapable: such research "mean[t] a political board [at the NSF]. It mean[t] someone concerned with promoting all the health legislation which someone m[ight] want, all the housing legislation . . .

and all the other matters which come in under the all-inclusive term of 'social sciences'. . . . Social sciences [we]re politics"; they were, therefore, not properly the responsibility of a nationally funded research agency.[29]

Within this pressure-cooked legislative environment, social scientists had every reason to be pessimistic about the prospects of their work being underwritten by a national research agency. There were nevertheless two arguments that commended themselves to advocates of social science funding, one of general applicability, the other uniquely conducive to the benefit of economists. The former emphasized areas of "convergence" between the natural and the social sciences, where basic research took on seemingly "objective," "verifiable," and of course "nonpartisan" characteristics. Indeed, it was this tactic that ultimately won over a recalcitrant cadre within the Senate; the NSF was allowed to support certain research activities in the social sciences, such as demography, communication, the history and philosophy of science, and mathematical economics and game theory, that apparently met this criterion. By contrast, the latter sought to link economic knowledge with the needs of a national security apparatus. Edwin G. Nourse of the Brookings Institution, who in but a few years would be the founding chair of the Council of Economic Advisers, put it best in his testimony before the Senate on Kilgore's NSF bill when he claimed that "an adequate defense hinge[d] on the strength of the industrial system, for which an understanding of economic principles and practices [wa]s fundamental." Not simply the abstract (and rigorous) examination of models of arbitrage and decision making but also the applied study of macroeconomic performance could now become part of a cold war agenda to preserve and protect the nation's security.[30]

It is therefore hardly surprising that federal and private foundation support for social science research disproportionately favored economics throughout the postwar era. From the late 1950s until the mid-1980s, just under 46 percent of the NSF funding allocated to the social sciences went to investigators in economics; for all federal funding agencies, the share garnered by economists was almost 60 percent. While there are less reliable data for foundation grants, the Social Science Research Council concluded in 1983 that "[o]f all the social science disciplines, the foundations . . . show[ed] a clear preference for economics" throughout the postwar era. To be sure, certain leading independent-sector agencies, such as the Rockefeller Foundation and the Russell Sage Foundation, tried, especially in the 1950s and 1960s, to steer a substantial amount of support to advanced study in political theory and sociology, but "the lure of economics' possible payoffs for [helping to manage the] economy, combined with the discernible methodology and the potential rigor of economic analysis, made it the favored object of foundation attention."[31]

Economists no doubt enjoyed the fact that they were, comparatively speaking, the social science darlings of the independent sector during the postwar years; nonetheless, like a favorite child who had exhausted the generosity of parents, they found themselves growing increasingly dependent, as time passed, on the kindness of others. In point of fact, from the end of the Great Depression through 1980, while private foundation funding of social science research had increased almost fifteenfold, it peaked rather quickly, and its rate of growth then tailed off. By contrast, colleges and universities expanded their support for social science research at an increasing rate; in this endeavor, they were of course bested by the federal government. If in 1940 foundations had granted $3 million to social science projects, and colleges and universities $12 million, with federal expenditure minuscule by comparison, by 1980 their $41 million in social science research disbursements paled in comparison with the $300 million committed by colleges and universities, not to mention the $524 million distributed by the federal government. Like a wealthy relative indeed, Uncle Sam had simply pushed other family members aside in winning the affections of a younger generation.[32]

A "discernible methodology" and a "potential rigor" of their scholarship thus placed economists in a relatively privileged position when it came to the extramural funding of their work. Yet like all American scholars at the time, irrespective of disciplinary field, their prospects and fortunes became ever more closely tied to the general nationalization of advanced study inspired by World War II and the ensuing cold war. In fact, the expansion in the support for academic research coming from colleges and universities themselves slowly but surely became hostage to that process of socialized provision. As Clark Kerr of the University of California had so accurately and succinctly implied some years later, what had been the "Land Grant College" funding strategies of the nineteenth century gave way to the "Federal Grant University" systems of the twentieth.[33]

Federal support of higher education and research during the cold war era was, of course, disproportionately focused on the life and physical sciences and on engineering. Above and beyond the political, diplomatic, cultural, and ideological manifestations of the conflict with the Soviet Union and the People's Republic of China, the struggle for superpower supremacy was first and foremost a military contest. The advent of the nuclear age had made clear that the physical sciences were of considerable importance in the determination to sustain armed superiority in an altogether new geopolitical environment. For all these reasons, Washington maintained a steady flow of resources, through its defense agencies and national laboratories, but also through direct grants to the nation's colleges and universities, so that American science would flourish and the nation's interests, as a matter of course, be protected. Further stimulated by Russia's successful test of an atomic bomb in September 1949 (and of a "super" or "hydrogen" bomb in the summer of 1953), the coming of war in the Korean peninsula the following year, and such challenges to America's aeronautical capabilities as the orbiting of a Russian earth satellite (the *Sputnik*) in October 1957, government support of science and engineering became the basis of yet a new (and more powerful) "arsenal of democracy."[34]

What with the modest dimensions of government support for social science research, relative to the commitments in science and engineering, during the cold war, the very large share that went to economists was impressive indeed. More to the point, along with other colleagues in the social sciences, the arts, and the humanities, economists benefited from the financial transformation caused by cold war research policy throughout the academic community. Federal research grants directly supported work in the sciences and engineering; in the collegiate and university setting they also indirectly provisioned the activities of scholars and artists across the campus. Grant contract surcharges that covered the "indirect cost" to an educational institution of maintaining the research facilities for investigators utilizing federal awards (such as laboratories, libraries, maintenance personnel, technical support staff, utilities, and site infrastructure) thus first emerged during World War II.

With the coming of the cold war, the fiscal dependence of American colleges and universities on the revenues generated by indirect-cost "taxes" imposed upon outside research grants grew by leaps and bounds. Academic administrators quickly recognized that these funds could also be employed to support work in areas not generally sustained by federal government interest—especially in the arts and humanities. Federal research funding thus became an essential component, through either direct or indirect allocative mechanisms, of virtually every facet of intellectual and creative activity taking place at the nation's colleges and universities at the time. Demographic trends serving to expand the eligible college-age population, rising expectations regarding appropriate levels of educational attainment, and public policy initiatives to provide substantial aid to the college-bound enhanced the demand for higher education and thus encouraged institutions in their metamorphosis into federalized entities. Economists may have been relatively privileged in securing federal support for their research during the cold war, but that dispensation was both cultivated and circumstantial. On the one side, their work held the special interest of particular federal agencies, and their relatively high success in winning direct grants, compared with other social scientists, exemplified that fact. On the other, like all their academic colleagues, independent of field and skill, economists were also the legatees of a peculiar system of public educational finance that had, as its cardinal tributary, the work of the weaponeers.[35]

Washington's cold war patronage of what was fast becoming one of the preeminent branches of the social sciences, not to mention the continuing support afforded by private foundations, encouraged a kind of self-confident professionalism among economists that earlier generations of scholars had only imagined. With satisfaction and pride, practitioners could now reflect upon the coming of age of a powerful new field that, in at least the formal sense of collegiate and university organization, was in most cases less than a half century old. Far beyond the prestige (and resources) federal and nonprofit-sector agencies bestowed upon specialists working in areas, like linear programming and game theory, which had what appeared to be a direct applicability to matters of national security, statist agendas also nurtured a broader kind of professional activism that touched all economists irrespective of field. In some cases this energy focused on the means by which a larger array of economic learning could be made useful to government; in others, it reckoned with the ideological and social implications of the cold war itself.

While striving to adhere to its strictures against partisan endorsements, a task made all the more difficult in the highly charged politics of the immediate postwar era, the leadership of the American Economic Association turned its attention to engagement with seemingly more "objective" needs of the national security state.[36] In these efforts, their work was paralleled by that of colleagues already assigned to some of Washington's highest echelons. Over the course of the 1950s, for example, government economists made frequent visits to the military service academies, and to such institutions as the War College of the Air Force and the Industrial College of the Armed Forces (of the National Defense University, Fort McNair, Washington D.C.) to discuss (and participate in conferences on) such matters as "mobilization of the national economy in the face of atomic attack," "economic stabilization after attack," "the economics of national security," "economic preparedness," and "domestic economies and their relation to national power."[37]

AEA officials also worked closely with colleagues on government duty to assist the national service academies in fully integrating an increasingly rigorous and operational discipline within their curricula. On behalf of the Armed Forces Institute, Secretary-Treasurer James Washington Bell coordinated the efforts of several scholars to oversee textbook selections in the field for cadets and midshipmen, thus "prov[iding] the Armed Forces of the United States with educational materials which [we]re in accord with the best civilian practices" in economics as a whole. By the midfifties it also became common for AEA functionaries to help designate particular professionals for work in special seminars on international organization and security convened by the transnational diplomatic and military alliance known as the North Atlantic Treaty Organization (NATO). It was a short step from these activities to involvement with the recruitment of undergraduate and graduate economics students for work within the now greatly expanded domain of the national security apparatus—including the Central Intelligence Agency (CIA).[38]

In the wake of the Korean War, and the exceedingly tense standoff that arose thereby between the United States and the Soviet Union across the central European plain and, along with China, across the Taiwan Strait and the Sea of Japan, the federal government believed civil defense planning and military preparedness to be necessary and prudent endeavors. Here, too, economists, in both official and consulting capacities, played their part. Late in 1954, it hardly seemed a waste of time for the staff of the Council of Economic Advisers to initiate a series of wide-ranging discussions on the matter of "emergency economic stabilization" in the event of a nuclear exchange. Edward Phelps, assistant director for stabilization in the Office of Defense Mobilization, suggested to his director, Arthur Flemming, that in the event of a nuclear attack civil defense authorities should be given the power to set wages, prices, and rents—as well as to ration goods and services. To be effective, plans for such a contingency would need to be set up in advance.

He felt Council and other government economists should begin the process of articulating such emergency arrangements. In cold war imagery that could not have been lost on his contemporaries, Phelps declared: "I do not envisage someone crawling out of the rubble waving a price regulation but I do suggest that certain minimum and simple rules of economic behavior may properly supplement other survival rules when it is time to move beyond the first instinctive or pre-arranged measures." Flemming agreed, and he received support from CEA chair Arthur Burns in detailing Council and Civil Defense Administration personnel to the task. CEA member Raymond Saulnier had a central role in the effort, representing the Council on the Defense Mobilization Board. The work was wide-ranging, spanning the most general issues of price and wage policies in the event of war to specific areas of concern such as the development of schedules for war-damage indemnification.[39]

If American economists, some in the most visible of official positions, others in academic environments better funded than ever before, found themselves increasingly caught up in the workings of the national security state, they were also soon confronted with yet another attribute of the cold war—the monitoring of intellectual communication and the actual suppression of certain ideas. Much like their counterparts in the physical sciences and engineering, those economists doing research of interest to the national defense establishment sometimes found avenues of scholarly interaction closed due to the perceived sensitivity of their work. Secrecy might have been an essential ingredient in the protection of military assets, but it was, by definition, the ultimate obstacle to the dissemination, evaluation, and critique of the results of any scholarly enterprise. Not infrequently, economists at RAND, at the Departments of Defense and State, in the Executive Office of the President, not to mention those working at colleges and universities with the support of federal contracts, found the immediate results of their investigations quarantined, awaiting publication approval from intelligence censors whose instincts and goals were, of course, hardly imbued with generous notions of academic freedom.[40]

Submission to the discipline of security clearances and research concealment was presumably an uncoerced choice for those recruited to the ranks of cold war service; for others, the condemnatory attentions of counterintelligence operatives, not to mention of unsympathetic colleagues and opportunistic politicians, were invasive and threatening. Hand in hand with the support of particular varieties of economic scholarship that the cold war inspired, there went an actual suppression of certain tendencies in economic analysis that were regarded as dangerous, wrongheaded, even treasonous. In this experience of the anti-Communist purges of the postwar era, the economics profession was hardly unique. The impact of McCarthyism throughout the American academy was profound and widespread.[41] Just as national security concerns privileged certain kinds of academic research by means of funding, and other signs of prestige and governmental approval, they also played no small part in the enfeeblement of other intellectual traditions. Either through the passive means of deprivation of support and encouragement, or by the active efforts of university and government authorities to deny employment and advancement to those deemed to be marginal to a discipline's dominant trajectory, cold war ideology powerfully framed the late-twentieth-century evolution of American scholarship.[42]

For those colleagues whose political activities, beliefs, or personal associations were taken to be evidence of their membership in a virtual "fifth column" of scholars, anticommunism put their careers as professional economists at grave risk. As early as the mid-1940s, the editors of the *American Economic Review* had been anxious to minimize the presence of articles and book reviews that focused on socialist and Marxist ideas. Paul T. Homan, a UCLA professor then serving as *AER* editor, rejected a proposed submission on the grounds that its publication would eventuate in the receipt of "another dozen pieces on revised and unrevised Marxism." Rejection, in this case, was to his mind the "only way of damming the expected flood" of undesired articles. If AEA secretary-treasurer James Washington Bell shared Homan's contempt for Marxist scholarship, he nevertheless masked his true feelings with condescension. In receipt of an outline for Raya Dunayevskaya's *State Capitalism and Marxism*, he found that he had no comments to make. "I did try to penetrate DAS KAPITAL [*sic*] in the original," he wrote the author in reply, "[but] I found it too abstract and Hagelian [*sic*]." He was, he concluded, "inclined to believe that an apostle must be mystical and incomprehensible to have a perennial or perpetual following."[43]

Even concerns with propriety and collegiality could not prevent individuals like Homan from tripping over themselves when it came to the work of scholars on the Left. When David Wright of the University of Virginia, in his review of Lawrence R. Klein's *The Keynesian Revolution*, mentioned that the author was "a socialist if not a Marxist," the *AER* editor found himself "disturbed about the personal reference." He told Wright that "[b]efore including it, [he] [w]ould need to have evidence that it was actually true." Homan also felt compelled to contact Klein himself; when the future Nobel Memorial Prize laureate wrote back to protest that "name-calling is entirely out of place in a review in a professional journal," Homan turned to "an independent source [for] confirmation of . . . Klein's left wing views." For his part, Wright did not believe "that anyone reading the text would retain any doubts as to whether Klein was a Marxist." After all, Klein "[wa]s a close friend of Paul Sweezy's [the well-known radical economist] and belong[ed] to the extreme left wing of socialism—as far as one c[ould] go without being a Communist." Having cleared the "personal reference" for publication, Homan told Klein "that it [wa]s almost the universal practice to call attention to such matters in reviews where there [wa]s any justification for doing so, not only in the case of leftist views but at any point across the ideological spectrum." Klein never wrote back, perhaps finding the editor's invocation of "universal practice" thoroughly disingenuous.[44]

Personal and professional ties, independent of political differences, sometimes worked to lessen the potential blows of the anticommunist purge among economists. When there was fear in 1950 that Robert A. Gordon might leave his position at Berkeley because of an investigation of left-wing faculty by the regents, Arthur Burns, then director of the National Bureau of Economic Research, stood by to offer Gordon a position in New York. In the end the gesture was unnecessary; it nonetheless spoke volumes about Burns's regard for Gordon given their rather deep differences regarding economic theory and policy. Of course, where an individual had neither the requisite stature nor patronage, allegations of ideological perfidy could prove much more troublesome. Raymond Saulnier, in the summer of 1956, was quite concerned to have thorough security checks of graduate students and new colleagues nominated for service on the staff of the Council of Economic Advisers given that some of these subalterns might have elsewhere "worked for people who [we]re under a cloud."[45]

The social and ideological pressures imposed by the cold war did not solely evoke among economists varying degrees of collaboration with (or resistance to) the instruments of political surveillance and enforced conformity. They aroused as well a sensitivity to the obligations of a professional community to a nation determined to demonstrate not simply the material (and military) but also the moral superiority of its way of life. In the great contest with the Soviet Union and China, the United States was to be judged as much by its commitment to democratic values as by the growth rate of its gross domestic product and the size of its conventional and nuclear arsenals. If economists, by reason of their training and skills, had something to contribute on matters of growth policy and defense planning and procurement, they also had a responsibility, as scholars and experts, to police their ranks for signs of bigotry and prejudice. In this context it was no accident that a leading member of the AEA, indeed a ranking scholar at a major southern university, would take the lead in the spring of 1957 to see to it that the Association avoided holding its annual meetings at hotels that refused accommodation to people of color. Segregation in a professional society, along dimensions other than those having to do with skill and accomplishment, had no place.[46]

Ethical principles and the moral imperatives of ideological conflict aside, the cold war mobilization of the American economics profession ineluctably rested upon the discipline's serviceability to the state. But that usefulness now far transcended the application of particular problem-solving techniques to the puzzles of military procurement, strategic choice, and the optimal allocation of matériel. It resonated as well with the far broader goal of macroeconomic management and control. High rates of growth, robust levels of employment, and stable prices were the standards by which a capitalist society could demonstrate its advantages over command economies premised upon socialist or communist designs. As the emblematic "Kitchen Debate" between Soviet premier Nikita Khrushchev and Vice President Richard Nixon had suggested in 1959, winning the cold war involved more than husbanding a credible nuclear deterrent, deploying fleets, garrisons, and air wings around the world, and utilizing special forces in counterinsurgency campaigns. It also required that an economic system deliver the goods to the people. Prosperity was an essential weapon in the struggle for the hearts and minds of any society.[47]

   Much like their colleagues in the physical sciences who served the needs of
the defense apparatus, American economists found themselves poised to participate in the realization of some of the most significant statist aims of the cold
war era. Indeed, their expertise placed them at a crucial intersection of those
objectives—a vigorous national economy was essential both to equip the armed
forces and to demonstrate the virtues of American capitalism. Guns *and* butter
were thus the protocol; a "New Economics" could provide the means to that end.
Both the experience of the Great Depression and the challenges of world war had
made clear to a new generation of specialists that the public sector occupied a
crucial niche in the mechanisms of the national economy. Properly managed and
monitored, that segment of the macroeconomy not only would provision an appropriate quantity and quality of public goods on its own behalf but also would afford
the private sector the wherewithal to expand output targets, enhance productivity,
and maintain employment. Interweaving public and private accumulation strategies, reckoning with the "mixed economy" of the postwar era, denoted the ascendancy of what was arguably the defining characteristic of the arguments of John
Maynard Keynes. Independent of specific policy initiatives, Keynesianism represented a new way of thinking about the economy as a whole, one that dovetailed
with broader governmental objectives tied to the struggle against Communism.
Whatever the intellectual foundations of the "Keynesian revolution," its historical
moorings were made fast by the exigencies of the cold war.[48]

Economists found the institutional zenith for their service to the national security
state of the cold war years in the Council of Economic Advisers within the Executive Office of the President. Created by the Employment Act of 1946, the CEA
was composed of three senior members appointed by the president upon the consent of the Senate. Assisted by a professional research staff, members had the
major responsibility of preparing an annual *Economic Report of the President* for
submission to the Congress. They were also expected to lend assistance and counsel in the formulation of economic policy. To this day the Council is regarded
as a demonstration of the inherent usefulness and importance of the economics
discipline; it stands as the only executive branch unit (other than the Office of the
Surgeon General) that, by the terms of its enabling legislation, represents a *specific* professional field in the White House.[49]

   The founding members of the CEA thus took office in the summer of 1946
amid high expectations regarding the value of economics to statecraft.[50] With the
globalist perspective of the Truman administration, as epitomized by the Truman
Doctrine that called for the attenuation of the military, political, and diplomatic
influence of the communist nations, the context within which postwar American
macroeconomic management would be undertaken was created. Geopolitical containment, and its first great test in the Korean peninsula in the early 1950s, confronted Washington with the need to finance a massive expansion in American
military capabilities. Under the aegis of the New Economics, this extraordinary

fiscal requirement, one ultimately exceeding that of World War II, was met. Ironically, that achievement was realized at the cost of creating enormous tensions within the professional community regarding the role of economists in government and the purpose of economic learning. Those conflicts, also exhibited in what became strained relations among the CEA's three original members, spoke directly to contested notions of, and expectations for, professional expertise that had characterized the history of the American economics discipline since the late nineteenth century.[51]

In the minds of its principal architects, the Council of Economic Advisers would provide scientific, objective, and disinterested service to the president. Through the calculation and evaluation of empirical data, its members could offer advice and counsel on the means best suited for the stated ends of government policy. In this respect it is no surprise that one of the leading historians of the rise of the American "mixed economy" has argued that the CEA was, in its very constitution, a *conservative* project of reform. An independent "board of experts" was preferable, in the eyes of both anti–New Deal Republicans and much of a business community intrigued by, yet suspicious of, Keynesian projects of centralized economic intervention, to highly politicized agencies either in the Executive Office Building or on Capitol Hill. Indeed, as the distinguished economist Theodore O. Yntema of the University of Michigan, a member of the highly influential Committee for Economic Development (CED), put it a year after the Council's creation: "We [i.e., the CED] ha[d] a strong preference for building a sound institutional structure [for economic advising] which w[ould] work automatically with a minimum of *ad hoc* government interference."[52]

With the appointment of Edwin G. Nourse as the first chair of the CEA, conservatives had every reason to believe that their formalistic (and minimalist) designs for the Council would be realized. Having studied economics and history at Cornell, Nourse received his graduate training at Chicago and took up his first teaching appointment at the Wharton School. He headed the economics departments at the University of South Dakota (1910–12) and the University of Arkansas (1915–18) before moving on to Iowa State, where he helped found what became a distinguished program in agricultural economics. In 1923, Nourse moved to Washington to join the Institute of Economics (later, the Brookings Institution), with which he remained identified until his death. Before becoming AEA president in 1942, he had served for three years as chair of the Social Science Research Council. While to a later CEA chair Nourse's appointment seemed "a puzzle," in large measure both his background and his political instincts appeared to be quite appropriate to the charge of his new office.[53]

On the one hand, Nourse's expertise in agricultural economics situated him within one of the most credentialed and technical of fields within the discipline as a whole. This no doubt comforted those who looked to the CEA to set a standard for professional probity and integrity in the nation's service. On the other, his personal convictions were characterized by a moderation that gave him an appeal to centrists of both major political parties; in his own words, he was a "liberal conservative" and a "conservative liberal." Here was a scholar who believed it essential "to avoid the dangers of an industrial economics of capital or a socialist economics of labor as well as an agrarian economics of land," a quiet and formal man who once declared that "[a] social agency, like a mechanical device, may be safe and useful in one man's hands or in certain circumstances and an engine of destruction as used by another." Nourse's notion of "an ideal economic society" embraced a "market structure which combined fluidity with order, and business mores that blended freedom with self-discipline." Like an allegory for the twentieth-century evolution of a profession of which he had become a most visible member, his career chronicled a rise from rigorously trained apprentice of price theory to preeminent policy expert on retainer to the nation's president.[54]

By drawing a parallel between a "social agency" and a "mechanical device," Nourse indulged perhaps in a most revealing trope. To his mind, the CEA was "a scientific agency of the federal government," its work focused on "fact-finding." There would be, he thus concluded, "no occasion for the Council to become involved in any way in the advocacy of particular measures or in the rival beliefs and struggles of the different economic and political interest groups." Insofar as economics "[wa]s a profession, not a branch of politics," it followed that members of the CEA, and most especially its chair, had to cultivate a nonpartisan practice akin to that of the Supreme Court. The example of the high court commended itself to Nourse precisely because the justices served life terms well beyond the limits set by national elections. Indeed, to a close colleague at the University of Michigan, he confided his belief that CEA appointments should in fact extend beyond each presidential term. Like a well-designed and properly calibrated engine, professional advising in the federal government should, in Nourse's view, run smoothly and dependably whatever the prevailing conditions. It followed that he "d[id] not accept the theory that the Council chairman should continue only when he [wa]s in full accord with Administration policy."[55]

So committed was the CEA's founding chair to the idea that the Council's "prime function [wa]s to bring the best available methods of social science to the service of the Chief Executive and of the Congress in formulating national policy" that he routinely refused invitations to testify before legislative panels on Capitol Hill, including the Joint Economic Committee (JEC) itself.[56] Such appearances, Nourse argued, ran the risk of entangling the Council in precisely the kinds of political controversies that he found antithetical to the purpose of the agency as a whole. In this further manifestation of his commitment to a positivist economics, Nourse perhaps unwittingly triggered what became a bitter and divisive quarrel within the Executive Office of the President. While Truman tried to stand above the fray, leaving to individuals the decision to appear on the Hill, Nourse's CEA colleagues John Clark and Leon Keyserling openly broke with their superior, often taking up the opportunity to meet with a variety of congressional committees. Over time, Nourse's worst fears were realized as Clark and Keyserling became more closely identified with Truman's particular policy strategies and Nourse himself became increasingly isolated. Inevitably the press exploited what often appeared to be, and in fact at times were, profound splits within the CEA itself on pressing matters of policy. For Nourse personally, the situation ultimately became intolerable as the Council, in his eyes, "shift[ed] its role from that of national economic physician to that of advocate for White House policy." He resigned his appointment in the fall of 1949, his short tenure as Council chair no doubt a galling indication of how far short the reality of presidential advising had fallen from his preconceived hopes.[57]

Less than a year before his resignation, in his letter to Senator Ralph Flanders, Republican of Vermont, Nourse detailed his objection to the more politicized vision of the CEA's work that evidently inspired the likes of his colleagues Clark and Keyserling.[58] Reacting to the suggestion that Council members should resign in the event of major policy differences with the president, Nourse found it hard to believe that the senator would "ask for a Council whose economics would change with the change of the President or even with the change of the President's thinking in response to any sort of influences non-economic in character." How could a science worthy of the name accept the notion that its most highly placed representatives would serve merely as temporary instruments of a partisan agenda? If appointment to the CEA was "the highest recognition to which any economist c[ould] aspire," did it not follow that "council members [had to] be above and beyond the temptation to make economic rationalization serve any predetermined conclusion or policy[?]"[59]

Unfortunately for Nourse, and those of like mind, for any president, "influences non-economic in character" would command as much attention as, if not more than, those falling precisely within the purview of the CEA. In the case of the Truman administration (not to mention its immediate successors), matters of national security, construed in either material or ideological terms, decisively animated economic policy choices, not the reverse. Whether it was the Soviet blockade of Berlin, the Korean War, China's belligerence toward Taiwan and its recognition of Ho Chi Minh's government in Vietnam, or the rapidly deteriorating situation in both eastern Europe and the Middle East, the perception emerged among the highest officials of the American government that the nation faced mobilization needs that would ultimately transcend those of World War II itself. As epitomized by the defining document of American cold war strategy we know as NSC 68 (National Security Council Memorandum No. 68), whatever the concerns of economists in the executive branch, military needs would be the budgetary "tail" that would wag the fiscal "dog." It was this "noneconomic" reality that so powerfully framed the work of the first Council of Economic Advisers. Indeed, it would do so for decades to come.[60]

Given the seemingly insatiable appetite of what was now called the national military establishment, the stage was set for a protracted struggle over the dimensions and impacts of the federal budget.[61] Among economists in particular, there emerged a dispute between those in the profession, like Nourse, who believed in keeping Washington's expenditures to modest dimensions, and those, often led by Keyserling, who linked projects of military procurement and deployment with increased domestic spending targets. These latter "inflationists," as Nourse called them, found in a diplomatic and military agenda, epitomized by NSC 68 and the

Truman Doctrine that gave it further concrete expression, the blueprint for a more aggressive pump-priming role for the federal government in general. Cold war doctrine thus set the terms of debate concerning macroeconomic management.[62]

While what would be the record-setting $12.5 billion budget deficit of the Eisenhower administration still lay some years in the future, the specter of permanent shortfalls in federal revenue, arising from military expenditures far exceeding tax receipts, inspired Nourse in his conviction that economic principles not be sacrificed to political necessity.[63] To be sure, it was hardly a simple anti-Keynesian perspective that provoked Nourse in his anxiety; in his mind it was an essential principle of the New Economics that budget deficits incurred in slack times (for the purposes of stimulatory federal spending) had to be liquidated by surpluses accumulated in prosperous ones. Far from a kind of standpat conservatism of the exchequer, Nourse's dismay with what he called "fiscal tricks" emerged from his fear of the inflationary bias inherent in government spending. That federal disbursements could drive up the price level in the absence of sustained productivity increases was, in his view, an obvious and incontrovertible finding of economic science. "We must recognize that we can't get more out of the economic system than we put into it," Nourse told the golden anniversary convention of the National Retail Farm Implement Dealers. How could any properly trained economist fail to appreciate that fact?[64]

For Nourse, engaging his colleagues in intellectual debate was one thing; persuading the president of the probity of his arguments was something else entirely. But months before his resignation, he wrote Truman of his "belief that dangers to the domestic economy from financing [defense] expenditures out of continuing deficits and with a growing national debt are no less real than . . . military and diplomatic dangers." Allowing that "[i]t [wa]s not within [his] province or competence to make categorical judgments in the military or diplomatic field," the CEA chair nonetheless believed the situation quite grave. Indeed, Nourse had already reached the breaking point, having made the still private decision to leave his post a week earlier. He had been reluctantly forced to conclude that "a truly professional and non-political Council" was a chimera; it would inevitably "be known for the political clap-trap it so largely [had become]."[65]

Despite the fact that Nourse regarded his departure from the CEA, and his replacement as chair by Leon Keyserling, as a triumph of a narrow-minded politics over a professional and disinterested expertise, other more powerful critics of the council did not share in that perception. For the formidable Senator Robert Taft of Ohio, the widely acknowledged leader of the conservative Republicans in Congress, the CEA had always represented the proverbial Trojan horse of New Deal liberalism. It was useless to counterpose political connivance to a purported science of economics, as Nourse had done, in reckoning with the problems of Truman's economic policies when, in fact, the entire enterprise of the CEA was fraudulent from the start. The man known as "Mr. Republican" delighted in hoisting the likes of Keyserling and his allies by their own petard when he would provocatively ask why, given that military spending could now guarantee full employment, the CEA or the 1946 Employment Act was even necessary? In a series of threatening yet ultimately unsuccessful attempts to eliminate the council's funding, Taft drove home the point that, outside the academy, splitting the hairs of economic reasoning obscured the far more important issues of choosing the ends of public policy. To one drawn from the rough-and-tumble world of political bargaining, the notion of a "coldly scientific and nonpolitical" CEA was at best an unfortunate delusion, at worst a self-serving fantasy of academic professionals determined to enhance their prestige and influence at the expense of genuine public debate.[66]

Ironically enough, in his contempt for those who held an enduring and uncritical faith in the virtues of professional skill, Senator Taft found unlikely supporters in Harry Truman and Leon Keyserling. In letting Nourse go, Truman knew he would garner the wrath of many impressed by the economist's credentials and reputation. On the other hand, as one contemporary noted, the president had grown "more and more uncomfortable as he looked over the shoulder of Dr. Nourse at the guiding spirit of the Science of Economics; it . . . made him as uneasy as it once made the Queen of Scots to hear the voice of God through the lips of John Knox." Whatever support Edwin Nourse might have received from professional colleagues and well-meaning admirers from across the country, he had lost the president's confidence rather quickly.[67]

As for Leon Keyserling, misgivings about the status of economics as a rigorous policy science and about economists themselves as an ingrown clique were deeply ingrained and strongly held. He found the discipline itself "remote from life" and thought it "ridiculous to pretend that there is 'neutrality' or a kind of scientific objectivity in economics." Academic credentials did not impress Keyserling as indications of capability in the council environment; he believed this, in large measure because "[t]he academic teaching of economics and the academic study of economics ha[d] very, very little to do with the real world." He fretted over the tendency for the CEA to become inbred, particularly because "recruitment [to the council and its staff] [wa]s almost entirely from one narrow school of professional economists." Coming from a student of Rexford G. Tugwell, these sentiments were not particularly surprising.[68] Nevertheless, they also masked an enduring defensiveness, on Keyserling's part, that he had never completed the doctorate, having gone "ABD" (all but dissertation) in the Columbia graduate program when he joined the Agricultural Adjustment Administration in 1933. Stung by the attacks of enemies who held up his lack of a terminal degree in economics as evidence of his incompetence, Keyserling mused that if he had "written an essay on bimetallism in Spain in the 16th century and gotten a Ph.D. for it, and for thirteen years had taught by routine a course in trade regulations, reading the same notes every year, then [he] would have [been] regarded . . . as a qualified economist."[69]

Professional exclusivity and arrogance notwithstanding, Keyserling very much became a lightning rod for the two sides to the debate over the purpose and practice of the Council of Economic Advisers. His champions and critics alike were drawn from across the ranks, both high and low, of the profession with which he had a love-hate relationship.[70] Apart from the implications it had for the trajectory of his career, Keyserling's notoriety also raised a host of thorny questions regarding the future of the council, in particular, and of economics in the public service in general. Many members of the profession, having contemplated the Nourse-Keyserling struggle in Washington, feared that the CEA had lost valuable capital and prestige. One colleague found council publications "at first noncontroversial and platitudinous" only to become, with Keyserling's accession to the chair, "controversial and platitudinous." Another thought the CEA lacked "clout" under Nourse and gained quite a bit more under Keyserling, albeit not necessarily for the best of reasons. With the appointment of Roy Blough to replace Nourse, one financial markets newsletter thundered that "[t]he CEA [wa]s no economic advisory group—it [wa]s a group deep in left field." Many members of the profession might have indeed wondered, as the Truman presidency drew to a close, if the great triumph of the Employment Act of 1946 had all gone for nought.[71]

While the creation of the Council of Economic Advisers had fostered in some the "fear of [an] invisible Rasputin whispering in the president's ear," it had also encouraged a professional elite in the cultivation not simply of its own importance and skill but also of highly visible and appropriate governmental venues within which to display its capabilities. The difficulties encountered in the inaugural CEA, epitomized by the bitter struggle between Nourse and Keyserling, would not be allowed to eliminate the promise of decades of genuine achievement and effort. From the Great War to the cold war, American economists had demonstrated an ever-more-impressive ability to serve the needs of the state while at the same time pushing forward the intellectual (and indeed institutional) sophistication of their discipline. If the Truman Council had seemingly squandered the opportunities bestowed on the field by the Employment Act, the fault lay not in the design nor in the intent but rather in the execution. Greater attention to professional deportment and practice would solve the problem. The demands of statecraft could thus be served without sacrifice of integrity or scientific principle. For American economists a season of remarkable self-confidence and prestige thus appeared on the horizon. Yet seasons come to pass.[72]

5

Statecraft and Its Retainers

> The economists in our universities and research institu-
> tions toil in the field of values as well as that of fact and
> theory. When they come to Washington, they cannot
> leave their ideologies behind.
> —ARTHUR M. OKUN (1969)[1]

RECAPTURING the presidency and the Congress in the election of 1952 encouraged many Grand Old Party stalwarts in the belief that the potent Democratic influence of two decades had, at long last, come to an end. Whatever the tenuous nature of their control on Capitol Hill—one seat in the Senate, nine seats in the House of Representatives—and despite the ideological moderation of Dwight Eisenhower, whose national popularity had prompted some of his champions to indulge fantasies of a bipartisan presidential endorsement, Republicans viewed with satisfaction the imminent opportunity to dismantle the most objectionable manifestations of the New Deal and the Fair Deal. The blurring of party differences wrought by the beginnings of the cold war, the marginalization of the Right by the victory of the Grand Alliance over fascism, the suppression of the Left by the gathering momentum of McCarthyism—all this emboldened the enemies of federalism, primarily but not solely Republicans, to settle accounts.[2]

To be sure, the run-up to the 1952 campaign had been an occasion for spirited and, at times, hot-tempered debate within the major parties themselves. Supporters of Senator Robert Taft of Ohio refused to make Eisenhower's nomination unanimous at the Republican national convention in Chicago. Harry Truman's decision to step down sparked a struggle for power among the Democrats as well—the wounds of the "Dixiecrat" rebellion still festering after the party's improbable victory in 1948. The president's choice of Illinois governor Adlai Stevenson as his successor eased tensions in the four-way race for the nomination that emerged between Averell Harriman (governor of New York), Estes Kefauver (senator from Tennessee), Richard Russell (senator from Georgia), and Stevenson himself. But in the final analysis, on election day, Eisenhower's thirty-three million votes, then the largest popular tally in a presidential canvass, signaled what some pundits referred to as "the revolt of the moderates" and the start of what the president-elect himself hoped would be a "Second Era of Good Feelings." No matter how the 1952 returns were read, it was clear that, in the wake of Roosevelt's reconfiguration of his party, one of the great transformations of American political history had taken hold: on the one side, the party of Jefferson, the defender of states' rights and localism, had in short order become the champion of

federal authority and centralized power; on the other, the party born of the nineteenth-century crisis of the Union, the vanguard of a modern administrative state,
stood as a resolute critic of Washington's increasing presence in almost every
aspect of the nation's life.[3]

That, in the protean political environment of the early 1950s, the Employment
Act of 1946 was a favorite target for the opponents of federalism (and of the New
Deal coalition as a whole) was hardly surprising. Controversial at the time of its
initial reading, the bill served as a kind of lightning rod for liberals and conservatives alike. Indeed, a brief yet passionate debate over the stipulation of "price
stability" as, along with "full employment," the goal of national economic policy
had provided a succinct mapping of the ideological gulf that separated them.
Periodic squabbles over the funding for the Council of Economic Advisers gave
further vent to their opposing convictions. By the winter of 1953, with the installation of the first Eisenhower cabinet, the prospect of eliminating the Council entirely did not seem unrealistic. Yet decades of an enterprising professionalism
served to muster a broad spectrum of economists in defense of what had already
become, internecine squabbles and particular disappointments notwithstanding, a
singular representation of their authority and influence.[4]

Of the increasingly strident contests between Leon Keyserling and Edwin
Nourse that had punctuated the operations of Truman's CEA, bad blood and pessimistic expectations for the continued salience of economic advising in the executive branch had been the primary result. For a brief period, the Council's critics
succeeded in holding up continued funding in the last days of the Truman presidency. There was, in fact, widespread expectation that the CEA would be either
entirely dismantled when Eisenhower assumed office or reduced both in its responsibilities and in its access to the president himself. A compromise was
reached in the early months of 1953 with the appointment of Arthur Burns as the
new Council chair. Refunded by a less than enthusiastic Republican Congress,
the CEA was also refashioned with greater authority vested in Burns himself. To
Council member Neil Jacoby of UCLA, both Burns's professionalism and the
president's insistence that policy advice be based on scientific judgments alone
set a high tone that arguably saved the CEA from extinction at a time when its
reputation was at a low ebb; he was hardly alone in this perception. Indeed, Burns
was widely admired as a quintessential professional, one capable of uniting many
economists arrayed along the political spectrum; as for Eisenhower, he resolutely
abhorred "pressure groups," and his vision of what one noted historian of the
period has called a "corporate commonwealth" included the ideal of a "depoliticized, administrative state." If Council antagonists were unrequited in their desire
to see the CEA disappear, they could at least, by the spring of 1953, take solace
in the idea that its pro-activist days—exemplified by the frenetic (and unabashed)
political energy of a Keyserling—were over.[5]

While an increasingly professionalized CEA played to ever-more-laudatory
reviews through the balance of the 1950s and early 1960s, the struggle between
"science" and "policy," between political virtue and intellectual conviction, remained. If muted by the impeccable academic credentials of new generations of

economists drawn to Washington, the debate first joined by Keyserling and Nourse over the proper place of economic expertise in the federal government remained nonetheless unresolved. Even as their discipline grew in stature, cultivating both research resources and prestige far in excess of that garnered by its cognate fields; even though their leading practitioners enjoyed a kind of public visibility unimagined by colleagues in the other social sciences; despite the unique distinction of having a new "Nobel Prize" created to celebrate their triumphs, economists remained diffident about the volatile intersection between their scholarship and their ideological beliefs.

For those who constituted the vanguard of the "New Economics" in the 1950s and the 1960s (and for the entire profession of which they were the most conspicuous representatives), service in Washington brought many benefits.[6] It also exacted a price. Discovering that their skills were nurtured "in the field of values as well as that of fact and theory," economists found themselves increasingly challenged to differentiate between what they took to be the scholarly and the political. The essential distinction rested, in their minds, on an appreciation of the "professional view" in any policy dispute. Yet, as Arthur Okun had put it in 1969 after several years of brilliant government service, to articulate that frame of reference "effectively require[d] the talents of a missionary, an outstanding pedagogue, and a super-sales[person.]" Given that these requirements were hardly those essential (if not inimical) to success in the academic and scientific world, the conundrums associated with any notion of "economics in the public service" were obvious. At the very moment that their fascination with statecraft reached its zenith, American economists thus found themselves forced ever more to reckon with the implications of being its retainers.[7]

Not least of the historical forces that shaped the continuing evolution of the American economics profession in the latter half of the twentieth century was the unique prosperity the nation enjoyed throughout the 1950s and 1960s. If the application of a new learning to the management of a "mixed economy" provided an exceptional opportunity for social scientific expertise to demonstrate its rigor and effectiveness, the context within which that display took place set the terms of both its practice and its success. Having proved its mettle in the extraordinary years of world war, and having continued to do so in the early stages of what would be an even longer cold war, modern economic theory was now deployed in an altogether novel exercise—the pursuit and maintenance of full employment growth in peacetime. That, owing to history itself, the national economy was singularly well positioned for sustained expansion in the postwar period made that task all the more tractable.

Unlike any other industrialized nation in the world at the time, the United States met the 1950s with an economy not only physically intact but also organizationally and technologically robust. The demographic echoes of war set the stage for an acceleration in the rate of population growth, while the labor market effects of demobilization surprisingly sparked a rise in wages and incomes. Rapid and profitable conversion to domestic production was further engrossed by foreign demand—most vividly and poignantly emanating from those regions most devastated by the war itself—for the products of American industry and agriculture. As for international finance, the nation stood as creditor virtually to the entire world, and the dollar, both by default and by a multilateral agreement first reached by the Allied nations at Bretton Woods, had become a kind of *numeraire* to a newly emergent system of global commerce. With no small justification, the fifties and sixties would come to be regarded as a golden age of American capitalism.[8]

Macroeconomic management, demanding under any circumstances, was made substantially easier for a postwar generation that found itself the beneficiaries of historical circumstance. Far from solving the cruel puzzle of idle capacity and widespread unemployment that had characterized the Great Depression, and unlike the challenge to rationalize allocation and maximize production in the emergency of war, the task that lay before American economists by the mid-1950s was both more straightforward and less difficult. More straightforward because, thanks to both the "Keynesian revolution" in economic thought and the policy experience derived from mobilization and war, the relationship between individual market behavior and aggregate outcomes was finally subject to systematic understanding. Less difficult because, given the sturdy rebound of the economy in the wake of World War II, there existed both the confidence (most especially exemplified by the moderate rates of return in the markets for Treasury bills and other government obligations) and the means (most vividly represented by rising income tax receipts) to realize fiscal spending targets with a minimum of redistributive implications.[9]

So optimistic were politicians and the vast majority of economists concerning the effectiveness of stabilization policy techniques that it became fashionable by the early 1960s to speak of the "end of the business cycle" and of the ability of policy makers to "fine-tune" macroeconomic performance. In the 1965 report of his Council of Economic Advisers, President Lyndon Johnson made it clear that he "d[id] not believe recessions [we]re inevitable." Similarly, in what was arguably the most influential economics textbook ever published, Paul Samuelson wrote that his colleagues "*kn[ew] how* to use monetary and fiscal policy to keep any recessions that br[oke] out from snowballing into *lasting* chronic slumps." He went on to claim that the business cycle was thus a thing of the past. Expert knowledge buttressed by a healthy and resilient economy could now make the periodic deprivation and hardship once believed to be the inevitable consequence of the cycle truly a thing of the past.[10]

Cultivating a politics of aggregate productivity and a discourse about sustained prosperity was not solely the result of professional self-assurance and self-promotion, nor was it simply the manifestation of a particular politician's (or a particular party's) strategy to procure votes. The focus on growth and accumulation so characteristic of the new economics of the postwar era represented as well a transformation in the nation's political culture that had been in the making for decades.

For nineteenth-century convictions regarding the probity of thrift and self-improvement, mid-twentieth-century Americans had swapped a fascination with, a virtual anxiety about the individuation and comfort associated with consumption. Production was no longer an end in itself, nor could it alone provide meaning and dignity to one's life. Rather, it was the goods and services of the material world that afforded freedom and amenities, setting one's self off from others and liberating all from both the overt and the hidden injuries of class, ethnicity, and gender. What came to be known as the "economic growthmanship" practiced by a new social scientific elite was, on the one side, a particular aspect of a stage in the evolution of a professional community; on the other, it distilled, within a set of seemingly unassailable aspirations and beliefs, a society's unself-conscious embrace of an altogether new set of cultural ideals.[11]

Within an economics of abundance and stability rested the ingredients of a prosperous commonwealth devoid of the class antagonisms and struggles over normative values that were a threat to both the legitimacy of social scientific policy making and social tranquillity and political cohesion. If an "emphasis on an ever-growing pie, rather than on slicing up a given pie in a new way, [wa]s well designed . . . to attract widespread support" for particular policies, it was also true that the depiction of the economy as a kind of positive-sum game from which all could benefit independent of their *relative* shares in particular outcomes was an essential part of the political-economic ideology of postwar America from the time of Truman's Fair Deal through that of Lyndon Johnson's Great Society, up to and including the early stages of Richard Nixon's New Federalism.[12] Their specific analytical differences aside, virtually all mainstream American economists both embraced and relied upon this "depoliticization" of the marketplace in their determination to separate positive economic "science" from normative assertions. So long as the profession could retain this image of its work as a calculation of optimal means to a given end rather than the comparison of different and possibly incompatible goals, its claims to the authority and influence devoutly sought since the late 1890s were secure. So soon as that archetype was jettisoned or challenged, modern economics would find itself in a world, not of rigor and logic, but rather of ideological belief and political power.[13]

What went hand in hand with the effort to make economics a "science" of statecraft during the postwar era was a conscious and systematic determination to standardize the training of new colleagues and homogenize the content of undergraduate and graduate curricula. Much like the rhetoric of prosperity and productivity that framed the pronouncements of the profession's most visible theoreticians and analysts, the increasing concern over the training of economists linked the evolution of particular theoretical and practical doctrines within the field with the broader social and political force of anticommunism. Containment of what were perceived to be threatening initiatives on a global scale expressed itself domestically in an overweening anxiety about enemies at home. For virtually all academic fields within the United States, economics being no exception, McCarthyism thus yoked together disciplinary evolution with socially constructed and politically molded agendas.[14]

Interestingly enough, and not surprisingly, concerns with the content and delivery of economics curricula emerged directly from the World War II experience. Wartime efforts on behalf of the National Roster of Scientific and Specialized Personnel (NRSSP) had made the leadership of the American Economic Association both particularly sensitive and responsive to requests for information about the discipline and its specialists. Moving from a focus on calculating the profession's numbers and activities, as the NRSSP had requested, to a self-conscious assessment of teaching methods, course content, and educational performance standards was altogether understandable and clear-cut. AEA initiatives in this regard were only further stimulated by the desire of the Veterans Administration and related agencies to facilitate the reentry of armed forces personnel to civilian life after World War II and the Korean conflict.[15]

Defining what an economist was, and what he or she did for a living, was one thing; stipulating how an economist was to be trained, not to mention evaluating his or her professional skills, was something else. In a series of studies, the first of which was launched in 1949, with follow-ups taking place throughout the 1950s, AEA task forces conducted wide-ranging surveys of undergraduate and graduate curricula throughout the country. Of particular importance to these committees were the "opinions of leaders in graduate training" in the field at the nation's foremost research institutions. Recognizing that "[t]he Association ha[d] a definite professional responsibility in this [regard]," the Ad Hoc Committee on Graduate Training in Economics made its first report to the AEA Executive Committee late in 1950. Determined to guide universities in the establishment and maintenance of "good graduate program[s] in economics at various levels," the committee particularly encouraged institutions to improve standards for the selection of incoming students, articulate precise objectives for advanced study in the field, and vet subject matter and course content with a view toward the rigorous training of new colleagues. Specifically, the committee believed that the "important tools" in all graduate economics instruction were "mathematics, accounting, statistics, history, logic, scientific method, and foreign language."[16]

Whether through general oversight or simply moral suasion, AEA officials were eager to engage the largest number of colleges and universities possible in the improvement and standardization of undergraduate and graduate instruction in economics.[17] Some brief attempts were even made, both in the fall of 1950 and a bit over a decade later, to look to the high school level as an appropriate venue in which to prepare students for formal introduction to the field when they entered college. By the summer of 1951, the Rockefeller Foundation was sufficiently impressed with the Association's work on curricular matters that it allocated the then impressive sum of $16,000 to the effort. Senior academic officers from around the country were grateful for the periodic reports and correspondence the AEA shared with them regarding economics training. Both AEA officials and

some of these campus administrators believed the work had more general applicability to graduate training in other disciplines. Even the United Nations Educational, Scientific, and Cultural Organization (UNESCO) expressed interest, scheduling a May 1951 conference on the teaching of economics in Egypt, France,
Great Britain, India, Mexico, Sweden, the United States, and Yugoslavia.[18]

Never far from the surface, in all their concern with the quality of training in
their discipline, was the anxiety many academic economists and AEA leaders felt
about the complicated and sometimes tortured connections between professional
qualifications and policy pronouncements. Engagement with contemporary public
policy issues clearly had the potential to undercut claims to professional objectivity. The matter was especially difficult given the ever-growing presence of the
federal government in the funding of advanced study in economics. Early in April
1959, in fact, a meeting of social science organizations in Washington noted, with
some trepidation, "[t]he influence which Government, especially through research
contracts, now exert[ed] on the developments [sic] of the disciplines [them-
selves.]" Indeed, as early as 1946, Joseph Spengler had urged the AEA Executive
Committee to discuss not simply minimum standards for the economics doctorate
but also "a related problem, namely, the ethical rules or standards o[f] [the] profession." He wondered if the discipline needed "a Hippocratic oath to guard against
government economists violating sound doctrine to follow [a] party line, or to
insure sound ethical practices on the part of counselors and nonteaching economists[.]" While Spengler's suggestion went unheeded, the concerns to which it
gave voice remained. A bit over a decade later, AEA secretary-treasurer James
Washington Bell could receive an irate letter that declared "[s]ome U.S. economists are quacks—out-and-out fakers." The missive closed with a taunting question: "While the Unions are cleaning out their Hoffas and Congressmen are
exposing nepotism,—what are *you* doing?" Bell never replied.[19]

The pursuit of disciplinary precision and professional rectitude during the postwar decades no doubt seemed, to economists at the time, a logical outcome of a
process of development stretching back to the late nineteenth century. Yet like all
historical mechanisms it also involved its opposite—the suppression of ideas and
methods believed to be deviant and thereby antithetical to the advancement of the
science as a whole. Celebrated cases of particular individuals either forced from
academic positions or mistreated and marginalized aside, the purge of non-neoclassical (and predominantly Marxist) ideas from the corpus of American economics during the cold war went mostly unchallenged. On the one side, new generations of students were denied exposure to heterodox or critical traditions in the
literature, thereby ensuring that, with the passage of time, the neoclassical viewpoint would predominate in the discipline. On the other, an older generation, either
cowed by McCarthyite tactics at their home or other institutions or predisposed
to an anti-Marxism that had been, along with personal conviction, schooled in
revulsion at such things as the 1939 Non-Aggression Pact between Germany and
the Soviet Union and the horrifying revelations regarding Stalinism that emerged
from the Twentieth (Soviet) Communist Party Congress of 1956, served to police
the community of economics scholars with no small amount of effectiveness.[20]

Even so, making the discipline of economics safe for a liberal capitalism was, with a few notorious exceptions, not something to be undertaken with passion and demagoguery but rather with composure and an emphasis on competence and rigor. Precisely because economists, regardless of their political persuasions, did work that touched upon some of the most significant and potentially divisive questions with which any society had to contend, the determination to make the field as "scientific" and "objective" as possible took on a special urgency during the cold war decades. Emphasizing the study of means rather than ends in economic life was an essential tool in the pursuit of that goal. Unlike the physical and life sciences, the humanities, and the arts, the social sciences in general and economics in particular allowed their practitioners comparatively little room with which to distinguish between political action per se and academic argument. While a physicist's opinion on matters of state or a sculptor's view of the Soviet Union was presumably an issue separable from his or her professional identity, for an economist such distinctions were far less clear. Ironically enough, such disciplinary and professional differences afforded social science faculties far more leeway to purge their ranks of those holding fast to unacceptable and unpopular doctrines. The homogenization of opinion within the social sciences often took place along the dimension of academic peer review rather than overt political repression. With the exception of a Paul Baran, a left-wing economist was rarely fired or harassed for "political" reasons during the McCarthyite hysteria; unlike, say, a mathematician expelled from a faculty appointment and ultimately imprisoned for refusing to answer questions about his political beliefs, an economist of radical loyalties could be denied promotion and advancement, left without research funding, and sequestered from journal editorial boards all on the basis of a professional "vetting" regarded as apolitical and rational. Determined to get rid of faculty colleagues in the sciences, an anti-Communist institution would have difficulty relating their political beliefs to their research. In the social sciences, the situation was quite reversed, so much so that to this day, while some campuses and individuals have regretted the political repression of various colleagues during the 1950s and 1960s, such remorse has rarely if ever been expressed with regard to those who had been unfortunate enough to be in the social sciences. If, for example, Marxian economic theory was "wrong," the firing of Marxist economists was something easily justified. In the physical and life sciences the situation was thoroughly different; presumably a colleague's Communist convictions, say, said nothing, for example, of his or her grasp of the third law of thermodynamics. Would a physics department be expected to retain a colleague who believed the earth was flat? Why, then, should an economics department apologize for ridding itself of those whose ideas and methods were at variance with the state of the art?[21]

If the "state of the art" in economics provided a systematic template with which to structure personnel decisions, especially but not solely during the cold war, defining that "state of the art" became an essential and momentous enterprise. While the specific ingredients of that act of identification found their roots in neoclassical theory, the use of that inventory was ever more focused on the advanced training of new generations of specialists. Throughout the 1950s, leading doctoral programs in economics emphasized the reading of journal articles and working papers among their matriculants. Like any science or engineering faculty, most American economics departments came to view graduate training as a process of exposure to the latest advancements in knowledge, not the cultivation of literacy in the classic texts, let alone controversial works.[22]

By no means was the effort to imitate the sciences in graduate instruction focused solely on the exclusion of Marxist principles from economics curricula. All manner of ideas and techniques considered to be insufficiently grounded in falsifiable propositions, or inadequately engaged with modern methods of hypothesis testing, came under suspicion. On the one side, this postwar evolution of the discipline merely brought to fruition a half-century-long effort to distance economics from what were viewed to be the questionable and even dangerous convictions of the "soft" social sciences (such as anthropology, political science, and sociology). On the other, it also swept up in its path heterodox approaches that not only had a fair number of proponents but hardly bore the stigma of Marxism. Gone from a rising number of nationally ranked graduate programs in economics, by the late 1950s, were agendas that acquainted the student with the work of a Thorstein Veblen, a Joseph Schumpeter, or a Karl Polanyi—not to mention a Karl Marx. In their place were "core" course sequences that emphasized neoclassical theory, most often in its mathematical representations. Like the training of chemists or physicians, the mentoring of new economists came to rely increasingly on a program of study focused and detailed by the profession's "leading lights" and best practice.[23]

It was also the case that the standardization of economics curricula, while ultimately successful to a remarkable degree, did not go unchallenged. By the early 1960s, taking inspiration from a reborn civil rights movement that had emerged in the preceding decade, galvanized by urban riots in Detroit, Los Angeles, Newark, and Washington D.C., inspired by a burgeoning feminist mobilization, committed to protesting the growing war in Vietnam, and (like virtually all Americans) shocked by a wave of political assassinations that punctuated the decade as a whole, a "New Left" emerged within the economics profession that would constitute the single most dramatic counterpoint to the neoclassical hegemony that had defined the discipline in the nation for over a century. In large measure, this anti-neoclassical resistance was as much premised upon classical and Marxian ideas as it was predominantly peopled by a younger generation of economists and their students.[24]

Determined to undermine what they believed to be the tendency of mainstream economic theory to apologize for rather than explain capitalism, New Left economists published stinging critiques of prevailing theory, mobilized colleagues through such organizations as the Union for Radical Political Economics (URPE), and sought to transform course content, especially at the undergraduate level, to encourage a more critical perception of economic life among their students.[25] Counterposed, of course, to this efflorescence of youthful criticism and subversion were the conservative instincts of an older generation that still held fresh in its memory what it took to be the worst expressions of politicized social thought history had to offer—German National Socialism and Soviet Communism. In the frenzied belief in a master race that the Nazis had epitomized and in the garbled hope for the construction of a "new economic person" that framed the five-year plans of Stalin, mainstream American economists (among others) believed they had encountered everything there was to fear in normative social theory. The challenges of the New Left might be tolerated; they might even be graciously taken up in a spirit of friendly debate.[26] But they would never be successful. Decades of professionalization and the harsh lessons of recent history, combined in the persons of a victorious wartime generation that now stood as the leaders in the discipline, would ensure this was so.

With their emphasis on competence and rigorous training, neoclassical economists of the postwar period were therefore particularly well equipped to fend off their radical antagonists. Liberal scholars could extol the virtues of open debate and a "free market" of ideas while at the same time insisting that anyone teaching or publishing in the field carry the credentials of a true professional. When, throughout the 1960s and 1970s, economics students would agitate for the inclusion of Marxian principles in their courses, the most frequent response from their faculty superiors was that it was exceedingly difficult to find anyone competent enough to teach the courses they sought. Given that almost no graduate programs in the country trained their students in non-neoclassical principles, this was hardly surprising. It was also virtually impossible to confront.[27] It was one thing for, say, a chemistry department to refuse to hire someone because he or she was opposed to the Vietnam War. In the turbulent political environment of the 1960s, such an action would have been roundly condemned as totalitarian, even illegal. Refusing to hire someone because his or her credentials and training were considered inadequate, as was so often the case when Marxists pursued appointment in economics faculties, was something else entirely. Perhaps it was true, as John Kenneth Galbraith declared during a struggle to promote Marxist economists at Harvard to tenured professorships in the early 1970s, that "[c]ompetency [wa]s always a disguise for something else" when a discipline's ranks were policed for uniformity. Nevertheless, the ability to frame the discourse about competence in ways that were seemingly professional and scientific allowed American economists, like almost no other group of social scientists in mid-twentieth-century America, to purge their institutions thoroughly of those whose work constituted a direct challenge both to their authority and influence and to some of their most deeply held ideological beliefs.[28]

Even where left-wing attacks on the neoclassical corpus resulted in telling wounds, the ability of mainstream practitioners to shift the terms of debate and thus preserve their dominance was not seriously weakened. To oft-repeated claims that mainstream economics ignored central questions regarding the distribution of income, the impact of racism and sexism in labor markets, and the wealth inequality of nations, neoclassical theorists could reply that such issues were more appropriately the subject matter of other fields such as anthropology, history, political science, and sociology. By thus defining critical questions as being outside the domain of their field, economists could preserve a rhetorical and methodological integrity that maintained professional rigor and objectivity. In other cases, mainstream arguments could insist that neoclassical *methods* could address non-neoclassical *problems*, thereby again preserving the discipline's theoretical conformity while admitting a bit more diversity in the form of its application.

Finally, on those occasions when anti-neoclassical critiques were powerfully framed within the vocabulary of modern (and increasingly mathematized) economic theory per se, the mainstream proved itself sufficiently flexible either to engage the arguments in more and more esoteric exchanges or to ignore them altogether. In a series of theoretical debates that transpired during the 1960s and 1970s, anti-neoclassical scholars, Joan Robinson most prominent among them, succeeded in exposing an array of logical inconsistencies in the core of the neoclassical framework. These "Cambridge controversies in the theory of capital," as they came to be known in the literature, constituted the high tide of the New Left offensive against the mainstream. Never resolved in a systematic way, these exchanges became increasingly recondite and formalistic. Neoclassical investigators dismissed the "Cambridge criticisms" as either "empirical" problems or theoretical curiosities. The "controversies" simply faded away; point and counterpoint in professional journals could not undo what history and circumstance had wrought over a century.[29]

Thus at the very moment that a New Economics of statecraft was established in Washington, American economists also succeeded in preserving what they took to be their profession's distinctive and scientific quality and in quarantining alternative doctrines in the field that they viewed as disruptive and dangerous. To the extent that dissenting points of view could and would remain part of the discipline, they would do so only in the handful of non-neoclassical graduate programs operating across the country and in the toleration, within mainstream programs, for research and teaching on the history of economic thought. For the overwhelming majority of doctoral candidates in the field, any genuine and substantive awareness of oppositional traditions in economics depended upon their exposure to classic and marginal texts—works that, by definition, did not constitute the core of a graduate training sequence. It was therefore hardly surprising that New Left students, and others less enthralled with neoclassical theory than the vast majority of their peers, tended to cluster in history-of-thought classes. There they gained not simply a literacy in venerable contributions to the evolution of economic doctrine but also an appreciation for the fact that, as with any discipline (or any human community, for that matter), outsiders and other liminal figures were "the most articulate conscious voices of values" that more often than not were left unexplored.[30]

Pockets of opposition notwithstanding, the preeminence of neoclassical economics remained an enduring feature of the social scientific landscape within the United States throughout the postwar period. While a general unease about the dogmatic quality of graduate instruction in the field would continue to animate the activities and research of a small number of scholars, their efforts would remain modest in both magnitude and impact. For all of its intellectual virtuosity and impressive activism, New Left economics changed little; its proponents never achieved any appreciable influence in professional associations, leading journal editorial boards, or prominent doctoral degree programs. If the historical sensibility affords the chance to renew or preserve heterodox visions obscured by time, its judgments nonetheless can be quite severe.[31]

This is all to say that by the latter half of the fifties, and continuing throughout the 1960s and 1970s, the predominant share of the American economics community was both wedded to and supportive of a professional practice inspired by the positivism of its neoclassical progenitors. Those ancestors, the "gentry social scientists" of the late nineteenth century, would have looked with great satisfaction on the New Economists of the late twentieth century, with whom they shared a belief in the notion of American exceptionalism and a faith that "[if] history generated change it [could] be controlled by scientific rationality, its wayward conflict reduced to the predictable consequences of social manipulation." What disputes and controversy remained had to do with arguments over the means of policy implementation. Only with the passage of time, and the emergence of an entirely new set of historical circumstances, would disputes over policy goals thrust themselves to center stage.[32] In the final analysis, the struggle for the soul of modern American economics would take place not within academic debates on college and university campuses nor in bursts of student activism at (among other places) Berkeley, Ithaca, Morningside Heights, San Francisco, and Port Huron but in Washington, D.C.[33]

It was with a great deal of pride and self-assurance that most economists regarded the evolution of professional policy advising in the federal government after Dwight Eisenhower first took office. Irrespective of differing opinions on specific public issues, the vast majority of economists could note with great satisfaction the high quality, painstaking professionalism, and impressive publicity that slowly but surely became linked in the public mind (and in the minds of elected officials) when considering the work of agencies such as the Council of Economic Advisers. In the Executive Office Building, the capabilities and usefulness of an entire discipline were now made apparent; in the management of America's "mixed economy," a professionalizing elite's ambitions, nurtured for almost a century, were seemingly fulfilled.[34]

Constructing and maintaining the CEA's reputation in public circles, especially in the wake of the almost fatal squabbles that had emerged within it during the Truman years, necessarily put a premium on the credentials of its servants. Only the most impeccable academic backgrounds, both for Council staff and for appointed members, could squelch the doubts, inflamed by the sniping that had gone on between Leon Keyserling and Edwin Nourse, that the agency's critics had voiced ever since the Employment Act had been signed into law. President Eisenhower's appointment of Arthur Burns as the new CEA chair had accomplished much in the way of silencing the naysayers. Liberal and conservative economists alike had the kind of respect for Burns that quickly swept away the ill feeling and bad taste left over from the inaugural Council's travails. At the same time, Burns's prestige facilitated the emergence of an informal yet well-organized network of peers with which CEA staffing could be impressively secured and its work well done.[35]

Like the head of any office within a new presidential administration, especially one that represented the coming to power of a party that had wandered in a political wilderness for twenty years, Burns faced the daunting task of sorting through an enormous number of résumés—both solicited and unsolicited—in his effort to assemble a CEA staff. He insisted that the Council be peopled by those "who ha[d] had rather specialized training in economics"; for that reason alone, he turned away many applications for appointment from those who (mistakenly) believed that political service in the recent election campaign alone might somehow win them federal patronage. He relied upon a network of correspondents, friends, and acquaintances in the profession with whom he had worked for decades, both to suggest appropriate recruits and to assist him in vetting those names that came his way. He thus instinctively turned to leading figures in major academic positions to re-create the Council of Economic Advisers itself.[36]

CEA personnel review did not, however, precisely because it could not, subsist within a vacuum. Along with the relative quality of their accomplishments, skills, and diplomas, individual prospects had to be ranked by other criteria that ranged from the sublime to the mundane.[37] There was, for example, a concern with geographic diversity in the appointments, most likely pursued with an eye toward appeasing the local sensibilities of senators and members of Congress. No small amount of negotiation with college and university authorities, not to mention with particular scholars themselves, was often necessary to wrestle a colleague away from campus and research obligations, as well as personal ties. Not infrequently, in a practice that would endure in Council operations thereafter, bargains would need to be struck to bring particular colleagues to Washington for rather specific amounts of time or to allow them to consult on various CEA projects from afar.[38]

Along with these fairly straightforward constraints upon and permutations within CEA staff decisions, Burns and his colleagues also contended with the far more delicate matter of private politics and individual identities. Simple party loyalty, of course, required that attention be paid to the particular side of the aisle on which a colleague sat. Indeed, this could occasion some hand-wringing as, in the words of one of Burns's contemporaries, "the supply of fairly distinguished academic economists who [we]re also Republicans (or at least not known as Democrats or leaning that way) [wa]s very sparse." There was nevertheless a distinct effort to avoid the recruitment of those with "a New Dealish flavor to their past." At the same time, above and beyond worrying about a candidate's party sympathies, the concern with political virtue, when it moved on to inquiries about membership in "civil liberties groups" and the contents of someone's "security file," easily extended itself to the pursuit of a McCarthyite agenda. Just as intrusive was the solicitation of information regarding a person's faith; Burns was certainly not above asking if one potential appointee was Jewish.[39]

Ideological approbation, when it was forthcoming, also embraced no small amount of institutional (and therefore doctrinal) self-promotion. When asked to suggest "the names of a few younger economists" for Council staff positions, the emergent dean of American anti-Keynesians, Milton Friedman, made clear that his selections were "of the 'liberal' persuasion—in the nineteenth century English sense of that term rather than its modern corruption." This meant, of course, that the individuals in question were not only "very sympathetic to the administration and cognizant of the importance of its success," but also that "all of those mentioned [we]re Chicago Ph.D.'s." Partly reflective of Friedman's particular academic location, his proposals also underscored both a desire to further the careers of his students (and thus the reputation of his campus) and "the fact that [the University of] Chicago ha[d] been the main single source of people with this viewpoint [of the 'liberal persuasion']" in the profession at large. A network of personnel review for executive service in the federal government could also become a means to further the prestige and impact of specific graduate institutions and of particular points of view in the discipline. With the exception of their colleagues in certain areas in the physical sciences and engineering—perhaps most notably physics and aeronautics—American economists were unique in their ability to deploy on their own behalf the image and clout of a presidential agency like the CEA.[40]

Along with a matrix of academic talent scouts, the Eisenhower CEA also sought to cultivate an array of contacts in the academic and business communities, as well as within the upper echelons of the organized labor movement, with whom to consult about and "troubleshoot" Council activities. Such efforts had not been uncommon during the Keyserling-Nourse years; indeed, the Employment Act of 1946 had envisioned such meetings between the Council and representatives of the private economy, but now they took on a far more systematic and routinized quality. They were, in some respects, reminiscent of earlier initiatives within the leadership of the American Economic Association to "focus informed public opinion" on major policy matters through the work of specifically tasked ad hoc committees. The decided focus of these intermittent gatherings, however, was mostly on garnering "the counsel of independent university economists." When approached, business executives were usually asked to share empirical information they had gathered about the operation of particular markets. As for labor leaders, while they were consulted on occasion, their involvement was fairly limited in ways hardly surprising while the Republican Party held sway in Washington.[41]

Needless to say, the work of Council members and staff was not simply part of an academic and private-sector community of interest but also of the political network within the nation's capital itself. Especially as the 1960 presidential election approached, CEA operatives became more and more involved in partisan assignments. They participated in formulating an economic program for the Republican Party Platform Committee; dissected, from their own special perspective, the speeches of Democratic nominee John Kennedy; and assisted the Republican standard-bearer, then vice president Richard Nixon, in his own campaign. Yet even before the enticements of the nation's quadrennial political revelry made themselves felt, the Eisenhower Council had linked its professional labors with the political agendas of its sovereigns. In September 1957, for example, Raymond Saulnier had tried to organize the views of a distinguished group of academics in support of what had by then become something of an eighth sacrament to conservatives: a proposed amendment to the Employment Act of 1946 that would have made price-level stabilization, along with full employment, a stipulated objective of national economic policy.[42]

Engagement with prevailing political concerns aside, those who, like Burns, Jacoby, and Saulnier, served on the CEA during the 1950s, were especially eager to avoid the miscues of Keyserling's regime. When it came to matters of formal advising, specifically those linked with the statutory obligations and responsibilities of the Council office, Eisenhower's CEA lieutenants were quick to relinquish a lively activism for what they construed to be a studied professionalism. They avoided press interviews when they believed they might disrupt the poised reception of scheduled economic forecasts; declined invitations to Republican National Committee fund-raisers; and refused to convey personal views on specific proposals under scrutiny on Capitol Hill, especially when approached to do so by those in the minority on a particular legislative committee. Saulnier even refused to issue a general statement about the economic importance of the nation's merchant fleet because he feared it would be used in unsuitable ways on behalf of a particular senator's constituents. All this was done out of a conviction concerning the right and proper conduct of scholars on official business.[43]

Yet along with specific notions concerning proprieties in the nation's executive service, the Eisenhower Council members also embraced distinct ideas about their duty to the public. Believing that he and his colleagues "[we]re members of an honorable profession that ha[d] certain standards and traditions," Council chair Arthur Burns thought an economist's usefulness rested on his or her capacity to think "scientifically" about jobs, prices, money, capital, and the like. While it was obvious that practitioners were "inevitably influenced by [their] philosophic and ethical attitudes," they were nonetheless singularly well trained "to distinguish between fact and opinion" in policy debates. As a consequence, economists were uniquely poised to "clarify the issues . . . that politicians debate[d] and [could thus] help to direct thought and eventual action along constructive channels." Essential to the success of such an enterprise was "common sense" and "good humor."[44]

Neil Jacoby similarly argued that "economists [could] play an important role in Federal policy making," especially with the powerful tool that was the Council of Economic Advisers. But "the primary factor in the prestige and value of the Council [wa]s the attitude of the President toward . . . competent and disinterested economic advice." Clearly if the chief executive privileged the work of the CEA, not only would presidential policy choice improve but also other departments of government would emulate the example. The demand for the services of professional economists would thus expand throughout Washington. Preserving the gains in authority and influence such a fortunate state of affairs would yield required only that colleagues avoid the corruption (and the temptation) of the political limelight.[45]

In large measure both Burns and Jacoby expressed opinions regarding the use of economics in the public service that would have been endorsed by an overwhelming proportion of their peers. Yet most strikingly, their sense of decorum in government counseling lacked specific attention both to the public at large and to their elected representatives. Jacoby was hardly reluctant to be explicit on this point. For CEA economists, he claimed, "[t]here [wa]s no injunction to advise Congress or the public." Indeed, to his mind, involvement with public policy debate jeopardized the quality and the dependability of professional expertise. Only "by making a minimum of public pronouncements, by limiting oral or written public statements, . . . and by . . . privately . . . influencing their colleagues in government" could the usefulness of economic wisdom be proved. The UCLA faculty member thus "th[ought] of the Council . . . as akin to the Board of Governors of the Federal Reserve System," an elite forum within which the best minds, shielded from the intrusions and premature exposure often afforded by the media, could utilize the best disciplinary practice in pursuit of state objectives. Any communication the CEA might have with senators, members of Congress, academics, and business leaders was best "carried on without fanfare or publicity." It followed that "[i]f the task of educating the public in economic analysis [wa]s an important one," nonetheless "it [wa]s *not* the Council's job."[46]

Still quite sensitive to what they perceived to be the damage done to the reputation of the CEA by the controversy that had precipitated Edwin Nourse's resignation, Burns and Jacoby were understandably determined to protect the professional image of the Council both in the volatile atmosphere of Washington and in the wider ambit of national politics itself. To an impressive degree they were quite successful in doing so. Nevertheless, making expert economics advising in government "coldly scientific and nonpolitical" was an enterprise fraught with difficulty and contradiction. If nothing else, events would drive that point home like no hypothetical argument ever could.[47]

———————

A remarkably prosperous decade in the United States, the 1950s were nevertheless punctuated by three recessions. Relatively brief and mild, these downturns stood as a sturdy challenge to mainstream macroeconomists who believed that a new learning could make such fluctuations a thing of the past.[48] They also assumed, especially in the case of the last slump (which occurred right on the eve of the 1960 presidential campaign), a growing significance in the minds of politicians eager to "score points" in electoral contests that had been, at least since the thirty-fourth president's reelection in 1956, fairly tame. For Massachusetts senator John F. Kennedy in the very closely contested presidential race of 1960, tarring his opponent, Vice President Richard Nixon, with the brush of the 1959 recession was a useful and ultimately successful, if decidedly opportunistic, tactic.[49]

By the winter of 1961, therefore, a sluggish national economy had become both a political liability for a new administration and a professional opportunity for a new cadre of economists in the Executive Office Building. On the one side, a new president faced a test that would, among others, ultimately determine if he might join Franklin Roosevelt and Woodrow Wilson as the only Democrats since Andrew Jackson to serve more than one consecutive term in the White House. On the other, Kennedy's experts had the chance to show what a New Economics could do; indeed, they might at last demonstrate, absent the distortions of depression and world war, the capacities of a modern industrial (and well-managed) peacetime economy. To this heady set of circumstances were brought the striking sophistication on economic matters of a new president and the powerful skills of analysis and persuasion of his handpicked CEA. For the economics profession as a whole, it was an exquisite moment of anticipation and confidence.

On the secure professional foundation bequeathed to them by their immediate predecessors, the economists of the New Frontier fashioned a spirit of unabashed activism.[50] Acknowledging that "policy-making [wa]s by no means an exact and objective science," Yale's James Tobin, who joined the CEA just after Kennedy's inauguration, firmly believed that "[a] neutral nonpartisan Council, if one could be imagined, would simply not provide advice of interest to the President." The chief executive, in his view, surely needed "professional" as well as "disinterested advice," but it necessarily had to come from those who "share[d] his objectives and his concern for the record of his Administration." Even more to the point, to the extent "economics ha[d] always been a policy-oriented subject," its application to "the urgent . . . issues of the day" was both appropriate and essential. Without it, the discipline "w[ould] become a sterile exercise, without use or interest." Not surprisingly, and in a fashion his Council colleagues Kermit Gordon and Walter Heller would have heartily endorsed, Tobin had no patience with those "who fear[ed] that economics w[ould] be discredited if it [wa]s applied" to contemporary debates; they "reminded [him] of a football coach who never play[ed] his star back for fear he might be injured."[51]

To a not insignificant degree, the pointed determination of Kennedy's advisers to locate themselves at the center of economic policy disputes had as much to do with personality and temperament as with particular convictions regarding professional obligation and opportunity. Gordon, for example, was a skilled administrator endowed with a fine sense of political trends and a wise perception of the president's concerns on any given topic. The Council chair, Walter Heller, had a remarkable gift for writing brief, insightful, and thoroughly convincing memorandums that not only captured Kennedy's attention for the CEA's work but also, over time, encouraged the president in the practice of turning to the Council ever more frequently for analysis and consultation. As one distinguished historian of the period put it, Heller's "pithy prose . . . carried a force in a page or two that the [Department of the] Treasury's tedious, bureaucratic reports could not match." Finally, while somewhat shy and diffident, Tobin possessed a powerful intellect that served, for his more gregarious and publicly visible colleagues, to ground the Council's work on the sturdiest possible analytical grounds. A remarkable team, Gordon, Heller, and Tobin have an exceedingly strong claim to have been the most impressive, and certainly the best publicly known, CEA ever to have served the chief executive.[52]

Yet above and beyond the fine synergy that animated their days in Washington, Kennedy's Council members also shared commonalties of experience and training of a more systematic sort. All three had begun their graduate work during the Great Depression, forced by circumstance thereby to bring to their introduction to the advanced study of economics a worldliness that made them impatient with abstraction for its own sake. At the same time, their own teachers and mentors were beginning to digest the withering attacks on orthodox theory fostered by the work of Keynes and his students, ultimately placing Gordon, Heller, and Tobin at the forefront of a new generation of Keynesian scholars in the United States. Perhaps even more important, like most of their generation, these men had been wrenched from their professional studies to serve the nation in World War II. In all three cases they became part of a vast apparatus of federal economic planning that not only had been born of necessity but also, most vividly, had worked well. It is hardly surprising that they could thus bring to Washington almost two decades later a faith in and commitment to macroeconomic management that was as determined as it was sophisticated.[53]

Coupled with the talents and experience that made his Council of Economic Advisers so effective was the patronage and support afforded by President Kennedy's receptiveness to economic argument. Indeed, it was this openness, a product of the "analytical mind" Kennedy brought to discussions of economic policy, that gave his CEA, especially in the person of Chair Heller, unique access to the Oval Office. While formally the activism of the Kennedy Council may have seemed fairly similar to the widely criticized politicization witnessed during Leon Keyserling's tenure as chair, Harry Truman had been far less aware of and interested in the work of the first CEA. The situation was altogether different in the winter of 1961 as the youngest president in the nation's history took office.[54]

Faced with an economy the insipid performance of which had left the unemployment rate around 7 percent, the new administration in Washington was also discomfited by middling productivity gains in the nation's workplaces that now weakened America's international trade position. What had been almost two decades of unchallenged national supremacy in world markets, a circumstance both facilitated and recognized by the Bretton Woods agreements of 1944, could no longer be sustained in the face of the revitalization of the economies of Western Europe and Japan. As they reestablished their international economic presence, nations like the Federal Republic of Germany and Japan exploited the advantages of an advanced technological base that was the outgrowth of the recent rebuilding of their major industries. Ironically enough, they also thrived because of their relative insulation, under international treaties and protocols (exemplified by the erection of a "nuclear umbrella" by the United States to forestall what was feared to be the potential for Soviet and Chinese aggression), from the burdens of defense spending. Consequently, their major manufacturing sectors—such as automobiles, electronics, and steel—became powerful competitors with their American counterparts. Whatever the concerns of President Kennedy's CEA with the domestic weaknesses of the national economy, the international context within which these difficulties emerged could not be ignored.[55]

Given these fairly stark international realities, it was hardly surprising that some of the most powerful policy makers in the Kennedy government sought to frame the nation's economic challenges with respect to global financial networks. Both Treasury secretary Douglas Dillon and his undersecretary for monetary affairs, Robert Roosa, regarded the growing imbalance between imports and exports, and the potential drain on national gold stocks of which it warned, to be the defining economic policy problem of the New Frontier.[56] In this assessment they were joined by William McChesney Martin, chair of the Federal Reserve System Board of Governors. As a central banker, Martin was further troubled by the inflationary bias that any deterioration in the value of the dollar (and thus in its "buying power") would engender. Both Treasury and the Fed were thus of like mind that relatively high interest rates were, by late 1961 and early 1962, a desirable and appropriate goal of administration economic policy.[57]

For President Kennedy's Council of Economic Advisers, however, no matter how customary and venerable the medicine, the proposed monetary cure was worse than the fiscal disease. If the productivity of enterprise could only be enhanced by new investment, and if unemployment could only be reduced by expenditures large enough, net of depreciation allowances, to expand capacity and output, raising the price of loanable funds would be both counterproductive and self-defeating. The solution lay, in the view of Walter Heller and his colleagues, in stimulating economic growth through deficit spending while accommodating such "pump priming" through flexible interest rates.[58] In peacetime the nation has rarely witnessed a more vivid confrontation between the goals of full-employment activism and traditional monetary propriety. Exemplified by the bureaucratic struggles that emerged between the CEA and the Fed, the debate over the proper "mix" of fiscal and monetary policy during the Kennedy administration would become emblematic of national policy discussions through the remainder of the century.[59]

Late in 1961, the members of the CEA began to formulate a plan to bring unemployment down to the 4 percent level—a target they believed both feasible and necessary to lift the economy out of the doldrums. In their view, the most efficient and politically expedient method to reach that target was through an income tax cut. By thus increasing the amount of discretionary funds available to producers and consumers alike, the tax reduction would, they believed, stimulate spending that would ultimately generate higher levels of employment and national product. The short-run deficits incurred by the loss of federal revenue would be redeemed in the longer run by a larger tax yield (even at lower tax rates) from a higher national income. Managing demand in the nation's marketplace in this fashion would cause an increase in the supply of goods and services (and thereby of incomes across the board) that would enable the economy to grow out of the initial red ink.[60]

In proposing the first deliberate peacetime indulgence of federal budget deficits, Kermit Gordon, Walter Heller, and James Tobin faced a formidable task of both persuasion (of the president and the Congress) and bureaucratic neutralization (of the Fed and its allies in the Treasury). To a large extent, the former was more daunting than the latter. Convincing the president that a tax cut was appropriate actually rekindled a debate that had begun shortly after the Democratic Party convention in the summer of 1960. An annual macroeconomic growth target of 5 percent had been made part of the party's convention platform at Los Angeles; on behalf of the Democratic Advisory Committee, Leon Keyserling had prepared a manifesto that claimed, among other things, that realizing the goal required large increases in direct federal spending. It was not a position with which Kennedy was particularly comfortable, especially given the vigorous counsel he had received from his father regarding the virtues of tight money and balanced budgets. He turned to his economics brain trust to sort through the issues, thus setting the stage for a policy debate that continued through the first two years of his presidency.[61]

Sensing the Democratic nominee's concern "that a kind of unmitigated Keyserling or old-style Democratic liberalism in regard to economics and fiscal policy wasn't going to pay off politically . . . during the campaign," James Tobin began formulating a tax reduction strategy to achieve the 5 percent growth target. While his arguments did not become part of Kennedy's campaign rhetoric, they did provide the foundation for discussions that would take place late in 1961 and early in 1962 within both the Executive Office Building and the Oval Office. Ironically enough, despite his agnosticism on the deficit question, during his campaign Kennedy did not avoid suggesting the need for an "easy money" policy as part of a growth package. The candidate's somewhat cavalier views on the matter caused a great deal of consternation at the Fed. As for the "fiscalists" in his inner circle, moving Kennedy beyond campaign speculation to presidential decision was another matter altogether.[62]

The president's relative degree of economic sophistication notwithstanding, it fell to his CEA advisers to make their case for a tax cut in a fashion that would both persuade and inspire.[63] For this purpose, Walter Heller's adroit skill in rendering policy argument as graceful prose linked up well with James Tobin's sharply honed analytical instincts. Turning to CEA staff economist Arthur Okun, Tobin asked his former Yale colleague to estimate, if possible, the relationship between the level of unemployment and the magnitude of the gross national product. Out of that statistical protocol emerged "Okun's law," a rather straightforward calculation which showed that for every 1 percent reduction in unemployment there could be garnered (through direct impacts on levels of output and indirect reductions in the "underemployment" of contracted labor in slack times) a 3 percent increase in national product. With that quantitative and rigorous demonstration of the virtues of a stimulatory fiscal policy, the Council captured John Kennedy's imagination. Here was a powerful rhetorical device, one that Heller could easily exploit both in memorandums for the president and in testimony before the Joint Economic Committee of the Congress, with which to justify a tax cut and hold both budgetary conservatives and monetary purists at bay.[64]

Taking on congressional and public opposition to deficit spending was a political task in which the CEA became thoroughly engaged. The same can be said for the less visible infighting that emerged with traditionalists at both the Fed and the Treasury. In ways that presumably would have delighted Leon Keyserling and disturbed Edwin Nourse, the economists of the New Frontier did not hesitate to make clear their conviction that the reduction of unemployment, rather than of federal deficits, was the true mission of good government and the most compelling goal of a well-chosen public policy. Their ultimate success in making their case rested squarely on their skill in linking the analytical propositions of the New Economics with a thinly veiled ideological argument that the costs of idleness (in both forgone national income and social fragility) far outweighed the burdens of short-run debt and potential pressure on the international value of the dollar.[65]

In President Kennedy, Heller and his colleagues found a sympathetic student of the New Economics, nervous all the same about its political implications; in William Martin of the Federal Reserve System, and to a lesser extent Douglas Dillon at Treasury, they encountered more problematic skeptics. The timidity of his first budget message to the Congress notwithstanding, the president had refrained from asking for a tax increase to supplement additional military expenditures (between $3 and $4 billion) in the wake of the Berlin crisis.[66] What solace the CEA might have taken from that forbearance on the part of the chief executive was tempered by the knowledge of his oft-repeated fear that he "would be kicked in the balls by the opposition" if he asked outright for a tax cut. At the same time, as the president became more and more persuaded of the probity of the CEA's analysis of the nation's economic ills, "he suggested that the Council do some serious thinking about how to use the White House as a pulpit for public education." It was within this context that Tobin had turned to Okun for his landmark statistical study of unemployment and gross national product. As for Heller, he would later note that the profession had made "no greater contribution" than "raising the level of [economic policy] discussion" as had been done during the debate over the Kennedy tax reduction. Arthur Okun wholeheartedly concurred.[67]

Taking the measure of the naysayers at Treasury and the Federal Reserve Board had, by contrast, less to do with persuasive argumentation premised on scholarly credentials than with straightforward and hardheaded struggles for the president's ear. By far, Douglas Dillon was the easier opponent for the New Frontiersmen of the CEA. A lone Republican in a Democratic cabinet, his freedom of maneuver was already quite constrained. More to the point, so profound was the mutual admiration between Heller and Undersecretary Roosa that the Kennedy Council enjoyed special access to the highest echelons in the Treasury Building. Here Walter Heller's gift for writing and his gracious interpersonal style truly paid off. Indeed, it was Dillon who had thrown crucial support to the CEA suggestion that the president avoid a tax increase for military purposes late in the summer of 1961.[68]

William McChesney Martin had neither the political obligations to President Kennedy nor the official responsibilities to the executive branch that constrained the conduct of Secretary of Treasury Dillon. The "independence" of the Fed from the executive branch was the result of both conscious intent in its founding legislation and decades of practice among a Board of Governors whose sensibilities were more attuned to the needs of the nation's banking industry than anything else.[69] As a consequence, maintaining a conformity between fiscal and monetary policy was (and is) always difficult. Presidents have, more often than not, had to rely on the goodwill of Fed chairs to oblige their fiscal policy goals, while the Fed itself has had to prevail upon the willingness of particular administrations to refrain from tampering with its bureaucratic singularity. All these traditions and expectations the economics of the New Frontier worked to test.

William Martin, steeped in time-honored Fed practice and bearing the imprimatur of a Republican conservatism on monetary affairs belied by his appointment as chair by the Democrat Harry Truman, fully believed that the decision making of the central monetary authority, and the appointment of its chief officers, should be "nonpolitical." It was for this reason that he had refused, contrary to the traditional script, to offer his resignation to the new president. That it was no less customary for the president to decline the offer made no difference, especially given rumors that Kennedy was more than ready to break with that habit. Martin, as early as January 1961, thus put Kennedy on notice of his intentions to buck the liberal tide in Washington. In Washington's activist climate in the early 1960s, the Fed chair's convictions were hardly immune to criticism. Even those predisposed to support Martin, given their earlier service to the Fed, found his obduracy inappropriate.[70]

Before he formally took office, Kennedy had anticipated difficulties with Martin and his colleagues. Indeed, the president-elect had conceived of James Tobin as a prospective administration appointee who could "have [had] a real crack at some of th[e] policies of Bill Martin's." Yet whatever his intentions, Kennedy ultimately chose a road paved with compromise, negotiation, and close attention to his right flank in Congress; he ultimately reappointed Martin as Fed chair, believing that he "need[ed] . . . Republicans [Martin and Douglas Dillon at Treasury] to maintain a strong front as far as the financial community [wa]s concerned." It was, however, more in the nature of a deal (however unacknowledged in public) than a surrender. By early 1963 the president encouraged his CEA to prepare, for inclusion in his 1963 budget message, the formal tax-cut proposal so long debated and which he believed the Fed (in the person of its chair, now comforted by his renewed term and authority) would, if not endorse, simply tolerate. Its ultimate legacy was the Revenue Act of 1964. Peacetime deficit spending as an explicit growth policy of the federal government had finally come home.[71]

While most conspicuous among them, the CEA's struggles with the Fed were but part of a wider problem encountered by the Kennedy administration concerning the coordination of national economic policy. Here, too, Walter Heller and his colleagues sought innovative and politically adept solutions. Born of their conviction that professional expertise had so much to offer the federal government, and given their own schooling in the sometimes rough context of inter-agency rivalry, these White House economists were eager to link the work of colleagues throughout the executive branch in ways that would avoid the misun-derstandings and sometimes self-defeating actions of disparate offices. Out of their desire emerged an idea to forge structured links between the Council, the Treasury, and the Bureau of the Budget.[72]

In what Walter Heller dubbed the "Troika," Kennedy administration officials from the Council of Economic Advisers, the Department of the Treasury, and the Bureau of the Budget periodically met both to share information and to interweave their respective agendas for policy formulation. The initial motivation for these meetings stemmed from the hope that Council forecasts of macroeconomic per-formance would be directly informed by annual revenue projections provided by Treasury and governmental expenditure estimates supplied from Budget. Over time, the sessions (held only when members had particular issues to place on a meeting docket) covered the entire range of policy questions facing the adminis-tration. After the struggles with McChesney Martin had been resolved, officials from the Fed were also included in an expanded format that was (less artfully) named the "Quadriad."[73]

To a large extent, and in ways that no doubt surprised its participants at least initially, the Quadriad arrangement worked well. Meetings went smoothly; opera-tional matters were discussed with courtesy, and disagreements resolved amica-bly. A bureaucratic counterpart to the détente that had emerged between the White House, the Treasury, and the Fed, the Quadriad served well through the balance of the Kennedy presidency and throughout the administration of Lyndon Johnson. Its very success masked a less obvious purpose, one even devious in design—the enhancement of the prestige and clout of the Council of Economic Advisers itself. By placing the CEA on an equal footing with Treasury, Budget, and the Federal Reserve System, the Quadriad setting officially lent the Council the kind of visi-bility and authority within the executive branch, akin to that of any cabinet office, that had been almost two decades in the making.[74] Indeed, this had been one of the concealed goals of Heller's gambit in the first place. Gardner Ackley would note years later that the Quadriad meetings were always conducted on terms set by the Council, with the other original "Troika" members—Budget and Treasury—following its lead. As for the Fed, its participation was, in his view, "a joke."[75] Besting President Kennedy in the battle over his reappointment, Fed Chair Martin had nonetheless lost the war.[76]

A bit over a year before he was murdered in Dallas, President Kennedy asked Congress to implement what would be (at that time) the largest income tax reduc-tion in the nation's history—a $13.5 billion decrease spread over three years. By early 1964 that proposal became law, coupled with a diminution in the levy im-posed on corporate profits and the implementation of more generous depreciation allowances in the revenue code.[77] Within a year the national unemployment rate fell to a bit over 4 percent, and the utilization of manufacturing capacity exceeded the 90 percent level in virtually all major sectors. By the fall of 1964 "the success of the tax cut" was so apparent that, in the words of Arthur Okun, "economists were riding about as high a crest of esteem and respect . . . as ha[d] ever been achieved." Perhaps it had been true, as Presidential Special Counsel Theodore Sorensen had told James Tobin in 1961, that "the most expendable thing" in the Kennedy White House had been the "reputations [of the CEA members] as professional economists." In the end, no matter how one valuated the stakes, the payoff to such gambles had been huge.[78]

If the apparent triumph of the New Economics brought immediate distinction to Heller and his Council colleagues, it also amassed honor for the profession as a whole. Across generational as well as political divides, economists from around the country shared in the accomplishments of their more visible colleagues in Washington "who brought the fruits of the Keynesion [sic] revolution firmly into the public field." Recent doctoral students could reflect with pleasure on the fact that the prestige of the CEA now brought "added luster to [the discipline] . . . and the[ir] degrees." Theoretical opponents, like Milton Friedman, hardly friends of the fiscal activism that had been practiced and now celebrated, could nonetheless take pride in the fact that they had anticipated that colleagues like Gordon, Heller, and Tobin would "acquit [their] responsibilities to the Administration & to the Profession . . . with integrity and competence." Similarly, Arthur Burns felt that Heller could "leave [his] post with a feeling of achievement and in the knowledge that [he] ha[d] earned the respect of economists, even when they disagreed with [him]." All members of the economics community had understood "that there [had been] a grave risk in the President surrounding himself with college professors," for "if they [had] failed they [would have] failed not only for themselves but for the group they represented." Yet their fears had been more than allayed. As a lead aide to Senator William Proxmire (Democrat of Wisconsin) had put it, before the Kennedy CEA had taken office, "economics was viewed generally among top policymakers, especially on Capitol Hill, as an esoteric field which could not bridge the gap to meet specific problems of concern." Heller and his associates "ha[d] almost single-handedly made the profession both respectable and useful in the eyes of government." Less than a century in the making, the professional community of American economists had every reason to be proud.[79]

So dramatic was the apparent success of the New Economics and so intoxicating the faith and self-esteem it fostered among its proponents, it was perhaps inevitable that its architects would contemplate taking on even more demanding challenges. On the eve of President Kennedy's reelection campaign, Walter Heller, inspired by discussions with certain key advisers and armed with a striking examination of recent changes in income distribution undertaken by a CEA staff member, began to formulate a strategy to eradicate poverty nationwide. The president's receptivity to the idea had been in large part enhanced by the very positive impressions he had of the work of Michael Harrington, arguably the leading American socialist of his time. Yet it was not simply a concern with the problems of the poor that facilitated the acceptance of a new policy initiative on their behalf;

the belief that modern macroeconomic management could both increase the growth rate and more equitably distribute its benefits was no small part of the optimism that characterized the final days of John Kennedy's presidency.[80]

A month before the president's fateful trip to Texas, the chair of his Council of Economic Advisers began work on an antipoverty policy agenda. The links between the goals of eradicating want and achieving full employment output seemed to Walter Heller to be both obvious and straightforward. At the same time, a burgeoning civil rights movement and the pressures it brought to bear on a traditional Democratic Party strategy of tolerating southern segregation in exchange for electoral loyalty—a practice that had its roots in the secession crisis of the previous century—further encouraged an economic activism in Washington that was unprecedented. To most of the New Economists, the Kennedy tax cut had been "a necessary, although not sufficient, condition for the elimination of discrimination in employment" and the progressive redistribution of wealth and income to the nation's most unfortunate citizens. Having been "greatly troubled by the prospect of a civil rights program . . . launched without an expansionary economic program," they believed it a logical step to follow the fiscal triumphs of 1963 with a federal offensive against both deprivation and disempowerment. "[H]aving mounted a dramatic program for one disadvantaged group (the Negroes), it was [now] both equitable and politically attractive to launch [a] specifically designed [one] to aid other disadvantaged groups." Suddenly far separated from abstruse debates about the relationship between fiscal and monetary policy, federal economists were now very much part of an effort to stimulate social and political change in modern American society that was as novel as it was complicated.[81]

No doubt inspired by the grief he nurtured during the long flight home from Love Field on the evening of 22 November 1963, Walter Heller went directly from Andrews Air Force Base to the Executive Office Building next door to the White House. He labored well into the night, preparing an extensive memorandum for President Lyndon Johnson that detailed both the current economic conditions facing the government and a blueprint for a national War on Poverty. His efforts were requited the next evening when the president, taking him aside after a general staff meeting, urged him to "move ahead on the poverty theme . . . full-tilt." Declaring himself to be "a Roosevelt New Dealer," Johnson had further assured his chief economic adviser that he was "no budget slasher." He "underst[oo]d that expenditures ha[d] to keep on rising to keep pace with the population and help the economy." Fiscal and social activism had now become inextricably joined; their integument was the New Economics.[82]

Yet as the confrontation over Berlin had so tellingly demonstrated, any and all decisions regarding economic and social policy were necessarily framed during the 1960s within the context of the cold war itself. Whatever domestic objectives he had set for himself, President Kennedy had continually been forced to reckon with the burdens imposed by a national security agenda that had emerged after 1945. The same was even more poignantly the case for his successor. In ways exquisitely ironic, the very defense apparatus that had provided such opportunity and resources to a social science regarded by the mid-1960s as "a great success" ultimately became a major part of that discipline's undoing. A civil war in the Indochinese peninsula in which the United States became embroiled for almost two decades was only the most vivid and costly example of that apostasy.

Edwin G. Nourse

Along with his colleagues John Clark and Leon Keyserling, Edwin Nourse was a member of the first Council of Economic Advisers to serve an American president. Indeed as the Council's first chair, he sought to frame the work of his office in ways that would herald its emergence as the institutional zenith for economists in public service. Nourse's strongly held convictions regarding professionalism and scientific deportment, as well as his political centrism (he once described himself as a "liberal conservative" and a "conservative liberal"), led him to conceive of the Council as a "scientific agency of the federal government," one that could rightly claim to be a "Supreme Court of economic advice." It was an aspiration that would go unfulfilled in the tumultuous environment of Washington, made impossible by the fiscal realities of domestic and foreign policy in his day. An embittered Nourse ultimately declared "a truly professional and non-political Council" a chimera; his words had a poignant resonance decades later. (The American Economic Association)

Robert Taft

Senator Robert Taft of Ohio was a powerful and determined critic of the creation of a Council of Economic Advisers in the Executive Office of the President. In his view, the Council was at best a bureaucratic mistake, at worst a kind of "Trojan horse" for the continuation of New Deal policies. In a series of threatening yet ultimately unsuccessful attempts to eliminate the agency's funding, Taft drove home the point that, outside the academy, splitting the hairs of economic reasoning obscured the far more important task of choosing the ends of public policy. To one drawn from the rough-and-tumble world of political bargaining, the notion of a "coldly scientific and nonpolitical" CEA was at best an unfortunate delusion, at worst a self-serving fantasy of academic professionals determined to enhance their prestige and influence at the expense of a genuinely public debate on policy issues. (The Ohio Historical Society)

Arthur F. Burns

As its second chair, Arthur F. Burns was determined to protect the professional image of the Council of Economic Advisers both in the volatile atmosphere of Washington, D.C., and in the wider ambit of national politics itself. He steadfastly rejected the claims of the Council's conservative detractors, who sought to dismantle it but a few years after its original establishment, and he did much to enhance the reputation and prestige of the agency. It was Burns's belief that preserving the authority and influence of economists in public service required only that colleagues avoid the corruption (and the temptation) of the political limelight. Even so, making expert economic advising in government "nonpolitical" was an enterprise fraught with difficulty and contradiction. If nothing else, events drove that point home like no hypothetical argument ever could. (The American Economic Association)

Walter Heller

Appointed chair of the Council of Economic Advisers by President John F. Kennedy, Walter Heller led what was arguably the most impressive, and certainly the best publicly known, CEA to have served the chief executive. Along with colleagues Kermit Gordon and James Tobin, he personified an unstinting faith in a "New Economics" that had been launched in a spirit of unabashed activism. Like his Council colleagues, Heller had begun his graduate work during the Great Depression, forced by circumstances to bring to the advanced study of economics a worldliness that made him impatient with abstraction for its own sake. With the advent of World War II, he witnessed the elaboration of a federal economic planning apparatus that not only had been born of necessity but also, most vividly, had worked well. It is hardly surprising that almost two decades later Heller brought to Washington a commitment to governmental management of the economy that was as determined as it was sophisticated. (The American Economic Association)

James Tobin

Possessed of a powerful intellect that situated the work of national economic advisers within a sturdy analytical framework, James Tobin nevertheless rejected the notion that such public service could ever be "neutral" or "nonpartisan." For a scholar who ultimately became a Nobel Memorial Prize laureate, it seemed obvious that, to the extent "economics ha[d] always been a policy-oriented subject," its application to the "the urgent issues of the day" was both appropriate and essential. Tobin thus had no sympathy with those colleagues worried that the discipline would suffer if it were resolutely engaged with contemporary debates. What he feared far more was the possibility that, in the absence of concrete applications, economics would become "a sterile exercise, without use or interest." Such anxiety proved to be far more prescient, and was subsequently realized in ways far more ironic, than Tobin ever anticipated. (The American Economic Association)

Arthur M. Okun

One of the finest applied economic analysts of his generation, Arthur Okun was a very prominent member of the cadre of economic experts who served the national government during the 1960s. Like many of his colleagues, he found himself increasingly challenged, during his appointment to the Council of Economic Advisers, to differentiate between the scholarly and the political. The essential distinction, Okun claimed, rested on an appreciation of the "professional view" in any policy dispute. Yet, as he put it after a brilliant and remarkably effective tenure in the Executive Office of the President of the United States, to articulate that frame of reference "require[d] the talents of a missionary, an outstanding pedagogue, and a super-sales[person]." Given that at least some of those requirements were hardly essential (if not inimical) to success in the academic and scientific world, the puzzles associated with any notion of "economics in the public service" were as obvious as they were disturbing. (The Brookings Institution)

Arthur Laffer

Arthur Laffer was one of the primary architects of what came to be known as "supply-side economics," a fairly eclectic array of ideas, assertions, and speculations focused on a common objective—the elimination of government intervention in the marketplace to sustain "full employment growth." He represented a new generation of economists who, reacting to the poor performance of the national economy during the 1970s, launched a wholesale assault not only on the intellectual foundations of what had once been called the "New Economics" but also on the professional ideal of a "public purpose" for the discipline that had so animated their professional forebears. In the final analysis, Laffer and his "supply-side" colleagues, whether they intended to do so or not, simply managed to provide a rationale for what became one of the most highly politicized and transparently unfair transformations in national policy in modern memory. Their unfortunate legacy remains to this day—and with it, the perilous progress of the profession they represent. (The University of Southern California)

6

Statecraft and Its Discontents

[D]o not let us overestimate the importance of the economic problem, or sacrifice to its supposed necessities other matters of greater and more permanent significance. It should be a matter for specialists—like dentistry. If economists could manage to get themselves thought of as humble, competent people, on a level with dentists, that would be splendid!
   —JOHN MAYNARD KEYNES (1930)[1]

AMERICAN ECONOMISTS in 1965 had a great deal about which to be pleased. Sustained growth over a five-year period had increased real national product by a third; unemployment, given the creation of 6.8 million new jobs, had fallen to almost 4 percent; the price level had risen at an annual rate of merely 2 percent. The innovative tax-cut strategy so aggressively pursued by President Kennedy's Council of Economic Advisers "had apparently worked as advertised." In Washington, the "New Economics had become official orthodoxy, and Walter Heller and his successors the acknowledged master architects of [national] policy." Even conservative critics of the new wisdom, scholars and politicians alike, had been forced to concede that some of their worst fears had never materialized. The budget deficits incurred in the initial tax reduction were well on the way to being redeemed by the ample receipts the Internal Revenue Service now garnered from a rapidly growing economy; by 1969 the federal ledger would be balanced, albeit for the last time in three decades.[2]

A robust expansion, and the self-confidence to manage it that the "New Economics" inspired, also encouraged a new presidential administration in the aggressive pursuit of the War on Poverty that had been first considered late in 1963. In this agenda of social remediation, one that so deftly linked a vision of civil rights reform not only to a strategy of material redistribution essential to its genuine success but also to the goal of ensuring the Democratic Party's majority electoral status for years to come, President Lyndon Johnson displayed a remarkable political savvy inculcated by decades of experience on Capitol Hill. At the same time, he represented a generation of political leaders and policy analysts who had come to believe that "the economic problem" and "its supposed necessities" could now be mastered. At last, "other matters of greater and more permanent significance" could be addressed while economic considerations provided the tools for, rather than the constraints upon, success.[3]

It was thus, in the Washington of the mid-1960s, that economics had seemingly become "a matter for specialists," an enterprise by which "humble, competent people" served the needs of the state and society. Whatever disagreements might emerge among professional economists regarding theoretical points of view, whatever internecine (and often recondite) disputes might be endured by analysts of varying schools of thought, there remained an irreducible belief in the scientific rigor and practical applicability of the field—a faith that subsisted in no small part on the success of the "Kennedy tax cuts." Yet professional pride need not and did not always translate into universal agreement; more to the point, events, having a logic of their own, served ultimately to delimit both the accomplishments and the salience of the New Economics. As had been the case throughout its modern history, a social science discipline that had, at times, capitalized on circumstances beyond its control and prospered in their wake also encountered the boundaries of their munificence. As a consequence, the statecraft that had made American economics preeminent among the social sciences in the mid–twentieth century also played parent, in later decades, to its discontents.

———————

With hindsight, it was the economy's performance in the last quarter of 1965 that forecast the end both of the nation's unprecedented postwar affluence and of the unique contexts within which fiscal interventionism had seemed so straightforward. During those three months, gross domestic product increased by the largest amount in history; the danger signs were to be found in the behavior of the price level. Within a year, the rate of inflation rose to almost 3 percent, increased to just under 4 percent by the second half of 1967, and accelerated toward 4.5 percent by the middle of 1968. None of the leading policy makers in Washington "realized then how stubbornly persistent the wage-price inflation ignited by the [economy's] overheating would prove to be." Theirs was an exquisitely ironic oversight; in the economic crisis that followed, during which "growth liberalism came a cropper and the American Century came to an end," the prestige and the confidence of the New Economists was also extinguished. The discipline, not to mention its leading disciples, would never be the same.[4]

On its face, the proximate cause of the inflationary spiral that unhinged the balanced growth of the 1960s was the escalating fiscal burden of the Vietnam War. It was, after all, in the spring of 1965 that the United States had initiated a bombing campaign against North Vietnam that would grow without cease for years to come. At the same time, the first regular army troops arrived in the South to begin the "search-and-destroy" missions that would characterize American ground tactics until peace negotiations began in Paris after the 1968 Tet offensive. By the summer of 1965, President Johnson had deployed 175,000 troops in the Indochinese peninsula; another 100,000 arrived in 1966. Of this unrelenting military commitment, and of the rapidly proliferating contracts let by the Pentagon to provide equipment and weapons to the expeditionary force, CEA, Bureau of the Budget, and Department of the Treasury economists were left surprisingly unaware. Whereas the Eisenhower administration had made the CEA chair an adjunct member of the National Security Council (NSC), and even though the CEA played an important role in NSC deliberations during the 1961 Berlin Crisis and the Cuban Missile Crisis the next year, no such liaison had been implemented in the Johnson White House. Budget and Treasury were similarly left out of the loop, and "things began to fall apart."[5]

Bureaucratic insulation was one thing; a foolhardy agnosticism and a forced professional detachment were something else entirely. In actuality, economists within and outside the government had grown increasingly nervous that fiscal stimulation had become excessive by late 1965. CEA chair Gardner Ackley paused in the summer of 1967 to reflect ruefully on the fact that the Council had been taken "totally by surprise" when Vietnam troop deployments escalated two years previously. The communication breakdown between the Executive Office of the President and the Pentagon had thus thrown the CEA's macroeconomic forecast for 1965 and 1966 way off. Whatever solace Ackley might have taken in the notion that the Council could not be held responsible for being kept in the dark was tempered by his conviction that he and his colleagues could rightfully "be blamed for not being more suspicious of the numbers [they] were getting" from the Department of Defense. Neil Jacoby, a rather conservative CEA member during the Eisenhower administration, was far more blunt in his assessment. That "the economic leaders of the Johnson Administration" failed "to apply fiscal restraint early [in 1966]" was, in his view, a cause for genuine "regret" and criticism.[6]

Having been excessively stimulated by a military mobilization that occurred precisely at the time major domestic spending initiatives had also begun, the national economy of the late 1960s strained to operate efficiently at its capacity ceiling. The accelerating inflation rates thus generated were an obvious justification, in the eyes of virtually the entire economics profession, for both fiscal and monetary restraint. Yet while financial policy changes were, at the time, "more flexible and mobile," alterations in federal disbursements and taxes were "generally very slow."[7] Perhaps more to the point, to the extent that fiscal policy could be formulated only in the political environment of the Congress, while monetary parameters could be altered in camera by the Federal Reserve Board of Governors, virtually the entire burden of adjustment now fell outside what the New Economics had argued was its most effective policy tool—the modulation of federal accounts. By the summer and early fall of 1967, CEA members turned to their influential academic colleagues and encouraged them in the circulation of petitions and letters to members of Congress in support of an anti-inflation tax increase. Much like their predecessors during the debate over the Smoot-Hawley Tariff some four decades earlier, this new generation of economists quickly discovered the limits of their influence. When the president and the Congress finally acted, imposing an income tax surcharge in June 1968, it was far too little and much too late. The economy had already embarked on an inflationary spiral from which it would not fully recover for over a decade.[8]

Small wonder it was that, confronted with the deteriorating performance of an economy they had only just recently believed subject to systematic control, many New Economists staunchly defended their professional prerogatives while condemning the political contexts that had sabotaged their best work. If the president "did not accept his economists' advice," the mistake was his, not the other way around. After all, early in 1964 it had appeared there was "light at the end of the tunnel" in Vietnam; there was little reason to expect nor data to predict the escalation of the conflict a year later. So long as the economic costs of the war were made clear to the president, and appropriate arguments made that the war be "financed responsibly and sensibly," then the discipline's most visible practitioners would have done their duty. The Council was obviously "never asked and . . . would not have been expected to have a vote or say or an opportunity to advise the President on what were essentially national security military decisions." If "Vietnam changed the entire budget posture [and] took all the elbow room away," it was also clear that "those [we]re not the considerations that [were] primary in whether a war [wa]s worth fighting." In the opinion of Lyndon Johnson's core economic advisers, if something was "worth shedding blood for, then it [wa]s worth a couple of points on the price index and the other headaches on the economic side."[9]

Struggling to retain a professional composure that the events of the late 1960s did much to undermine, several of the New Economists found a perverse affirmation in the "fiscal fiasco of the Vietnam period." As James Tobin put it, "The validity of New Economics as science [wa]s . . . not impaired but rather reinforced by the fact that bad things happened as predicted when the advice of its practitioners was rejected. The economic efficacy of fiscal policy [wa]s confirmed, not refuted, by the powerful stimulus that Vietnam deficit spending delivered to the economy." It was, moreover, clear that the difficulty lay not in the analytics of a social science but in a political milieu in which raising taxes was far more problematic than lowering them. Even more troublesome was persuading a legislature to impose "a tax increase on the faith of [a] forecast." The fisc was indeed a peculiar animal, one fed from revenues generated by a tax system that had many of the characteristics of a ratchet wheel. It easily moved in one direction—downward; political detents prevented it from just as easily retracing its steps.[10]

None of these contemplations of the relationship between politics and professional economic analysis were, nor would they have been, news to President Johnson. His reluctance to seek a formal declaration of war against the Democratic Republic of Vietnam from the Congress, an act that no doubt would have facilitated a wartime tax policy of appropriate dimensions, bespoke his conviction that the conflict's unpopularity had significant magnitude. His oft-repeated unwillingness to sacrifice Great Society programs that benefited the poor, the sick, and the disadvantaged to the economic exigencies of war represented merely an effort to mask the fact that he was in fact doing just the opposite. For the first time in its history, the United States government thus eschewed the traditional means of war finance—income and excise tax increases, sales of government bonds, and direct rationing of essential commodities—and relied instead almost entirely on the seemingly uncomplicated expedient of printing money and its corollary, the "hidden tax" of inflation. This was strikingly ironic, for the profession that had once helped guide the state in the judicious and efficient mobilization of wartime resources now became a witness to its once-prized pupil's utter failure.[11]

Johnson administration economists thus found themselves in something of a quandary. On the one side, highly politicized criteria now framed the most important decisions made with regard to national economic policy; on the other, the professional cadre entrusted with the formulation of that policy instinctively avoided the political spotlight. Indeed, the rise of an authoritative community of economists since the turn of the century had rested perforce on the cultivation of a scientific detachment from normative agendas. Close involvement with affairs of state was thus a fine line to tread. To remain focused on a supposedly "objective" set of issues risked being left without influence on decisions that would have dramatic economic impacts. Yet to engage in the full array of White House policy debates would, at best, seem an intrusion on the responsibilities (and authority) of other administration officials; at worst, it could inject an apparently dangerous ideological cast to high-level economic advising itself. Was it not in fact true that modern American economists had succeeded, unlike their colleagues in virtually all the other social sciences, in constructing themselves as the practitioners of a rigorous, dispassionate, and apolitical discipline? How could the prestige attendant upon that achievement be preserved if partisan views substituted for analytical discourse? Genuine answers to these difficult questions had perhaps deeper historical roots, in the increasing willingness of CEA members, for example, to involve themselves in the work of presidential campaigns and party politics. Whether the conundrum of professionalized statecraft had indeed that sort of pedigree or, in fact, was a specific outgrowth of the tumult of the Vietnam era, it was clear that agencies like the CEA had come a very long way, some would have said a frightening distance, from Edwin Nourse's vision of a "Supreme Court" of economic advice.[12]

For the vast majority of the New Economists, the paradox of situating professional expertise within a highly charged political environment could be squarely faced only with great difficulty. Many of them resolved the puzzle by resort to notions of duty and obligation that those who toiled in the Senior Executive Service ostensibly owed their ultimate superior. Whatever their individual views of the dangerous financing undertaken for the Vietnam War, for example, "loyal advisers to the President . . . could not express them publicly." Their only outlet would have been resignation. None chose that course, although presumably the option must have been often on their minds.[13]

Squaring professional (and personal) commitments to the highest echelons of the federal government with one's own values, not to mention with the need to preserve and protect one's professional reputation outside of Washington, was no doubt a painful if not impossible task. Perhaps only once, according to archival records, did a CEA member specifically pose the question of the relationship between the agency's work and the broader political context within which it was done. James S. Duesenberry, an eminent specialist in applied macroeconomics and econometrics who served as a Council member from February 1966 through June 1968, suggested to his colleague Arthur Okun that a strongly worded memorandum be prepared for the president noting the enormous economic costs of the Vietnam War and the ways in which they obstructed the realization of other policy goals. The Harvard professor was particularly concerned that a failure to communicate such sentiments to Johnson would in fact raise a serious question as to "whether [the CEA] w[as] meeting [its] responsibilities and obligations." Far from trying to separate economic issues from a broader set of political concerns, Duesenberry wondered if they should not be joined at the hip. Okun demurred, claiming the president "would not at all be receptive to such an obviously hortatory position." However strained or complicated, the political quarantine envisioned as an essential part of a professional economics in governmental service would nonetheless, if not in fact then in principle, be upheld at all costs.[14]

It was of course not simply the undisciplined financing of war that had placed the government's professional economic policy advisers in such frustrating and disturbing straits. Domestic initiatives had also brought pressures to bear on the Treasury that further bedeviled the efforts of experts to keep the economy on a balanced and measured course. In his determination to erect "a social consciousness in concrete," President Johnson was entirely unreceptive to policy proposals that, to his mind, ran the risk of depleting the funding for his Great Society programs. Despite his apparent awareness of the need for a tax increase as early as 1966, for example, the president worried that placing a surcharge bill before the Congress would simply provide social conservatives the ammunition they needed to dismantle the structures of reform. Indeed, in that year, rather than embrace the increasing anxieties of his chief economic advisers, LBJ instead secured a $290 million increase in the budget for the Office of Economic Opportunity (OEO), the primary institutional venue for the prosecution of his War on Poverty. Even though he understood the "fiscal situation wa[s] abominable," he was absolutely committed to preserving the domestic liberalism that was the defining characteristic of his presidency.[15]

While the failure to finance the Vietnam War through appropriate tax policies led directly to the increasing federal deficits of the late 1960s, military expenditures were not solely responsible for the continued fiscal imbalance that spanned the 1970s. Indeed, of the $86 billion by which federal spending rose from 1969 through 1973, almost $78 billion were allocated to "transfer payments" such as Social Security, Medicare, housing assistance, and educational subsidies. These latter expenditure "echoes" of the Great Society worked to leave Washington in red ink well after war disbursements trended downward. For the same five-year period, in fact, Vietnam War spending fell almost $14 billion. In the absence of the rising transfers of these years, given the current tax rates in effect and given the endgame under way in Vietnam, it is conceivable there would have been a federal surplus by 1970. Thus, it is more than plausible to argue "it was 'butter,' not 'guns' which was the source of [President Richard] Nixon's fiscal problems."[16]

Conservatives were more than willing, therefore, to blame the nation's enduring fiscal problems in the wake of the Vietnam era on the Great Society programs themselves. That the war had destabilized federal finance from the start and, more to the point, that conservatives had refused to underwrite the war adequately unless domestic spending programs were drastically cut, was conveniently forgotten. In point of fact, transfer disbursements were just that—the reallocation of tax receipts from one set of citizens to another. Using Vietnam as a political weapon against the president, conservatives in the Congress succeeded in separating such transfer commitments from their tax base. Political expediency aside, this revolt against "New Deal liberalism" became especially potent precisely because the logic of Keynesianism—that the intertemporal flexibility of public finance could both stimulate growth and ultimately requite its debts—was subverted at its source.[17]

Ironically enough, while the careful judgments and prognostications of the highest-ranking economists in the CEA, the Bureau of the Budget, and the Treasury were ignored, the technical skills of other professionals were used to further the dimensions of Johnson's social programs. Having witnessed, for example, the successful implementation of the Planned-Programming-Budgeting System (PPBS) at the Pentagon, the president insisted that similar methods be employed at OEO and other domestic agencies. Political and military considerations might interfere with the utilization of an unalloyed expertise when it came to worrying about growth rates and inflation; at the more middling federal echelons, by contrast, state-of-the-art professional methods were welcome and encouraged. If the economy could not be "fine-tuned" by its most visible policy advisers, nonetheless the constituent parts of the executive branch bureaucracy could be as well managed as contemporary professional practice might allow.[18]

Wishful thinking cannot of course last forever; the imperatives of arithmetic ultimately forced the president's hand, his fear that a request for a tax surcharge would encourage the right wing in Congress to demand domestic spending cuts in exchange notwithstanding. It was not a Republican opponent, but rather the Democratic chair of the House Ways and Means Committee, Wilbur Mills of Arkansas, who made Johnson's anxious expectation a reality. By the fall of 1967, Mills succeeded in bottling up in his committee the proposed 10 percent tax increase that the White House had reluctantly been forced to send to the Hill. The wrangling over spending cuts as political payment for the tax rise continued for months; the surtax itself did not go into effect until almost a year later. By that point, the inflationary momentum the economy had gained reached a magnitude well beyond the corrective potential of what had become a rather timid gesture toward fiscal rectitude.[19]

Although subsequent events, the rapid rise in world oil prices that began in October 1973 most prominent among them, would make the inflation of the late 1960s seem quite modest in retrospect, the ineffectiveness of the 1968 income tax surcharge marked the beginning of the most unstable economic performance witnessed in the United States since the Great Depression. It also signified the demise of the New Economics. Suggestions that social scientific expertise could enable government to "fine-tune" the nation's markets, "constantly and precisely adjusting dials to keep the economy on track," rather than the rallying cry of a new generation of practitioners, instead became an aiming point for critics and detractors. Never mind that the New Economists themselves had never felt comfortable with the phrase. The very fact that the public had been kept unaware of the true views of economists in the highest echelons of government now made it easy for them, pundits and reporters, conservatives and naysayers alike, to assume the worst.[20]

Inflation, which accelerated throughout the late 1960s and 1970s, was now easily (if inaccurately) viewed as the direct result of fiscal interventionism and "big government." Military miscalculation and dissembling, political grandstanding, cold war ideology taken to an extreme that was as unprecedented as it was undebated within a Congress denied the opportunity to consider a formal declaration of war, and (perhaps most important) the determination of Washington conservatives to hold effective economic policy hostage to an anti–Great Society agenda—not to mention an equal determination by most liberals to refuse the ransom demand—all these essential ingredients of the "fiscal fiasco" were resolutely forgotten. Perhaps this was just; in their conviction that professional probity not be exposed to political infighting within the Beltway nor the glare of its attendant publicity, the New Economists had also unwittingly armed their most aggressive opponents in a great struggle to come. Over the next two decades, those who wished to defend an activist posture for the discipline were placed in the position of defending virtually all of their analytical and professional claims. Rather than being enabled to show how political connivance had ruined a capable expertise in service to the state, the New Economists were increasingly placed on the defensive, trying to justify macroeconomic management of any sort.

To be sure, the counterattack upon compensatory fiscal policy, and the Keynesian doctrines that had inspired it, was not initially staged upon a broad front; probing reconnaissance and brief but violent forays were first undertaken at particular points in the line. The most vulnerable of these salients was of course the issue of inflation itself, and it was here that a conservative retrenchment in the economics discipline found its most durable axis. With a rising national price level, it was an uncomplicated task to shift public attention from the growth rhetoric of the New Economists, and its attendant claims regarding the elimination of poverty and related social ills, to the apparent links between low unemployment and high inflation. Moreover, since inflation ostensibly hurt everyone, while unemployment burdened a relatively small yet unfortunate proportion of the labor force, the substitution of price stability for high employment as a national economic policy objective was as well a rather straightforward exercise in revanchist sloganeering.

Whatever the political maneuvering engaged in by liberal and conservative politicians in the wake of the "economic crisis of 1968," by means of a professionalizing discourse now almost a century old, economists quickly and adroitly made the debate their own. As early as 1958, A. William Phillips, a New Zealander who had originally trained in electrical engineering and later took up a position at the London School of Economics, had published an empirical study of the rate of change in wages and the rate of unemployment in Great Britain. The inverse relationship he detected between these two variables had been derived from data that spanned almost a century, a statistical robustness that, when generalized to the rate of change of the price level as a whole, encouraged the profession to speak of a "Phillips curve" that mapped a trade-off between inflation and unemployment. Were government to choose low unemployment as a policy goal, the Phillips curve predicted more rapid price rises; conversely, toleration of higher unemployment would yield, under the same rubric, lower inflation. What government could not choose, according to the argument, was high employment and low inflation at the same time.[21]

Focusing on the "Phillips trade-off problem," social science expertise remained true to its professional ideal. Economists could generate and analyze data from which the Phillips Curve could be derived, all with due attention to standards of scholarly precision and authority. An analytical project like this was something entirely different from an impassioned and highly charged exchange about the relative virtues of high employment as distinct from price stability. That latter debate had already of course punctuated the congressional discussion that had surrounded the passage of the Employment Act of 1946 and the reorganization of the CEA office during the Eisenhower administration. It had hardly been the stuff of journal articles and conference proceedings, nor had it been embraced by professional economists as particularly edifying. It fell to the "public," then, to argue "about which point on the Phillips trade-off [a government] should aim for."[22]

In the altogether different political environment of the late 1960s, the juxtaposition of unemployment and inflation thus became in large measure a new, defining paradigm in macroeconomics itself. For one founding member of the Council of Economic Advisers, contemplating that development from the perspective of retirement, this shift in the preoccupations of his colleagues constituted "a crime." While he stood more or less alone in this ungenerous assessment, Leon Keyserling nevertheless had a point. What had been, as a consequence of the largely surreptitious escalation of an undeclared war on the other side of the globe, a wholly contrived manipulation of economic policy undertaken outside of the skilled evaluation that could be afforded by some of the profession's leading and most visible members, served as justification for the wholesale reorientation of the field. Rather than staunchly attack what were arguably the institutional and ideological roots of their discipline's disrepute, economists turned their instruments of criticism inward. By doing so, they succeeded less in a project of remediation than in furthering a particular, and highly politicized agenda. In their determination to avoid politics, as a medium subversive of the scientific rigor they took to be the sine qua non of their professional aspirations, economists thus made themselves its captives.[23]

Even in their determination to reconstitute an economics of state intervention, one sensitive to an apparent inflation-unemployment dilemma, within a framework of dispassionate empirical study and theoretical analysis, the New Economists made notional concessions to their critics that only furthered the dismantling of the kind of engaged social scientific practice they had labored so hard to construct in the first place. Neither a conscious nor a contrived intention, nevertheless disputes over the precise empirical characterization of the Phillips curve swept the idea of full employment targets from the domain of professional macroeconomic discourse. Some investigators, typically labeled conservatives, increasingly spoke of a "natural rate" of unemployment—a magnitude specified by the number of individuals at any given point in time looking for jobs paying more than the prevailing wage in a given market or temporarily "exiting" the labor force— below which policy initiatives geared toward jobs creation would only generate rapidly rising rates of inflation. Others, usually of a more liberal outlook, eschewed the implications of the word "natural" and spoke instead of a "non-accelerating inflation-rate of unemployment," or "NAIRU," below which intervention in labor markets would similarly work at cross-purposes with the goal of price stability. Determining the particular unemployment rate one might label as "natural" or not prone to accelerate inflation, let alone implementing appropriate policy measures to realize that target value, thus framed the agenda for applied macroeconomic analysis as a whole. This was a far cry from the agenda Congress had articulated for a statist economics when it had declared, a quarter century earlier, that "it [wa]s the continuing policy and responsibility of the Federal Government . . . to foster . . . conditions under which there w[ould] be afforded useful employment opportunities . . . for those able, willing, and seeking to work, and to promote maximum employment, production, and purchasing power."[24]

If by 1970 the entire analytical framework within which most American economists thought about policy matters had dramatically changed, it was also the case that the profession's transformation in this regard did not take place independent of events and material circumstances. The postwar expansion that had left the national economy globally dominant was fast proving itself at an end—nowhere more strikingly than in the nation's factories. Early in the 1950s, American manufacturing had generated levels of output roughly four times that of its nearest competitors; investment in the industrial sector had been greater than in the rest of the world, total employment virtually twice as large as that of Britain and even greater with reference to Japan. In 1969, national employment in manufacturing began to shrink from a bit over fourteen million workers to a bit under twelve million by 1986. Rates of growth in output similarly trended downward; by 1980 the United States produced less than 30 percent of the world's manufactured goods, a share much reduced from the 40 percent levels achieved in the early 1960s. A comparable deterioration took place in the American share of world manufacturing exports. From the time Lyndon Johnson assumed the presidency to the celebration of the nation's bicentennial, the proportion fell one-fifth. Whatever the scholarly dimensions of their professional controversies, American economists also faced the harsh realities of an increasingly anemic and volatile national commerce.[25]

Coupled with the inflationary environment created by the Vietnam War, changes in the world oil market in the early 1970s further weakened the American economy and eviscerated most of the prosperity bequeathed by the New Frontier and the Great Society. When on 17 October 1973 the Organization of Petroleum Exporting Countries (OPEC) announced its intention to cut production by 5 percent per month for the next two years, energy prices worldwide took off. Crude oil prices immediately rose by two-thirds; in January 1974 they doubled. Not surprisingly, as a result, average annual inflation rates for the national economy throughout the 1970s stood at roughly 9 percent. For the decade 1972–82, it is estimated that the total change in the American cost of living was approximately 133 percent. Poor crop yields in 1971 and 1972 due to drought conditions in the nation's agricultural regions only made the inflationary spiral worse. As the costs of production acceler-ated upward, the national unemployment rate also began to rise; from almost 5 percent in 1973, idleness increased to a bit over 8 percent of the labor force two years later. By 1982 that rate rose toward 10 percent. For the 1970s, the decennial average was just below 7 percent. Within a very short time, the American economy now exhibited the worst of both worlds—high inflation and high unemployment. Professional economists had every reason to be perplexed.[26]

Oddly enough, the OPEC price shock, while different in form and etiology, had many of the same consequences as the 1929 New York stock market debacle. Real incomes fell dramatically. The values of bank, private, and corporate invest-ment portfolios were seriously imperiled. With consumer and investor confidence thus dealt a serious blow, aggregate investment declined as firms became hesitant about the future and households postponed major expenditures. Profit margins shrank as the costs of production rose. Capacity utilization and employment con-sequently shrank. The cumulative oil price increases of the 1970s also had a devastating impact on the national balance of international payments—a $40 bil-lion deficit in fuel imports alone emerged by decade's end. Macroeconomic growth rates deteriorated. This combination of apparent stagnation and high in-flation gave rise to a new entry in the manual of economic pathology—"stagfla-tion." With the description of this novel malady completed, economists and pun-dits alike also devised a new diagnostic—the "misery index," a sum of the rates of inflation and unemployment. Throughout most of the seventies that index flirted with the 20 percent range; its disconcerting message helped lay the founda-tions for a major transformation in American economic policy in the decades to come.[27]

Not surprisingly, as the macroeconomic volatility of the 1970s worsened, the intellectual foundations of economic policy similarly shifted. With the demise of the Bretton Woods system of fixed exchange rates and with the perceived disappearance of a determinate Phillips curve relationship tying high unemploy-ment rates to lower inflation, confidence in the Keynesian revolution in economic thought diminished. Whatever ingredients might have thus existed for a consensus among policy analysts dissolved. Spending by the government was increasingly excoriated, although countercyclical action was now condemned not so much for its alleged inflationary bias as for its possibly negative impacts on the incentives for risk-bearing and productive behavior in the marketplace. As noted by one astute observer of the American economic profession, himself a vigorous and accomplished champion of Keynesian methodology, by 1980 it was very difficult indeed "to find an American academic macroeconomist under the age of 40 who professed to be a Keynesian." Thus was accomplished "an astonishing intellectual turnabout in less than a decade."[28]

To be sure, the end of a Keynesian consensus, such as it existed among American economists at the time, was not solely a scholarly enterprise. After all, acceptance of interventionist fiscal policy in the early 1960s had been linked with the emergence of a majority political coalition supportive of both increased defense spending and the implementation of redistributive measures linked with civil rights reform. As that bipartisan association was undermined—for a variety of political and social reasons—the commitment to Keynesianism also waned. Yoked to a reaction against redistribution and federalism was thus a vigorous and cogent revival of old-fashioned policy thinking. Classical monetary theory, so much inspired by the work of Milton Friedman, reemerged as a powerful and legitimate counterpart to the wisdom and learning of what had been the New Economics of the 1960s. With a beachhead against compensatory fiscal policy now secured by monetarism, an even more aggressive attack upon a statist economics could be joined.

If rapid inflation subverted the political foundations of a successful Keynesianism, it also directly challenged the intellectual authority of the New Economics by demonstrating the inability of spending policy to halt the rise in the cost of living. Indeed, throughout much of the 1970s and 1980s, Keynesian theorists could propose little in the way of anti-inflation measures other than what some have called "fiscalism in reverse"—the reduction of public expenditures as a whole. This allowed for a monetarist proposal for the elimination of countercyclical spending and the imposition of fixed (and preannounced) policy targets for key monetary variables (most importantly the rate of growth in the money supply itself) to take center stage in Washington. Keynes's "General Theory" of economic processes was thus relegated to the status of a specific argument concerning the Great Depression; it was hardly applicable, in the minds of a new generation of specialists, to an altogether novel situation in which high inflation, high unemployment, and low growth rates all prevailed at the same time. In place of Keynes's apparently outmoded message, late-twentieth-century American economists sought to erect an altogether new paradigm.[29]

Once the battle ensign of a supremely confident social science community enlisted in the service of the state, Keynesianism stood instead by the late 1960s as a gravestone for the dashed expectations of the New Economists. With what had once been the blueprint for economic statecraft in tatters, investigators turned their attention to the reconstruction of first principles. If fiscal interventionism had proved itself a failure, no matter that the genesis of that debacle had little to do with analytical errors and far more to do with political manipulation, it was necessary nonetheless to rescue economics from the nonscientific discourse of partisan debate and refashion the rigor and reliability that had made the field one of the great academic success stories of the century. It was within this context that a "new classical macroeconomics" came to dominate the professional literature, an anti-Keynesian initiative that substituted behavioral assumptions drawn from microdata for the aggregative approach emphasized in the New Economics. This "new macroeconomics" posed an emphasis on expectations formation as the key to understanding economic mechanisms rather than the fallacy of composition that Keynes himself had believed the essential axiom of modern social theory.[30]

So eager were mainstream economists to disassociate themselves from the purported inadequacies of Keynesian theory that, in very large numbers, they uncritically embraced a simple, some critics would ultimately say tautological, assumption—the "rational expectations" hypothesis. Central to this proposition was the idea that market actors would behave in conformity with a "rational" assessment of all available information. If this were true, all economic outcomes—prices, wages, interest rates, and so forth—were necessarily the result of the sum total of individual actions that were themselves premised upon a cogent and self-seeking prediction of possible market results. In other words, market movements (whether in individual sectors or for the economy as a whole) obtained as a result of individual behaviors guided by informed calculation. Economic performance was thus the result of the rationally generated expectations of individuals; to be otherwise, such individual behaviors could not be rational. The obvious circularity of the argument garnered less comment than the seemingly powerful analytical tools it could provide in the pursuit of a new, scientific macroeconomics.[31]

Rational expectations theory beckoned toward a variety of methodological and analytical implications that dramatically transformed both the research agenda and the public posture of the American economics profession. On the one side, it suggested that estimating the impacts of particular policies was far more complicated than originally believed. If public policy measures actually changed both the behavioral and the structural characteristics of the economy, quantification of their effects would be distorted as a consequence. In some degree this suggestion applied to economics Werner Heisenberg's "uncertainty principle" in quantum mechanics, which held that instruments of observation and measurement themselves altered the objects of analysis. While this notion provided grist for the mills of theoretical econometricians for decades to come, yet another conclusion derived from the rational expectations argument struck directly at the idea that economic science could provide any useful techniques for statecraft itself.[32]

In what came to be known as the "policy ineffectiveness proposition," rational expectations theorists took their assault upon Keynesian doctrine a step further. Assuming that a notional individual in the marketplace had both access to the same data as government and the instinct to act rationally with respect to economic objectives, they argued it necessarily followed that any alteration in fiscal or monetary policy would be effectively anticipated by all economic agents. This being the case, policy initiatives would be nullified as rational individuals adjusted their behavior in accordance with the available information. Say the government chose to increase its spending on goods and services, all with a view toward increasing the level of national output—one of the major weapons of the Keynesian arsenal. Rational individuals would react to the announcement of this new policy by increasing their savings rates in anticipation of the rise in future tax liabilities that increased federal spending would eventually necessitate. By reducing consumption, higher savings rates would offset the expansionary potential of the fiscal effort. It followed that compensatory economic policy was impotent; if market outcomes were the necessary and inevitable result of rational individuals pursuing their self-interest, macroeconomic management was an exercise in futility. Thus did the articulation of a new, seemingly rigorous approach to economic analysis set the stage for "th[e] retreat of modern economic theory from the policy arena[,] the single most important [development] in the discipline since Keynesianism was driven from center stage."[33]

For the "new classical" theorists, it mattered little that their core propositions seemed unrealistic, even fanciful. To the criticism that few individuals had access to the kinds of information that would make their rational expectations model accurate, they countered with the rhetoric of deductive science. To the claim that the vast majority of Americans were rarely in a position to make the kinds of contractual and transactional maneuvers in response to policy changes that animated the ineffectiveness proposition, they asserted the primacy of theory over applied analysis. To the suggestion that the rational expectations approach merely constituted a resurrection of outmoded principles derived from turn-of-the-century texts, they pointed to the apparent failures of Keynesian theory in its effort to substitute new concepts for those of more venerable vintage. Finally, to the speculation that a "new classical" discipline would evolve into the "sterile exercise, without use or interest" of which James Tobin had warned in 1963, the rational expectations theorists replied with the confidence of recent proselytes. Competitive markets, with amply distributed information on the basis of which actors were sufficiently skilled and inclined to make informed and rational decisions, did not require the intervention of a well-meaning yet ill-equipped and self-defeating government to achieve optimal ends. Indeed, most efforts at official remediation of market outcomes merely made matters worse. An economics capable of demonstrating these truths was hardly jejune.[34]

It was hardly apolitical either. Whatever their personal convictions and values, whether by intention or indifference, the new classical macroeconomists of the 1970s became significant collaborators in an ideological project that would endure for decades to come. Only in its most specific and sometimes esoteric manifestations would this agenda reveal itself as "supply-side economics." Its actual dimensions far transcended the professional discourse of a particular academic discipline and, in fact, would subsequently touch upon almost every facet of the nation's social and political life. Perhaps there was a harsh yet fair justice in this denouement. Having desired and cultivated public influence and authority for a century or more, mainstream American economists had seen their wish requited in the statism born of World War II and the cold war. Exquisitely sensitive to professional protocols, yet always eager to take up some of the most vexing and difficult problems of modern government, the New Economists of the postwar era saw their hopes rise and fall with the best and the worst that the New Deal Order had had to offer. A flight from politics, a reconsideration of first principles, an "inward turn" were all likely and inevitable postures for a profession now bewildered and confused. Yet, ironically enough, the retreat from statecraft and its attendant politics was nothing of the sort. On the contrary, those who most earnestly condemned what they believed to be the unscientific and inappropriately normative agenda of Keynesianism merely set the stage for the most dramatic yet least apparent politicization of economic analysis and practice in over a century.[35]

A recasting of the theoretical bearing and public influence of American economists in the years after the Vietnam War did not, of course, take place in a vacuum. Independent of the technical skirmishes that punctuated the pages of leading journals and inflamed the proceedings of many conferences, the controversies in which the profession's mainstream now found itself caught up drew much of their brio from political contests transacted on a much larger stage. High unemployment and rapid inflation, owing to the material insecurity and deprivation they caused, served as accelerants for a political blaze that would ultimately consume much of the social initiatives of the New Frontier and the Great Society. A backlash against civil rights reform magnified by the fear and anger that emerged from the urban insurrections of the late 1960s and that only hardened as the coalition for change grew to include immigration and homosexual rights activists; counterattacks upon a resurgent feminism that had been in no small measure sparked by the civil rights movement itself; intergenerational strife that had for several years pitted young against old and that ultimately portrayed the student movement(s) of the 1960s as the worst manifestation of an undisciplined, hedonistic, and coddled youth duped by the New Left; and the growing wariness of both the corporate world and much of organized labor regarding the goals of environmental protection—all these were essential ingredients in a rightward shift in the national political spectrum that proved as decisive a force in the transformation of American economic policy practice as any scholarly argument.[36]

If a late-twentieth-century American politics of reaction and resentment rested upon foundations that far transcended matters of economic doctrine and practice, nevertheless, to the extent conservative rhetoric successfully cast government as the patron of liberal reform gone reckless, an immensely powerful link could then be drawn between economic instability, on the one side, and statist interventionism, on the other. An adroit if disingenuous tactic was this, for it played upon rising middle-class anxieties about the tax burdens of federalism while at the same time avoiding any honest reckoning with the proximate causes of a volatile price level and slack labor markets. Resolutely ignored was the fact that the era's persistent inflation, and the attendant unemployment it fostered, arose predominantly from exogenous circumstances—runaway Pentagon spending during the Vietnam War, poor crop yields in the wake of an extraordinary period of drought, and the manipulation of the world oil market by a powerful and determined cartel. Conservative rhetoric could nonetheless frame the economic turmoil of the times as a direct outgrowth of a muscle-bound and irresponsible public sector. When coupled with the cynicism and outrage cultivated by the scandals that surrounded

Washington after Republican Party operatives broke into the Democratic National Committee's "Watergate" offices in the spring of 1972—events that led two years later to President Richard Nixon's forced resignation under threat of impeachment—the avenging contentions became virtually irresistible.[37]

Misery loves company. By the midseventies, conservative politicians desperate to reverse the high tide of federal interventionism epitomized by the New Frontier and the Great Society, middle-class Americans increasingly hard-pressed by deteriorating incomes and rising taxes, and an array of constituencies determined to strike back at the liberal reforms of the preceding two decades found common cause in economic reaction. Two specific developments during 1978, each rooted in what were perceived to be the past failures of public policy, signaled the beginning of a return to economic practices that predated the New Deal.

One was a popular movement, termed a "taxpayers' revolt," to limit government spending and tax revenues by statute. While the ultimate goal of this mobilization, the ratification of a constitutional amendment requiring balanced federal budgets—precisely the sort of practice Keynes and the New Economists argued was both unnecessary and counterproductive—remains unrealized to this day, certain notable successes at the state and local level gave its leaders heart. Arguably the most influential of these triumphs was the 1978 passage of a statewide proposition in California that limited property tax assessments. As momentum gained at the local level, national leaders jumped on the bandwagon of economy in government in order to push further proposals that would inflexibly limit federal employment and spending.[38]

The second development resulted from the battering of the dollar in foreign exchange markets that emerged after Richard Nixon left office. Holders of dollars worldwide sold them in large amounts throughout the late 1970s because they feared that American economic policies would continue to cause "stagflation," weak capital formation, and limited real economic growth. In response, the Federal Reserve Board moved to support the dollar through monetary stringency, and President Jimmy Carter promulgated a wide-ranging program that included voluntary guidelines for wage and price increases, further measures to support the dollar's international value, and a renewed pledge to hold down government employment and spending in order to reduce the large federal deficits that had, now for close to a decade, become annual events. All of these initiatives expressed a growing belief among some national leaders and many voters that government policies requiring significant spending, deficit financing, and money creation (to ease the interest-rate pressures that deficits would otherwise create) were more a cause of economic instability than a cure.[39]

Ronald Reagan's stunning landslide victory over Jimmy Carter in the 1980 presidential election formally signaled the transition from Keynesian-style demand management in Washington to the allegedly new, yet in fact strikingly old, strategies of "supply-side economics." Believing that the fundamental source of the problems facing the contemporary American economy had to do with supply problems rather than demand fluctuations, the supply-side theorists focused their policy proposals on the means by which macroeconomic supply conditions might be improved. Increasing the output of goods and services, it was presumed, would alleviate the twin problems of stagnation and inflation that had troubled the economy since the late 1960s.

Supply-side theory drew attention to what were believed to be the distortions created by high levels of government spending, high taxation of income, and extensive governmental regulation of economic affairs. Excessive income taxation, it was argued, stifled productive effort, for example, by discouraging overtime work. It robbed individuals of the fruits of enterprise and risk-bearing. Finally, it distorted economic decision making so as to slow growth and create the very fiscal pressures that contributed to the problems of "stagflation" in the first instance. The solution would involve a radical reduction in taxes, a systematic shrinking of government spending programs and, thus, federal agency budgets, and the elimination of costly regulatory measures.

In February 1981, the newly elected Reagan administration presented its Program for Economic Recovery to the Congress. Inspired by the arguments of supply-side economists, the proposal called for the control of federal spending, the reduction or elimination of a wide variety of social entitlement and redistributive schemes that had their roots in the politics of the New Frontier and the Great Society, and the aggressive reduction of tax rates on incomes. In particular, it called for 10 percent annual reductions in marginal income tax rates for three years beginning in the summer of 1981. Along with this economic platform, the president's program also provided for the implementation of investment incentives for private business (by means of accelerated depreciation schedules), for the streamlining or elimination of a host of regulatory codes, and for monetary stringency. The hope, along with the expectation that such measures would stimulate growth through investment, jobs creation, and greater labor productivity, was that the federal budget might be balanced within three years; concomitant savings on interest payments and a lessening of the loanable funds shortages caused by the massive government presence in the nation's capital markets would be only the most immediate benefits of the new policies.

By August, the Economic Recovery Tax Act became law, implementing, in the form of income tax reduction, a major component of the supply-side protocol. Over the next three years, major cuts were also made in such federal programs as unemployment insurance, food stamps, Aid to Families with Dependent Children, Medicaid, student loans, retirement benefits, grants for mass transportation, and benefits to import-affected industries. Paralleling these transformations in fiscal policy was a strict anti-inflationary monetary posture. The results were mixed. On the one side, inflation was strikingly reduced. From 9 percent in 1981, the annual rate of increase in the price level fell to 3.5 percent by the end of Reagan's first presidential term. Unemployment, after rising to 9.7 percent in 1982, fell to 7.5 percent in 1984–85, and to 5 percent by the end of 1988. Yet consistent with their belief that an "inflation threshold" existed, Reagan administration officials did not seek to press job idleness below the 1988 mark. In this, what came to be known as "Reaganomics" sharply distinguished itself from the

Keynesian-style full-employment commitments of both its Democratic and Republican predecessors.

During the 1980 presidential campaign, Ronald Reagan had asked members of the American electorate if they were "better off [then] than they [had been] four years ago." For a vast majority, this had been a most persuasive rhetorical quip given that the rates of inflation and unemployment had remained quite high throughout the Carter presidency itself. Yet ironically enough, the passionate response that Reagan's interrogatory evoked expressed itself almost entirely in an antistatist fashion. In the highly charged political environment of the 1980 campaign, tax reduction became not an instrument of countercyclical policy tooled by a professional expertise but rather a symbol of relief for a populace hardpressed by economic instability itself. Far from being a measured response to unemployment and excess capacity, as had been the case with the "Kennedy round" of tax cuts, the downward revision of the revenue schedules undertaken in 1981 was a crude sop in an election year. No doubt Keynes himself would have been appalled at this opportunistic manipulation of what he had believed to be one of the finer achievements of a "general theory" of economics. That the Reagan tax cuts were disproportionately favorable to the wealthiest segments of society, and thus at variance with the redistributive objectives of Keynesian practice, was simply an obvious (yet accurate) manifestation of their genuine intent.[40]

That supply-side economics was less a new wisdom brought to bear on matters of public policy than a catechism devised by those with other, more blatantly political, fish to fry was made strikingly clear in the fiscal policy choices it ostensibly encouraged. Chief among these, of course, was the scheme for income tax reduction; unlike the arguments derived from applied macroeconomics that had militated in favor of the use of revenue policy as a means to stabilize consumption spending over the business cycle, those used to justify this linchpin of "Reaganomics" were premised on assertions rather than econometric evidence. In their efforts to persuade both the public and the Congress of the probity of their tax plan, Reagan administration officials invoked the work of a previously obscure analyst, Arthur Laffer.[41]

Rather than focus on the aggregate impacts of changes in levels of discretionary expenditure, as had been the Keynesian method, Laffer took the novel approach of seeking to relate tax revenues to changes in tax rates. He did so by resort to a series of claims regarding the microeconomic effects of changing taxation rules. Rising tax rates, Laffer argued, would generate increasing tax revenues up to some threshold level beyond which higher rates would actually result in lower revenues due to individuals' substitution away from taxable effort in the marketplace. Less overtime work, avoidance of highly taxed returns on particular investment instruments, and greater resort to compensation in kind (that was not subject to assessment) or "under the table" was, in his view, the rational and understandable response of an economically energetic population resisting greater tax burdens. This was a subtle yet clever deduction, for it construed high rates of income taxation to be not simply onerous in some abstract sense but actually counterproductive from the standpoint of the public treasury. Why would any government seek to push tax rates so high as to jeopardize aggregate receipts? Tax cutting was, therefore, not only a popular but also a rational strategy for statecraft itself.

The "Laffer curve," a hypothetical mapping of tax revenues against tax rates, presumably described some optimal configuration at which total revenues would be maximized. There was some point on the graph where the "best" income tax rate could be discerned; it was the selection of that rate which was supposedly the goal of the fiscal agenda articulated in the Program for Economic Recovery. Needless to say, Reagan administration officials claimed that the extant tax schedules exceeded the optimal settings implied by Laffer's research. There was, however, a not inconsiderable difficulty with the claim. No reliable estimates had been made in an effort to verify the construction of the Laffer curve; both its shape and the exact location along its span at which the American economy was "located" were never empirically demonstrated.

Debates over national fiscal policy, within the context framed by Laffer's investigations, took on a decidedly abstract quality—so much so that one of Ronald Reagan's main opponents in the Republican Party primaries of 1980 ridiculed the entire supply-side agenda as "voodoo economics." Assertions that contemporary tax rates exceeded the Laffer "optimum" were countered with similar declarations that they fell short of that value. Comparisons with other industrialized nations, most of whose tax rates far exceeded those of the United States, whose revenues were apparently unaffected by them, and whose economic performance at the time was often relatively robust, were rarely if ever attempted. Instead, specious reasoning superseded debate grounded in evidence; high tax rates were assumed to be "bad" and lower rates "good." Similarly, federal deficits were excoriated in principle and the generally high level of national debt bemoaned. Economic analysis, now grounded in the unsubstantiated rhetoric of the "Laffer curve," apparently afforded simple policy remedies for national ills.[42]

Exactly what symptoms the therapies were in fact capable of alleviating was never made clear. At the same time that the first round of Reagan tax cuts was implemented, the largest peacetime increase of American armed forces and weapons systems began. Indeed, the stimulatory impacts of so unrestrained an indulgence in federal spending prompted many supply-side advocates to claim (erroneously) that the tax-cut strategy had done its job. So dramatic was President Reagan's military buildup, a strategy epitomized by his determination to create a six-hundred-ship navy, that by the end of the 1980s the national economy allocated close to $300 billion annually to the Pentagon—an increase of approximately 120 percent for the decade as a whole. The fiscal consequences of defense spending in the 1980s were such that the purported budgetary benefits of supply-side economics could never be measured. During the first Reagan term, the annual federal deficit grew from 2.7 percent to 5.2 percent of gross domestic product. If fiscal balance had been the central promise of the new departures in policy practice undertaken in 1981, the federal ledger became, by 1983, an indelible record of failure. By 1989, the total national debt stood at some $2 trillion; in this regard, Ronald Reagan stood alone as one of the most profligate peacetime spenders in the history of the Republic.[43]

Perhaps it was quite fitting that supply-side theory had painted itself into the corner of federal deficits much as the New Economics had done. Indeed, the entire idea of peacetime military expansion after World War II had been sold in part to the Congress and local public officials on the basis of all the resources and funding that would flow their way. Military bases brought jobs to local communities and profits to local businesses. Defense spending in general created better-paying jobs that provided higher purchasing power for the other products of domestic industry. Compensatory demand management, in fact, had counted in its bag of tools the potentially stabilizing influence of Pentagon procurement (not to mention of other public goods disbursements) in the face of the business cycle. Seven successive post–New Deal presidential administrations had also embraced that logic. The exigencies of the cold war had combined with the domestic politics of the "mixed economy" in forging that kind of bipartisan commitment to public spending. Why should Reaganomics have been any different?

Yet it was, in ways that were quite profound. Keynesian-style demand management had always grounded itself on the assumption that budget deficits incurred in bad times would be redeemed with higher tax receipts in the boom. Moreover, as a surging economy approached its capacity ceiling, the reimposition of higher tax rates would be justified as an instrument of further security. In stark contrast, Reaganomics made no such claim upon the future. Tax reduction as a political strategy, especially when coupled with increased spending on federal operations such as defense, carried no guarantees of subsequent restoration. Quite the contrary. To the extent that revenue cuts became fixed by a kind of political inertia, and insofar as the tax base itself had been more or less permanently eroded by reductions in tax *rates*, the very tools of Keynesian fiscal policy were blunted. Thus it was, in an exquisite historical irony, that Ronald Reagan's immediate successors in the White House—George Bush and William Clinton—faced the sheer impossibility of implementing countercyclical fiscal measures even had they wished to do so. In this sense, although the Reagan administration practiced a kind of Keynesianism in its dramatic expansion of military spending while at the same time reducing federal taxes, supply-side economics did unambiguously achieve one particular policy objective: it made the future use of Keynesian spending policies entirely problematic, if not impossible.

Warnings about the absolute magnitude of the national debt, deployed as justifications for anti-Keynesian policy initiatives, had been well-worn canards. Often accused of simply espousing a reckless overspending that would lead to permanent indebtedness, Keynesian analysts could not repeat enough their view that just as taxes should be cut in recession, they should be raised in robust expansion. They were similarly ignored when they pointed out that timely growth stimulation today would yield higher incomes and wealth tomorrow from which greater tax receipts could be earned at lower proportionate cost. Suggestions that it was not the size of the national debt but the share of the domestic product it represented that was the crucial policy variable also fell on deaf ears.

So thorough had been the disgrace of Keynesianism that the most rigorous appeals to common sense and evidence in defense of the New Economics, not to mention the indications of the failures of Reaganomics, came to naught. Even thoughtful liberal Democratic allies in the Congress, enacting on an individual basis what ultimately happened to the economic principles that animated their party as a whole, mouthed the rhetoric of supply-side theory. Nine months before Ronald Reagan's first election to the presidency, Senator William Proxmire of Wisconsin took the New Economists to task for "views [that could] not be justified either politically or economically." Furious that federal shortfalls had not ultimately been made good by surpluses, he told Arthur Okun that "[n]either the President, the Congress, nor the public c[ould] accept the consensus of the professional economists that a deficit [wa]s justified in almost every year." In Proxmire's view, "to maintain its credibility, [the profession had to] do better than that." Okun's retort, that "elected officials [had to] do better than climbing on bandwagons of uninformed public opinion," was a clear indication not so much of an individual's pique but rather of a professional community's mortification and growing ineffectuality.[44]

Not the least of the consequences of the national economy's unfortunate performance throughout the 1970s, and the attendant fracturing of the broad-based analytical consensus that had characterized the predominant part of the American economics profession for decades, was the havoc wrought in policy discussion itself. Gone were both the self-confident agreement about first principles and the interpersonal comity that more often than not went with it. Walter Heller, whose tenure as the nation's ranking economics official epitomized more halcyon days for both the economy and the profession that studied it, was quickly struck by the lack of consensus that characterized members of Richard Nixon's Council of Economic Advisers. In a display of generous understanding during the president's first term, he expressed concern that Nixon was continually put in the position of having "to finally cut the Gordian knot" because of conflicting reports and recommendations received from colleagues at the CEA, Treasury, and the Fed. If President Johnson had failed to keep his economic advisers fully apprised of the workings of his government, in the turmoil and confusion that consequently enveloped the nation's markets, economists increasingly failed those who followed him in the Oval Office.[45]

Rare is the professional who admits to being out of his or her depth. Far from squelching the optimism of most economists that their discipline had something of genuine value to offer to statecraft, the difficulties of the 1970s provoked further efforts to ensure that expertise had a place in government. Yet with a consistency that was, at the time, as unremarked as it was insidious, economists in public life (not to mention many of their colleagues in the academic and corporate worlds) made themselves the servants of a highly partisan politics uniquely indifferent to the complexities and the puzzles of the "science." If it was not, in certain individual cases, so much a matter of being explicit instruments of a political

agenda, the fact remains that as a profession the overwhelming majority of economists found themselves unable or unwilling to speak out in opposition. Theirs,
more often than not, became not so much a collaboration of intent as one of
silence.

Cutting the tax lifeline of federal economic policy practice during the 1980s
was as effective a conservative strategy of political retrenchment as it was manipulative of public sentiment. In place of the Keynesian argument that more equitably distributed incomes and wealth, effected by the tax system itself, would generate higher aggregate consumption and thus more robust economic growth, the
"new classical" economists posed a simpler view of the market system. Tax cuts,
which would necessarily place proportionately more discretionary income in the
hands of the wealthiest portions of the population, they claimed, would encourage
investment, which in turn would enhance employment. Thus would the benefits
of fiscal austerity "trickle down" through the income distribution. That greater
tax savings for the rich would stimulate investment was a proposition that directly
contravened Keynes's claim that it was investment, through its impact on employment and production (and thus incomes), which ultimately garnered rises in savings. Overall, taxes could thus be condemned as the mortal enemy of incentives
to work and to invest. Lost from view was the Keynesian rejoinder—that judicious tax policy, through the enhancement of consumption and investment it
would procure, could guarantee the profits of enterprise and thereby the prosperity
of the whole.[46]

So widely shared was the passion for tax cuts as a kind of "Holy Grail" of a
"new classical" economics that even the major political parties, toward the end
of Ronald Reagan's second presidential term, could find little about which to
disagree on that score. All that was left was political pandering to targeted constituencies. For the Republicans that meant emphasizing the usefulness of tax reduction for upper-income groups and the broadening of the argument to include proposals for reductions in the prevailing levy on capital gains; for the Democrats
the riposte was to focus on what was so beguilingly labeled "middle-class tax
relief." Both parties flirted with radical suggestions to eliminate the entire structure of income taxation itself, usually toying with half-baked ideas concerning the
implementation of a single-rate income tax or a national sales tax. With genuine
justification, an observer new to the scene might have concluded, during the 1988
presidential campaign especially, that John Maynard Keynes (not to mention his
like-minded colleagues and students) had never published a word.

Like most nostrums, tax reduction created more problems than it solved. Federal spending, whether engrossed by military initiatives such as those undertaken
during the Reagan presidency or propelled by transfer-payment programs long
on the books, rose both in absolute terms and on a per capita basis throughout the
1980s and early 1990s. A rising national debt only seemed to make more obvious
the failures (and the failings) of supply-side economics and its attendant pieties.
It was hardly surprising, therefore, that conservatives increasingly focused their
attention on disbursements themselves. Within this context arose the next offen-

sive against economic statecraft, the second prong of the attack originally launched by the Reagan tax cuts—the proposal for a balanced budget amendment to the United States Constitution.

A hardy perennial in the garden of conservative economic ideas, the balanced budget amendment became decidedly fashionable in 1985 when the National Governors Association passed a resolution favoring its adoption. Ever since, it has been the catalyst for a great deal of campaign posing and a regular addition to the list of bills pending before each Congress. Although it has consistently failed of passage, it remains a talisman of the Right, appropriately so given the fact that it would, by statute, eliminate the essential instrument of Keynesian fiscal policy from use by the Treasury, a kind of final nail in the Keynesian coffin. No wonder, then, that it has been and remains an object of great admiration among conservatives, equally loathsome to liberals. Far more striking than the obvious reactions it has provoked across the political spectrum have been, like the debate around the tax-cut strategies of the 1980s and 1990s, the muddled claims proffered in its defense—arguments that have made and that continue to make a mockery of the ideal of professionalized economic expertise in service to the state.[47]

Balanced budget advocates throughout the 1980s and 1990s utilized particular conceptions of government accounting practices, standards of measurement of debt burdens, assumptions regarding mechanisms of debt liquidation, and notions of state finance either completely inaccurate or thoughtless. In response, both professional economists and liberal protagonists were strikingly timid and, oftentimes, ineffective. Ignored in almost every discussion of the balanced budget idea was the peculiar design of the national accounts. Included in every annual budget in Washington were (and are) capital expenditures; separating these from operating expenses, save for depreciation allotments, had always been the standard practice of business enterprise. Doing so would, in the federal case, have generally reduced deficit levels considerably. There were, in fact, even beyond the relatively simple matter of balance sheet preparation, more trenchant criticisms to be made of deficit and debt measurement in the public sector.[48]

For fairly obvious political reasons, critics of Keynesian-style spending techniques focused their attacks on absolute levels of indebtedness. Large numbers, especially those rendered in red, were impressive instruments of persuasion in the dismantling of the mixed economy. Yet as any banker, let alone economic specialists, knew, debt burden could only be meaningfully evaluated with reference to the ultimate ability to pay. In this context, the national debt, representing a claim on the wealth and income streams of future generations, necessarily had to be measured with reference to the gross domestic product (GDP) itself. As a share of annual income, debt reveals its true lading. By this measure, American public finance, while obviously deranged in the wake of the Vietnam era, had since the early 1980s shown tangible improvement—not surprisingly, because the ratio of annual deficits to the GDP had fallen steadily from a high of 6.3 percent in 1983 to 1.4 percent in 1996. Looking at the debt as a whole, in 1995 the national shortfall stood at $3.6 trillion, just over 50 percent of a $7 trillion GDP. This compared quite favorably with a debt-GDP proportion of over 100 percent at the end of World War II—interestingly enough, the beginning of a period of growth and expansion in the national economy that was historically unprecedented. In this context, the central target variable would link any rate of growth in the debt to the rate of growth of the macroeconomy, a notion altogether obscured in the public debates surrounding a balanced budget amendment.

The sheer obtuseness of the public discussions concerning government finance in the late 1980s and early 1990s prompted a fair number of professional economists to act. In January 1997, James Tobin (then emeritus at Yale University and a Nobel laureate) led an effort to petition Congress on the matter. Calling the proposed balanced budget amendment "unsound and unnecessary," the document was ultimately signed by twelve hundred colleagues (eleven of them Nobel Memorial Prize winners). At the end of that month, it was presented on Capitol Hill. Above and beyond the misunderstandings the petition sought to expose, it also expressed the conviction that "[t]he Constitution [wa]s not the place to put specific economic policy." Reaction to this professional foray into the realm of public debate was inconsequential. The signatories of the "Economists' Statement Opposing the Balanced Budget Amendment" found themselves prophets with neither honor nor influence.

Yet the debate over the national debt held within it an important if fairly unwelcome lesson for social scientists who coveted a place in public affairs. Instruments of economic policy, most especially those having to do with government finance, were clearly first and foremost political creations. No public outcry, for example, shook Washington in the fall of 1945 when the financial obligations incurred in the wake of four years of international conflict assumed dimensions that, in the short run, altogether dwarfed the productive capacity of the nation's markets. A remarkable degree of political solidarity concerning war aims had prevented it. Similarly, throughout the 1980s and 1990s, it was politics rather than economics that not only framed policy outcomes but, more to the point, set the terms of public debate. If economists found themselves demoralized and confused by the indifference that met their arguments and prognostications, they might have been forgiven their lament. Theirs was a discipline, the product of a century of intellectual and social evolution, that fostered in its practitioners the notion that they could decisively separate ideology from analysis.

In point of fact, the transformation of the nation's political landscape in the wake of the Vietnam era had subverted the very foundations of the liberalism that had made sense out of the New Economics. An emphasis on political economic issues that had framed the high tide of activist government since the New Deal had provided a community of professionals with both the means and the ends to deploy their expertise. As soon as social issues concerning opportunity and equality occupied center stage, most dramatically in the formulation of the War on Poverty, American liberalism ran headlong into the abiding national puzzle of race and ethnicity. A backlash was the inevitable result, one that shifted a dynamic emphasis on productivity and plenty during the 1950s and 1960s to a static refrain concerning the costs and benefits, the winners and losers in market outcomes during the 1980s and 1990s. So dependent had the promise of liberalism been upon sustained growth as a vehicle of redistributive betterment and justice that the first signs of macroeconomic instability robbed it of its voice and its authority. Indeed, by the last years of the century, the New Deal order was dead, and with it the hopes and achievements of the New Economics.[49]

Perhaps it was predictable, given the rightward turn of American politics in the late twentieth century, that professional economics would itself regress and retrench. A kind of naïveté coupled with an unbridled enthusiasm had propelled the discipline's leading lights to make claims on its behalf it could not redeem. Once events, and the ideological shifts they provoked, overtook the statecraft economists had so painstakingly fashioned, their flanks were wholly exposed to an unrelenting and unparalleled assault. Reversion to classic principles, a rejection of heterodox notions, an insistence on a professional deportment unable and unwilling to join with the ideological issues in dispute, and a contentment with a return to scholarly detachment were understandable if pathetically timid reactions.[50]

It has long been a conviction of those who study the history of the sciences that moribund intellectual traditions may only be overcome by the effective articulation of alternatives. For modern American economics the possibilities for such a restructuring were by the late 1990s, precisely because of the effectiveness of the professionalizing processes that had obtained since the turn of the century, few and far between. A select group at leading colleges and universities continued to wield enormous influence over the distribution of research grants, their own ranks replenished from a hiring process disproportionately focused on the graduates of a small number of highly regarded training programs, including their own. Any examination of publication practices in the field would demonstrate as well that the dissemination of research results remained powerfully concentrated in the hands of an elite few. It is a striking yet hardly surprising finding that, at the height of the economic instability occasioned by the Vietnam War, the OPEC oil price shocks, and the downward trends in productivity enhancement experienced throughout the 1970s, alumni of only seven graduate programs in the discipline authored well over half the scholarly articles published in the nation's three leading economics journals. Such disciplinary inbreeding was hardly conducive to the elaboration of alternative paradigms.[51]

If, by the 1990s, economics was a social scientific discipline fast retreating from a public role it had sought for decades, it was clearly not the case that the influence of all of its practitioners was on the wane. Supply-side theorists, in ways far out of proportion with their achievements, continued to enjoy a prominence and an authority in economic debate that was virtually hegemonic. Anti-Keynesian rhetoric became ever more fashionable; calls for parsimony in governmental expenditure policy, often phrased in ways approximating a morality play, went virtually unchallenged. No better signal of the sea change that had taken place could be found than the news, broadcast in the fall of 1997, that N. Gregory Mankiw, a young economics professor at Harvard University, would receive a $1.25 million advance from a major textbook publisher to produce a new volume in which Keynes's name barely appeared once. As advance copies of the text made their way into the hands of reviewers, even *Business Week* magazine could express alarm at the widening popularity of what it derisively called "feel-good economics."[52]

There was, of course, a genuine logic to the whole process. Linked with the marvelously abstract claims of rational expectations theory, supply-side economics had succeeded in making a compelling case for the ineffectiveness of national policies that sought to intervene in the nation's markets. Indeed, the argument had been taken a step further by claiming that, even if the government sought to manipulate economic outcomes, it would only succeed in generating perverse results: stimulatory spending would ultimately reduce consumption, steps to increase employment would actually generate more idleness, aggregate policies to enhance technological change and productivity would in the end reduce the total supply of goods and services. Thus situated within the analytical domain of supply-side theory, economic statecraft was stymied. Why do anything when activism brought no appreciable benefits? A new laissez-faire doctrine found the largest possible audience, and the hope for a reorientation of economic analysis that would have made sense of the disturbing events of the 1970s and 1980s, while remaining true to a commitment that had characterized the profession since the 1930s, went unrequited.

Over three decades ago, the distinguished historian William Appleman Williams, reflecting upon the entire span of the nation's past, noted that policy appeals based on the principle of laissez-faire were, more often than not, actually premised on a slightly different conviction—that of laissez-nous-faire. Arguments militating in favor of less government involvement in economic life usually reduced themselves to strategies, on the part of particular elites, to secure opportunities with which to exercise greater control over resources, the workforce, and households. Williams's thesis had particular relevance with respect to the transformations in economic thinking that prevailed in the United States after the early 1970s. As the Keynesian consensus of the postwar era dissolved, and as it was replaced by an increasingly detached social theory that actively condemned governmental activism in the marketplace, the economics profession became less and less an engaged social scientific community in the public service and more and more a mouthpiece for a particular, interest-based agenda. No longer ministers to statist power, many economists reinvented themselves as privy councillors to private wealth.[53]

Since the economic turmoil of the early 1970s, indicting government for the nation's material woes had become an ever-more-expansive enterprise. Dismantling the Keynesian apparatus of the federal government had been only part of this project. Eager to ferret out any plausible cause of inefficiency and inflated costs in the national economy, analysts, political leaders, policy advocates, and pundits became increasingly preoccupied with the perceived burdens of governmental regulation in the marketplace. Deconstructing a variety of federal statutes and agencies, along the lines specified by an offensive against such statist intervention in economic affairs, became a significant parallel strategy in the eradication of Keynesian practice. Proponents of what was dubbed "privatization" argued that such reforms in the ways government did business would lead to greater efficiency in the allocation of scarce resources. By leaving decisions to businesspeople and other expertly trained individuals in the private sector, it was claimed, an appropriate system of incentives and capabilities would yield a more optimal distribution of services and a more inspired utilization of scarce public monies.[54]

Deregulation had a bipartisan gestation, its birth facilitated by the antitaxation attitudes fostered during the economic uncertainties of the 1970s. It was Jimmy Carter's presidential administration, building upon some initial and tentative steps taken by Gerald Ford's White House, that launched the first systematic efforts to reassess and ultimately eliminate to whatever extent possible federal oversight in the finance, telecommunications, and transportation sectors. The initial forays were focused predominantly in the aviation industry, culminating in the closure of the Civil Aeronautics Administration when Congress passed the 1978 Airline Deregulation Act. Fast on the heels of that landmark legislative decision came the 1982 settlement between the Antitrust Division of the Department of Justice and the American Telephone and Telegraph Corporation (AT&T), an agreement that began the systematic deregulation of the nation's telecommunications infrastructure. Shortly thereafter, the Reagan administration began reconfiguring the government's role in the nation's banking industry, an effort that had profound consequences in the savings and loan sector for years to come. By the time George Bush took office, the momentum of the deregulatory process had grown very strong indeed. Declaring a moratorium on all new federal regulations early in 1992, the president also asked his deputy, Vice President Dan Quayle, to chair the new Council on Competitiveness as an informal "superarbiter" of national regulatory issues.[55]

While the Quayle Council lasted only a year, liquidated in its infancy by Democrat William Clinton in one of his first acts as president, the political movement of which it stood as a striking exemplar continued. So irresistible was the appeal of deregulation rhetoric that policy initiatives were proposed and often enacted without due consideration of either their justification or their consequences. Increasingly, mainstream American economists made themselves part of this process—often eager to formulate techniques for its implementation, rarely willing to confront many baseless assertions deployed on its behalf. Nowhere was this strange reality made more manifest than in the transformation of the regulatory environment within which the nation's banking industry did its work.[56]

Beginning with the Ford and Carter presidencies, operational rules for banks, brokerage houses, and savings and loan institutions were relaxed. Among brokerages, deregulation resulted in a proliferation of discount offices that allowed investors to avoid the expenses and commissions associated with more traditional houses. Among banks, the elimination of many restrictions on the geographic range of their operations stimulated competitive entry throughout many states, although by the early 1990s a reconcentration of assets through bank mergers began in earnest. In the savings and loan industry, however, deregulation contributed to a crisis of mammoth proportions.[57]

It was in the period before deregulation, when rising interest rates and the proliferation of money market investment funds made it increasingly difficult for savings banks to offer depositors competitive rates of return, that the savings and loan catastrophe had its roots. As the rates paid on such alternative investments as money market funds dramatically increased (in no small measure pushed upward by the process of inflation that began in 1973), "Regulation Q," a federal rule limiting the maximum rate of interest that could be paid on savings and other demand deposits, made it virtually impossible for savings and loan institutions (S&Ls) to attract funds. Ironically, interest rate regulation had begun in 1933 when the Federal Reserve System implemented its first version of Regulation Q. The goal had been precisely to prevent the competitive shopping around for interest returns and to encourage depositors to place their funds in institutions selected on the basis of reputations for solvency and safety.

Banking industry lobbyists, not surprisingly, wished to eliminate Regulation Q. In 1980, the Carter administration, ostensibly seeking to aid a troubled industry, eased interest rate restrictions by means of the Depository Institutions Deregulation and Monetary Control Act (known, by insiders, as the "Diddymac"). The new law abolished geographic restrictions on the investment activities of S&Ls, thereby bringing a national market within the purview of individual institutions that had operated locally for decades. It also provided for deposit insurance of up to $100,000 for every savings account in the system—tendered by the Federal Savings and Loan Insurance Corporation (FSLIC), a derivative of the Federal Deposit Insurance Corporation (FDIC). S&Ls were no longer tied to deposits generated in their immediate communities but rather could attract deposits from far away by offering through brokers the high rates of interest made possible by deregulation itself.

Geographic deregulation created a national market in unregulated savings deposits—as, for the first time, S&Ls were allowed to offer account and credit privileges and other banking services nationwide. FSLIC guarantees simultaneously created a false sense of security within the S&L industry itself. The thrifts responded by investing in speculative commercial ventures in the hopes of shoring up their profitability—profitability that had been compromised for over a decade by Regulation Q. Thrifts' net income, as a share of their total assets, had averaged only 0.5 percent throughout the late 1970s; it fell to 0.1 percent by 1980 and turned negative in 1981 and 1982. Home mortgage business, the mainstay of the industry since the Great Depression, dropped off. Indeed, it became increasingly (and uncharacteristically) common for the S&Ls to provide full financing for a broad spectrum of investments with little or no down payment.[58]

A further difficulty emerged in this reformed environment. Thrifts found that the interest they earned on traditional mortgages provided insufficient funds to pay the higher interest rates they were now allowed to offer on an array of financial instruments. Some institutions thus began to use up their own liquid reserves to make good the difference. By 1982, fifty thrifts nationwide failed—a rate unprecedented since World War II. Congress, reflecting bipartisan concern for the S&L sector, responded with another revision of law. The Garn–St. Germain Bill, signed into law by President Ronald Reagan in 1982, having gone "through Congress like a dose of salts, with virtually no hearings in either Senate or House Banking committees," further loosened the restrictions on the kinds of investments S&Ls could make. The Federal Home Loan Bank Board, later reconstituted as the Office of Thrift Supervision, also participated in this strategy by reducing, virtually to zero, the minimum amount of capital that a bank was required to have on hand to underwrite particular investments.[59]

In the savings and loan industry, the deregulation of the 1970s and 1980s generated hasty, at times foolish and even corrupt, decision making. Operating in unrestricted and almost unknown territory, S&Ls became involved in questionable investment schemes, many of them unsecured, some very risky. Moreover, in the late 1980s, as the real estate market softened (especially in the South and the Southwest due to troubles in the oil, mining, and aviation industries), thrifts found even their traditional avenues of investment painfully encumbered. Thus began a series of savings and loan failures that had no equal since the 1930s. Unable to make good their obligations to depositors, S&Ls exhausted their deposit insurance and approached the Congress for relief. The full dimensions of the "bailout" ultimately necessary to restore the industry to firm footing were nothing short of mind-boggling.

Deregulation, at least in the financial sector, thus failed its proponents. Undertaken at the behest of an energetic and vocal academic and political constituency, it created vast costs in addition to its purported benefits. Regulatory reform, in this sense, responded far less to the lobbying of public-interest groups than to the efforts of cadres of new entrepreneurs (such as Carl Icahn in aviation, and Charles Keating and Michael Milken in finance) and academic practitioners (such as Alfred Kahn, the Cornell University economist who was one of the original architects of airline deregulation) to gain access to particular markets and to enjoy and exploit new levels of statist influence and visibility. There were no mass demonstrations in state capitals and in Washington, D.C., to deregulate major sectors of American industry. In the hands of a smaller cadre, deregulation became an essential part of the doctrine of laissez-nous-faire.

The savings and loan debacle did nothing to stem the ardor of public officials for continued deregulation of the banking industry as a whole. By the spring of 1997, Clinton administration specialists prepared legislative proposals to allow insurance companies, banks, and securities firms to do business in one another's markets. A practice long banned by the Glass-Steagall Act of 1933, which had been fashioned in response to the reckless management of investment funds that had helped make the crash of 1929 a catastrophe, the intermingling of banking and other financial operations had remained under close federal scrutiny for decades. The legislative passage of these proposals was secured in 1999. Meanwhile, the potentially anticompetitive and dangerous aspects of the proposed overhaul—such as the "tie-in" sale of mortgages and mortgage insurance, or the use of deposit funds in high-risk investments in which a bank had taken a particularly aggressive position—went mostly unremarked.[60]

It was, to be sure, not simply the financial sector in which the consequences of deregulation expressed themselves in such negative ways—nor where the vast majority of the economics profession continued to stand mute, except in those contexts in which it could facilitate the deregulatory process itself. In the airline industry, where deregulation advocates had long pointed to apparent successes in the expansion of service and the lowering of fares, such that an ever-growing proportion of the nation's population used air transport year after year, elimination of the Civil Aeronautics Administration generated a less than impressive record of economic accomplishment. From the early 1980s until 1988, the number of independent airline companies fell by more than half; the number of independent regional airlines declined from 250 to 170. In the same time period, over three hundred small towns lost commercial aviation service altogether. As major companies, in the deregulated environment, created "hub" facilities, price competition in those particular markets virtually disappeared. Concerns about hard-pressed firms skirting safety regulations, manipulating labor practices, and delaying maintenance schedules proliferated nationwide. By the late 1990s, the industry had reconcentrated itself in the wake of significant mergers. Complaints about price-fixing thus escalated. While many transportation economists had been quick to applaud the implementation of airline deregulation, virtually none of them spoke up about the problems that emerged in the newly configured industry.[61]

Telecommunications afforded a particularly large and complex territory for deregulatory initiatives, especially given the dissemination of new technologies (ranging from the personal computer to remote cellular phones to digital television to the Internet) throughout the business world and a large proportion of the nation's households. By ending the AT&T monopoly of the nation's telephone and telegraph market, the 1982 consent decree clearly led to a rapid drop in long-distance toll rates. Much like the immediate impacts of airline deregulation, the divestiture led to a marked increase in the nation's use of long-distance telephony. At the same time, and again ignored by economists who had mobilized in favor of the breakup of AT&T, the cross-subsidization of local phone costs by long-distance revenues, long claimed by AT&T itself, was lost. Local phone service became increasingly expensive; by the late 1990s, the costs of installing household phones had run sufficiently high as to cause consternation on the part of advocates of lower-income groups. Pay phone access was similarly restricted through both higher per-call costs and the reduction in the number of phones available for public use. Fees were imposed for the use of directory assistance for the first time. Many consumer groups were left wondering if the nation's households were left better off or not. No such self-interrogation appears to have occurred in the economics community.[62]

Deregulation of the telecommunications sector also brought a massive restructuring of firms within it.[63] Liberalization of ownership laws, which for decades had sought to mitigate the potential for oligopolistic control, was the proximate cause. New auction rules, implemented by the Federal Communication Commission (FCC) to allocate spectrums for wireless technologies, among other innovations, furthered the easing of governmental oversight of the industry as a whole. Allegations of bid rigging emerged almost as soon as the FCC arbitrage began. The economic expertise that had fostered the creation of these new auction procedures was absent efforts to police its equitable enforcement. Meanwhile, the many smaller companies spawned by the AT&T antitrust decision began, by the late 1990s, a merger initiative to reclaim both market share and its attendant control. The difference, this time, was that the federal regulatory apparatus to oversee such newly constituted large industry actors was gone.[64]

In the health care industry, deregulation was less an issue, with the exception of proposals to reform product safety codes, than the pursuit of strategies to make the delivery of care more market-based than practice-based. With respect to the former, allegations that the Food and Drug Administration (FDA) had become "hostile" to business and a fetter on profitability in the pharmaceuticals industry dovetailed well with suggestions that new-product testing become more privately based. In response to industry complaints that FDA reviews were too costly and time-consuming, friendly politicians—no doubt inspired by the rhetoric of an economics profession increasingly opposed to government intervention in markets—took up the cause. Led by Senator James Jeffords, Republican of Vermont, the Congress began consideration of a bill to privatize FDA operations in the summer of 1997. That bill, if it had become law, would have allowed pharmaceutical companies to submit new products for inspection to private laboratories they themselves would have designated. So obvious were the corporate intentions behind this effort, the epitome of a laissez-nous-faire attitude grown more and more popular, that the relative silence of industrial organization economists on the matter was startling.[65]

As for medical care delivery itself, the drive toward deregulation and privatization revealed a series of contradictions that remained unresolved throughout the 1980s and 1990s. Basing medical practice on a cost-benefit calculus, framing it within the for-profit institutional setting of the health maintenance organization (HMO) and of "managed care," raised a series of disturbing ethical questions and fostered increasing amounts of resistance on the part of consumers. Ironically enough, this in turn stimulated some efforts to reregulate the industry, although the outcome of those initiatives remained unclear. Leading medical economists, such as Uwe Reinhardt of Princeton University, along with their claim that only by imposing free-market incentives would the costs of medical care come down over time, increasingly attacked what they described as the "entitlement mentality" of Americans on the subject of health care. In this rhetorical design, of course, these scholars (even if unwittingly) linked their arguments with those of conservatives opposed to the welfare state agendas of earlier decades. No small part of the movement to render the health care industry more like its private-sector counterparts were the rising costs of Medicare itself in a nation in which the age composition of the population rose steadily from the 1970s onward. Suggestions that greater proportions of Medicare practice be "profit-based" and that means tests be imposed on Medicare recipients only made more acceptable what had become a more and more common strategy of a federal government strapped for revenues—the imposition of "user fees" for various services once guaranteed to all under a progressive income tax system. Here again, the budgetary problems of the post–Vietnam War era provided the substratum within which a virtual revolution in both social policy and social science expertise (not to mention public attitudes) could take place.[66]

Advocates of market-based practices in social policy also turned their attention to matters of environmental protection. Here, too, substantial segments of the American business community, by the 1980s, complained of an "overregulation" with respect to air and water quality, as well as occupational and consumer product safety, that excessively jeopardized the profitability of enterprise. That significant proportions of the workforce could be mobilized in this antigovernment stance was testimony more to the anxiety working Americans had regarding the security of their employment than to powerfully held convictions about the virtues of free markets. Economic theorists again became indispensable participants in the conversation. The notion that direct regulation of "externalities" tied to particular economic activities was necessary precisely because no private allocation of liability was immediately possible in the unregulated marketplace was subjected to growing criticism. In its place the discourse of exchange took center stage. Specialists suggested that externalities be, like all commodities, instruments of commerce. They argued that firms whose production processes generated effluents or toxic waste, for example, should be free to bargain, both with government and with private households, as to acceptable levels of discharge. A polluter could then in principle pay a subsidy for environmental damage; those eager to protect the environment, in parallel fashion, might bargain over an agreed-upon level of payments to an establishment to cease and desist from particular activities. Inspired by this kind of reasoning, in 1994 the Air Quality Management District in the Los Angeles region instituted a program of "smog credits" whereby companies could accumulate points allowing for particular levels of air pollution in exchange for other environmental remediation (such as paying for the scrapping of old cars without catalytic converters). The general idea was market based: let pollution be bargained over like any other product. Private parties to that transaction, acting on rational incentives, would generate "optimal" outcomes.[67]

There is no more passion to be found than among those of the recently converted. American economists became increasingly enthralled with the idea of "market-driven" solutions to the problem of externalities. In their enthusiasm, many theorists overlooked historical and political legacies that made this part of the deregulatory strategy particularly clumsy. None of these were more apparent than the processes of industrial location that tended to concentrate dangerous operations in neighborhoods and regions more heavily populated by the poor. Their lack of access to effective legal representation made these communities only more susceptible to the worst that the dismantling of environmental regulation could offer. By the late 1990s, it became obvious to a growing number of community activists that privatized markets in, for example, pollution credits yielded higher concentrations of pollutants in certain areas while more affluent communities reaped the benefits. That the dimensions of class, in these cases, were often paralleled by those of race and ethnicity made the results all the more obnoxious. "Environmental racism" thus became not simply a rallying cry for a new generation of local organizers but also a particularly disturbing label for a policy outcome hardly contemplated by its most ardent architects.[68]

As an instrument of alleged social reform, the free market became a canonical device in the hands of late-twentieth-century economic policy analysts. Deregulation of electricity transmission, privatization of prisons, proposals for "tax vouchers" to create a private market in schooling, the renewed construction of toll roads, suggestions that the postal service be eliminated, trial programs to let private corporations run state welfare systems, experimentation with the privatization of social security accounts, contracting out local services to private firms—ranging from parks maintenance to air traffic control to public library networks—even the notion that various parts of the national security and defense apparatus be contracted out to the highest private bidder, all became and remain parts of a new economic "discourse" in contemporary America.[69]

Yet, in perhaps the greatest irony of all, the profession that had once prided itself on the refinement of the idea of "opportunity cost" had (and continues to have) virtually nothing to say of substance regarding the "opportunity costs" of privatization.[70] On the one side, deregulated markets fostered the expenditure of vast sums of money on new promotional efforts to encourage consumers to shift services from one provider to another. Daily mail deliveries and frequent evening phone calls became the advance guard of a tidal wave of sales efforts and "come-ons" that presumably fostered competition in previously monopolized services but that also consumed greater and greater amounts of both company resources and households' time and energy. At best, deregulation prompted confusion among targeted populations; at worst, it provided a venue within which corrupt practices could flourish.[71] To respond in reasoned and informed ways to every proposal would have forced consumers to allocate ever-increasing amounts of already scarce time to their evaluation. For a vast majority of consumers it was not unreasonable to assume that the avalanche of competitive market information became an incoherent and often bothersome babble. Models of "rational expectations" were clearly not equal to the task of explaining this strange new reality. In this context, the warning of the ages—caveat emptor—took on an altogether poignant meaning.[72]

On the other side, deregulation restructured markets in ways that often stifled competition. By the early 1990s, local governments began to examine the practices of new entrants in major utilities sectors that seemed decidedly manipulative, if not based on overt conspiracies to restrain trade. In certain instances, proposals to "reregulate" industry met with attentive hearings in local government agencies. Over time it is conceivable that certain sectors may indeed by subject to new regulatory discipline, although such intervention will take place in the wake of a complete redistribution of particular markets among a new set of industrial actors. Viewed from this broad, historical perspective, deregulation in the late-twentieth-century United States was actually nothing of the sort. Far from an inspired political process of liberation, whereby an overweening state apparatus was chased from the field of energetic competitive enterprise, deregulation was actually an essential moment in the reregulation of the nation's markets for the benefit of new corporate constituencies. Of this most remarkable development in economic affairs, the discipline that, more than any other, helped initiate the process has had nothing of importance to say.[73]

Privatization also generated productivity losses and cost inefficiencies owing to the burdens it imposed on communities negatively affected by market restructuring. For example, in central urban areas where banking deregulation led to the liquidation of large numbers of branches, whole neighborhoods found themselves without banking service. In many cases this then prompted the proliferation of check-cashing and gyro-account storefronts that imposed high fees for their services. The same was true of the increasing use of automated banking machines. Aside from the direct cost consequences of these developments, the additional indirect burdens loomed large. Individuals might spend half to all of a day taking care of a variety of transactions that once could have been quickly secured at a local banking branch. In health care and day care, similar problems emerged in the wake of deregulation—serving only to increase the number of lost working days for a population already paying ever-higher fees for services once provided on a more universalized and thus cheaper basis. Perhaps in this sense, contemporary markets should not be understood to have been "privatized" but rather to have been "anomized" or "disassociated." For a significant portion of the nation's population, the effort to decollectivize the assignment of cost liability for an array of social "goods" had a significant impact on styles (and qualities) of life and levels of economic welfare.[74]

By the late 1990s, no more dramatic example of the wholesale reorientation in the attitude of mainstream professional economists toward public policy strategies had emerged than that concerning information and statistics. The impulse to "deregulate" market environments quickly extended itself to the domain of data generation and distribution; with it, the urge to halt the government's participation in the provisioning of timely and accurate information regarding economic performance followed as a matter of course. To the extent that economic statistics could themselves be conceived of as a commodity, it seemed logical to argue that their "production" and utilization should be privatized. Suggestions that the statistical reporting activities of federal agencies such as the Department of Commerce, Department of Labor, and Council of Economic Advisers be terminated were seriously entertained. Individuals, households, and firms (not to mention government offices themselves) could, it was argued, purchase economic information from private econometrics practices. Superior statistical work would be rewarded, in such a market setting, while inaccurate and unreliable products would ultimately be driven out by the discipline of competitive enterprise. An econometric "shop" capable of delivering effective forecasts of, say, inflation, unemployment, and other significant parameters would find its services much sought after by consumers (within both households and corporations) eager to make appropriate allocative decisions. The converse would of course be true for those statistical operations less skilled and capable. This suggestion, that the statistical activities of government be replaced by the private venues of "normal" commerce, had the added virtue, in the eyes of its champions, of encouraging further shrinkage in the size and cost of governmental agencies themselves.[75]

At the same time that proposals for the privatization of statistical reporting emerged, political leaders launched an ever-widening array of attacks on the actual process of economic forecasting within the federal government itself. Inflation-rate projections came under increasing scrutiny as their implications, for the payment of social security assistance, the adjustment of income tax brackets, the renegotiation of federal contracts over time (as well as the modification of private-sector wage and price agreements), all captivated a Congress, and ostensibly a public, determined to reduce federal expenditures. Here, too, decades of criticism and cynicism about the economic activities of government took their toll. By early 1997, Senate leaders called for the establishment of an independent panel of "experts" to review and improve the ways in which inflation was measured. That for decades the Council of Economic Advisers, the Department of Commerce, the Department of Labor, and the Treasury had been entrusted with this important task, and that this new proposal was almost universally accepted, only gave further testimony to how frayed federal agency reputations had become toward the end of the century. No doubt Edwin Nourse (and, to be sure, virtually all of his successors) would have been humiliated—far from remaining a wellspring of reliable economic expertise, federal offices like the CEA had become mere punching bags in a series of political slugfests.[76]

For some future chronicler it might no doubt make sense that, in its apparent maturity, a profession committed to the understanding of the workings of the market would find some of its members ultimately placed in the position of arguing for the application of laissez-faire principles to the creation of economic information itself. Even so, the particularities of the historical forces accounting for that outcome would also force resort to a more critical assessment. Policy doctrines, of any sort and at any time, are themselves the product of a complicated past. In the case of the American economics profession, contemporary prescriptions for a public purpose, far from being the distillation of an objective body of theory, are the manifestation of a far more complex heritage. It is the legacies of that provenance that matter the most.[77]

Over a century ago, American scholars eager to understand the economic world in which they lived embraced a project of both theoretical and social import. In doing so, they yoked the insights of an intellectual revolution in the ways social scientists understood human behavior in commercial settings to a specific agenda of professional advancement. A late-nineteenth-century transformation in economic thought afforded these investigators a powerful and versatile set of tools with which to situate human rationality at the center of a remarkable and immensely influential human institution—the marketplace. A "science" of individual behavior and social organization was thus established, the implications of which played no small part in the creation of a respected and ultimately quite accomplished community of professional experts.

But an authoritative community does not, precisely because it cannot, subsist on its own. American economists were most eager to place their skills at the service of the state. Here history proved both a blessing and a curse, for the profession's great achievements of the twentieth century, especially but not solely during years of global conflict and war, were also paralleled by failures and betrayals emanating from the same source. Indeed, it would be these negative moments in the century-long progress of their self-realization that would drive economists and their discipline farther and farther from engagement with the affairs of state in favor of an increasingly introverted and surprisingly opaque discourse. At the same time, eager like most professionals to retain an influence and visibility in public affairs that would cultivate a continued appreciation of their virtues and skills, later generations of economists would make themselves—whether consciously or not—useful servants of those, in both the political and the commercial worlds, who had an altogether different view of public purpose and of the appropriate role of government.[78]

Speculative yet serious-minded late-twentieth-century proposals to privatize the creation and dissemination of economic data brought this fascinating and intricate history to a symbolic close. For professional American economists the essential mechanism in the working of a modern market system was the liberation of individual rationality, armed with the benefit of accurate and reliable information, to pursue chosen ends. Further, they argued, so long as rationality was not somehow distorted or "bounded" in illegitimate ways, and provided that market information was consistently accessible to all, the outcome of competitive bargains would be the best possible for the largest number of market participants. Leaving the very instrument of rationality itself, information and data, to the competitive discipline of the market emerged as a logical and coherent extrapolation of the essential argument in the first place.

Yet in the very effort to idealize the market and its operation, contemporary American economists had left aside the other part of the equation—the history that had seemingly made their ideas and practice relevant to and important for a public purpose. When, for example, Herbert Hoover had insisted that government should provide free and accurate economic information for an enterprising and rational people, he had merely sought to operationalize some of the more rarefied claims of a modern economics itself. A half century later, in headlong retreat from the demands of a statist social science, American economists turned Hoover's insight on its head. In doing so, they substituted a crucial *precondition* of the proper workings of an unfettered market system for the product of the system itself. Human rationality, and the intelligence and statistics that were its necessary components, thus became not the distinctive premise of a modern science of society but rather mere articles of commerce themselves. American economists thus made products of what had been, for their discipline for many decades, their starting axioms. Economic science had, at last, become sophistry.

Reduced to arguing (if, up to now, only in hypothetical fashion) that the ingredients of rationality might best be things to be bought and sold, contemporary economic theorists seemed blissfully unaware of both the irony and the implications
of the historical journey of which they stood as the result. Their ancestors, the
"offspring of mixed parentage—European scholarship and Yankee social reform,"
had found much of merit in a neoclassical theory with which they had become
infatuated. The rigor and systematicness that doctrine brought to their field encouraged them to covet influence in a larger and more demanding world of policy.
So determined were they in pursuit of this goal that, for a not inconsiderable
period of time, they believed it was not their responsibility "to teach business
[people] how to do their job," but rather to examine critically both the workings
and the remediation of economic practice as a whole. In the great armed conflicts
of the twentieth century, they became for a time the heroes of what some called
"the economist's war," and they showed themselves to be uniquely skilled at the
"military application" of their expertise that was part "historical accident" and
part "sociological" phenomenon.

By the second half of the twentieth century, these celebrated social scientists
found themselves firmly entrenched in a growing and powerful governmental
apparatus. Those who labored in the highest echelons of government were not
reluctant to admit that they worked "in the field of values as well as that of fact
and theory." But the history that had privileged them also deceived. The world of
politics and power ultimately took matters out of their hands, and they, determined
to remain true to a professional and an intellectual code that had grown only more
venerable with time, assiduously cultivated alternatives of an altogether different
sort. These "humble, competent people" applied themselves to these new agendas
with the same capability and determination that had distinguished the efforts of
generations of their forebears. Yet this time there was a difference, for in their
scholastic introversion, in their thoughtless alliance with new business elites determined to use public policy for private rather than communal ends, in their
pursuit of a dessicated market paradigm that ran the risk of rendering the very
foundations of a democratic and free commerce as themselves objects of profit
making and accumulation, this new generation of specialists refashioned a social
science apparently disconnected from and seemingly unengaged with the social
and political world in which they lived. The most formative and exciting century
in the evolution of the American economics profession had come to this.

Epilogue

Being Ignored (Reprise)

> [T]he age of chivalry is gone. That of sophisters, econo-
> mists, and calculators, has succeeded; and the glory of
> [the world] is extinguished for ever.
> —EDMUND BURKE (1790)[1]

ON A BRISK, partly cloudy day in October 1975, the secretary-general of the Royal Swedish Academy of Sciences, Carl Gustav Bernhard, took up the happy task of notifying two scholars they would share the next Nobel Memorial Prize in Economic Science. He sent one letter westward to New Haven, Connecticut; the other he posted in the opposite direction, across the Gulf of Finland, to Leningrad. "[F]or their contribution to the theory of [the] optimum allocation of resources," Tjalling C. Koopmans of Yale University and Leonid V. Kantorovich of the Soviet Union's Academy of Sciences thus became the only economists ever honored at Stockholm whose work contemporaneously spanned the geopolitical and ideological divide of the cold war.[2]

Bernhard's notification was particularly gratifying to Koopmans, who was "delighted to . . . shar[e] the award with Academician Kantorovich, whom [he] ha[d] known personally for a number of years, and whom [he] h[e]ld in the highest esteem, as a person and for his scientific contributions." It also heralded, in the opinion of the editorial staff of the *New York Times*, a "revolution in economics" that demonstrated "the fact that . . . despite their many differences, both capitalist and Communist economies . . . ha[d] important similarities in the problems to be solved and in the tools available for [their] solution." There arguably could be no greater claim to the scientific rigor and dispassionate professionalism of a discipline than this—that two investigators, separated by one of the most violent and costly ideological confrontations in history, "renewed, generalized and developed[,] largely independently of one another," fundamental methods of analysis of universal applicability.[3]

Kantorovich and Koopmans had in fact surreptitiously cultivated a professional and personal relationship for almost two decades, leading up to the occasion of their Nobel triumph. Indeed, in the fall of 1956, Koopmans had seen a copy of what would become a celebrated paper by Kantorovich "On the Translocation of Masses," an investigation of what was essentially a classic linear programming problem in the use of transportation resources. So impressed was the Yale economist with the Russian's efforts that he wrote him directly, telling Kantorovich that he had clearly "paralleled but in greater part [had] anticipated a development . . .

in the United States which ha[d] stretched out over the period from 1941 . . . and [wa]s still continuing." Koopmans expressed the hope that his letter "m[ight] lead to an exchange of information" between the two scholars.[4]

Kantorovich's investigations had begun at the same time as Koopmans's, in the late 1930s, when the Soviet had been tasked "to recommend ways of scheduling operations on a fixed installation of machine tools in the plywood industry." But it was not until the mid-1950s that Kantorovich's research became known outside of his homeland. It was nevertheless clear in Koopmans's mind that the Russian "ha[d] priority over most" of the work in linear programming done in the United States in the interwar period. While several colleagues disputed Koopmans's conclusion in this regard, some describing the Soviet work as "a direct borrowing from activity analysis" in this country, Koopmans would have none of it. He described the "translocation of masses" essay as "simply amazing" and "extremely perceptive," a fine example of "mathematicians perceiving economic truth that had escaped economists in their environment." Carefully and resolutely establishing contacts with Kantorovich was, therefore, a matter of high scientific principle.[5]

Less concerned with self-aggrandizing disputes over the timing of their mutual work, Koopmans was far more anxious about the impact of notoriety in Western academic circles on Kantorovich's political position at home. While he "ha[d] the impression that mathematicians enjoy[ed] somewhat greater freedom from prevailing [Soviet] doctrines, probably because no one expect[ed] them to collide with economic doctrines," he nonetheless believed that Kantorovich and his colleagues "stake[d], if not their lives, then certainly their careers" on the appropriate reception of their work at home. When Koopmans's Yale colleague Raymond Powell met Kantorovich in Leningrad late in the summer of 1957, the Soviet scholar had been quite nervous, indeed strikingly uncommunicative. Powell, admitting that "a personality quirk" might have had something to do with the strained meeting, believed "the press of external circumstances" weighed heavily on Kantorovich, all the more exacerbated by the fact "that Kantorovich [wa]s almost certainly a Jew, and a Jew in Leningrad." Koopmans's anxieties in this regard were only intensified when word emerged a year later that Kantorovich had been attacked within the Soviet Union for departures, in his research, from Marx's labor theory of value.[6]

No doubt emboldened by concerns over the political fate of his Soviet colleague, Koopmans redoubled his efforts to bring Kantorovich's work to the attention of the West. The Yale economist saw to the translation of more work by the Soviet mathematician, turning often for help to his friend and colleague Robert Campbell at the University of Southern California. He facilitated the exchange of journals, working papers, and books with Kantorovich and, in return, had Soviet publications reviewed in Western serials. On several occasions, Kantorovich expressed his gratitude for the manner in which Koopmans played intellectual midwife to the emergence of a trans–cold war collaboration. In similar vein, C. West Churchman, a Berkeley faculty member and editor in chief of *Management Sci-*

ence in 1960, credited Koopmans with the "excellent groundwork [he had] laid
. . . for . . . continuing . . . cooperat[ion] with the Russian people[.]"[7]

By the time Kantorovich and Koopmans met face-to-face in Stockholm, they
had become close colleagues and friends. What admiration and esteem was the
foundation of this relationship also served to support the gratitude Kantorovich
must have felt for Koopmans's agency in bringing his work to a worldwide audience. Indeed, it is safe to say that without the intervention of the Yale scholar, the
Soviet mathematician may have labored in obscurity for the rest of his career. For
both intellectual and personal reasons, it was therefore more than just that the two
men mixed up their Nobel medals, Kantorovich taking home Koopmans's prize,
Koopmans finding the name "Kantorovich" inscribed on his when he returned to
New Haven. It took close to two years for the medals to be exchanged—returned
to their rightful owners through the good services of the Swedish ambassadors to
the Soviet Union and the United States.[8]

The intellectual and personal friendship sustained by Kantorovich and Koopmans personified (and indeed personalized) what had been a more deep-seated
historical process of the postwar period. For some decades after World War II,
Western social scientists had commented on the potential for "convergence" in
the economic practices of capitalist nations with those of the Soviet Union. After
all, Russia had faced exceptional problems with respect to national mobilization,
first during Stalin's program of collectivization in the interwar period (at which
time Kantorovich had begun his pathbreaking research), later with respect to
military mobilization in the face of Germany's "Operation Barbarossa" that had
commenced in the summer of 1941. With the advent of the cold war, the need
for systematic allocative methods only increased as the military contest with the
United States and the European member nations of the North Atlantic Treaty
Organization intensified. Similarly, with the coming of World War II, the United
States and other Allied nations faced dramatic needs for appropriate methods
to manage mobilization; it was in this context that Koopmans had made his
crucial discoveries on behalf of British and American merchant shipping administrators. Again, during the cold war era, the importance and usefulness of the
work that Koopmans and later researchers executed only became more and more
apparent.

Even so, for economists the seeming convergence of ideas in their disciplines,
from East and West, appeared to be less the result of particular historical and
political forces than the outcome of intellectual trends of longer gestation. As
another Yale economist put it shortly after Koopmans won the Nobel Memorial
Prize, "The techniques of activity analysis [perfected by Kantorovich and Koopmans both] exemplif[ied] the pure theory of decision-making, and, as such,
[we]re remarkably indifferent to economic institutions and organizational forms."
It was thus "one of the great achievements of this methodological revolution"
that "economists of the East and the West" could enjoy "continued dialogue—
free of ideological overtones." Scientific rigor and objectivity had at long last
triumphed over sectarian posturing; an "age of sophisters, economists, and calcu-

lators" had indeed emerged, but contrary to the late-eighteenth-century skepticism of an Edmund Burke, it potentially signaled a new era of understanding, comity, and peace.[9]

Speculation concerning the apparent similarities of advanced economic practice in the East and the West disappeared as soon as the Soviet Union collapsed in December 1991. In its place emerged an unabashed smugness about the virtues of capitalist markets as engines of growth and rising material welfare. The shared Nobel Memorial Prize in Economic Science of 1975 thereby stood less as a symbol of intellectual parallelism than of an older, albeit inspired, statism that had spanned the great contest of the cold war itself. Reversing the timing of scientific priority that Koopmans himself had been so scrupulous to preserve, commentators cavalierly declared the triumph of capitalist over socialist principles, suggesting that "the pure theory of decision-making" exemplified by such techniques as linear programming was a Western discovery that had then penetrated to the East.[10] Intellectual precision and with it historical sensitivity were now replaced by an unrelenting triumphalism grounded in dogma rather than fact.

If an awareness of the peculiar historical roots of a professionalized economics in the United States was lost in the celebration of Soviet devolution, it was also the case that the role of economists in public policy making had been by the same token dramatically transformed. Indeed, the latter process had been unfolding for some time prior to the advent of *perestroika*. The fiscal debacle of the Vietnam War era had set in train a series of changes in economic doctrine that were ultimately paralleled by alterations in institutional practice in Washington itself. Its authority and standing compromised by the distressing economic history of the 1960s and 1970s, the Council of Economic Advisers was ever more powerfully challenged in the realm of policy making. Perceiving both the CEA and the Bureau of the Budget as powerful examples of executive power run amok, Congress established its own Budget Office in 1974 to provide an alternative source of economic forecasts and policy prescriptions. It thus indulged in the kind of politicization of advising that a Leon Keyserling might have genuinely admired; no doubt Edwin Nourse would have been shocked. The consequent proliferation of points of view might rightfully be understood as an inevitable response of the legislative branch to the rise of the imperial presidency (not to mention a reaction to the Watergate scandals of the Nixon era); by contrast, for those hopeful to maintain an unimpeachable reputation for professional economic opinion, it represented their worst fears.

What went hand in hand with the declining cachet of economists in the executive branch was the shift in the "balance of power" between the CEA and the Board of Governors of the Federal Reserve System that also began in the 1970s. In no small degree, this resurgence of the Fed as a (if not the) major arbiter of economic policy making had everything to do with a rightward shift in Washington that found its roots in the election of 1972 when Richard Nixon handily defeated George McGovern. Turning its back on the interventionist strategies of the Kennedy and Johnson years, the Nixon administration initiated the process by which price stabilization rather than full employment would become the central goal of national policy. In this task, the Fed became the essential instrument of realization; ironically enough, it fell to Nixon's Democratic successor, Jimmy Carter, to appoint the grand architect of the Fed's restoration—Paul Volcker.

On another level, however, the eclipse of fiscal policy (and its practitioners) by the monetarist predilections of the Fed Board of Governors was also symptomatic of a new intellectual trajectory in the economics discipline, an evolution that left Keynesianism in a shambles and replaced it with the nostrums of rational expectations theory and supply-side policy prescriptions. A unique combination of political circumstances and a shifting professional discourse thus served to reorient national economic policy making in ways William McChesney Martin, not to mention Benjamin Strong, would have found familiar and desirable. Price stability became once again the goal of macroeconomic management; compensatory fiscal policy did not merely fade from view but fell into outright disrepute. A virtual century of increasingly statist preoccupations and practices culminated in a series of ever-more-damaging critiques that rendered statism itself a feeble and uninspiring creed. Far from enjoying center stage in Washington, economists within the Executive Office of the President were systematically outflanked by a closed cadre of central bankers who, while originally appointed by presidents, were beholden to no one but themselves.[11]

Predictably enough, the full implementation of the monetarist policy formula under the Carter administration pushed the economy into a major recession, one that fully obscured the prosperity of the 1960s and set the stage for Ronald Reagan's landslide electoral victory of 1980.[12] First by reducing the money supply, then by raising both bank-reserve requirements and the interest charged on Federal Reserve loans to member institutions, the Fed brought the economy to a virtual standstill. Mortgage rates rose beyond 15 percent, and the prime rate reached a historic high of 20 percent. While it would take some time, and a new administration, to see inflation completely wrung out of the system, the reconfiguration of authority with respect to national economic policy making was immediate. Indeed, throughout the years of the Reagan presidency, the Council of Economic Advisers drifted into obscurity, its members unknown to the public in ways Walter Heller and his colleagues would have found quite strange. The Fed reigned, and would continue to reign, supreme.

So thorough and relentless was the Fed's attack upon inflationary bias in the late-twentieth-century American economy that its champions and critics alike found ample justifications for their particular points of view. Conservatives lauded what they took to be the "depoliticization" of economic policy, crafted now within the closed deliberations of the Federal Reserve Board Open Market Committee, that allowed for the first successful assault on price volatility in almost two decades. Liberals complained of the Fed's "independence" from political processes that could make it more accountable to constituencies more concerned with employment growth and job security. Whatever their differences, however, all "Fed watchers" throughout the 1980s and 1990s had to agree that the Board of Governors had become the final arbiters of national economic policy. Perhaps more to the point, with his appointment as chair of the board in 1987 by President Ronald Reagan (and his reappointments in 1992, 1996, and 2000), Alan Greenspan, who had served as CEA chair under President Gerald Ford, became the most powerful economic policy maker in Washington. Indeed, a future secretary of labor put it more dramatically a few years later: the Fed chair had become "the most powerful man in the world."[13]

With the return of the Democratic Party to the White House in 1992, the Fed's authority had grown so robust that the Clinton administration made more formal and bureaucratic what had been, since 1980, a fait accompli. Despite calls from within his own party to replace Fed chair Greenspan and reassess the procedures of the Board of Governors itself, President Clinton renewed Greenspan's tenure and declined to support House Banking Committee chair Henry B. Gonzalez (Democrat of Texas) in his effort to place Federal Reserve reform legislation before the Congress in its first 1993 session. Adding to the perception that the new administration had accepted a shift in the relative influence of the CEA and the Treasury vis-à-vis the Fed, the creation of the new National Economic Council (NEC) left muddled and confused the lines of authority regarding economic policy running from the Executive Office of the President to other branches of the federal government. While pundits compared the influence wielded by CEA chair Laura Tyson, Labor Secretary Robert Reich, and NEC chair Robert Rubin, the apparent "troika" of lead economic advisers in the White House, the Fed's sway in Washington steadily increased.[14]

Midway through Bill Clinton's first presidential term, the inevitable occurred. Regarding the proliferation of economic advising functions in the executive branch as redundant and wasteful, critical of the president's appointments to those posts, and wholly impressed by the veracity and utility of the Fed's macroeconomic policies, Republican members of the House Appropriations Committee pushed through a bill to eliminate funding for the Council of Economic Advisers. Popular in the Congress, the bill ultimately died in the Senate. Its symbolism was, however, strikingly clear. In a mere half century, the institutional foundations of economic "fine-tuning" in the federal government had been swept away. The dream of an unchallenged repository of economic skills in the executive branch had been outflanked, its highly visible professionalism and the prestige that went with it replaced by the in camera proceedings of a faceless gathering of bankers. Economic statecraft had abandoned the limelight of the public arena for the proverbial smoke-filled room.[15]

At century's end, the discipline so powerfully shaped by the epoch's tumultuous history and by the statecraft it both inspired and deployed to its own advantage was confronted with a remarkable paradox. On the one side, the very prestige and influence of economics as a social science had been built upon statist agendas stretching back to the Great War. Yet on the other, the contemporary profession had turned inward, spurning the fiscal activism and frank political engagement of its forebears, preferring a more withdrawn posture that ostensibly depoliticized its work while at the same time it made more and more practitioners mere shills for particular corporate elites eager to seize upon public assets now increasingly "privatized." Eschewing the lessons to be won from a frank assessment of both the triumphs and the failures of statism, the vast majority of American economists in the late twentieth century abandoned the very inclinations and practices that had brought their field to such prominence in the first place.

Hand in hand with the retreat of economists from the open arena of state policy went the increasing disengagement of the public from genuine debate over fiscal and monetary affairs. In no small measure, the seeming withdrawal of the electorate from concrete disputes over economic policy formation, and its growing obsession with trivialities of image and deportment invented by "spin doctors" serving political leaders of all sorts, had everything to do with the homogenization of information gathering and the "corporate takeover of public expression" characteristic of an age in which the media had become mere subsidiaries of multinational firms marketing a wide array of products.[16] Yet it also had everything to do with a professional strategy, literally spanning a century, that sought to replace public contests over policy making with the refined and relatively closed research and analysis of a credentialed elite.

It is one of the supreme ironies of the "information revolution" of the late twentieth century that a public offered access to larger and larger sets of data is, at the same time, less and less capable of judging their veracity and using them effectively.[17] In no instance is this more obvious than in the case of economic numeracy. Independent of the fact that the vast majority of Americans have no grasp of the ways in which economic data are estimated (let alone how, for example, the various tax deductions from their paychecks are calculated), survey results demonstrate that well more than half of the citizenry are unaware, at any given point in time, of the magnitudes of core economic variables that frame public policy discussion.[18] This social reality refracts the influence and impact of policy-making professionals in an altogether different way than early-twentieth-century notions of disinterested expertise in the public service once claimed. For rather than linking expert knowledge to the deployment of informed popular choice in elections, contemporary economic discourse takes on the form of a private conversation among a select few who enjoy privileged access to political officials. Where such discussion ties the assertions of economists themselves to the interests of particular corporate elites, as became so characteristic of the "Reagan revolution" in national policy making, the antidemocratic consequences of this historical development become particularly obvious. Even more to the point, the rigor and scientific precision that economists claim are characteristic of their discipline serve to silence, through the substitution of arguments over ends with those over means, the genuine political debate that has (and will) always surround economic policy formulation as a whole. An enlightened citizenry, mobilized in political debate and expression, the essential foundation of Progressivist designs for reform early in the twentieth century, has now become increasingly rare.[19]

In a strange and arguably unintended fashion, American economists thus find themselves once again being ignored. Yet this time, at the turn of the century, the disengagement of the public from the methods and learning of a social science derives less from an uncertainty about its usefulness and virtues than from a political and historical evolution that has placed economic debate beyond the comprehension and interest of the large mass of the people. It is an extraordinary irony that this process of detachment has had as much to do with the professionalizing strategies and impulses of economists themselves as with larger social and political forces beyond their control.[20] In this regard, the middle-class professionalism of which economics has been a striking example has revealed itself to be stunningly two-faced. To the one side are its "human dedication," "personal nobility," "social idealism," "service to society," and "discovery of great knowledge." On the other are encountered its "degradation," "pettiness," and "rank self-interest" that coalesce in a "shameless exploitation of [learning] for profit." For all these reasons, the "culture of professionalism" in modern American "has existed only at the edge of personal cynicism and duplicity."[21]

Of the historical genesis of that "cynicism and duplicity," most professionals, especially but not solely economists, have been thoroughly ignorant. Lacking a historical sensibility that would force them to reckon with the role of events, institutions, and individuals in generating particular intellectual and policy-oriented results, they erroneously conclude that the evolution of their expertise has transpired on the basis of analytical trajectories inherent in the discipline itself. In this context, what has happened within a profession's past is viewed either as part of a continuum of advancement or as an unfortunate and wasteful diversion. It is not conceived of in terms of an array of political and social relationships, involving power and status, between people.

Iconography of course has its virtues, not the least of which is the building of morale, but critical awareness is certainly not one of them. Like victims of amnesia, economists construct a narrative of their past that has less to do with a concrete reality than with present concerns to legitimate particular forms of conduct and privilege. Out of that imagination, inspired as it is by social and political forces themselves, emerges less a genuine history than a myth. While that legend may "continue for several generations almost as an inherited set of attitudes," only time will tell if it "eventually may be restructured under the impact of an incongruous environment."[22]

Not the least of the consequences born of a century of professionalization in economics has been the determination of its mainstream practitioners to rid it of what they take to be political overtones. In place of the unabashed partisanship of its earliest and most illustrious architects—François Quesnay, Adam Smith, David Ricardo, Karl Marx, John Stuart Mill, León Walras, Alfred Marshall, and John Maynard Keynes, to name some—contemporary economists have fashioned a method of inquiry and a style of argument that reifies the workings of a "free market" to the status of a natural law. Yet unlike their colleagues in the life sciences who, in their study of the structure and function of organisms, understand pathology and decay to be inherent in their subjects, these social scientists conceive the object of their study to abide in an immutable and generally healthy fabric born of what they believe to be "human nature." It has been the strange logic of this particular doctrinal evolution that its proponents have increasingly argued against therapeutic intervention when markets have performed poorly. Allowing markets to function "naturally" has been their more common prescription—so unlike their counterparts in medicine and physiology who for centuries have honed instruments and techniques specifically intended to divert nature from its course.

Needless to say, the generally antistatist posture of the contemporary economics profession, and the policy frameworks it thus empowers and inspires, are not simply the products of imagination or will but rather the outcomes of long-lived historical forces that have indeed spanned all of the last century. That today most economists believe in allocative outcomes—such as rising levels of material welfare, high rates of employment, stable price structures, and vibrant patterns of technical progress—that the market cannot generate and indeed has never generated on its own is but the mirror image of the fact that, in its unregulated and unmanipulated operation, the market only betrays all that economists have ever imagined. Indeed, it is *this* reality that has, over the ages, inspired the discipline's greatest advances in theory and method.[23]

From the mid–eighteenth century through the nineteenth century, economic inquiry had been premised upon an appreciation of the class basis of society—epitomized by the tripartite division of a community into landowners, capitalists, and laborers. The major works in the field that emerged through these years, Smith's *The Wealth of Nations*, Ricardo's *Principles of Political Economy and Taxation*, Marx's *Capital*, Mill's *Principles of Political Economy*, all were linked by their grounding in a set of convictions concerning class, property, and power. They were concerned with "the rightness or wrongness, the inevitability or malleability, of the[se] arrangements of power and prestige [to be] discover[ed] in all human societies."[24]

Even with the rise of neoclassical economic theory at the turn of the last century, the deployment of such politically contextualized ideas in economic analysis did not wane—although, to be sure, the focus on individualized decision making and exchange relations would ultimately and powerfully disturb the a priori postulates of the classical tradition. For those investigators for whom a focus on allocative choice became the central object of economics, a set of assumptions concerning possessive individualism and participatory democracy was of decisive importance. Whatever the suitability or failings of these (or any) particular ideals regarding the social world under study, the point is that at different moments in history a broad array of economists shared them; what is more, and most probably of greater importance, they were *self-consciously aware* of them.

The loss of a deliberate and acknowledged engagement with political and social issues that characterizes economics today has been the product of a long and indeed poignant history. Economists found their voice in the twentieth century by mobilizing for war and by taking up the challenges and burdens of statism. Yet in the corridors of power this professional elite, so intent on elaborating and sustaining a scientific rigor it believed unique, also encountered the corruptions of ideology, the interference of institutions and beliefs, the volatility and unpredictability of events. In headlong retreat from the statecraft that had been their special birthright, and obviously influenced by political and social changes themselves stimulated by the failures of economic interventionism, American economists demobilized their expertise and pursued an increasingly privatized and introverted agenda, one that encouraged the vast majority of Americans to distrust and condemn statism itself. It may very well then make sense to say that economics has failed the polity from which it once drew its strength.[25]

A smug confidence in the presumed superiority of "free markets" and "deregulated" economic environments cannot and does not substitute for a genuine grasp of the history that has framed particular policy outcomes. In point of fact, it was statism and centralized economic policy practice that had brought economists and their discipline to the prominence and influence they enjoyed through the latter half of the twentieth century. As the quite special ties between Leonid Kantorovich and Tjalling Koopmans so clearly portrayed at the height of the cold war itself, economic statecraft even bridged some of the rifts between capitalist and socialist doctrines in the modern era.

By the end of the twentieth century, capitalism had apparently prevailed over its opponents. Even so, the seeming victory manifested itself primarily in formal terms alone; substantively, the "defeated versions" of economics represented the most inspired (and historically grounded) qualities of their triumphant adversary.[26] Their own expertise and enterprise now unswervingly joined with an ongoing celebration of the merits of "free markets," American economists ignore the implications and the meanings of the special circumstances that fostered their influence in the first place. Yet these forces, this history inexorably framed the evolution of this most consequential of the social sciences. Today, the withdrawal from engaged debate over the ends of national policy and the cultivation of a scholastic discourse that has increasingly separated economics and its practitioners from the arena of genuinely public decision making have become more and more widespread. This disciplinary and professional evolution, this perilous progress, has brought economics, and with it the very nature and quality of the public policy debate on which it has always subsisted and thrived, to the point of extinction.

Notes

Prologue
Being Ignored

1. John Desmond Bernal, *Science in History* (London: Watts, 1957), 707.

2. On the history of the Smoot-Hawley Tariff, some of the leading references are Elmer E. Schattschneider, *Politics, Pressures and the Tariff: A Study of Free Private Enterprise in Pressure Politics, as Shown in the 1929–1930 Revision of the Tariff* (Hamden, Conn.: Prentice-Hall, 1935); Sidney Ratner, *The Tariff in American History* (New York: Van Nostrand, 1972); and, more recently, Edward S. Kaplan, *American Trade Policy, 1923–1995* (Westport, Conn.: Greenwood, 1996); and Barry Eichengreen, "The Political Economy of the Smoot-Hawley Tariff," *Research in Economic History* 12 (1989), 1–43. For the circumstances surrounding the submission of the economists' petition to President Hoover, the broader correspondence the president had with experts during the debate over the tariff bill, as well as the direct quotations from Wilcox's letter to Hoover, see Wilcox to Hoover, 2 May 1930, Box 410 (Folder: "American Eagle-Emb 1929–1932"); Irving Fisher (Yale University) to Hoover, 2 June 1930, Box 562 (Folder: "Irving Fisher 1929–1932"); Thomas Walker Page (U.S. Tariff Commission) to Hoover, 14 October 1929, Box 280 (Folder: "Tariff Commission—Correspondence 1929 October 11–31"); all in the Hoover Presidential Subject Files [hereafter HPSF], (Herbert Hoover Presidential Library, West Branch, Iowa).

3. There is today a large literature condemning the Smoot-Hawley Tariff for its deleterious impacts on the interwar global economy. See, for example, my *Great Depression: Delayed Recovery and Economic Change in America, 1929–1939* (New York: Cambridge University Press, 1987), chap. 7; as well as Barry Eichengreen, *Golden Fetters: The Gold Standard and the Great Depression, 1919–1939* (New York: Oxford University Press, 1992).

4. Readers may find of interest a recent study of the contemporary evolution of the economics profession that, above and beyond its focus on the scholarly literature per se, has many affinities with the themes of this work. See Robert L. Heilbroner and William Milberg, *The Crisis of Vision in Modern Economic Thought* (New York: Cambridge University Press, 1995). An eminent historian has recently articulated an appreciation of the impact of statism on the evolution of the contemporary social sciences that also powerfully resonates with some of the arguments advanced here. See Carl E. Schorske, "The New Rigorism in the Human Sciences, 1940–1960," *Daedalus* 126 (1997): 289–309.

5. Any student of the history of the American economics profession is indebted to the pathbreaking work of A. W. Coats. Much of his extensive corpus is referenced in the pages that follow. Here note should be made of his masterwork, *The Sociology and Professionalization of Economics*, 2 vols. (London: Routledge, 1993).

6. There is a vast literature on Progressivism and the political aspirations of liberal American elites in the twentieth century. See, for example, Richard Hofstadter's classic study *The Age of Reform: From Bryan to F.D.R.* (New York: Random House, 1955); James Weinstein, *The Corporate Ideal in the Liberal State, 1900–1918* (Boston: Beacon, 1960); and Daniel T. Rodgers, "In Search of Progressivism," *Reviews in American History* 10 (1982): 113–32. No one has written with more insight nor critical purchase on the matter of the American middle class and professional ideals than the late Christopher Lasch. See, for example, *The True and Only Heaven: Progress and Its Critics* (New York: Norton, 1991), and his study *The Revolt of the Elites and the Betrayal of Democracy* (New York: Norton, 1995). Also see Steven Brint, *In an Age of Experts: The Changing Role of Professionals in Politics and Public Life* (Princeton, N.J.: Princeton University Press, 1994). More recent assessments of the collapse of the "liberal ideal" are Alan Brinkley, *The End of Reform: New Deal Liberalism in Recession and War* (New York: Knopf, 1995); Gary Gerstle, "The Protean Character of American Liberalism," *American Historical Review* 99 (1994): 1043–73; Daniel Yergin and Joseph Stanislaw, *The Commanding*

Heights: The Battle between Government and the Marketplace That Is Remaking the Modern World (New York: Simon and Schuster, 1998); Steve Fraser and Gary Gerstle, eds., *The Rise and Fall of the New Deal Order, 1930–1980* (Princeton, N.J.: Princeton University Press, 1989); and James C. Scott, *Seeing Like a State: How Certain Schemes to Improve the Human Condition Have Failed* (New Haven, Conn.: Yale University Press, 1998).

7. It was, of course, Max Weber who speculated about the seemingly rootless quality of attitudes toward wealth accumulation in the United States. See *The Protestant Ethic and the Spirit of Capitalism*, trans. Talcott Parsons (New York: Scribner's, [1904–05] 1958), 182.

8. For a particularly sensitive and beautifully written history, deployed in the genre of biography, of liberal politics in the age of American hegemony in the wider world, see Ronald Steel, *Walter Lippmann and the American Century* (Boston: Little, Brown, 1980).

9. Throughout the book I have tried to explain the reasons why particular bodies of evidence have been used. It is worth noting here, however, that with respect to archival materials drawn from presidential libraries, research was confined to the use of archives in which the relevant data had already been cataloged and cleared for public access. There is also some use of oral history transcripts, but the focus of the research was less on prosopography than on the fashioning of a political and social history overall. For an excellent example, however, of the historical perceptions of leading figures in economics today, see the following articles, all published in a special number of *Daedalus* 126 (1997): Robert M. Solow, "How Did Economics Get That Way and What Way Did It Get?," 39–58; David M. Kreps, "Economics: The Current Position," 59–86; and William J. Barber, "Reconfigurations in American Academic Economics: A General Practitioner's Perspective," 87–104.

10. I have undertaken a preliminary discussion of this matter in my "Knowledge Production, Professional Authority, and the State: The Case of American Economics during and after World War II," in *What Do Economists Know? New Economics of Knowledge*, ed. Robert Garnett (London: Routledge, 1999), 103–23. Also see, in this regard, Frederick Cooper and Randall Packard, *International Development and the Social Sciences: Essays on the History and Politics of Knowledge* (Berkeley: University of Califor-

nia Press, 1998); and Nahid Aslanbeigui and Verónica Montecinos, "Foreign Students in U.S. Doctoral Programs," *Journal of Economic Perspectives* 12 (1998), 171–82.

Introduction
Professional Expertise as a Historical Problem

1. George Bernard Shaw, *The Doctor's Dilemma: A Tragedy* (London: Constable and Company, [1906] 1920), 28.

2. See Dwight D. Eisenhower, "Farewell to the Nation," in *The Eisenhower Administration, 1953–1961: A Documentary History*, ed. R. L. Branyan and L. H. Larsen (New York: Random House, 1971), vol. 2, 1376.

3. See John Maynard Keynes, *The General Theory of Employment, Interest and Money* (New York: Harcourt, Brace, 1936), preface.

4. The quotation is from the core work of one of the best-known historians of this type, Burton J. Bledstein, *The Culture of Professionalism: The Middle Class and the Development of Higher Education in America* (New York: Norton, 1976), 90. Of clear inspiration to Bledstein's particular outlook are David Riesman, *The Lonely Crowd: A Study of the Changing American Character* (New Haven, Conn.: Yale University Press, 1950); and C. Wright Mills, *White Collar: The American Middle Classes* (New York: Oxford University Press, 1951). The sociological taxonomy of scientific characteristics is, of course, Robert K. Merton's from essays reprinted in his *Sociology of Science: Theoretical and Empirical Investigations* (Chicago: University of Chicago Press, 1973), 267–78.

5. From Thorstein Veblen, *The Higher Learning in America: A Memorandum on the Conduct of Universities by Business Men* (New York: Kelley, [1918] 1965), 42. Michael A. Dennis has specifically noted the complications, for Merton's model of scientific norms, posed by the institutional contexts within which research is performed. See his "Accounting for Research: New Histories of Corporate Laboratories and the Social History of American Science," *Social Studies of Science* 17 (1987), 492. David F. Noble has provided a striking assessment of the importance of the corporate framework for an appreciation of the evolution of professional expertise and scientific knowledge. See his *America by Design: Science, Technology, and the Rise of Corporate Capitalism* (New York: Knopf, 1977).

6. In part, this is precisely the burden of an argument made by Martin J. S. Rudwick in his "A Year in the Life of Adam Sedgwick and Company, Geologists," *Archives of Natural History* 15 (1988), 243–68. Rudwick explains in his introduction: "The commercial allusion in the title has a . . . meaning. Companies produce goods and services by means of processes operated by personnel. It would be useless to try to understand the work of an industrial firm merely by analysing its finished and packaged products. Yet until recently, much of what passed for history of science was just such an analysis of polished publications, with little attention to the processes by which they were produced or to the practice of the scientists themselves."

7. See Thomas S. Kuhn, *The Structure of Scientific Revolutions* (Chicago: University of Chicago Press, [1962] 1966); and Kuhn, *The Essential Tension: Selected Studies in Scientific Tradition and Change* (Chicago: University of Chicago Press, 1977). Parsons's links with the "Mertonian" conception of the scientific enterprise are made clear in "The Present Position and Prospects of Systematic Theory in Sociology," in his *Essays in Sociological Theory* (New York: Free Press, [1945] 1954), 212–37. The philosophical foundations of Merton's and Parsons's views of science are clearly articulated in the epistemological work of Karl Popper. See his *Poverty of Historicism* (New York: Harper and Row, 1961); *Conjectures and Refutations: The Growth of Scientific Knowledge* (New York: Basic Books, 1962); and *Objective Knowledge: An Evolutionary Approach* (Oxford: Clarendon Press, 1972). In this regard, Parsons's determination to make sociology a "science" is significant. See, for example, Charles Camic, "The Making of a Method: A Historical Reinterpretation of the Early Parsons," *American Sociological Review* 52 (1987), 421–39. Roger E. Backhouse has more recently situated debates in economics itself within controversies in the theoretical literature on the sociology and philosophy of science. See, for example, his *Explorations in Economic Methodology: From Lakatos to Empirical Philosophy of Science* (New York: Routledge, 1998), a study clearly inspired by a very well known essay by Mark Blaug, "Kuhn versus Lakatos, or Paradigms versus Research Programmes in the History of Economics," *History of Political Economy* 7 (1975), 399–433. Also see, in this regard, Martin Bronfenbrenner, "The 'Structure of Scientific Revolutions' in Eco-

nomic Thought," *History of Political Economy* 3 (1971), 136–51.

8. Some well-known examples of the "network theory" approach are Bruno Latour, *The Pasteurization of France* (Cambridge: Harvard University Press, 1988); Michel Callon and John Law, "On Interests and Their Transformation: Enrolment and Counter-Enrolment," *Social Studies of Science* 12 (1982), 615–25; and Steve Woolgar, "Interests and Explanation in the Social Study of Science," *Social Studies of Science* 11 (1981), 365–94. Studies of "laboratory life" were inspired by the pathbreaking work of Latour and Woolgar. See their *Laboratory Life: The Construction of Scientific Facts* (Princeton, N.J.: Princeton University Press, 1988). The efflorescence of work on conflict among communities of scientific "interests" found its roots, to some extent (and interestingly enough), in the earlier work of Karl Mannheim. See his *Ideology and Utopia: An Introduction to the Sociology of Knowledge*, trans. Louis Wirth and Edward Shils (New York: Harcourt Brace Jovanovich, [1929] 1936). Leading contributions in this genre are David Bloor, *Knowledge and Social Imagery* (Chicago: University of Chicago Press, 1976); Steven Shapin, "Pump and Circumstance: Robert Boyle's Literary Technology," *Social Studies of Science* 14 (1984), 481–520; Steven Shapin and Simon Schaffer, *Leviathan and the Air-Pump: Hobbes, Boyle, and the Experimental Life* (Princeton, N.J.: Princeton University Press, 1985); as well as Shapin, *A Social History of Truth: Civility and Science in Seventeenth-Century England* (Chicago: University of Chicago Press, 1992); and Barry Barnes and Donald Mac-Kenzie, "On the Role of Interests in Scientific Change," in *On the Margins of Science: The Social Construction of Rejected Knowledge*, ed. R. Wallis (Keele: University of Keele Press, 1979), 49–66. Yet another striking and quite influential example of the new "social" approach to the study of science is Michael Lynch, *Scientific Practice and Ordinary Action: Ethnomethodology and Social Studies of Science* (Cambridge: Cambridge University Press, 1993).

9. An appreciation of the dichotomous quality of research on the exclusionary character of professions may be garnered from Thomas Haskell, *The Emergence of Professional Social Science: The American Social Science Association and the Nineteenth-Century Crisis of Authority* (Urbana: University of Illinois Press, 1977); Bledstein, *The Culture of Professionalism*; and

Magali Sarfatti Larson, *The Rise of Professionalism: A Social Analysis* (Berkeley: University of California Press, 1977). Also see Jeffrey L. Berlant, *Professions and Monopoly* (Berkeley: University of California Press, 1975); and Eliot Freidson, *Professional Dominance* (Chicago: Aldine, 1970). Some of this literature emphasizes a class-based approach not simply to the rise of professions but of an intellectual elite as a whole. See, for example, Alvin W. Gouldner, *The Future of Intellectuals and the Rise of the New Class* (New York: Oxford University Press, 1981); Russell Jacoby, *The Last Intellectuals: American Culture in the Age of Academe* (New York: Basic Books, 1987); J. Ben-David, "Professions in the Class System of Present Day Societies," *Current Sociology* 12 (1963), 247–98; and Charles Derber, William A. Schwartz, and Yale Magrass, *Power in the Highest Degree: Professionals and the Rise of a New Mandarin Order* (New York: Oxford University Press, 1990). The classic work by Carr-Saunders and Wilson on the functionalist approach to professionalization is their *The Professions* (Oxford: Oxford University Press, [1933] 1964). Their contribution is, of course, closely identified with the investigations of Parsons, as well as with those of Harold Wilensky, "The Professionalization of Everyone?" *American Journal of Sociology* 70 (1964), 137–58; and Everett Hughes, "Professions," *Daedalus* 92 (1963), 655–68.

10. From Pierre Bourdieu, *Outline of a Theory of Practice*, trans. Richard Nice (New York: Cambridge University Press, 1977), 22. Also see, in this regard, Michel Foucault, "The Discourse on Language," an appendix to his *The Archaeology of Knowledge*, trans. A. M. Sheridan Smith (New York: Harper and Row, 1972), 215–37. Consideration of the significance of professional discourse for an understanding of the authority of experts is provocatively explored, in the case of economics, by Dierdre McCloskey in her "The Rhetoric of Economics," *Journal of Economic Literature* 21 (1983), 434–61; "The Literary Character of Economics," *Daedalus* 203 (1984), 97–119; "The Standard Error of Regressions," *Journal of Economic Literature* 34 (1996), 97–114; and "The Loss Function Has Been Mislaid: The Rhetoric of Significance Tests," *American Economic Review* 75 (1985), 201–5. The contributions of literary critics have also been uniquely influential, as in the case of Stanley Fish, *Is There a Text in This Class? The Authority of Interpretive Communities* (Cambridge: Harvard University Press, 1980); and Jane Tompkins, *Sensational Designs: The Cultural Work of American Fiction, 1790–1860* (New York: Oxford University Press, 1985). Also of interest, in this regard, are T. F. Gieryn, "Boundary Work and the Demarcation of Science from Non-Science," *American Sociological Review* 48 (1983), 781–95; and W. J. Goode, "Encroachment, Charlatanism, and the Emerging Profession," *American Sociological Review* 25 (1960), 902–14. It is in the work of Andrew Abbott that one finds the foundations of the "systems" approach to professionalization. See *The System of Professions: An Essay on the Division of Expert Labor* (Chicago: University of Chicago Press, 1988); and "The Sociology of Work and Occupations," *Annual Review of Sociology* 19 (1993), 187–209. Also see John B. Cullen, *The Structure of Professionalism* (New York: Petrocelli, 1978); and Randall Collins, *The Credential Society* (New York: Academic Press, 1979).

11. What has become a virtually classic treatment of the eclectic approach to professionalization characteristic of historical scholarship is R. W. Gordon, "Legal Thought and Legal Practice in the Age of American Enterprise: 1870–1920," in *Professions and Professional Ideology in America*, ed. Gerald L. Geison (Chapel Hill: University of North Carolina Press, 1983), 4–82. Also see, in this regard, a more recent study by Laura Kalman undertaken from the perspective of legal scholarship itself: *The Strange Career of Legal Liberalism* (New Haven, Conn.: Yale University Press, 1996). In his massive treatment of intellectual and cultural history, Peter Gay notes the increasing centrality of analyses of professionalism for a historical understanding of the modern world. See *The Cultivation of Hatred*, vol. 3 of *The Bourgeois Experience: Victoria to Freud* (New York: Norton, 1993), 484–91.

12. The quotations are from the highly regarded study by Paul Starr, *The Transformation of American Medicine* (New York: Basic Books, 1982), 3. Historians have, of course, turned the critical lens of social history on the evolution of their own profession, as best exemplified by Peter Novick, *That Noble Dream: The "Objectivity Question" and the American Historical Profession* (New York: Cambridge University Press, 1988). An excellent example of the perspective on professionalization afforded by attention to institutional contexts, unique for its focus on philanthropy, is E. Richard Brown, *Rockefeller Medicine Men: Medicine and Capi-*

talism in America (Berkeley: University of California Press, 1979). A more tendentious assessment of the social and political foundations of expertise is offered by Edward T. Silva, and Sheila A. Slaughter, *Serving Power: The Making of the Academic Social Science Expert* (Westport, Conn.: Greenwood, 1984). Chandra Mukerji provides a fascinating argument about government institutions creating a "reserve army" of scientific labor to be utilized in moments of emergency and mass mobilization. See her study *A Fragile Power: Scientists and the State* (Princeton, N.J.: Princeton University Press, 1989). A consideration of the celebration of quantification as an index of a field's rigor and objectivity is undertaken in my "Numerable Knowledge and Its Discontents," *Reviews in American History* 18 (1990), 151–64. Also see Theodore M. Porter, *Trust in Numbers: The Pursuit of Objectivity in Science and Public Life* (Princeton, N.J.: Princeton University Press, 1995).

13. Along with the classic work of Wiebe, *The Search for Order, 1877–1920* (New York: Hill and Wang, 1967), some of the essential contributions to an understanding of Progressivism are Richard Hofstadter, *The Age of Reform: From Bryan to F.D.R.* (New York: Random House, 1955); Gabriel Kolko, *The Triumph of Conservatism: A Reinterpretation of American History* (Glencoe, Ill.: Free Press, 1963); and Daniel T. Rodgers, "In Search of Progressivism," *Reviews in American History* 10 (1982), 113–32. An equally significant contribution to the understanding of the ties between expertise, Progressivism, and early-twentieth-century American history is Louis Galambos, "The Emerging Organizational Synthesis in Modern American History," *Business History Review* 44 (1970), 279–90.

14. The corporatist nature of much of Progressive thought is analyzed in James Weinstein's pathbreaking study *The Corporate Ideal in the Liberal State, 1900–1918* (Boston: Beacon, 1960); as well as Martin J. Sklar, *The Corporate Reconstruction of American Capitalism, 1890–1916: The Market, the Law, and Politics* (New York: Cambridge University Press, 1988). Also see Stephen Skowronek, *Building a New American State: The Expansion of National Administrative Capacities, 1877–1920* (New York: Cambridge University Press, 1982); Morton Keller, *Regulating a New Society: Public Policy and Social Change in America, 1900–*

1933 (Cambridge: Harvard University Press, 1994); Clarence E. Wunderlin Jr., *Visions of a New Industrial Order: Social Science and Labor Theory in America's Progressive Era* (New York: Columbia University Press, 1992); John M. Jordan, *Machine-Age Ideology: Social Engineering and American Liberalism, 1911–1939* (Chapel Hill: University of North Carolina Press, 1994); and Mark C. Smith, *Social Science in the Crucible: The American Debate over Objectivity and Purpose, 1918–1941* (Durham, N.C.: Duke University Press, 1994). Some of the more ungenerous appraisals of the Progressives' major opponents, the Populists, are found in the work of Richard Hofstadter, *The Progressive Movement, 1900–1915* (Englewood Cliffs, N.J.: Prentice-Hall, 1963); and H. L. Mencken, *Heathen Days, 1890–1936* (New York: Knopf, 1943); as well as his *Notes on Democracy* (New York: Knopf, 1926). Edward Bellamy's *Looking Backward, 2000–1887* (Boston: Houghton Mifflin, 1888) afforded both a far more sympathetic view of the anti-Progressive tradition and an enduring critique of an America in thrall to corporate liberalism.

15. Strikingly perceptive, although dated, are Lewis Corey's considerations of the political and social influence of the middle class in history. See his study *The Crisis of the Middle Class* (New York: Covici Friede, 1935). William Whyte's landmark investigation of the personality of the middle-class manager and professional remains as cogent and incisive as it was almost a half century ago. See *The Organization Man* (New York: Simon and Schuster, 1956). Equally resilient in its perceptive power is Barbara Ehrenreich, *Fear of Falling: The Inner Life of the Middle Class* (New York: Pantheon, 1989). In many respects, the work of Corey, Whyte, and Ehrenreich builds on the study of nineteenth-century cultural ideals advanced in George M. Frederickson's *Inner Civil War: Northern Intellectuals and the Crisis of the Union* (New York: Harper and Row, 1965). There is a vast literature on the history of professions and professionalization that inspires the claims made here. See, for example, Carlo Cipolla, "The Professions: The Long View," *Journal of European Economic History* 2 (1973), 37–51; Terry N. Clark, *The French University and the Emergence of the Social Sciences* (Cambridge: Harvard University Press, 1973); Fritz K. Ringer, *The Decline of the German Mandarins: The German Academic Community, 1890–1933* (Cambridge: Harvard

University Press, 1969); Rodney Coe, "The Process of the Development of Established Professions," *Journal of Health and Social Behavior* 11 (1970), 59–67; Charles E. McClelland, *The German Experience of Professionalization: Modern Learned Professions and Their Organizations from the Early Nineteenth Century to the Hitler Era* (New York: Cambridge University Press, 1991); Maria Malatesta, ed., *Society and the Professions in Italy, 1860–1914* (Cambridge: Cambridge University Press, 1995); Elliott A. Krause, *Death of the Guilds: Professions, States, and the Advance of Capitalism, 1930 to the Present* (New Haven, Conn.: Yale University Press, 1996); and D. Duman, "The Creation and Diffusion of a Professional Ideal in Nineteenth Century Britain," *Sociological Review* 27 (1979), 113–38.

16. A most interesting, recent challenge to the point of view advanced here, one that sees in more recent history a resurgence of public claims against the authority of professionals, is Brian Balogh, *Chain Reaction: Expert Debate and Public Participation in American Commercial Nuclear Power, 1945–1975* (New York: Cambridge University Press, 1991). Also on matters of professional authority and public life, see L. Braude, "Professional Autonomy and the Role of the Layman," *Social Forces* 39 (1961), 297–301; Thomas L. Haskell, ed., *The Authority of Experts* (Bloomington: Indiana University Press, 1984); Terence J. Johnson, *Professions and Power* (London: Macmillan, 1967); D. Portwood, and A. Fielding, "Privilege and the Professions," *Sociological Review* 29 (1981), 749–73; and Michael R. Rubin, *The Knowledge Industry in the United States, 1960–1980* (Princeton, N.J.: Princeton University Press, 1986).

17. Particularly compelling demonstrations of the insights won by a perspective such as this are found in recent studies of the history of the earth sciences: Robert Marc Friedman, *Appropriating the Weather: Vilhelm Bjerknes and the Construction of a Modern Meteorology* (Ithaca, N.Y.: Cornell University Press, 1989); Naomi Oreskes, "Science and Security before the Atomic Bomb: The Loyalty Case of Harald Sverdrup," *Studies in the History and Philosophy of Modern Physics* 3 (2000): 309–69; as well as Naomi Oreskes and Ronald E. Doel, "Physics and Chemistry of the Earth," in *The Cambridge History of Science*, vol. 5, *Modern Physical and Mathematical Sciences*, ed. Mary J. Nye (Cambridge: Cambridge University Press, forthcoming). Arguably one of the most influential studies of science from the

broad perspective of social and political history is Daniel Kevles, *The Physicists: The History of a Scientific Community in Modern America* (New York: Knopf, 1977). Also see A. Fielding and D. Portwood, "Professions and the State," *Sociological Review* 28 (1980), 23–53; Roy MacLeod, ed., *Government and Expertise: Specialists, Administrators, and Professionals, 1860–1919* (New York: Cambridge University Press, 1988); and David Moss, *Socializing Security: Progressive-Era Economists and the Origins of American Social Policy* (Cambridge: Harvard University Press, 1996).

18. For a thought-provoking consideration of the ways in which economics has, throughout the twentieth century, become an ever-more-prominent facet in both the intellectual evolution of other disciplines and the practices of public and private institutions, see Jack Hirshleifer, "The Expanding Domain of Economics," *American Economic Review* 75 (1985), 53–68.

Chapter 1
Shaping an Authoritative Community

1. Irving Fisher to E.R.A. Seligman, 20 February 1902, Box 8 (Folder: "President Seligman's Correspondence 1902"), Records of the American Economic Association [hereafter RAEA], (Northwestern University Library—Special Collections, Evanston, Illinois). A commanding figure in the modern history of his profession, Irving Fisher (1867–1947) is considered one of the most important contributors to the development of the neoclassical theory of capital and interest. During a long and prominent career at Yale University, he did more (in the opinion of most historians of economic thought) to further the elaboration of a mathematically rigorous (and therefore "scientific") economics in the United States than almost any other contemporary. Nobel laureate Paul Samuelson once referred to Fisher as "perhaps the greatest single name in the history of American economics" in his "Irving Fisher and the Theory of Capital," in *Ten Economic Studies in the Tradition of Irving Fisher*, by William Fellner et al. (New York: Wiley, 1967), 17. See Robert Loring Allen, *Irving Fisher: A Biography* (Cambridge: Blackwell, 1993); Irving Norton Fisher, *My Father, Irving Fisher* (New York: Comet Press, 1956); Dorothy Ross, *The Origins of American Social Science* (New York: Cambridge University Press, 1991),

173, 180–82; and Irving Fisher, *The Nature of Capital and Income* (London: Macmillan, 1906).

2. The AEA charter was ratified on 9 September 1885 at Saratoga, New York. The definitive work on the early struggles over the establishment of the AEA is, of course, Mary O. Furner, *Advocacy and Objectivity: A Crisis in the Professionalization of American Social Science, 1865–1905* (Lexington: University Press of Kentucky, 1975), esp. chap. 3. But also see Ross, *The Origins of American Social Science*, 63, 110, 159; A. W. Coats, "The Political Economy Club: A Neglected Episode in American Economic Thought," *American Economic Review* 51 (1961), 624–37; as well as "The First Two Decades of the American Economic Association," *American Economic Review* 50 (1960), 555–74; and Robert L. Church, "Economists as Experts: The Rise of an Academic Profession in the United States, 1870–1920," in *The University in Society*, vol. 2, *Europe, Scotland, and the United States from the 16th to the 20th Century*, ed. Lawrence Stone (Princeton, N.J.: Princeton University Press, 1974), 571–609. Disputes among the founders of the AEA were primarily provoked by Richard T. Ely and his professed goal of seeing the Association become a consortium of reformers—activists focused on contemporary policy questions. See his "Past and Present of Political Economy," *Johns Hopkins University Studies in History and Political Science* 2 (1884), 143–202; as well as his "The Founding and Early History of the American Economic Association," *American Economic Review* 26 (1936), 144; and his autobiographical *Ground under Our Feet* (New York: Macmillan, 1938), 134, 137; and Benjamin G. Rader, *The Academic Mind and Reform: The Influence of Richard T. Ely in American Life* (Lexington: University Press of Kentucky, 1966). As Dorothy Ross notes in *The Origins of American Social Science*, 159, reformist agendas, among a variety of social science groups at the turn of the century, were such that "professional claim[s] to objectivity continued to be vulnerable." Also see, in this regard, Magali Sarfatti Larson, *The Rise of Professionalism: A Social Analysis* (Berkeley: University of California Press, 1977), chaps. 1 and 2.

3. See A. W. Coats, "The American Economic Association, 1904–1929: Prologue," 1–5, and chap. 8: "Associations with Other Associations," 104–6; RAEA, Box 0 (Folder 1).

4. I am here invoking the words of the leading expert on the ideological struggles that framed the first two decades of the American Economic Association. See Furner, *Advocacy and Objectivity*, 322. Peter Novick has written a similarly pathbreaking analysis regarding the rise of a professional history discipline in the United States throughout this century; see his *That Noble Dream: The "Objectivity Question" and the American Historical Profession* (New York: Cambridge University Press, 1988). Also see Dorothy Ross, "The Development of the Social Sciences," in *The Organization of Knowledge in Modern America, 1860–1920*, ed. A. Oleson and J. Voss (Baltimore: Johns Hopkins University Press, 1979), 109, 116, 131; and her "The Liberal Tradition Revisited and the Republican Tradition Addressed," in *New Directions in American Intellectual History*, ed. John Higham and Paul K. Conkin (Baltimore: Johns Hopkins University Press, 1979), 120. There is a growing literature on the struggles over the achievement of "objectivity" in the social sciences in early twentieth-century America. See, for example, John M. Jordan, *Machine-Age Ideology: Social Engineering and American Liberalism, 1911–1939* (Chapel Hill: University of North Carolina Press, 1994); Mark C. Smith, *Social Science in the Crucible: The American Debate over Objectivity and Purpose, 1918–1941* (Durham, N.C.: Duke University Press, 1994); Robert C. Bannister, *Sociology and Scientism* (Chapel Hill: University of North Carolina Press, 1987); and James Allen Smith, *The Idea Brokers: Think Tanks and the Rise of the New Policy Elite* (New York: Free Press, 1991), who traces these debates to the middle of the nineteenth century as exemplified by the creation of the American Association for the Promotion of Social Science in 1865.

5. I embrace here the widely accepted convention of referring to the immediate forebears of modern economics—most prominently Adam Smith, David Ricardo, and Karl Marx (and their followers)—as "classical" investigators. Those whose research reoriented the field of economics at the turn of the twentieth century are thus said to have initiated the "neoclassical" approach. See my essay "A New Agenda for a New Century: American Economists and the 'Marginalist Revolution' in Textual and Historical Perspective" (unpublished manuscript, Department of History, University of California, San Diego).

6. On the manner in which "American exceptionalism" molded the evolution of the modern American social sciences, see Ross, *The Origins of American Social Science*.

7. It would be a gross oversimplification to suggest that there were not powerful and eloquent critics, within the community of professional American economists, who challenged the move toward seeming "objectivity" and scientism in their field. Most prominent among these was Thorstein Veblen, who maintained his critical stance throughout his career. See *The Engineers and the Price System* (New York: Huebsch, 1921); and his masterwork, *The Place of Science in Modern Civilization* (New York: Viking, 1919), which includes his inspired essays "Why Is Economics Not an Evolutionary Science?" [1898], (56–81); "The Preconceptions of Economic Science" [1899–1900], (82–179); and "The Limitations of Marginal Utility" [1909], (231–51). Yet it is a profound commentary on the evolution of the field (and on the historical process that is the core focus of this book) that students of economics in the United States, at least since World War II, can complete an entire undergraduate major (let alone a graduate program) without hearing Veblen's name mentioned once.

8. From Joseph C. Kiger, *American Learned Societies* (Washington, D.C.: Public Affairs Press, 1963), 39–40. The continuing resonance of the controversies joined over the founding of the AEA expressed itself most vividly in the celebrated academic freedom alarms raised during the trial of Richard Ely for subversive activity at Wisconsin in 1894, as well as those raised in the wake of the forced resignation of Edward W. Bemis from the University of Chicago in 1895. In both cases, as subsequent discussion in this chapter will show, the separate issues of professional competence and the individual right to political advocacy were conflated. Ironically enough, Ely submitted to discipline and, for the remainder of his career, avoided the overt teaching of "radical ideas" along with his earlier active efforts on behalf of striking labor unions. Bemis, on the other hand, saw his career ruined, never to be repaired. See Burton Bledstein, *The Culture of Professionalism: The Middle Class and the Development of Higher Education in America* (New York: Norton, 1976), 302–3, 328–29; as well as the classic study by Richard Hofstadter and Walter P. Metzger, *The Development of Academic Freedom in the United States* (New York: Columbia University Press, 1955), 397, 426–36. Roger L. Geiger argues, in *To Advance Knowledge: The Growth of American Research Universities, 1900–1940* (New York: Oxford University Press, 1986), 284, that this early period in the

evolution of the modern American economics profession has been viewed in three major ways: one approach, identified with the work of Mary Furner in *Advocacy and Objectivity*, claims that the "wide acceptance of the professional norm of objectivity drew economists away from advocacy of social policy"; another, linked with the research of Robert Church in "Economists as Experts," holds that "professionalization was pursued primarily to allow economists to continue social advocacy behind the cloak of expertise"; and, finally, a third, argued by Thomas Haskell in *The Emergence of Professional Social Science: The American Social Science Association and the Nineteenth-Century Crisis of Authority* (Urbana: University of Illinois Press, 1977), "stresses the necessary causes and continuous operation of the imperatives of professionalization." Haskell, interestingly enough, makes a particularly strong claim that the controversies surrounding the rise of the AEA were "epiphenomenal" (see page 187, footnote 48). In this view he is not joined by the large majority of historians of the Association. See Furner, *Advocacy and Objectivity*, chap. 2. Also see John Higham, Leonard Krieger, and Felix Gilbert, *History* (Englewood Cliffs, N.J.: Prentice-Hall, 1965), 109.

9. Patten to Ely, 22 October 1909; RAEA, Box 10 (Folder: "Correspondence EA–LZ 1909"). Also see A. W. Coats, "The American Economic Association, 1904–1929: Prologue," 15 in RAEA, Box 0 (Folder 1). Coats notes that, despite the effort to secure a broad membership drive, AEA leaders worried often about the need to set "stringent standards" for the admission of those from the business community. One unidentified official even suggested that such standards be modeled along those of the American Actuarial Association. (A published version of Coats's essay may be found as "The American Economic Association 1904–1929," *American Economic Review* 54 [1964], 261–85.)

10. Carver to Clarence E. Bowen, 10 November 1909, RAEA, Box 10 (Folder: "Correspondence A–Dz 1909").

11. Nelson W. Evans (of Evans and Crawford, Attorneys-at-Law) to Carver, 2 November 1910; and Carver to Evans, 7 November 1910; both in RAEA, Box 11 (Folder: "Correspondence EA–HZ 1910").

12. See "Report of the Secretary of the American Economic Association," 17 December 1914, RAEA, Box 13 (Folder: "Reports Annual Meeting 1914"). Also see Carver to F. H. Dixon (Pro-

fessor of Economics, Dartmouth College), 14 April 1911, RAEA, Box 11 (Folder: "Correspondence Aa–Kz 1911"). Carver stated in this communication: "We have pretty nearly exhausted the academic field [for members], and have practically all the teachers of economics in the Association now, though occasionally we find a new one." He thought it essential that the Association continue to push for new participants in the business world.

13. See, for example, Young to F. R. Fairchild (Yale University), 24 April 1914; Young to F. H. Dixon (Dartmouth College), 1 May 1914; Young to H. J. Davenport (University of Missouri–Columbia), 23 April 1914; Young to Ira B. Cross (Stanford University), 24 April 1914; Young to E. L. Bogart (University of Illinois–Urbana Champaign), 25 April 1914; Young to David Friday (University of Michigan), 23 April 1914; and Young to L. H. Haney (University of Texas–Austin), 23 April 1914; all in RAEA, Box 13 (Folder: "Correspondence Aa–Mz"). On the need to focus on "junior staff," see Davis R. Dewey (Massachusetts Institute of Technology) to Young, 10 February 1914, RAEA, Box 60 (Folder: "1914"). On the initiation of the membership campaign, see Young to Annie E. Gardner (AEA staff secretary), 18 January 1914, RAEA, Box 13 (Folder: "Correspondence Na–Zz 1914").

14. See Davenport to Young, 11 May 1914, RAEA, Box 13 (Folder: "Correspondence Aa–Mz 1914"); and Charles L. Reed to Young, 3 December 1914, RAEA, Box 13 (Folder: "Correspondence Na–Zz 1914").

15. See Dewey to Young, 15 April 1914, RAEA, Box 13 (Folder: "Correspondence Dewey 1914"); as well as "Report of the Secretary of the AEA," 17 December 1914, RAEA, Box 13 (Folder: "Reports Annual Meeting 1914").

16. E. E. Pratt to Young, 8 November 1915, RAEA, Box 13 (Folder: "Correspondence Dewey 1915"); Pratt to Young, 11 November 1915, RAEA, Box 13 (Folder: "Correspondence LA–Zz 1915"); Hoadley to Carver, 7 February 1914, RAEA, Box 13 (Folder: "Correspondence Az–Mz 1914"). Young evidently shared his correspondence with Pratt with Davis Dewey. Having read it, Dewey feared Pratt had a point and suggested that some thought be given to the idea of creating two classes of AEA membership for academics and businesspeople. Nothing came of it. See Dewey to Young, 15 November 1915, RAEA, Box 13 (Folder: "Correspondence

Dewey 1915"). Needless to say, it is not surprising that there are so few letters in the AEA files explaining member resignations—even in those years, such as 1913 and 1914, when the rate of separation was high. A decision to leave a membership organization was (and is) no doubt most often expressed simply in the failure to renew the payment of dues.

17. Young to A. M. Sakolski (Delaware and Hudson Company of Albany), 24 May 1915; Sakolski to Young, 23 September 1915; Young to Sakolski, 25 September 1915; all in RAEA, Box 13 (Folder: "Correspondence LA–Zz 1915"). Sakolski, in his suggestion to raise membership standards, had urged Young to consider the example of the American Society of Civil Engineers, where licensure was the core issue. Such a high barrier to entry in the AEA was necessary, in his view, in order to "shut out the pseudo-economists, statisticians, 'industrial engineers,' 'efficiency experts,['] etc, etc who advertise[d] their membership in the American Economic Association as recognition of their scientific standing."

18. Young to Emery Marvel MD, 9 May 1916, RAEA, Box 14 (Folder: "Correspondence GA–SZ 1916"). On concerns about charges of an "inner circle," see Young to E.R.A. Seligman, 15 October 1915, RAEA, Box 13 (Folder: "Correspondence LA–Zz 1915"; and Young to Dewey, 20 July 1915, RAEA, Box 13 Folder: "Correspondence Dewey 1915"). Struggles over the direction and control of the American Historical Association at this point in time are given systematic context by Peter Novick in *That Noble Dream*, chap. 4. On AEA membership goals in 1915, see "Report of the Secretary for the Year Ending December 1915," RAEA, Box 13 (Folder: "Meetings 1915").

19. From A. W. Coats, "The American Economic Association, 1904–1929: A Prologue," 25. Also see the confident report, regarding AEA membership, given some years later in a letter from the Association's secretary-treasurer to the engineering editor of *Steel—The Iron Trade Review*; James Washington Bell to E. F. Ross, 11 September 1939, RAEA, Box 28 (Folder: "Correspondence M–Z 1939").

20. Fisher to Seligman, 20 February 1902, RAEA, Box 8 (Folder: "President Seligman's Correspondence 1902"). Also, for general background, see RAEA, Box 8 (Folder 10: "Correspondence regarding the proposition for the American Economic Association to establish an

economic journal. Compiled by J. H. Hollander, Chmn., Publications Committee, and Frank Fetter, Sec'y., AEA, April 28, 1902").

21. See A. W. Coats, "Part III: Publications: The Pre-history of the American Economic Review," and "The American Economic Review," 203–4, all from "The American Economic Association, 1904–1929," RAEA, Box 0 (Folder 1).

22. The general draft of Fetter's letter to the Executive Council is found in RAEA, Box 60 (Folder 2: "AEA Correspondence re establishment of an economic journal"). While the draft is undated, the replies indicate that the letter must have gone out early in January 1902.

23. Ely to Jacob H. Hollander, 5 February 1902, RAEA, Box 60 (Folder 2: "AEA Correspondence re establishment of an economic journal"). While Fetter sent the initial request for input, Hollander, a Johns Hopkins University faculty member and future AEA president, was tasked by the Executive Council to receive and collate replies. The first issue of the *American Economic Review* appeared in March 1911.

24. James T. Young to Hollander, 28 April 1902; H. T. Newcomb to Hollander, 7 April 1902; and H. H. Powers to Hollander, 4 March 1902; all in RAEA, Box 60 (Folder 2: "AEA Correspondence re establishment of an economic journal").

25. Carl C. Plehn to Hollander, 25 February 1902; and Henry W. Lamb to Hollander, 7 April 1902; both in RAEA, Box 60 (Folder 2: "AEA Correspondence re establishment of an economic journal"). Plehn became AEA president in 1923.

26. Adams to Hollander, 11 February 1902); and Stephen F. Weston to Hollander, 29 March 1902; both in RAEA, Box 60 (Folder 2: "AEA Correspondence re establishment of an economic journal").

27. J. H. Arnold to Hollander, 2 April 1902; James H. Hamilton to Hollander, 20 March 1902; and Kinley to Hollander, 26 February 1902; all in RAEA, Box 60 (Folder 2: "AEA Correspondence re establishment of an economic journal").

28. H. C. Emery (of the *Yale Review*) to Hollander, 17 April 1902; and Dewey to Hollander, 25 April 1902; both in RAEA, Box 60 (Folder 2: "AEA Correspondence re establishment of an economic journal"). Born in 1858, a brother of the eminent philosopher John Dewey, the founding editor of the *American Economic Review* Davis Dewey managed the journal for thirty years from its establishment in 1911. A member

of the economics faculty at the Massachusetts Institute of Technology for a half century before his retirement in 1933, Dewey died in 1942. See an unattributed clipping of one of Dewey's obituaries in RAEA—Box 30 (Folder: "Correspondence A–L 1942").

29. Carver to Seligman, 15 May 1902 and Adams to Seligman, 16 May 1902; both in RAEA, Box 8 (Folder: "President Seligman's Correspondence 1902"). Also see Carver to Dewey, 11 August 1910, RAEA, Box 60 (Folder: "AER 1910, Davis R Dewey, Corr re founding AE Review and his early editorship").

30. Dewey to Francis Y. Edgeworth, 26 January 1911; Dewey to Clinton Rodgers Woodruff, 15 December 1910; Dewey to W. J. Ashley, 9 January 1911; all in RAEA, Box 60 (Folder: "AER 1910, Davis R Dewey, Corr re founding AE Review and his early editorship"); Minutes of the Executive Committee of the AEA, 30 November 1906, RAEA, Box 1 (Folder 5). Also see a letter from Dewey to Clive Day (of Yale University), 2 March 1915, RAEA, Box 62 (Folder: "AER 1914–1917 Editors"), in which Dewey notes: "[T]here is some criticism in regard to the proportion of leading articles devoted to current problems and questions of the day and that the Review would be doing a greater service if it gave more space to economic articles of purely technical professional interest." Also see Dewey to Young, 31 March 1915, RAEA, Box 13 (Folder: "Correspondence Dewey 1915") regarding the "mix" between theoretical and applied articles in the *Review*.

31. Meeker to E. W. Kemmerer (Princeton University and AEA President), 21 February 1926, RAEA, Box 20 (Folder: "Kemmerer 1926"); E. S. Cowdrick to Frederick S. Deibler (Northwestern University and AEA Secretary-Treasurer), 22 January 1929, RAEA, Box 23 (Folder: "Correspondence A–L 1929").

32. Fisher to Carver, 7 November 1916, RAEA, Box 14 (Folder: "Correspondence Aa–Fz 1916"); as well as Young to Gray, 27 May 1914, RAEA, Box 13 (Folder: "Correspondence Gray 1914"); Fetter to Young, 24 June 1914, RAEA, Box 13 (Folder: "Correspondence Aa–Mz 1914"). Fisher, in his position on the AAAS issue, anticipated future developments. By the end of the interwar period, AEA president Jacob Viner (of Princeton University) regarded membership in the AAAS to be an essential ingredient in the maintenance of the prestige and visibility

of economics as a rigorous social science—thereby endorsing a position long advocated by, among others, Wesley Mitchell of Columbia University and the National Bureau of Economic Research. See Viner to Bell, 11 January 1939, RAEA, Box 28 (Folder: "Jacob Viner 1939").

33. Young to Parry, 18 October 1916, RAEA, Box 14 (Folder: "Correspondence Aa–Fz 1916"). Listing, in the *American Economic Review*, the annual granting of doctoral degrees in the field along with the titles of successfully defended dissertations was another part of the effort to professionalize new generations of students and young faculty. See a draft of Davis Dewey's letter to academic economics departments beginning this practice, 17 December 1914, RAEA, Box 13 (Folder: "Correspondence Dewey 1915").

34. There had been, of course, in both the eighteenth and nineteenth centuries, significant exceptions to the tendency of economic theorists to ignore the domestic realm in their investigations, but they were just that, exceptions. Most notable among them, perhaps, was Friedrich Engels, *The Origin of the Family, Private Property and the State, in the Light of the Researches of Lewis H. Morgan* (New York: International Publishers, [1891] 1942). The philological irony inherent in the determination of professional economists to avoid investigations of the domestic sphere is also conspicuous, albeit less so than in the Greek, in a late Latin name for the field—*Studiis Commeatalibus* (studies of provisions [or supplies]).

35. The AHEA was established in 1908. Some of the leading figures in the professionalization of home economics in the early twentieth century were Martha van Rensselaer (Cornell University), Ellen Swallow Richards (Massachusetts Institute of Technology), Marion Talbot (Wellesley College and the University of Chicago), and Mary Schenck Woolman (Columbia University and Simmons College). For a thought-provoking assessment of their efforts, see Phyllis Palmer, *Domesticity and Dirt: Housewives and Domestic Servants in the United States, 1920–1945* (Philadelphia: Temple University Press, 1989), chap. 5. Also see Helen Pundt, *AHEA: A History of Excellence* (Washington, D.C.: American Home Economics Association, 1980); and Linda Marie Fritschner, "The Rise and Fall of Home Economics" (Ph.D. diss., University of California–Davis, 1973). On Dew-

ey's fiat, see A. W. Coats, "The American Economic Review," RAEA—Box 0 (Folder 1), p. 204. On the intellectual implications of the exclusion of feminist categories from economic analysis, see Marilyn Waring, *If Women Counted: A New Feminist Economics* (New York: HarperCollins, 1988).

36. Palmer, *Domesticity and Dirt*, 90. Also see Christine Delphy, *Close to Home: A Materialist Analysis of Women's Oppression*, trans. and ed. D. Leonard (Amherst: University of Massachusetts Press, 1984), 176. In ways both ironic and poignant, specialists in home economics pursued similar strategies of prestige enhancement, "exclusivity," and professionalization that their male colleagues deployed against them in fields like economics. Aside from the unequal status in the community of professions that even their best efforts could obtain, these women would ultimately suffer from male entry into the home economics field itself. This "male influx was accompanied by a new name, human ecology, that indicated the transformation of the discipline from home-centeredness to human-centeredness, from female to male." See Margaret W. Rossiter, *Women Scientists of America: Struggles and Strategies to 1940* (Baltimore: Johns Hopkins University Press, 1982), 187. At Cornell University, for example, what had been the School of Home Economics eventually became the College of Human Ecology. Similarly, at the University of Chicago, the former Department of Household Administration ultimately evolved into the School of Social Service Administration. In recent years the impact on women of a variety of professionalizing processes in the United States has received increasing attention from scholars. See, for example, Virginia Drachman, *Hospitals with a Heart: Women Doctors and the Paradox of Separatism at the New England Hospital, 1862–1969* (Ithaca, N.Y.: Cornell University Press, 1984); Regina Morantz-Sanchez, *Sympathy and Science: Women Physicians in American Medicine* (New York: Oxford University Press, 1985); Ellen Fitzpatrick, *Endless Crusade: Women Social Scientists and Progressive Reform* (New York: Oxford University Press, 1990); Mary Jo Deegan, *Jane Addams and the Men of the Chicago School, 1892–1918* (New Brunswick, N.J.: Rutgers University Press, 1988); and Jacqueline Goggin, "Challenging Sexual Discrimination in the Historical Profession: Women Historians and the American Historical Associa-

tion, 1890–1940," *American Historical Review* 97 (1992), 769–802. Also see Joan Wallach Scott, "American Women Historians, 1884–1984," in her *Gender and the Politics of History* (New York: Columbia University Press, 1988), 178–98.

37. From A. W. Coats, "The American Economic Review," RAEA, Box 0 (Folder 1), 204, 205ff.

38. Dewey to Henry G. Bradlee, 27 February 1922, RAEA, Box 60 (Folder: "1922"); as well as A. W. Coats, "The American Economic Review," RAEA, Box 0 (Folder 1), 221–22.

39. Carver to Dewey, 9 June 1911; RAEA—Box 60 (Folder: "1911"). Regrettably, the archives of the *American Economic Review* do not include all the typescripts of materials evaluated for possible publication. Even so, the correspondence remains a rich collection of evidence concerning the attitudes and goals of this early generation of professionalizing economists.

40. Fetter to Dewey, 20 March 1916; Dewey to Fetter, 16 March 1916; Fetter to Dewey, 15 October 1915; all in RAEA, Box 63 (Folder: "AER 1910–1917 Frank A. Fetter (Pres., AEA, 1912) with Davis R. Dewey.").

41. Hotchkiss to Dewey, 4 June 1921, RAEA, Box 60 (Folder: "1921"); and Lewis H. Haney to Dewey, 25 October 1919, RAEA, Box 60 (Folder: "1919"). It is striking that the issue of mathematical exegesis perplexed Dewey and his referees for many years. Rejecting an article from Raymond Garver of UCLA, Dewey explained that referees found it too technical for inclusion in the *Review*. Garver wrote back in frustration: "In any science, proofs can be deduced only from assumptions[.] If I consider the problem of a falling body, and disregard air resistance, I am not necessarily an ignoramus. It may be that I am merely considering a reasonable approximation." See Garver to Dewey, 29 April 1935; and Dewey to Garver, 23 April 1935; both in RAEA, Box 60 (Folder: "1935").

42. Dewey to Veblen, 16 March 1915, RAEA, Box 13 (Folder: "Correspondence LA–Zz 1915"). Veblen apparently did not reply to Dewey's invitation. Also see Dewey to Fetter, 18 July 1917, RAEA, Box 62 (Folder: "AER 1914–1917 Editors"); and Dewey to Young, 26 September 1914, RAEA, Box 13 (Folder: "Correspondence Dewey 1914"). In addition, see Dewey to Young, 31 March 1915, RAEA, Box 13 (Folder: "Correspondence Dewey 1915").

43. H. C. Taylor, "Statement on book reviews for the American Economic Review" (although undated, this statement was presumably circulated in 1911 given its inclusion in the 1911 file of Davis Dewey's correspondence), RAEA, Box 60 (Folder: "1911"). Also see Fetter to Dewey, 24 May 1911, RAEA, Box 60 (Folder: "1911"). The distinctive nature of book reviewing in professional journals, relative to the refereeing of submitted essays, would also explain the greater abundance of correspondence in *AER* records concerning book review controversies.

44. Farnam to Dewey, 6 April 1911, RAEA, Box 63 (Folder: "AER 1911–1917 Henry W. Farnam with Davis R. Dewey"). Matters of printing costs and quality of product concerned AEA officials for several years after the *Review* began publication. In May 1916, for example, one article author (who happened to be the vice-president of the Rumford Press of Concord, New Hampshire) conveyed to AEA secretary-treasurer Allyn Young his contempt for the printing job done on his piece. Young could only agree with the complaint. Referring to the academic publisher responsible for the *Review* at that time, he "agree[d] . . . that the Princeton Press is no print shop." See W. S. Rossiter to Young, 2 May 1916, RAEA, Box 14 (Folder: "Correspondence Aa–Fz 1916").

45. Dewey to Calhoun, 21 August 1930; and Means to Dewey, 25 September 1930; both in RAEA, Box 60 (Folder: "1930"); Dewey to Douglas, ?1925, RAEA, Box 60 (Folder: "1925"). While the full date of Dewey's missive to Douglas is obscured in the files, its inclusion in the 1925 folder is clear. Also see Fetter to Dewey, 3 January 1912, RAEA, Box 60 (Folder: "1912"). The new work in question, by Taussig, was his *Principles of Economics* (New York: Macmillan, 1911); that of Hawtrey, his *Good and Bad Trade: An Inquiry into the Causes of Trade Fluctuations* (London: Constable, 1913).

46. Ray B. Westerfield(?) to Dewey, 27 January 1925, RAEA, Box 19 (Folder: "Correspondence N–Z 1925"); it was Westerfield who wrote Dewey to express Professor Putnam's concerns.

47. Dewey to Kinley, 23 October 1913, RAEA, Box 60 (Folder: "1913"); Dewey to Young, 1 October 1915, RAEA, Box 13 (Folder: "Correspondence Dewey 1915"). Dewey made the comment about "cultivating radicals" with reference to his decision to send complimentary copies of the *AER* to the Chicago Arbeiter-Zei-

tung Publishing Company, printers of the left-wing daily *Chicagoer Arbeiter-Zeitung*.

48. R. M. Hudson (Chief, Division of Simplified Practice, U.S. Department of Commerce) to Westerfield, 4 April 1925, to which, in Westerfield to Hudson, 14 April 1925, the reply was made that "the American Economic Association is a scientific society and is not interested in propaganda"; both in RAEA, Box 19 (Folder: "Correspondence N–Z 1925"); Dewey to Harvey N. Chase, 2 February 1914, RAEA, Box 61 (Folder: "Harvey N. Chase from Davis R. Dewey"); Everett J. House to Young, 17 November 1914, RAEA, Box 13 (Folder: "Correspondence Na–Zz 1914"); Alton B. Parker (Chairman, League to Enforce Peace) to Young, 24 April 1916, RAEA, Box 1 (Folder: "Correspondence GA–Sz 1916"). Also see Coats, "The American Economic Association, 1904–1929," 18–20, 24. Professor Coats notes that the concern with impartiality even prompted the AEA leadership to reject a proposed link with the Institute for Economic Research in Washington, D.C. (forerunner of the Brookings Institution); nor did the Association endorse an appeal from Irving Fisher for members of the AEA to support both the War Savings Committee and the League of Nations.

49. The Ely, Bemis, and Ross disputes are discussed in detail by Richard Hofstadter and Walter P. Metzger in *The Development of Academic Freedom in the United States*, 423–45. Hofstadter and Metzger note the confrontation discussed at the time, by Thorstein Veblen, between the "culture of science" and the "culture of business." See Veblen's *Higher Learning in America: A Memorandum on the Conduct of Universities by Business Men* (New York: Kelley, [1918] 1957), 24–34, 70, passim. Also see Furner, *Advocacy and Objectivity*, 165–98, 235–59; Ross, *The Origins of American Social Science*, 133, 176, 230–32, 318; Edward Ross, *Seventy Years of It: An Autobiography* (New York: Appelton-Century, 1936), 64–68, 80–86, 101–3, 230, 290, 317–19; and Warren Samuels, "The Firing of E. A. Ross from Stanford," *Journal of Economic Education* 22 (1991), 183–90.

50. No doubt Association officials were quite discomfited by the potential for difficult publicity surrounding any involvement in the Ross matter. When Secretary-Treasurer Young was asked by the National Office of the Socialist Party, in Chicago, to provide it with a copy of the special AEA committee report on the Ross case, Young made clear that no such formal document ex-

isted. He went further in pointing out that the committee itself really had no "official" existence. See Etheleryn (?) Mills to Young, 29 June 1915; and Young to Mill, 1 July 1915; both in RAEA, Box 13 (Folder: "Correspondence LA–Zz 1915"). On the Joint Committee with the APSA and ASA, see RAEA, Box 13 (Folder: "Reports Annual Meeting 1914"). For the AEA, the Joint Committee members were Richard Ely, Frank Fetter, and E.R.A. Seligman; for the APSA, Herbert Croly, J. Q. Dealey, and F. N. Judson; for the ASA, James Lichtenberger, Roscoe Pound, and U. G. Weatherly.

51. See a special folder on the "AER 1913 Willard C. Fisher—Shankin controversy—Wesleyan College of Feb, 1913," RAEA, Box 63. For Young's observations, see Young to Seligman, 7 July 1915; and, additionally, Seligman to Young, 16 April 1915; Young to Seligman, 21 April 1915; all in RAEA, Box 13 (Folder: "Correspondence LA–Zz 1915").

52. On the Nearing case, see Dewey to Fetter, 15 September 1915; and Fetter to Dewey, 19 September 1915; both in RAEA, Box 63 (Folder: "AER 1910–1917 Frank A. Fetter with Davis R. Dewey"). Also see Nearing's personal testimony, *The Making of a Radical: A Political Autobiography* (New York: Harper and Row, 1972), esp. 76–96. On the Dartmouth case, see Young to G. C. Cox, 27 July 1915; also see Adams to Young, 26 April 1915; and Young to Adams, 5 May 1915; all in RAEA, Box 13 (Folder: "Correspondence Aa–Kz 1915"). The apparent reluctance of an organization like the AEA to involve itself in specific personnel cases in academia stood in quite interesting contrast to the posture of those groups, like the American Bar Association and the American Medical Association, that created specific machinery—a board of medical examiners or a professional conduct and ethics committee—to police the conduct and standing of its individual members. Of course, the central distinction in this regard involves that of licensure. Lawyers and physicians, in turn-of-the-century America, submitted to the authority of the state, in matters of entry to the profession, in exchange for which their own professional leaderships became part of the apparatus of standards enforcement. Where licensure did not exist, as in the case of economics, matters of conduct and standing would involve not simply particular professional groups but also employers—most notably college and university officials, trustees, and alumni—refracted through the institution of

tenured appointment. Perhaps it is for this reason that in those academic specialties lacking licensure, the relationship between practitioners and employers often became, and still remains, an arena of struggle and contested authority. Even so, it seems clear that the licensed professions, as epitomized in the legal notion of malpractice, focus their personnel disputes less on matters of what their discipline does than on questions of how things are most properly done. The nonlicensed academic fields, by contrast, must reckon as much with questions of substance as of form.

53. From Ross, "The Development of the Social Sciences," 123, 126, 138. Roger L. Geiger, in his *To Advance Knowledge*, vii and 2, provides a definitive account of how the war affected the institutional evolution of a "university research system" in the United States—establishing "patterns of structure, intellectual organization, and financing that are still recognizable today." Similarly, Carol S. Gruber notes the improvement in the status of academic professions that the war occasioned. Prior to it, "[t]he social status of the newly professionalized professoriate was uncertain, reflecting the ambivalence of American society to the life of the mind." See her *Mars and Minerva: World War I and the Uses of the Higher Learning in America* (Baton Rouge: Louisiana State University Press, 1975), 44.

54. Young to Houston, 4 May 1914, RAEA, Box 13 (Folder: "Correspondence Aa–Mz 1914"). That agricultural matters provided one context within which AEA leaders could pursue an intervention in governmental affairs was perhaps not entirely fortuitous. Agricultural economics, after all, was a specialty that had, since the middle of the nineteenth century, firmly established itself as an empirically grounded and rigorously defined enterprise. Its links with the natural sciences, in particular agronomy and biology, no doubt greatly helped in this regard. Moreover, insofar as agriculture had been (and arguably still is) the most heavily regulated and managed segment in the American economy—in sharp distinction from the experience of virtually all other nations—the federal administrative apparatus in agriculture was one of the most highly developed agencies in the executive branch. This peculiar historical circumstance, as well, most likely encouraged and facilitated the interest of professional economists in the DOA in the early 1900s. For an exceedingly important investigation of the historical and political implications of American agriculture's special position in na-

tional statecraft, see Theda Skocpol and Kenneth Finegold, "State Capacity and Economic Intervention in the Early New Deal," *Political Science Quarterly* 97 (1982), 255–78.

55. W. F. Wilcox to Gray, 13 June 1914, RAEA, Box 13 (Folder: "Correspondence Gray 1914"); Koren to Young, 21 May 1914; Houston to Young, 11 May 1914; and Young to Houston, 4 May 1914; all in RAEA, Box 13 (Folder: "Correspondence Aa–Mz 1914").

56. J. B. Moore (U.S. Department of State) to Gray and Young, 16 February 1914, RAEA, Box 13 (Folder: "Correspondence Aa–Mz 1914"); also see a copy of the AEA resolution in question in Box 13 (Folder: "Correspondence Na–Zz 1913"). Also see Ruth Evans (Office of the Mayor; Boston, Massachusetts) to Carver, 8 January 1914; Carver to Evans, 15 January 1914; Edward A. Fitzpatrick (APSA) to Young, 7 January 1914; Young to Fitzpatrick, 14 January 1914; all in RAEA, Box 13 (Folder: "Correspondence Aa–Mz 1914").

57. LeRossignol to Young, 13 March 1917, RAEA, Box 14 (Folder: Correspondence Aa–Mz 1917); and Perrin to Young, 26 November 1915, RAEA, Box 13 (Folder: "Correspondence LA–Zz 1915").

58. See Young to Silas L. Egley, 8 October 1917; Egley to Dewey, 2 October 1917; and McIlhenny to Young, 8 October 1917; all in RAEA, Box 14 (Folder: "Correspondence Aa–Mz 1917"). Also see Coats, "The American Economic Association, 1904–1929," 15. Needless to say, several professional and scientific societies were approached by the civil service authorities. In this respect, the war was a transformative event for a broad spectrum of the nation's occupational elite. See, for example, in this regard, Gruber, *Mars and Minerva*; David M. Kennedy, *Over Here: The First World War and American Society* (New York: Oxford University Press, 1980); Burl Noggle, *Into the Twenties: The United States from Armistice to Normalcy* (Urbana: University of Illinois Press, 1974); Ronald Schaffer, *America in the Great War: The Rise of the War Welfare State* (New York: Oxford University Press, 1991); and Jerry Israel, *Building the Organizational Society: Essays on Associational Activities in Modern America* (New York: Free Press, 1972). For a most interesting and recent investigation of the war's impact on the professionalization of the field of chemistry, see Hugh R. Slotten, "Human Chemistry or Scientific Barbarism? American Responses to World

War I Poison Gas, 1915–1930," *Journal of American History* 77 (1990), 476–98; as well as the work of David J. Rhees, "The Chemists' Crusade: The Rise of an Industrial Science in Modern America, 1907–1922 (Ph.D. diss., University of Pennsylvania, 1987); and Arnold Thackray et al., *Chemistry in America, 1876–1976* (Boston: Reidel Publishing/Kluwer Academic Publishers, 1985), 98–102.

59. It was with the assistance of Henry Farnam, a Yale faculty member and former AEA president, that Commons won support to form nine such committees on Finance and Currency, Agriculture and Food Production, Labor and Labor Legislation, the Conservation of Natural Resources, Corporation Finance and Regulation, the Cost Accounting of Government Contracts, the Control of War Prices and Combinations and the Distribution of Products, and the Distribution of Income and Wealth as Affected by the War. See Commons to Executive Committee, 11 May 1917, RAEA, Box 14 (Folder: "Correspondence Aa–Mz 1917"). These groups managed to do little in the one year of the war's duration after their establishment, but Association support for them was strong. In only three months leading up to the war's end, Young managed to raise, by a general appeal to the AEA membership, a bit over $1,100 to sustain their work. Even so, the fundraising initiative also elicited critical replies from businesspeople who expressed their concern that the Association have more "practical men" in its membership ranks. See Young to Seligman, 9 October 1918; Erastus W. Bulkley (Spencer Trask and Company, New York) to Young, 15 July 1918; Young to Bulkley, 22 July 1918; Lessing Rosenthal (Attorney-at-Law, Chicago) to Young, 15 July 1918; Young to Rosenthal, 2 August 1918; Young to William C. Graves (Secretary to Julius Rosenthal, Chicago), 9 December 1918; and Calvin Tomkins to Young, 28 August 1918; all in RAEA, Box 15 (Folder: "Correspondence 1918").

60. See Edward T. Silva and Sheila A. Slaughter, *Serving Power: The Making of the Academic Social Science Expert* (Westport, Conn.: Greenwood, 1984), appendix, table 5. The sample by which Silva and Slaughter investigated the federal war agency work of leading social scientists included the War Department, the War Industries Board, the War Labor Policies Board, the War Trade Board, the War Fuel Administration, the War Shipping Board, the Excess Profits Advisory Board, the United States Food Admin-

istration, the Advisory Tax Board, the Price Fixing Commission, the Sugar Equalization Board, the War Savings Committee of the Department of the Treasury, the Advisory Commission on the Peace, and various Interallied Conference groups. Also see the United States Library of Congress, *The United States at War: Organizations and Literature* (Washington, D.C.: U.S. Government Printing Office, 1917), 19, 30–31; and Robert D. Cuff, *The War Industries Board: Business-Government Relations during World War I* (Baltimore: Johns Hopkins University Press, 1973). On the special AEA committees formed during the war years, see Commons to Executive Committee, 11 May 1917, RAEA, Box 14 (Folder: "Correspondence Aa–Mz 1917"). On the civil service canvass, see "Report of the [AEA] Secretary for Year Ending 18 December 1917," RAEA, Box 14 (Folder: "Correspondence Na–Zz 1917"); as well as Clark to Young, 12 May 1917; and McIlhenny to Young, 8 October 1917; both in RAEA, Box 14 (Folder: "Correspondence Aa–Mz 1917"); and McIlhenny to Young, 13 June 1918, RAEA, Box 15 (Folder: "Correspondence 1918").

61. On the national research clearinghouse idea and on the need to make economists' work "effective," see Hamilton to Fisher, 27 April 1918; Fisher to Hamilton, 1 May 1918; Young to Fisher, 8 May 1918; Young to Fisher, 18 June, 1918; Fisher to Young, 1 May 1918; all in RAEA, Box 15 (Folder: "Correspondence Fisher 1918"). On involvement with the work of the Census Bureau, see Fisher to Young, 21 November 1918, RAEA, Box 15 (Folder: "Correspondence Fisher 1918"). On membership appeals attendant upon war-related work, see Fisher to Members of the National Institute of the Social Sciences (no date); and W. P. Goemann to Fisher, 18 May 1918; both in RAEA, Box 15 (Folder: "Correspondence Fisher 1918"). Fisher actually extended his appeal for new members to the American Bar Association, believing the war work of economists would capture the imagination of attorneys. See Young to Gardner, 22 May 1918, RAEA, Box 15 (Folder: Correspondence Fisher 1918"). Fisher also engaged in activist agendas, even those that skirted the Association injunction against partisan posturing in its name. In the second week of May 1918, for example, he wrote all AEA members urging them to contribute to the national Thrift Campaign to help finance the war. He took pains to note that his "appeal [wa]s to the members individually," lest

he violate Association rules. See Fisher to Members Circular, 9 March 1918, RAEA, Box 15 (Folder: "Correspondence Fisher 1918").

62. From Irving Fisher, "Economists in Public Service," *American Economic Review* 9 (1919), 7, 18–21; and Wesley Mitchell, "The Prospects of Economics," in *The Trend of Economics*, ed. Rexford G. Tugwell (New York: Crofts, [1924] 1932, 23. These remarks by Fisher and Mitchell are noted in William J. Barber's excellent study, *From New Era to New Deal: Herbert Hoover, the Economists, and American Economic Policy, 1921–1933* (New York: Cambridge University Press, 1985), 2–3. The title of Fisher's speech, of course, evoked that of a famous article by Woodrow Wilson (then president of Princeton University): "Princeton in the Nation's Service," *Forum* 22 (1896), 450–66. There were obvious and dramatic parallels in the impact of World War I on both economists and specialists in the physical sciences—especially with regard to the creation of institutional links between the needs of the state and scholarly research agendas. See, for example, F. B. Jewett, "The Genesis of the National Research Council and Millikan's World War I Work," *Review of Modern Physics* 20 (1948), 1–6; and V. Kellogg, "The National Research Council," *International Conciliation* 154 (1920), 423–30.

63. From Gruber, *Mars and Minerva*, 44–45, 257–59. As Gruber notes, there have been a number of fine interventions in the literature concerning the contradictions faced by intellectuals in times of national crisis. See, for example, C. Angoff, "The Higher Learning Goes to War," *American Mercury* 11 (1927), 179–91; Merle Curti, "The American Scholar in Three Wars," *Journal of the History of Ideas* 3 (1942), 241–64; and Robert L. Beisner, *Twelve against Empire: The Anti-imperialists, 1898–1900* (Chicago: University of Chicago Press, 1985). Of singular importance, in this regard, is George M. Frederickson, *The Inner Civil War: Northern Intellectuals and the Crisis of the Union* (New York: Harper and Row, 1968), not to mention the remarkable literary contribution of Edmund Wilson, *Patriotic Gore* (New York: Oxford University Press, 1962).

64. On the proliferation of academic freedom cases during the war years, the classic reference is of course Hofstadter and Metzger, *The Development of Academic Freedom in the United States*, 495–506. Ely's move from radical reformer to unquestioning patriot is discussed in

Gruber, *Mars and Minerva*, 116, 256; his Germanophobia is given free rein in *The World War and Leadership in a Democracy* (New York: Macmillan, 1918). That Nearing became a lightning rod for economists committed to the war effort is vividly shown in an irate letter sent to AEA secretary-treasurer Allyn Young in the winter of 1917. The assistant freight traffic manager of the Atchison, Topeka, and Santa Fe Railroad terminated his Association membership when he discovered that Nearing was a member. "[A]t this time when every man is tested as to his patriotism," J. S. Bartle declared, "it seems to me [Nearing's] activities should be resented in every way possible by real Americans . . . it would be better for the country as a whole if he could be silenced once and for all. . . ." See Bartle to Young, 3 December 1917, RAEA, Box 14 (Folder: "Correspondence Aa–Mz 1917").

65. Young to Perrin, 28 January 1916, RAEA, Box 13 (Folder: "Correspondence LA–Zz 1915"); and Fisher to Seligman, 20 January 1902, RAEA, Box 8 (Folder: "President Seligman's Correspondence 1902").

66. The words are Woodrow Wilson's, from his war message to the Congress on 2 April 1917. See Arthur S. Link, ed., *The Papers of Woodrow Wilson* (Princeton, N.J.: Princeton University Press, 1983), vol. 41, 526.

Chapter 2
Prospects, Puzzles, and Predicaments

1. Arthur C. Pigou, "Empty Economic Boxes: A Reply," *Economic Journal* 32 (1922), 463. For thirty-five years a professor of political economy at Cambridge University, Arthur C. Pigou (1877–1959) figured prominently in the professionalization of economics in Great Britain. A gifted teacher, he is widely acknowledged to have inspired whole generations of students in his unabashed admiration for the work of Alfred Marshall—arguably the dominant figure in British economics from the 1890s until his death in 1924. It was Marshall's professorship that Pigou, then but thirty years old, assumed at Cambridge in 1908. Best known, through the ages, for his influential *Economics of Welfare* (London: Macmillan, 1920), Pigou's *The Economics of Stationary States* (London: Macmillan, 1935) also had a dramatic impact on his peers. Remarkably prolific, having by the age of fifty published nine books and destined to write nine more before his

death, Pigou served, in the formal example of his *Theory of Unemployment* (London: Macmillan, 1933), as the main antagonist for Keynes's revolutionary critique of neoclassical economics in the 1930s. Subsequent decades have shown that Keynes was not altogether fair in his published assaults upon Pigou's work, overlooking Pigou's anticipation of some of the most enduring aspects of Keynesianism itself. See David Collard, "A. C. Pigou, 1877–1959," in *Pioneers of Modern Economics in Britain*, ed. D. P. O'Brien and J. R. Presley (New York: Macmillan, 1981); and Mark Blaug, *Great Economists before Keynes: An Introduction to the Lives and Works of One Hundred Great Economists of the Past* (New York: Cambridge University Press, 1986), 189–91.

2. From Ellis Hawley, "Economic Inquiry and the State in New Era America: Antistatist Corporatism and Positive Statism in Uneasy Coexistence," in *The State and Economic Knowledge: The American and British Experiences*, ed. Mary O. Furner and Barry Supple (New York: Cambridge University Press, 1990), 288–89. Hawley notes that World War I properly dates the first utilization of "credentialed professionals" for purposes of "economic inquiry" by the national government. He further documents that, other than the work of some specialists in agencies created by the Congress (such as the National Monetary Commission of 1908–12) and the executive branch (such as the Interstate Commerce Commission and the Tariff Commission), the first permanent apparatus of the federal government to retain a staff of professional economists was the Board of Governors of the Federal Reserve System. On the "hundreds" of economists involved in government work during the war years, see Robert L. Church, "Economists as Experts: The Rise of an Academic Profession in the United States, 1870–1920," in *The University in Society*, vol. 2, *Europe, Scotland, and the United States from the 16th to the 20th Century*, ed. Lawrence Stone (Princeton, N.J.: Princeton University Press, 1974), 599. Also see Leonard White, *Trends in Public Administration* (New York: McGraw-Hill, 1933), 271–72, who counted 25 "economic and political science" specialists in federal government employment in 1896—a number that rises, in his calculation, to 848 during Herbert Hoover's presidency. On the formation and work of the Central Bureau of Planning and Statistics, headed by Harvard economics professor Edwin F. Gay, see Guy Alchon, *The Invisible Hand of Planning: Capitalism, Social Science, and the State in the 1920s* (Princeton, N.J.: Princeton University Press, 1985), 26–32; Herbert Heaton, *A Scholar in Action: Edwin F. Gay* (Cambridge: Harvard University Press, 1952), 98–129; and Zenas L. Potter, "The Central Bureau of Planning and Statistics," *Quarterly Publications of the American Statistical Association* 16 (1919), 275–85.

3. On the rapid demobilization after the world war, see Burl Noggle, *Into the Twenties: The United States from Armistice to Normalcy* (Urbana: University of Illinois Press, 1974), 46–65; Robert F. Himmelberg, "The War Industries Board and the Antitrust Question," *Journal of American History* 52 (1965), 59–74; Alchon, *The Invisible Hand of Planning*, 35–37; and Hawley, "Economic Inquiry and the State in New Era America," 290–91. It was Princeton's Frank Fetter who, in 1925, indulged in some hyperbole when he spoke of the war's impact on the "popular esteem" of the economics discipline. In his essay "The Economists and the Public," *American Economic Review* 15 (1925), 13, he went on to say, "Business men who had seen the work of economists during the war paid them the sincere flattery of outbidding the universities and opening economic research departments. Various governmental departments retained economists who had been given leave of absence from college duties during the war, and created new positions for them as economic advisers."

4. It is a striking irony that Pigou's conviction, that a fully professionalized economics was necessarily divorced from the practicalities of the business world and the vagaries of market practice, has in the past half century been entirely reversed in the minds of most of his colleagues. Indeed, the assumption that modern economic analysis is directly applicable to the activities of commercial enterprise, and that in fact it can provide insights for the effective "privatization" of public sector operations, is a powerful component of the contemporary theoretical identity of the discipline. A conceptual and historical assessment of the process by which this reversal in professional self-awareness has taken place is one of the core goals of this study.

5. A vast and impressive literature has, for several years now, addressed the distinctive nature of American political culture from the turn of this century to World War II. See, for some classic references, James Weinstein, *The Corporate Ideal in the Liberal State, 1900–1918* (Bos-

ton: Beacon, 1960); Jeffrey Lustig, *Corporate Liberalism* (Berkeley: University of California Press, 1982); Robert Wiebe, *The Search for Order, 1877–1920* (New York: Hill and Wang, 1967); Samuel Haber, *Efficiency and Uplift: Scientific Management in the Progressive Era, 1890–1920* (Chicago: University of Chicago Press, 1964); Daniel T. Rodgers, *The Work Ethic in Industrial America, 1850–1920* (Chicago: University of Chicago Press, 1974); Richard Hofstadter, *The Age of Reform: From Bryan to F.D.R.* (New York: Random House, 1955); Ellis Hawley, "Herbert Hoover, the Commerce Secretariat, and the Vision of an 'Associative State,' 1921–1928," *Journal of American History* 61 (1974), 116–40; David Montgomery, *Workers' Control in America* (New York: Cambridge University Press, 1979); and, more recently, Martin J. Sklar, *The Corporate Reconstruction of American Capitalism, 1890–1916: The Market, the Law, and Politics* (New York: Cambridge University Press, 1988); John M. Jordan, *Machine-Age Ideology: Social Engineering and American Liberalism, 1911–1939* (Chapel Hill: University of North Carolina Press, 1994); Lizabeth Cohen, *Making a New Deal: Industrial Workers in Chicago, 1919–1939* (New York: Cambridge University Press, 1990); and Jerry Israel, *Building the Organizational Society: Essays on Associational Activities in Modern America* (New York: Free Press, 1972). On the ideological appeal of isolationism, despite its obvious contravention in actual economic policy and activities, the classic work remains that of William Appleman Williams, *Tragedy of American Diplomacy* (Cleveland: World Publishing, 1959), as well as his *Contours of American History* (Cleveland: World Publishing, 1961).

6. The stunted nature of the federal administrative apparatus in the modern United States has been quite intelligently investigated by political scientists, most notably Theda Skocpol and her colleagues and students. See, for example, Theda Skocpol and Kenneth Finegold; "State Capacity and Economic Intervention in the Early New Deal," *Political Science Quarterly* 97 (1982), 255–78; and Theda Skocpol, *Protecting Soldiers and Mothers: The Political Origins of Social Policy in the United States* (Cambridge: Harvard University Press, 1992). Also see Ellis W. Hawley, *The New Deal and the Problem of Monopoly: A Study in Economic Ambivalence* (Princeton, N.J.: Princeton University Press, 1966); Ira Katznelson and Bruce Pietrykowski, "Rebuilding the

American State: Evidence from the 1940s," *Studies in American Political Development* 5 (1991), 301–39; and Stephen Skowronek, *Building a New American State: The Expansion of National Administrative Capacities, 1877–1920* (New York: Cambridge University Press, 1982). For especially useful comparative perspectives on this issue, see Peter Gourevitch, *Politics in Hard Times: Comparative Responses to International Economic Crises* (Ithaca, N.Y.: Cornell University Press, 1986); and Charles Maier, ed., *The Changing Boundaries of the Political: Essays on the Evolving Balance between the State and Society, Public and Private in Europe* (New York: Cambridge University Press, 1987).

7. Ellis Hawley makes this point in a particularly compelling way in his "Economic Inquiry and the State in New Era America," 293–99. Also see Harry C. McDean, "Professionalism, Policy, and Farm Economists in the Early Bureau of Agricultural Economics," *Agricultural History* 57 (1983), 64–82; Donald L. Winters, *Henry Cantwell Wallace as Secretary of Agriculture* (Urbana: University of Illinois Press, 1970), 109–16; John M. Gaus and Leon Wolcott, *Public Administration and the United States Department of Agriculture* (Chicago: Public Administration Service, 1940), 35–50; A. G. Black, "Agricultural Policy and the Economist," *Journal of Farm Economics* 18 (1936), 311–19; Lloyd S. Tenny, "The Bureau of Agricultural Economics in the Early Years," *Journal of Farm Economics* 29 (1947), 1017–26; and K. A. Fox, "Agricultural Economists in the Econometric Revolution: Institutional Background, Literature and Leading Figures," *Oxford Economic Papers* 41 (1989), 53–70. Given the long-standing interventionist strategies of the federal government in agriculture, the case of agricultural economics—as an example of the links between professionalizing strategies and statism—stands in sharp contrast to that of general economics itself. There were, of course, no counterparts in the industrial, service, and trade sectors of the economy to the land-grant colleges, experiment stations, and farm agent networks created for agriculture from the mid–nineteenth century onward. In this century, agricultural economists were thus able to capitalize on long-standing ties between farmers and federal agencies in their own pursuit of professional standing and influence. Powerful intellectual resonances between agricultural economic theory and natural scientific fields such as biology, genetics, and agronomy—not to men-

tion engineering—further served to differentiate these practitioners from their colleagues in economics as a whole. It is hardly surprising, for all these reasons, that agricultural economics has maintained (and further deepened) its separation from the discipline of economics through the creation and maturation of separate faculties, degree programs, and professional societies. Also see Henry Charles Taylor, *A Farm Economist in Washington, 1919–1925*, ed. Dawn Danz-Hale (Madison: University of Wisconsin–Madison, Department of Agricultural Economics, 1992). William Parker speculated some decades ago that interventionism in American agriculture was the direct result of dispersed and relatively modest patterns of landholding (as compared, for example, to the European case) that made support for agricultural improvement, research, and training a necessarily *collective* task. The impact of Jeffersonian ideology in that historical process was also clearly of singular importance. See Parker's "Slavery and Agricultural Development: An Hypothesis and Some Evidence," *Agricultural History* 44 (1970), 115–25.

8. From Roger L. Geiger, *To Advance Knowledge: The Growth of American Research Universities, 1900–1940* (New York: Oxford University Press, 1986), 147–48. Also see Donald T. Critchlow, *The Brookings Institution, 1916–1952: Expertise and the Public Interest in a Democratic Society* (DeKalb: Northern Illinois University Press, 1985), 56–76.

9. Ultimately, the National Bureau became a powerhouse in fund-raising, enjoying steady support from not only the Carnegie Corporation but also the Rockefeller Foundation, the Social Science Research Council, various federal government agencies, and some private corporations. Allen Weinstein, in *The Decline of Socialism in America, 1912–1925* (New York: Monthly Review Press, 1967), examines the part foundation funding played in steering social science research away from socialist agendas.

10. See Hawley, "Economic Inquiry and the State in New Era America," 302; Alchon, *The Invisible Hand of Planning*, 52–59; and N. I. Stone, "The Beginnings of the National Bureau of Economic Research," in *The National Bureau's First Quarter Century*, ed. Wesley Mitchell (New York: National Bureau of Economic Research, 1945). Also see Lucy Sprague Mitchell, *Two Lives: The Story of Wesley Clair Mitchell and Myself* (New York: Simon and Schuster, 1953). The original board of directors of the

NBER included Mitchell, Gay, and other well-known economists such as Thomas S. Adams, John R. Commons, and Allyn Young. The American Economic Association, the American Statistical Association, the American Engineering Council, the American Bankers Association, the American Federation of Labor, and the American Federation of Farm Bureaus also had, by charter, representation on the Bureau's board, along with five universities, which had claim to "Directorships by University Appointment"—Chicago, Columbia, Harvard, Wisconsin, and Yale. The National Industrial Conference Board, the Chamber of Commerce of the United States, and the American Bar Association were initially proposed to have board representation. They were quickly dropped, however, and the American Management Association and the National Publishers Association were added. No doubt the reputation for partisanship that the Institute of Economics won early in its life contributed to the decision of officials in the American Economic Association to refuse a formal link between the two organizations in 1919. See A. W. Coats, "The American Economic Association, 1904–1929: Prologue," RAEA, Box 0 (Folder 1), 22–23.

11. This work was organized under the aegis of the Advisory Committee on Statistics within the Department of Commerce that Secretary Hoover convened when he assumed his cabinet post in 1921. Along with Edwin Gay and Wesley Clair Mitchell, the committee included Edwin R. A. Seligman of Columbia, Allyn Young of Harvard, Walter F. Willcox of Cornell, Carroll W. Doten of MIT, and William S. Rossiter of the Census Bureau. As one historian of this group's work has noted, the committee "was a formidable assemblage of talents which embraced some of the most respected names in American academic economics. But it was surely no accident that the membership was leavened by veterans of wartime work in government." See William J. Barber, *From New Era to New Deal: Herbert Hoover, the Economists, and American Economic Policy, 1921–1933* (New York: Cambridge University Press, 1985), 8.

12. See Hawley, "Economic Inquiry and the State in New Era America," 304, 300–303. Indeed, with Hoover's assistance, the NBER received support from the Carnegie Corporation for all of the cyclical instability and unemployment research. Also see Alchon, *The Invisible Hand of Planning*, 71–85. From its earliest in-

come account investigations, the NBER published *Income in the United States: Its Amount and Distribution, 1909–1919* (New York: National Bureau of Economic Research, 1921); and *Distribution of Income by States in 1919* (New York: National Bureau of Economic Research, 1922). For the President's Conference on Unemployment, the NBER produced *Business Cycles and Unemployment, Including an Investigation Made under the Auspices of the National Bureau of Economic Research* (New York: McGraw-Hill, 1923). Hawley notes that Secretary Hoover and the NBER leadership believed the business cycle study to have been "the most important economic investigation ever undertaken" (305), comparable to that of the National Monetary Commission, which, in 1912, proposed the creation of the Federal Reserve System. In its study of business cycles, the Bureau ultimately published several famous volumes: *Income in the Various States* (1924); *Migration and the Business Cycle* (1926); *Business Annals* (1926); *The Behavior of Prices* (1927); and *Business Cycles: The Problem and Its Setting* (1927).

13. For a discussion of the historical interconnections between the philanthropic community, academia, and public policy in the United States, see Barry D. Karl and Stanley N. Katz, "The American Private Philanthropic Foundation and the Public Sphere, 1890–1930," *Minerva* 19 (1981), 236–70. A classic study of the links between philanthropic strategies and professional development is E. Richard E. Brown, *Rockefeller Medicine Men: Medicine and Capitalism in America* (Berkeley: University of California Press, 1979). Of similar interest is Donald Fisher, *Fundamental Development of the Social Sciences: Rockefeller Philanthropy and the United States Social Science Research Council* (Ann Arbor: University of Michigan Press, 1993); as well as Fisher, "The Role of Philanthropic Foundations in the Reproduction and Production of Hegemony: Rockefeller Foundations and the Social Sciences," *Sociology* 17 (1983), 206–33; and D. Grossman, "American Foundations and the Support of Economic Research: 1913–1929," *Minerva* 20 (1982), 59–82. Also see Hawley, "Economic Inquiry and the State in New Era America," 301; and Donald T. Critchlow, "Think Tanks, Antistatism, and Democracy: The Nonpartisan Ideal and Policy Research in the United States, 1913–1987," in *The State and Social Investigation in Britain and America*, ed. Michael J.

Lacey and Mary O. Furner (Cambridge: Cambridge University Press, 1993), 279–322. More recent investigations of these issues may be found in James Allen Smith, *The Idea Brokers: Think Tanks and the Rise of the New Policy Elite* (New York: Free Press, 1991); and Ellen Condliffe Lagemann, *The Politics of Knowledge: The Carnegie Corporation, Philanthropy, and Public Policy* (Middletown, Conn.: Wesleyan University Press, 1989).

14. From Church, "Economists as Experts," 605. Also see Herbert Heaton, *A Scholar in Action: Edwin F. Gay* (Cambridge: Harvard University Press, 1952), passim; and Wallace B. Donham and Esty Foster, "The Graduate School of Business Administration, 1908–1929," in *The Development of Harvard University since the Inauguration of President Eliot, 1869–1929*, ed. Samuel Eliot Morison (Cambridge: Harvard University Press, 1930), 533–48.

15. See Church, "Economists as Experts," 606; Blaug, *Great Economists before Keynes*, 168–70; and Mitchell, *Two Lives*, passim. Also see Simon Kuznets, "The Contribution of Wesley C. Mitchell," in *Institutional Economics: Veblen, Commons, and Mitchell Reconsidered*, by C. E. Ayres, Neil W. Chamberlain, Joseph Dorfman, Robert A. Gordon, and Simon Kuznets (Berkeley: University of California Press, 1963), 95–122.

16. Some other leading figures in the articulation of an institutionalist economics were, at the time, Clarence Ayres (Amherst College), John R. Commons (University of Wisconsin), Morris Copeland (Michigan), Walton Hamilton (Amherst College), Frederick Mills (Columbia University), and Adolph Wolfe (New School for Social Research). See, for example, Clarence Ayres, *The Problem of Economic Order* (New York: Farrar and Rinehart, 1938); as well as Ayres, "The Co-ordinates of Institutionalism," *American Economic Review* 41 (1951), 47–55; and John R. Commons, *Institutional Economics: Its Place in Political Economy* (New Brunswick, N.J.: Transaction Publishers, [1934] 1990). Sometimes regarded as the first econometrician, Henry Ludwell Moore (Columbia University) also had a decisive influence on the evolution of institutionalism. In this regard, see Philip Mirowski, "Problems in the Paternity of Econometrics: Henry Ludwell Moore," *History of Political Economy* 22 (1990), 587–609. Another exceedingly influential contribution to the institutional-

ist canon is Gunnar Myrdal, *The Political Element in the Development of Economic Theory*, trans. Paul Streeten (London: Routledge and Kegan Paul, 1953). A classic examination of the history of thought in institutionalist economics is Allan G. Gruchy, *Modern Economic Thought: The American Contribution* (New York: Prentice-Hall, 1947). There are powerful historical and intellectual links between institutionalist economics and the field of industrial relations; see Bruce E. Kaufman, *The Origins and Evolution of the Field of Industrial Relations* (Ithaca, N.Y.: ILR Press–Cornell Studies in Industrial and Labor History, 1993).

17. Veblen (1857–1929) received a Ph.D. in philosophy from Yale University in 1884. Seven years later he enrolled as a graduate student in economics at Cornell, where he studied under James L. Laughlin. He held his first faculty appointment at the University of Chicago (1892–1906) and later moved on to Stanford University (1906–9). From 1911 to 1918 he taught at Missouri. Taking early retirement at the end of World War I, he was an adjunct faculty member at the New School for Social Research in New York until his death. Rick Tilman has embarked on a three-volume study of Veblen's life and work, the first part of which has been published as *Thorstein Veblen and His Critics, 1891–1963: Conservative, Liberal, and Radical Perspectives* (Princeton, N.J.: Princeton University Press, 1992). Also see Peter Rutkoff and William Scott, *New School: A History of the New School for Social Research* (New York: Free Press, 1986).

18. From Thorstein Veblen, "Why Is Economics Not an Evolutionary Science?" in *The Place of Science in Modern Civilization* (New York: Viking, [1898] 1919), 56, 67; and, in the same volume, both "The Preconceptions of Economic Science" [1899–1900], 177; and "The Limitations of Marginal Utility" [1909], 231–51. Also see a fascinating discussion by O. H. Taylor, "Economic Theory and Certain Non-economic Elements in Social Life," in his *Explorations in Economics: Notes and Essays in Honor of F. W. Taussig* (New York: Kelley, [1936] 1967), 380–90.

19. See Paul T. Homan, *Contemporary Economic Thought* (New York: Harper, 1928), 440, 446; and Harry Landreth, *History of Economic Thought* (Boston: Houghton Mifflin, 1976), 325. On Mitchell's claims regarding the proper ways to understand cyclical fluctuations, see Hawley,

"Economic Inquiry and the State in New Era America," 303; Wesley Clair Mitchell, *Business Cycles* (Berkeley: University of California Press, 1913); and Arthur F. Burns, "Wesley Mitchell and the National Bureau," in National Bureau of Economic Research, *Twenty-ninth Annual Report* (1949), 23–26, 36–44. Also see Philip A. Klein, "The Neglected Institutionalism of Wesley Clair Mitchell: The Theoretical Basis for Business Cycle Indicators," *Journal of Economic Issues* 17 (1983), 867–99.

20. See Lionel Robbins, *An Essay on the Nature and Significance of Economic Science* (London: St. Martin's, 1969), 16, 38, 77, 106, 109–10—to this day, arguably the finest and most straightforward explanation of the neoclassical approach to economic studies. Also see Alfred Marshall, *Principles of Economics* (London: Macmillan, [1890] 1961), 42, 38—one of the most influential texts in modern economic theory that both provided a systematic summing-up of the major intellectual trends in the field at the time and that powerfully influenced generations of investigators, perhaps most notably John Maynard Keynes.

21. See Veblen, "The Limitations of Marginal Utility"; Wesley C. Mitchell, "The Rationality of Economic Activity I," *Journal of Political Economy* 18 (1910), 97–113; as well as Mitchell, "The Rationality of Economic Activity II," *Journal of Political Economy* 18 (1910), 197–216; and Mitchell, "The Prospects of Economics," in *The Trend of Economics*, ed. Rexford G. Tugwell (New York: Crofts, [1924] 1935), 25–28. Also see Walton H. Hamilton, *Industrial Policy and Institutionalism: Selected Essays* (Clifton, N.J.: Kelly, [1915–18] 1974). In this discussion of American institutionalist economics, I have been much informed by the work of Yuval Yonay, *The Struggle over the Soul of Economics: Institutionalist and Neoclassical Economists in America between the Wars* (Princeton, N.J.: Princeton University Press, 1998). Yonay argues that institutionalism had quite a dramatic impact on the evolution of American economics and that its influence remains palpable to this day. Also see his "When Black Boxes Clash: Competing Ideas of What Science Is in Economics, 1924–39," *Social Studies of Science* 24 (1994), 39–80. In this conviction he is joined by an eminent historian of the profession, William Barber, who has specifically noted (in "The Divergent Fates of Two Strands of 'Institutionalist' Doctrine during the New Deal

Years" [unpublished manuscript, Department of Economics, Wesleyan University, n.d.]) the enduring visibility of certain institutionalist ideas pursued during the 1930s. With all due respect for their scholarship, I am not persuaded by Barber's and Yonay's findings—especially given, as subsequent chapters of this study will show, the impact of World War II and the cold war on the further evolution of neoclassical doctrine and the maintenance of its intellectual hegemony not simply in economics in particular but in the social sciences generally.

22. Indeed, while this theoretical conundrum was apparent almost from the start, it was not until the 1960s work of Nobel laureate Kenneth Arrow that it found its most sophisticated and authoritative treatment. In his articulation of an "incommensurability theorem," Arrow demonstrated that the explicit measurement and aggregation of individual preferences was impossible. See Arrow, "A Difficulty in the Concept of Social Welfare," *Journal of Political Economy* 58 (1950); as well as his *Social Choice and Individual Values* (New York: Wiley, 1951). Arrow's claims paralleled those of others who noted that utility could be understood only in ordinal, not cardinal, terms. That interpersonal comparisons and quantification of utility was an intractable problem for neoclassical theory was also acknowledged by Paul Samuelson in his classic essay "Consumption Theory in Terms of Revealed Preference," *Economica* 15 (1948), 243–53.

23. See Tjalling C. Koopmans, "Measurement without Theory," *Review of Economics and Statistics* 29 (1947), 164, 172, 162. The volume under review was the work of Arthur F. Burns and Wesley C. Mitchell, *Measuring Business Cycles* (New York: National Bureau of Economic Research, 1946). The finest overview and evaluation of Koopmans's debate with Burns and Mitchell is Philip Mirowski's "The Measurement without Theory Controversy: Defeating Rival Research Programs by Accusing Them of Naive Empiricism," *Economies et Sociétés: Serie Oeconomia* 23 (1989), 109–31. Mirowski persuasively notes that, while surely not the only attack on the institutionalist approach to appear in print, Koopmans's review essay became, in the eyes of neoclassical economists, the canonical and decisive blow to institutionalism as a whole. Some ten years later Koopmans would rigorously formulate and explicate his convictions about the scientific probity of the neoclassical agenda in

his remarkable *Three Essays on the State of Economic Science* (New York: McGraw-Hill, 1957). E. Roy Weintraub also provides insight regarding the interdependent histories of neoclassical economic theory and of econometrics in his *General Equilibrium Analysis: Studies in Appraisal* (New York: Cambridge University Press, 1985), 80–86. Thoughtful explorations of the complex links between theory and empirical methodology that emerge in the work of economic statisticians are offered by David Hendry, "Econometrics: Alchemy or Science?" *Economica* 47 (1980), 387–406; and by Edward Leamer, "Let's Take the Con Out of Econometrics," *American Economic Review* 73 (1983), 31–43. Another view of the Koopmans-Mitchell controversy is provided by Mary S. Morgan, *The History of Econometric Ideas* (New York: Cambridge University Press, 1990), 55–56, 252.

24. See Frank H. Knight, "The Limitation of Scientific Method in Economics," in *The Trend of Economics*, ed. Rexford G. Tugwell (New York: Crofts, [1924] 1934), 259, 264; and Mitchell, "The Prospects of Economics," 19. Also see Frank H. Knight, *On the History and Method of Economics: Selected Essays* (Chicago: University of Chicago Press, 1963). One of the most enduring legacies of institutionalism was a commitment to survey research not simply in economics per se but in the social sciences as a whole. By the 1930s, in fact, the United States was clearly a world leader in the execution of survey research protocols. In large measure the interest in compiling vast quantities of behavioral data was derived not only from the empiricist techniques of an institutionalist economics but also from the interests of corporate enterprise in understanding its markets as thoroughly as possible. I am grateful to my colleague Dan Schiller (of the Department of Communication at the University of California, San Diego) for illuminating discussion on this point. As early as 1917, the J. Walter Thompson Company of New York had corresponded with the leadership of the American Economic Association regarding an ongoing project to gather information on annual clothing expenditures in the United States. See Young to J. Walter Thompson Company, 6 February 1917; and J. Walter Thompson Company to Young, 2 February 1917; both in RAEA, Box 14 (Folder: "Correspondence Na–Zz 1917"). That market survey research was both methodologically and conceptually linked to the data-gathering proclivities of the federal bureaucracy

in the interwar period is suggestively explored by Jackson Lears in "The Ad Man and the Grand Inquisition: Intimacy, Publicity, and the Administrative State in America, 1880–1940" (paper presented at the Davis Center for Historical Studies, Princeton University, 30 March 1990).

25. McAdoo to Wilson, 2 August 1917, Box 523 (Folder: "2 August 1917"), Papers of William Gibbs McAdoo [thereafter PWGM], Manuscript Division, Library of Congress (Washington, D.C.). A particularly well-informed and succinct portrait of McAdoo is provided by the late Jordan A. Schwarz in *The New Dealers: Power Politics in the Age of Roosevelt* (New York: Knopf, 1993), 3–31. McAdoo's special access to the President and the close attention Wilson paid to the sentiments of his Treasury secretary were the result of many years of political cooperation and the fact that McAdoo was Wilson's son-in-law.

26. Wilson to McAdoo, 17 April 1913, PWGM, Box 517 (Folder: "17 April 1913").

27. Woodrow Wilson's tenure as the chief executive has increasingly been understood by historians to herald the beginning of an "administrative state" in twentieth-century America. World War I is similarly grasped as having played an essential part in this transformative process. What is striking, however, is the high degree of informality in the policy advising process that appears to have characterized his administration. The dearth of federal agencies, not to mention practices, encouraging and allowing for the intimate participation of professional economists in government in the early part of this century is clearly apparent in a consideration of executive branch correspondence. In the case of the Wilson years, see, for example, McAdoo to Wilson, 14 April 1913, PWGM, Box 517 (Folder: "14 April 1913") on the opinions of a "Mr. Palmer" and a "Mr. Barry" on the pending "Currency Bill" (eventually the Federal Reserve Act of 1913)— some of which McAdoo found to be not "at all sound"; Wilson to McAdoo, 7 June 1913, PWGM, Box 517 (Folder: "7 June 1913") regarding the views of "Major Higginson" of Boston on the establishment of a Federal Reserve network; and similarly McAdoo to Wilson, 17 June 1913, noting the views of "many prominent people" with whom he had recently met about extension of the Aldrich-Vreeland Act (passed in the spring of 1908 to facilitate expansion of the national money supply); McAdoo to Wilson, 2 July 1913, reporting the concerns of a small

banker with the proposed Federal Reserve Act; and McAdoo to Wilson, 5 August 1913, on the "strongly" held convictions of various senators; all in PWGM, Box 517 (folder designations are by date of the relevant letter).

28. See James Livingston, *Origins of the Federal Reserve System: Money, Class, and Corporate Capitalism, 1890–1913* (Ithaca, N.Y.: Cornell University Press, 1986), esp. chap. 3, 71–102, and passim. Also see Sayre E. Dykes, "The Establishment and Evolution of the Federal Reserve Board: 1913–1923," *Federal Reserve Bulletin* 75 (1989), 227–43.

29. Seligman to Wilson, 13 September 1913, PWGM, Box 527 (Folder: "13 September 1913"); and Hadley to Wilson, 1 July 1913, PWGM, Box 527 (Folder: "1 July 1913"). The Owen-Glass Act became law just before Christmas in 1913; a seven-member Board of Governors assumed duties the following summer, and the Federal Reserve Banks opened for business in November 1914.

30. See McAdoo to Wilson, 17 May 1914, PWGM, Box 518 (Folder: "17 May 1914"); McAdoo to Wilson, 10 March 1914, PWGM, Box 518 (Folder: "10 March 1914"); and Wilson to McAdoo, 10 January 1914, PWGM, Box 518 (Folder: "10 January 1914"), all on the matter of Federal Reserve Board appointments. See McAdoo to Wilson, 21 July 1913, PWGM, Box 517 (Folder: "21 July 1913"); and McAdoo to Wilson, 3 June 1913, PWGM, Box 517 (Folder: "3 June 1913") on internal revenue districting.

31. On the Smoot-Hawley "fiasco," see the preface to this study. Also see McAdoo to Wilson, 9 March 1917, PWGM, Box 522 (Folder: "9 March 1917") on Taussig's appointment and the statutory provisions regarding the political composition of the Tariff Commission; McAdoo to Wilson, 28 December 1916, PWGM, Box 521 (Folder: "28 December 1916") again on Taussig's appointment; McAdoo to Wilson, 26 December 1916, PWGM, Box 521 (Folder: "26 December 1916") on the appointment of "Miss Ida Tarbell"; McAdoo to Wilson, 11 November 1916, PWGM, Box 521 (Folder: "11 November 1916") on the appointment of Irving Fisher; McAdoo to Wilson, 16 October 1916, PWGM, Box 521 (Folder: "16 October 1916") on members of the commission drawn from the business community; Hurley to Wilson, 13 October 1916, PWGM, Box 521 (Folder: "13 October 1916") on the need for business and economics professionals on the commission; McAdoo to Wilson, 6 October 1916,

PWGM, Box 521 (Folder: "6 October 1916") on Taussig; and McAdoo to Wilson, 4 October 1916, PWGM, Box 521 (Folder: "4 October 1916") on "Judge Wallace of Missouri."

32. See McAdoo to Wilson, 2 September 1914, PWGM, Box 519 (Folder: "2 September 1914"); and McAdoo to Wilson, 3 September 1914, PWGM, Box 519 (Folder: "3 September 1914"). McAdoo's first estimate of the revenue losses due to the disruption of international trade was $100 million.

33. The proponent of the land tax idea was George L. Record, an attorney in New Jersey who had known Wilson briefly during the latter's tenure as president of Princeton University. See Record to Wilson, 3 May 1917; and Wilson to McAdoo, 8 May 1917; both in PWGM, Box 522 (Folder: "8 May 1917"). On the need to control inflation and impose centralized planning mechanisms, see McAdoo to Wilson, 16 May 1917, PWGM, Box 522 (Folder: "16 May 1917"); McAdoo to Wilson, 30 April 1917, PWGM, Box 522 (Folder: "30 April 1917"); McAdoo to Wilson, 22 April 1917, PWGM, Box 522 (Folder: "22 April 1917"); and McAdoo to Wilson, 16 July 1917, PWGM, Box 523 (Folder: "16 July 1917"). On the lending requirements for the allies, see McAdoo to Wilson, 18 July 1917, PWGM, Box 523 (Folder: "18 July 1917").

34. See Strong to McAdoo, 15 February 1918; and McAdoo to Wilson, 19 February 1918; both in PWGM, Box 524 (Folder: "19 February 1918").

35. The unique nature of the allocative pressures occasioned by war was noted in a letter from Wilson to McAdoo, 24 November 1918, PWGM, Box 525 (Folder: "24 November 1918"). On the bureaucratic struggles over troop movements and the use of the national railroad network, as well as McAdoo's efforts to utilize the skills of Baruch, see McAdoo to Wilson, 9 September 1918, PWGM, Box 525 (Folder: "9 September 1918"); McAdoo to Wilson, 25 March 1918; McAdoo to Wilson, 2 March 1918; McAdoo to Baker, 2 March 1918; Wilson to McAdoo, 26 February 1918; Hoover to Wilson, 19 February 1918; Wilson to McAdoo, 20 February 1918; and McAdoo to Wilson, 23 February 1918; all in (with relevant file folder designations by date) PWGM, Box 524.

36. See Commons to Wilson, 21 March 1917; and Sprague to Wilson, 12 April 1917; both in PWGM, Box 528 (Folder: "21 March 1917"). An outstanding narrative of the work of professional economists in formulating wartime taxation policy during the Wilson presidency is found in W. Elliot Brownlee, "Economists and the Formation of the Modern Tax System in the United States: The World War I Crisis," in *The State and Economic Knowledge: The American and British Experience*, ed. Mary O. Furner and Barry Supple (New York: Cambridge University Press, 1990), 401–35. Brownlee notes that it was Yale economist Thomas S. Adams who was the central professional figure at Treasury dealing with the taxation issue.

37. I am inspired here by the crucially important work of Ellis Hawley, especially his "Herbert Hoover, the Commerce Secretariat, and the Vision of an 'Associative State,'" 116–40.

38. Carver to Taft, 24 December 1912, RAEA, Box 12 (Folder: "Correspondence Ta–Zz 1912"). The American Political Science Association established a public service training committee at the same time. See RAEA, Box 12 (Folder: "Correspondence Kinley 1913").

39. Young to Cannan, 11 May 1915, RAEA, Box 13 (Folder: "Correspondence Aa–Kz 1915"). Young's frustration at the time was no doubt exacerbated by the membership losses that had beset the AEA. See Dewey to Young, 15 February 1915; and Young to Dewey, 18 February 1915; both in RAEA, Box 13 (Folder: "Correspondence Dewey 1915").

40. See Adams to Young, 4 April 1916; and Carver to Young (no date, but the text indicates the letter was sent early in March 1916); both in RAEA, Box 14 (Folder: "Correspondence Aa–Fz 1916"); and "Minutes of Business Meeting at Richmond" (December 27–28, 1918), RAEA, Box 15 (Folder: "Correspondence Aa–Gz 1919"). Indeed, the end of World War I elicited only a handful of apposite project proposals from AEA members. Davis Dewey and Carl Plehn (of the University of California) sought to pool information about economists leaving public service, in particular at the War Industries Board, with a view toward recruiting them into academic positions. Allyn Young coordinated the gathering of books and back issues of the *American Economic Review* for distribution to scholarly libraries in Europe damaged by combat. Henry Gardner (of Brown University) circulated an open petition to Association members calling for congressional endorsement of membership in the League of Nations. See Dewey to Plehn, 30 November 1918, RAEA, Box 60 (Folder: "1918"); Herbert Putnam (of the Library of Con-

gress) to Young, 14 November 1919), RAEA, Box 15 (Folder: "Correspondence Ha–Zz 1919"); and Gardner to AEA Members, 12 January 1919, RAEA, Box 15 (Folder: "Correspondence Aa–Gz 1919").

41. See Schwarz, *The New Dealers*, 34, and his pithy summary of Hoover's political career on pages 32–56. Some of the most influential portraits of Hoover, especially with regard to the extraordinary work he did as commerce secretary, have been provided by Ellis Hawley. See his "Herbert Hoover, the Commerce Secretariat, and the Vision of an 'Associative State,'" as well as his edited anthology *Herbert Hoover as Secretary of Commerce: Studies in New Era Thought and Practice* (Iowa City: University of Iowa Press, 1981). Also see Joan Hoff Wilson, *Herbert Hoover: Forgotten Progressive* (Boston: Little, Brown, 1975); Evan Metcalf, "Secretary Hoover and the Emergence of Macroeconomic Management," *Business History Review* 59 (1975), 60–80; James S. Olson, *Herbert Hoover and the Reconstruction Finance Corporation 1931–1933* (Ames: Iowa State University Press, 1977); and Albert U. Romasco, *The Poverty of Abundance: Hoover, the Nation, the Depression* (New York: Oxford University Press, 1965). George Nash has been engaged in a systematic study of Hoover's life, the published book products of which to date are: *The Life of Herbert Hoover* (New York: Norton, 1983) and *Herbert Hoover and Stanford University* (Stanford, Calif.: Hoover Institution Press, 1988). Powerfully overshadowed, in life and death, by Franklin Delano Roosevelt, Hoover remains a most enigmatic figure, especially given the seeming paralysis of his presidency in the face of the Great Depression itself. Nothing in his career up until the fall of 1929 would have suggested that Hoover would have been anything but one of the most activist presidents in modern memory. The judgement of history has, in his case, been harsh, and the taciturnity, some would even say the bitterness, that characterized his years in retirement did not help those, champions and critics alike, who sought in later years to redress the balance.

42. See Lowell to Hoover, 10 April 1922; and Hoover to Lowell, 10 March 1922, Box 131 (Folder: "Commerce Department Foreign & Domestic Commerce Dr. Julius Klein 1922 March–June"), Commerce Papers of Herbert Hoover [hereafter CPHH], Herbert Hoover Presidential Library, West Branch, Iowa. Also see Taussig to Hoover, 27 (?) June 1921, CPHH, Box 595

(Folder: "Prof. F. W. Taussig 1921–1927"). On Mitchell's systematic involvement with Hoover, see CPHH, Box 618 (Folder: "Unemployment Business Cycles 1921") and later discussion here.

43. Two years later, Hoover would explain to H. G. Moulton, the director of the Institute for Government Research: "I, and I believe most business [people] and economists in the country, are impressed with the necessity for the maintenance and improvement in [statistical] services for being the primary foundation to business stability in the elimination of speculation, the reduction of the hazards of business, and in the provision of fundamental material upon which economic thought must resolve." See Hoover to Moulton, 25 May (?) 1923, CPHH, Box 575 (Folder: "Statistics 1921–1928"). Drew E. Vande Creek has examined the impact of Emory Johnson, Solomon Huebner, and Joseph Willits, all of the Wharton School at the University of Pennsylvania, in contributing to the fulfillment of part of Hoover's vision with regard to the proper relationship between the state, the private sector, and private research organizations. See "The Construction of Economic Expertise in Philadelphia, 1890–1940" (Ph.D. diss., University of Virginia, 1995).

44. See Hoover to Taussig, 23 June 1921; Taussig to Hoover, 27 (?) June 1921; Taussig to Hoover, 14 July 1921; and Hoover to Taussig, 20 July 1921; all in CPHH, Box 595 (Folder: "Prof. F. W. Taussig 1921–1927"). When the first issue of the *Survey* was released at the end of September 1921, Hoover was eager to solicit continuing advice from professionals in order to improve the publication. Alonzo Taylor, an economist then director of the Food Research Institute at Stanford University, was, for example, engaged to evaluate the quality of the reporting on agricultural products. Noting that the "data of one year ha[d] been used as a base line" for the inaugural issue, Taylor was greatly concerned that the promulgation of such simple time series was "for crops [at least] a particularly vicious practice." His proposal that a five-year moving average be employed was immediately accepted. See Taylor to Christian Herter (Assistant to the Secretary, Department of Commerce), 29 September 1921; and Herter to Taylor, 11 October 1921; both in CPHH, Box 596 (Folder: "Alonzo E. Taylor 1921").

45. See Moulton to Hoover, 1 June 1923; and W. C. Mullendore (Assistant to the Secretary) to Moulton, 28 August 1923; as well as Hoover to

Moulton, 25 May (?) 1923; all in CPHH, Box 575 (Folder: "Statistics 1921–1928"). Also see Hoover to Owen D. Young, 9 March 1925, CPHH, Box 719 (Folder: "Owen D. Young 1925–1926"). Hoover worked closely with Dana Durand, director of the Bureau of the Census, in reorganizing and amplifying the statistical activities of the Commerce Department. To assist Durand he appointed Willford King, a well-known applied economist, as special agent of the census. See Hoover to Durand (via memorandum), 8 March 1922, CPHH, Box 618 (Folder: "Unemployment Business Cycles 1922 January–March").

46. See Hunt to Pritchett, 29 December 1921, CPHH, Box 655 (Folder: "Unemployment National Bureau of Economic Research 1921"). See Hunt's "Memorandum for Secretary Hoover," 2 November 1921; Gay to Hoover, 25 October 1921; Mitchell to Hunt, 20 October 1921; all in CPHH, Box 618 (Folder: "Unemployment Business Cycles 1921"). The extent to which the Federal Reserve Board was responsible for timely action to contain and reverse the recession of 1920 is a matter open to debate. Some economic historians have argued that the brevity of that slump was due less to policy choices made in Washington than to swift readjustments tied to postwar demobilization. Regarding Mitchell's consultative work with the Conference on Unemployment, see the correspondence between Mitchell and Hunt, spanning September through November of 1921, all in CPHH, Box 654 (Folder: "Unemployment Wesley C. Mitchell 1921").

47. See Hunt to F. P. Keppel (of the Carnegie Corporation), 26 October 1927; Hunt, "Memorandum for Secretary Hoover," 15 September 1927; Hoover to Miller, 3 April 1923; Berridge to Hunt, 5 April 1923; Hunt to Berridge, 7 April 1923; and Hunt to Berridge, 19 April 1923; all in CPHH, Box 618 (Folder: "Unemployment Business Cycles 1923 april [sic]"). Also see Hunt, "Memorandum for Secretary Hoover," 20 October 1921, CPHH, Box 618 (Folder: "Unemployment Business Cycles 1921").

48. See Hunt to Mitchell, 6 December 1921; Mitchell to Hunt, 10 December 1921; both in CPHH, Box 654 (Folder: "Unemployment Wesley C. Mitchell 1921"); Dixon to Otto T. Mallery (staff member of the Study of Business Cycles group), 2 June 1922; and Hunt to Mitchell, 10 June 1922; Hunt to Michell, 29 September 1922;

all in CPHH, Box 654 (Folder: "Unemployment Wesley C. Mitchell 1922 May–September").

49. See Young to Mitchell, 20 November 1922; and Hunt to Mitchell, 26 October 1923; both in CPHH, Box 655 (Folder: "Unemployment Wesley C. Mitchell 1922 October–December"); Hunt to Mitchell, 10 August 1922, CPHH, Box 654 (Folder: "Unemployment Wesley C. Mitchell 1922 May–September"); and Mitchell to Hunt, 28 February 1922, CPHH, Box 654 (Folder: "Unemployment Wesley C. Mitchell 1922 January–March").

50. See Mitchell to Otto T. Mallery (Commerce Department Assistant to the Conference on Unemployment), 4 February 1922; Hunt to Mitchell, 6 February 1922; both in CPHH, Box 654 (Folder: "Unemployment Wesley C. Mitchell 1922 January–March"). The legislation in question was known as the Kenyon Bill and proposed the long-range planning and scheduling of public works expenditures with a view toward minimizing idleness.

51. See Arch W. Shaw (President, the Shaw Company) to Hoover, 29 May 1923; and Shaw to Hoover, 28 April 1923; both in CPHH, Box 556 (Folder: "Arch W. Shaw 1923"); and Harold Phelps Stokes to Shaw, 10 December 1924, in CPHH, Box 556 (Folder: "Arch W. Shaw 1924"). It is now widely acknowledged by economic historians that the interwar years witnessed the emergence of an altogether "new era" of product diversification, technical change, and competitive interaction among firms. In this sense, Hoover's "waste elimination" initiatives, while plausible from an engineering perspective, stood in direct conflict with prevailing trends in the economic development of the national economy at midcentury. See Alchon, *The Invisible Hand of Planning*. A not insignificant aspect of Hoover's vision in this regard had to do with efforts to conserve natural resources—efforts that carried over to the New Deal years. See, for example, Marion Clawson, *New Deal Planning: The National Resources Planning Board* (Baltimore: Johns Hopkins University Press, 1981).

52. See Dewey to Thomas Walker Page (Institute of Economics, Washington, D.C.), 26 March 1924, RAEA, Box 18 (Folder: "Correspondence N–Z 1924"). In 1995, at the time of its 110th anniversary, the American Economic Association listed no less than one hundred possible subclassifications of expertise (arrayed among nineteen core fields) in its membership directories (and ancillary publications).

53. See Chester Harvey Rowell to Hoover, 25 January 1927; Hoover to Rowell, 29 January 1927; Rowell to Hoover, 15 January 1927; all in CPHH, Box 528 (Folder: "Henry M. Robinson 1927–1928"); and Robinson to Hoover (via telegram), 26 December 1923, CPHH, Box 525 (Folder: "Henry M. Robinson 1921–1923"). The 1924 conference on German reparations and reconstruction was convened due to Germany's default in December 1922 and January 1923. A commission, headed by former U.S. Bureau of the Budget director Charles G. Dawes, formulated a revised payment schedule that operated until the spring of 1930, at which time a final settlement of the issue was instituted under the terms of a plan whose chief architect was Owen D. Young. By 1932, with the crisis of the Great Depression in full swing and with the impending collapse of German democracy, over 90 percent of the payments to have been made under the so-called Young Plan were canceled.

54. See "The McNary-Haugen Plan as Applied to Wheat: Operating Problems and Economic Consequences" and "The McNary-Haugen Plan as Applied to Wheat: Limitations Imposed by the Present Tariff," published as nos. 4 and 6, respectively, of *Wheat Studies of the Food Research Institute* 3 (February–March 1927), Stanford University, copies of which are lodged in CPHH, Box 596 (Folder: "Alonzo E. Taylor 1927–1928 & undated"). Also see Leo C. Monahan (Secretary to Herbert Hoover) to Elizabeth Brand (Secretary to Taylor), 9 September 1925; and Brand to Hoover, 24 August 1925; both in CPHH, Box 596 (Folder: "Alonzo E. Taylor 1925"); and Taylor to Hoover, 6 March 1924; Taylor to Hoover (via telegram), 2 April 1924, both in CPHH, Box 596 (Folder: "Alonzo E. Taylor 1924").

55. See President's Committee on Recent Economic Changes, Conference on Unemployment, *Recent Economic Changes in the United States* (New York: McGraw-Hill, 1929). A fine overview of the study's final report is provided by William Barber in *From New Era to New Deal*, 65–68.

56. From President's Committee on Recent Economic Changes, *Recent Economic Changes*, I:81. Also see Barber, *From New Era to New Deal*, 67–68; and a copy of a press release regarding the work of the "Committee on Recent Economic Changes," CPHH, Box 188 (Folder: "Economic Situation in Russia-Ecuador 1922–1928 & undated"). The members of the commit-

tee were Hoover (as chair), Walter F. Brown (assistant secretary of commerce), William Green (president, American Federation of Labor), John Lawrence (president, New England Council), Max Mason (President, University of Chicago), Adolph C. Miller (Board of Governors, Federal Reserve System), Lewis E. Pierson (president, U.S. Chamber of Commerce), John J. Raskob (vice president, General Motors Corporation), A. W. Shaw (president, Shaw Company), Louis J. Tabler (master, National Grange), Daniel Willard (president, Baltimore and Ohio Railroad), George McFadden (president, George H. McFadden and Brothers), Clarence M. Woolley (board chair, American Radiator Company), and Owen D. Young (board chair, General Electric Corporation). The technical staff of the committee, as was by now common practice, comprised economists hired as consultants under the auspices of the National Bureau of Economic Research. These analysts, under the direction of Wesley Mitchell, included some of the most prominent academicians in the field at the time, such as John Maurice Clark (who examined cyclical changes), Morris T. Copeland (marketing trends), Ralph C. Epstein (business profits), Edwin F. Gay (secular trends), Frederick C. Mills (prices), Edwin G. Nourse (agricultural trends), Willard L. Thorp (industrial trends), and Leo Wolman (population and labor), among others. See Shaw to French Strother (of the White House staff), 14 February 1931, HPSF, Box 120 (Folder: "Economics—Correspondence 1931").

57. The words concerning Hoover's ascension to the presidency are William Barber's in *From New Era to New Deal*, 65.

58. See Brown to Hoover, 26 January 1931; and Hoover to Brown, 30 January 1931; both in HPSF, Box 120 (Folder: "Economics—Correspondence 1931").

59. While the crash of the New York stock market on 29 October 1929 is usually taken to be the beginning of the Great Depression in the United States, concerns about the national economy had emerged well over a year before. A softness in construction activity was apparent in 1928; indices of industrial production had started to drop by the spring of 1929. Interestingly enough, that the American economy had significantly weakened before the stock market crash was ultimately demonstrated in a study undertaken by the National Bureau of Economic Research after World War II. See Geoffrey H. Moore, *Statistical Indications of Cyclical Reviv-*

als and Recessions, NBER Occasional Paper 31 (New York: National Bureau of Economic Research, 1950).

60. See Fisher to Hoover, 24 April 1929; Hoover to Fisher, 25 April 1929; both in HPSF, Box 334 (Folder: "Unemployment—Correspondence 1929, January–May"); Hoover to Hunt, 29 July 1930; Hunt to Hoover, 30 July 1930; and Hoover to Hunt, 8 August 1930; all in HPSF, Box 336 (Folder: "Unemployment—Advisory Committee on Employment Statistics 1930, May–July"). The research staff for the unemployment survey included Leo Wolman of the NBER, Mary Van Kleeck of the Russell Sage Foundation, and Harold F. Browne of the National Industrial Conference Board (NICB). John Maurice Clark and Sumner Slichter played an advisory role. On the formation of the research staff and its early work, see Shaw to Hoover, 29 July 1930; Hoover to H. W. Laidler (President, NBER), 30 July 1930; Hoover to Wolman, 12 August 1930; Wolman to Hoover, 16 August 1930; Hoover to Magnus W. Alexander (of the NICB), 30 July 1930; and Alexander to Hoover, 4 August 1930; all in HPSF, Box 336 (Folder: "Unemployment—Advisory Committee on Employment Statistics 1930, May–July"). Hoover, when creating the Advisory Committee on Employment Statistics, also consulted with William Butterworth (president of the U.S. Chamber of Commerce), P. W. Litchfield (president of the Goodyear Tire and Rubber Company), John Edgerton (president of the National Association of Manufacturers), and William Green (president of the American Federation of Labor). See Hoover to Butterworth, 30 July 1930; Butterworth to Hoover, 11 August 1930; Hoover to Litchfield, 22 August 1930; Litchfield to Hoover, 18 August 1930; Hoover to Edgerton, 30 July 1930; and Hoover to Green, 30 July 1930; all in HPSF, Box 336 (Folder: "Unemployment—Advisory Committee on Employment Statistics 1930, May–July"). At the same time, the Hoover administration worked with the Social Science Research Council to undertake a systematic "investigation of the consumption habits and cost of living of the American people." Officials of both the American Economic Association and the American Statistical Association lent their endorsement to this project; as early as the summer of 1928, the AEA had gone on record, in a formal resolution, calling for such a survey. See F. S. Deibler (Secretary-Treasurer of the AEA) to Herbert Lord (Director, U.S. Bureau of the Budget), 27

July 1928, RAEA, Box 22 (Folder: "Correspondence A–M 1928"); as well as Mitchell to Hoover, 7 May 1929; Mitchell to Ray Lyman Wilbur (Secretary of the Interior), 23 September 1929; Willfred I. King (American Statistical Association) to Hoover, 3 January 1930; all in HPSF, Box 864 (Folder: "Social Science Research Council 1929–1933"); and Gay (on behalf of the AEA) to Hoover, 14 January 1930, HPSF, Box 410 (Folder: "American Eag–Emb 1929–1932").

61. This generalization emerges from perusal of hundreds of letters lodged in the Hoover Presidential Subject Files at the Herbert Hoover Presidential Library. It was in April 1931 that Hoover's secretary, French Strother, asked J. Frederic Dewhurst, then the acting chief of the Division of Statistical Research in the Bureau of Foreign and Domestic Commerce, to recommend some reading for "the Chief" on depressions and related economic issues. Dewhurst provided a list that included *Business Annals* by Willard L. Thorp, *Economic History of the American People* by E. L. Bogart, *Tariff History of the United States* by Frank W. Taussig, and *Financial History of the United States* by Davis Dewey. He also recommended Wesley Mitchell's entry "Business Cycles" in the *International Encyclopaedia of the Social Sciences* for the president's consideration. See Dewhurst to Strother, 6 April 1931, HPSF, Box 120 (Folder: "Economics—Correspondence 1931").

62. A particularly fine history of the Reconstruction Finance Corporation (RFC), which distributed loans and subsidies totaling $10.6 billion by 1935, is James S. Olson, *Saving Capitalism: The Reconstruction Finance Corporation and the New Deal, 1933–1940* (Princeton, N.J.: Princeton University Press, 1988). Olson shows that the RFC had its institutional and procedural roots in the establishment of the War Finance Corporation in 1918—an effort by the Wilson administration to facilitate defense mobilization headed, predictably enough, by William Gibbs McAdoo. The financing of economic recovery after 1929 was, in Hoover's mind, the central means toward the alleviation of economic distress. By July 1932, the Emergency Relief and Construction Act reoriented some of the activities of the RFC toward relief. Yet an overweening bureaucracy and a pitifully inadequate amount of funding made Hoover appear, in Olson's words, "cold, apathetic, and stingy, willing to loan billions to banks while millions of people starved" (21). Franklin Roosevelt ap-

preciated Hoover's capabilities quite well. When, within five working days of his inauguration, Roosevelt declared a bank holiday, he "institutionalized his reputation as a man of action and Hoover's as a hopeless conservative" (30). What Roosevelt had actually done, of course, was send up to Capitol Hill a proposal that had been under consideration in the Hoover administration; he presented a suggested emergency banking act as a legislative initiative of his own. Clearly Hoover was no heartless leader wedded to simplistic notions of laissez-faire, nor was Roosevelt entirely original in his ideas regarding state economic intervention.

63. The temporary measures suggested would have essentially allowed banks more liquid reserves with which to do business. Not only would rediscounting have expanded the volume of loanable funds on hand; the use of such notes as security for note circulation would have released the intolerable pressures that had built up on gold reserves. In essence, the proposal outlined an aggressive strategy of monetary expansion.

64. See Hoover to Meech, 6 October 1931; and Meech to Hoover, 5 October 1931, Box 111 (Folder: "Financial Matters 1929–33"), Hoover Presidential Personal File [hereafter HPPF], Herbert Hoover Presidential Library, West Branch, Iowa. On advice concerning the financial needs of the Reconstruction Finance Corporation, see Fisher to Hoover (via telegram), 16 July 1932, HPSF, Box 246 (Folder: "Reconstruction Finance Corp. correspondence, 1932 July 16–30"); and on expansionary monetary policy and the ideas of Irving Fisher, see James A. Frear (Member of Congress) to Hoover, 15 July 1932, HPSF, Box 120 (Folder: "Economics—Correspondence 1932"). Fisher's many communications with Hoover regarding the need to reflate through monetary mechanisms include Fisher to Hoover, 9 May 1931; Fisher to Hoover, 15 July 1931; Hoover to Fisher, 16 July 1931; Fisher to Hoover, 10 July 1931; Fisher to Hoover, 21 December 1931; Fisher to Hoover, 11 April 1932; as well as Fisher to Frederic C. Walcott [senator from Connecticut], 4 May 1932; all in HPSF, Box 562 (Folder: "Irving Fisher 1929–1932"); and finally Fisher to Hoover (via telegram), 31 January 1932, HPSF, Box 543 (Folder: "Economic, R 1930–1933"). Also on monetary expansion, see King to Hoover, 21 May 1931, HPSF, Box 470 (Folder: "Business Depression 1931 January–June"); on bank failures, see Tom L. Popejoy (Department of Economics, University

of New Mexico) to Hoover, 13 October 1931, HPSF, Box 560 (Folder: "Financial 1931 October 16–31"); and on a proposed relief program, see W. C. Schluter (Wharton School of Finance and Commerce, University of Pennsylvania) to Hoover, 22 March 1932, HPSF, Box 809 (Folder: "Reconstruction Finance Corporation 1932 March–1933").

65. See Hoover to Shaw, 17 February 1933, HPPF, Box 207 (Folder: "Arch W. Shaw 1930–33"); and, concerning the conference at the University of Chicago, Fisher to Frederic C. Walcott, 4 May 1932, CPHH, Box 562 (Folder: "Irving Fisher 1929–1932"). Interestingly enough, Fisher opposed the spending suggestions of his colleagues at Chicago. At the same time, he conceded that "Hoover ha[d] . . . little or no chance of re-election unless great reflation occur[red] before November." See Thomas F. Cargill, "Irving Fisher: Comments on Benjamin Strong and the Federal Reserve in the 1930s," *Journal of Political Economy* 100 (1992), 1273–77. Even after his November 1932 defeat, Hoover continued to receive suggestions from economists—including a joint letter urging him to support "the development of barter exchange as a means of alleviating unemployment," signed by almost two dozen leading authorities such as John Bates Clark (Columbia), Morris A. Copeland (Michigan), Paul H. Douglas (Chicago), Frank A. Fetter (Princeton), Walton H. Hamilton (Yale), Wilford I. King (NYU), Richard A. Lester (Princeton), Broadus Mitchell (Johns Hopkins), Sumner H. Slichter (Harvard), Leo Wolman (Columbia), and Irving Fisher himself. See J. Douglas Brown (Director, Industrial Relations Section; Department of Economics, Princeton University) to Hoover, 18 January 1933; and Lawrence Richey (Secretary to Hoover) to Brown, 19 January 1933, in which Richey states that "[t]he President . . . is very much interested in the entire [idea]"; both in HPPF, Box 212 (Folder: "Unemployment; Unemployment Relief 1929–33"). Also see Paul H. Douglas, *In the Fullness of Time: The Memoirs of Paul H. Douglas* (New York: Harcourt Brace Jovanovich, 1971).

66. There is a large literature on the activism of the New Deal that situates Roosevelt's many economic policy goals within the context of his political reconfiguration of the constituency of his party. There is no more telling demonstration of the highly politicized nature of New Deal spending policy, for example, than Gavin Wright, "The Political Economy of New Deal

Spending: An Econometric Analysis," *Review of Economics and Statistics* 56 (1974), 262–81. Wright shows that federal disbursements for relief and recovery during the thirties were disproportionately focused in western states, where Roosevelt's concerns with stabilizing voter support, in what had been predominantly Republican strongholds, outweighed more prudent assessments of those sites in the national economy where the stimulatory impacts of federal spending would have been greatest. Also see David C. Colander and Harry Landreth, eds., *The Coming of Keynesianism to America: Conversations with the Founders of Keynesian Economics* (Cheltenham, England: Elgar, 1996)—in particular the interview with trusted Roosevelt aide Leon Keyserling, who argues that few of the ideas that framed the New Deal were derived directly from the work of Keynes. On the general ineffectiveness of New Deal recovery policy, see my *Great Depression: Delayed Recovery and Economic Change in America, 1929–1939* (New York: Cambridge University Press, 1987), chap. 7 ("New Deal Economic Policy and the Problem of Recovery"); as well as Michael M. Weinstein, *Recovery and Redistribution under the NIRA* (New York: Elsevier North-Holland, 1980).

Chapter 3
The Mobilization of Resources and Vice Versa

1. Paul A. Samuelson, "A Warning to the Washington Expert," *New Republic*, 11 September 1944, 298, as quoted in Barry M. Katz, *Foreign Intelligence: Research and Analysis in the Office of Strategic Services, 1942–1945* (Cambridge: Harvard University Press, 1989), 103. Samuelson (1915–) is widely regarded as one of the most influential and accomplished neoclassical economists of this century, the first American to receive, in 1970, the Nobel Memorial Prize in Economic Science. In a remarkable 1941 doctoral dissertation completed at Harvard University when he was twenty-six, "Foundations of Economic Analysis" (subsequently published by Harvard University Press in 1947), Samuelson sought to demonstrate that all economic action could be understood as an effort to maximize some objective (such as utility or output) subject to constraints (such as budgetary limitations or resource availability)—all framed in the language of the differential and integral calculus.

But a few years later he received the first John Bates Clark Medal from the American Economic Association—given for the most distinguished work by an economist under the age of forty. In *Linear Programming and Economic Analysis* (New York: McGraw-Hill, 1958), which he co-authored with Robert Dorfman and Robert Solow, Samuelson continued this line of inquiry, formulating rigorous techniques by which an array of previously disparate specialties within economics, for example, price theory and growth theory, could be conceptually linked. His elementary *Economics: An Introductory Analysis*, first published in 1948 (New York: McGraw-Hill), has been one of the most successful and influential textbooks in the field, credited by many with facilitating the introduction of neoclassical ideas to generations of students in the United States and elsewhere. When he received his Ph.D., Samuelson was considered by many to be a likely candidate for professorial appointment at his alma mater; his surprising departure was taken by many contemporaries to be a sign of the anti-Semitism widely believed to be so common at Harvard. Moving across town to help strengthen what has remained one of the principal competitors of Harvard in the field of economics, in 1941 Samuelson joined the faculty at the Massachusetts Institute of Technology, where he remains to this day. The author of scores of now-classic articles that span a striking number of topics in economics, Samuelson has also served on the U.S. War Production Board (during World War II), and at the Treasury Department, the Bureau of the Budget, the Board of Governors of the Federal Reserve System, and the Council of Economic Advisers. See A. Kendry, "Paul Samuelson and the Scientific Awakening of Economics," in *Twelve Contemporary Economists*, ed. J. R. Shackleton and G. Locksley (London: Macmillan, 1981); Leonard Silk, *The Economists* (New York: Basic Books, 1976), chap. 1; and Mark Blaug, *Great Economists since Keynes: An Introduction to the Lives and Works of One Hundred Modern Economists* (New York: Cambridge University Press, 1985), 213–16.

2. On the gold standard petition, see Frederick A. Bradford (Lehigh University) to Davis R. Dewey (Editor, *American Economic Review*), 23 November 1933, RAEA, Box 60 (Folder: "1933"). With regard to the general macroeconomic impacts of the Great Depression in the United States, see Peter Temin, *Did Monetary Forces Cause the Great Depression?* (New York: Nor-

ton, 1976); Broadus Mitchell, *Depression Decade: From New Era through New Deal, 1929–1941* (New York: Rinehart, 1955); Lester V. Chandler, *America's Greatest Depression: 1929–41* (New York: Harper and Row, 1970); and my *Great Depression: Delayed Recovery and Economic Change in America, 1929–1939* (New York: Cambridge University Press, 1987).

3. Smith to Deibler, 19 December 1932, RAEA, Box 24 (Folder: "Correspondence M–Z 1932"); and Hermann F. Arendtz (United Business Service, Boston) to Deibler, 20 July 1933, RAEA, Box 24 (Folder: "Correspondence A–L 1933"). The outlook of AEA officials in the early 1930s was not brightened by the fact that the depression caused an immediate drop in membership as hard-pressed unfortunates failed to renew their dues payments. Ironically enough, while this decline in the Association census tapered off quickly, the net result was a further homogenization of the ranks. Those most able to maintain or initiate membership in hard times tended to be securely placed academics at leading colleges and universities nationwide. See, for example, Deibler to R. B. Westerfield (Yale University), 2 November 1934, RAEA, Box 25 (Folder: "Correspondence M–Z 1934"), as well as much of the general correspondence held in the files for 1932 and 1933 in RAEA—Box 24.

4. That American institutionalist economics fared well during the depression era is the burden of William J. Barber's "The Divergent Fates of Two Strands of 'Institutionalist' Doctrine during the New Deal Years," *History of Political Economy* 26 (1994), 569–87; as well as his exemplary *Designs within Disorder: Franklin D. Roosevelt, the Economists, and the Shaping of American Economic Policy 1933–1945* (New York: Cambridge University Press, 1996), 1–3, 64–67, 108–12, 117–120, 120–31, and passim. An appreciation of the theoretical eclecticism that often characterized New Deal economic policy discussions in Washington may be won from John Morton Blum, *From the Morgenthau Diaries: Years of Crisis, 1928–1938* (Boston: Houghton Mifflin, 1959). On the development of "stagnation theories" concerning the performance of mature economies, see my "Explaining America's Greatest Depression: A Reconsideration of an Older Literature," *Revista di Storia Economica*, 2d ser. (1985), 155–74. Also useful in this regard is William E. Stoneman, *A History of the Economic Analysis of the Great Depression in America* (New York: Garland, 1979). Keynes's dramatic attack upon neoclassical theory is found, of course, in *The General Theory of Employment, Interest, and Money* (New York: Harcourt, Brace). Expansion in the number of Ph.D. economists being trained at the nation's universities continued throughout the 1930s. By 1939, the leading institution in this regard was Harvard.

5. See Lewis H. Haney (New York University Business School) to Dewey, 11 October 1935, RAEA, Box 60 (Folder: "1935"). Also see Luther Gulick (Director of Research, Commission of Inquiry on Public Service Personnel) to Deibler, 25 March 1935; and Deibler to Morris A. Copeland (Department of Economics, University of Michigan), 29 November 1935; both in RAEA, Box 56 (Folder: "AEA 1935–36 Committee on Public Personnel Report—Corr. with Deibler, Sec."); as well as Minutes of Executive Committee, 5 May 1933, RAEA, Box 60 (Folder: "1933").

6. I discuss this issue at some length in my *Great Depression*, chap. 7. Also see Ellis W. Hawley, *The New Deal and the Problem of Monopoly: A Study in Economic Ambivalence* (Princeton, N.J.: Princeton University Press, 1966), especially chap. 2. William Barber deftly portrays the eclecticism of economic policy debate in the Roosevelt administration in his "Government as a Laboratory for Economic Learning in the Years of the Democratic Roosevelt," in *The State and Economic Knowledge: The American and British Experiences*, ed. Mary O. Furner and Barry Supple (New York: Cambridge University Press, 1990), 103–37. Roosevelt's declaration of the need for "bold, persistent experimentation" in national policy came in his first presidential campaign. See Franklin D. Roosevelt, *The Public Papers and Addresses of Franklin D. Roosevelt* (New York: Macmillan, 1941), vol. 5, 233–34.

7. See Jordan A. Schwarz, *The New Dealers: Power Politics in the Age of Roosevelt* (New York: Knopf, 1993), 185–86. For an important contribution regarding the breadth and diversity of debates that transpired among New Deal economists, see Theodore Rosenof, *Economics in the Long Run: New Deal Theorists and Their Legacies, 1933–1993* (Chapel Hill: University of North Carolina Press, 1997). Also see Roger Sandilands, *The Life and Political Economy of Lauchlin Currie: New Dealer, Presidential Adviser, and Development Economist* (Durham, N.C.: Duke University Press, 1990).

8. The movement of the Roosevelt government between opposing notions of appropriate industrial recovery policy is the central ingredient in the traditional perception of a "first" and a "second" New Deal, the former focused on planning and regulation, the latter emphasizing antitrust enforcement, improved labor relations, and compensatory fiscal spending. The notion of two New Deals was first formulated by Basil Rauch in *The History of the New Deal: 1933–1938* (New York: Creative Age Press, 1944), vi. The highly politicized nature of Roosevelt's spending decisions is most ably documented by Gavin Wright, "The Political Economy of New Deal Spending: An Econometric Analysis," *Review of Economics and Statistics* 56 (1974), 262–81. The conception of the "multiplier" effects of fiscal spending, that each dollar disbursed in government purchases will generate far more than a dollar in total revenues as orders reverberate through the nation's labor and product markets, is a central theme in Keynesian theory. See, for example, Paul A. Samuelson, "Interaction between the Multiplier Analysis and the Principle of Acceleration," *Review of Economics and Statistics* 21 (1939), 75–78. That New Deal fiscal spending was quite low and, on balance, often contractionary is discussed by E. Cary Brown, "Fiscal Policy in the 'Thirties: A Reappraisal," *American Economic Review* 46 (1956), 857–79. As pointed out by Alvin Hansen, in fact, aggregate public works expenditures during the 1930s (for federal, state, and local governments combined) did not equal their precrash levels until 1938. See Hansen's "Was Fiscal Policy in the Thirties a Failure?" *Review of Economics and Statistics* 45 (1963), 320–23. One of the best discussions of Roosevelt's unanticipated gambit at the 1933 World Economic Conference, taking the nation off gold, is to be found in Albert U. Romasco, *The Politics of Recovery: Roosevelt's New Deal* (New York: Oxford University Press, 1983), 44–45.

9. Ironically enough, where a particular economic expertise had pride of place in the New Deal was in the agricultural recovery agencies and programs. The focus and success of New Deal agricultural policy stand in sharp contrast to the mixed record elsewhere. A particularly fine exploration of the evidence in this regard is Sally Clarke's *Regulation and the Revolution in United States Farm Productivity* (New York: Cambridge University Press, 1994). It seems safe to say that once again the nation's greater experience with centralized agricultural regulation, along with the very strong intellectual trajectory of the agricultural economics field, made the difference. The Tennessee Valley Authority was another success story in this regard, garnering international attention from as far away as Palestine as other nations sought advice on how to develop and revitalize rural areas. See Schwarz, *The New Dealers*, 120; and David E. Lilienthal, *The Journals of David E. Lilienthal: The TVA Years 1939–1945* (New York: Harper and Row, 1964), 594–95.

10. This impression emerges from a consideration of the correspondence Fisher maintained with Roosevelt throughout the 1930s. See, for example, Fisher to Roosevelt, 2 March 1933; Fisher to Roosevelt, 24 November 1933; Fisher to Roosevelt, 30 April 1933; Fisher to Roosevelt, 19 March 1933; Fisher to Roosevelt, 23 October 1934; Fisher to Roosevelt, 30 August 1934; Fisher to Roosevelt, 29 April 1935; Fisher to Roosevelt, 21 August 1935; Fisher to Roosevelt, 30 March 1938; and Fisher to Roosevelt, 22 November 1944; all in Box 1 (Folder: "Fisher, Irving; Fragmentary Papers, 1933–1944; MS68-7"), the papers of Irving Fisher [hereafter PIF], Franklin Delano Roosevelt Library, Hyde park, New York. The president's replies were always courteous yet brief, assuring Fisher that he "appreciate[d] [Fisher's] continued interest in letting [his] views on current economic problems" be known. See Roosevelt to Fisher, 14 April 1938; as well as Roosevelt to Fisher, 16 April 1938; Roosevelt to Fisher, 28 June 1938; Roosevelt to Fisher, 12 September 1938; Roosevelt to Fisher, 13 March 1939; Roosevelt to Fisher, 21 April 1939; and Roosevelt to Fisher, 29 June 1939; all in PIF, Box 1 (Folder: "Fisher, Irving; Fragmentary Papers, 1933–1944; MS68-7"). Much more of an insider than Fisher ever was, Princeton's Jacob Viner, having served in the Treasury Department during Roosevelt's first two terms, nevertheless ultimately felt compelled to resign when he could no longer accept the wage-setting strategies of the National Industrial Recovery Act and their attendant financial implications. See Viner to Alexander Sachs (Vice-President, the Lehman Corporation, and recent Director of the Division of Research and Planning of the National Recovery Administration), 25 May 1934 in the Papers of Alexander Sachs, Franklin Delano Roosevelt Library, Box 85 (Folder: "Viner, Jacob"); and Viner to Henry Morgenthau, Jr. (Secretary of the Treasury), 14 April 1938, in the Papers of Henry Morgenthau, Jr., Franklin Del-

ano Roosevelt Library, Box 301 (Folder: "Viner, Jacob and Family 1935–1943").

11. See the excellent survey of the historical process by which national accounting became a government function in Mark Perlman, "Political Purpose and the National Accounts," in *The Politics of Numbers* ed. William Alonso and Paul Starr (New York: Russell Sage Foundation, 1987), 133–51. Also see Joseph W. Duncan and William C. Shelton, *Revolution in United States Government Statistics, 1926–1976* (Washington, D.C.: United States Department of Commerce, 1978); as well as Carol S. Carson, "The History of the United States National Income and Products Accounts: The Development of an Analytical Tool," *Review of Income and Wealth* 21 (1975), 153–81. Kuznets's enterprise was pursued under the aegis of the Commerce Department's Bureau of Foreign and Domestic Commerce. The bureau was essentially led by Willard Thorp and Robert F. Martin, both of whom were assisted by Winfield Riefler, then chair of the Central Statistical Board. The initial national product calculations, made at the Senate's request, were published in the January, August, and November 1935 issues, as well as the July 1936 issue, of the *Survey of Current Business*. See Perlman, "Political Purpose and the National Accounts," 139.

12. See Perlman, "Political Purpose and the National Accounts," 140. Keynes's inability to persuade Franklin Roosevelt to his point of view, regarding recovery policy, has been much remarked upon by historians and biographers. An excellent consideration of that impasse is offered in Barber, "Government as a Laboratory for Economic Learning," 106–17. One of the best surveys of the early intellectual history of Keynesian doctrine is Peter Clarke, *The Keynesian Revolution in the Making, 1924–1936* (Oxford: Clarendon Press, 1988). Also of interest is David C. Colander and Harry Landreth, eds., *The Coming of Keynesianism to America: Conversations with the Founders of Keynesian Economics* (Cheltenham, England: Elgar, 1996).

13. According to one of his most famous biographers, Roosevelt himself was, with the onset of the depression of 1937, Japan's ongoing yet undeclared war with China, and Germany's earlier seizure of the Rhineland, quite self-conscious of the need to transform his public image from that of "Dr. New Deal" to "Dr. Win-the-War." See James MacGregor Burns, *Roosevelt: The Lion and the Fox* (New York: Harcourt, Brace,

1956), epilogue. William Leuchtenberg, in a now-classic article "The New Deal as Analogue of War," reprinted in his *The FDR Years: On Roosevelt and His Legacy* (New York: Columbia University Press, 1995), 35–75, noted the several ways in which New Deal programs built upon and emulated the federal bureaucracies created to prosecute World War I. Indeed, in several cases, the same personnel were recruited to work within those New Deal agencies that, in Leuchtenberg's words, served as virtually direct analogues of those they had served during the Great War. It is not surprising, therefore, that such a historical continuity could carry forward to World War II.

14. See Perlman, "Political Purpose and the National Accounts," 144. As Perlman shows, Kuznets and Nathan initially calculated that for 1942 the national economy could produce 40,000 tanks, 50,000 airplanes, and 7 million tons of merchant shipping capacity. FDR, upon being informed of these estimates, raised the "promised" levels to 45,000 tanks, 60,000 planes, and 8 million tons of shipping capacity. He went further, posing the following goals for 1943: 75,000 tanks, 125,000 planes, and 20 million tons of shipping. Perlman offers as well a more general and thought-provoking observation concerning the impact of World War II on the economics profession when he writes: "If the war gave the medical profession antibiotics, it gave economists new tools and techniques and comparable optimism about what their future role would be" (146). An excellent discussion of the work of Kuznets and Nathan is provided by Michael Edelstein, "The Size of U.S. Armed Forces during WWII" (unpublished manuscript, Department of Economics, Queens College, City University of New York, 1997).

15. Again, see the excellent discussion by Perlman, "Political Purpose and the National Accounts," 144–45. That the American military was at first quite hostile to the efforts of Kuznets and Nathan is discussed by Perlman and by John E. Brigante, *The Feasibility Dispute: Determination of War Production Objectives for 1942 and 1943* (Washington, D.C.: Committee on Public Administration Cases, 1950). Also see Merton J. Peck and Frederic M. Scherer, *The Weapons Acquisition Process: An Economic Analysis* (Boston: Harvard University Graduate School of Business, 1962), for insight into the enduring influence of the World War II research on military-industrial feasibility issues and procurement strategies.

16. Wartime economic expertise was also impressively displayed in the coordination of international finance (among the Allies) and, ultimately, the postwar management of exchange-rate policies. While not focused upon in this study, the impact of the work of international economists on governmental practice, not to mention the effect that American geopolitical commitments and interests had on their work, are also important parts of the twentieth-century history of the profession. Indeed, within the U.S. State Department, there emerged by the late 1940s a cadre of specialists, dubbed "The Economists" by their detractors, who became intimately involved with the postwar implementation of such things as the Bretton Woods agreements, the General Agreement on Tariffs and Trade (the GATT), the European Recovery Program (the Marshall Plan), and the economic aspects of the occupations of Germany and Japan. Perhaps most prominent among these individuals was Willard Thorp, who maintained close ties with the academic wing of the discipline throughout his public career. In this regard, see, for example, Georg Schild, *Bretton Woods and Dumbarton Oaks: American Economic and Political Postwar Planning in the Summer of 1944* (New York: St. Martin's, 1995); Richard S. Sayers, *Financial Policy: 1939–45* (London: HMSO, 1956); William S. Borden, *The Pacific Alliance: United States Foreign Economic Policy and Japanese Trade Recovery, 1947–1955* (Madison: University of Wisconsin Press, 1984); and Michael Schaller, *The American Occupation of Japan: The Origins of the Cold War in Asia* (New York: Oxford University Press, 1985). The postwar international context is further and most ably surveyed in Diane B. Kunz, *Butter and Guns: America's Cold War Economic Diplomacy* (New York: Free Press, 1997).

17. See, for example, United States Bureau of the Budget, War Records Section, *The United States at War: Development and Administration of the War Program by the Federal Government* (Washington, D.C.: U.S. Government Printing Office, n.d.), 521–29—part of a series of "Historical Reports on War Administration" issued by the Bureau of the Budget. Interestingly enough, the war also breathed new life into that unique product of the policy imagination bequeathed by the Hoover administration, the Reconstruction Finance Corporation (RFC). The exigencies of war allowed the RFC to be even more aggressive

and flexible in its activities than had the pressures of the depression. Between 1940 and 1945, the RFC disbursed $39.5 billion to manufacturing and extractive industries of crucial importance to the success of the mission of the armed services. See James S. Olson, *Saving Capitalism: The Reconstruction Finance Corporation and the New Deal, 1933–1940* (Princeton, N.J.: Princeton University Press, 1988), 216–27. Robert D. Cuff, in "War Mobilization, Institutional Learning, and State Building in the United States," in *The State and Social Investigation in Britain and the United States*, ed. Michael J. Lacey and Mary O. Furner (Cambridge: Cambridge University Press, 1993), 388–425, demonstrates how experienced World War I administrators were effectively used in the far more demanding context of World War II.

18. From Katz, *Foreign Intelligence*, 8–9, and chap. 4. Katz notes that the hiring of Paul Sweezy required a preliminary interview of the young graduate student by the director of OSS, General William Donovan. Also of interest, in this regard, are *Oral History Memoir of Charles P. Kindleberger* (16 July 1973, by Richard D. McKinzie, Cambridge, Massachusetts), Harry S. Truman Library; Independence, Missouri, passim; *Oral History Interview with Edward S. Mason* (17 July 1973, by Richard D. McKinzie, Cambridge, Massachusetts), Harry S. Truman Library; Independence, Missouri, 2–3; Robin W. Winks, *Cloak and Gown: Scholars in the Secret War, 1939–1961* (New York: William Morrow, 1987). The "Secret War" generated other impacts that would have an enduring influence on the evolution not simply of economics but of virtually all fields in the engineering, life, natural, and social sciences—all attendant upon the stimulus it gave to the development of high-speed methods of computation. In the work of American cryptanalysts on the communication codes of the Japanese, and in the celebrated success of Alan Turing and his colleagues in cracking the German "Enigma" cypher at their Bletchley Park facility in Britain, World War II also facilitated the birth of the computer. It would be hard to overemphasize the significance, for the later twentieth-century evolution of mathematical economics and econometrics, of this wartime advancement in the creation of artificial intelligence.

19. The economic notion of "opportunity cost," as that value (measured in money or goods and services) surrendered for something in order

to secure it in competition with other uses and needs, is one of the core precepts of neoclassical doctrine.

20. See United States Bureau of the Budget, War Records Section, *The United States at War*, 113. Employing neoclassical concepts in the investigation of allocative choice problems also set the stage for the application of similar ideas to problems of strategic choice during the cold war. These matters are taken up in detail in the next chapter of this study.

21. Further discussion of the significant impact of Koopmans's wartime research on the trajectory of the economics discipline in the postwar era is taken up in the next chapter. On Koopmans's early career in the United States, see E. Roy Weintraub, *General Equilibrium Analysis: Studies in Appraisal* (New York: Cambridge University Press, 1985), 90. The history of the Cowles Foundation itself is relevant to these issues; particularly informative are Kenneth J. Arrow, "Cowles in the History of Economic Thought," and Gerard Debreu, "Mathematical Economics at Cowles," both in *Cowles Fiftieth Anniversary: Four Essays and an Index of Publications* (New Haven, Conn.: Cowles Foundation for Research in Economics, 1991), 1–24 and 25–48, respectively; as well as Clifford Hildreth, *The Cowles Commission in Chicago, 1939–1955* (New York: Springer-Verlag, 1986). Also see Carl F. Christ, "The History of the Cowles Commission," in *Economic Theory and Measurement: A Twenty Year Report, 1932–1952* (Chicago: Cowles Commission for Research in Economics, 1952), 3–66; Christ, "The Cowles Commission's Contributions to Econometrics at Chicago, 1939–1955," *Journal of Economic Literature* 32 (1994), 30–59; and Lawrence R. Klein, "Econometrics at Cowles, 1944–47," *Banco Nazionale del Lavoro Quarterly Review* 177 (1991), 107–17. Also see United States Bureau of the Budget, War Records Section, *The United States at War*, chap. 6 (esp. pp. 143–54), "Transporting the Goods."

22. From Katz, *Foreign Intelligence*, 198. There can be no doubt that much of the historical picture sketched here concerning the economics profession could be reproduced with respect to most, if not all, other professional fields. For example, during World War II, the Manhattan Project clearly transformed physics, and the needs of the armed forces spawned dramatic changes in medical science and practice. But again, in more academic areas, similar forces (and opportunities) came to bear on practitioners. The work of anthropologists for the navy in the Pacific archipelagoes, survey research on draftees and enlistees conducted by sociologists concerned to facilitate the adjustment of civilians to military life, studies of the ingredients of democratic stability undertaken by political scientists for army occupation authorities, and intelligence analyses executed by historians for the OSS are but a few cases in point. See, for example, Daniel Kevles, *The Physicists: The History of a Scientific Community in Modern America* (New York: Knopf, 1977); Albert E. Cowdrey, *Fighting for Life: American Military Medicine in World War II* (New York: Free Press, 1994); and P. Buck, "Adjusting to Military Life: The Social Sciences Go to War, 1941–1950," in *Military Enterprise and Technological Change: Perspectives on the American Experience*, ed. Merritt Roe Smith (Cambridge: MIT Press, 1985), 203–52. Peter Novick offers a striking portrait of the historical profession during both World War II and the succeeding cold war in *That Noble Dream: The "Objectivity Question" and the American Historical Profession* (New York: Cambridge University Press, 1988), chap. 10. With respect to the natural sciences, and contemporary sources, also of interest are George W. Gray, *Science at War* (New York: Harper and Brothers, 1943); Irvin Stewart, *Organizing Scientific Research for War* (New York: Little, Brown, 1948); and Roy F. Nichols, "War and Research in Social Science," *American Philosophical Society Proceedings* 87 (1944), 361–64. A more personalized reflection upon the profound influence of the wartime experience on the economics profession is found in John Kenneth Galbraith, *A Life in Our Time* (London: Deutsch, 1981).

23. Some excellent contemporary narratives concerning the economic and logistical achievements of the national war effort are Seymour E. Harris, *Price and Related Controls in the United States* (New York: McGraw-Hill, 1945); Bruce Catton, *The War Lords of Washington* (New York: Harcourt, Brace, 1948); Eliot Janeway, *The Struggle for Survival: A Chronicle of Economic Mobilization in World War II* (New Haven, Conn.: Yale University Press, 1951); Donald M. Nelson, *Arsenal of Democracy: The Story of American War Production* (New York: Harcourt, Brace, 1946); and United States Civilian Production Administration, *Industrial Mobilization for*

War: History of the War Production Board and Predecessor Agencies, 1940–1945 (Washington, D.C.: U.S. Government Printing Office, 1947).

24. The special meeting of the AEA Executive Committee was held on 23 March 1940. See James Washington Bell (AEA Secretary-Treasurer) to Paul Homan (Cornell University), 4 April 1940; James W. Angell (Columbia University) to Bell, 20 April 1940; Homan to Bell, 11 July 1940; all in RAEA, Box 57 (Folder: "1940–1944 Classification of Personnel").

25. Carl C. Brigham (Chair, Social Science Research Council) to Bell, 10 October 1940; Brigham to Bell, 15 October 1940; Bell to Paul Homan (Cornell University), 4 April 1940; James W. Angell to Bell, 20 April 1940; Homan to Bell, 11 July 1940; all in RAEA, Box 57 (Folder: "1940–1944 Classification of Personnel").

26. Records of the Special Executive Committee Meeting on Classification, 23 March 1941 and 24 March 1941, Bell to Special Executive Committee and the Editorial Board of the *American Economic Review*, 22 February 1940. Some Association members were not unmindful of the fact that wartime mobilization and deployment of personnel would not directly address deeper questions concerning categorization. Frederick Mills of Columbia University wrote Homan on 19 October 1940 that the "appropriate classification of economists, economic activities and economic publications is a broader matter than is the special problem we face right now"; RAEA, Box 57 (Folder: "1940–1944 Classification of Personnel").

27. Leonard Carmichael (Director, National Resources Planning Board) to Bell, 17 June 1941; Steuart Henderson Britt (National Roster of Scientific and Specialized Personnel) to Sumner Slichter, 27 November 1941; both in RAEA, Box 57 (Folder: "1940–1944 Classification of Personnel"); Copeland (now of Office of Production Management) to Slichter, 8 December 1941; Slichter to AEA Executive Committee, 23 December 1941; Bell to Slichter, 1 May 1941; all in RAEA, Box 29 (Folder: "Correspondence A–L 1941"); Clyde E. Holmes (Office of Production Management) to Bell, 3 October 1941, RAEA, Box 29 (Folder: "Correspondence M–Z 1941").

28. Britt to Presidents and Secretaries of Professional Societies, 31 January 1942, RAEA, Box 57 (Folder: "Classification of Personnel"); V. H. Yahnke (U.S. Civil Service Commission) to AEA, 29 May 1943); Bell to Yahnke, 13 July

1943; both in RAEA, Box 31 (Folder: "Correspondence A–L 1943"); Carmichael (now of War Manpower Commission) to Bell, 12 August 1943, RAEA, Box 32 (Folder: "Correspondence M–Z 1943").

29. Lloyd E. Blauch (Federal Security Agency) to Bell, 9 August 1943; Bell to Blauch, 11 August 1943; both in RAEA, Box 31 (Folder: "Correspondence M–Z 1943"); Edwin G. Nourse to Bell, 1 July 1942; Bell to Nourse, 3 July 1942; Bell to Nourse, 21 April 1942; Nourse to Bell, 18 April 1942; all in RAEA, Box 30 (Folder: "Edwin G. Nourse 1942"). The Harvard University Department of Economics, only months after Germany's attack on Poland, established a course for undergraduates and graduate students on "war economics," seeking the advice of government officials regarding curricular content. See, for example, Seymour E. Harris (Harvard University) to Richard Gilbert (Director of Research, U.S. Department of Commerce), 10 January 1940, as well as Gilbert to Harris, 17 January 1940, in the Papers of Richard Gilbert, Franklin Delano Roosevelt Library (Hyde Park, New York), Box 8 (Folder: "Harris, Seymour E. 1940–42").

30. Edward S. Mason to Homan, 19 October 1940; Homan to Mason, 25 October 1940; Homan to Aaron Director (Brookings Institution), 3 October 1940; Director to Homan, 15 October 1940; Homan to Slichter, 16 October 1940; Slichter to Homan, 13 November 1940; Homan to Slichter, 18 November 1940; R. B. Heflebower to Homan, 22 July 1941; Homan to Heflebower, 10 August 1941; all in RAEA, Box 91 (Folder: "AER 1940–41 Defense Program"). All the more interesting because it was written well over a year before the nation's formal entry into the war, Mason's letter to Homan, of 19 October 1940, provided a systematic list of the kinds of topics he thought appropriate for making the *Review* more relevant to wartime concerns, such as national income and defense expenditures, the national capacity to produce military equipment, production priorities scheduling, defense plant location economics, defense plant amortization methods, defense labor economics, consumer economics, governmental contracting techniques for war, wartime price controls, and the problem of excess profits in defense production. In the summer of 1941, Homan directly approached Simon Kuznets at the University of Pennsylvania, suggesting he do a *Review* article

on the nation's war potential modeled on similar work done by Keynes in Great Britain. Kuznets declined. See Homan to Kuznets, 15 August 1941; and Kuznets to Homan, 15 September 1941; both in RAEA, Box 91 (Folder: "AER 1940–41 Defense Program").

31. "Report on Wartime Changes in Economics Curriculum," 7 July 1943 and 15 July 1943, RAEA, Box 32 (Folder: "Correspondence M–Z 1943").

32. Ibid. The United States Department of Agriculture spearheaded particular efforts to revise graduate training in agricultural economics in light of wartime needs and concerns. Mordecai Ezekiel, then an economic adviser to the chief of the Bureau of Agricultural Economics in the DOA, facilitated the enterprise. See, for example, Frederick W. Waugh (Social Sciences Department Chair, USDOA Graduate School) and Lewis H. Rohrbaugh (Director, USDOA Graduate School) to Ezekiel, 29 November 1945; in the Papers of Mordecai Ezekiel; Franklin Delano Roosevelt Library (Hyde Park, New York), Box 1 (Folder: "Agriculture. U.S. Department of: Graduate School, Advisory Committee on General Economics [1945–46]").

33. Horace Taylor to the AEA Executive Committee, 16 December 1944; J. S. Davis to Taylor, 22 May 1944; Davis to Joseph Spengler, 19 May 1944; Davis to Paul M. O'Leary, 19 May 1944; Bell to Taylor, 20 September 1944; Davis to Taylor, 22 and 28 September and 7 October 1944; Taylor to Bell, 18 October 1944; Bell to Taylor, 23 October 1944; M. M. Knight to Bell, 28 January 1945; Leonard L. Watkins to Taylor, 8 March 1945; Claude E. Hawley (Federal Security Agency) to Bell, 11 September 1950; Bell to Hawley, 20 September 1950; all in RAEA, Box 58 (Folder: "AEA 1944–1951 Committee on Undergraduate Teaching of Economics and Training of Economists"); Davis to AEA Executive Committee, 19 April 1944, RAEA, Box 32 (Folder: "Joseph S. Davis"). Also see Report by the "(Ad Hoc) Committee on Graduate Training in Economics" to the AEA Executive Committee, 1 December 1950; Bell to Howard R. Bowen, 30 October 1950 and 17 April 1951 and 9 May 1951 and 6 June 1951; Bell to Spengler, 14 September 1951; Bowen to Bell, 8 October 1953; Herbert E. Longenecker (Dean, University of Pittsburgh) to Bell, 8 December 1953; Harold L. Hazen (Dean, Massachusetts Institute of Technology) to Bell, 8 December 8 1953; Joseph H. Park (Dean, New

York University) to Bell, 22 December 1953; all in RAEA, Box 58 (Folder: "AEA 1950–53 (Ad Hoc) Committee on Graduate Training in Economics"). Invited to be "scrutineers" of the final committee report sent to university officials were Milton Friedman, I. L. Sharfman, and Joseph Spengler. Also see "The Committee on the Undergraduate Teaching of Economists and the Training of Economists," *American Economic Review* 40 (1950); "Economics in General Education: Roundtable on Report of the Committee on the Teaching of Elementary Economics," *American Economic Review* 41 (1951), 697–716; and Howard Bowen, "Graduate Education in Economics," *American Economic Review* 43 (1953), 1–23.

34. RAEA, Box 57 (Folder: "AEA 1944 Committee on Focusing of Informed Opinion").

35. RAEA, Box 57 (Folder: "AEA 1944–1945 Committee to Draft Consensus Report on Function of Government in the Postwar American Economy"). Also see Herbert Feis to Emanual Goldenweiser, 23 February 1944; Goldenweiser to Feis, 24 February 1944; and Stephen Enke (UCLA) to Goldenweiser, 5 May 1944; all in the Papers of E. A. Goldenweiser, Manuscript Division, Library of Congress, Washington, D.C., Box 1 (Folder: "Correspondence 1940–52").

36. RAEA, Box 57 (Folder: "AEA 1944–1945 Committee to Draft Consensus Report on Function of Government in the Postwar American Economy"). In June 1945, Willford King, working on a "Handbook of Accepted Economics," found that "on average" at least 90 percent of the members of the AEA endorsed his material. "[I]t seems," he believed, "that [he had] proved conclusively that economists d[id] agree on most . . . primary principles." See RAEA, Box 57 (Folder: "AEA 1945–1946 Committee on Consensus Reports"). Also see Bell to I. L. Sharfman, 15 March 1945, RAEA, Box 33 (Folder: "Pres. I. L. Sharfman, 1945"). The Webb-Pomerene Act, passed in 1918, exempted such antitrust violations as price-fixing from prosecution provided they were related to export sales.

37. Bell to National Roster of Scientific and Specialized Personnel, 12 March 1948; Hawley to Bell, 5 May 1950; Bell to Hawley, 28 June 1950; all in RAEA, Box 58 (Folder: "AEA 1948–50 National Roster of Scientific and Specialized Personnel"). Concerns about educating veterans

to the nature of the economics profession persisted into the Korean War years. See Bell to Dean E. McIntire (Veterans Administration; Kansas City, Missouri), 20 December 1954; McIntire to Bell, 16 December 1954; both in RAEA, Box 39 (Folder: "American Economic Assoc. Corr. 1954, M–Z"); and Olin S. Lutes (Veterans Administration) to Bell, 11 July 1952, RAEA, Box 37 (Folder: "American Economic Assoc. Corr. 1952, M–Z"). In August 1945 the Association was approached by the army with regard to veterans of a different sort. German prisoners of war at Concordia, Kansas, had been receiving the *American Economic Review* because it was held that this "served a useful purpose indeed in the[ir] re-education . . . to the realities of the situation and toward a Democratic conception of life." The prison camp headquarters wished to know if it might translate the journal for use by a greater number of its prisoners. This would be "useful to [the army's] purposes for the balance of the time [the] Prisoners . . . remain[ed] in this country . . . [and would] be helpful in promoting a proper mental attitude among the German people and therefore . . . promote likewise the cause of lasting peace." The Association had no objection. Karl C. Teufel (U.S. Army Captain, Headquarters—Prisoner of War Camp, Concordia-Kansas) to the Association, 25 August 1945; Bell to Teufel, 11 September 1945; both in RAEA, Box 32 (Folder: "Correspondence M–Z 1945"). Also of interest in this regard is Ron Robin, *The Barbed-Wire College: Re-educating German POWs in the United States during World War II* (Princeton, N.J.: Princeton University Press, 1995).

38. Kenneth R. Shaffer (American Book Center for War Devastated Libraries) to Bell, 8 August 1946; John O. Coppock (U.N. Relief and Rehabilitation Administration—Greece Mission) to the Association, 13 August 1946; Joseph D. Coppock (U.S. Department of State) to E. A. Goldenweiser, 7 October 1946; all in RAEA, Box 33 (Folder: "Correspondence A–L 1946"). Robert Outsen (U.S. Army Colonel) to the Association, 3 May 1951; Bell to Outsen, 18 May 1951; both in RAEA, Box 36 (Folder: "American Economic Assoc. Corr. 1951, M–Z"). Also see Bell to Devereaux C. Josephs (Carnegie Corporation), 26 December 1946; Bell to Taylor, 2 March 1948; Paul H. Douglas to Bell, 8 April 1948; all in RAEA, Box 58 (Folder: "AEA 1948–1949 Committee on Aid to Foreign Scholars"). The generational consequences of Ameri-

can involvement in the restructuring of foreign economics departments are most telling with respect to Japan. Most of those Japanese economists who had resisted militarism were left-wing. By the 1960s the rather strange result had emerged whereby young students of economics in Japan were considerably more conservative than their professors. Not surprisingly, many talented young Japanese then pursued their doctoral degrees in the United States, where their political convictions and interests were closer to those of their supervisors. Of course, in the United States and much of Europe the opposite intergenerational political split emerged between students and faculty in the sixties. A more systematic discussion of the transnational influence and authority the American economics profession came to enjoy in the later twentieth century is taken up in my "Knowledge Production, Professional Authority, and the State: The Case of American Economics during and after World War II," in *What Do Economists Know? New Economics of Knowledge*, ed. Robert Garnett (London: Routledge, 1999), 103–23.

39. RAEA, Box 93 (Folder: "AER July 1944 AEA-ALA Book List on Economics for European Libraries"). On the role of postwar reconstruction in the twentieth-century Americanization of Europe and Asia, see, for example, Michael J. Hogan, "American Marshall Planners and the Search for a European Neocapitalism," *American Historical Review* 90 (1985), 44–72; Charles S. Maier, "The Politics of Productivity: Foundations of American International Economic Policy after World War II," *International Organization* 31 (1977), 607–33; Armin Rappaport, "The United States and European Integration: The First Phase," *Diplomatic History* 5 (1981), 121–49; Borden, *The Pacific Alliance*; David Horowitz, ed., *Corporations and the Cold War* (New York: Monthly Review Press, 1969); Charles L. Mee Jr., *The Marshall Plan: The Launching of the Pax Americana* (New York: Simon and Schuster, 1984); and Alan S. Milward, *The Reconstruction of Western Europe, 1945–1951* (London: Methuen, 1984).

40. Maurice C. Mackey, Jr. (U.S. Air Force Lieutenant, Air Force Academy) to Bell, 5 November 1956; and Bell to Mackey, 19 November 1956; both in RAEA, Box 41 (Folder: "American Economic Assoc. Corr.-1956, M–Z"). Also see Lee Nichols (U.S. Information Agency) to Bell, 13 April 1959; Nichols to Bell, 30 March 1959; Bell to Nichols, 14 April 1959; all in RAEA, Box

45 (Folder: "American Economic Assoc. 1959 Correspondence, M–Z"). "Linear programming" (or, as it was sometimes called, "activity analysis") was the formal term for the allocative modeling undertaken by Tjalling Koopmans and others. "Input-output analysis" involved the mathematical simulation of all of the activities taking place within the macroeconomy as a whole. One of the groundbreaking contributions to this research was made by Harvard's Wassily Leontieff in *The Structure of American Economy, 1919–1939: An Empirical Application of Equilibrium Analysis* (New York: Oxford University Press, 1951).

41. A complicated exception to this generalization would apparently be that of Keynesianism insofar as Keynes's critique of neoclassical thinking was also seemingly legitimated by the experiences of World War II. In point of fact, the extent to which Keynesian theory is indeed "antineoclassical" is open to debate, and the speed with which Keynesian ideas were ultimately reabsorbed into the neoclassical corpus, in the postwar period, a telling historical challenge to the original premise. These matters are taken up in further detail in subsequent chapters of this study.

42. A sense of the anxieties some colleagues, especially institutionalists during the interwar years, had about the broadening domain of mathematics in economics may be won from the correspondence of the editors of the *American Economic Review*. See, for example, A. B. Wolfe (Ohio State University) to Davis R. Dewey, 6 March 1935, RAEA, Box 85 (Folder: "AER 1935 MSS. Returned"); John Ise (University of Kansas) to Dewey, 1 February 1939, RAEA, Box 60 (Folder: "1939"); Lewis Haney (New York University) to Dewey, 1939?, RAEA, Box 89 (Folder: "AER 1939 H"); and Walton Hamilton to Dewey, 9 February 1939, RAEA, Box 89 (Folder: "AER 1939 Hamilton-Mund Controversy"). Also see Lewis Haney to Paul T. Homan, 16 January 1941, RAEA, Box 91 (Folder: "AER 1940–41 Editorial Policy").

43. See Dewey to Smith, 27 December 1932, RAEA, Box 60 (Folder: "1932").

44. It is not surprising, in this context, to note that the eminent British economist Joan Robinson could argue in 1975 that neoclassical economics had more applicability in a planned or wartime economy than in a decentralized market setting. See her "Consumer Sovereignty in a Planned Economy," in her *Collected Economic Papers* (Oxford: Blackwell, 1975), vol. 3, 70–81. Armed conflict brings a necessary centralization of control within societies, along with a powerful "simplification of objectives" by which leaders and the public can quickly and efficiently make decisions. As a corollary to this well-documented social and political impact of war there emerges an attenuation of political conflict and economic contestation as societies make efforts to position themselves adequately with respect to a common enemy. Modern American economics, viewed in this light, emerges as the product of an effort to understand and interact with an altogether unique and contingent set of circumstances—conditions that have little, if anything, to do with a peacetime economy structured to foster the accumulation of private wealth in decentralized market settings. On war as a "simplification of objectives," see Lionel Robbins, *The Economic Problem in Peace and War: Some Reflections on Objectives and Mechanism* (London: Macmillan, 1947); as well as Forest H. Capie and Geoffrey E. Wood, "The Anatomy of a Wartime Inflation: Britain, 1939–1945," in *The Sinews of War: Essays on the Economic History of World War II*, ed. Geoffrey T. Mills and Hugh Rockoff (Ames: Iowa State University Press, 1993), 21–42.

45. Data on foundation support of academic research during the 1930s may be gathered from Raymond Rich Associates, *American Foundations and Their Fields*, vols. 2–5 (New York: Twentieth Century Fund, 1931–42; as well as Roger L. Geiger, *To Advance Knowledge: The Growth of American Research Universities, 1900–1940* (New York: Oxford University Press, 1986), 253–64. The shortfall in independent-sector grants was all the more dramatic and disconcerting given the fact that the number of operating foundations, during the same years, rose by roughly a third. Rebecca S. Lowen, in *Creating the Cold War University: The Transformation of Stanford* (Berkeley: University of California Press, 1997), 17–42, provides a compelling portrait of the transformative impact of the 1930s experience on the institutional perceptions and funding strategies of university administrators and faculty investigators. Also of interest in this regard is Samuel Klausner and Victor Lidz, eds., *The Nationalization of the Social Sciences* (Philadelphia: University of Pennsylvania Press, 1986); and V. Ray Cardozier, *Colleges and Universities in World War 2* (Westport, Conn.: Praeger, 1993).

Chapter 4
On Behalf of the National Security State

1. From the introduction to Tjalling C. Koopmans, ed., *Activity Analysis of Production and Allocation: Proceedings of a Conference* (New York: Wiley, 1951). Koopmans (1910–84), who received the 1975 Nobel Memorial Prize in Economic Science, originally trained in mathematics and physics at the University of Utrecht and the University of Leiden. By 1936 his interests had turned toward economics and econometrics, stimulated in part by work he did for the League of Nations in Geneva on the abstract analysis of economic time series and the applied study of merchant shipping networks. His experience with the League served him well when, on his emigration to the United States in 1940, he undertook his remarkable service for the Combined Shipping Adjustment Board in Washington, D.C. At the end of World War II, Koopmans moved to the Cowles Commission at the University of Chicago (which subsequently became the Cowles Foundation at Yale University). Within these venues he executed the research on "activity analysis" that had such a dramatic impact on the trajectory of modern economic thought in the latter part of the century. Throughout the remainder of his career he sought to apply the insights of this earlier research to the problem of resource allocation over time, making decisive contributions to the development of an altogether new branch of economics itself—optimal growth theory (see, for example, his "Economic Growth at a Maximal Rate," *Quarterly Journal of Economics* 78 [1964], 355–94). Koopmans's 1957 book, *Three Essays on the State of Economic Science* (New York: McGraw-Hill), provided a systematic overview of the links between his recent work on activity analysis and the "standard" corpus of neoclassical economic theory as a whole. The volume remains a singularly clear and concise summary of the conceptual posture of the discipline at midcentury. A gifted musician, Koopmans served as president of the Econometric Society in 1950 and president of the American Economic Association in 1978. See L. Werin and K. G. Jungenfelt, "Tjalling Koopmans' Contributions to Economics," in *Contemporary Economists in Perspective*, ed. H. W. Spiegel and Warren J. Samuels (Greenwich, Conn.: JAI Press, 1984), 1; and Mark Blaug, *Great Economists since Keynes: An Introduction to the Lives*

and Works of One Hundred Modern Economists (New York: Cambridge University Press, 1985), 119–21.

2. I discuss the ingredients of the nation's postwar economic success in some detail in my "Understanding American Economic Decline: The Contours of the Late-Twentieth-Century Experience," in *Understanding American Economic Decline*, ed. Michael A. Bernstein and David Adler (New York: Cambridge University Press, 1994), 3–33. A particularly compelling account of the misgivings that economists and members of the business community had, as the end of World War II approached, may be found in Robert M. Collins's outstanding study *The Business Response to Keynes: 1929–1964* (New York: Columbia University Press, 1981).

3. A recent and definitive economic history of international monetary arrangements throughout this century is Barry Eichengreen's remarkable *Golden Fetters: The Gold Standard and the Great Depression, 1919–1939* (New York: Oxford University Press, 1992), esp. 395–99. America's dominant international position in the "Bretton Woods system" of world trade, not to mention its robust prosperity of the postwar years, persisted until the economic pressures of the Vietnam War, coupled with the dramatic rises in the price of crude oil implemented by the Organization of Petroleum Exporting Countries in the early 1970s, profoundly weakened the nation's markets. These matters are discussed in greater detail in the following chapters of this study.

4. Tjalling Koopmans himself noted, in reference to research in economics, one of the most striking "sociological" characteristics of the immediate postwar years. In the introduction to his edited volume *Activity Analysis of Production and Allocation*, he declared "that governmental agencies, for whatever reason, have so far provided a better environment and more sympathetic support for the systematic study, abstract and applied, of principles and methods of allocation of resources than private industry." He went on to observe that there was as well "more mobility of scientific personnel between government and universities, to the advantage of both." A mere three decades after Koopmans wrote these words, it would become far more popular to claim that it was the private rather than the public sector that could provide a "more sympathetic" arena for the advanced study of resource alloca-

tion problems, not to mention for the application of rational choice theory to decision making. Whatever the ideological motivations behind the notion, history belies the argument. In Michael A. Bernstein and Allen Hunter, eds., *The Cold War and Expert Knowledge: New Essays on the History of the National Security State* (special issue of the *Radical History Review* 63 [1995]), several investigators report on the impacts of cold war culture on a variety of disciplines, including economics, political science, and psychology. For vivid portrayals of similar effects on such fields as the physical sciences, computer science, even ecology, see, respectively, Stuart W. Leslie, *The Cold War and American Science: The Military-Industrial-Academic Complex at MIT and Stanford* (New York: Columbia University Press, 1993); Paul N. Edwards, *The Closed World: Computers and the Politics of Discourse in Cold War America* (Cambridge: MIT Press, 1996); and Sharon E. Kingsland, *Modeling Nature: Episodes in the History of Population Ecology* (Chicago: University of Chicago Press, 1985).

5. On the notion and definition of the national security state, see, for example, K. Nelson, "The 'Warfare State': The History of a Concept," *Pacific Historical Review* 40 (1971), 127–43; Fred J. Cook, *The Warfare State* (New York: Macmillan, 1962); Norman A. Graebner, ed., *The National Security: Its Theory and Practice, 1945–1960* (New York: Oxford University Press, 1960); and Irving L. Horowitz, *The War Game: Studies of the New Civilian Militarists* (New York: Ballantine, 1962). I have also benefited greatly from reading an essay by Michael Dennis, " 'Our First Line of Defense': Two University Laboratories in the Postwar American State," *Isis* 85 (1994), 427–55; and the fine piece by Robert J. Leonard, "War as a 'Simple Economic Problem': The Rise of an Economics of Defense," in *Economics and National Security: A History of Their Interaction*, ed. Craufurd D. Goodwin (Durham, N.C.: Duke University Press, 1991), 261–83, that has inspired no small part of the discussion in this chapter as a whole. One of the best and most thoughtful studies of the impact of the cold war on the nation's cultural life is Paul Boyer, *By the Bomb's Early Light: American Thought and Culture at the Dawn of the Atomic Age* (New York: Pantheon, 1985). Also see Lary May, ed., *Recasting America: Culture and Politics in the Age of the Cold War* (Chicago: University of Chicago

Press, 1989); and George Lipsitz, *Class and Culture in Cold War America: A Rainbow at Midnight* (Westport, Conn.: Greenwood, 1981).

6. It should be added that the extension of these techniques to business decision making also seemed quite straightforward. If one could describe the production activities of a firm in mathematical form, it would then clearly be possible to develop methods to maximize, for example, output subject to the constraints of resource availability, labor costs, and technical capabilities. See, for example, Richard P. Levin and Rudolph P. Lamone, *Linear Programming for Management Decisions* (Homewood, Ill.: Richard Irwin, 1969); as well as Herbert A. Simon, *The New Science of Management Decision* (New York: Harper, 1960). Examples of the generalizable implications of methods for calculating constrained maximums and minimums in an objective problem may be found in Kenneth J. Arrow and Leonid Hurwicz, "Gradient Methods for Constrained Maxima," *Operations Research* 5 (1957), 258–65; and Marguerite Frank and Philip Wolfe, "An Algorithm for Quadratic Programming," *Naval Research Logistics Quarterly* (1956), 95–110.

7. The major (and most famous) publication to come out of the Chicago meetings was the anthology edited by Koopmans, *Activity Analysis of Production and Allocation.* Interestingly enough, Koopmans's work at the Shipping Board had been carried on in isolation from the equally significant wartime investigation by Frank L. Hitchcock, "The Distribution of a Product from Several Sources to Numerous Localities," *Journal of Mathematics and Physics* 20 (1941), 224–30. As to the significance of Koopmans' research, John S. Maclay of the British Merchant Shipping Mission wrote him two months after V-E Day to say that the work "contributed enormously to the effective prosecution of the War." See Maclay to Koopmans, 29 July 1944, Box 17 (Folder 311: "Personal 1939–50"), Papers of Tjalling C. Koopmans [hereafter PTCK], Sterling Memorial Library, Yale University, New Haven, Connecticut. On the Chicago conference, also see the penetrating discussion by E. Roy Weintraub, *General Equilibrium Analysis: Studies in Appraisal* (New York: Cambridge University Press, 1985), 90–94; as well as his "On the Existence of a Competitive Equilibrium: 1930–1954," *Journal of Economic Literature* 21 (1983), 1–39.

8. From an interview with Professor Emeritus George B. Dantzig, 3 May 1989, Department of Operations Research, Stanford University, at Palo Alto. Dantzig was a central figure in the development of linear programming—work he had undertaken in the late forties for the U.S. Air Force. His classic essay "Maximization of a Linear Function of Variables Subject to Linear Inequalities" was a central piece of the Koopmans conference volume. While he had no formal training in economics, Dantzig nonetheless had "some exposure" to economics problems during a brief stint, early in his career, as an applied statistician in the Bureau of Labor Statistics of the Department of Commerce. It was, in Dantzig's view, the need to "mechanize" linear programming problems by bringing in the notion of an "objective" (to be minimized or maximized) that made clear the links between economics and his research in applied mathematics.

9. See Lionel Robbins, *An Essay on the Nature and Significance of Economic Science* (London: St. Martin's, 1969); and Robert Dorfman, Paul A. Samuelson, and Robert M. Solow, *Linear Programming and Economic Analysis* (London: McGraw-Hill, 1958), chaps. 1–3. While the research of early neoclassical theorists had gained increasing respectability since the 1870s, earlier (and quite famous) works in this tradition had had a distinctly polemical, usually anti-Marxist, quality. That tone was sharply distinguished from the apparently objective, apolitical, and elegant formulations of mid-twentieth-century mathematical economic theorists. See, for example, Eugen von Böhm-Bawerk, *Karl Marx and the Close of His System*, ed. P. M. Sweezy (London: Merlin Press, 1975); and John Bates Clark, *The Distribution of Wealth: A Theory of Wages, Income and Profits* (New York: Kelley, 1967).

10. See, for example, David Novick, *Efficiency and Economy in Government through New Budgeting and Accounting Procedures* (RAND Corporation, Report R-254, February 1, 1954); Tibor Scitovsky, Edward S. Shaw, and Lorie Tarshis, *Mobilizing Resources for War* (New York: McGraw-Hill, 1951); Stephen Enke, "An Economist Looks at Air Force Logistics," *Review of Economics and Statistics* 40 (1958), 230–39; Charles J. Hitch, "Economics and Military Operations Research," *Review of Economics and Statistics* 40 (1958), 199–209; L. J. Sterling, "Decision Making in Weapons Development," *Harvard Business Review* 38 (1958), 127–36; Horst Mendershausen, "Economic Problems in

Air Force Logistics," *American Economic Review* 48 (1958), 632–48; A. Charnes, W. W. Cooper, and B. Mellon, "Blending Aviation Gasolines: A Study in Programming Interdependent Activities in an Integrated Oil Company," *Econometrica* 20 (1952), 135–59; Harold C. Levinson, "Experiences in Commercial Operations Research," *Journal of the Operations Research Society of America* 2 (1953), 220–39; and Martin S. Feldstein, "Economic Analysis, Operational Research, and the National Health Service," *Oxford Economic Papers*, n.s., 15, no. 1 (1963), 19–31. On the work of the Weapons Systems Evaluation Group, see Timothy W. Stanley, *American Defense and National Security* (Washington, D.C.: Public Affairs Press, 1956), 89; as well as George E. Pugh, "Operations Research for the Secretary of Defense and the Joint Chiefs of Staff," *Journal of the Operations Research Society of America* 8 (1960), 839–40. Alain C. Enthoven, in "Economic Analysis in the Department of Defense," *American Economic Review* 53 (1963), 413–23, concluded an insightful discussion with a humorous (while, like most good jests, revealing) comment: "[T]he tools of analysis that we use are the simplest, most fundamental concepts of [the] economic theory . . . most of us learned as sophomores. The reason Ph.D.'s are required is that many economists do not believe what they have learned until they have gone through graduate school and acquired a vested interest in [the] analysis" (422).

11. Dorfman, Samuelson, and Solow give an excellent summary of the essential ideas of game theory in their *Linear Programming and Economic Analysis*: "[T]he theory of games rests on the notion that there is a close analogy between parlor games of skill, on the one hand, and conflict situations in economic, political, and military life, on the other. In any of these situations there are a number of participants with incompatible objectives, and the extent to which each participant attains his [or her] objective depends upon what all the participants do. The problem faced by each participant is to lay his plans so as to take account of the actions of his opponents, each of whom, of course, is laying his own plans so as to take account of the first participant's actions. Thus each participant must surmise what each of his opponents will expect him to do and how these opponents will react to these expectations" (2). Significant examples of the impact that game-theoretic work had on general conceptions of economic decision making are Gerhard

Tintner, "The Theory of Choice under Subjective Risk and Uncertainty," *Econometrica* 9 (1941), 298–304; Martin Shubik, "Game Theory as an Approach to the Theory of the Firm," *American Economic Review* 50 (1960), 560–64; and Herbert A. Simon, "Theories of Decision-Making in Economics and Behavioral Science," *American Economic Review* 49 (1959), 253–83. Simon ultimately won the 1978 Nobel Memorial Prize in Economic Science for his work in modern decision theory.

12. See von Neumann and Morgenstern's classic work, *Theory of Games and Economic Behavior* (Princeton, N.J.: Princeton University Press, 1947). Also see R. Duncan Luce and Howard Raiffa, *Games and Decisions* (New York: Wiley, 1958); Albert W. Tucker and R. Duncan Luce, eds., *Contributions to the Theory of Games* (Princeton, N.J.: Princeton University Press, 1959); as well as Morgenstern's "Economics and the Theory of Games," *Kyklos* 3 (1949), 294–308. Leonid Hurwicz explored some of the broader implications of game theory for economic thought as a whole in his influential essay "The Theory of Economic Behavior," *American Economic Review* 35 (1945), 909–25. More recent efforts to explain the significance of game theory for the late-twentieth-century development of the economics discipline are Franklin Fisher, "Games Economists Play: A Noncooperative View," *Rand Journal of Economics* 20 (1989), 113–24; David M. Kreps, *Game Theory and Economic Modelling* (Oxford: Oxford University Press, 1990), esp. 6–7, 30–31, 36; and Roy Radner, "Hierarchy: The Economics of Managing," *Journal of Economic Literature* 30 (1992), 1382–415. Richard Stone's article "The Theory of Games," *Economic Journal* 58 (1948), 185–201, introduced game theory to the mainstream community of economics scholars in Great Britain. Many of those scholars who made crucial contributions to the development of game theory brought a wide array of political commitments to their work. For some, especially those for whom World War II remained a gruesome memory, game theory held out the promise of establishing a means to codify and resolve human conflict in ways less irrational, passionate, and brutal than war. There was even the hope that strategic gaming might demonstrate the ultimate irrationality of mutually assured destruction in a nuclear exchange. As von Neumann and Morgenstern had claimed in their classic work, it might conceivably be possible "to find the math-

ematically complete principles which define[d] 'rational behavior' " (31), to reduce the welter of psychological impulses and instincts for violence to understandable and therefore presumably malleable dimensions. For a stimulating discussion on this matter, I am grateful to my colleague Tracy Strong of the Department of Political Science at the University of California, San Diego. Robert W. Dimand and Mary Ann Dimand have recently published the first volume of a systematic, textual history of the development of game theory, one that traces the roots of the idea back to the seventeenth century. See their *History of Game Theory*, vol. 1, *From the Beginnings to 1945* (New York: Routledge, 1997), 1, 7.

13. Within microeconomics, the branch of the discipline that focused on the study of firm and household behavior, dealing with monopolistic and oligopolistic competition (rather than with the abstract "baseline" of perfectly competitive markets) had proved difficult and confusing. Where competition took the form of a very large number of competitors, economic theorists found themselves well on the way to crafting mathematical proofs of the tendency of prices to gravitate toward stable (or "equilibrium") positions. Yet in highly concentrated markets, in which there were a small number of competitors (oligopoly) or two dominant firms (duopoly) or a single giant (monopoly), the mathematics were far less tractable, and the outcomes they described were far less determinate (or, at times, reasonable). Edward H. Chamberlin's *The Theory of Monopolistic Competition* (Cambridge: Harvard University Press, [1933] 1962); and Joan Robinson's *The Economics of Imperfect Competition* (London: St. Martin's, [1933] 1961) had squarely posed the conundrums with which "realistic" market structures confronted theorists. Paul Sweezy had also demonstrated the ways in which oligopolistic competition subverted the traditional neoclassical theory of markets in his "Demand under Conditions of Oligopoly," *Journal of Political Economy* 47 (1939). Game theory inspired an altogether new approach to the problem, allowing theorists to conceptualize competitive behavior in concentrated market settings in ways both rigorous and more directly linked to neoclassical notions of maximizing behavior. A most influential contribution in this regard was William Fellner's *Competition among the Few* (New York: Kelley, 1960). Marc Trachtenberg, in his vastly interesting *History and Strategy* (Princeton, N.J.: Princeton University Press,

1991), 15, makes the point that Fellner's book also inspired the work of strategic theorists. Also see Martin Shubik, *Strategy and Market Structure: Competition, Oligopoly, and the Theory of Games* (New York: Wiley, 1959).

14. Again, see Dorfman, Samuelson, and Solow, *Linear Programming and Economic Analysis*, 2. Philip Mirowski affords an excellent summary of the early history of game theory development and a compelling documentation of the singularly important role that military funding played in that process, in his "When Games Grow Deadly Serious: The Military Influence on the Evolution of Game Theory," in *Economics and National Security: A History of Their Interaction*, ed. Craufurd D. Goodwin (Durham, N.C.: Duke University Press, 1991), 227–55. Equally impressive is an article by Robert J. Leonard, "From Parlor Games to Social Science: Von Neumann, Morgenstern, and the Creation of Game Theory: 1928–1944," *Journal of Economic Literature* 33 (1995), 730–61, which emphasizes the significance (and historical contingency) of the von Neumann–Morgenstern collaboration. Simply put, it was Morgenstern, the economist, who framed the rigorous language of game theory, as developed by the extraordinary mathematician von Neumann, in ways that facilitated both its engagement with and its reformulation of neoclassical concepts. See Mohammed Dore, Sukhamoy Chakravarty, and Richard Goodwin, eds., *John von Neumann and Modern Economics* (New York: Oxford University Press, 1989); and S. Ulam, "John von Neumann, 1903–1957," *Bulletin of the American Mathematical Society* 64 (1958), 1–49. Also of interest in this regard is Leonard's "Creating a Context for Game Theory," *History of Political Economy* 24 (1992), 29–76; as well as Philip Mirowski's "What Were von Neumann and Morgenstern Trying to Accomplish?" *History of Political Economy* 24 (1992), 113–47—the entire journal number, in fact, is devoted to the history of game theory. A striking representation of the permeation of the work of nuclear strategists by the conceptual apparatus of game theory is, of course, Herman Kahn's *On Thermonuclear War* (Princeton, N.J.: Princeton University Press, 1960), esp. 162–89; as well as his *Thinking about the Unthinkable* (New York: Avon, 1962). Also see Philip Green, *Deadly Logic: The Theory of Nuclear Deterrence* (Columbus: Ohio State University Press, 1966); and Oskar Morgenstern, *The Question of National Defense* (New York: Random House,

1959). In the summer of 1959, Tjalling Koopmans recalled that his discussions with von Neumann concerning game theory had a tremendous impact on his further work in the field of linear programming and activity analysis. See Koopmans to A. H. Taub (School of Mathematics, Institute for Advanced Study), 24 July 1959; Taub to Koopmans, 20 July 1959; and Taub to Koopmans, 27 July 1959; all in PTCK—Box 17 (Folder 307: "T 1956, 1959").

15. See Albert Wohlstetter, "The Delicate Balance of Terror," *Foreign Affairs* 39 (1959), 211–34. It was this essay, perhaps more than any other scholarly product, that gave rigorous expression to the aspiration of many game theorists that, properly handled, strategic gaming might prevent nuclear conflict through systematic demonstration of the potential for mutually assured destruction. Marc Trachtenberg, in *History and Strategy*, 20, called Wohlstetter's essay "probably the single most important article in the history of American strategic thought." Another influential work that conveys a sense of the impact of economic thinking on strategic theory is Walter Isard, *Arms, Arms Control, and Conflict Analysis: Contributions from Peace Science and Peace Economics* (New York: Cambridge University Press, 1988). Also see Deborah Welch Larson, "Deterrence Theory and the Cold War," *Radical History Review* 63 (1995), 86–109; and Stephen P. Waring, "Cold Calculus: The Cold War and Operations Research," *Radical History Review* 63 (1995), 28–51.

16. From an interview with Herbert Scarf, who worked at RAND from 1954 to 1957, now professor emeritus of economics at Yale University, 15 May 1989, at New Haven. Scarf joined RAND immediately after completing his Ph.D. in mathematics at Princeton University in 1954. Although, as a junior staff member, he was not directly privy to the funding arrangements for the corporation's economists, he nevertheless had the distinct impression that the Office of Naval Research was the key benefactor. In Scarf's view, Wohlstetter was instrumental in moving game theory down "its strategic road." A most thought-provoking, and characteristically heterodox, consideration of the intellectual ramifications of defense economics is Kenneth E. Boulding, "Towards a Pure Theory of Threat Systems," *American Economic Review* 53 (1963), 424–34; as well as his *Conflict and Defense* (New York: Harper and Row, 1962), esp. 332ff.

17. It was the Office of Naval Research (ONR), interestingly enough, that provided the core funding for the writing of *Games and Decisions* by Howard Raiffa and Duncan Luce. A significant proportion of the research done by von Neumann and Morgenstern at Princeton (not to mention work undertaken by graduate students who would ultimately go on to very distinguished careers in the field, such as Martin Shubik, John Nash, and Lloyd Shapley) was also underwritten by the navy. ONR further sustained projects to build computers tasked specifically to solve games with military applications. All of these matters are noted by Philip Mirowski in "When Games Grow Deadly Serious," 242. Also see Joseph Gani, ed., *The Craft of Probabilistic Modelling* (New York: Springer Verlag, 1986), 17; Sylvia Nasar's biography of John Nash, *A Beautiful Mind* (New York: Simon and Schuster, 1998); and Oskar Morgenstern, ed., *Economic Activity Analysis* (New York: Wiley, 1954), 505. George Dantzig remembers that Dorfman, Samuelson, and Solow received substantial support from both ONR and the RAND Corporation in the research that culminated in the publication of *Linear Programming and Economic Analysis*; from the Dantzig interview, 3 May 1989.

18. From Office of Naval Research, Department of the Navy, *Office of Naval Research: Forty Years of Excellence in Support of Naval Science*, ed. F. E. Saalfeld (n.p., n.d.); and also see Office of Aerospace Research, U.S. Air Force, *Air Force Research Objectives: 1969*, ed. J. Seiden (n.p., n.d.); and Office of Aerospace Research, U.S. Air Force, *Air Force Research Objectives: 1968* (Arlington, Va.: U.S. Air Force, n.d.). On the army's relatively slow acceptance of the new research agendas and planning techniques, see S. I. Gilman, "Operations Research in the Army," *Military Review* 36 (1956), 54–64. According to the Army Research Office of the U.S. Army Laboratory Command (Research Triangle Park, North Carolina), "research in economics has never been an area supported by [that] office." Letter to the author from W. Davis Hein (Army Research Office), 16 August 1988. Similarly, with the exception of operations research per se, the Air Force Office of Scientific Research (AFOSR) "ha[s] never supported any research concerning economics." Letter to the author from John O. Dimmock (AFOSR), 18 August 1988. The key service arm in the support of modern economics research was (and has clearly been) the U.S. Navy. This is a somewhat ironic

finding given the fact that economists had, during World War II, played a significant role in the Strategic Bombing Survey undertaken for the Army Air Force. See J. Steinhardt, "The Role of Operations Research in the Navy," *U.S. Naval Institute Proceedings* (May 1946); as well as Samuel Eliot Morison, *The Two-Ocean War* (Boston: Little, Brown, 1963), 102–9. Ronald Clark, in *The Rise of the Boffins* (London: Phoenix House, 1962), shows that the British army similarly was slow, relative to the Royal Air Force and the Royal Navy, to embrace operations research as a tool; yet, once persuaded, the Imperial General Staff took up the challenge with more vigor and determination than their American counterparts. A more recent scholarly article provides a fine example of the application of game theory to rational choice in strategic decision making. See Robert P. Wolff, "Maximization of Expected Utility as a Criterion of Rationality in Military Strategy and Foreign Policy," *Social Theory and Practice* 1 (1970), 99–111.

19. From Bruce L. R. Smith, *The RAND Corporation: Case Study of a Nonprofit Advisory Corporation* (Cambridge: Harvard University Press, 1969), 111–12. Bellman eventually spearheaded the application of linear programming to allocative problems over time, thereby "dynamizing" the technique. It was indeed not surprising that, during Kennedy's tenure as president, the "whiz kids" of the national security and defense agencies came to prominence in the media. Their primary representative was, of course, the brilliant Secretary of Defense Robert McNamara. Of interest in this regard is Fred Kaplan, *The Wizards of Armageddon* (New York: Simon and Schuster, 1983); and William W. Kaufmann, *The McNamara Strategy* (New York: Harper, 1964). Martin Feldstein, in his "Economic Analysis, Operational Research, and the National Health Service," 21, noted with approval the appointment of Charles J. Hitch, a prominent specialist on defense economics, as assistant secretary of defense (and Pentagon comptroller) during the Kennedy and Johnson administrations. The appointment of the former head of the Economics Division at RAND and future president of the University of California was, in Feldstein's view, "indicative of the growing acceptance of the usefulness of economic analysis in th[e] area of public expenditure." Hitch's *The Economics of Defense in the Nuclear Age*, which he coauthored with Roland N. McKean (Cambridge: Harvard University Press, 1960), became a classic in its

field; also highly regarded were his essays "Sub-optimization in Operations Problems," *Journal of the Operations Research Society of America* 1 (1953), 87–89; and "Economics and Military Operations Research," 199–209. Henry E. Rowen and Alain C. Enthoven joined Hitch in the transformation of the Pentagon's utilization of economic analysis. Also see Hans Speier and Herbert Goldhamer, "Some Observations on Political Gaming," *World Politics* 12 (1959), 71–83; Sidney Verba, "Simulation, Reality, and Theory in International Relations," *World Politics* 16 (April 1964), as cited in Smith, *The RAND Corporation*; and William Poundstone, *Prisoner's Dilemma* (New York: Doubleday, 1992), a deft explanation of the essential principles of game theory and their ultimate application to the puzzles of nuclear strategy.

20. From Smith, *The RAND Corporation*, 12–13. Smith makes the provocative point that some scholars have discovered the origins of the military applications of operations research and gaming techniques in the late nineteenth and early twentieth centuries. He cites such work as Frederick W. Lanchester, *Aircraft in Warfare: The Dawn of the Fourth Army* (London: Constable, 1916); and William R. Livermore, *The American Kriegspiel: A Game for Practising the Art of War upon a Topographical Map* (Boston: Houghton Mifflin, 1882). In the spring of 1954, RAND economists, led by Henry Rowen and Albert Wohlstetter, began a study for the air force that utilized linear programming techniques to assist the chief of staff in formulating an order of battle for the nation's strategic bomber fleet. According to Smith, *The RAND Corporation*, 200ff., four alternative deployments were evaluated with respect to their cost of operation and their usefulness in completing their combat missions: (1) systematic overseas basing; (2) overseas basing solely in times of war; (3) U.S.-based squadrons utilizing air refueling; and (4) U.S.-based squadrons utilizing ground refueling at overseas bases. The analytical methods that had emerged from the work of Dantzig, Koopmans, and others proved especially effective in deriving results from a bewildering array of data involving direct and indirect costs, the capabilities of extant aviation technology, and the vulnerability to enemy attack of alternative basing schemes. "Strategic Bases Study (RAND Report R-266)," as this special RAND investigation came to be known in its published form, ultimately recommended the fourth option. The resulting disposition of the

Strategic Air Command prevailed for some time, a component of the "New Look" nuclear arsenal of the Eisenhower administration. On the notion of the "New Look," see, for example, Robert A. Divine, *Eisenhower and the Cold War* (New York: Oxford University Press, 1981); John Lewis Gaddis, *Strategies of Containment: A Critical Appraisal of Postwar American National Security Policy* (New York: Oxford University Press, 1982); H. W. Brands, "The Age of Vulnerability: Eisenhower and the National Insecurity State," *American Historical Review* 94 (1989); and R. M. Saunders, "Military Force in the Foreign Policy of the Eisenhower Presidency," *Political Science Quarterly* 100 (1985). In time, technological change (that affected the flight performance and carrying capacity of both bombers and aerial tankers), alterations in the nation's geopolitical alliances (that affected the availability of overseas bases), the evolution of strategic doctrine (that tended to shift greater proportions of the nuclear weapons stockpile from bombers to land-based and sea-based missiles), and the volatile admixture of interservice rivalry (that powerfully influenced the choice of particular weapons systems) all conspired to make RAND Report R-266 obsolete. Even intraservice antagonisms had their effects, pitting, within the air force, for example, those who favored "big bombers" against their colleagues who championed smaller and faster aircraft. Within the navy there were analogous disagreements among submariners (not to mention between the "silent service" and naval aviators) over the best ways to deploy nuclear ordnance—either in smaller, faster "attack boats" primarily oriented toward fleet operations or in larger, potentially more vulnerable "boomers" dedicated entirely to the launching of intercontinental ballistic rockets. See Michael S. Sherry, *Preparing for the Next War: American Plans for Post-war Defense, 1941–1945* (New Haven, Conn.: Yale University Press, 1977); as well as Sherry, *The Rise of American Air Power: The Creation of Armageddon* (New Haven, Conn.: Yale University Press, 1987).

21. See Charles Hitch, "Plans, Programs, and Budgets in the Department of Defense," *Journal of the Operations Research Society of America* 2 (1963), 1–17; Alain C. Enthoven and K. Wayne Smith, *How Much Is Enough? Shaping the Defense Program, 1961–1969* (New York: Harper and Row, 1971), 32–33; Enthoven, "Economic Analysis in the Department of Defense," 413–23;

Samuel A. Tucker, ed., *National Security Management: A Modern Design for Defense Decision: A McNamara-Hitch-Enthoven Anthology* (Washington, D.C.: Industrial College of the Armed Forces, 1966); Jacob A. Stockfish, ed., *Planning and Forecasting in the Defense Industries* (Belmont, Calif.: Wadsworth, 1962); J. Sterling Livingston, "Decision Making in Weapons Development," *Harvard Business Review* 36 (1958), 127–36; Allen Schick, "The Road to PPBS: The Stages of Budget Reform," *Public Administration Review* 26 (1966), 243–58; and the comprehensive overview provided by Joint Economic Committee, Congress of the United States, *Hearings, The Planning-Programming-Budgeting System: Progress and Potentials* (90th Cong., 1st sess., 1967). On the significant role of the RAND Corporation in the development of PPBS, see Smith, *The RAND Corporation*, 112ff.

22. Professor Harry N. Scheiber (University of California, Berkeley), letter to the author, 29 December 1991. Perhaps the single most dramatic cause of the collapse of the PPBS protocols in 1969 was the increasing economic damage caused by the Vietnam War. See, for example, W. R. Cook, "Whatever Happened to PPBS?" *International Review of Administrative Sciences* 52 (1986), 223–41. PPBS, with its emphasis on the systematic calculation of the costs and benefits of proposed policy initiatives, was also used in the evaluation of social programs during the Kennedy and Johnson administrations.

23. The words are Enthoven's and Smith's from their *How Much Is Enough?* 33. One of the foremost critics of the PPBS initiative was political scientist Aaron Wildavsky. See his "Rescuing Policy Analysis from PPBS," Subcommittee on National Security and International Operations, Committee on Government Operations, United States Senate, *Planning-Programming Budgeting: Rescuing Policy Analysis from PPBS* (91st Cong., 1st sess., 1969) [reprinted from *Public Administration Review* 29 (1969)]; "The Practical Consequences of the Theoretical Study of Defense Policy," *Public Administration Review* 25 (1965), 90–103; and "The Political Economy of Efficiency," *Public Administration Review* 26 (1966), 298–302. The burden of Wildavsky's argument was that PPBS could never substitute for (although it could obscure) the *political* choices that necessarily delimited any decisions about the appropriate means to realize a given end of public policy.

24. From Thomas C. Schelling, "PPBS and Foreign Affairs," memorandum prepared at the request of the Subcommittee on National Security and International Operations, Committee on Government Operations, United States Senate (90th Cong., 1st sess., 1968), 2.

25. From Smith, *The RAND Corporation*, 16. Smith also notes that, as a paid RAND consultant, Thomas Schelling wrote another classic text in game theory and economic analysis, *The Strategy of Conflict* (Cambridge: Harvard University Press, 1960). Also see Schellings's "Bargaining, Communication, and Limited War," *Journal of Conflict Resolution* 1 (1957), 19–36; as well as John Cross, "On Professor Schelling's Strategy of Conflict," *Naval Research Logistics Quarterly* 8 (1961), 421–26. Interestingly enough, Schelling's approach to the analytics of "bargaining" was, in large measure, inspired by William Fellner's theory of oligopoly as presented in *Competition among the Few*. See Trachtenberg, *History and Strategy*, 15.

26. See, for example, the work Ellsberg did at RAND, "The Crude Analysis of Strategic Choices," *American Economic Review* 51 (1961), 472–78, in which the U.S.-Soviet postwar confrontation was described by a two-by-two gaming matrix giving each superpower two choices—"wait" or "strike." Also see Daniel Ellsberg, "Risk, Ambiguity, and the Savage Axioms," *Quarterly Journal of Economics* 75 (1961), 643–69, an essay that reported on some of Ellsberg's work as a graduate student at Harvard. A particularly striking essay, "The Theory of the Reluctant Duelist," *American Economic Review* 46 (1956), 909–23, argued that a major inadequacy of game theory concerned its assumption that players (or "duelists") would always, in fact, play a game. Ellsberg, quite significantly, asked in that piece: "Why bother to play [a] game at all, if one prefers the certainty of zero to the chance of winning or losing?" The implication of Ellsberg's argument, one that subverted the initial axioms of game theory as a whole, was that in certain contexts "the only winning move [in a contest] [wa]s not to play." It is too easy, of course, to read into this iconoclastic article some anticipation of Daniel Ellsberg's ultimate "defection" from the cold war during one of the most celebrated scandals surrounding the Vietnam War. Revealed to the public on 13 June 1971, a seven-thousand-page Department of Defense document, colloquially referred to as the "Pentagon Papers," portrayed a two-decade cam-

paign of dissimulation and obfuscation concerning the nation's political objectives and military
tactics in Indochina. It was Ellsberg, with the
benefit of security clearances he held as a DOD
and RAND Corporation analyst, who had gained
access to the papers and "leaked" them to the
New York Times and the *Washington Post.* The
public outcry that ensued played no small part
in the evisceration of whatever domestic support
remained for the nation's involvement in a long
and bloody war. It also gave rise to a series of
legal battles concerning the public's access to information and the purported prerogatives of the
executive branch of the federal government. A
rather large literature has emerged concerning
the Pentagon Papers. One of the most recent and
best executed studies is by David Rudenstine,
*The Day the Presses Stopped: A History of the
Pentagon Papers Case* (Berkeley: University of
California Press, 1997).

27. The words are Marc Trachtenberg's from
his *History and Strategy,* 15. Trachtenberg goes
on to note that Washington's interest in the analytics of strategic choice created a "market . . .
for ideas from economics"—a circumstance that
privileged certain kinds of research over others.
In this regard it is most interesting to note the
suggestion of L. W. Martin that, at the same time
in Great Britain, a "lack of adequate linkage between the formal government establishment and
outside critics and lay strategists" hampered the
effective evolution of British postwar military
doctrine. See his essay "The Market for Strategic
Ideas in Britain," *American Political Science Review* 56 (1962), 23–41. Also see Gene M. Lyons
and Louis Morton, *Schools for Strategy: Education and Research in National Security Affairs*
(New York: Praeger, 1965). On the lack of evidence to support a claim that game theory powerfully shaped American strategy, see Trachtenberg, *History and Strategy,* 14 n. 21, as well as
the book review he notes by Thomas Schelling,
of Anatol Rapoport's *Strategy and Conscience*
(New York: Schocken, 1964), published in the
American Economic Review 54 (1964), 1082–88.

28. The general data on federal funding for research activities are reported in Office of Naval
Research, Department of the Navy, *Windows to
the Origins* (n.p., n.d.), 7, 12. A thorough history
of ONR is Harvey M. Sapolsky, *Science and the
Navy: The History of the Office of Naval Research* (Princeton, N.J.: Princeton University
Press, 1990). A comprehensive sense of the
background against which developments in pub-

lic research funding took place may be won from
A. Hunter Dupree, *Science in the Federal Government: A History of Policies and Activities to
1940* (Cambridge: Harvard University Press,
1957).

29. See J. Merton England, *A Patron of Pure
Science: The National Science Foundation's
Formative Years, 1945–57* (Washington, D.C.:
National Science Foundation, 1982), 54, 108. An
excellent narrative and analysis of the founding
of the National Science Foundation is provided
by Mark Solovey, "The Politics of Intellectual
Identity and American Social Science, 1945–
1970" (Ph.D. diss., University of Wisconsin–
Madison, 1996), esp. chap. 2; along with his article (coauthored with Daniel Lee Kleinman) "Hot
Science/Cold War: The National Science Foundation after World War II," *Radical History Review* 63 (1995), 110–39. Kleinman's monograph
*Politics on the Endless Frontier: Postwar Re-
search Policy in the United States* (Durham,
N.C.: Duke University Press, 1995) is quite useful as well, as is Dael Wolfle, *Renewing a Scientific Society: The American Association for the
Advancement of Science from World War 2 to
1970* (Washington, D.C.: American Association
for the Advancement of Science, 1989). Also see
Harry Alpert, "The National Science Foundation
and Social Science Research," *American Sociological Review* 19 (1954), 208–11; "The Social
Sciences and the National Science Foundation,
1945–1955," *American Sociological Review* 22
(1955), 653–61; as well as his "Congressmen,
Social Scientists, and Attitudes toward Federal
Support of Social Science Research," *American
Sociological Review* 23 (1958), 682–86. Struggles over the continuing involvement of the NSF
in social science research endured well into the
1960s and would reappear with every debate
over proposed NSF budgets in Congress. Indeed,
in March and April 1981, when such a dispute
was under way on Capitol Hill, Nobel economics
laureate James Tobin, along with twenty-one colleagues, wrote various members of Congress and
Philip Handler, then president of the National
Academy of Sciences, to call for an avoidance
of cuts in the Division of Social and Economic
Science at the NSF. Tobin argued that the NSF
was the "main source for support of *basic* research in social science," and he noted as well
the crucial role the foundation played in the development of such things as linear programming—a field that now had wide applications,
"for example, in oil refineries and transportation

networks." See Tobin to Handler, 19 March 1981, and a copy of the open letter to the Congress, dated 3 April 1981; both in PTCK, Box 21 (Folder 403: "National Science Foundation Budget alarms 1981"). The resonance of the debates over the NSF enabling legislation with more recent quarrels over the funding of the National Endowment for the Arts (NEA) and the National Endowment for the Humanities (NEH) is striking, especially so given that opponents of the NEA and the NEH typically invoke agencies like NSF as pristine examples of uncomplicated (albeit expensive) claims upon the public purse.

30. See England, *A Patron of Pure Science*, 26, 33, 232–33; and D. J. Kevles, "The National Science Foundation and the Debate over Postwar Research Policy, 1942–1945: A Political Interpretation of *Science—The Endless Frontier*," *Isis* 68 (1977), 5–26. *Science—The Endless Frontier* was the name of the exceedingly influential report on the future place of the federal government in the nation's scientific research and development prepared for President Harry Truman in July 1945 by Vannevar Bush. Milton Lomask, in *A Minor Miracle: An Informal History of the National Science Foundation* (Washington, D.C.: National Science Foundation, 1975), 43, makes the interesting point that the original proposals to create the NSF emphasized the goal of improving the nation's standard of living through scientific advancement. In that context it was obviously not that much of a leap to consider federal funding for abstract research in economics. It is hardly surprising that given the final compromise over the NSF's commitment to social science research, the work of Kenneth Arrow and Gerard Debreu, for example, on the modeling of competitive equilibria in economic transactions was supported by the Office of Naval Research as part of its program in "Mathematical and Physical Sciences." See Kenneth J. Arrow and Gerard Debreu, "Existence of an Equilibrium for a Competitive Economy," *Econometrica* 20 (1954), 265–90; Kenneth J. Arrow and Frank H. Hahn, *General Competitive Analysis* (San Francisco: Holden Day, 1971); Gerard Debreu, *Theory of Value* (New York: Wiley, 1959); and Gerard Debreu and Herbert Scarf, "A Limit Theorem on the Core of an Economy," *International Economic Review* 4 (1963), 235–46. It was, of course, the notion that social scientific research could be "neutral" or "impartial" that came under withering attack a few years later at the hands of the late sociologist Alvin W. Gouldner in *The Coming Crisis of Western Sociology* (New York: Basic Books, 1970). His book echoed some of the arguments in the classic text of Robert S. Lynd, *Knowledge for What? The Place of Social Science in American Culture* (New York: Grove Press, 1939). Also see Terence Ball, "The Politics of Social Science in Postwar America," in *Recasting America: Culture and Politics in the Age of the Cold War*, ed. Lary May (Chicago: University of Chicago Press, 1989), 76–92; Otto N. Larsen, *Milestones and Millstones: Social Science at the National Science Foundation, 1945–1991* (New Brunswick, N.J.: Transaction Publishers, 1992); Robert Franklin Maddox, "The Politics of World War II Science: Senator Harley M. Kilgore and the Legislative Origins of the National Science Foundation," *West Virginia History* 41 (1979), 20–39; and Robert P. McCune, "Origins and Development of the National Science Foundation and Its Division of Social Sciences, 1945–1961" (Ph.D. diss., Ball State University, 1971).

31. See Social Science Research Council, "Research Support and Intellectual Advance in the Social Sciences," *Items* 37 (1983), 35–7; and the National Science Foundation, *Federal Funds for Research and Development, 1967–83* (Washington, D.C.: National Science Foundation, 1983), 2, 24, 28, 50. The links between the Social Science Research Council (SSRC) and the Rockefeller Foundation are systematically explored in the most recent work of one of the leading experts on independent-sector funding of academic research, the sociologist Donald Fisher, in *Fundamental Development of the Social Sciences: Rockefeller Philanthropy and the United States Social Science Research Council* (Ann Arbor: University of Michigan Press, 1993).

32. See Social Science Research Counci, "Research Support and Intellectual Advances in the Social Sciences," table 1, 36. With regard to rates of growth, from 1940 to 1980, colleges and universities increased their support for social science research some twenty-five-fold; the federal government, almost twentyfold (from a base, on the eve of World War II, of virtually zero). In contrast, foundations increased their funding twelvefold, but by the early 1970s the rate of expansion had dwindled to nothing. Yet, as the SSRC notes, "[I]f the postwar story is one that portrays a dogged but shrinking role for foundations [in social science research], it also contains some moments of high drama" (36), the principal

actor being the Ford Foundation. Between 1951 and 1956, Ford granted $40 million to an array of projects in the "behavioral sciences." Most prominent of the recipients of those funds were the Center for Advanced Study in the Behavioral Sciences at Palo Alto (which the Ford grant created), the Institute for Social Research and the Research Center for Group Dynamics at the University of Michigan, the Laboratory for Social Relations at Harvard University, and the Bureau of Applied Social Research at Columbia University. See Bernard Berelson, "Behavioral Sciences," *International Encyclopedia of the Social Sciences*, ed. David L. Sills (New York: Free Press/Macmillan, 1968), vol. 2, 41–45. Also of interest is Gene M. Lyons, *The Uneasy Partnership: Social Science and the Federal Government in the Twentieth Century* (New York: Russell Sage Foundation, 1969).

33. See Clark Kerr, *The Uses of the University* (Cambridge: Harvard University Press, 1963), 68–69. Kerr's trope played upon the memory of the Land Grant College Act (or Morrill Act) of 1862, which gave each state thirty thousand acres of public land (or the equivalent in scrip) for each representative and each senator it had in the Congress to assist in the establishment of higher educational institutions. Originally intended to foster the creation of schools of agriculture and mechanical arts, the act ultimately played a central role in the emergence of public universities in every state of the union. The practice of allocating land grants to support education had a venerable heritage; under the Articles of Confederation the first such grants were authorized, within the context of the Land Ordinance of 1785, for public school networks in the states.

34. These emblematic incidents of the cold war uniformly stimulated dramatic increases in federal support of particular military-industrial research projects. When the Soviets, for example, developed their first nuclear weapon, President Truman initiated the drive to develop a thermonuclear device; similarly, the *Sputnik* incident provoked debates about a possible "missile gap" between the Soviet Union and the United States, with attendant decisions to funnel resources into the development of new bomber aircraft and ballistic rocket systems. Some excellent, recent narratives of these events may be found in Melvyn P. Leffler, *A Preponderance of Power: National Security, the Truman Administration, and the Cold War* (Stanford, Calif.: Stanford University Press, 1992), esp. chaps. 8–10; and Martin Walker, *The*

Cold War: A History (New York: Henry Holt, 1993), esp. chaps. 4–5. One of the leading historians of American foreign relations during the cold war era, John Lewis Gaddis, has now published the first volume of a two-volume history of the period that takes advantage of recently released Soviet archives. See his *We Now Know: Rethinking Cold War History* (New York: Oxford University Press, 1997).

35. A particularly vivid and detailed portrayal of the many ways in which cold war research funding transformed American colleges and universities is Rebecca S. Lowen, *Creating the Cold War University: The Transformation of Stanford* (Berkeley: University of California Press, 1997). Lowen's fine research also reveals the impact of cold war administrative agendas on curricula, the relationship between teaching and research activities on campus, and student achievement. A further appreciation of the ways in which the rise of the "Federal Grant University" affected every aspect of American higher education may be won from the autobiographical essays contained in Noam Chomsky et al., *The Cold War and the University: Toward an Intellectual History of the Postwar Years* (New York: New Press, 1997); and John Trumpbour, "Harvard, the Cold War, and the National Security State," in *How Harvard Rules: Reason in the Service of Empire*, ed. John Trumpbour (Boston: South End Press, 1989), 51–128. On the development of "indirect cost" budgetary strategies, see Dennis, "'Our First Line of Defense,'" 427–55; as well as Michael Aaron Dennis, "A Change of State: The Political Cultures of Technical Practice at the MIT Instrumentation Laboratory and the Johns Hopkins University Applied Physics Laboratory, 1930–1945" (Ph.D. diss., Johns Hopkins University, 1990). One of the leading historians of the modern American university establishment has more recently published the second volume of his survey of the twentieth-century rise of research institutions, one that pays particular attention to the impact of public and foundation funding; see Roger L. Geiger, *Research and Relevant Knowledge: American Research Universities since World War II* (New York: Oxford University Press, 1993). Also see his earlier essay "Science, Universities, and National Defense: 1945–70," *Osiris* 7 (1992), 26–48. Dependence on federal funding became so significant by the 1980s, especially in the public universities, that with the devolution of the Soviet Union, and the attendant reduction in defense spending (especially in

those areas not directly linked with frontline deployments), a fiscal crisis emerged in American higher education. Whether through drastic retrenchment, the forging of altogether new links with the corporate sector, or rapid increases in tuition and fees, most institutions have yet to find the antidote to the addiction nurtured by military-industrial funding that began over a half century ago. The surge in the demand for a college education was of course linked with the coming of age of the baby boom caused by World War II. It was also stimulated by the allocation of generous support for college tuition payments authorized, for example, by the GI Bill and the National Defense Education Act of 1958.

36. In the fall of 1947, for example, the AEA secretariat refused to endorse publicly the proposed European Recovery Program (popularly known as the "Marshall Plan"). Enacted in April of the following year, the program was placed under the control of the Economic Cooperation Administration and tasked to restore agricultural and industrial output levels in Europe to their prewar magnitudes. Over the ensuing four years, the United States appropriated some $12 billion in what was a highly successful effort that also had the dramatic political impact of shoring up Western (Allied) European governments in the face of what were horrendous economic conditions in the wake of World War II. On the Marshall Plan itself, see Michael J. Hogan, *The Marshall Plan: America, Britain, and the Reconstruction of Western Europe, 1947–1952* (New York: Cambridge University Press, 1987). Of more specific interest, in this regard, is the memoir of Charles P. Kindleberger, *Marshall Plan Days* (Winchester, Mass.: Allen and Unwin, 1987). AEA officials even turned down an invitation to participate in the Conference on Human Rights and the Freedom of Information to be held at the Department of State in Washington in March 1948. See Ada M. Stoflet to James Washington Bell (AEA Secretary-Treasurer), 19 November 1947, RAEA, Box 34 (Folder: "Correspondence M–Z 1947"); and Francis H. Russell (Director, Office of Public Affairs, U.S. Department of State) to Bell, 13 February 1948, RAEA, Box 34 (Folder: "Correspondence A–L 1948").

37. See, for example, Raymond J. Saulnier (Chair, Council of Economic Advisers) to Major General Richard H. Carmichael (Commandant of the War College of the Air University, Maxwell Air Force Base, Alabama), 1 March 1960, Box 24 (Folder: "Chron[ological File]; January, Feb-

ruary and March 1960"), Records of the Office of the Council of Economic Advisers, 1953–61 [hereafter CEA Records], Dwight D. Eisenhower Library, Abilene, Kansas. Also see Saulnier to Major General Max S. Johnson (Commandant, U.S. Army War College, Carlisle Barracks), 14 April 1958, CEA Records, Box 25 (Folder: "Chron; April, May and June 1958"); Saulnier to Admiral E. T. Wooldridge (Commandant, National War College), 28 January 1958, CEA Records, Box 25 (Folder: "Chron; January, February and March 1958"); Saulnier to Major General R. P. Hollis (Commandant of the Industrial College of the Armed Forces, Washington D.C.), 6 May 1957, CEA Records, Box 25 (Folder: "Chron; January to June, 1957"); Saulnier to Colonel Robert F. McDermott (Dean of Faculty, U.S. Air Force Academy), 9 October 1956; and McDermott to Arthur F. Burns (Chair, Council of Economic Advisers), 2 October 1956; both in CEA Records, Box 25 (Folder: "Chron; July to December, 1956"); Saulnier to the Publications Division of the Industrial College of the Armed Forces, 10 August 1955, CEA Records, Box 26 (Folder: "Chron; July to December, 1955"); and Neil H. Jacoby (Member, Council of Economic Advisers) to Rear Admiral W. McL. Hague (Commandant of the Industrial College of the Armed Forces), 18 May 1954, CEA Records, Box 26 (Folder: "Chron; January to June 1954"); and Vice-Admiral Fitzhugh Lee (Commandant, National War College) to Arthur F. Burns (then at the National Bureau of Economic Research), 20 June 1967; Lee to Burns, 5 July 1966; Burns to Lee, 19 July 1966; and Burns to Lee, 26 June 1967; all in CEA Records, Box 38 (Folder: "U.S. Gov't.—Defense Department"). Needless to say, economics, at the same time, became an increasingly important part of the curricula at the Air Force Academy (Colorado Springs), the Military Academy (West Point), and the Naval Academy (Annapolis).

38. See Edward L. Allen (Deputy Director, Research and Reports—CIA) to Arthur F. Burns (then at Columbia University), 24 October 1966, CEA Records, Box 38 (Folder: "U.S. Gov't.—Central Intelligence Agency"); Bell to Harry D. White (U.S. Armed Forces Institute); 18 February 1952; Bell to Edwin E. Witte (Wisconsin), 29 February 1952; Bell to William Bethke (LaSalle Extension University), 29 February 1952; Witte to Bell, 18 March 1952; Bell to Baldwin M. Woods (Berkeley), 24 March 1952; and White to Bell, 11 April 1952; all in RAEA, Box 59 (Folder

2: "AEA 1952 Armed Forces Institute—Corr. of J. W. Bell, Sec"). Also see file on "AEA 1955–1956 Committee to Select U.S. Representatives to Oxford NATO Seminar," 14–28 July 1956, RAEA, Box 59 (Folder 12); as well as Lieutenant Maurice C. Mackey, Jr. (U.S. Air Force Academy) to Bell, 5 November 1956; and Bell to Mackey, 19 November 1956; both in RAEA, Box 41 (Folder: "American Economic Assoc. Corr.—1956, M–Z"). AEA work with the Armed Forces Institute had actually begun a bit over a month after V-J Day. See Major Glenn L. McConagha to Bell, 26 September 1946; and Bell to McConagha, 3 October 1946; both in RAEA, Box 33 (Folder: "Correspondence M–Z 1946"). The primary focus of economics research within the CIA was (and remains to this day) the estimation of industrial capacity and war-making potential in other nations. As for activities under the aegis of NATO, economists ultimately became (and remain) involved with work on strategic deterrence theory and decision making under uncertainty and conflict. For example, in the March 1987 issue of the *American Economic Review* (vol. 77, p. 237), NATO placed an announcement calling for research proposals to be funded under a new program focused on "games with incomplete information and bounded rationality decision models." Interestingly enough, in 1956, Lincoln Gordon explored NATO coalition dynamics with reference to the theory of games. See his "Economic Aspects of Coalition Diplomacy: The NATO Experience," *International Organization* 10 (1956), 529–43.

39. Memorandum on the "Stabilization Program," Phelps to Flemming, 20 December 1954, Box 15 (Folder: "Stabilization Policy Committee"), Office of the Chairman, Council of Economic Advisers, Records: 1953–61 [hereafter OCCEA], Dwight D. Eisenhower Library, Abilene, Kansas. Also see Phelps to Flemming, 21 January 1955; Phelps to Burns, 24 January 1955; and Flemming to Burns, 24 January 1955; all in OOCEA, Box 15 (Folder: "Stabilization Policy Committee"). Also see Saulnier to Flemming, 4 January 1956, CEA Records, Box 26 (Folder: "Chron File; January to June, 1956"); Saulnier to Phelps, 11 July 1955, CEA Records, Box 26 (Folder: "Chron File; July to December, 1955"); and Neil Jacoby (Council of Economic Advisers) to Irving Siegel (Civil Defense Administration), 30 March 1954, CEA Records, Box 26 (Folder: "Chron File; January to June 1954"). On the general contours of the federal government's plans

for civil defense during the cold war, see Laura McEnaney, *Civil Defense Begins at Home: Militarization Meets Everyday Life in the Fifties* (Princeton, N.J.: Princeton University Press, 2000).

40. See, for example, a letter from Neil Jacoby (of the CEA) to Stephen Enke (then working at RAND) that mentions a journal article of Enke's which Jacoby "[was] somewhat surprised—though delighted—to find . . . clear[ed] for publication." From Jacoby to Enke, 14 June 1954, CEA Records, Box 26 (Folder: "Chron File; January to June 1954"). Struggling with the security implications of academic research linked to military needs had, of course, been a challenge for American scholars ever since World War I. With the emergence of the "Manhattan Project" during World War II, the issue became a dominant one in the life of the academy. I have explored some of these issues, with respect to one institution's experience, in my "To Win the War: Defense Research at Yale University, 1939–1950," *Yale Scientific* 49 (1975), 4–8.

41. That impact has now begun to receive impressive attention from historical scholars. The most recent contribution in this regard is Ellen W. Schrecker's *No Ivory Tower: McCarthyism and the Universities* (New York: Oxford University Press, 1986); and also see, of specific interest, John E. King, *Economic Exiles* (New York: St. Martin's, 1988). Also see Sigmund Diamond, *Compromised Campus: The Collaboration of Universities with the Intelligence Community, 1945–55* (New York: Oxford University Press, 1992); and Lionel S. Lewis, *Cold War on Campus: A Study of the Politics of Organizational Control* (New Brunswick, N.J.: Transaction Books, 1988). More general investigations of the impact of the cold war on a variety of disciplines are Samuel A. Klausner and Victor N. Lidz, eds., *The Nationalization of the Social Sciences* (Philadelphia: University of Pennsylvania Press, 1986); Bernstein and Hunter, *The Cold War and Expert Knowledge*; Chomsky et al., *The Cold War and the University*; and Allen Hunter, ed., *Rethinking the Cold War: Essays on Its Dynamics, Meaning, and Morality* (Philadelphia: Temple University Press, 1998). Also see, for comparative examples, Steve J. Heims, *Constructing a Social Science for Postwar America: The Cybernetics Group, 1946–53* (Cambridge: MIT Press, 1991); Dennis Thomison, *A History of the American Library Association: 1876–1972* (Chicago: American Library Association, 1978); and

Redmond Kathleen Molz, *National Planning for Library Service: 1935–1975* (Chicago: American Library Association, 1984).

42. In the case of economics, one of the best assessments of the impact of the postwar "Red scare" on the discipline is Lawrence Lifschultz, "Could Karl Marx Teach Economics in the United States?" originally published in *Ramparts*, 12 April 1974, 27–30, 52–59); reprinted in *How Harvard Rules: Reason in the Service of Empire*, ed. John Trumpbour (Boston: South End Press, 1989), 279–86. How certain branches of a field are rejected and, more important, how the notion of "deviant science" emerges in a given discipline is of course a topic for investigation in and of itself. See, for example, Roy Wallis, ed., *On the Margins of Science: The Social Construction of Rejected Knowledge*, Sociological Review Monograph 27 (Keele: University of Keele, 1979). In the case of the American economics profession, anticommunism was a fundamental part of the process that defined what was (and what was not) "scientific" in the field. Of course, as Lifschultz's provocative title suggests, the aversion to Marxist and socialist ideas in the study of economic life had been quite characteristic of the profession since the turn of the century, when neoclassical theorists took up the challenges of the classical political economists and of Marx himself.

43. See Bell to Dunayevskaya, 6 December 1956, RAEA, Box 41 (Folder: "American Economic Assoc. Corr. 1956, A–L"); Guenter Reimann to Homan, 22 April 1945; and Homan to Reimann, 7 May 1945; both in RAEA, Box 94 (Folder: "AER 1945 O–R").

44. See Homan to Klein, 9 December 1947; Klein to Homan, 2 December 1947; Homan to Wright, 18 November 1947; Wright to Homan, 1 November 1947; and Homan to Wright, 29 October 1947; all in RAEA, Box 94 (Folder: "AER 1947–1948").

45. See Raymond F. Mikesell (?) to Saulnier, 20 June 1956, CEA Records, Box 2 (Folder: "[Administrative, CEA], Pending Personnel Matters"); and Gordon to Burns, 26 July 1950, Box 132 (Folder: "[Personnel—Directors]—R. A. Gordon, [1959–68]"), Arthur F. Burns Papers, 1928–69 [hereafter AFBP], Dwight D. Eisenhower Library, Abilene, Kansas. There is no evidence that Saulnier ever rejected a nominee on political grounds, but it is interesting that one of his staff members, Boris C. Swerling, had had to defend himself, upon his initial appointment,

for having "Communist activity or affiliation" in his background. Evidently, in earlier work Swerling had done at Stanford's Food Research Institute, he had received funding from the Institute of Pacific Relations, which some regarded as a suspect organization. Moreover, during a previous tenure at the University of Toronto, Swerling had collaborated with a colleague, a former Canadian army officer, who later was connected with atomic espionage. See Saulnier to Swerling, 28 May 1958; and Swerling to Burns, 9 April 1956; both in CEA Records, Box 1 (Folder: "[Administrative, CEA], Personnel (CEA Staff and Prospects)"). Perhaps the most celebrated cases involving the harassment of Marxist economists during the cold war involved the distinguished scholars Paul Baran and Paul Sweezy. Baran, a professor at Stanford University, whose book *The Political Economy of Growth* (New York: Monthly Review Press, 1957) is a classic in its field, was repeatedly denounced in public and private venues by university officials. President Wallace Sterling of Stanford referred to him, on one occasion in the spring of 1961, as a "sworn enemy of the United States." While protected by his tenured status, Baran saw his salary frozen for close to a decade by vindictive administrators; not infrequently he was assigned teaching loads double those of his colleagues. On the Baran case, also see King, *Economic Exiles*, 176. Sweezy was denied tenured promotion at Harvard University in 1947 and left formal academic employment for good. He was (and remains) one of the most accomplished Marxist theoreticians in the United States. His books *The Theory of Capitalist Development: Principles of Marxian Political Economy* (New York: Monthly Review Press, [1942] 1968) and *Monopoly Capital: An Essay on the American Economic and Social Order* (New York: Monthly Review Press, 1966), which he coauthored with Baran, are considered two of the most important contributions to Marxist economic theory in the twentieth century. See Lifschultz, "Could Karl Marx Teach Economics in America?" 268, 283, 286.

46. The colleague in question was Joseph Spengler of Duke University. See, in particular, Spengler to Bell, 3 April 1957, RAEA, Box 42 (Folder: "American Economic Assoc. Corr. 1957, M–Z"). Spengler, interestingly enough, was particularly concerned that the Association be wary of segregation in northern cities as "this problem [wa]s about as common in the North as it [wa]s in the South." In 1944, Bell had made

clear to Broadus Mitchell, Edward A. Ross, and Pearl Buck, all of whom had written him on behalf of the American Civil Liberties Union (ACLU), that the AEA did not bar African Americans from membership. See ACLU to Bell, 21 November 1944; and Bell to ACLU, 20 March 1945; both in RAEA, Box 32 (Folder: "Correspondence A–L 1945"). That cold war ideology had no insignificant part in mobilizing sentiment on behalf of the civil rights movement of the postwar era has become a central theme of a large and impressive literature. When federal troops, in the 1950s and again in the 1960s, were deployed in the South, for example, to enforce school desegregation and protect African Americans seeking to register to vote, there is no doubt that official Washington, no matter the personal convictions of individual leaders involved, was also particularly anxious to deprive Communist states of the propaganda value afforded by Jim Crow. Among students of the civil rights movement itself, the divide between an older generation of African Americans and their children who, in the 1940s, had served with great honor and sacrifice in a war against racial tyranny in Europe and East Asia, figures prominently in explaining the postwar advent of this "Second Reconstruction." Notorious scandals involving the superior treatment that German prisoners of war received in detention centers in the South, relative to their (often) black warders, only served to heighten the sensitivity to racial injustice both in the region and nationwide. More recent studies of the cold war experience of the Latino American community have arrived at similar conclusions. The primary exceptions to the experience of the racial liberalization occasioned by the cold war era (at least during its early years) appear to have been those of the Japanese Americans, whose unjustified World War II internment by the Roosevelt government would be (monetarily) compensated only decades later, and of the indigenous peoples of North America.

47. On the "Kitchen Debate," a much-discussed colloquy between Khrushchev and Nixon before an exhibit of American household appliances, see, for example, "Two Worlds: A Day-Long Debate," *New York Times*, 25 July 1959, 1, 3; and "Encounter," *Newsweek*, 3 August 1959, 15–19. No doubt, for many American political leaders, the connection between economic deprivation and the popular appeal of Communist principles had been amply demonstrated during the Great Depression, when the Communist

Party of the United States enjoyed its largest membership. Moreover, the success of the Marshall Plan in ameliorating exceedingly harsh postwar economic conditions was widely viewed as having played an essential part in "saving" Western Europe from Communism. See Leffler, *A Preponderance of Power*, 157–67. Indeed, as John Steinbeck had written in *The Grapes of Wrath* (New York: Penguin, [1939] 1992), 206, his epic novel of deprivation and politicization during the 1930s, it was necessary, when contemplating political upheaval, to "separate causes from results [because] Paine, Marx, Jefferson, Lenin, were results, not causes." This was a lesson hardly lost on the postwar opponents of Communism; the searing lessons of the Great Depression and World War II made clear the connections between want and social instability. Indeed, in more recent years, the view has been widely held that the ultimate collapse of the Soviet Union, and of Communist governments throughout Eastern Europe, had as much to do with the economic failures of these regimes as with any other proximate cause.

48. Some of the most useful works on the idea of a "Keynesian revolution" in economic thought and policy making are Alan Booth, *British Economic Policy, 1931–1949: Was There a Keynesian Revolution?* (New York: Harvester Wheatsheaf, 1989); Lawrence R. Klein, *The Keynesian Revolution* (New York: Macmillan, 1947); Peter Clarke, *The Keynesian Revolution in the Making, 1924–1936* (New York: Oxford University Press, 1988); and Robert W. Dimand, *The Origin of the Keynesian Revolution: The Development of Keynes' Theory of Employment and Ouput* (Aldershot: Elgar, 1988). See, for some recent examples of scholarship linking the Keynesian revolution with military-industrial priorities, Jonathan Soffer, "The Moral Economy of Military Keynesianism" (paper presented at the annual meeting of the American Historical Association, January 1997, New York); and William S. Borden, "Keynesianism and Military Spending: 1950–1969" (unpublished manuscript, Mathematica Policy Research, October 1991). A staunch critic of specific policy proposals that emerged from Keynesian theorists, Milton Friedman nonetheless conceded in his AEA presidential address of 1967 that, with respect to the perspective on national economic structure and function that Keynesianism provided, economists had all become Keynesians in the end. His declaration represented a powerful consensus of

opinion among American economists, independent of political preferences, that prevailed well into the 1970s. See Milton Friedman, "The Role of Monetary Policy," *American Economic Review* 58 (1968), 1–22. For a deft consideration of the political factors that framed the Keynesian revolution, one that seeks to demonstrate the paucity of purely intellectual explanations of that development, see Marc Trachtenberg, "Keynes Triumphant: A Study in the Social History of Economic Ideas," *Knowledge and Society: Studies in the Sociology of Culture Past and Present* 4 (1983), 17–86. Certainly the experience of World War II must have inspired economists and policy makers in the belief that increased military production was possible while maintaining or expanding consumer product output. In this regard see Harold Vatter, "The Material Status of the U.S. Civilian Consumer in World War II: The Question of Guns or Butter," in *The Sinews of War: Essays on the Economic History of World War II*, ed. Geoffrey T. Mills and Hugh Rockoff (Ames: Iowa State University Press, 1993), 219–42, who argues that, rationing and particular product shortages aside, the American standard of living improved with the 1940s military mobilization. John Morton Blum offers a vivid portrait of the extent to which American consumers during World War II were, especially in a comparative international context, quite "spoiled" in their material expectations and experience. See his *V Was for Victory: Politics and American Culture during World War II* (New York: Harcourt, Brace, 1976), chap. 3, esp. 92–105.

49. While the Employment Act did not specify that members of the Council be "economists" per se, it did require that each appointee would, "as a result of training, experience, and attainments," be "exceptionally qualified to analyze and interpret economic developments . . . and to formulate and recommend national economic policy to promote employment, production, and purchasing power under free competitive enterprise." See "Employment Act of 1946," Public Law 304 (79th Cong., 2d sess.), 2. With one exception, every member of the Council has been an economist who holds the doctorate. There is a vast literature on the history of the creation of the CEA, and of its operations over time. Sharp debate prevailed for some time regarding the ultimate structure of the Council. Some political leaders argued for the creation of an "ivory tower" group outside the government; others sought the appointment of an individual who

would serve as a personal adviser to the president. Still others considered the creation of an independent panel modeled on the Federal Trade Commission or the Board of Governors of the Federal Reserve System. See, for example, Herbert Stein, *The Fiscal Revolution in America, 1929–1964* (Chicago: University of Chicago Press, 1969), chap. 9; as well as his more recent update that extends the survey through 1994, *The Fiscal Revolution in America: Policy in Pursuit of Reality* (Washington, D.C.: AEI Press, 1996); Stephen K. Bailey, *Congress Makes a Law: The Story behind the Employment Act of 1946* (New York: Columbia University Press, 1950); Hugh S. Norton, *The Employment Act and the Council of Economic Advisers, 1946–1976* (Columbia: University of South Carolina Press, 1977); and Edwin G. Nourse, *Economics in the Public Service: Administrative Aspects of the Employment Act* (New York: Harcourt, Brace, 1953). A fine discussion of the policy practice that emerged in the early years of the Council is Robert M. Collins, "The Emergence of Economic Growthmanship in the United States: Federal Policy and Economic Knowledge in the Truman Years," in *The State and Economic Knowledge: The American and British Experiences*, ed. Mary O. Furner and Barry Supple (New York: Cambridge University Press, 1990), 138–70. Also see Walter S. Salant, *Some Intellectual Contributions of the Truman Council of Economic Advisers to Policy-Making* (Washington, D.C.: Brookings Institution, 1973). In commemoration of the fiftieth anniversary of the Employment Act, the *Journal of Economic Perspectives* (10 [1996], 3–53) commissioned symposium articles, two of which, written by former chairs of the CEA, understandably provided clear testimony to the pride and confidence economists have nurtured regarding the Council. For example, Herbert Stein, who served the CEA from 1969 to 1974, in "A Successful Accident: Recollections and Speculations about the CEA," argued "that the CEA ha[d] given the government and the public economic advice as good as the economics profession . . . had to offer" (20). In "The CEA: An Inside Voice for Mainstream Economics," Charles L. Schultze, who served the CEA from 1977 to 1981, concluded that the Council "[wa]s an institution that ha[d] served the country well" (39).

50. They were John Clark, an economist and attorney serving as dean of the College of Business Administration at the University of Nebraska; Leon Keyserling, an attorney from Wash-

ington, D.C., and New York with extensive New Deal experience in economic affairs; and the founding CEA chair, Edwin G. Nourse, an agricultural economist who for many years had been resident at the Brookings Institution.

51. Again, the best recent study of the foreign policy of the Truman presidency is Leffler's *Preponderance of Power*. In chapter 6, Leffler specifically addresses some of the policy challenges faced under the Truman Doctrine. An added pressure with respect to American economic performance in the immediate postwar period was derived from the needs of the Military Assistance Program (MAP) that sought to provide weapons and other equipment to the armed forces of the nation's allies. In fiscal year 1951 alone, MAP required almost $1.5 billion in funding. See Chester Pach Jr., *Arming the Free World: The Origins of the United States Military Assistance Program, 1945–1950* (Chapel Hill: University of North Carolina Press, 1991).

52. Interestingly enough, congressional conservatives were eager to minimize the influence of "New Dealers" in an agency that already, in their minds, bore much of the New Deal's legacy. In Nourse, founding chair, they had an actual opponent of the New Deal, although, to be sure, in Clark and Keyserling they had just the opposite. With the chairship of Arthur Burns, during Dwight D. Eisenhower's first presidential term, the Council took on a decidedly academic aspect, one that enabled Republicans more effectively to police the ranks of the CEA. The general rule of thumb was to select individuals from faculties far removed from Washington—the general notion being that such distance was usually correlated with the absence of New Deal experience. Herbert Stein, in "A Successful Accident," 4–6, has some telling observations in this regard. Overall, the Council created jobs for and lent prestige to members of but a few, major departments of economics across the country. On conservative attitudes toward the Council and the notion that the CEA was a "conservative" reform project, see Collins, "The Emergence of Economic Growthmanship in the United States," 145–56. Created in 1942, the Committee for Economic Development (CED) brought together powerful representatives of the business and academic community who advocated the use of compensatory fiscal spending policies. Collins's *Business Response to Keynes*, the only systematic study of its kind, documents the crucially important role the CED played in the early stages not only of the Keynes-

ian revolution in economic thought but also of the postwar mixed economy in the United States. Also see, in this regard, Karl Schriftgeisser, *Business and Public Policy: The Role of the Committee for Economic Development, 1942–1967* (Englewood Cliffs, N.J.: Prentice-Hall, 1967), which focuses on the impact of the CED on public perceptions of the usefulness of Keynesian policy techniques. Mark Solovey provides a concise and very useful overview of the scientistic attitudes early members of the CEA brought to their work. See his "The Politics of Intellectual Identity and American Social Science," 152–73.

53. See Stein, "A Successful Accident," 4. While at Brookings, Nourse was actively involved in the writing of the interwar classics of applied American economics, *America's Capacity to Produce* (Washington, D.C.: Brookings Institution, 1934); and *America's Capacity to Consume* (Washington, D.C.: Brookings Institution, 1934). The biographical sketch of Nourse is based on a typescript memoir he placed in his files when they were lodged in the Harry S. Truman Library (Independence, Missouri): "The Professional Background of the First Chairman of the Council of Economic Advisers," Box 1 (Folder: CEA Staff File Nourse, Edwin—Biograph. Info. Nourse"), 1, 4, 13–14, Papers of Edwin G. Nourse [hereafter PEGN], Truman Library.

54. From "The Professional Background of the First Chairman of the Council of Economic Advisers," PEGN, Box 1 (Folder: "CEA Staff File Nourse, Edwin—Biograph. Infor. Nourse"), 3, 8. Also see *Oral History Interview with Edwin G. Nourse* (7 March 1972, by Jerry N. Hess, Washington, D.C.), Harry S. Truman Library, Independence, Missouri, 79.

55. See Nourse's "Memo for the Record," 17 October 1949, PEGN, Box 6 (Folder: "Daily Diary 1949–98"); "Economists in Politics," *Business Week* (26 March 1949) clipping, PEGN, Box 6 (Folder: "Daily Diary 1949–33"); Nourse to President Harry S. Truman, 29 July 1946; Truman to Nourse, 31 July 1946; both in PEGN, Box 3 (Folder: "Daily Diary 1946–2 E.G.N. letter accepting chairmanship of Council of Economic Advisers July 29, 1946 Nourse Papers"). President Truman accepted Nourse's description of the role of the Council in this latter exchange of letters. Also see Nourse to William Haber (University of Michigan), 23 August 1946, PEGN, Box 1 (Folder: "CEA Staff File Appointments, 1946–47 Nourse").

56. Originally known as the Joint Committee on the Economic Report (of the President), the JEC was created as well by the Employment Act of 1946. Composed of seven senators and seven members of Congress, the JEC was particularly charged to receive the *Economic Report of the President* annually, assess its findings, and hold hearings as it saw fit. Needless to say, from its inception, members of the JEC were eager to hear testimony from the members of the CEA, particularly its chair.

57. Nourse's struggles with Clark and Keyserling, and indirectly with President Truman, are vividly documented in the archival evidence. See, for example, William W. Remington (Office of International Trade, U.S. Department of Commerce) to Nourse, 21 October 1949; Nourse to Truman, 29 July 1946; Nourse "Memorandum of Personal Consultation with the President," 14 January 1947, 4; all in PEGN, Box 3 (Folders: "Alphabetical File Resignation, Corresp. Re E. G. Nourse;" "Daily Diary 1946–2 E.G.N. letter accepting chairmanship of Council of Economic Advisers July 29, 1946 Nourse Papers," respectively); Nourse "Memo," 6 November 1947; Nourse to Senator Ralph E. Flanders (Vermont), 4 December 1948; J. A. Livingston, "Economic Advisers Disagree on Staying Shy of Congress," *Washington Post* clipping, 25 November 1947; J. A. Livingston, "Truman's Economic Advisers Take the Veil, Not the Cash," *Washington Post* clipping, 3 February 1947; Clark to John R. Steelman (White House staff), 22 January 1948; "Bureau of the Budget Memo" to Nourse, 15 January 1948; all in PEGN, Box 4 (Folders: "Daily Diary 1947–34 Memorandum in re invitation to testify before the Sen. Foreign Relations Comm. November 6, 1947 Nourse Papers," "Daily Diary 1947–36 E.G.N. reply to Sen. Flanders December 4, 1947 Nourse Papers," "Daily Diary 1947–37 J. A. Livingston, Wash. Post, 'Economic Advisers Disagree on Staying Shy of Congress' November 25, 1947 Nourse Papers," "Daily diary 1947–39," "Daily diary 1947–40a," respectively); Truman to Nourse, 3 August 1948; copy of Keyserling testimony before the Joint Economic Committee of Congress, 8 February 1949; both in PEGN, Box 5 (Folders: "Daily diary 1948–30b," "Daily Diary 1949–7," respectively); Nourse to Senator Claude Pepper (Democrat of Florida), 8 April 1949; Truman to Nourse, 8 April 1949; Nourse to Senator John L. McClellan, 31 May 1949; all in PEGN, Box 6 (Folders: "Daily Diary 1949–42," "Daily Diary 1949–44,"

"Daily Diary 1949–51," respectively). The one exception Nourse made to his policy of refusing to testify before the Congress was when he was invited to present the CEA's office budget request to the Appropriations Committee of the House. By his last year in office, Nourse was so beaten down by the "invitations controversy" that he stopped answering such requests with explanations for his absence and instead turned them over to Clark and Keyserling. As for Keyserling, very much Nourse's bête noire on the first CEA, the opportunity to testify before the JEC was most welcome. As he told his Columbia University mentor, the distinguished New Deal economist Rexford Tugwell, the JEC "were deeply interested and they certainly want the Council and the Joint Committee to maintain a close liaison." He was "not worried about how risky [that liaison] m[ight] be to members of the Council, who [were] expendable." See Keyserling to Tugwell, 16 February 1949, Papers of Rexford G. Tugwell [hereafter PRGT], Franklin Delano Roosevelt Library, Hyde Park, New York, Box 12 (Folder: "Keyserling, Leon H.").

58. Interestingly enough, the differences between Clark and Keyserling, on the one side, and Nourse, on the other, concerning the *practice* of the Council did not necessarily conform to general expectations about the differences, among the three, concerning *policy*. Many leading figures in the profession, to be sure, believed Nourse would be the centrist on the Council, with Keyserling to his left; yet Clark was expected to provide "balance" from the right. In the end, Clark and Keyserling were allies in a dispute that eventually forced Nourse off the Council. See, for example, Robert A. Gordon (Berkeley) to Nourse, 30 July 1946; and Nourse to Gordon, 3 August 1946; both in PEGN, Box 1 (Folder: "CEA Staff File Appointments, 1946–47 Nourse"). Keyserling and Nourse both insisted, for the remainder of their lives, that their confrontation in the late forties never became personalized. They socialized together long after Nourse left the Council and Keyserling succeeded him as chair. See *Oral History Interview with Edwin G. Nourse*, 39; and *Oral History Interview with Leon H. Keyserling* (3, 10, and 19 May 1971, by Jerry N. Hess, Washington, D.C.), Harry S. Truman Library, Independence, Missouri, 109, 113. Keyserling specifically recalled that his differences with Nourse "did not arise out of the economic issues, they arose out of the

question of whether we should represent the President on the Hill."

59. Nourse to Flanders, 4 December 1948, PEGN, Box 4 (Folder: "Daily Diary 1947–36 E.G.N. reply to Sen. Flanders December 4, 1947 Nourse Papers"). Also see Edwin G. Nourse, "Why I Had to Step Aside," *Collier's*, 18 February 1950; microfilm copies of the Papers of Edwin G. Nourse in the John M. Olin Research Library (Cornell University; Ithaca, New York), Reel 3. Also see Nourse to Joseph C. O'Mahoney (Democratic Senator from Wyoming, Chair of the JEC), 9 February 1949, Box 8 (Folder: "Statement by Edwin G. Nourse to Chairman, Joint Committee on Economic Report"), Papers of Leon Keyserling [hereafter PLK], Harry S. Truman Library, Independence, Missouri. Keyserling rejected Nourse's reasoning. Years later he wondered: "Suppose the Joint Chiefs of Staff disagreed with the President on a weapon; or the Director of the Budget on an appropriation; or the Secretary of State on a foreign policy; or the head of HEW [the Department of Health, Education, and Welfare] on a health program?" The answer, he believed, was simple—either one resigned or followed the president's lead. See *Oral History Interview with Leon H. Keyserling*, 52.

60. Again, a masterful narrative of these foreign affairs events and their domestic policy impacts during the Truman presidency is Leffler, *A Preponderance of Power*, esp. chaps. 6 and 8. Prepared in the spring of 1950 by Paul Nitze and the Policy Planning Staff of the Department of State, NSC 68 explicitly detailed the implications of containment strategy and the commitments of the Truman Doctrine. Premised on the idea that the Soviet Union sought to establish "absolute authority over the rest of the world," the memorandum identified American foreign policy goals having to do with the attenuation of Soviet influence along "its periphery," the support of independent governments in eastern Europe and East Asia, and the ultimate transformation of the Soviet system. In addition, NSC 68 detailed the need for covert operations, improvements in domestic security practices, and international intelligence activities. Overall, it is regarded as one of the most, if not the most, revealing representations of American cold war perceptions and strategies. See Leffler, *A Preponderance of Power*, 355–56; and NSC 68, "United States Objectives and Programs for National Security," 14 April 1950, the full text of which was first published in *Naval War College Review* 27 (1975), 51–108;

reprinted in Thomas Etzold and John Lewis Gaddis, eds., *Containment: Documents on American Policy and Strategy, 1945–1950* (New York: Columbia University Press, 1978), 385–442. No doubt the thinking behind NSC 68 was dramatically influenced by George Kennan's assessment of Soviet intentions distilled during his tour of duty in the American mission and later embassy in Moscow, where he had served as third secretary in 1933, second secretary in 1935, minister-counselor in 1945, and ambassador from 1952 to 1953. See Kennan, "The Sources of Soviet Conduct," *Foreign Affairs* 25 (1947), 566–82. The outstanding and important work of Michael S. Sherry has been instrumental in explicating the postwar defense planning process in the United States and its broader political and social impacts. See, in addition to *Preparing for the Next War* and *The Rise of American Air Power*, his *In the Shadow of War: The United States since the 1930s* (New Haven, Conn.: Yale University Press, 1996). Also of interest in this regard is Peter Karsten, ed., *The Military in America: From the Colonial Era to the Present* (New York: Free Press, 1980).

61. The National Security Act of 1947 reorganized the army and the navy, designated the air force for the first time as a separate service branch, and constituted them all within a single national military establishment (NME) headed by a secretary of defense. It also created the National Security Council and, within it, the Central Intelligence Agency (replacing the Office of Strategic Services and other intelligence units that emerged from World War II). Amended in 1949, the act renamed the NME the Department of Defense.

62. The narrative constructed here is based on a general assessment of the evidence in PEGN, along with specific citations as noted. In recent years there have been fascinating contributions to the literature on the impact of the cold war on American ideology and on the strategies deployed by government leaders to maintain public support for the "war effort." Two very able studies in this regard are Allan Winkler, *Life under a Cloud: American Anxiety about the Atom* (New York: Oxford University Press, 1993); and Guy Oakes, *The Imaginary War: Civil Defense and American Cold War Culture* (New York: Oxford University Press, 1994).

63. For purposes of comparison, it is worth noting that by the end of World War II the total national *debt* stood at almost $259 billion. Tru-

man succeeded in somewhat reducing that figure before the Korean War reversed the trend. Throughout the Eisenhower years, the debt rose, reaching $289 billion just before John F. Kennedy took office. Absolute growth notwithstanding, the 1960 figure represented the lowest per capita arrearage since the major war offensives of 1944 in Normandy, the Marshalls, Marianas, Carolines, and Palaus archipelagoes, and in the Philippines. Interestingly enough, during the Great Depression, many economists and most financiers had confidently argued that the nation's money markets could not sustain a national debt of more than $100 billion.

64. Nourse spoke before the Farm Implement Dealers on 18 October 1949. See PEGN, Box 6 (Folder: "Daily Diary 1949–99 News Story on Natl. Retail Farm Assoc. Oct 18, 1949 Nourse Papers"). Needless to say, Keyserling did not share Nourse's qualms. When he completed his tour of duty on the Council, in January 1953, Keyserling told President Truman: "We have ample resources to continue the defense effort at whatever pace the best-informed and most responsible people deem necessary; to maintain a standard of living which will give our people hope for the future as well as satisfaction in the present; to help realistically with the further economic and military strengthening of the free world; and, above all, to continue to expand our own productive facilities for meeting the ever-growing tasks of the future. Every major economic policy should converge on this overwhelming purpose." See "News release for January 1953," PLK, Box 10 (Folder: "Tobin, James—Keynsian [sic] Economic Theory"). When, in the fall of 1948, President Truman asked Nourse to prepare an "anti-inflation program" in light of the nation's military and diplomatic initiatives, the Richmond Times Dispatch scoffed in an editorial: "Mr. Truman is handing Dr. Nourse an empty bucket with which to put out a fire on which he himself is squirting gasoline." See the clipping of 25 November 1948 in PEGN, Box 5 (Folder: "Daily Diary 1948–33"). On the Eisenhower administration budget deficit as an "upper bound" record for its day, see James Tobin, The New Economics One Decade Older (Princeton, N.J.: Princeton University Press, 1974), 3. On page 15, Tobin makes the perceptive point that the debate between Keyserling and Nourse had less to do with the general idea of countercyclical fiscal policy than with disagreements over means. Keyserling believed the public sector to be underfunded and looked to direct government spending as the mechanism by which full employment output could be achieved. Nourse, by contrast, envisioned the use of tax and monetary policy to stimulate private-sector investment spending, thus driving the economy to its capacity ceiling without running perpetual federal deficits. Overall the analytical difference turned on varying estimations of the relative importance of public and private accumulation strategies. The most recent and rigorous assessment of the deficit financing techniques used to pursue cold war objectives is provided by Michael Edelstein, "What Price Cold War? Military Spending and Private Investment in the United States, 1946–1979," Cambridge Journal of Economics 14 (1990), 421–37. Also see his "War and the American Economy in the 20th Century," in Cambridge Economic History of the United States, vol. 3, ed. Stanley Engerman and Robert Gallman (New York: Cambridge University Press, forthcoming).

65. See Nourse's memo for the record, 9 August 1949. PEGN, Box 6 (Folder: "Daily Diary 1949–72"); and Nourse to Truman, 15 August 1949, PEGN, Box 6 (Folder: "Daily Diary 1949–92"). In fact, Nourse told Truman, on 9 August, of his intention to resign. But the decision was not announced until October. See Nourse to Truman, 9 August 1949, PEGN, Box 6 (Folder: "Daily Diary 1949–73"); Nourse's memo for the record, 12 August 1949, PEGN, Box 6 (Folder: "Daily Diary 1949–74"); Nourse's memo for the record, 22 October 1949, PEGN, Box 6 (Folder: "Daily Diary 1949–102"); and Nourse's memo for the record, 23 October 1949, PEGN, Box 6 (Folder: "Daily Diary 1949–103"). Nourse's habit of writing for the record appears to have been born of both his need to vent his feelings and his desire to see his side of the story preserved. The encouragement of his former SSRC colleague, University of Pennsylvania history professor Roy Nichols, was also important. See Nichols to Nourse, 5 November 1949, PEGN, Box 3 (Folder: "Alphabetical File Resignation, Corresp. Re E. G. Nourse"); as well as Nourse to Nichols, 30 December 1946, PEGN, Box 2 (Folder: "Alphabetical File Annual Report of Council of Econ. Advis. Dec. 1946 Nourse"), in which Nourse committed himself to keeping a personal record for "the future student—if history professors are so short of subjects as to assign this topic."

66. See James Tobin, "Academic Economics in Washington," *Ventures* [a magazine of the Yale University Graduate School] 2 (1963), 26; reprinted in James Tobin, *National Economic Policy* (New Haven, Conn.: Yale University Press, 1966), chap. 18; Nourse to Taft, 26 August 1948, PEGN, Box 5 (Folder: "Daily Diary 1948–30b"); Memo from Nourse to CEA Staff, 10 May 1948, PEGN, Box 5 (Folder: "Daily Diary 1948–15"); Memo from Nourse to CEA Staff, 5 June 1948, PEGN, Box 5 (Folder: "Daily Diary 1948–28"); and "Council of Economic Advisers Budget Justification for Fiscal Year 1951," 26 September 1951, PEGN, Box 2 (Folder: "Alphabetical File Budget of Council of Econ. Advisors 1951 Nourse"). It remains exceedingly difficult for Americans, of any generation and of all political persuasions, to render dispassionate assessments of Robert A. Taft. Reviled by many for his adroit sponsorship of the 1947 Labor-Management Relations Act (that bore his name with that of co-sponsoring Representative Fred Hartley of New Jersey), condemned by others for his objection to the Nuremberg Trials, tarred with the brush of isolationism by many historians, the senator remains one of the most complex and challenging figures of the cold war era. Viewed in hindsight, his anxieties over New Deal and Fair Deal liberalism, his temerity in confronting hagiographic portrayals of the Allies and their cause relative to the Axis powers, his questioning of the nation's role in the postwar world, and indeed his condemnation of "scientific" policy elites in Washington reflect a far more complicated and intriguing public life than extant historiography has allowed.

67. From Don K. Price, *Government and Science: Their Dynamic Relation in American Democracy* (New York: New York University Press, 1954), 182. Walter S. Salant, a member of the CEA staff during the Truman years, remembered that Nourse felt particularly aggrieved that the president paid, in his view, so little attention to him. By contrast, Keyserling seemed very much part of the White House inner circle. Special Assistant to the President John R. Steelman concurred in this judgment and noted that Keyserling, early on, became part of the tight-knit group that planned Truman's 1948 campaign. Truman's special counsel, Charles S. Murphy, and his administrative assistant (and ultimately director of the Bureau of the Budget from 1950 to 1953), Frederick J. Lawton, confirmed this assessment, as did William L. Batt Jr., the director of research

for the Democratic National Committee in the 1948 election. See the following oral history transcripts lodged in the Harry S. Truman Library: *Oral History Interview with Walter S. Salant* (30 March 1970, by Jerry N. Hess, Washington, D.C.), 53; *Oral History Interview with John R. Steelman* (15 January 1963, by Charles T. Morrissey, Washington, D.C.), 34; *Oral History Interview with Charles S. Murphy* (2 May, 3 June, and 24 July 1963; 21 May, 24 June, 15 July, and 25 July 1965; 19 May 1970, by Charles T. Morrissey and Jerry N. Hess, Washington, D.C.), 121–23; *Oral History Interview with Frederick J. Lawton* (17 June and 9 July 1963, by Charles T. Morrissey, Washington, D.C.), 14, 16, 23; *Oral History Interview with William L. Batt, Jr.* (26 July 1966, by Jerry N. Hess, Washington, D.C.), 1–2. On Keyserling's active involvement in White House political planning, assistance in drafting State of the Union Messages, and related activities, see Keyserling to Clark Clifford (Special Counsel to the President), 5 October 1948; Keyserling memo to Clifford, 3 March 1949; Keyserling memo to Clifford, 30 September 1949; all in PLK, Box 8 (Folder: "White House Contacts—Clark M. Clifford, 1946–1952 [1 of 2]"); Keyserling to Murphy, 13 December 1950; Keyserling to Murphy, 5 January 1951; Murphy to Keyserling, 21 May 1951; Keyserling to Murphy, 6 June 1951; and Keyserling memo to Murphy, 2 January 1952; all in PLK, Box 8 (Folder: "White House Contacts—Charles S. Murphy").

68. Indeed, seventeen months into his tenure on the CEA, Keyserling wrote his mentor concerning the state of the economics discipline and its role in policy making. "An economist is not a slot machine," he told Rexford Tugwell, "who can turn out 'objective analyses' with equal celerity for policy makers of diametrically opposite views. An economist advising a Chief of State must and should have an economic and social viewpoint, and be willing under appropriate circumstances to unveil it. Any other course seems to me a combination of the very type of cowardliness, self-deception, and dissimulation which you have on many occasions quite appropriately scored." See Keyserling to Tugwell, 25 March 1948, PRGT, Box 12 (Folder: "Keyserling, Leon H.").

69. See *Oral History Interview with Leon H. Keyserling*, 5, 86 (the word "ridiculous" has been transposed to the beginning of the sentence in which it is used), 127, 131–32. Late in January 1950, the Republican senator from Nebraska, Hugh Butler, had inserted into the *Congressional*

Record an editorial from the 20 January issue of the *Omaha Evening World Herald* titled "The Quack." It was a vicious attack on Keyserling, which noted, among other things, that he had been refused membership in the American Economic Association for years and was ultimately admitted when he was appointed to the CEA by Truman. The distinguished Amherst College economist (later at Princeton University) Lester V. Chandler put it directly to Donald Dawson of the White House staff in a letter sent in the spring of 1950 that condemned Keyserling's elevation to CEA chair. Declaring that Keyserling was not an economist, Chandler concluded that Keyserling's "advice on specific economic policies should carry no more weight than that of any other citizen." See Chandler to Dawson, 20 April 1950; and memo from "J.V.F." (Secretary of the Navy James V. Forrestal) to Steelman, 25 January 1950; both Box 1566 (Folder: "Official File, File: 985-A Endorsements G–L"), in Papers of Harry S. Truman [hereafter PHST], Harry S. Truman Library, Independence, Missouri. That CEA recruitment was a fairly hidebound process is amply documented by archival evidence. While the appointment of Council members involved presidential prerogative (with the chair having crucial input as to the selection of his or her two compeers), the assembling of a staff involved the exploitation of a private network that spanned a select group of elite colleges and universities. Additional research assistantships were also distributed among worthy graduate students close to finishing their dissertations. See, for example, Nourse to Haber, 23 August 1946; Nourse to I. L. Sharfman (Chair, Department of Economics; University of Michigan), 27 September 1946; Sharfman to Nourse, 4 October 1946; Nourse to John D. Sumner, 14 March 1947; Nourse to William Leonard Crum (Harvard University), 31 July 1946; Crum to Nourse, 6 August 1946; Nourse to Robert Warren (Institute for Advanced Study), 8 August 1946; Warren to Nourse, 14 August 1946; Nourse to Walter W. Stewart (Institute for Advanced Study), 12 September, 1946; Stewart to Nourse, 14 September 1946; and Nourse to Warren, 16 October 1947; all in PEGN, Box 1 (Folder: "CEA Staff File Appointments, 1946–47 Nourse").

70. The eminent Keynesians Alvin H. Hansen and Seymour E. Harris (both of Harvard University) vigorously supported Keyserling's appointment as CEA chair, arguing in a telegram to Truman: "Some economists may not put the trade union stamp of approval on [Keyserling] since he is not a Ph.D. in Economics; but he knows more than enough theoretical economics to perform exceedingly well in the proposed post." See their Night Letter to Truman, 24 October 1949, as well as Salant to Murphy, 26 October 1949, which refuted rumors that some members of the CEA staff were contemplating resignation if Keyserling assumed the chair; both in PLK, Box 6 (Folder: "Congratulatory Messages"). Equally as renowned, Robert A. Gordon of Berkeley, with a determination similar to that of Hansen and Harris, protested Nourse's departure and replacement by Keyserling. See Gordon to Nourse, 25 October 1949, PEGN, Box 3 (Folder: "Alphabetical File Resignation, Corresp. Re E. G. Nourse"). Among White House officials, Keyserling was of course quite well regarded, both for his energy and for his versatility. As William K. Divers of the Federal Home Loan Bank Board observed: "Keyserling was one of the most able men that I have ever run into, in or out of Government . . . one-third economist, one-third lawyer, and one-third politician." See *Oral History Interview with William K. Divers* (18 December 1969; 12 March, 19 March, 2 April, 16 April, and 21 April 1970; by Jerry N. Hess, Washington, D.C.), 58, 67.

71. See the "Gould-Financial Letter" of 12 May 1950 regarding the Blough appointment. The unsigned piece expressed considerable (and, in retrospect, inexplicable) dismay that Blough came from the University of Chicago, "long a hot bed of left wing thinking and teaching." Clipping in Box 15 (Folder: "Clippings—Roy Blough Council of Economic Advisers May 1950–August 1952"), Papers of Roy Blough [hereafter PRB], Harry S. Truman Library, Independence, Missouri. Also see Edward Ames (Department of Economics, Amherst College), Letter to the Editor, *New York Times*, 26 May 1950; and *Oral History Interview with Edward S. Mason* (17 July 1973, by Richard D. McKinzie, Cambridge, Massachusetts), 36.

72. See Stein, "A Successful Accident," 3. With the 1952 general election, the Republicans captured both the White House and the Congress. Responding to conservative pressures within his own party, President Eisenhower at first appointed one economic adviser, Arthur Burns, to undertake the duties of the CEA. A consummate academic and professional with an outstanding reputation, admired by virtually all of his colleagues, Burns succeeded in persuading the pres-

ident to retain the Council structure as originally imagined in the Employment Act. Nevertheless, the chair was given greatly increased powers to appoint the Council staff and tasked alone with the responsibility to report CEA views to the president. As Stein puts it, "the reorganization plan seems hardly to have been necessary, but it served as public notice that the Nourse-Keyserling situation was not going to be repeated" (9).

Chapter 5
Statecraft and Its Retainers

1. Arthur M. Okun, *The Political Economy of Prosperity* (Washington, D.C.: Brookings Institution, 1969), 23. One of the greatest applied macroeconomists of his generation, Arthur Okun (1928–80) was one of the most influential figures ever to serve on the Council of Economic Advisers. A Jersey City native, he trained at Columbia University under the supervision of Arthur Burns and in 1952 took up an academic appointment at Yale University, where he rose to the rank of professor eleven years later. In 1961, Okun assumed duties as a staff economist with the CEA. From 1964 to 1968 he served the Council as a member; from 1968 to 1969 he was its chair. Having completed his CEA tenure, Okun became a senior fellow at the Brookings Institution, where he remained until his premature death. His major publications included *The Political Economy of Prosperity* (1970); *Equality and Efficiency: The Big Tradeoff* (Washington, D.C.: Brookings Institution, 1975); and the posthumous *Prices and Quantities: A Macroeconomic Analysis* (Oxford: Blackwell, 1982). At Brookings, Okun coedited the *Brookings Papers on Economic Activity*, a quarterly that rapidly became one of the most respected journals in its field. His 1962 essay "Potential GNP: Its Measurement and Significance" (first published in the American Statistical Association, *Proceedings of the Business and Economics Section* and reprinted as an appendix to *The Political Economy of Prosperity*, 132–45) had a tremendous impact not simply on policy formulation and implementation but also on the arguments employed by economists and executive branch officials in their dealings with the Congress during the presidential administrations of John F. Kennedy and Lyndon Johnson. The calculation, in that essay, of a statistical relationship between the level of national unemployment and amounts of forfeited national product was so empirically robust that it quickly became known as "Okun's law." By demonstrating that, for every 1 percent increase in unemployment, the gross national product fell 3 percent, Okun placed in the hands of policy makers and politicians alike a powerful analytic and rhetorical device. Articulation of this "law" was (and is) widely regarded as one of the most important moments in the history of the "Keynesian revolution" in the United States. See Mark Blaug, *Great Economists since Keynes: An Introduction to the Lives and Works of One Hundred Modern Economists* (New York: Cambridge University Press, 1985), 188–89.

2. The term "federalism" is used here to refer to the centralization of political and economic power in Washington in the wake of the New Deal and World War II. Needless to say, this is a somewhat idiosyncratic usage given the more complex connotations the word evokes for both legal theorists and political scientists. See Wallace E. Oates, "An Essay on Fiscal Federalism," *Journal of Economic Literature* 37 (1999), 1120—49, esp. footnote 2.

3. Placed in a slightly different historical context, the "flip-flop" of the major parties in the mid–twentieth century could be characterized thus: the Democratic Party, with its Jeffersonian vision of individual liberty and economic competence, increasingly embraced Hamiltonian means to achieve its ends; the Republican Party, far more comfortable with Alexander Hamilton's vision of the nation's political-economic future, after years in the political wilderness of the New Deal and the Fair Deal, exhibited more and more a kind of Jeffersonian timidity about statist agendas of all sorts—save for defense. Eisenhower's hope for a new "Era of Good Feelings" resonated with the phrase, coined by a Boston newspaper (the *Columbian Centinel*) in the summer of 1817, used to describe the two-term presidency of James Monroe. Interestingly enough, Monroe's broad popularity, epitomized by his reelection in 1820 with all but one vote in the electoral college, was premised upon the recent demise of the Federalist Party. The "Dixiecrat" Party formed in July 1948; it was composed of southern Democrats disaffected over Truman's civil rights initiatives. Their revolt culminated in the nomination of South Carolina governor Strom Thurmond for the presidency. Along with the splintering of the Democrat's Left occasioned by ousted commerce secretary Henry Wallace's decision to pursue a third-party candidacy, the

"Dixiecrat" episode reflected the deep divisions within Roosevelt's "Grand Coalition" that would plague the Democratic Party throughout the remainder of the century.

4. Postwar anxieties about inflation, the brief episode of accelerated price rises in the wake of the dismantling of the controls of the World War II era notwithstanding, might seem peculiar given a generation of experience with devastating *deflation* during the Great Depression. But the fact remains that, along with the typical concerns of bankers, creditors, and merchants dependent upon foreign trade with stable currency values, the vivid example of the political consequences of runaway inflation afforded by the collapse of the Weimar Republic in 1933 no doubt haunted many. The singular role of inflation in destabilizing German interwar democracy is discussed, for example, in David Abraham, *The Collapse of the Weimar Republic: Political Economy and Crisis* (Princeton, N.J.: Princeton University Press, 1981); and Gerald Feldman's comprehensive study *The Great Disorder: Politics, Economics, and Society in the German Inflation, 1914–1924* (New York: Oxford University Press, 1993).

5. The now-classic reference regarding Eisenhower's political-economic views is Robert Griffith, "Dwight D. Eisenhower and the Corporate Commonwealth," *American Historical Review* 87 (1982), 87–122. Also see John Patrick Diggins, *The Proud Decades: America in War and Peace, 1941–1960* (New York: Norton, 1988), 130–31. Diggins's work has some links with the revisionist literature on Eisenhower such as Fred I. Greenstein, *The Hidden-Hand Presidency: Eisenhower as Leader* (New York: Basic Books, 1982); Vincent P. De Santis, "Eisenhower Revisionism," *Review of Politics* 38 (1976), 190–207; and Arthur Schlesinger Jr., "The Ike Age Revisited," *Reviews in American History* 11 (1983), 1–11. Needless to say, in his admiration for an "administrative state," Eisenhower had much in common with another midwesterner, Herbert Hoover. Neil Jacoby's recollection is found in *Oral History Interview with Neil H. Jacoby* (November–December 1970, by James V. Mink for the Columbia University Oral History Project), transcript at the Dwight D. Eisenhower Library, Abilene, Kansas, 11–12, 17. Also see *Oral History Interview with Raymond J. Saulnier* (7 August 1967, by John Luter for the Columbia University Oral History Project), transcript at the Eisenhower Library, vol. 1, 1, 18; and "Adminis-

trative History of the Council of Economic Advisers," Records of the Lyndon Baines Johnson Library [hereafter RLBJL], Box 1 (Folder: "Volume I Administrative History [1 of 2]"), Lyndon Baines Johnson Library, Austin, Texas.

6. While Seymour E. Harris had, in 1947, published the influential anthology *The New Economics* (New York: Knopf), the phrase "new economics" gained popular currency in 1962 as the Council of Economic Advisers under President Kennedy pursued its tax-cut strategy with the Congress. See James Tobin, *The New Economics One Decade Older* (Princeton, N.J.: Princeton University Press, 1974), 7 n. 4, where Tobin specifically notes an article in *Newsweek* (16 July 1962), "Question: Is a Tax Cut What the Country Needs?"

7. From Okun, *The Political Economy of Prosperity*, 23, 30.

8. See, for example, Michael J. Webber and David L. Rigby, *The Golden Age Illusion: Rethinking Postwar Capitalism* (New York: Guilford, 1996); Stephen A. Marglin and Juliet B. Schor, eds., *The Golden Age of Capitalism* (Oxford: Clarendon Press, 1990); and my "Understanding American Economic Decline: The Contours of the Late-Twentieth-Century Experience," in *Understanding American Economic Decline*, ed. Michael A. Bernstein and David Adler (New York: Cambridge University Press, 1994), 3–33. Also see Harold Vatter and John Walker, eds., *History of the U.S. Economy since World War II* (Armonk, N.Y.: Sharpe, 1996). Needless to say, military spending itself provided another source of growth for the economy as a whole. See, for example, George Hildebrand et al., "Impacts of National Security Expenditures upon the Stability of the American Economy," in *Federal Expenditure Policy for Economic Growth and Stability*, Joint Economic Committee of the Congress, 5 November 1957 Washington, D.C.: U.S. Government Printing Office, 1957), 523–41. In retrospect, the surprising rise in wages in postwar labor markets had much to do with the relaxation of wartime controls, a decline in the labor force participation rate of women, and the decision by many veterans to utilize their benefits to attend college.

9. As James Tobin, CEA member from 1961 to 1962, put it in retrospect, "The practitioners of the New Economics did not have to confront distributive issues squarely. It was apparent in advance that if their macro-economic policies took effect and succeeded, recovery and growth

... would do much more to lift the incomes of the poor and disadvantaged than any conceivable redistribution and would be much less politically and socially divisive." See his *The New Economics One Decade Older*, 53. Indeed, this notion of "a rising tide lifting all boats" was of singular importance to the War on Poverty launched by the Johnson administration in 1963. In her new monograph *Poverty Knowledge* (Princeton, N.J.: Princeton University Press, 2001), Alice O'Connor systematically explores the relationship between the Keynesian outlook of a new generation of economic theorists and the tendency, throughout the 1960s, to sidestep the redistributive issues inherent in any consideration of incomes policy.

10. See Paul A. Samuelson, *Economics: An Introductory Analysis* (New York: McGraw-Hill, 1972), 250. First published in 1948, the Samuelson text remains in print to this day, thirteen editions and millions of sold volumes later. President Johnson's declaration is found in United States Council of Economic Advisers, *Economic Report of the President: 1965* (Washington, D.C.: U.S. Government Printing Office, 1965), 10. It was Walter Heller, CEA chair from 1961 to 1964, who first spoke of "fine-tuning" the national economy through the adroit mix of fiscal and monetary policies. The label quickly became the target of powerful satire in the hands of conservative critics—so much so that Heller eventually conceded (in Milton Friedman and Walter W. Heller, *Monetary vs. Fiscal Policy* [New York: Norton, 1969], 34) that his choice of words was a worthy installation in "the gallery of gaffes in economic-policy semantics." See, for example, Charles B. Reeder, "Business Economists and National Economic Policy," *Business Economics* 3 (1967), 7–10; and George Terborgh, *The New Economics* (Washington, D.C.: Machinery and Allied Products Institute, 1968), 166–72. Even Arthur Okun found himself uneasy with the phrase. See his *The Political Economy of Prosperity*, 111.

11. On the origins and elaboration of "economic growthmanship" in American policy making, see Robert M. Collins, "The Emergence of Economic Growthmanship in the United States: Federal Policy and Economic Knowledge in the Truman Years," in *The State and Economic Knowledge: The American and British Experiences*, ed. Mary O. Furner and Barry Supple (New York: Cambridge University Press, 1990), 138–70; as well as his *People of More: Economic Growth in Postwar America* (New York: Oxford

University Press, 2000). There is a vast literature on the cultural watershed epitomized by the advent of "consumerism" in mid-twentieth-century America. Some of the best-known contributions in this regard are Jackson Lears, *No Place of Grace: Antimodernism and the Transformation of American Culture, 1880–1920* (New York: Pantheon, 1981); as well as his *Fables of Abundance: A Cultural History of Advertising in America* (New York: Basic Books, 1994); Stuart Ewen and Elizabeth Ewen, *Channels of Desire: Mass Images and the Shaping of American Consciousness* (New York: McGraw-Hill, 1982); Warren Susman, *Culture as History: The Transformation of American Society in the Twentieth Century* (New York: Pantheon, 1984); William H. Whyte, *The Organization Man* (New York: Simon and Schuster, 1956); Herbert Gans, *Popular Culture and High Culture: An Analysis and Evaluation of Taste* (New York: Basic Books, 1974); and Robert Lynd and Helen Lynd, *Middletown: A Study in American Culture* (New York: Harcourt, Brace, 1956). The singular importance of the economic experience of the interwar decades in facilitating this cultural shift is made clear in the work of Roland Marchand, *Advertising and the American Dream: Making Way for Modernity, 1920–1940* (Berkeley: University of California Press, 1985); and Martha L. Olney, *Buy Now, Pay Later: Advertising, Credit, and Consumer Durables in the 1920s* (Chapel Hill: University of North Carolina Press, 1991). In his thoughtful study *Pragmatism and the Political Economy of Cultural Revolution, 1850–1940* (Chapel Hill: University of North Carolina Press, 1994), 170, James Livingston notes the significant ties between Keynesianism and consumerism and further suggests links between these twentieth-century ideas and those of the neoclassical theorists in the late nineteenth century. Joyce O. Appleby, in her *Liberalism and Republicanism in the Historical Imagination* (Cambridge: Harvard University Press, 1992), 34–90, finds harbingers of the modern consumerist ethic in the seventeenth century.

12. Needless to say, an "ever-growing pie" would yield increasing *absolute* shares independent of the ways in which the whole was distributed. A national product of fixed dimensions, let alone a shrinking one, would on the other hand powerfully charge any and all discussions of its division. For the Truman era, this argument is persuasively made by Alonzo Hamby in "The Vital Center, the Fair Deal, and the Quest for a

Liberal Political Economy," *American Historical Review* 77 (1972), 653–78; for the Eisenhower years, by Griffith in "Dwight D. Eisenhower and the Corporate Commonwealth," 87–122. Also see John W. Sloan, *Eisenhower and the Management of Prosperity* (Lawrence: University Press of Kansas, 1991); and William Fellner, "The Economics of Eisenhower: A Symposium," *Review of Economics and Statistics* 38 (1956), 373–75.

13. On the bipartisan consensus that emerged concerning the "politics of prosperity," see, for example, Collins, "The Emergence of Economic Growthmanship in the United States"; and Hamby, "The Vital Center, the Fair Deal, and the Quest for a Liberal Political Economy," 653–78. In a striking collection of essays by historians and political scientists, Peter J. Katzenstein, ed., *Between Power and Plenty: Foreign Economic Policies of Advanced Industrial States* (Madison: University of Wisconsin Press, 1978), the transnational nature of the postwar tendency to "depoliticize" economic policy decisions is vividly demonstrated. The observation concerning the political tactic of emphasizing an "ever-growing pie" is made by James Tobin, *National Economic Policy: Essays* (New Haven, Conn.: Yale University Press, 1966), 42.

14. The most thorough contribution in this regard is Ellen W. Schrecker, *No Ivory Tower: McCarthyism and the Universities* (New York: Oxford University Press, 1986). Also see my "American Economics and the National Security State, 1941–1953," *Radical History Review* 63 (1995), 8–26.

15. AEA action in response to federal agency requests in this regard is amply documented in the archives. See, for example, James Washington Bell (AEA Secretary-Treasurer) to NRSSP, 12 March 1948; Claude E. Hawley (Federal Security Agency) to Bell, 5 May 1950; and Bell to Hawley, 28 June 1950; all in RAEA, Box 58 (Folder 6: "AEA 1948–50 National Roster of Scientific and Specialized Personnel"). Also see Bell to Dean E. McIntire (Veterans Administration, Kansas City), 20 December 1954; McIntire to Bell, 16 December 1954; and Bell to Carl F. Wehrwein (U.S. Department of Agriculture), 8 March 1954; all in RAEA, Box 39 (Folder: "American Economic Assoc. Corr. 1954, M–Z"). In his letter to Wehrwein, Bell noted that, in his capacity as an AEA official, he had been first approached to draft a description of the "profession

of economist" by the War Manpower Commission (WMC) in 1944.

16. See the committee's report in RAEA, Box 58 (Folder 12: "AEA 1950–53 (Ad Hoc) Committee on Graduate Training in Economics"). In its focus on mathematics training, the committee's report resonated with the findings of a study undertaken in the summer of 1949 at the behest of the memberships of the Mathematical Association of America, the Institute of Mathematical Statistics, and the Econometrics Society. See the memorandum of 30 August 1949, "Committee on Mathematical Training of Social Scientists"; along with Bell to William G. Madow (Department of Mathematics, University of Illinois–Urbana/Champaign), 15 June 1950; both in RAEA, Box 35 (Folder: "Committee on Mathematical Training of Social Scientists").

17. See Howard Bowen, "Graduate Education in Economics," *American Economic Review* 43 (1953), 1–23; J. E. Sargent, "Are American Economists Better?" *Oxford Economic Papers*, n.s., 15 (1963), 1–7; and Bruno S. Frey, Werner W. Pommerehne, Friedrich Schneider, and Gilbert Guy, "Consensus and Dissension among Economists: An Empirical Inquiry," *American Economic Review* 74 (1984), 986–94. Also see A. W. Coats, "Changing Perceptions of American Graduate Education in Economics, 1953–1991," *Journal of Economic Education* 23 (1992), 341–52.

18. On the reaction of academic officers and AEA officials, see Harold L. Hazen (Dean, MIT Graduate School) to Bell, 8 December 1953; Joseph H. Park (Dean, New York University Graduate School) to Bell, 22 December 1953; and Herbert E. Longenecker (Dean, University of Pittsburgh Graduate School) to Bell, 8 December 1953; on forming the graduate instruction committees and the support of the Rockefeller Foundation, see Bell to Howard R. Bowen (Illinois), 17 April 1951; Bell to Bowen, 30 October 1950; Bell to Joseph Spengler (Duke), 14 September 1951; Bell to Bowen, 6 June 1951; and Bowen to Bell, 8 October 1953; and on the interest of UNESCO, see Horace Taylor (Columbia) to Bell, 1 May 1951; all in RAEA, Box 58 (Folder 12: "AEA 1950–53 (Ad Hoc) Committee on Graduate Training in Economics"). On the assessment of the teaching of economics at the high school level, see "A Report by a Special Textbook Study Committee of the Committee on Economic Education of the American Economic Association" in RAEA—Box 53 (Folder: "Economics in the

Schools"); and see Hawley to Bell, 11 September 1950; and Bell to Hawley, 20 September 1950; both in RAEA, Box 58 (Folder 6: "AEA 1948–50 National Roster of Scientific and Specialized Personnel"). On the roots of some of these initiatives in the 1940s, see Frederick A. Bradford (Lehigh) to Taylor, 24 May 1949, RAEA, Box 57 (Folder 11: "AEA 1944–1951 Committee on Undergraduate Teaching of Economics and Training of Economists").

19. See C. A. Castle to Bell, 16 April 1959; and Castle to Bell, 26 August 1959; both in RAEA, Box 45 (Folder: "American Economic Assoc. 1959 Correspondence A–L"). In mentioning Teamster Union president Jimmy Hoffa, Castle invoked the example of the Labor Management Reporting and Disclosure Act of 1959 (sometimes known as the Landrum-Griffin Act) that sought to suppress the influence of organized crime in the labor movement. On Spengler's musings, see Bell to Emanuel A. Goldenweiser (then AEA President), 2 December 1946, RAEA, Box 33 (Folder: "Executive Committee—Winter Meeting"). That Spengler chose to invoke the example of the medical profession's Hippocratic oath was, of course, revealing for it implicitly raised the ever-recurring question of licensure for practicing economists. On the April 1959 social sciences meeting in Washington, D.C., see Fritz Maclup (AEA representative) to Arthur F. Burns (then AEA President), 16 April 1959, RAEA, Box 46 (Folder: "Recognition of the Social Sciences Conference").

20. Maintaining an economics curriculum devoid of Marxist (and other heterodox) influences also involved recasting the history of economic thought in ways that minimized both the influence and the importance of non-neoclassical traditions. Many generations of students were taught to regard the work of Marx and other non-neoclassical theorists as dead ends or detours off the main route of progress for the field as a whole. George Stigler, in *Essays in the History of Economics* (Chicago: University of Chicago Press, 1956), 59, put it well when he wrote that "a believer in the labor theory of value could not get a professorship at a major American university [because] professors could not bring themselves to believe that he was both honest and intelligent."

21. The example of the "mathematician" invokes the celebrated case of Chandler Davis at the University of Michigan. Called before the House Committee on Un-American Activities, Davis invoked a First Amendment privilege in an effort to avoid being questioned about his political beliefs. Found in contempt, he was sentenced to prison, and he lost his academic position in Ann Arbor. He ultimately went on to a distinguished career at the University of Toronto. A notable exception to the generalization drawn in the text involves the case of Moses Finley. Separated, as a junior faculty member, from Rutgers University, Finley moved to the University of Cambridge, where he ultimately became the Regius Professor of Ancient History. Rutgers's officials have always insisted that Finley's firing had nothing to do with his left-wing political activity during the 1950s and was instead the result of his being found to be deficient as a professional historian.

22. These developments did not go unremarked or uncontested. Even as influential a member of the profession as Russell C. Leffingwell could find fault with the transformation of graduate training in economics that took place after World War II. Noting, in the winter of 1952, that their curriculum emphasized the reading of later works at the expense of original and earlier contributions, he expressed concern that Yale University economists thought "it [wa]s all right for the boys [*sic*] to be reading [Paul] Samuelson and [others], who [we]re competent mediocrities." By contrast, Leffingwell believed "the boys should be reading Adam Smith and [David] Ricardo and [John Stuart] Mill and [Alfred] Marshall and [John Maynard] Keynes." See Leffingwell to C. D. Dickey, 18 February 1952, Russell C. Leffingwell Papers, Manuscripts and Archives, Sterling Memorial Library, Yale University, New Haven, Connecticut, Series I, Box 7 (Folder: "150"). Leffingwell, a former assistant Treasury secretary during the Wilson presidency, and later (1948) the board chair of J. P. Morgan and Company, was considered by many to be one of the "deans" of the American financial community of his day. His less than enthusiastic attitude toward changes in graduate economics training no doubt had much to do with his nonacademic career. I am grateful to my colleague Jane Knodell of the University of Vermont for this reference. To be sure, there were exceptions to the wholly "scientistic" reconfiguration of economics curricula. James Tobin of Yale, for example, always insisted that his students read Keynes in the original. But these unique practices were just that—exceptions.

23. Some of the classic works thus lost from graduate economics curricula were Joseph A.

Schumpeter, *Business Cycles: A Theoretical, Historical, and Statistical Analysis of the Capitalist Process* (New York: McGraw-Hill, 1939); as well as his *Imperialism and Social Classes* (New York: Kelley, 1951); Thorstein Veblen, *The Engineers and the Price System* (New York: Hebisch, 1921); as well as his *Instinct of Workmanship, and the State of the Industrial Arts* (New York: Kelley, 1914); and Karl Polanyi, *The Great Transformation* (Boston: Beacon, 1944). To be sure, in some cases the work of many heterodox theorists would endure in special and unique environments—such as the New School for Social Research in New York or, later, the University of Massachusetts–Amherst—that devoted themselves to maintaining older traditions in the field. In other cases, these marginalized intellects would be resurrected in later years, although almost always in a new, neoclassical garb. This was especially the case with the work of Joseph Schumpeter, which, in the 1970s and 1980s, enjoyed a revival as a device with which to understand the rise and fall of business enterprise as a process of economic "natural selection." See, for example, Richard Nelson and Sidney Winter, *An Evolutionary Theory of Economic Change* (Cambridge: Harvard University Press, 1982). Needless to say, even in the uniformly neoclassical environment of the 1960s and later decades, many graduate programs would seek to "differentiate" their product by emphasizing particular approaches to neoclassical concerns: monetarist concepts, for example, at the University of Chicago; Keynesian concepts at MIT. This rather quickly led to a kind of *Methödenstreit* among most American economics faculties that sought to sharpen these conceptual differences. Observing this development in 1985, Dierdre McCloskey could write, in *The Rhetoric of Economics* (Madison: University of Wisconsin Press, 1985): "Sales people for university textbooks in the United States complain that an economics professor simply will not look at a text that does not come from the right church (184)."

24. One of the best sources on the New Left challenge in the economics discipline remains Lawrence Lifschultz, "Could Karl Marx Teach Economics in the United States?" *Ramparts*, 12 April 1974, 27–30, 52–59; reprinted in *How Harvard Rules: Reason in the Service of Empire*, ed. John Trumpbour (Boston: South End Press, 1989), 279–86. On the generational nature of the revolt, and offering a much broader perspective on this historical phenomenon in modern United States history, three classic texts are Paul Goodman, *Growing Up Absurd: Problems of Youth in the Organized System* (New York: Vintage, 1960); Kenneth Keniston, *Young Radicals: Notes on Committed Youth* (New York: Harcourt, Brace, 1968); and Sara Evans, *Personal Politics: The Roots of Women's Liberation in the Civil Rights Movement and the New Left* (New York: Vintage, 1979).

25. Three vastly influential members of URPE constructed a textbook that, for a time, enjoyed success as a heterodox supplement to more traditional readings used in introductory economics courses during the 1970s. See Richard C. Edwards, Michael Reich, and Thomas E. Weisskopf, *The Capitalist System: A Radical Analysis of American Society* (Englewood Cliffs, N.J.: Prentice-Hall, [1972] 1986).

26. A fine example of the seriousness with which mainstream economists took the New Left challenge, and of the willingness to take up its critique point for point, is Tobin's book *The New Economics One Decade Older*, 41–57.

27. This makes all the more ironic the decision, at the 1973 annual meeting of the American Economic Association (at Toronto), to pass a resolution condemning political discrimination in hiring in economics departments. In almost every respect, the resolution had virtually no impact given its focus on freedom of political expression as distinct from intellectual diversity in the discipline.

28. See Lifschultz, "Could Karl Marx Teach Economics in the United States?" 286. The specific cases at Harvard to which Galbraith referred involved Samuel Bowles and Herbert Gintis. Denied promotion, both moved to the University of Massachusetts–Amherst, where they assisted in constructing a distinctive, left-wing graduate program. Along with the New School for Social Research, the University of California–Riverside, and the University of Utah, Massachusetts is one of a handful of programs where anti-neoclassical traditions in economics have been preserved. The future of some of these programs, more recently, has come into doubt as funding becomes ever more strained and the profession ever more homogeneous. No matter how successful they have been, they have nevertheless often remained, in the eyes of the profession that marginalizes them, intellectual ghettos.

29. The opening salvo in the "Cambridge controversies" was launched by Joan Robinson

in "The Production Function and the Theory of Capital," *Review of Economic Studies* 21 (1953–54), 81–106. For the most thorough overview of the debate, see Geoffrey C. Harcourt, *Some Cambridge Controversies in the Theory of Capital* (Cambridge: Cambridge University Press, 1972). Also see A. Bhaduri, "On the Significance of Recent Controversies on Capital Theory: A Marxian View," *Economic Journal* 79 (1969), 532–39; Luigi Pasinetti, "Switches of Technique and the 'Rate of Return' in Capital Theory," *Economic Journal* 79 (1969), 508–31; and Paul A. Samuelson, "Parable and Realism in Capital Theory: The Surrogate Production Function," *Review of Economic Studies* 29 (1962), 193–206; as well as Samuelson, "A Summing Up," *Quarterly Journal of Economics* 80 (1966), 568–83.

30. See Victor Turner, *Dramas, Fields, and Metaphors: Symbolic Action in Human Society* (Ithaca, N.Y.: Cornell University Press, 1974), 17–28. Some very interesting observations on the role of marginal figures in history are offered by Tetsuo Najita in "Introduction: A Synchronous Approach to the Study of Conflict in Modern Japanese History," in *Conflict in Modern Japanese History: The Neglected Tradition*, ed. Tetsuo Najita and J. Vicotr Koschmann (Princeton, N.J.: Princeton University Press, 1982), 3–21.

31. One of the finest examples of the continuing anxiety about the nature of graduate economics education is found in the work of David Colander and his collaborators. See, for example, David C. Colander and Arjo Klamer, *The Making of an Economist* (Boulder, Colo.: Westview, 1990). In the research for their book, Colander and Klamer surveyed graduate students at the six top-ranked programs in the country. When asked if an awareness of economics literature was important to success in the field, 3 percent of their respondents said yes; 68 percent said no. When asked if a knowledge of economic institutions was similarly significant, 10 percent said yes; 43 percent said no. In contrast, 57 percent of their respondents stated that strong mathematical skills were essential to success. Also see David C. Colander and Reuven Brenner, eds., *Educating Economists* (Ann Arbor: University of Michigan Press, 1992); as well as Colander's "Economists Don't Teach Students What They Need to Know," *Chronicle of Higher Education*, 13 November 1991, A52.

32. Strangely enough, the New Left's criticism of mainstream economics would ultimately resonate with a conservative counterattack against Keynesianism and the functioning of the "mixed economy" of the late twentieth century. In their assault on what they took to be the "capitalist apologetics" of neoclassical economics, New Left activists would contribute to a more general loss of confidence in the statist agendas pursued in Washington in the 1960s and 1970s. This would help to pave the way for an antistatist revolt not only of the electorate but also of many social science policy analysts. What would distinguish the antistatism of the Right from that of the Left, however, would be its continuing use of the rhetoric of rigor and competency in mainstream professional discourse—a strategy that would bear fruit in the "supply-side revolution" in American economic policy making during the 1980s. These matters are taken up in more detail both in the next chapter and in the epilogue of this study.

33. Allusions in the text are made, respectively, to the Free Speech Movement that emerged in 1964 on the founding campus of the University of California, the armed seizure of a Cornell University administration building by African-American students in 1968, the dramatic takeover of the Columbia University campus by student activists in the same year, a police clash with student protestors at San Francisco State College, also in 1968, and the defining 1962 national convention of the Students for a Democratic Society held on Michigan's eastern shore. The quoted words in the text are from Dorothy Ross, *The Origins of American Social Science* (New York: Cambridge University Press, 1991), 96.

34. This is the general burden of the arguments advanced in many fine narrative histories of the Council of Economic Advisers itself. See Stephen K. Bailey, *Congress Makes a Law: The Story behind the Employment Act of 1946* (New York: Columbia University Press, 1950); E. Ray Canterbery, *The President's Council of Economic Advisers: A Study of Its Functions and Its Influence on the Chief Executive's Decisions* (New York: Exposition Press, 1961); Edward S. Flash Jr., *Economic Advice and Presidential Leadership: The Council of Economic Advisers* (New York: Columbia University Press, 1965); Hugh S. Norton, *The Employment Act and the Council of Economic Advisers, 1946–1976* (Columbia: University of South Carolina Press, 1977); and Herbert Stein's magisterial book *The Fiscal Revolution in America, 1929–1964* (Chicago: University of Chicago Press, 1969).

35. Ultimately Burns was widely regarded as having been the catalyst for the professional transformation of the CEA. Some of his contemporaries even suggested that, in his hands, the "Nourse view" of the Council's functioning prevailed over Keyserling's freewheeling and aggressive style. Whether Burns himself was comfortable with these characterizations is not clear; while he held convictions about professionalism that would no doubt have incurred Keyserling's wrath, he was far more willing to be involved in the day-to-day political jousting in Washington than Nourse ever was. For an interesting discussion of these matters, see Corinne Silverman's typescript, dated "December 1958," AFBP, Box 12 (Folder: "C.E.A. [Council of Economic Advisers]—Inter-University Case Program Study").

36. In all these regards, Burns (who served as Council chair from 1953 to 1956) was supported by his colleagues on the Eisenhower CEA (listed here with their years of service): Neil H. Jacoby (1953–55), Walter W. Stewart (1953–55), Raymond J. Saulnier (1955–56, 1957–61 as chair), Joseph S. Davis (1955–58), Paul W. McCracken (1956–59), Karl Brandt (1958–61), and Henry C. Wallich (1959–61). Throughout the personnel files of the Council during his tenure as chair, Burns left résumés of unsuccessful applicants for positions with marginalia such as "probably too specialized," "only banking experience," "not much training in academic economics," and so forth. On rejecting proposed appointments of political operatives with insufficient training, see Robert Gray (Special Assistant to the President) to Saulnier, 21 November 1956; and Saulnier to Gray, 26 November 1956; both in Records of the Office of the Council of Economic Advisers, 1953–61 [hereafter ROCEA], Dwight D. Eisenhower Library, Abilene, Kansas, Box 1 (Folder: "Administrative, CEA, Personnel Matters"). Some examples of the "academic network" Burns activated for CEA personnel decisions are found in the following correspondence: Saulnier to Moses Abramovitz (Stanford University), 16 December 1955; and Saulnier to Aaron Gordon (Berkeley), 16 December 1955; both in ROCEA, Box 1 (Folder: "[Administrative], CEA, Personnel Matters"). Also see Saulnier to Gordon, 9 April 1957 (telegram); Saulnier to Donald S. Thompson (Federal Reserve Bank—Cleveland), 13 April 1955; Jacoby to Burns, 11 December 1953 (memorandum); Jacoby to Burns, 28 September 1953 (memorandum); all in ROCEA, Box 1 (Folder: "[Administrative, CEA, Person-

nel, Prospects for Council Staff"]; and James Washington Bell (Northwestern) to Burns, 25 February 1955; Geoffrey H. Moore (National Bureau of Economic Research) to Burns, 17 March 1955; Henry M. Oliver (Indiana) to Moore, 1 February 1955; Richard A. Lester (Princeton) to Moore, 15 March 1955; all in ROCEA, Box 2 (Folder: "[Administrative, CEA], Pending Personnel Matters"). Also see Milton Friedman (Chicago) to Burns, 1 July 1953; and W. L. Crum (Berkeley) to Burns, 1 July 1953; both in AFBP, Box 94 (Folder: "Appointments Correspondence [re C.E.A. Positions], 1953–1955 (2)").

37. It should be emphasized, of course, that the foundation upon which Council personnel decisions were based was built on the core principles of mainstream economic theory. As Neil Jacoby would recall, consideration of nominees turned on establishing that they "had shown through [their] public statements and . . . writings that [they were] a person in the neo-classical ideological tradition." To his mind this required that the candidate believed in the virtues of market competition, private property, and a government of limited functions. "For this reason," Jacoby noted, the CEA leadership "did not consider it efficient to go out and deliberately look for people who might be labeled as radicals. This would [have] introduce[d] inharmonious elements." He also remembered that the vast majority of economics advisers and appointees throughout the executive branch had been recruited through academic networks. See *Oral History Interview with Neil H. Jacoby*, 44–46, 86.

38. Ironically enough, far from being deferential to the "needs of the state" when asked for nominations to the Council, some colleagues indicated that if they were aware of a distinguished individual potentially available for service in Washington, they would rather try to recruit him or her to their own institutions. See, for example, Collis Stocking (CEA Administrative Officer) to Saulnier, 22 June 1956; ROCEA, Box 2 (Folder: "[Administrative, CEA], Personnel, International Economics"). On the occasional struggles with campus administrators regarding leaves for government service, as well as the implementation of special consulting arrangements when necessary, see Jacoby to Melvin G. de Chazeau (Cornell), 9 February 1954, ROCEA, Box 1 (Folder: "[Administrative], CEA, Personnel Matters"); Albert N. Jorgensen (President, University of Connecti-

cut) to Saulnier, 22 May 1956; Saulnier to Jorgensen, 15 May 1956; Saulnier to Philip E. Taylor (Connecticut), 9 May 1956; all in ROCEA, Box 1 (Folder: "[Administrative, CEA], Personnel (CEA Staff and Prospects"); Saulnier to John H. Hoagland (Michigan State), 10 February 1959, ROCEA, Box 1 (Folder: "Chron File; January, February and March 1959"); Saulnier to Edward H. Chamberlin (Harvard), 25 November 1958, ROCEA, Box 25 (Folder: "Chron File; October, November and December 1958"); Saulnier to Chamberlin, 16 September 1958; Saulnier to Hoagland, 11 July 1958; and Julius Shiskin (Department of Commerce) to Hoagland, 9 July 1958; all in ROCEA, Box 25 (Folder: "Chron File; July, August, and September 1958"); Saulnier to Kenneth D. Roose (Oberlin), ROCEA, Box 26 (Folder: "Chron File; January to June, 1956"). Also see Saulnier to Millicent C. McIntosh (President, Barnard College), 9 May 1955, ROCEA, Box 26 (Folder: "Chron File; January to June, 1955"); as well as Jacoby to de Chazeau, 9 February 1954; and Ernest K. Lindley (Washington Editor, *Newsweek*) to Jacoby, 20 January 1954; both in ROCEA, Box 26 (Folder: "Chron File; January to June 1954"). On the desire to distribute CEA appointments geographically, see Crum to Burns, 25 February 1955; and Bell to Burns, 25 February 1955; both in ROCEA, Box 1 (Folder: "[Administrative, CEA, Personnel], Prospects for Council Membership]").

39. Perhaps Burns, himself a Jew, was especially sensitive on the issue of religion, fearing that, were several Jews to serve on the CEA at the same time, the agency would be made vulnerable to anti-Semitic critics. After all, linking American Jewry with the New Deal had been a not uncommon invention during the thirties— whether in the minds of conservative opponents of Roosevelt's "Grand Coalition" or of hysterical racists eager to invoke well-worn canards about the imaginary "Protocols of the Elders of Zion." On this concern and on the issue of "security files," see Friedman to Burns, 25 May 1953; Raymond F. Mikesell (?) to Saulnier, 20 June 1956; both in ROCEA, Box 2 (Folder: "[Administrative, CEA], Pending Personnel Matters"). On the anxiety about those Council prospects sympathetic to the New Deal, see Jacoby to Howard S. Ellis (Berkeley), 1 April 1954; and Ellis to Jacoby, 9 April 1954; both in ROCEA, Box 2 (Folder: "[Administrative, CEA], Personnel, International Economics"]. Jacoby, lacking an international affairs specialist on the CEA

staff, had been utilizing Robert Triffin of Yale on a consulting basis, but he was worried that Triffin was "a New Dealer." On the desire to avoid Democrats in the appointment process and on the dearth of Republican academics suitable for recruitment, also see Gabriel Hauge (White House Staff) to Burns, 11 August 1953 (memorandum); and Crum to Burns, 25 February 1955; both in ROCEA, Box 1 (Folder: "[Administrative, CEA, Personnel], Prospects for Council Memberships"].

40. It is thus not surprising that, by 1969, American economists could also imitate certain branches of the physical and life sciences in enjoying the fame of a new "Nobel Prize" in their discipline. This matter is taken up in the epilogue of this study. On Milton Friedman's perceptions, see Friedman to Hauge, 26 July 1956, ROCEA, Box 1 (Folder: "[Administrative], CEA, Personnel, Prospects for Council Staff"). Institutional imprimaturs could also, of course, work in reverse. Insofar as the vast majority of economists at UCLA, for example, were believed to be Democrats, with the notable exception of Neil Jacoby himself, little effort was expended on recruiting Council members or staff from Westwood. See Bell to Burns, 25 February 1955.

41. See Saulnier to J. A. Beirne (President, Communications Workers of America), 14 March 1958, ROCEA, Box 25 (Folder: "Chron File; January, February and March 1958"); and Saulnier to Warren J. Bilkey (Notre Dame), 23 March 1959; ROCEA, Box 25 (Folder: "Chron File; January, February and March 1959"). On requests for business information, see Saulnier to George Cline Smith (F. W. Dodge Corporation), 5 October 1960 seeking data on the "Dodge Index of Construction Contracts," ROCEA, Box 24 (Folder: "Chron File; October, November, December 1960"); and Saulnier to J. C. Swartley (Chief Statistician, American Telephone and Telegraph Corporation), 19 May 1960, seeking assistance in measuring business activity by information on business phone installations and toll call volume, ROCEA, Box 24 (Folder: "Chron File; April, May and June 1960"). On meetings with academic economists and concern with their "counsel," see Saulnier to J. Steele Gow (Falk Foundation), 24 January 1957; Robert D. Calkins (Brookings Institution), 4 January 1957; and a form letter from Saulnier to all the participants in the "Conference with Academic Economists" held on 26 November 1956; all in ROCEA, Box 5 (Folder: "Brookings Institution,

Conferences, CEA and academic economists, 1954–57"). At that session, in attendance were V. Lewis Bassie (Illinois), Karl Brandt (Stanford), Robert Calkins (Brookings), William Fellner (Yale), Milton Friedman (Chicago), Aaron Gordon (Berkeley), William Haber (Michigan), Neil Jacoby (then of UCLA), Richard Musgrave (Michigan), Albert Rees (Chicago), Paul Samuelson (MIT), George Terborgh (Machinery and Allied Products Institute), and John Williams (Harvard). CEA members and staff were also eager to participate in national conferences in both the business world and the academy. See, for example, Saulnier to Alan T. Waterman (Director, National Science Foundation), 30 October 1957; and Saulnier to Robert Lipsey (National Bureau of Economic Research), 16 September 1957; both in ROCEA, Box 25 (Folder: "Chron File; July to December 1957").

42. Nothing came of Saulnier's initiative nor of the proposed amendment. His form letter on the matter, dated 6 September 1957, went out to a virtual who's who of the profession's academic wing: Gardner Ackley (Michigan), Roy Blough (Columbia), Arthur Burns (then returned to the National Bureau of Economic Research), John Dunlop (Harvard), William Fellner (Yale), Milton Friedman (Chicago), John Galbraith (Harvard), Robert A. Gordon (Berkeley), Seymour Harris (Harvard), Walter Heller (Minnesota), Calvin Hoover (Duke), Neil Jacoby (UCLA), D. Gale Johnson (Chicago), Frank Knight (Chicago), Simon Kuznets (Johns Hopkins), Charles Lindblom (Yale), Edward Mason (Harvard), Frederick Mills (Columbia), Richard Musgrave (Michigan), Albert Rees (Chicago), Paul Samuelson (MIT), Theodore Schultz (Chicago), I. L. Sharfman (Michigan), Sumner Slichter (Harvard), Arthur Smithies (Harvard), George Stigler (then of Columbia), Jacob Viner (Princeton), Henry Wallich (Yale), and Edwin Witte (Wisconsin). He also contacted Leon Keyserling and Edwin Nourse. See ROCEA, Box 25 (Folder: "Chron File; July to December 1957"). On work for Nixon's campaign, see Saulnier to Nixon, 27 September 1960 (memorandum); Saulnier to Nixon, 16 September 1960 (memorandum); Saulnier to John Hamlin (Headquarters, Nixon for President), 13 September 1960; Saulnier to Agnes Waldron, 9 September 1960; Saulnier to Pat Gray (Headquarters, Nixon for President), 25 August 1960 (with attached "Memorandum for the Vice-President"); all in ROCEA, Box 24 (Folder: "Chron File; July, August, September

1960"). On work for the Republican Platform Committee, see Saulnier to Clarence Randall (Special Assistant to the President), 29 June 1960, ROCEA, Box 24 (Folder: "Chron File; April, May and June 1960").

43. Saulnier also, on a rare occasion when he accepted an invitation to give a speech (in this case at Vassar College), demanded that the address be strictly "off the record." On the merchant fleet and Vassar incidents, see Saulnier to Margaret G. Myers (Chair, Department of Economics, Sociology, and Anthropology, Vassar College), 6 February 1958; and Saulnier to John Marshall Butler (Republican Senator from Maryland), 4 December 1957; both in ROCEA, Box 25 (Folders, respectively: "Chron File; January, February and March 1958" and "Chron File; July to December 1957"). Also see, for example, Saulnier to Thruston B. Morton (Chair, Republican National Committee), 20 August 1959; Saulnier to William Proxmire (Democratic Senator from Wisconsin), 8 July 1959; both in ROCEA, Box 25 (Folder: "Chron File; July, August and September 1959"). Also see Saulnier to Prescott Bush (Republican Senator from Connecticut), 2 March 1959; and Saulnier to Thomas B. Curtis, 2 March 1959; both in ROCEA, Box 25 (Folder: "Chron File; January, February and March 1959").

44. See the text of Burns's speech before the Columbia University Club of Washington, D.C., on 19 October 1955 ("An Economist in Government"), and before the Columbia Associates Luncheon on 14 May 1957 ("An Economist's Reflections on a Career in Government"); in AFBP, Box 75 and 76, respectively.

45. See Jacoby to Blough (then Principal Director, Department of Economic Affairs of the United Nations), 30 June 1954, ROCEA, Box 26 (Folder: "Chron File; January to June 1954").

46. Ibid.

47. It was James Tobin, in his "Academic Economics in Washington," *Ventures* [a magazine of the Yale University Graduate School] 2 (winter 1963), 26; reprinted in his *National Economic Policy* (New Haven, Conn.: Yale University Press, 1966), chap. 18, who had used the phrase "coldly scientific and nonpolitical" to describe Edwin Nourse's attitude regarding the work of the CEA—but it could be used equally as well to summarize the aspirations of Burns and Jacoby. Some thought-provoking ideas on these matters are raised by Henry C. Wallich in his fascinating comparative study, "The Ameri-

can Council of Economic Advisers and the German *Sachverstaendigenrat*: A Study in the Economics of Advice," *Quarterly Journal of Economics* 82 (1968), 349–79.

48. The three slumps notwithstanding, weekly earnings for American workers rose throughout the decade. Living standards for most greatly improved. A clear majority of the nation's population worked shorter hours and enjoyed the amenities of a much broader array of durable and nondurable goods than their forebears. Before World War II, for example, approximately a quarter of the nation's farm households had electricity; by 1959, over 80 percent of them did and as a consequence they also had, for example, telephones, televisions, and refrigerators. See United States Department of Labor, *Economic Forces in the U.S.A.* (Washington, D.C.: U.S. Government Printing Office, 1960), 73, 80; and United States Department of Commerce, *Statistical Abstract of the United States* (Washington, D.C.: U.S. Government Printing Office, 1960), 336. John Patrick Diggins provides a concise and vivid overview of the nation's economic welfare during the fifties in *The Proud Decades*, chap. 6. Also see my "Understanding American Economic Decline," 3–33. Another fine survey of the nation's experience in the three decades after World War II is James T. Patterson's *Grand Expectations: The United States, 1945–1974* (New York: Oxford University Press, 1996).

49. Kennedy's campaign mantra that he would get the country "moving again" adroitly played to anxieties aroused by the recession. Some historians of the era have marshaled evidence to suggest that Nixon was particularly irritated with Eisenhower's unwillingness to increase federal spending before the election. Such a "pump-priming" strategy would presumably have taken the economic issue out of the Democrats' hands; it stood, however, at variance with the president's determination to maintain a balanced federal budget. As for the 1960 vote itself, the results were a testimony to how close the issue had been: Kennedy received less than half of the popular vote, approximately 120,000 ballots more than Nixon, while winning a decisive majority in the electoral college (303 to 219, with 15 votes cast for Virginia's Harry Byrd). On all these matters, see, for example, John Morton Blum, *Years of Discord: American Politics and Society, 1961–1974* (New York: Norton, 1991), 20–21, who also notes that "Kennedy's narrow

victory, as Nixon saw it, owed more to dissatisfaction with the economy than to the Democratic campaign"; Stephen E. Ambrose, *Eisenhower: The President* (New York: Simon and Schuster, 1984); as well as his *Nixon: The Education of a Politician* (New York: Simon and Schuster, 1987); Arthur Schlesinger Jr., *A Thousand Days: John F. Kennedy in the White House* (Boston: Houghton Mifflin, 1965); Diggins, *The Proud Decades*, 340–43; and Theodore H. White, *The Making of the President: 1960* (New York: Atheneum, 1961).

50. The original members of the Kennedy Council of Economic Advisers were Kermit Gordon of Williams College, a Swarthmore alumnus and former Rhodes scholar; Walter Heller (the Council chair) of the University of Minnesota, who had received his professional training at Wisconsin, been chief of Internal Finance for the United States Military Government in Germany, and served on the Economic Cooperation Administration mission to Germany; and James Tobin of Yale University, who had trained at Harvard University, received the distinguished John Bates Clark Medal of the American Economic Association in 1955, and served as president of the Econometric Society in 1958.

51. See Tobin, "Academic Economics in Washington," 26.

52. The words are John Morton Blum's from his *Years of Discord*, 56.

53. Kermit Gordon first entered government service with the Office of Price Administration in 1941 and moved on to serve in the economics section of the Office of Strategic Services for the remainder of the war. Along with his work at the Treasury during World War II, and later with the military occupation authorities in Germany, Walter Heller helped fashion the income tax withholding system instituted in 1942. Forced to interrupt his graduate study at Harvard, James Tobin worked in the Office of Price Administration and at the War Production Board before serving as an officer in the Naval Reserve.

54. That the activist posture of the Kennedy Council bore striking similarities to that of Truman's is candidly discussed in an exchange of letters between Leon Keyserling and James Tobin in the early 1970s. See Tobin to Keyserling, 5 August 1971; and Keyserling to Tobin, 21 July 1971; both in PLK, Box 10 (Folder: "Tobin, James—Keynsian [*sic*] Economic Theory"). The issue is further discussed, along with observa-

tions concerning Truman's lack of engagement with the work of the Council, by Keyserling. See *Oral History Interview with Leon H. Keyserling* (3, 10, and 19 May 1971, by Jerry N. Hess, Washington, D.C.), Harry S. Truman Library, Independence, Missouri, 161–72, 190–94. On Kennedy's "analytical mind," see *Oral History Interview with Walter S. Salant* (30 March 1970 by Jerry N. Hess, Washington, D.C.), Harry S. Truman Library, Independence, Missouri, 44–45. Salant, who had previously worked at the Treasury, the Securities and Exchange Commission, the Office of Price Administration, and the Economic Stabilization Administration, served as a staff economist for the CEA from 1946 to 1952. His essay "Some Intellectual Contributions of the Truman Council of Economic Advisers to Policy-Making," *History of Political Economy* 5 (1973), 36–49, argues that some of the policy innovations attributed to the Kennedy Council were in fact anticipated by the first CEA. Unabashed in his admiration for the president's grasp of economic ideas, Walter Heller once called Kennedy "the first economist in the White House." James Tobin, when asked by the president-elect in December 1960 to join the CEA, at first demurred with the comment that he was simply an "ivory-towered economist." Kennedy evidently replied: "That's the best kind. I'm an ivory-towered President." See Heller's personal memorandum for the record, 23 December 1960, in Box 5 (Folder: "Appointment of Heller 1960–1964 and undated"), Papers of Walter Wolfgang Heller [hereafter PWWH], John Fitzgerald Kennedy Library, Boston, Massachusetts; as well as Emil Despres to Heller, 23 November 1963, PWWH, Box 6 (Folder: "Sympathy Letters—Assassination 11/23/63–12/11/63").

55. During the 1960s and 1970s, the American share of real national product devoted to defense procurement and operations was almost double that of West Germany and (not surprisingly, given the provisions of the Security Treaty), close to six and one-half times larger than that of Japan. I discuss the mechanisms accounting for the economic renaissance of those nations devastated by World War II, and their consequence for American economic performance, in my "Understanding American Economic Decline," 16–24. By the late 1970s, it was not uncommon for American workers, especially in the automobile, steel, and textile industries, to employ equipment several decades older than

that engaged in foreign production. The consequences in poor productivity growth were painfully obvious. See my "Economic Pessimism and Material Prosperity," in *The Humanities and the Art of Public Discussion*, vol. 2 (Washington, D.C.: Federation of State Humanities Councils, 1990), 19–27.

56. On the one side, in large part due to the less competitive position American industry enjoyed in world trade by the early 1960s, the nation began to import more goods from overseas than it sold in exports. On the other, American investment expenditures abroad continued to increase along with a steady stream of payments for the maintenance of military bases and troop deployments worldwide. As a consequence, large reserves of dollars accumulated in both Asia and Europe as foreign governments, corporations, and individuals were further engrossed with American disbursements. Under the provisions of the Bretton Woods conference, the United States was in principle obligated to convert these dollar accounts into gold at the fixed (and increasingly undervalued) rate of thirty-five dollars per ounce. To be sure, throughout most of the sixties, the nation's trading partners abstained from insistence on this conversion as they recognized it would destabilize the value of the dollar, thereby undercutting America's demand for their exports, and antagonize Washington, which was, after all, providing military protection from perceived Communist threats in Eastern Europe, Latin America, and East Asia. (U.S. foreign aid grants in the form of weapons systems and training for counterinsurgency operations within their borders no doubt also explained their patience in this regard.) Nevertheless, the "dollar drain" represented a potentially catastrophic liability that could, in its liquidation, decimate United States gold reserves. Indeed, by the late 1960s, France refused to accept dollars in payment on foreign account. Fearing other nations would follow suit, President Richard Nixon closed the "gold window" in 1971, thus abrogating the Bretton Woods currency provisions and ultimately allowing the dollar to "float" in value against all other monetary instruments.

57. Dillon, Roosa, and Martin thus embraced a common prescription suggested by traditional monetary theory: higher domestic rates of return would discourage the drain of dollars into overseas investments (that presumably generated lower earnings) while at the same time attenuat-

ing inflationary pressures by raising the costs of both consumer and investor borrowing at home. A succinct and straightforward narrative of these early debates over economic policy in the Kennedy cabinet is offered by John Morton Blum in his *Years of Discord*, 53–57.

58. Needless to say, the public deficits envisioned by the Kennedy CEA as a necessary policy instrument had the potential to encourage the Fed in its pursuit of a "tight" monetary stance. Larger federal government borrowing requirements would, in the view of most members of the Board of Governors, require higher interest rates as the relative supply of loanable funds to the private sector was reduced to meet public sector needs. Such "disintermediation" in the nation's capital markets was (and is) another oft-repeated explanation for the tendency of fiscal and monetary policy to clash.

59. It is safe to say that, with the inflationary price shocks of the 1970s, the influence of the Fed over the implementation of national economic policy steadily increased, ultimately eclipsing both the visibility and the role of the CEA in the executive branch. These matters are discussed in greater detail in the next chapter and the epilogue of this study. That the effectiveness of domestic fiscal policy might be vitiated by international financial flows was a paradox appreciated by John Maynard Keynes himself. In 1942, Keynes told Roy Harrod that "the whole management of the domestic economy depends upon being free to have the appropriate rate of interest without reference to the rates prevailing elsewhere in the world." He concluded that "[c]apital control [wa]s a corollary to this." See John Maynard Keynes, *Activities 1940–1944: Shaping the Post-war World; The Clearing Union*, vol. 25 of *The Collected Writings of John Maynard Keynes*, ed. Donald Moggridge (New York: Macmillan, 1980), 148–49]. Also see James R. Crotty, "On Keynes and Capital Flight," *Journal of Economic Literature* 21 (1983), 59–65; John Maynard Keynes, "National Self-Sufficiency," *Yale Review* 22 (1933), 755–69; and Jeffrey Williamson, "On the System in Bretton Woods," *American Economic Review* 75 (1985), 74–79.

60. A particularly clear and concise statement of the fiscal objectives of the Kennedy Council is provided by James Tobin's "Growth through Taxation," *The New Republic*, 25 July 1960; reprinted in his *National Economic Policy*, 78–88. Ironically enough, some two decades later, the

notion that the economy could be stimulated sufficiently to grow out of federal deficits became a mainstay in arguments concerning the "supply-side" policies proposed by Ronald Reagan's administration.

61. See *Oral History Interview with Walter Heller, Kermit Gordon, James Tobin, Gardner Ackley, and Paul Samuelson* (interview conducted at Fort Ritchie, Maryland, 1 August 1964, by Joseph Pechman), John Fitzgerald Kennedy Library (Boston, Massachusetts), 34, 36–37, 72–73. On page 47, Pechman notes the special influence Joseph Kennedy had on his son's economic policy views.

62. See ibid., 62.

63. In their joint oral history interview, Walter Heller, Paul Samuelson, and James Tobin all noted Kennedy's interest in and strong grasp of mainstream economic principles. Samuelson recalled a postconvention briefing in Hyannisport where the distinguished Harvard economist Seymour Harris began a rapid and highly detailed presentation for the nominee. When an aide (Archibald Cox) suggested Harris slow down and think of his talk as "Ec A," the Harvard professor protested that "Jack's had Ec A." Kennedy then jokingly interjected: "It's true I did, but it was in 1940, and I got a C in the course." See ibid., 32, 44, 72–73, 146, 251, 303–4, 309–10. Also see an appendix of notes to the interview that Tobin provided after reviewing the original typescript, esp. notes 4 and 4a.

64. See Okun, "Potential GNP," 132–45. When his statistical work on unemployment and output was presented to the president, Okun was asked directly by Kennedy if he would ever be able to present a balanced budget to the Congress. Okun replied that the more appropriate question was whether there would ever be 5 percent unemployment. Along with the complete report submitted to the Joint Economic Committee on Okun's study, the arguments of CEA members and staff did much to allay the president's fear "that [an] unbalanced budget was more of a political and public opinion threat . . . than unemployment." In Heller's view, Okun's law "was probably one of the milestones in the education of the president on economic matters." See *Oral History Interview with Walter Heller, Kermit Gordon, James Tobin, Gardner Ackley, and Paul Samuelson*, 289, 292, 298.

65. See Heller to Nourse, 4 March 1966, Records of the Council of Economic Advisers: 1961–1968 (ROCEA: 1961–1968), Lyndon

Baines Johnson Library (Austin, Texas), Microfilm Roll 36 (Folder: "Walter Wolfgang Heller
(WWH)—thru October 1965"); as well as Keyserling to Lyndon Baines Johnson, 25 May 1963;
Heller to Keyserling, 30 April 1963; Keyserling
to Heller, 13 May 1963; all in ROCEA: 1961–
1968—Microfilm Roll 37 (Folder: "Leon Keyserling"). Also see Jacoby to Burns, 17 July
1967; and Burns to Jacoby, 3 August 1967; both
in AFBP, Box 12 (Folder: "Neil J. Jacoby [1]");
as well as Mordecai Ezekiel (then of the Food
and Agriculture Organization) to Arthur Smithies (Harvard University), 13 January 1962, Papers of Mordecai Ezekiel (PME), Franklin D.
Roosevelt Library (Hyde Park, New York), Box
7 ("Ezekiel, Mordecai: Personal, 1962–63").

66. In mid-August 1961, the German Democratic Republic—under orders from Moscow—
erected a wall dividing the eastern and western
zones of occupation of Berlin. This direct contravention of the agreement among the Allied powers, in the wake of World War II, to preserve open
access to the entire city brought the military
forces of both the United States and the Soviet
Union to full-alert status. While the immediate
crisis passed without incident, save for the killing
of many East Berliners who sought to cross the
line of demarcation to the West, it led to the
expansion of the American garrison in Central
Europe for decades to come. On the $3 to $4 billion projection and Kennedy's anxieties about it,
see *Oral History Interview with Walter Heller,
Kermit Gordon, James Tobin, Gardner Ackley,
and Paul Samuelson*, 377–78.

67. On the other hand, a conservative like
Neil Jacoby would presumably not have been
pleased. See ibid., 179, 219–20. Also see Heller
to Robert F. Wallace (School of Business Administration, Montana State University), 7 June
1963; PWWH—Box 50 (Folder: "W–Wehrle").
Heller also acknowledged the important help of
professional colleagues outside of Washington in
the "public education" effort. During the debate
over the tax-cut plan, for example, the distinguished welfare economist Francis Bator (of
MIT) wrote the chair of the House Committee
on Ways and Means, Wilbur Mills, and business
leader David Rockefeller to support the CEA
proposal. Heller was particularly grateful for the
effort, especially Bator's statement to Rockefeller "that the government [wa]s not a household
and that it [could] not and should not operate by
rules drawn from every-day notions of personal
rectitude." See Heller to Bator, 13 August 1962;

Bator to Mills, 27 July 1962; Bator to Heller, 9
July 1962; and Bator to Rockefeller, 6 July 1962;
all in ROCEA: 1961–1968, Box 12 (Folder:
"Francis M. Bator"). Arthur Okun later emphasized the exceedingly important work done in
this regard by Walter Heller himself. He said in
1969: "[T]he largest emphasis of the Council's
activity [during the Kennedy years] was on the
salesmanship of a product rather than on the development of a superior product[.] And I think
it's fortunate historically that Walter's personality and talents fitted in immensely well for that.
He's a great publicist; he's a great salesman. No
one can put across ideas in more simple and lucid
form than he can." See *Oral History Interview
with Arthur M. Okun* (conducted 20 March 1969,
by David McComb, Washington, D.C.), Lyndon
Baines Johnson Library, Austin, Texas, 20, as
well as 5–11, 15.

68. Arthur Okun ultimately credited Heller
with winning the president's support in the struggle over possible tax increases associated with
the Berlin standoff. See *Oral History Interview
with Arthur M. Okun* (20 March 1969), 12. Heller
recalled that he and James Tobin were so concerned about what the president would do on the
military spending issue that they asked Paul Samuelson to make a special trip to Hyannisport to
meet with Kennedy and encourage him to avoid
a tax surcharge. See *Oral History Interview with
Walter Heller*, II-32. Paul Samuelson remembered that Heller's appointment as CEA chair
may have been motivated in large part by the
president-elect's desire to counterbalance Dillon
as a more conservative presence in the cabinet.
See *Oral History Interview with Walter Heller,
Kermit Gordon, James Tobin, Garner Ackley,
and Paul Samuelson*, 117. Shortly before Kennedy took office, Heller, preparing to leave Minnesota for Washington, wrote Roosa (then at the
Federal Reserve Bank of New York) that he "was
delighted to see that [Roosa] had accepted the
post as Undersecretary of the Treasury . . . [given
that the] prospects of a constructive and cooperative working relationship between the Council
[of Economic Advisers] and the Treasury [we]re
very considerably strengthened [there]by." See
Heller to Roosa, 3 January 1961, PWWH, Box
47 (Folder: "University of Minnesota 1/3/61–9/
10/61"). Again, thanks to professional pedigrees
that were respected and admired across the spectrum of mainstream economic opinion, Heller
could capitalize on the goodwill originally fostered by Arthur Burns for the Council's work.

See, for example, Saulnier to Heller, 22 August 1964, ROCEA: 1961–1968—Microfilm Roll 39 (Folder: "Raymond J. Saulnier"). In the opinion of Seymour Harris of Harvard University, Heller's tenure in Washington witnessed the beginning of a CEA influence that would steadily eclipse that of Treasury, reaching a zenith during the Johnson administration. See *Oral History Interview with Professor Seymour E. Harris, Senior Consultant to the Secretary of the Treasury* (conducted 16 and 17 June 1964), John Fitzgerald Kennedy Library (Boston, Massachusetts), 71. Treasury secretary Dillon's ultimate support for the tax cut notwithstanding, it was difficult to bring the entire bureaucracy into line. Early in 1963, with the benefits of tax reduction but a few months away, officials at Treasury responsible for the Savings Bond Program began a radio and television ad campaign to encourage citizens to place their tax savings into United States Bonds. This "tomfoolery," of course, tended to weaken the spending stimulus that the tax cuts created. The confusion among offices at the Treasury was never fully cleared up. See Robert Dorfman (Harvard University) to Heller, 22 January 1963; and Heller to Dorfman, 26 January 1963; both in PWWH, Box 48 (Folder: "D").

69. On the creation of the Federal Reserve System, the most recent and thorough contribution is James Livingston, *Origins of the Federal Reserve System: Money, Class, and Corporate Capitalism, 1890–1913* (Ithaca, N.Y.: Cornell University Press, 1986). Also see my article "The Contemporary American Banking Crisis in Historical Perspective," *Journal of American History* 80 (1994), 1382–96. Among all industrialized nations, the United States is virtually unique in this separation of banking policy from the regular contours of the executive branch—as exemplified by the fact that the nation has no Central Bank operating under the control of a financial ministry. The Board of Governors of the Fed is composed of seven people, each appointed every two years for a fourteen-year term. The president appoints the chair from this group for a four-year term that begins approximately two years before each presidential tenure.

70. See James Tobin, "The Future of the Fed," *Challenge* (January 1961); reprinted in his *National Economic Policy*, 136. On Martin's surprising refusal to submit his resignation, see *Oral History Interview with Walter Heller, Kermit Gordon, James Tobin, Gardner Ackley, and Paul Samuelson*, 188–89, in which Tobin speculated

that a large part of the Fed chair's reluctance had to do with his suspicion that his pro forma submission would in fact be accepted. Samuelson, on page 185, noted Kennedy's frustration when Martin in fact did not tender his withdrawal; the president joked, at one point, about the possibility of turning off the heat and pulling the phones at the Federal Reserve System headquarters.

71. See *Oral History Interview with Walter Heller, Kermit Gordon, James Tobin, Gardner Ackley, and Paul Samuelson*, 136, 195. On the delicate diplomacy that Walter Heller thought essential "[to] the interest of getting the maximum cooperation from the 'independent' Federal Reserve," see Heller to Paul H. Douglas (Democratic Senator from Illinois), 10 July 1961, PWWH, Box 47 (Folder: "Copies of Outgoing Letters 3/24/61–7/24/61"). In forging the modus operandi that eventually emerged between the White House and the Fed, John Kenneth Galbraith evidently played an important role—especially in a personal appeal to William McChesney Martin. See Heller to Galbraith (then Ambassador to India), 6 August 1961, PWWH, Box 47 (Folder: "Copies of Outgoing Letters 8/5/61–11/14/63").

72. In addition to this initiative within the executive branch, the Kennedy Council (and its successors) also carried on in the tradition of the Eisenhower advisers in periodically scheduling an array of consultative meetings with academic colleagues, business leaders, trade union officials, and consumer advocacy groups. More than ample documentation of these practices is found in the CEA records at both the John Fitzgerald Kennedy Library and the Lyndon Baines Johnson Library. It should also be noted that, in its interaction with professional colleagues, the CEA quickly became a virtual clearinghouse for the sharing of research in progress that was relevant to the articulation of national economic policy. Council members were as well often asked to vet essays submitted to leading journals and to comment on the dissertation work of doctoral candidates. Needless to say, Council consultants and their students were assiduously encouraged to continue research agendas that had relevance for the CEA's mission. In all these respects, the Council played a powerful role in framing the intellectual trajectory (and procreation) of the economics discipline, one that would ultimately be imitated by other federal agencies in which economists were prominent such as the Treasury and the Federal Reserve System. Indeed, in the

opinion of officials in the Johnson White House, the CEA "seem[ed] better 'plugged in' to its profession than other groups." See Memorandum to the CEA Staff from Charles B. Warden, Jr. (Staff Assistant to the CEA Chair), 6 May 1967, ROCEA: 1961–1968—Microfilm Roll 66 (Folder: "May 19, 1967—'Young Economists' visit to Exec. Office"). Obvious analogies to the life and physical sciences could be drawn with respect to the impact of agencies like the Department of Agriculture, the Department of Defense, the National Aeronautics and Space Administration, the National Institutes of Health, the National Institutes of Mental Health, and the Centers for Disease Control and Prevention.

73. See *Oral History Interview with Walter Heller, Kermit Gordon, James Tobin, Gardner Ackley, and Paul Samuelson*, 326, 328, 330–31. Walter Heller recalled that the Quadriad was originally known as the Financial Summit Meeting. Also see *Oral History Interview with Charles L. Schultze* (conducted 28 March 1969, by David McComb, Washington, D.C.) [Lyndon Baines Johnson Library (Austin, Texas)], I-7. Formation of the Troika and the Quadriad is also discussed in Box 1 (Folder: "Chapter 1: The Council as an Organization"), the *Administrative History of the Council of Economic Advisers* [hereafter AHCEA], 14–15, and appendix including a copy of a memorandum from Heller to President Johnson, 1 December 1963, 3–4, Lyndon Baines Johnson Library, Austin, Texas. The AHCEA was part of the larger Departmental Histories Project of the LBJ years that covered the period from October 1963 through January 1969. Several boxes of the records of the project remain closed under Johnson Library rules (presumably until the deaths of all participants), including three boxes of Council records alone.

74. As the CEA, and other economics policy-making units like the Fed, became situated ever more clearly in the public eye, their recruitment practices came under the scrutiny of the first liberal Democratic government to serve since the decision in *Brown v. Board of Education* and the mobilization of U.S. Army troops in Little Rock, not to mention the first administration to create a President's Commission on the Status of Women. Administration economists and consultants were eager to improve the representation of women and minority scholars in the work of their offices. Yet their very sensitivity to these matters also served, precisely because it brought the issue of professional integration into the open like never

before, to expose the unexamined presumptions and indiscretions that made diversity so difficult to achieve. It was as easy, for example, to assume that a talented black colleague would "be a useful man on African economic development" as it was to include comments about a female candidate being "charming" and "attractive" in a letter of recommendation for a Council staff posting. One would look in vain through the literally hundreds of letters in CEA records regarding staff appointments for comparable suppositions and observations about white male recruits. As for actual leadership positions, even good intentions could not overcome deeply ingrained bias. When President Johnson thought seriously about appointing a woman to the Federal Reserve Board of Governors, he thought it logical that she would be "consumer-minded." His advisers and consultants were more direct and blunt in their preconceptions: Paul Samuelson opined that "[w]omen [we]re very estimable but the Federal Reserve [wa]s not necessarily the best place for them." See Max M. Kampelman to Heller, 5 April 1961; and Heller to Kampelman, 24 April 1961; both in PWWH, Box 49 (Folder: "K"); and Walt W. Rostow (Special Presidential Assistant for National Security Affairs) to Henry R. Labouisse (Director, International Cooperation Administration), 13 March 1961; Papers of John F. Kennedy (Presidential Papers—White House Staff Files, Walt W. Rostow File) [John Fitzgerald Kennedy Library (Boston, Massachusetts)], Box 3 (Folder: "WA–WH"). Samuelson reports on Johnson's idea and on his own reaction to it in *Oral History Interview with Walter Heller, Kermit Gordon, James Tobin, Gardner Ackley, and Paul Samuelson*, 366–67. On the concern of the Kennedy and Johnson administrations with the diversity of appointed staff, see Heller's Memorandum for the President, 1 February 1964, PWWH, Box 13 (Folder: "2/64").

75. See *Oral History Interview with Gardner Ackley* (conducted 13 April 1973 by Joe B. Grantz at Ann Arbor) [Lyndon Baines Johnson Library (Austin, Texas)], II-20-1. It was Ackley's frank opinion that a large reason for the exclusion of the Fed from authentic participation in the work of the Quadriad was the incompetence of chair Martin whom he described, at II-6, as "absolutely zero as an economist." He went on to say that it was unlikely the nation would "ever have a chairman of the Federal Reserve who [like Martin] [wa]s so completely out of the mainstream of economics." Interestingly enough, the

Kennedy years mark a watershed in the history of the Fed as the Board of Governors thereafter became ever more thoroughly professionalized. Up until the mid-1960s the majority of the governors were always drawn from the business and banking communities, few of them with professional degrees in economics—indeed, in 1961 none of the seven members held such credentials. Since then the situation has been quite the reverse. Indeed, by the time of the "Reagan revolution" in economic policy making in the 1980s, the Fed had become arguably the most visible and influential outpost of the profession in federal government service, assuming a role in the implementation of economic policies that places it very much at the "head of the table," with the CEA, Treasury, and Budget following its lead. Some implications of this development are discussed in the next chapter, but it is striking to note here that to the extent professional economists have now found the Fed a worthy and sturdy venue from which to participate in the work of government, they have done so within a bureaucracy whose separation from the political oversight of the president and the Congress remains a point of continuing debate. One might, therefore, speak of the profession insulating itself, within the domain of the Federal Reserve, from political life in ways both unimaginable to individuals like Kermit Gordon, Walter Heller, and James Tobin and simply not possible prior to the 1980s. Even so, what was regarded as thoughtful criticism of the Fed's "independence" coming from the mainstream of both the profession and the government in the 1960s—in, for example, the person of James Tobin—is today more likely regarded as a strident and implausible call for radical reform.

76. Heller was later quite forthcoming about his ulterior motives in the Quadriad's formation in *Oral History Interview with Walter Heller* (conducted 20 February 1970 by David McComb at the University of Minnesota), Lyndon Baines Johnson Library, Austin, Texas, II-1-2. Although the Bureau of the Budget did not have formal cabinet status during the Kennedy administration, it had understandable influence over White House decision making. It was reorganized as the Office of Management and Budget in 1971, and its director was formally given cabinet status by President Richard Nixon. On the effective operations of the Quadriad, see *Oral History Interview with Walter Heller, Kermit Gordon, James Tobin, Gardner Ackley, and Paul Samuelson*, 329. Cre-

ation of the Quadriad rekindled discussions about the usefulness of a proposed "National Economic Council" that would bring all of the economic policy units of the federal government together in formal consultation. Briefly discussed during the debate over the Full Employment and Stabilization Act itself, the idea languished until the mid-1960s, although even then it received little genuine consideration. See, for example, Heller to Henry H. Villard (New York City), 26 March 1964; and Villard to Heller, 25 February 1964, both in PWWH, Box 50 (Folder: "V"). Exasperated by the Fed in January 1961, James Tobin had brought the matter up again, suggesting that "Congress could establish a coordinating committee for economic policy similar to the National Security Council." See Tobin, "The Future of the Fed," 136. In the final analysis the idea of a "National Council" faded away, although William Clinton created a facsimile during his first presidential term that commenced in 1993, one notable for its lack of influence, prestige, and effectiveness.

77. Kennedy's request was ultimately pared down to a $12 billion decrease. The speed and enthusiasm with which Lyndon Johnson took up the economic agenda of his predecessor was a matter of both pride and admiration for Walter Heller. But weeks after he had taken the oath of office aboard *Air Force One*, Johnson was, in Heller's words, "fully committed to the tax cut" and "taking hold well on the economic side." See Heller to Roy Blough (Graduate School of Business, Columbia University), 5 January 1964; PWWH—Box 47 (Folder: "Block-B").

78. On Tobin's chat with Sorensen, see *Oral History Interview with Walter Heller, Kermit Gordon, James Tobin, Gardner Ackley, and Paul Samuelson*, 235. Okun's observation is made in *Oral History Interview with Arthur M. Okun* (20 March 1969), 14. Perhaps Walter Heller's alma mater, Oberlin College (where he had been a member of the class of 1935), best portrayed the risks its distinguished alumnus had borne so well in the citation included with his honorary doctor of laws degree: "Next to the Presidency itself, the chairmanship of the Council [of Economic Advisers] is the most exposed office in our government. Not everyone in the country professes expertness in military and foreign affairs, but no one of our 200 million men, women, children and infants will concede to any other greater expertness than his own in economic public policy."

The undated document is included in PWWH, Box 49 (Folder: "Heller–Herzog").

79. See Roy E. Moor (Administrative Assistant to William Proxmire) to Heller, 10 October 1964, PWWH, Box 49 (Folder: "M"); Burns to Heller, 11 May 1964, AFBP, Box 12 (Folder: "Council of Economics Advisers—Walter W. Heller"); Friedman to Heller, 30 December 1960; and Rashi Fein (Brookings Institution) to Heller, 16 September 1963; both in PWWH, Box 48 (Folder: "F"); Marcus Alexis (DePaul University) to Heller, 19 January 1961, PWWH, Box 47 (Folder: "A"); and Leroy S. Wehrle (US AID Mission to Laos) to Heller, 8 July 1964, PWWH, Box 50 (Folder: "W–Wehrle").

80. Heller's central role in the emergence of the antipoverty strategy is attested to by an array of testimony from members of the administration. Then director of the Bureau of the Budget (and future CEA chair under President Jimmy Carter), Charles Schultze, who had noted the president's high regard for Harrington, also credited Heller as the individual "who probably first put the idea [of a poverty policy] in Kennedy's head." See *Oral History Interview with Charles L. Schultze* (28 March 1969), I-38-9. Similar recollections are provided by both Gardner Ackley and Robert Lampman. See *Oral History Interview with Gardner Ackley*, I-9; and *Oral History Interview with Robert Lampman* (24 May 1983, by Michael L. Gillette, Madison, Wisconsin) Lyndon Baines Johnson Library, Austin, Texas, I-1-3. As for Harrington's work, the president had evidently read his most recent book, *The Other America: Poverty in the United States* (New York: Macmillan, 1962). A CEA staff member, Robert Lampman had generated the estimates of skewed wealth and income distribution (exhibited in data drawn from the early 1960s) that so struck Heller. Lampman remembered, on page I-4, that Heller specifically asked that a "simplified version" of the econometrics memorandum be prepared for the president's consideration. A graduate school classmate of Heller's and later a professor of economics at the University of Wisconsin–Madison, Lampman wrote a chapter of the *Economic Report of the President: 1964* dealing specifically with the proposed War on Poverty. When Lapman died in 1997, James Tobin called him "the intellectual architect of the war on poverty." See *New York Times*, 8 March 1997, 11, 52.

81. From Walter Heller's "Confidential Notes on Meeting with the President, October 21,

1963," 2, PWWH, Box 13 (Folder: "10/18/63–10/31/63"). Heller indicated that his briefing of the president followed up on a "memo of last summer." Regarding the links between the tax-cut policy and efforts to end employment discrimination, see Lloyd Ulman (Director, Institute of Industrial Relations, University of California–Berkeley) to Heller, 3 July 1963, PWWH, Box 12 (Folder: "7/2/63–7/20/63"). On Heller's meeting with the president before the trip to Dallas, see *Oral History Interview with Robert Lampman*, I-14. At that time, Kennedy evidently indicated that the antipoverty theme would be an essential part of his 1964 campaign. African-American voters began to abandon the Republican Party—the "Party of Lincoln"—during the New Deal. One of the few studies of this historical sea change is Nancy Weiss, *Farewell to the Party of Lincoln: Black Politics in the Age of FDR* (Princeton, N.J.: Princeton University Press, 1983). Yet it was not until the civil rights rebellion of the postwar era that the Democratic Party leadership began to take explicit account of this remarkable change in the nation's electoral composition. Throughout the Truman presidency, of course, and well into the first year of the Kennedy administration, temporizing with the "Dixiecrats" below the Mason-Dixon line was all too common. The "Solid South" that had supported Democratic presidential candidates since the late 1850s had always been "lily white." Transformed by a grassroots uprising in the 1950s and 1960s, the region's white voters would become targets for a "southern strategy," first successfully utilized by Richard Nixon in the 1968 presidential campaign, that would see the Republican Party carry southern states for the first time since Reconstruction.

82. See Heller's "Notes on Meeting with President Johnson, 7:40 p.m., Saturday, November 23, 1963," 1–3, PWWH, Box 13 (Folder: "11/16/63–11/30/63"). Regarding the flight from Dallas to Washington on *Air Force One* and Heller's preparation for the meeting with Johnson, see *Oral History Interview with Joseph A. Pechman* (interview conducted by David G. McComb, 19 March 1969, at Washington, D.C.) [Lyndon Baines Johnson Library (Austin, Texas)], 24. Pechman noted that the president was exceedingly impressed by Heller's professionalism and hard work in the immediate days after the Kennedy assassination. One of the finest surveys of the work of professional social scientists in the prosecution of the War on Poverty is

Henry Aaron's *Politics and the Professors: The Great Society in Perspective* (Washington, D.C.: Brookings Institution, 1978). Also see Robert H. Haveman, *Poverty Policy and Poverty Research: The Great Society and the Social Sciences* (Madison: University of Wisconsin Press, 1987).

Chapter 6
Statecraft and Its Discontents

1. John Maynard Keynes, "Economic Possibilities for Our Grandchildren," in his *Essays in Persuasion* (New York: Harcourt, Brace, 1932), 373. Almost universally regarded as the greatest economist of the twentieth century, Keynes (1883–1946) is best known for the withering critique of mainstream theory that he advanced in his *General Theory of Employment, Interest and Money* (1936). While the *General Theory* is most widely understood to have inspired new departures in policy making exemplified by the interventionist practices of the New Deal, the fact remains that the work is first and foremost a theoretical one, a quality consistent with Keynes's earlier (and similarly influential) scholarly forays in mathematics (e.g., *A Treatise on Probability* [1921]) and monetary economics (e.g., *A Treatise on Money* [1930]). The inaccurate perception of Keynes as a policy analyst rather than as a theorist most likely derives in part from the many well-received publications he issued on pressing contemporary issues during the course of his career—such as *Indian Currency and Finance* (1913), *The Economic Consequences of the Peace* (1919), and *A Tract on Monetary Reform* (1923)—as well as from the central (and quite visible) role he played in the Bretton Woods Conference of 1944. A gifted polymath who had studied classics and mathematics at King's College, Cambridge, Keynes was also a fine and broadly published essayist who enjoyed the respect and company of the celebrated Bloomsbury group, the British intellectual circle that included the likes of Bertrand Russell, Lytton Strachey, and Virginia Woolf. An adviser to the British Treasury for many years, chair of a major insurance company, and editor of the flagship *Economic Journal*, Keynes also served as bursar of King's College some years after receiving appointment as a fellow, a post in which his economic acumen yielded prodigious material benefits for his alma mater. Keynes perceived in neoclassical theory a transformation in

the analytical focus of economics that did little to improve the discipline's applicability both to the workings of modern capitalist economies and to everyday policy problems. See Roy F. Harrod, *The Life of John Maynard Keynes* (London: Macmillan, 1951); Donald E. Moggridge, *Keynes* (New York: Fontana/Collins, 1976); Mark Blaug, *Great Economists before Keynes: An Introduction to the Lives and Works of One Hundred Great Economists of the Past* (New York: Cambridge University Press, 1986), 106–9; and Robert Skidelsky's two-volume biography, *John Maynard Keynes: A Biography* (New York: Macmillan, 1983, 1996).

2. The quotations are from James Tobin, *The New Economics One Decade Older* (Princeton, N.J.: Princeton University Press, 1974), 34.

3. Charles Schultze, who ultimately served as CEA chair under President Jimmy Carter, recalled that Johnson was always impatient with long-run budgetary planning and economic policy analysis. When confronted with advisers' concerns about the costs of a particular program, for example, the president might say: "Can't you get this program in? It will only cost fifty million the first year, don't bother me about the rest." See *Oral History Interview with Charles L. Schultze* (conducted 10 April 1969 by David McComb at Washington, D.C.) [Lyndon Baines Johnson Library (Austin, Texas)], II-48. For LBJ, clearly, politics set the economic agenda, not the other way around. It should be noted, of course, that the president's electoral agenda, by which he envisioned securing majority status for his party through the impacts of both civil rights reform and a successful antipoverty program, was not simply a product of his own strategic decision making. It also derived from the powerful political pressure both Congress and the executive branch felt at the hands of a dramatic localized mobilization, especially but not solely taking place in the southern states, against de jure and de facto racial segregation.

4. On the turning point of 1965 and the end of "growth liberalism and the American Century," see Robert M. Collins, "The Economic Crisis of 1968 and the Waning of the 'American Century,'" *American Historical Review* 101 (1996), 401, 422; as well as his "Growth Liberalism in the Sixties: Great Societies at Home and Grand Designs Abroad," in *The Sixties: From Memory to History*, ed. David Farber (Chapel Hill: University of North Carolina Press, 1994), 11–44. On the surprise of "stubbornly persistent" infla-

tion, see Tobin, *The New Economics One Decade Older*, 36. A more recent study of the turmoil that the Vietnam War provoked in the federal apparatus is Robert Buzzanco, *Masters of War: Military Dissent and Politics in the Vietnam Era* (New York: Cambridge University Press, 1996).

5. The quotation is Tobin's in *The New Economics One Decade Older*, 34. On the divergence in practice between the Johnson administration and its immediate predecessors, see Walter Heller's memorandum for presidential aide Jack Valenti, 7 August 1964, PWWH, Box 3 (Folder: "The Role of the Council 9/20/62–8/7/64 + undated"). CEA involvement in national security matters had also been facilitated, in the past, by its formal representation on the Civil and Defense Mobilization Board (CDMB) in the Executive Office of the President. See Frank B. Ellis (Director, CDMB) to Heller, 16 May 1961; and Heller to Ellis, 12 May 1961; Records from the CEA: 1961–1968 (RCEA: 1961–1968), Lyndon Baines Johnson Library, Austin, Texas, Microfilm Roll 4 (Folder: "Civil Defense Mobilization Board CEA Membership—Misc. Correspondence, etc."). On the escalation of the Vietnam War and its dramatic economic implications, see Collins, "Growth Liberalism in the Sixties," passim; Jack Valenti, *A Very Human President* (New York: Norton, 1975), 345; Larry Berman, *Planning a Tragedy: The Americanization of the War in Vietnam* (New York: Norton, 1982); and George Kahin, *Intervention: How America Became Involved in Vietnam* (New York: Knopf, 1986), 347–401. Most recently, H. R. McMaster has argued that the Joint Chiefs of Staff, in particular their chair from 1962 to 1964—army general Maxwell Taylor—consciously misled Presidents Kennedy and Johnson about their genuine views of the military dimensions of the Vietnam War. See his *Dereliction of Duty: Lyndon Johnson, Robert McNamara, and the Joint Chiefs of Staff, and the Lies That Led to Vietnam* (New York: HarperCollins, 1997).

6. See Jacoby (Dean of the School of Business Administration, UCLA) to Arthur Burns (Columbia University and the National Bureau of Economic Research [NBER]), 16 August 1966; and Ackley to Burns, 12 June 1967; both in Arthur F. Burns Papers, Dwight D. Eisenhower Library, Abilene, Kansas, Box 12 (Folders: "Neil H. Jacoby (1)" and "Council of Economic Advisers," respectively). James Tobin, in *The New Economics One Decade Older*, 34, similarly blames DOD for failing to keep the CEA, the Bu-

reau of the Budget, and the Department of Treasury fully apprised of the magnitude of the military buildup in Indochina. As for the actual costs of the Vietnam War, the definitive discussion is now provided by Michael Edelstein, "War and the American Economy in the 20th Century," in *Cambridge Economic History of the United States*, vol. 3, ed. Stanley Engerman and Robert Gallman (New York: Cambridge University Press, forthcoming). Looking solely at the *direct* costs of the conflict (that is, expenditures for labor, capital, and the goods and services to engage in combat and supply the combat effort), Edelstein (using as his benchmark dates, August 1964 through January 1973) estimates a total burden of a bit over $313 billion in 1982 dollars, representing $3.1 billion per month. While considerably less than the direct costs of, say, World War II (which Edelstein estimates at almost $55 billion per month in 1982 dollars), the total is nonetheless arresting. Edelstein based his very careful calculations on the work of Thomas Riddell, "A Political Economy of the American War in Indo-China: Its Costs and Consequences" (Ph.D. diss., American University, 1975); and Robert Warren Stevens, *Vain Hopes Grim Realities* (New York: New Viewpoints/Franklin Watts, 1976). Needless to say, such cost accounting of the burdens of war ignores the additional direct costs of human conflict attendant upon lost lives, permanent injury and disability, and the destruction of land and capital.

7. Early in 1966, it was the Fed that took up the challenge of inflation, raising discount rates in an effort to stifle the economy's hyperactivity. In some respects, the policy worked. Residential construction, for example, fell 25 percent during that year. But business investment remained robust. Ironically enough, monetary "tightening" then threatened to precipitate a recession in 1967. Restoration of an earlier investment tax credit, in the spring of that year, forestalled that outcome.

8. The Revenue and Expenditure Control Act of 1968 imposed an additional 10 percent levy on corporate and personal incomes. On the petitions regarding the need for a tax surcharge, see the memorandums from Gardner Ackley to President Lyndon Johnson, 24 July 1967, 25 July 1967, 16 August 1967, and 11 September 1967, AHCEA, all in Box 1 (Folder: "Volume II, Doc. Supplement Part I [1 of 2]"). Some of the powerful and influential figures in the profession—a few of whom had seen service with the CEA or other government agencies—who lent their

names to these petition and letter-writing efforts were Moses Abramovitz (Stanford), E. Cary Brown (MIT), John Dunlop (Harvard), Otto Eckstein (Harvard), Robert Eisner (Northwestern), William Fellner (Yale), John Kenneth Galbraith (Harvard), Aaron Gordon (Berkeley), Kermit Gordon (Brookings Institution), Walter Heller (Minnesota), Leon Keyserling (private practice), Abba Lerner (Berkeley), John Lintner (Harvard), Paul McCracken (Michigan), John Meyer (Harvard), Geoffrey Moore (NBER), Joseph Pechman (Brookings Institution), Richard Ruggles (Yale), Robert Solow (MIT), Joseph Spengler (Duke), and George Terborgh (Machinery and Allied Products Institute). Former CEA member James Tobin went one step further, publishing an "op-ed" piece in the *Washington Post* (8 October 1967) on the need for a tax increase. Ackley was particularly pleased with his effort. See Ackley to Tobin, 9 October 1967, Records of the Council of Economic Advisers: 1961–1968 (ROCEA: 1961–1968), microfilm roll 40 (Folder: "James Tobin"). On the limitations of fiscal policy relative to its monetary counterpart, see Tobin, *The New Economics One Decade Older*, 37.

9. See *Oral History Interview with Arthur Okun* (15 April 1969, by David G. McComb, Washington, D.C.), Lyndon Baines Johnson Library, Austin, Texas, 4–5; *Oral History Interview with Gardner Ackley* (13 April 1973, by Joe B. Grantz, Ann Arbor, Michigan), Lyndon Baines Johnson Library, Austin, Texas, I-10-11; and Joseph Pechman (then visiting at Yale University) to Herbert Stein (Committee for Economic Development, Washington D.C.), 11 May 1967, ROCEA: 1961–1968, microfilm roll 38 (Folder: "Joseph A. Pechman"). Also see Collins, "The Economic Crisis of 1968 and the Waning of the 'American Century,'" 401ff.

10. On the problems of legislation "by forecast," see *Oral History Interview with Charles L. Schultze*, 28 March 1969, II-20. Tobin reflects upon the ironic confirmation of the New Economics during the late 1960s in *The New Economics One Decade Older*, 36. Also see Arthur M. Okun, "The Fiscal Fiasco of the Vietnam Period," in his edited anthology, *The Battle against Unemployment* (New York: Norton, 1972), 150–63. So politically unattractive was an anti-inflationary tax rise that in the fall of 1967 a petition of professional economists calling on the Congress for such a surcharge garnered a mere 260 signatories, some 2.5 percent of the total membership of the American Economic Association at the time. See Arthur M. Okun, *The Political Economy of Prosperity* (Washington, D.C.: Brookings Institution, 1969), 18. On the general history of American taxation policy, and of the problematic political constraints within which it has been formulated, the work of W. Elliot Brownlee is exceedingly important. See his *Federal Taxation in America: A Short History* (New York: Cambridge University Press, 1996); and his edited anthology, *Funding the Modern American State, 1941–1995: The Rise and Fall of the Era of Easy Finance* (New York: Cambridge University Press, 1996).

11. See *Oral History Interview with Gardner Ackley*, II-16. On LBJ's reluctance to seek a formal war declaration, see, for example, Robert Dallek, *Lyndon Johnson and His Times, 1961–1973* (New York: Oxford University Press, 1998); Robert A. Caro, *The Years of Lyndon Johnson* (New York: Knopf, 1982); and Eric Goldman, *The Tragedy of Lyndon Baines Johnson* (New York: Knopf, 1969).

12. With each passing presidential administration, the involvement of CEA members and their research staffs in partisan activity increased. On the acceleration of this development during the Kennedy and Johnson administrations, and on the antagonisms it produced among academic and official economists, see, for example, Aaron Gordon (Berkeley) to Gardner Ackley, 9 June 1965; ROCEA: 1961–1969—microfilm roll 36 (Folder: "R. Aaron Gordon"); Richard Fulton (Democrat of Tennessee, member of the House Ways and Means Committee) to Walter Heller, 30 November 1967; and Heller to Fulton, 6 December 1967; both in ROCEA: 1961–1968, microfilm roll 36 (Folder: "Walter Wolfgang Heller (WWH)—thru October 1965"); *Oral History Interview with Gardner Ackley*, I-19; and *Oral History Interview with Arthur Okun*, 20 March 1969, 5, 12.

13. See Tobin, *The New Economics One Decade Older*, 36.

14. See *Oral History Interview with Arthur Okun*, 15 April 1969, 5–6.

15. See Collins, "The Economic Crisis of 1968 and the Waning of the 'American Century,'" 416, 418; as well as Lloyd C. Gardner, *Pay Any Price: Lyndon Johnson and the Wars for Vietnam* (Chicago: I. R. Dee, 1995). Further appreciation of the aggressive dimensions LBJ envisioned for his reform agenda may be won from considering that in 1964 the *total* federal budget

the president had put before the Congress was $98 billion. His OEO funding request two years later thus constituted by itself almost 30 percent of that figure. The growth in the food stamps component of the Aid to Families with Dependent Children (AFDC) program is also illustrative: $36 million in such stamps were distributed to approximately 600,000 people in 1965; within ten years the figures had grown to $4 billion allocated among 17 million persons. Similarly, public housing subsidies paid by the federal government rose from an annual total of $236 million to $1.2 billion in the same time period.

16. See Edelstein, "War and the American Economy in the 20th Century," 58–61.

17. It cannot be emphasized enough that the conservative attack on Keynesianism relied to a very large extent on the specious comparison of government finance with household ledgers. For Keynes and his followers, however, the essential issue was that governments, given their virtually infinite time horizons, could indeed do what households could not—take on debt with an assurance that *in the long run* it could be liquidated. Indeed, assuming future generations would be more prosperous (in no small part due to the inspired policy choices of their forebears), the burden of such liquidation would be proportionally smaller. Perhaps even more to the point, also forgotten in antideficit diatribes was the fact that the vast proportion of the national debt had been and is held by the public—to whom the United States Treasury paid and pays valuable interest payments in compensation for their risk-bearing. In other words, the debt was and is an obligation while at the same time it was and is an asset—to millions of people and institutions. On the collapse of the "New Deal Order" owing, in part, to these transformations in the perception of state capabilities in finance, see Steve Fraser and Gary Gerstle, eds., *The Rise and Fall of the New Deal Order, 1930–1980* (Princeton, N.J.: Princeton University Press, 1989).

18. On the president's fascination with the use of PPBS in the War on Poverty, see *Oral History Interview with Charles L. Schultze* (28 March 1969, by David McComb, Washington, D.C.), Lyndon Baines Johnson Library, Austin, Texas, I-52; and *Oral History Interview with Robert Lampman* (24 May 1983, by Michael L. Gillette, Madison, Wisconsin), Lyndon Baines Johnson Library, Austin, Texas, I-34–35.

19. See John Morton Blum, *Years of Discord: American Politics and Society, 1961–1974* (New York: Norton, 1991), 250–51; Collins, "The Economic Crisis of 1968 and the Waning of the 'American Century,'" 412; Robert Eisner, "Fiscal and Monetary Policy Reconsidered," *American Economic Review* 59 (1969), 897–905; as well as his "What Went Wrong?" *Journal of Political Economy* 79 (1971), 629–41. That the tax surcharge did little to stem the inflationary tide was also linked with an easing of monetary policy that took hold in 1968, which, adding insult to injury, had been implemented initially out of concern that fiscal restraint might overshoot its mark and generate excessive unemployment. Efforts to correct *that* problem, by raising the discount rate, only encouraged inflows of short-term funds from overseas (and efforts by banks to increase their loanable assets by borrowing on dollar accounts overseas). These international liquidity flows further frustrated efforts to use higher interest rates as a brake on the accelerating inflation of the late 1960s.

20. See Milton Friedman and Walter W. Heller, *Monetary vs. Fiscal Policy* (New York: Norton, 1969), 34. Also see Okun, *The Political Economy of Prosperity*, 111, where he declared: "We have never claimed or attempted to engage in the practice known as 'fine-tuning.'" On the instability of the national economy after 1968, see my "Understanding American Economic Decline: The Contours of the Late-Twentieth-Century Experience," in *Understanding American Economic Decline*, ed. Michael A. Bernstein and David E. Adler (New York: Cambridge University Press, 1994), 3–33. An explicit comparison of the economic difficulties experienced in the United States in the 1930s and the 1970s is offered in my "Economic Instability in the United States in the 1930s and the 1970s: An Essay in Historical Homology," in *The Great Depression of the 1930s and Its Relevance for the Contemporary World*, ed. Ivan Berend and Knut Borchardt (Budapest: Karl Marx University of Economics, 1986), 35–60

21. Phillips's pathbreaking study was published as "The Relation between Unemployment and the Rate of Change of Money Wage Rates in the United Kingdom, 1861–1957," *Economica*, n.s., 25 (1958), 283–99. His calculations suggested that with an unemployment rate of 2.5 percent, Britain's wages rose approximately 2 percent per year. The price level would remain stable, Phillips claimed, assuming that productivity also rose at a yearly rate of 2 percent. Generalization of Phillips's findings to the price level

as a whole was first undertaken by Richard G. Lipsey two years later in his "The Relation between Unemployment and the Rate of Change of Money Wage Rates in the United Kingdom, 1862–1975: A Further Analysis," *Economica*, n.s., 27 (1960). Further extension of the argument, in an article that brought the British research to a wider academic audience in the United States, was undertaken by Paul A. Samuelson and Robert A. Solow in their "Analytical Aspects of Anti-inflation Policy," *American Economic Review* 50 (1960), 177–94.

22. See Tobin, *The New Economics One Decade Older*, 38–39.

23. A revealing example of the transformation in the discourse of macroeconomics is afforded by Arthur Okun's publication of *Equality and Efficiency: The Big Tradeoff* (Washington, D.C.: Brookings Institution, 1975). This volume, produced by one of the leading architects and most eloquent proponents of the New Economics, posited the counterposition of unemployment and inflation as one of the central "economic problems" of the contemporary era. On Keyserling's reproachful contemplation of his colleagues' work in the wake of the Johnson presidency, see *Oral History Interview with Leon H. Keyserling* (9 January 1969, by Stephen Goodell, Washington, D.C.), Lyndon Baines Johnson Library, Austin, Texas, 6, 39.

24. From the "Employment Act of 1946," 79th Cong., 2d sess., 20 February 1946, Section 2. The shift in attitudes regarding not simply the responsibilities of the federal government in the nation's labor markets but also the possibilities of even achieving "full employment" itself also affected perceptions of the poor. It became increasingly fashionable to argue that idleness was more an individual than a social problem, and a variety of weakly substantiated claims were advanced that poor relief actually exacerbated the problem. What went hand in hand with this strategy was the determination to assert that the social spending programs of the Johnson years had had no positive impacts. In fact, just the opposite was the case—the gap between African-American and white American wealth and incomes, for example, was never smaller than by the late 1960s—but the political realities of the moment made a vast majority of political leaders and citizens alike indifferent to the evidence. See, for example, Charles Murray, *Losing Ground: American Social Policy, 1950–1980* (New York: Basic Books, 1984); and Allen Matusow, *The Unravel-*

ing of America: A History of Liberalism in the 1960s (New York: Harper and Row, 1984). Thus ensued the end of the War on Poverty and the beginning of the "War on Welfare." On the very positive impacts of the 1960s antipoverty programs, see Rebecca M. Blank, *It Takes a Nation: A New Agenda for Fighting Poverty* (Princeton, N.J.: Princeton University Press, 1998). A striking symbol of the political and intellectual transformations thereby realized, it was a Democratic president who, in the late 1990s, would ultimately oversee a dramatic dismantling of federal assistance to the poor—William Clinton. See Michael B. Katz, *The Undeserving Poor: From the War on Poverty to the War on Welfare* (New York: Pantheon, 1989), chaps. 7–8. On the burgeoning literature concerning the "natural" and "NAIRU" rates of unemployment, see James Tobin, "The Wage-Price Mechanism: Overview of the Conference," in *The Econometrics of Price Determination*, ed. Otto Eckstein (Washington, D.C.: Board of Governors of the Federal Reserve System, 1972); and Arthur Okun, "Fiscal-Monetary Activism: Some Analytical Issues," *Brookings Papers on Economic Activity* (1972:1), 123–72.

25. See Michael J. Webber and David L. Rigby, *The Golden Age Illusion: Rethinking Postwar Capitalism* (New York: Guilford, 1996), 306; as well as Michael L. Dertouzos, Richard K. Lester and Robert M. Solow, *Made in America: Regaining the Productive Edge* (Cambridge: MIT Press, 1989); Peter Dicken, *Global Shift* (London: Chapman, 1992); H. D. Watts, *Industrial Geography* (Harlow, Essex: Longman, 1987); and P. Varaiya and M. Wiseman, "Investment and Employment in Manufacturing in U.S. Metropolitan Areas," *Regional Science and Urban Economics* 11 (1981), 431–69. Also see William J. Baumol and Kenneth McLennan, *Productivity Growth and U.S. Competitiveness* (New York: Oxford University Press, 1985); Barry Bluestone and Bennett Harrison, *The Deindustrialization of America: Plant Closings, Community Abandonment, and the Dismantling of Basic Industries* (New York: Basic Books, 1982); and Robert B. Reich, *The Next American Frontier* (New York: Penguin, 1983).

26. See Angus Maddison, "Economic Stagnation since 1973, Its Nature and Causes: A Six Country Survey," *De Economist* 131 (1983), 585–608; United States Council of Economic Advisers, *Economic Report of the President: 1984* (Washington, D.C.: U.S. Government

Printing Office, 1984), selected tables; Stanley Lebergott, *Manpower in Economic Growth: The American Record since 1800* (New York: McGraw-Hill, 1964), selected tables; Organization for Economic Cooperation and Development (OECD), *Labour Force Statistics: 1960–71* (Paris: OECD, 1973), 72–73; OECD, *Labour Force Statistics: 1966–77* (Paris: OECD, 1979), 78–79; and Michael A. Bernstein, *The Great Depression: Delayed Recovery and Economic Change in America, 1929–1939* (New York: Cambridge University Press, 1987), 208–14. The 1971 collapse of the Bretton Woods system of fixed exchange rates worsened the inflationary bias of the economy. As the American dollar fell in value, given the weakening of the American economy then under way, the real cost of imports, most especially of fuel, rose further still. See my "Understanding American Economic Decline," 18–24.

27. On the powerful influence such rhetorical devices as the "misery index" brought to bear on political discussion during the 1970s, see Douglas A. Hibbs Jr., *The Political Economy of Industrial Democracies* (Cambridge: Harvard University Press, 1987).

28. From Alan S. Blinder, "The Fall and Rise of Keynesian Economics," *Economic Record* 64 (1988), 278. Also see Josef Steindl, "Reflections on the Present State of Economics," *Banca Nazionale del Lavoro Quarterly Review* 148 (1984), 3–14; Maddison, "Economic Stagnation since 1973," 598–608; and Alan R. Sweezy, "The Keynesians and Government Policy: 1933–39," *American Economic Review* 62 (1972), 116–24.

29. The classical monetarism that Milton Friedman did so much to resurrect in governmental policy circles is perhaps best represented by his masterwork, coauthored with Anna J. Schwartz, *A Monetary History of the United States, 1867–1960* (Princeton, N.J.: Princeton University Press, 1963). Also see his *Essays in Positive Economics* (Chicago: University of Chicago Press, 1953); as well as his presidential address to the American Economic Association, published as "The Role of Monetary Policy," *American Economic Review* 58 (1968), 1–22. This latter contribution by Friedman was challenged a few years later in James Tobin's presidential address to the AEA, "Inflation and Unemployment," *American Economic Review* 62 (1972), 1–18. Also see Harry G. Johnson, "The Keynesian Revolution and the Monetarist Counter-Revolution," *American Economic Re-*

view 61 (1971), 1–14. On the relegation of Keynes's arguments to the status of exceptions to the general neoclassical view, see John R. Hicks, *The Crisis of Keynesian Economics* (New York: Basic Books, 1975); Michael Bleaney, *The Rise and Fall of Keynesian Economics: An Investigation of Its Contribution to Capitalist Development* (London: Macmillan, 1985); and Nina Shapiro, "Keynes and Equilibrium Economics," *Australian Economic Papers* 31 (1978), 207–23. Ironically enough, many historians of economic thought argue that, in a vastly influential interwar era essay, Hicks provided some of the essential ammunition to those who would ultimately work to reabsorb Keynesian principles within a more generalized neoclassical apparatus. See his "Mr. Keynes and the 'Classics': A Suggested Interpretation," *Econometrica* 5 (1937), 147–59.

30. The "fallacy of composition," that a whole cannot be understood as merely the sum of its parts, framed much of Keynes's critique of prevailing doctrines in economics dating from the turn of the century. In his *General Theory* he noted, for example, that "rational" behavior on the part of individuals—say, saving substantial portions of income during a recession—could generate "irrational" results in the aggregate, in this case, a reduction in total consumption spending that would merely make the recession worse.

31. It is now widely accepted that the "rational expectations" hypothesis first systematically emerged in R. F. Muth, "The Demand for Non-Farm Housing," in *The Demand for Durable Goods*, ed. A. C. Hargerger (Chicago: University of Chicago Press, 1960), 29–96—a research article reporting on investigations that were, interestingly enough, partially funded by the Office of Naval Research. Muth pursued the issue further in his "Rational Expectations and the Theory of Price Movements," *Econometrica* 29 (1961), 315–35. Its application to a "new macroeconomics" took form in the influential work of Robert E. Lucas Jr.—scholarship for which Lucas received the Nobel Memorial Prize in 1995. See, for example, Lucas, "An Equilibrium Model of the Business Cycle," *Journal of Political Economy* 83 (1975), 1113–44; Lucas, "Understanding Business Cycles," in *Stabilization of the Domestic and International Economy*, ed. Karl Brunner and Allan H. Meltzer (New York: North-Holland, 1977), 7–29; as well as his "Methods and Problems in Business Cycle Theory," in his *Studies in Business Cycle Theory* (Cambridge: MIT Press, 1980), 271–96. Equally significant, in this

regard, was the work of Thomas Sargent and Neil Wallace. See, for example, their "Rational Expectations, the Optimal Monetary Instrument and the Optimal Money Supply Rule," *Journal of Political Economy* 83 (1975), 241–55. Excellent synthetic treatments of rational expectations theory are found in Steven Sheffrin, *Rational Expectations* (New York: Cambridge University Press, 1983); and Sheila Dow, *Macroeconomic Thought: A Methodological Approach* (Oxford: Blackwell, 1985). As for the tautological quality of the hypothesis, see Phillip Cagan, "Reflections on Rational Expectations," *Journal of Money, Credit and Banking* 12 (1980), 826–32; James Tobin, "How Dead Is Keynes?" *Economic Inquiry* 15 (1977); and Robert L. Heilbroner and William Milberg, *The Crisis of Vision in Modern Economic Thought* (New York: Cambridge University Press, 1995), 74–77.

32. Again, it was Robert Lucas who first articulated the notion that the statistical estimation of policy effects was highly problematic. See his "Econometric Policy Evaluation: A Critique," *Journal of Monetary Economics* 1 (1976), 19–46. Also see Robert E. Lucas Jr. and Thomas J. Sargent, eds., *Rational Expectations and Econometric Practice* (Minneapolis: University of Minnesota Press, 1981). From a more traditional monetarist perspective, Don Patinkin, the eminent Israeli economist, had for decades made similar criticisms of the Keynesian model. See, for example, his "Keynes and Econometrics: On the Interaction between the Macroeconomic Revolutions of the Interwar Period," *Econometrica* 44 (1976), 1091–123. Useful as a general guide to these developments in the field of econometrics is Mary S. Morgan, *The History of Econometric Ideas* (New York: Cambridge University Press, 1992). From a perspective sympathetic to Keynesianism, E. Roy Weintraub provided a thorough exploration of the deeper theoretical issues posed by the critical attack upon it of the rational expectations school in his *Microfoundations: The Compatibility of Microeconomics and Macroeconomics* (Cambridge: Cambridge University Press, 1979).

33. The words are those of Heilbroner and Milberg, *The Crisis of Vision in Modern Economic Thought*, 96. On the policy ineffectiveness proposition, see Robert E. Lucas Jr., "Some International Evidence on Output-Inflation Trade-Offs," *American Economic Review* 63 (1973), 326–34; and Bennet McCallum, "The Current State of the Policy Ineffectiveness Debate,"

American Economic Review 69 (1979), 240–45; as well as his "New Classical Macroeconomics: A Sympathetic Account," *Scandinavian Journal of Economics* 91 (1989), 223–52. On the treatment of information and expectations formation in the "new classical" tradition, see, for example, Sanford Grossman, "On the Efficiency of Competitive Stock Markets Where Traders Have Diverse Information," *Journal of Finance* 31 (1976), 573–85. With regard to the implications of the "new classical macroeconomics" for an understanding of scientific progress, see Rodney Maddock, "Rational Expectations Macrotheory: A Lakatosian Case Study in Program Adjustment," *History of Political Economy* 16 (1984), 291–310.

34. See James Tobin, "Academic Economics in Washington," *Ventures* 2 (winter 1963), reprinted in his *National Economic Policy* (New Haven, Conn.: Yale University Press, 1966), 204.

35. The phrase "inward turn" is borrowed from Heilbroner and Milberg, *The Crisis of Vision in Modern Economic Thought*, chap. 5.

36. On the activist "movements" of the 1960s and their subsequent demise, see, for example, Taylor Branch, *Parting the Waters: America in the King Years, 1954–63* (New York: Simon and Schuster, 1988); as well as his *Pillar of Fire: America in the King Years, 1963–65* (New York: Simon and Schuster, 1998); Sara Evans, *Personal Politics: The Roots of Women's Liberation in the Civil Rights Movement and the New Left* (New York: Vintage, 1979); James Miller, *"Democracy Is in the Streets": From Port Huron to the Siege of Chicago* (New York: Simon and Schuster, 1987); Aldon Morris, *The Origins of the Civil Rights Movement: Black Communities Organizing for Change* (New York: Free Press, 1984); Clayborne Carson, *In Struggle: S.N.C.C. and the Black Awakening of the 1960s* (Cambridge: Harvard University Press, 1981); Maurice Isserman, *If I Had a Hammer: The Decline of the Old Left and the Rise of the New Left* (New York: Basic Books, 1987); Alan Brinkley, *The End of Reform: New Deal Liberalism in Recession and War* (New York: Knopf, 1995); Kevin P. Phillips, *The Politics of Rich and Poor: Wealth and the American Electorate in the Reagan Aftermath* (New York: Random House, 1990); Kirkpatrick Sale, *Power Shift: The Rise of the Southern Rim and Its Challenge to the Eastern Establishment* (New York: Random House, 1975); and Jonathan Rieder, *Canarsie: The Jews*

and Italians of Brooklyn against Liberalism (Cambridge: Harvard University Press, 1985).

37. On the exogenous nature of the 1970s inflation, see Alan S. Blinder, "The Anatomy of Double-Digit Inflation in the 1970s," *Inflation: Causes and Effects*, ed. Robert E. Hall (Chicago: University of Chicago Press, 1982). The most thorough narrative concerning the Watergate scandals is Stanley I. Kutler, *The Wars of Watergate: The Last Crisis of Richard Nixon* (New York: Norton, 1992).

38. California's Proposition 13, placed on the ballot in the wake of the tireless efforts of Howard Jarvis and Paul Gann, was a significant example of the links between the conservative offensives of the 1970s and 1980s and nonprofit organizations committed to conservative agendas. Independent-sector organizations like the American Enterprise Institute, the Cato Institute, and the Heritage Foundation all served (and continue to serve) to direct funding not simply toward the political work of conservative activists but also toward the scholarly work of economists and other social scientists now embarked on an anti-Keynesian protocol. See Howard Jarvis, with Robert pack, *I'm Mad as Hell: The Exclusive Story of the Tax Revolt and Its Leader* (New York: Times Books, 1979). The role of American nonprofit organizations in the articulation of a professional economics has been particularly important in this century; their participation in the reorientation of the field in the 1970s and 1980s is still incompletely understood and more than worthy of systematic consideration. In this regard, see James Allen Smith, *The Idea Brokers: Think Tanks and the Rise of the New Policy Elite* (New York: Free Press, 1991); J. David Hoeveler, *Watch on the Right: Conservative Intellectuals in the Reagan Era* (Madison: University of Wisconsin Press, 1991); and David M. Ricci, *The Transformation of American Politics: The New Washington and the Rise of Think Tanks* (New Haven, Conn.: Yale University Press, 1993).

39. See, for example, Anthony S. Campagna, *Economic Policy in the Carter Administration* (Westport, Conn.: Greenwood Press, 1995). As to the changing international contexts within which economic policy was implemented in the late twentieth century, see Harold James, *International Monetary Cooperation since Bretton Woods* (New York: Oxford University Press, 1996).

40. That the income tax reductions of the Program for Economic Recovery put before the Congress by President Reagan were, in fact, a political contrivance to benefit the most privileged in the electorate is strikingly demonstrated in the memoirs of the president's director of the Office of Management and Budget, David Stockman. Stockman in particular referred to the budget strategy as a "Trojan horse" deployed on behalf of the rich. See his *Triumph of Politics: How the Reagan Revolution Failed* (New York: Harper and Row, 1986), 5–6, 8. Also see Joseph Pechman, *Who Paid the Taxes, 1966–85?* (Washington, D.C.: Brookings Institution, 1986); and Francis Fox Piven and Richard Cloward, *The New Class War* (New York: Pantheon, 1982).

41. See Arthur B. Laffer, *The Economics of the Tax Revolt: A Reader* (New York: Harcourt, Brace, 1979). Some two decades later, Laffer and his work are again obscure; one searches in vain today for major citations to his research.

42. The most obvious and telling cases for comparison were those of the member states of the Organization for Cooperation and Development (OECD). Created in September 1961, when it replaced the Organization for European Economic Cooperation that had administered the Marshall Plan, OECD was originally composed of the twenty largest (and most prosperous) industrialized states of Asia, Europe, and North America. Indeed, even by 1997, the highest marginal tax rates in the United States (39.6 percent for a married couple with an adjusted gross income greater than $263,750) were well below those of Canada (55 percent), France (56 percent), Germany (53 percent), Great Britain (55 percent), and Japan (65 percent). The quip regarding "voodoo economics" was uttered by George Bush. While clearly a product of the high feelings generated during the hard-fought 1980 primary season, the label became a source of no small amount of embarrassment when Bush accepted Ronald Reagan's offer of the vice presidency at the Republican National Convention in Detroit. Historical works that provide useful summaries of the policy changes of the period are Nicholas Spulber, *Managing the American Economy from Roosevelt to Reagan* (Bloomington: Indiana University Press, 1989); Martin Feldstein, ed. *American Economic Policy in the 1980s* (Chicago: University of Chicago Press, 1994); and Robert C. Wood, *Whatever Possessed the President? Academic Experts and Presidential Policy, 1960–1988* (Amherst: University of

Massachusetts Press, 1993). Also of interest is Paul W. McCracken, "Economic Policy in the Nixon Years," *Political Science Quarterly* 26 (1996), 165–77.

43. See Bernstein, "Understanding American Economic Decline," 22–24. Another example of the sheer magnitude of the military spending strategies embraced by the Reagan administration is afforded by comparative data on proportionate commitments to defense. By the end of the 1980s, the United States distributed 6.1 percent of national product to defense. France, by comparison, allocated 3.5 percent; the Federal Republic of Germany, 3.1 percent; and Japan, a bit less than 1 percent. A good example of the illegitimate claim by proponents of supply-side economics that the Reagan tax cuts had stimulated recovery is Lawrence Lindsey, *The Growth Experiment: How the New Tax Policy Is Transforming the U.S. Economy* (New York: Basic Books, 1990).

44. See Proxmire to Okun, 22 February 1979; Okun to Proxmire, 26 February 1979; Okun to Proxmire, 9 February 1979; and Proxmire to Okun, 1 February 1979; all in the Papers of Arthur Okun (PAO), Lyndon Baines Johnson Library, Austin, Texas, Box 20B (Folder: "O P"). At the very time that supply-side theorists succeeded in condemning Keynesianism as a recipe for runaway deficit spending, the share of annual gross domestic product represented by the federal deficit fell from 6.3 percent in 1983 to 1.4 percent by 1996. In another telling demonstration of the hyperbole utilized in the discussion of contemporary public finance, it could be demonstrated that by 1989 the wealthiest five hundred thousand American households could have liquidated the entire national debt with the *increase* in their total wealth over the previous ten years. The striking inability of liberals to counter the rhetoric of supply-side theorists was at no time better demonstrated than during the presidency of Jimmy Carter. In this regard, see Bruce Schulman, "Slouching toward the Supply Side: Jimmy Carter and the New American Political Economy," in *The Carter Presidency: Policy Choices in the Post–New Deal Era*, ed. Gary Fink and Hugh Graham (Lawrence: University Press of Kansas, 1998).

45. See *Oral History Interview with Walter Heller* (conducted 20 February 1970 by David McComb at the University of Minnesota), [Lyndon Baines Johnson Library (Austin, Texas)], II-6. Arthur Okun took a more jaundiced view of

President Nixon's difficulties, noting that the construction of a White House "enemies list" (which included his name) led to the systematic ostracism of certain professionals, believed to be ideologically incompatible with the administration, from policy consultations and other meetings with government officials. See Okun to David Marcus, 6 February 1978, PAO, Box 20B (Folder: "Mc M").

46. In *The Business Response to Keynes: 1929–1964* (New York: Columbia University Press, 1981), Robert Collins vividly demonstrates how the American business community had once been entirely persuaded by Keynes's view of the interactions between enterprise, households, and individual decision making in the marketplace. As for Keynes's notion of the causal links between investment and savings, there was perhaps no better summary of its essential logic than that offered by Michal Kalecki (1899–1970), a Polish expatriate whose inspired theoretical and statistical work both in Warsaw and, for the majority of his career, at the University of Cambridge anticipated, in the opinion of many, the work of Keynes himself. In his *Studies in the Theory of Business Cycles, 1933–39* (New York: Kelley, 1966), 14, 44, Kalecki advanced the central idea that workers spent what they received in wages while capitalists received, in the form of growing sales revenue, what they spent in investment.

47. In its most typical renditions, the proposed amendment would mandate a three-fifths majority in the Congress to pass any exceptions to a balanced budget in any given year—a legislative threshold that would effectively cripple any efforts toward deficit spending save for those in times of national emergency or war.

48. Virtually alone among his colleagues, the late Robert Eisner of Northwestern University provided the most systematic critique of both contemporary government accounting practices and, thereby, conservative assertions regarding public finance. See his *How Real Is the Federal Deficit?* (New York: Macmillan, 1986).

49. A particularly compelling discussion of the century's progress of American liberalism, framed more with reference to intellectual rather than political economic contexts, is Gary Gerstle's essay "The Protean Character of American Liberalism," *American Historical Review* 99 (1994), 1043–73. Also see Brinkley, *The End of Reform*; and Fraser and Gerstle, *The Rise and Fall of the New Deal Order*.

50. See John B. Taylor, "Changes in American Economic Policy in the 1980s: Watershed or Pendulum Swing?" *Journal of Economic Literature* 33 (1995), 777–84; as well as Richard M. Alston, J. R. Kearl, and Michael B. Vaughan, "Is There a Consensus among Economists in the 1990s?" *American Economic Review* 82 (1992), 203–20. American Economic Association president Gerard Debreu offered interesting speculations about the tendencies of modern economists to indulge an excessively introverted formalism in his presidential address in 1991: "The Mathematization of Economic Theory," *American Economic Review* 81 (1991), 1–7.

51. The authorship "shares" reported in a 1983 study for the period 1973–78 were, respectively, 54 percent in the *American Economic Review*, 58 percent in the *Journal of Political Economy*, and 74 percent in the *Quarterly Journal of Economics*. See E. Ray Canterbery and Robert Burkhardt, "What Do We Mean by Asking If Economics Is a Science?" in *Why Economics Is Not Yet a Science*, ed. Alfred Eichner (Armonk, N.Y.: M. E. Sharpe, 1983), 15–40. On the articulation of alternative scientific "paradigms," the classic reference is Thomas S. Kuhn, *The Structure of Scientific Revolutions* (Chicago: University of Chicago Press, [1962], 1966).

52. See Peter Coy, "Let's Not Take Feel-Good Economics Too Far," *Business Week*, 20 October 1997. Mankiw's text, *Principles of Economics*, was issued by Harcourt, Brace.

53. It is interesting to consider that at the very time that such changes in the outlook of the profession took place, opportunities for the employment of economists in the private sector increased dramatically. No doubt a parallel development, in this regard, was the transition in the aspirations of new generations of students who sought out careers in the corporate world rather than, as their predecessors had done a few decades before, positions in the government service. Equally intriguing is the fact that the anti-statism of this new cadre of young economists had close formal (if not substantive) similarities with that of an earlier generation who, in the 1960s most especially, as a New Left had excoriated government professionals as servants of a malicious power elite. On the notion of laissez-nous-faire, see William Appleman Williams, *The Contours of American History* (Chicago: World Publishing, 1961).

54. A particularly vivid, if strident, representation of these arguments is Susan Lee, *Hands Off: Why the Government Is a Menace to Economic Health* (New York: Simon and Schuster, 1996). A historical perspective on American attitudes regarding regulation is provided by Rudolph J. R. Peritz, *Competition Policy in America, 1888–1992: History, Rhetoric, Law* (New York: Oxford University Press, 1996).

55. See, for example, James Risen and Douglas Jehl, "Bush to Call for Freeze on New Regulations," *Los Angeles Times*, 21 January 1992, A1, A14; Edwin Chen, "White House Pushes Deregulation," *Los Angeles Times*, 31 January 1992, D4; and James Risen, "Clinton Kills Controversial Quayle Panel," *Los Angeles Times*, 23 January 1993, A14. Thomas Petzinger Jr. provides a thorough survey of the impacts of deregulation in the American aviation industry in his *Hard Landing: The Epic Contest for Power and Profits That Plunged the Airlines into Chaos* (New York: Times Business, 1996).

56. Most obvious among the unevidenced claims made in support of deregulation concerned costs. Contrary to perceptions, however, regulatory costs in the United States were (and are) consistently lower than those imposed by other governments in, for example, the OECD. By far the greatest number of such assertions came from business enterprises, but the relative silence of the American economics profession on the issue was quite striking.

57. Much of this argument, and that which follows, is derived from my essay "The Contemporary American Banking Crisis in Historical Perspective," *Journal of American History* 80 (1994), 1382–96.

58. Data on thrifts' income were generated by the Federal Home Loan Bank Board and the Office of Thrift Supervision. See Lawrence J. White, *The S&L Debacle: Public Policy Lessons for Bank and Thrift Regulation* (New York: Oxford University Press, 1991), 19.

59. The words are those of Martin Mayer in *The Greatest-Ever Bank Robbery: The Collapse of the Savings and Loan Industry* (New York: Collier, 1990), 61.

60. See, for example, Robert A. Rosenblatt, "Financial Laws May Face Major Overhaul," *Los Angeles Times*, 22 May 1997, D1, D13. Interestingly enough, it has been suggested that financial deregulation in this context arose as a compromise with the industry when the government needed banks to contribute more funds to the federal deposit insurance system in the wake of the savings and loan crisis. By helping to res-

cue the nation's savings and loan sector, commercial banks were thus offered the opportunity to gain access to wholly new markets. See Robert A. Rosenblatt, "U.S. Seeks Bank Levy to Aid FDIC," *Los Angeles Times*, 18 December 1990, A1, A28; and Robert A. Rosenblatt, "Congress OKs Rescue Plan for S&L Fund," *Los Angeles Times*, 1 October 1996, D2, D19. In the final analysis, it was estimated that the cost of "bailing out" the failed S&Ls of the 1980s would come to $500 billion with interest. Needless to say, this fiscal burden only added to the arguments of those invoking a budgetary crisis as justification for the systematic scaling down of federal operations and practices. See James S. Granelli, "Judge Throws Out Keating Conviction in S& L Fraud Case," *Los Angeles Times*, 3 December 1996, A1, A30. Yet another anxiety that emerged in the wake of financial deregulation was the possible "redlining" of particular communities and neighborhoods by banks no longer subject to systematic federal oversight.

61. By 1996, the nation's airways were dominated by three major carriers—American, Delta, and United. This was hardly the scenario envisioned (or extolled) by the proponents of deregulation two decades earlier. On these matters see James F. Peltz, "Airline Mergers '90s-Style Might Stand a Better Chance This Time," *Los Angeles Times*, 5 December 1996, D1, D9; and "Justice Dept. Reviews Claims of Airlines' Price Squeeze," *Los Angeles Times*, 12 February 1997, D1, D3.

62. See, for example, Susan Moffat, "Right Call? 10 Years Later, AT&T Split Favors Business," *Los Angeles Times*, 7 January 1992, D1, D7; Jube Shiver Jr., "New Rules Will Let Pay Phone Rates Climb," *Los Angeles Times*, 9 November 1996, A1, A19; Jube Shiver Jr., "Deregulation of Phones Stirs Hornet's Nest," *Los Angeles Times*, 28 April 1997, D1, D4; Jube Shiver Jr., "New Federal Rules Expected to Result in Pay Phone Hikes," *Los Angeles Times*, 7 October 1997, D1, D22; and Nancy Rivera Brooks, "PacBell Hikes Coin-Call Rate," *Los Angeles Times*, 18 October 1997, D1, D3.

63. Indeed, beginning in the mid-1980s, a new merger wave took place in major sectors of American industry. These consolidations represented some of the most significant and telling outcomes of "deregulation." Gulf Oil completed a $13.4 billion alliance with Standard Oil of California in 1984; Kraft merged with Philip Morris in 1988 in a deal similarly valued; RJR Nabisco

bought Kohlberg Kravis Roberts in a $25 billion negotiation in 1989; and Warner Communications absorbed Time, Inc. for $14.11 billion two years later. In 1996, there was a virtual "merger fever" that witnessed the consummation of six major takeovers: Bell Atlantic Corporation appropriated Nynex Corporation for $22.7 billion; Disney Company, Capital Cities/ABC for $19 billion; SBC Communications, the Pacific Telesis Group for $16.7 billion; WorldCom, MFS Communications for $14.4 billion; Wells Fargo, the First Interstate Bancorp for $14.2 billion; and Boeing, McDonnell Douglas for $13.3 billion. Through the end of the twentieth century, this "great merger wave" continued unabated; in 1999, no fewer than eight major concentrations were either announced or completed, the most prominent of which was the $122 billion union of MCI WorldCom and Sprint. The largest merger in the nation's history (to date) was announced in January 2000, when America Online and Time Warner reached agreement on a $165 billion combination.

64. See, for example, "Court Blocks Rule on Local Phone Rivalry," *Los Angeles Times*, 16 October 1996, D1, D6; Jube Shiver Jr., "Justice Dept. Approves Merger of PacTel, SBC Communications," *Los Angeles Times*, 6 November 1996, D1, D9; "FCC May Loosen Ownership Rules," *Los Angeles Times*, 8 November 1996, D4; "FCC to Auction Wireless Licenses," *Los Angeles Times*, 12 March 1997, D3; "Merger of Baby Bells Clears Hurdle," *Los Angeles Times*, 25 April 1997, D10; Jube Shiver Jr., "U.S. Probes Alleged Fixing of Bids for FCC Licenses," *Los Angeles Times*, 1 May 1997, D1, D5; Jube Shiver Jr., "AT&T Rate Cut Clears Way for FCC Reforms," *Los Angeles Times*, 5 May 1997, D1, D2; and Karen Kaplan and Thomas S. Mulligan, "Telephone Giants AT&T, SBC Discuss $50-Billion Merger," *Los Angles Times*, 28 May 1997, A1, A18. By the end of October 1997, the Federal Communications Commission (FCC) had completed the auction of 525 wireless licenses, with bids totaling $13.07 billion. Needless to say, rhetorical justification for auction processes like this one emphasized the revenue enhancement they could also generate to help balance the federal budget. See "Also . . . ," *Los Angeles Times*, 29 October 1997, D3. Paul Milgrom was one of the leading economists who designed auction processes used by the FCC. See his *Auction Theory for Privatization* (New York: Cambridge University Press, 1996). William

Vickrey of Columbia University received the 1996 Nobel Memorial Prize in Economic Science, in part, for work he had done on auction theory—work that helped the FCC structure its 1997 license sale.

65. See, for example, Robert Kuttner, "Medical Firms Take a Scalpel to the FDA," *Los Angeles Times*, 31 August 1997, M5. It should also be noted that proponents of FDA privatization consistently ignored the record. The time taken for FDA new-product reviews in fact fell from 1992 onward.

66. See, for example, Jacob S. Hacker, *The Road to Nowhere: The Genesis of President Clinton's Plan for Health Security* (Princeton, N.J.: Princeton University Press, 1997); Richard A. Epstein, *Mortal Peril: Our Inalienable Right to Health Care?* (Reading, Mass.: Addison-Wesley, 1997); Timothy Egan, "Oregon Lists Illnesses by Priority to See Who Gets Medicaid Care," *New York Times*, 3 May 1990, A1, A10; Carl Ginsburg, "The Patient as Profit Center: Hospital Inc. Comes to Town," *The Nation*, 18 November 1996, 18–22; David R. Olmos, "Ruling Expands Medicare Patients' Rights," *Los Angeles Times*, 12 March 1997, D3; Alain C. Enthoven and Sara J. Singer, "Perspective on Medicare: 2010 Will Be Too Late to Reform," *Los Angeles Times*, 12 March 1997, B9; Jonathan Peterson, and Janet Hook, "Clinton Comes to Defense of Medicare Means Testing," *Los Angeles Times*, 23 July 1997, A16; and David R. Olmos, "Survey Finds Wide Distrust of HMO Care," *Los Angeles Times*, 6 November 1997, A1, A18. By the fall of 1997, widespread anxiety over the quality of "managed health care" led President Clinton to accept the suggestion of a special commission he established that a "bill of rights" for patients be endorsed by the federal government. Ironically, while the proposed guidelines sought to redress a perceived imbalance between the ability of care providers and patients to protect their interests, no formal mechanisms of governmental oversight and enforcement were established. See Alissa J. Rubin, "Panel to Propose 'Bill of Rights' for Health Care," *Los Angeles Times*, 19 November 1997, A1, A18. Along with Reinhardt, one of the leading professional figures in the debate over the privatization of health care delivery (especially with respect to Medicare) was Alain C. Enthoven of Stanford—the singularly talented scholar who, earlier in his career, had undertaken research on the economics of defense that had been almost entirely inspired

(and funded) by statist rather than free-market protocols.

67. Perhaps no individual has been more influential in transforming the way both economists and attorneys think about these issues than Federal Circuit Court Judge Richard A. Posner, whose books afford a profound example of the core intellectual tenets of the deregulation movement. See his *Economic Analysis of Law* (Boston: Little, Brown, 1972); *The Economics of Justice* (Cambridge: Harvard University Press, 1981); and (with William M. Landes), *The Economic Structure of Tort Law* (Cambridge: Harvard University Press, 1987).

68. See, for example, Marla Cone, "Civil Rights Suit Attacks Trade in Pollution Credits," *Los Angeles Times*, 23 July 1997, A1, A19; Chris Kraul, "This Commodity's Smokin': Companies Trade Smog Credits on Online Exchange," *Los Angeles Times*, 30 April 1997, D2; and Frank Clifford, "Approval of Smog Credits Is Suspended," *Los Angeles Times*, 28 August 1997, A26. A particularly arresting example of the logic of the new environmental economics was provided by Lawrence Summers in the spring of 1992. Then a chief economist with the World Bank (and later a deputy secretary and secretary of the Treasury), Summers suggested that, in a global context, the dumping of toxic waste should be focused in those regions where the potential loss due to injury or death was lowest. Given that wages were the best proxy for the monetary value of such loss, the strategy suggested was clear: such dumping should be concentrated in those regions and countries with the lowest wages. While posing his argument merely as a thought experiment, Summers nevertheless chose a most revealing (and disturbing) context in which to indulge his penchant for hypothetical reasoning, one that spoke volumes about the nature of the contemporary economics discipline. See Doug Henwood, "Toxic Banking," *The Nation*, 2 March 1992, 257.

69. See, for example, Trudy Lieberman, "Social Insecurity: The Campaign to Take the System Private," *The Nation*, 27 January 1997, 11–17; Richard B. Anderson, "When Government Joins the Market Frenzy, We All Are at Risk," *Los Angeles Times*, 27 January 1997, B5; Dave Lesher, "Privatization Emerges as New Welfare Option," *Los Angeles Times*, 27 January 1997, A1, A16; Chris Kraul, "PUC Opens State to Competition for Energy Customers," *Los Angeles Times*, 7 May 1997, A1, A22; Susan Essoyan, "A

Word of Caution on Pitfalls of Privatization," *Los Angeles Times*, 15 May 1997, A5; Chris Kraul, "The State's New Power Brokers," *Los Angeles Times*, 15 August 1997, A1, A21; Ken Silverstein, "Privatizing War: How Affairs of State Are Outsourced to Corporations beyond Public Control," *The Nation*, 28 July/4 August 1997, 11–17; "Inmate-Abuse Suit Filed by Missouri," *Los Angeles Times*, 26 August 1997, A15; and "Inmate Abuse Is Said Worse Than Reported," *Los Angeles Times*, 28 August 1997, A18.

70. To be sure, an increasing array of economics scholarship has focused on the question of "transactions costs" associated with particular forms of bargaining. But this work has been disproportionately focused on the concerns and needs of firms contracting for labor, supplies, and marketing services. It has rarely, if ever, focused on consumers, and it has certainly not been applied in any systematic way to the "transactions costs" of deregulation. For one of the finest examples of the transactions costs literature, see Oliver Williamson, *The Economic Institutions of Capitalism: Firms, Markets, and Rational Contracting* (New York: Free Press, 1985).

71. The best-known cases of malfeasance in this regard involved "slamming," whereby new entrants in the telephonic communications market would shift household accounts without notifying the responsible parties.

72. This is especially evident in those markets, such as that for health care, where consumers do not have the expertise to make rational choices. As one journalist put it recently, "When you are a patient, it's not like buying a Toyota. Patients don't know how to choose their own anesthetic." See David Shenk, "Money + Science = Ethics Problems on Campus," *The Nation* 268 (1999), 17.

73. On local government investigations of the potential need for new regulatory intervention in utilities markets, the example of the cable-television industry is perhaps most apt. As particular cable-TV firms have captured large markets, rates for their service have risen dramatically. This in turn has prompted calls for renewed governmental oversight. See, for example, Leonard Bernstein, "San Diego Takes Step toward Increasing Cable TV Competition," *Los Angeles Times*, 31 January 1991, B1, B5.

74. In recent years, a "feminist economics" has emerged in the hands of certain scholars— one that has encouraged examination of such issues as the costs (both direct and indirect) of pri-

vatized health care and child care, not to mention of domestic labor in general. See, for example, Marianne A. Ferber and Julie A. Nelson, eds., *Beyond Economic Man: Feminist Theory and Economics* (Chicago: University of Chicago Press, 1993); and Julia A. Nelson, *Feminism, Objectivity and Economics* (New York: Routledge, 1997). Strikingly enough, this new research powerfully resonates with the activism of an earlier generation who, before and after World War I, campaigned for collectivized day care and domestic-labor arrangements in urban settings, arguing that the costs of "nuclear" family provision of such services were excessive. See Dolores Hayden, *The Grand Domestic Revolution: A History of Feminist Designs for American Homes, Neighborhoods, and Cities* (Cambridge: MIT Press, 1981). Joâo Vargas, now of the University of Texas at Austin, recently completed a dissertation at the University of California, San Diego, that focused on, among other things, the ethnographic and economic history of South-Central Los Angeles. He has been able to show the enormous amounts of time the residents of this part of the city now expend on the cashing of checks, the paying of bills, and the fulfillment of other transactions in an area more or less stripped of banking service in the wake of deregulation. See his "Blacks in the City of Angels' Dust" (Ph.D. diss., University of California, San Diego, 1999).

75. A particularly arresting portrayal of this argument is found in Michael Shrage, "U.S. Should Privatize Economic Statistics," *Los Angeles Times*, 27 July 1997, D4.

76. See "Lott Urges Expert Study of Inflation Adjustment," *Los Angeles Times*, 25 February 1997, A10. The budgetary implications of inflation rate calculations are best demonstrated by the fact that, by 1997, a downward adjustment of the annual inflation rate by a bit over 1 percentage point would have saved Washington some $1 trillion over the next decade. That sum of money evidently proved irresistible to budget "hawks" who spearheaded the effort to create an independent inflation-data commission. By contrast, critics of these initiatives argued that downward adjustments of inflation projections were part of a wider project to deprive Americans of the full value of social security and other pension-related entitlements. See, for example, Kevin Phillips, "(E)Con Artists," *Los Angeles Times*, 15 December 1996, M1, M3.

77. A contemporary example of the disjunction between the historical contexts within which policy analysis and implementation subsist and the self-regard by which professional economists explain specific proposals emerged with the 1994 implementation of the North American Free Trade Agreement (NAFTA). With virtual unanimity, American economists argued that NAFTA, by creating a "free-trade" zone between Canada, Mexico, and the United States, would enhance growth and employment within all three nations. Public perceptions were quite different, tending to focus on NAFTA's potential for "exporting" high-wage jobs in the United States to Mexico, for allowing corporations to escape environmental and occupational health and safety codes by moving their plants abroad, and for facilitating import competition for major sectors in agriculture and manufacturing. In fact, NAFTA's effects have been uneven and, in many cases, unpredictable. A growing segment of the population has come to the conclusion that most economists' projections of NAFTA's positive influence were either mistaken or disingenuous. More to the point, a sense that NAFTA represented a policy revision cultivated by corporate entities in pursuit of particular interests, independent of the public welfare, ultimately left President Clinton unable to persuade a reluctant Congress, in the fall of 1997, to grant him so-called fast-track authority to negotiate similar trade alliances with other regions. Again, in 1999, strikingly disruptive (and at times quite violent) demonstrations against a major meeting of the World Trade Organization (WTO) further demonstrated how professional rhetoric could run afoul of political realities. The WTO was a leading transnational agency in the pursuit of free-trade agendas widely endorsed by professional economists. The "Battle of Seattle," waged by a startling coalition of labor unions, socialist groups, environmental protection activists, and civil rights organizations, was as surprising as it was unexpected.

78. A compelling sense of just how dramatically the views of mainstream economists regarding their role in public affairs have changed since the 1970s may be distilled from a recent symposium that brought together contemporary members of the Council of Economic Advisers. See Martin Feldstein, "The Council of Economic Advisers: From Stabilization to Resource Allocation," *American Economic Review* 87 (1997), 99–102; Roger B. Porter, "Presidents and Economists: The Council of Economic Advisers,"

American Economic Review 87 (1997), 103–6; and Joseph Stiglitz, "Looking Out for the National Interest: The Principles of the Council of Economic Advisers, *American Economic Review* 87 (1997), 109–13. Also see, in this regard, R. H. Nelson, "The Economic Profession and Public Policy," *Journal of Economic Literature* 25 (1987): 49–91.

Epilogue
Being Ignored (Reprise)

1. Edmund Burke, *Reflections on the Revolution in France and on the Proceedings in Certain Societies in London Relative to That Event in a Letter to Have Been Sent to a Gentleman in Paris*, ed. J. G. A. Pocock (Cambridge, England: Hackett, [1790] 1987), 66.

2. Bernhard to Koopmans, 14 October 1975, PTCK, Box 21 (Folder 416: "Nobel Prize 1969– 1975 Nov").

3. See "Le Prix Nobel," an undated sheet of paper in Koopmans's hand in PTCK, Box 21 (Folder 417: "Nobel Prize 1975 Dec - 1981, n.d."); "Revolution in Economics," *New York Times*, 16 October 1975 (the clauses in the quotation have been transposed from the original); and Koopmans to Bernhard, 22 October 1975; both in PTCK, Box 21 (Folder 416: "Nobel Prize 1969–1975 Nov").

4. Koopmans to Kantorovitch [*sic*], 12 November 1956, PTCK, Box 13 (Folder 237: "Leonid V. Kantorovich, 1956–59").

5. See Koopmans to Robert W. Campbell (University of Southern California), 25 February 1957; and Koopmans to Campbell, 27 March 1958; both in PTCK, Box 13 (Folder 237: "Leonid V. Kantorovich, 1956–59"). On the dispute concerning "priority" between the Soviet and the American research, see Campbell to Koopmans, 13 February 1957; Koopmans to Wassily Leontief, 28 April 1959; and Leontief to Koopmans, 9 June 1959; all in PTCK, Box 13 (Folder 237: "Leonid V. Kantorovich, 1956–59"). Campbell had become aware of Kantorovich's work "through a CIA [Central Intelligence Agency] translation." The paper in question, that so captivated Koopmans's attention, was ultimately published in English as "On the Translocation of Masses," *Management Science* 5 (1958), 1–4. Also see L. V. Kantorovich, "Mathematical Methods of Organizing and Planning Production," *Management Science* 6 (1960), 363–422;

as well as L. Johansen, "L. V. Kantorovich's Contribution to Economics," *Scandinavian Journal of Economics* 18 (1976), 61–80—the latter an appreciation of the Russian's work in the wake of the award of his Nobel Memorial Prize.

6. See Harry Schwartz, "Soviet Economist Veers from Marx," *New York Times*, 6 November 1958, 6:1. Also see Leontief to Koopmans, 9 June 1959; Koopmans to Campbell, 25 February 1957; and Powell to Koopmans, 19 August 1957; all in PTCK, Box 13 (Folder 237: "Leonid V. Kantorovich, 1956–59"). Whatever the nature of the attacks upon Kantorovich, in the spring of 1958, *Pravda* had reported his election to the Academy of Sciences of the USSR. See Campbell to Koopmans, 11 April 1958, PTCK, Box 13 (Folder 237: "Leonid V. Kantorovich, 1956–59"). For a general overview of the career of Kantorovich, see Roy Gardner, "L. V. Kantorovich: The Price Implications of Optimal Planning," *Journal of Economic Literature* 28 (1990), 638–48.

7. See W. H. Marlow (George Washington University) to Koopmans, 26 March 1958; Marlow to Koopmans, 21 January 1959; both in PTCK, Box 13 (Folder 237: "Leonid V. Kantorovich, 1956–59"). Also see Koopmans to Gerhard Tintner (Iowa State College and Editor of *Econometrica*), 10 February 1960; Tintner to Koopmans, 15 February 1960; Koopmans to Les Livres Etrangers (Paris), 2 February 1960; Kantorovich to Koopmans, 24 January 1960; Kantorovich to J. M. Montias, 16 May 1960; Churchman to Koopmans, 10 June 1960; Koopmans to John Wiley and Sons (New York), 12 June 1964; and Koopmans to Kantorovich, 12 June 1964; all in PTCK, Box 13 (Folder 238: "Leonid V. Kantorovich, 1960–78, n.d.").

8. See Kantorovich to Koopmans, 14 August 1977; and Kantorovich to Koopmans, 13 August 1978; both in PTCK, Box 13 (Folder 238: "Leonid V. Kantorovich, 1960–78, n.d."). Also see Koopmans to Kantorovich, 24 July 1978; Koopmans to Stig Ramel (President of the Nobel Foundation), 24 July 1978; and Ramel to Koopmans, 23 August 1978; all in PTCK, Box 21 (Folder 417: "Nobel Prize 1975 Dec—1981, n.d."). As Ramel put it to Koopmans, "[T]he diplomats will find a solution to this most complicated international problem [i.e., the swapped medals]."

9. See Herbert E. Scarf, "The 1975 Nobel Prize in Economics: Resource Allocation," *Science* 190 (1975), 712.

10. I explore some issues surrounding the manner in which mainstream economic thought "crossed borders" in the post–World War II period in my "Academic Research Protocols and the Pax Americana: American Economics during the Cold War Era," in *Rethinking the Cold War: Essays on Its Dynamics, Meaning, and Morality*, ed. Allen Hunter (Philadelphia: Temple University Press, 1998), 257–70.

11. In his presidential address to the annual meeting of the American Economic Association in 1971, James Tobin put it well when he noted that fiscal policy alone could stimulate growth and unemployment; monetary policy could merely slow down expansion by the implementation of higher interest rates or (what amounted to the same thing) restrictions in the rate of growth of the money supply. The Fed could thus "pull on a string" to slow things down, but it could not "push" on it to speed things up. In this pithy metaphor, Tobin well summarized the difference between Keynesian-style activists in his profession and standpat monetarists. Perhaps even more to the point, former Fed chair Martin once described Federal Reserve responsibility as having the sole task of "leaning against the wind" of fiscal demand management. See James Tobin, "Inflation and Unemployment," *American Economic Review* 62 (1972), 1–18.

12. Bernard D. Nossiter, in his *Fat Years and Lean: The American Economy since Roosevelt* (New York: Harper and Row, 1990), 131, described Paul Volcker as having convinced President Carter to implement "good monetary medicine" at the cost of his political suicide.

13. The words are Robert B. Reich's from his *Locked in the Cabinet* (New York: Knopf, 1997), 80. The Open Market Committee of the Federal Reserve Board, composed of the Board of Governors and the presidents of Reserve System regional banks, exercises direct control over the national money supply (and thus prevailing rates of interest) through its weekly decisions regarding the purchase and sale of government securities. As to the varied and numerous assessments of the Fed's role and impact in the national economy in recent years, a sense of the controversy may be won from Bernard D. Rossiter, "The Myth of an Independent Fed," *The Nation*, 31 December 1990, 837–38; "Greenspan Rejects Calls to Reform Fed," *Los Angeles Times*, 14 October 1993, D1, D5; Keith Bradsher, "A Split over Fed's Role," *New York Times*, 29 August 1994, D1, D4; Robert Sherrill, "The Inflation of

Alan Greenspan: The Real Story behind Clinton's Fateful Choice," *The Nation*, 11 March 1996, 11–15; Martin S. Feldstein and Kathleen Feldstein, "Fed's Record Justifies Its Independence," *Los Angeles Times*, 8 November 1996, B9; Art Pine, "Fed Hikes Interest Rates Moderately to Deter Inflation," *Los Angeles Times*, 26 March 1997, A1, A27; Robert Kuttner, "Greenspan's Quarry Is Imaginary," *Los Angeles Times*, 30 March 1997, M5; James K. Galbraith, "Fixing the Fed," *The Nation*, 2 June 1997, 5; Art Pine, "Fed Putting a Crimp on Economy, Critics Say," *Los Angeles Times*, 11 August 1997, A1, A12; and Alan S. Blinder, "What Central Bankers Could Learn from Academics—and Vice Versa," *Journal of Economic Perspectives* 11 (spring 1997), 3–19.

14. See Jonathan Peterson, " 'Clintonomics' to Guide Economy," *Los Angeles Times*, 6 November 1992, A28–A29; "Clinton Is Economical with the Economists," *International Herald Tribune*, 21 December 1992, 7; and "Greenspan Rejects Calls to Reform Fed," D1, D5. A particularly thoughtful history of the relationship between the Fed and the executive branch in recent decades is provided by Gerald A. Epstein and Juliet B. Schor, "The Federal Reserve–Treasury Accord and the Construction of the Postwar Monetary Regime in the United States," *Social Concept* 8 (1995), 7–48. A broader historical context may be found in Nathaniel Beck, "Domestic Political Sources of American Monetary Policy: 1955–82," *Journal of Politics* 46 (1984), 786–817; and James Livingston, *Origins of the Federal Reserve System: Money, Class, and Corporate Capitalism, 1890–1913* (Ithaca, N.Y.: Cornell University Press, 1986). In the spring of 1997, a new Labour government in Great Britain was evidently inspired by the American example in monetary management. Breaking with three centuries of tradition, newly elected Prime Minister Tony Blair (Labour) granted the Bank of England independent authority to set interest rates. In the past, the Bank had always taken as its lead in policy matters the decisions and preferences of the Exchequer. The radical reform was, at the time, noted for the extent to which it "move[d] the venerable bank closer in character to the U.S. Federal Reserve and the independent central banks of Britain's European partners." See William D. Montalbano, "Bank of England Gets Rate-Setting Powers," *Los Angeles Times*, 7 May 1997, D1, D4.

15. See James Risen, "Panel Votes to Cut President's Economic Aides," *Los Angeles Times*, 7 December 1995, A17; and James Risen, "Economists Watch in Quiet Fury," *Los Angeles Times*, 8 January 1993, A1, A20–A21. On the controversies that erupted with almost every appointment President Clinton made to the CEA and the NEC, see Jonathan Peterson, "West Coast Economists Forge Axis with D.C.," *Los Angeles Times*, 21 August 1994, D1, D3; David M. Gordon, "With Tyson's Appointment to Economic Chair, a Harvest of Sour Grapes," *Los Angeles Times*, 24 January 1993, D2; Peter Passell, "More Advisers, Less Council?" *New York Times*, 17 December 1992, C2; and Louis Uchitelle, "An Appointment That Draws No Fire," *New York Times*, 7 January 1997, D3. Interestingly enough, the steady enhancement of the Fed's influence was paralleled by a growing celebration of its wisdom relative to the econometric forecasting engaged in by the private sector. David Romer and Christina Romer, members of the economics faculty at the University of California–Berkeley, undertook a study for the National Bureau of Economic Research early in 1997 that found the Fed's data-gathering and statistical simulation to be consistently superior to that of private consulting firms. See Art Pine, "It's Confirmed: Fed's Crystal Ball Is the Clearest of All," *Los Angeles Times*, 10 April 1997, A5. By the same token, most media organizations increasingly ignored those occasions when members of the CEA, let alone of the NEC, went to Capitol Hill to testify before the Joint Economic Committee. By contrast, whenever Fed chair Greenspan responded to a congressional invitation, it was a leading news item the next day.

16. With apologies to my late friend and colleague Herbert I. Schiller, *Culture, Inc.: The Corporate Takeover of Public Expression* (New York: Oxford University Press, 1989).

17. See my "Numerable Knowledge and Its Discontents," *Reviews in American History* 18 (1990), 151–64.

18. A Louis Harris poll of 1,255 adults in the spring of 1995, for example, found that 67 percent of the respondents did not know the current inflation rate, and 57 percent could not identify the prevailing rate of unemployment. See "Poll Shows Public Doesn't Follow Economic Data," *Los Angeles Times*, 23 May 1995, D2.

19. A relatively recent survey of the literature on this aspect of Progressivism may be found in John M. Cooper Jr., *Pivotal Decades: The United*

States, 1900–1920 (New York: Norton, 1990). One of the most sophisticated historical treatments of the relationship between numeracy and economic and political action is afforded by Patricia Cline Cohen, *A Calculating People: The Spread of Numeracy in Early America* (Chicago: University of Chicago Press, 1982). Also see, in this regard, William Alonso and Paul Starr, *The Politics of Numbers* (New York: Russell Sage Foundation, 1987).

20. See, for example, David M. Levy, *The Economic Ideas of Ordinary People: From Preference to Trade* (New York: Routledge, 1992); and Amos Kiewe and Davis W. Houck, *A Shining City on a Hill: Ronald Reagan's Economic Rhetoric, 1951–1989* (New York: Praeger, 1991).

21. The words are from Burton Bledstein's classic study *The Culture of Professionalism: The Middle Class and the Development of Higher Education in America* (New York: Norton, 1976), 334.

22. From David F. Musto, "Continuity across Generations: The Adams Family Myth," in *New Directions in Psychohistory: The Adelphi Papers in Honor of Erik H. Erikson*, ed. M. Albin, R. Devlin, and G. A. Heeger (Lexington, Mass.: Heath, 1980), 128. The notion of a "collective amnesia" that animates a profession's self-examination of its own past informs the work of Yuval Yonay, *The Struggle over the Soul of Economics: Institutionalist and Neoclassical Economists in America between the Wars* (Princeton, N.J.: Princeton University Press, 1998).

23. One of the truly classic considerations of these ideas, from the perspective of the Great Depression and World War II years, is John Kenneth Galbraith, *Economics and the Public Purpose* (Boston: Houghton Mifflin, 1973). A more recent memoir that offers an ambivalent assessment of statist policy in the late twentieth century is Daniel Patrick Moynihan, *Miles to Go: A Personal History of Social Policy* (Cambridge: Harvard University Press, 1996).

24. From Robert L. Heilbroner and William Milberg, *The Crisis of Vision in Modern Economic Thought* (New York: Cambridge University Press, 1995), 14.

25. An insightful contemplation of the complex relationship between scientific discourse and public policy debate is found in Yaron Ezrahi, *The Descent of Icarus: Science and the Transformation of Contemporary Democracy*

(Cambridge: Harvard University Press, 1990). Also of interest in this regard are Edward Purcell Jr., *The Crisis of Democratic Theory: Scientific Naturalism and the Problem of Value* (Lexington: University Press of Kentucky, 1973); and Robert M. Solow, "Science and Ideology in Economics," *The Public Interest* 21 (1970), 94–107. Earlier and quite remarkable assessments of the puzzling relationship between social science and political choice, specifically focused on economic matters, are Ian Malcolm and David Little, *A Critique of Welfare Economics* (Oxford: Oxford University Press, 1950); and Tibor Scitovsky, *The Joyless Economy: An Inquiry into Human Satisfaction and Consumer Dissatisfaction* (New York: Oxford University Press, 1976). Also see Ronald G. Walters, ed., *Scientific Authority and Twentieth-Century America* (Baltimore: Johns Hopkins University Press, 1997); and James Allen Smith, *The Idea Brokers: Think Tanks and the Rise of the New Policy Elite* (New York: Free Press, 1991).

26. The ahistorical celebration of the apparent triumph of the "market" in contemporary societies is well demonstrated in Daniel Yergin and Joseph Stanislaw, *The Commanding Heights: The Battle between Government and the Marketplace That Is Remaking the Modern World* (New York: Simon and Schuster, 1998); not to mention in the altogether inept book by Francis Fukuyama, *The End of History and the Last Man* (New York: Free Press, 1992). These superficial investigations are to be sharply counterposed to the quite thoughtful work of, for example, James C. Scott, *Seeing Like a State: How Certain Schemes to Improve the Human Condition Have Failed* (New Haven, Conn.: Yale University Press, 1998); William Reddy, *The Rise of Market Culture: The Textile Trade and French Society, 1750–1900* (New York: Cambridge University Press, 1984); and Michael Perelman, *The End of Economics* (New York: Routledge, 1996). Also see William Greider, *One World Ready or Not: The Manic Logic of Global Capitalism* (New York: Simon and Schuster, 1997); and Robert Kuttner, *Everything for Sale: The Virtues and Limits of Markets* (New York: Knopf, 1997). A novel point of view on these questions is afforded by a psychologist, Barry Schwartz, in *The Costs of Living: How Market Freedom Erodes the Best Things in Life* (New York: Norton, 1994).

Bibliography ──────────────────────

and Reference Abbreviations

Glossary of Abbreviations

AFBP Arthur F. Burns Papers, Dwight D. Eisenhower Library, Abilene, Kansas

AHCEA *Administrative History of the Council of Economic Advisers*, Lyndon Baines Johnson Library, Austin, Texas

CEA Records Records of the Office of the Council of Economic Advisers, 1953–61, Dwight D. Eisenhower Library, Abilene, Kansas

CPHH Commerce Papers of Herbert Hoover, Herbert Hoover Presidential Library, West Branch, Iowa

HPPF Hoover Presidential Personal File, Herbert Hoover Presidential Library, West Branch, Iowa

HPSF Hoover Presidential Subject Files, Herbert Hoover Presidential Library, West Branch, Iowa

OCCEA Office of the Chairman, Council of Economic Advisers, Records: 1953–61, Dwight D. Eisenhower Library, Abilene, Kansas

PEGN Papers of Edwin G. Nourse, Harry S. Truman Library, Independence, Missouri

PGRT Papers of Rexford G. Tugwell, Franklin Delano Roosevelt Library, Hyde Park, New York

PHST Papers of Harry S. Truman, Harry S. Truman Library, Independence, Missouri

PIF Papers of Irving Fisher, Franklin Delano Roosevelt Library, Hyde Park, New York

PLK Papers of Leon Keyserling, Harry S. Truman Library, Independence, Missouri

PRB Papers of Roy Blough, Harry S. Truman Library, Independence, Missouri

PTCK Papers of Tjalling C. Koopmans, Sterling Memorial Library, Yale University, New Haven, Connecticut

PWGM Papers of William Gibbs McAdoo, Manuscript Division, Library of Congress, Washington, D.C.

PWWH Papers of Walter Wolfgang Heller, John Fitzgerald Kennedy Library, Boston, Massachusetts

RAEA Records of the American Economic Association, Northwestern University Library—Special Collections, Evanston, Illinois

RLBJL Records of the Lyndon Baines Johnson Library, Lyndon Baines Johnson Library, Austin, Texas

ROCEA Records of the Council of Economic Advisers: 1961–68, Lyndon Baines Johnson Library, Austin, Texas

Manuscript Archives

Administrative History of the Council of Economic Advisers. Lyndon Baines Johnson Library, Austin, Texas.

Arthur F. Burns Papers. Dwight D. Eisenhower Library, Abilene, Kansas.

Commerce Papers of Herbert Hoover. Herbert Hoover Presidential Library, West Branch, Iowa.

Hoover Presidential Personal File. Herbert Hoover Presidential Library, West Branch, Iowa.

Hoover Presidential Subject Files. Herbert Hoover Presidential Library, West Branch, Iowa.

Microfilm Copies of the Papers of Edwin G. Nourse. John M. Olin Research Library, Cornell University, Ithaca, New York.

Office of the Chairman, Council of Economic Advisers, Records: 1953–61. Dwight D. Eisenhower Library, Abilene, Kansas.

Papers of Roy Blough. Harry S. Truman Library, Independence, Missouri.

Papers of Mordecai Ezekiel. Franklin Delano Roosevelt Library, Hyde Park, New York.

Papers of Irving Fisher. Franklin Delano Roosevelt Library, Hyde Park, New York.

Papers of Richard Gilbert. Franklin Delano Roosevelt Library, Hyde Park, New York.

Papers of E. A. Goldenweiser. Manuscript Division, Library of Congress, Washington, D.C.

Papers of Walter Wolfgang Heller. John Fitzgerald Kennedy Library, Boston, Massachusetts.

Papers of John F. Kennedy. Presidential Papers, John Fitzgerald Kennedy Library, Boston, Massachusetts.

Papers of Leon Keyserling. Harry S. Truman Library, Independence, Missouri.

Papers of Tjalling C. Koopmans. Sterling Memorial Library, Yale University, New Haven, Connecticut.

Papers of William Gibbs McAdoo. Manuscript Division, Library of Congress, Washington, D.C.

Papers of Henry Morgenthau Jr. Franklin Delano Roosevelt Library, Hyde Park, New York.

Papers of Edwin G. Nourse. Harry S. Truman Library, Independence, Missouri.

Papers of Alexander Sachs. Franklin Delano Roosevelt Library, Hyde Park, New York.

Papers of Harry S. Truman. Harry S. Truman Library, Independence, Missouri.

Papers of Rexford G. Tugwell, Franklin Delano Roosevelt Library, Hyde Park, New York.

Records of the American Economic Association. Northwestern University Library—Special Collections, Evanston, Illinois.

Records of the Council of Economic Advisers: 1961–68. Lyndon Baines Johnson Library, Austin, Texas.

Records of the Lyndon Baines Johnson Library. Lyndon Baines Johnson Library, Austin, Texas.

Records of the Office of the Council of Economic Advisers, 1953–61. Dwight D. Eisenhower Library, Abilene, Kansas.

Russell C. Leffingwell Papers. Manuscripts and Archives, Sterling Memorial Library, Yale University, New Haven, Connecticut.

Walt W. Rostow File. John Fitzgerald Kennedy Library, Boston, Massachusetts.

White House Staff Files. John Fitzgerald Kennedy Library, Boston, Massachusetts.

Oral History Interviews

Interview with Professor Emeritus George B. Dantzig. Department of Operations Research, Stanford University, 3 May 1989, at Palo Alto, California.

Interview with Professor Emeritus Herbert Scarf. Department of Economics, Yale University, 15 May 1989, at New Haven, Connecticut.

Oral History Interview with Gardner Ackley (13 April 1973, by Joe B. Grantz, at Ann Arbor). Lyndon Baines Johnson Library, Austin, Texas.

Oral History Interview with William L. Batt, Jr. (26 July 1966, by Jerry N. Hess, at Washington, D.C.). Harry S. Truman Library, Independence, Missouri.

Oral History Interview with William K. Divers (18 December 1969; 12 March, 19 March, 2 April, 16 April, and 21 April 1970; by Jerry N. Hess, at Washington, D.C.). Harry S. Truman Library, Independence, Missouri.

Oral History Interview with Professor Seymour E. Harris, Senior Consultant to the Secretary of the Treasury (conducted 16 and 17 June 1964; n.n., n.p.). John Fitzgerald Kennedy Library, Boston, Massachusetts.

Oral History Interview with Walter Heller (conducted 20 February 1970, by David McComb, at the University of Minnesota). Lyndon Baines Johnson Library. Austin, Texas.

Oral History Interview with Walter Heller, Kermit Gordon, James Tobin, Gardner Ackley, and Paul Samuelson (conducted 1 August 1964, by Joseph Pechman, at Fort Ritchie, Maryland). John Fitzgerald Kennedy Library, Boston, Massachusetts.

Oral History Interview with Neil H. Jacoby (November–December 1970, by James V. Mink, for the Columbia University Oral History Project, n.p.). Dwight D. Eisenhower Library, Abilene, Kansas.

Oral History Interview with Leon H. Keyserling (conducted 9 January 1969, by Stephen Goodell, at Washington, D.C.). Lyndon Baines Johnson Library, Austin, Texas.

Oral History Interview with Leon H. Keyserling (3, 10, and 19 May 1971, by Jerry N. Hess, at Washington, D.C.). Harry S. Truman Library, Independence, Missouri.

Oral History Memoir of Charles P. Kindleberger (16 July 1973, by Richard D. McKinzie, at Cambridge, Massachusetts). Harry S. Truman Library, Independence, Missouri.

Oral History Interview with Robert Lampman (conducted 24 May 1983, by Michael L. Gillette, at Madison, Wisconsin). Lyndon Baines Johnson Library, Austin, Texas.

Oral History Interview with Frederick J. Lawton (17 June and 9 July 1963, by Charles T. Morrissey, at Washington, D.C.). Harry S. Truman Library, Independence, Missouri.

Oral History Interview with Edward S. Mason (17 July 1973, by Richard D. McKinzie, at Cambridge, Massachusetts). Harry S. Truman Library. Independence, Missouri.

Oral History Interview with Charles S. Murphy (2 May, 3 June, and 24 July 1963; 21 May, 24 June, 15 July, and 25 July 1965; 19 May 1970, by Charles T. Morrissey and Jerry N. Hess, at Washington, D.C.). Harry S. Truman Library, Independence, Missouri.

Oral History Interview with Edwin G. Nourse (conducted 7 March 1972, by Jerry N. Hess, at Washington, D.C.). Harry S. Truman Library, Independence, Missouri.

Oral History Interview with Arthur M. Okun (conducted 20 March 1969, by David McComb, at Washington, D.C.). Lyndon Baines Johnson Library, Austin, Texas.

Oral History Interview with Arthur M. Okun (conducted 15 April 1969, by David G. McComb, at Washington, D.C.). Lyndon Baines Johnson Library, Austin, Texas.

Oral History Interview with Joseph A. Pechman (conducted 19 March 1969, by David G. McComb, at Washington, D.C.). Lyndon Baines Johnson Library, Austin, Texas.

Oral History Interview with Walter S. Salant (conducted 30 March 1970, by Jerry N. Hess, at Washington, D.C.). Harry S. Truman Library, Independence, Missouri.

Oral History Interview with Raymond J. Saulnier (conducted 7 August 1967, by John Luter, for the Columbia University Oral History Project, n.p.). Dwight D. Eisenhower Library, Abilene, Kansas.

Oral History Interview with Charles L. Schultze (conducted 28 March 1969, by David McComb, at Washington, D.C.). Lyndon Baines Johnson Library, Austin, Texas.

Oral History Interview with Charles L. Schultze (conducted 10 April 1969, by David McComb, at Washington, D.C.). Lyndon Baines Johnson Library, Austin, Texas.

Oral History Interview with John R. Steelman (conducted 15 January 1963, by Charles T. Morrissey, at Washington, D.C.). Harry S. Truman Library, Independence, Missouri.

Books, Monographs, and Anthologies

Aaron, Henry. *Politics and the Professors: The Great Society in Perspective.* Washington, D.C.: Brookings Institution, 1978.

Abbott, Andrew. *The System of Professions: An Essay on the Division of Expert Labor.* Chicago: University of Chicago Press, 1988.

Abraham, David. *The Collapse of the Weimar Republic: Political Economy and Crisis.* Princeton, N.J.: Princeton University Press, 1981.

Adams, James Ring. *The Big Fix: Inside the S&L Scandal: How an Unholy Alliance of Politics and Money Destroyed America's Banking System.* New York: Wiley, 1991.

Alchon, Guy. *The Invisible Hand of Planning: Capitalism, Social Science, and the State in the 1920s.* Princeton, N.J.: Princeton University Press, 1985.

Allen, Robert Loring. *Irving Fisher: A Biography.* Cambridge: Blackwell, 1993.

Alonso, William, and Paul Starr, eds. *The Politics of Numbers.* New York: Russell Sage Foundation, 1987.

Ambrose, Stephen E. *Eisenhower: The President.* New York: Simon and Schuster, 1984.

———. *Nixon: The Education of a Politican.* New York: Simon and Schuster, 1987.

Appleby, Joyce. *Liberalism and Republicanism in the Historical Imagination.* Cambridge: Harvard University Press, 1992.

Arrow, Kenneth J. *Social Choice and Individual Values.* New York: Wiley, 1951.

Arrow, Kenneth J., and Frank H. Hahn. *General Competitive Analysis.* San Francisco: Holden Day, 1971.

Ayres, Clarence. *The Problem of Economic Order.* New York: Farrar and Rinehart, 1938.

Backhouse, Roger E. *Explorations in Economic Methodology: From Lakatos to Empirical Philosophy of Science.* New York: Routledge, 1998.

Bailey, Stephen K. *Congress Makes a Law: The Story behind the Employment Act of 1946.* New York: Columbia University Press, 1950.

Balogh, Brian. *Chain Reaction: Expert Debate and Public Participation in American Commercial Nuclear Power, 1945–1975.* New York: Cambridge University Press, 1991.

Bannister, Robert C. *Sociology and Scientism.* Chapel Hill: University of North Carolina Press, 1987.

Baran, Paul. *The Political Economy of Growth.* New York: Monthly Review Press, 1957.

Baran, Paul, and Paul Sweezy; *Monopoly Capital: An Essay on the American Economic and Social Order.* New York: Monthly Review Press, 1966.

Barber, William J. *From New Era to New Deal: Herbert Hoover, the Economists, and American Economic Policy, 1921–1933.* New York: Cambridge University Press, 1985.

———. *Designs within Disorder: Franklin D. Roosevelt, the Economists, and the Shaping of American Economic Policy 1933–1945.* New York: Cambridge University Press, 1996.

Baumol, William J., and Kenneth McLennan. *Productivity Growth and U.S. Competitiveness.* New York: Oxford University Press, 1985.

Becker, Gary S. *A Treatise on the Family.* Cambridge: Harvard University Press, 1981.

Beisner, Robert L. *Twelve against Empire: The Anti-Imperialists, 1898–1900*. Chicago: University of Chicago Press, 1985.

Bellamy, Edward. *Looking Backward, 2000–1887*. Boston: Houghton Mifflin, 1888.

Berlant, Jeffrey L. *Professions and Monopoly*. Berkeley and Los Angeles: University of California Press, 1975.

Berman, Larry. *Planning a Tragedy: The Americanization of the War in Vietnam*. New York: Norton, 1982.

Bernal, John Desmond. *Science in History*. London: Watts, 1957.

Bernstein, Michael A. *The Great Depression: Delayed Recovery and Economic Change in America, 1929–1939*. New York: Cambridge University Press, 1987.

Bernstein, Michael A., and Allen Hunter, eds. *The Cold War and Expert Knowledge: New Essays on the History of the National Security State* [special issue of *Radical History Review* 63 (1995)].

Blackmar, Frank W. *Economics*. New York: Macmillan, 1900.

Blank, Rebecca M. *It Takes a Nation: A New Agenda for Fighting Poverty*. Princeton, N.J.: Princeton University Press, 1998.

Blaug, Mark. *The Methodology of Economics; or, How Economists Explain*. Cambridge: Cambridge University Press, 1980.

———. *Economic Theory in Retrospect*. Cambridge: Cambridge University Press, 1985.

———. *Great Economists since Keynes: An Introduction to the Lives and Works of One Hundred Modern Economists*. New York: Cambridge University Press, 1985.

———. *Great Economists before Keynes: An Introduction to the Lives and Works of One Hundred Great Economists of the Past*. New York: Cambridge University Press, 1986.

Bleaney, Michael. *The Rise and Fall of Keynesian Economics: An Investigation of Its Contribution to Capitalist Development*. London: Macmillan, 1985.

Bledstein, Burton J. *The Culture of Professionalism: The Middle Class and the Development of Higher Education in America*. New York: Norton, 1976.

Bloor, David. *Knowledge and Social Imagery*. Chicago: University of Chicago Press, 1976.

Bluestone, Barry, and Bennett Harrison. *The Deindustrialization of America: Plant Closings, Community Abandonment, and the Dismantling of Basic Industries*. New York: Basic Books, 1982.

Blum, John Morton. *From the Morgenthau Diaries: Years of Crisis, 1928–1938*. Boston: Houghton Mifflin, 1959.

———. *V Was for Victory: Politics and American Culture during World War II*. New York: Harcourt, Brace, 1976.

———. *Years of Discord: American Politics and Society, 1961–1974*. New York: Norton, 1991.

Böhm-Bawerk, Eugen von. *Capital and Interest*. New York: Kelley, [1890] 1957.

———. *Karl Marx and the Close of His System*. Ed. P. M. Sweezy. London: Merlin Press, 1975.

Booth, Alan. *British Economic Policy, 1931–1949: Was There a Keynesian Revolution?* New York: Harvester Wheatsheaf, 1989.

Borden, William S. *The Pacific Alliance: United States Foreign Economic Policy and Japanese Trade Recovery, 1947–1955*. Madison: University of Wisconsin Press, 1984.

Boulding, Kenneth E. *Conflict and Defense*. New York: Harper and Row, 1962.

Bourdieu, Pierre. *Outline of a Theory of Practice*. Trans. Richard Nice. New York: Cambridge University Press, 1977.

Boyer, Paul. *By the Bomb's Early Light: American Thought and Culture at the Dawn of the Atomic Age*. New York: Pantheon, 1985.

Branch, Taylor. *Parting the Waters: America in the King Years, 1954–63*. New York: Simon and Schuster, 1988.

———. *Pillar of Fire: America in the King Years, 1963–65*. New York: Simon and Schuster, 1998.

Brigante, John E. *The Feasibility Dispute: Determination of War Production Objectives for 1942 and 1943*. Washington, D.C.: Committee on Public Administration Cases, 1950.

Brinkley, Alan. *The End of Reform: New Deal Liberalism in Recession and War*. New York: Knopf, 1995.

Brint, Steven. *In an Age of Experts: The Changing Role of Professionals in Politics and Public Life*. Princeton, N.J.: Princeton University Press, 1994.

Brown, E. Richard. *Rockefeller Medicine Men: Medicine and Capitalism in America*. Berkeley and Los Angeles: University of California Press, 1979.

Brownlee, W. Elliot. *Federal Taxation in America: A Short History*. New York: Cambridge University Press, 1996.

———. *Funding the Modern American State, 1941–1995: The Rise and Fall of the Era of Easy Finance*. New York: Cambridge University Press, 1996.

Bukharin, Nikolai. *The Economic Theory of the Leisure Class*. London: Lawrence, 1927.

Bullock, Charles J. *Introduction to the Study of Economics*. Boston: Silver, Burdette, 1897.

Burke, Edmund. *Reflections on the Revolution in France and on the Proceedings in Certain Societies in London Relative to That Event in a Letter to Have Been Sent to a Gentleman in Paris*. Ed. J.G.A. Pocock. Cambridge: Hackett, [1790] 1987.

Burns, Arthur F., and Wesley C. Mitchell. *Measuring Business Cycles*. New York: National Bureau of Economic Research, 1946.

Burns, James MacGregor. *Roosevelt: The Lion and the Fox*. New York: Harcourt, Brace, 1956.

Buzzanco, Robert. *Masters of War: Military Dissent and Politics in the Vietnam Era*. New York: Cambridge University Press, 1996.

Cairncross, Alec. *Economic Ideas and Government Policy: Contributions to Contemporary Economic History*. New York: Routledge, 1996.

Calavita, Kitty, Henry N. Pontell, and Robert H. Tillman. *Big Money Crime: Fraud and Politics in the Savings and Loan Crisis*. Berkeley and Los Angeles: University of California Press, 1997.

Caldwell, Bruce. *Beyond Positivism: Economic Methodology in the Twentieth Century*. Boston: Allen and Unwin, 1982.

Campagna, Anthony S. *Economic Policy in the Carter Administration*. (Westport, Conn.: Greenwood Press, 1995.

Canterbery, E. Ray. *The President's Council of Economic Advisers: A Study of Its Functions and Its Influence on the Chief Executive Decisions*. New York: Exposition Press, 1961.

Cardozier, V. Ray. *Colleges and Universities in World War 2*. Westport, Conn.: Praeger, 1993.

Caro, Robert A. *The Years of Lyndon Johnson*. New York: Knopf, 1982.

Carr-Saunders, Alexander M., and Paul A. Wilson. *The Professions*. Oxford: Oxford University Press, [1933] 1964.

Carson, Clayborne. *In Struggle: S.N.C.C. and the Black Awakening of the 1960s*. Cambridge: Harvard University Press, 1981.

Carver, Thomas N. *Elementary Economics*. Boston: Ginn, 1919.

Catton, Bruce. *The War Lords of Washington*. New York: Harcourt, Brace, 1948.

Chamberlin, Edward H. *The Theory of Monopolistic Competition*. Cambridge: Harvard University Press, [1933] 1962.

Chandler, Lester V. *America's Greatest Depression: 1929–41*. New York: Harper and Row, 1970.

Chomsky, Noam, et al. *The Cold War and the University: Toward an Intellectual History of the Postwar Years*. New York: New Press, 1997.

Clark, John Bates. *The Distribution of Wealth: A Theory of Wages, Income and Profits*. New York: Kelley, [1899] 1967.

Clark, Ronald. *The Rise of the Boffins*. London: Phoenix House, 1962.

Clark, Terry N. *The French University and the Emergence of the Social Sciences*. Cambridge: Harvard University Press, 1973.

Clarke, Peter. *The Keynesian Revolution in the Making, 1924–1936*. Oxford: Clarendon Press, 1988.

Clarke, Sally. *Regulation and the Revolution in United States Farm Productivity*. New York: Cambridge University Press, 1994.

Clawson, Marion. *New Deal Planning: The National Resources Planning Board*. Baltimore: Johns Hopkins University Press, 1981.

Clay, Henry. *Economics: An Introduction for the General Reader*. London: Macmillan, 1919.

Coats, A. W. *Reflections on the Professionalisation of Economics*. Newcastle: Newcastle Lecture in Political Economy, 1980.

———. *The Sociology and Professionalization of Economics*. 2 vols. New York: Routledge, 1993.

Cohen, Lizabeth. *Making a New Deal: Industrial Workers in Chicago, 1919–1939*. New York: Cambridge University Press, 1990.

Cohen, Patricia Cline. *A Calculating People: The Spread of Numeracy in Early America*. Chicago: University of Chicago Press, 1982.

Colander, David C., and Arjo Klamer. *The Making of an Economist*. Boulder, Colo.: Westview Press, 1990.

Colander, David C., and A. W. Coats, eds. *The Spread of Economic Ideas*. New York: Cambridge University Press, 1989.

Colander, David C., and Reuven Brenner, eds. *Educating Economists*. Ann Arbor: University of Michigan Press, 1992.

Colander, David C., and Harry Landreth, eds. *The Coming of Keynesianism to America: Conversations with the Founders of Keynesian Economics*. Cheltenham, England: Elgar, 1996.

Collins, Randall. *The Credential Society*. New York: Academic Press, 1979.

Collins, Robert M. *The Business Response to Keynes, 1929–1964*. New York: Columbia University Press, 1981.

Commons, John R. *Institutional Economics: Its Place in Political Economy*. New Brunswick, N.J.: Transaction Publishers, [1934] 1990.

Cook, Fred J. *The Warfare State*. New York: Macmillan, 1962.

Cooper, Frederick, and Randall Packard. *International Development and the Social Sciences: Essays on the History and Politics of Knowledge*. Berkeley and Los Angeles: University of California Press, 1998.

Cooper, John M., Jr. *Pivotal Decades: The United States, 1900–1920*. New York: Norton, 1990.

Corey, Lewis. *The Crisis of the Middle Class*. New York: Covici Friede, 1935.

Cornford, Francis M., trans. *The Republic of Plato*. Oxford: Clarendon Press, 1948.

Cowdrey, Albert E. *Fighting for Life: American Military Medicine in World War II*. New York: Free Press, 1994.

Critchlow, Donald T. *The Brookings Institution, 1916–1952: Expertise and the Public Interest in a Democratic Society*. DeKalb: Northern Illinois University Press, 1985.

Cuff, Robert D. *The War Industries Board: Business-Government Relations during World War I*. Baltimore: Johns Hopkins University Press, 1973.

Cullen, John B. *The Structure of Professionalism*. New York: Petrocelli, 1978.

Dallek, Robert. *Lyndon Johnson and His Times, 1961–1973*. New York: Oxford University Press, 1998.

Darman, Richard. *Who's in Control? Polar Politics and the Sensible Center*. New York: Simon and Schuster, 1996.

Davenport, Herbert J. *Outlines of Elementary Economics*. New York: Macmillan, 1897.

Davies, Gareth. *From Opportunity to Entitlement: The Transformation and Decline of Great Society Liberalism*. Lawrence: University Press of Kansas, 1996.

Deane, Phyllis. *The Evolution of Economic Ideas*. Cambridge: Cambridge University Press, 1978.

Debreu, Gerard. *Theory of Value*. New York: Wiley, 1959.

Deegan, Mary Jo. *Jane Addams and the Men of the Chicago School, 1892–1918*. New Brunswick, N.J.: Rutgers University Press, 1988.

Deibler, Frederick S. *Principles of Economics*. New York: McGraw, Hill, 1936.

Delphy, Christine. *Close to Home: A Materialist Analysis of Women's Oppression*. Trans and ed. D. Leonard. Amherst: University of Massachusetts Press, 1984.

De Marchi, Neil. *The Popperian Legacy in Economics*. Cambridge: Cambridge University Press, 1988.

De Marchi, Neil, and Christopher Gilbert, eds. *History and Methodology in Economics*. Oxford: Clarendon Press, 1989.

Derber, Charles, William A. Schwartz, and Yale Magrass. *Power in the Highest Degree: Professionals and the Rise of a New Mandarin Order*. New York: Oxford University Press, 1990.

Dertouzos, Michael L., Richard K. Lester, and Robert M. Solow. *Made in America: Regaining the Productive Edge*. Cambridge: MIT Press, 1989.

Devine, Edward T. *Economics*. New York: Macmillan, 1898.

Diamond, Sigmund. *Compromised Campus: The Collaboration of Universities with the Intelligence Community, 1945–55*. New York: Oxford University Press, 1992.

Dicken, Peter. *Global Shift*. London: Chapman, 1992.

Diggins, John Patrick. *The Proud Decades: America in War and Peace, 1941–1960*. New York: Norton, 1988.

Dimand, Robert W. *The Origin of the Keynesian Revolution: The Development of Keynes' Theory of Employment and Output*. Aldershot: Elgar, 1988.

Dimand, Robert W., and Mary Ann Dimand. *A History of Game Theory*. Vol. 1, *From the Beginnings to 1945*. New York: Routledge, 1997.

Divine, Robert A. *Eisenhower and the Cold War*. New York: Oxford University Press, 1981.

Dobb, Maurice H. *Theories of Value and Distribution since Adam Smith*. Cambridge: Cambridge University Press, 1973.

Dore, Mohammed, Sukhamoy Chakravarty, and Richard Goodwin, eds. *John von Neumann and Modern Economics*. New York: Oxford University Press, 1989.

Dorfman, Joseph. *The Economic Mind in American Civilization*. New York: Viking, 1946–59.

Dorfman, Robert, Paul A. Samuelson, and Robert M. Solow. *Linear Programming and Economic Analysis*. London: McGraw-Hill, 1958.

Douglas, Paul H. *In the Fullness of Time: The Memoirs of Paul H. Douglas*. New York: Harcourt Brace Jovanovich, 1971.

Dow, Sheila. *Macroeconomic Thought: A Methodological Approach*. Oxford: Blackwell, 1985.

Drachman, Virginia. *Hospitals with a Heart: Women Doctors and the Paradox of Separatism at the New England Hospital, 1862–1969*. Ithaca, N.Y.: Cornell University Press, 1984.

Dumont, Louis. *Homo Hierarchicus: An Essay on the Caste System*. Trans. Mark Sainsbury. Chicago: University of Chicago Press, 1970.

———. *From Mandeville to Marx: The Genesis and Triumph of Economic Ideology*. Chicago: University of Chicago Press, 1977.

Duncan, Joseph W., and William C. Shelton. *Revolution in the United States Government Statistics, 1926–1976*. Washington, D.C.: United States Department of Commerce, 1978.

Dupree, A. Hunter. *Science in the Federal Government: A History of Policies and Activities to 1940*. Cambridge: Harvard University Press, 1957.

Eatwell, John, et al., eds. *Palgrave Dictionary of Economics*. London: Macmillan, 1987.

Edgeworth, Francis Y. *Mathematical Psychics*. London: Routledge, 1881.

———. *Papers Relating to Political Economy*. London: Macmillan, 1925.

Edie, Lionel. *Principles of the New Economics*. New York: Thomas Y. Crowell, 1926.

Edwards, Paul N. *The Closed World: Computers and the Politics of Discourse in Cold War America*. Cambridge: MIT Press, 1996.

Edwards, Richard, Michael Reich, and Thomas E. Weisskopf. *The Capitalist System: A Radical Analysis of American Society*. Englewood Cliffs, N.J.: Prentice-Hall, [1972] 1986.

Ehrenreich, Barbara. *Fear of Falling: The Inner Life of the Middle Class*. New York: Pantheon, 1989.

Eichengreen, Barry. *Golden Fetters: The Gold Standard and the Great Depression, 1919–1939*. New York: Oxford University Press, 1992.

Eisner, Robert. *How Real Is the Federal Deficit?* New York: Macmillan, 1986.

———. *The Misunderstood Economy: What Counts and How to Count It*. Boston: Harvard University Business School, 1994.

Ely, Richard T. *Outlines of Economics*. New York: Macmillan, 1893.

———. *The World War and Leadership in a Democracy*. New York: Macmillan, 1918.

———. *Ground under Our Feet*. New York: Macmillan, 1938.

Engels, Friedrich. *The Origin of the Family, Private Property and the State, in the Light of the Researches of Lewis H. Morgan*. New York: International Publishers, [1891] 1942.

England, J. Merton. *A Patron of Pure Science: The National Science Foundation's Formative Years, 1945–57*. Washington, D.C.: National Science Foundation, 1982.

Enthoven, Alain C., and K. Wayne Smith. *How Much Is Enough? Shaping the Defense Program, 1961–1969*. New York: Harper and Row, 1971.

Epstein, Richard A. *Mortal Peril: Our Inalienable Right to Health Care?* Reading, Mass.: Addison-Wesley, 1997.

Etyold, Thomas, and John Lewis Gaddis, eds. *Containment: Documents on American Policy and Strategy, 1945–1950*. New York: Columbia University Press, 1978.

Etzioni, Amitai. *The Semi-Professions and Their Organization*. New York: Free Press, 1969.

Evans, Sara. *Personal Politics: The Roots of Women's Liberation in the Civil Rights Movement and the New Left*. New York: Vintage, 1979.

Ewen, Stuart, and Elizabeth Ewen. *Channels of Desire: Mass Images and the Shaping of American Consciousness*. New York: McGraw-Hill, 1982.

Ezrahi, Yaron. *The Descent of Icarus: Science and the Transformation of Contemporary Democracy*. Cambridge: Harvard University Press, 1990.

Fairchild, Fred R. *Elementary Economics*. New York: Macmillan, 1930.

Feiwel, George R., ed. *Joan Robinson and Modern Economic Theory*. New York: New York University Press, 1989.

Feldman, Gerald. *The Great Disorder: Politics, Economics, and Society in the German Inflation, 1914–1924*. New York: Oxford University Press, 1993.

Feldstein, Martin, ed. *American Economic Policy in the 1980s*. Chicago: University of Chicago Press, 1994.

Fellner, William. *Competition among the Few*. New York: Kelley, 1960.

Ferber, Marianne A., and Julie A. Nelson, eds. *Beyond Economic Man: Feminist Theory and Economics*. Chicago: University of Chicago Press, 1993.

Ferguson, Charles. *The Neoclassical Theory of Production and Distribution*. London: Cambridge University Press, 1969.

Fetter, Frank A. *Principles of Economics with Applications to Practical Problems*. New York: Century, 1904.

Fish, Stanley. *Is There a Text in This Class? The Authority of Interpretive Communities*. Cambridge: Harvard University Press, 1980.

Fisher, Donald. *Fundamental Development of the Social Sciences: Rockefeller Philanthropy and the United States Social Science Research Council*. Ann Arbor: University of Michigan Press, 1993.

Fisher, Glenn W. *The Worst Tax? A History of the Property Tax in America*. Lawrence: University Press of Kansas, 1996.

Fisher, Irving. *Mathematical Investigations into the Theory of Value and Price*. New York: Kelley, [1892] 1961.

——. *The Nature of Capital and Income*. London: Macmillan, 1906.

——. *Elementary Principles of Economics*. New York: Macmillan, 1911.

——. *The Theory of Interest*. New York: Kelley, [1930] 1965.

Fisher, Irving Norton. *My Father, Irving Fisher*. New York: Comet Press, 1956.

Fisher, Robert M. *The Logic of Economic Discovery*. Brighton: Wheatsheaf, 1986.

Fitzpatrick, Ellen. *Endless Crusade: Women Social Scientists and Progressive Reform*. New York: Oxford University Press, 1990.

Flash, Edward S., Jr. *Economic Advice and Presidential Leadership: The Council of Economic Advisers*. New York: Columbia University Press, 1965.

Fox, Daniel M. *The Discovery of Abundance: Simon N. Patten and the Transformation of Social Theory*. Ithaca, N.Y.: Cornell University Press, 1967.

Fraser, Steve, and Gary Gerstle, eds. *The Rise and Fall of the New Deal Order, 1930–1980*. Princeton, N.J.: Princeton University Press, 1989.

Frederickson, George M. *The Inner Civil War: Northern Intellectuals and the Crisis of the Union*. New York: Harper and Row, 1965.

Freidson, Eliot. *Professional Dominance*. Chicago: Aldine, 1970.

Friedman, Milton. *Essays in Positive Economics*. Chicago: University of Chicago Press, 1953.

Friedman, Milton, and Walter W. Heller. *Monetary vs. Fiscal Policy*. New York: Norton, 1969.

Friedman, Milton, and Anna J. Schwartz. *A Monetary History of the United States, 1867–1960.* Princeton, N.J.: Princeton University Press, 1963.

Friedman, Robert Marc. *Appropriating the Weather: Vilhelm Bjerknes and the Construction of a Modern Meteorology.* Ithaca, N.Y.: Cornell University Press, 1989.

Fukuyama, Francis. *The End of History and the Last Man.* New York: Free Press, 1992.

Furner, Mary O. *Advocacy and Objectivity: A Crisis in the Professionalization of American Social Science, 1865–1905.* Lexington: University Press of Kentucky, 1975.

Gaddis, John Lewis. *Strategies of Containment: A Critical Appraisal of Postwar American National Security Policy.* New York: Oxford University Press, 1982.

———. *We Now Know: Rethinking Cold War History.* New York: Oxford University Press, 1997.

Galbraith, John Kenneth. *Economics and the Public Purpose.* Boston: Houghton Mifflin, 1973.

———. *A Life in Our Time.* London: Deutsch, 1981.

Gani, Joseph, ed. *The Craft of Probabilistic Modelling.* New York: Springer Verlag, 1986.

Gans, Herbert. *Popular Culture and High Culture: An Analysis and Evaluation of Taste.* New York: Basic Books, 1974.

Gardner, Lloyd C. *Pay Any Price: Lyndon Johnson and the Wars for Vietnam.* Chicago: I. R. Dee, 1995.

Garver, Frederic B., and Alvin H. Hansen. *Principles of Economics.* Boston: Glin, 1928.

Gaus, John M., and Leon Wolcott. *Public Administration and the United States Department of Agriculture.* Chicago: Public Administration Service, 1940.

Gay, Peter. *The Cultivation of Hatred.* Vol. 3 of *The Bourgeois Experience: Victoria to Freud.* New York: Norton, 1993.

Geiger, Roger L. *To Advance Knowledge: The Growth of American Research Universities, 1900–1940.* New York: Oxford University Press, 1986.

———. *Research and Relevant Knowledge: American Research Universities since World War II.* New York: Oxford University Press, 1993.

Gemmill, Paul F. *Fundamentals of Economics: A Textbook for Introductory College Courses in Economic Principles.* New York: Harper and Brothers, 1930.

Gide, Charles, and Charles Rist. *A History of Economic Doctrines.* Boston: D. C. Heath, [1913] n.d.

Godelier, Maurice. *Rationality and Irrationality in Economics.* New York: Monthly Review Press, 1972.

Goldman, Eric. *The Tragedy of Lyndon Baines Johnson.* New York: Knopf, 1969.

Goodman, Paul. *Growing Up Absurd: Problems of Youth in the Organized System.* New York: Vintage, 1960.

Gouldner, Alvin W. *The Coming Crisis of Western Sociology.* New York: Basic Books, 1970.

———. *The Future of Intellectuals and the Rise of the New Class.* New York: Oxford University Press, 1981.

Gourevitch, Peter. *Politics in Hard Times: Comparative Responses to International Economic Crisis.* Ithaca, N.Y.: Cornell University Press, 1986.

Graebner, Norman A., ed. *The Nationl Security: Its Theory and Practice, 1945–1960.* New York: Oxford University Press, 1960.

Gram, Harry, and Vivian Walsh. *Classical and Neoclassical Theories of General Equilibrium.* New York: Oxford University Press, 1980.

Gray, George W. *Science at War.* New York: Harper and Brothers, 1943.

Green, Philip. *Deadly Logic: The Theory of Nuclear Deterrence*. Columbus: Ohio State University Press, 1966.

Greenstein, Fred I. *The Hidden-Hand Presidency: Eisenhower as Leader*. New York: Basic Books, 1982.

Greider, William. *One World Ready or Not: The Manic Logic of Global Capitalism*. New York: Simon and Schuster, 1997.

Gruber, Carol S. *Mars and Minerva: World War I and the Uses of the Higher Learning in America*. Baton Rouge: Louisiana State University Press, 1975.

Gruchy, Allan G. *Modern Economic Thought: The American Contribution*. New York: Prentice-Hall, 1947.

Haber, Samuel. *Efficiency and Uplift: Scientific Management in the Progressive Era, 1890–1920*. Chicago: University of Chicago Press, 1964.

Hacker, Jacob S. *The Road to Nowhere: The Genesis of President Clinton's Plan for Health Security*. Princeton, N.J.: Princeton University Press, 1997.

Hadley, Arthur T. *Economics: An Account of the Relations between Private Property and Public Welfare*. New York: G. P. Putnam's Sons, 1896.

Hahn, Frank H. *On the Notion of Equilibrium in Economics*. Cambridge: Cambridge University Press, 1973.

Hamilton, Walton H. *Industrial Policy and Institutionalism: Selected Essays*. Clifton, N.J.: Kelly, [1915–18] 1974.

Harcourt, Geoffrey C. *Some Cambridge Controversies in the Theory of Capital*. Cambridge: Cambridge University Press, 1972.

———. *The Social Science Imperialists*. London: Routledge and Kegan Paul, 1982.

Harrington, Michael. *The Other America: Poverty in the United States*. New York: Macmillan, 1962.

Harris, Donald. *Capital Accumulation and Income Distribution*. Stanford, Calif.: Stanford University Press, 1978.

Harris, Seymour E. *Price and Related Controls in the United States*. New York: McGraw-Hill, 1945.

———. *The New Economics*. New York: Knopf, 1947.

Harrod, Roy F. *The Life of John Maynard Keynes*. London: Macmillan, 1951.

Haskell, Thomas L. *The Emergence of Professional Social Science: The American Social Science Association and the Nineteenth-Century Crisis of Authority*. Urbana: University of Illinois Press, 1977.

———, ed. *The Authority of Experts*. Bloomington: Indiana University Press, 1984.

Haveman, Robert H. *Poverty Policy and Poverty Research: The Great Society and the Social Sciences*. Madison: University of Wisconsin Press, 1987.

Hawkins, Hugh. *Pioneer: A History of the Johns Hopkins University, 1874–1889*. Ithaca, N.Y.: Cornell University Press, 1960.

Hawley, Ellis W. *The New Deal and the Problem of Monopoly: A Study in Economic Ambivalence*, Princeton, N.J.: Princeton University Press, 1966.

———. *Herbert Hoover as Secretary of Commerce: Studies in New Era Thought and Practice*. Iowa City: University of Iowa Press, 1981.

Hawtrey, Ralph G. *Good and Bad Trade: An Inquiry into the Causes of Trade Fluctuations*. London: Constable, 1913.

Hayden, Dolores. *The Grand Domestic Revolution: A History of Feminist Designs for American Homes, Neighborhoods, and Cities*. Cambridge: MIT Press, 1981.

Heaton, Herbert. *A Scholar in Action: Edwin F. Gay*. Cambridge: Harvard University Press, 1952.

Hegel, Georg W. F. *Philosophy of Right*. Trans. T. M. Knox. Oxford, Clarendon Press, [1821] 1942.

Heilbroner, Robert L. *The Worldy Philosophers: The Lives, Times and Ideas of the Great Economic Thinkers*. New York: Simon and Schuster, 1972.

Heilbroner, Robert L., and William Milberg. *The Crisis of Vision in Modern Economic Thought*. New York: Cambridge University Press, 1995.

Heims, Steve J. *Constructing a Social Science for Postwar America: The Cybernetics Group, 1946–53*. Cambridge: MIT Press, 1991.

Henry, John F. *John Bates Clark: The Making of a Neoclassical Economist*. New York: St. Martin's, 1995.

Herbst, Jurgen. *The German Historical School in American Scholarship*. Port Washington, N.Y.: Kennikat Press, 1972.

Hibbs, Douglas A., Jr. *The Political Economy of Industrial Democracies*. Cambridge: Harvard University Press, 1987.

Hicks, John R. *Value and Capital*. Oxford: Oxford University Press, 1939.

———. *The Crisis of Keynesian Economics*. New York: Basic Books, 1975.

Hicks, John R., and W. Weber, eds. *Carl Menger and the Austrian School of Economics*. Oxford: Oxford University Press, 1973.

Higham, John, Leonard Krieger, and Felix Gilbert. *History*. Englewood Cliffs, N.J.: Prentice-Hall, 1965.

Hildreth, Clifford. *The Cowles Commission in Chicago, 1939–1955*. New York: Springer-Verlag, 1986.

Hitch, Charles J., and Roland N. McKean. *The Economics of Defense in the Nuclear Age*. Cambridge: Harvard University Press, 1960.

Hobbes, Thomas. *Leviathan* Ed. C. B. Macpherson. New York: Penguin, [1651] 1968.

Hoeveler, J. David. *Watch on the Right: Conservative Intellectuals in the Reagan Era*. Madison: University of Wisconsin Press, 1991.

Hofstadter, Richard. *The Age of Reform: From Bryan to F.D.R.*. New York: Random House, 1955.

———. *The Progressive Movement, 1900–1915*. Englewood Cliffs, N.J.: Prentice-Hall, 1963.

Hofstadter, Richard, and Walter P. Metzger. *The Development of Academic Freedom in the United States*. New York: Columbia University Press, 1955.

Hogan, Michael J. *The Marshall Plan: America, Britain, and the Reconstruction of Western Europe, 1947–1952*. New York: Cambridge University Press, 1987.

Homan, Paul T. *Contemporary Economic Thought*. New York: Harper, 1928.

Horowitz, David, ed. *Corporations and the Cold War*. New York: Monthly Review Press, 1969.

Horowitz, Irving L. *The War Game: Studies of the New Civilian Militarists*. New York: Ballantine Books, 1962.

Hoxie, R. Gordon, et al., eds. *A History of the Faculty of Political Science, Columbia University*. New York: Columbia University Press, 1955.

Hunter, Allen, ed. *Rethinking the Cold War: Essays on Its Dynamics, Meaning, and Morality*. Philadelphia: Temple University Press, 1998.

Hutchinson, Terence W. *The Significance and Basic Postulates of Economics*. New York: Kelley, [1938] 1960.

———. *On Revolutions and Progress in Economic Knowledge*. Cambridge: Cambridge University Press, 1978.

Isard, Walter. *Arms, Arms Control, and Conflict Analysis: Contributions from Peace Science and Peace Economics*. New York: Cambridge University Press, 1988.

Israel, Jerry. *Building the Organizational Society: Essays on Associational Activities in Modern America*. New York: Free Press, 1972.

Isserman, Maurice. *If I Had a Hammer: The Decline of the Old Left and the Rise of the New Left*. New York: Basic Books, 1987.

Jacoby, Russell. *The Last Intellectuals: American Culture in the Age of Academe*. New York: Basic Books, 1987.

Jaffe, William, ed. *The Correspondence of Leon Walras and Related Papers*. Amsterdam: North-Holland, 1965.

James, Harold. *International Monetary Cooperation since Bretton Woods*. New York: Oxford University Press, 1996.

Janeway, Eliot. *The Struggle for Survival: A Chronicle of Economic Mobilization in World War II*. New Haven, Conn.: Yale University Press, 1951.

Jarvis, Howard, with Robert Pack. *I'm Mad as Hell: The Exclusive Story of the Tax Revolt and Its Leader*. New York: Times Books, 1979.

Jevons, William S. *The Theory of Political Economy*. New York: Macmillan, [1888] 1957.

Johnson, Alvin. *Introduction to Economics*. Boston: D. C. Heath, 1909.

Johnson, Terence J. *Professions and Power*. London: Macmillan, 1967.

Jordan, John M. *Machine Age Ideology: Social Engineering and American Liberalism, 1911–1939*. Chapel Hill: University of North Carolina Press, 1994.

Kadish, Alon, and Keith Tribe, eds. *The Market for Political Economy: The Advent of Economics in British University Culture, 1850–1905*. London: Routledge, 1993.

Kahin, George. *Intervention: How America Became Involved in Vietnam*. New York: Knopf, 1986.

Kahn, Herman. *On Thermonuclear War*. Princeton, N.J.: Princeton University Press, 1960.
———. *Thinking about the Unthinkable*. New York: Avon, 1962.

Kalecki, Michal. *Studies in the Theory of Business Cycles, 1933–39*. New York: Kelley, 1966.

Kalman, Laura. *The Strange Career of Legal Liberalism*. New Haven, Conn.: Yale University Press, 1996.

Kalmer, Arjo. *Conversations with Economists: New Classical Economists and Opponents Speak Out on the Current Controversy in Macroeconomics*. Totowa, N.J.: Rowman and Allanheld, 1984.

Kaplan, Edward S. *American Trade Policy, 1923–1995*. Westport, Conn.: Greenwood Press, 1996.

Kaplan, Fred. *The Wizards of Armageddon*. New York: Simon and Schuster, 1983.

Karsten, Peter, ed. *The Military in America: From the Colonial Era to the Present*. New York: Free Press, 1980.

Katouzian, H. *Ideology and Method in Economics*. New York: New York University Press, 1980.

Katz, Barry M. *Foreign Intelligence: Research and Analysis in the Office of Strategic Services, 1942–1945*. Cambridge: Harvard University Press, 1989.

Katz, Michael B. *The Undeserving Poor: From the War on Poverty to the War on Welfare*. New York: Pantheon, 1989.

Katzenstein, Peter J., ed. *Between Power and Plenty: Foreign Economic Policies of Advanced Industrial States*. Madison: University of Wisconsin Press, 1978.

Kaufman, Bruce E. *The Origins and Evolution of the Field of Industrial Relations*. Ithaca, N.Y.: ILR Press–Cornell Studies in Industrial and Labor History, 1993.

Kaufmann, William W. *The McNamara Strategy*. New York: Harper, 1964.

Keller, Morton. *Regulating a New Society: Public Policy and Social Change in America, 1900–1933*. Cambridge: Harvard University Press, 1994.

Keniston, Kenneth. *Young Radicals: Notes on Committed Youth*. New York: Harcourt, Brace, 1968.

Kennedy, David M. *Over Here: The First World War and American Society*. New York: Oxford University Press, 1980.

Kerr, Clark. *The Uses of the University*. Cambridge: Harvard University Press, 1963.

Kevles, Daniel. *The Physicists: The History of a Scientific Community in Modern America*. New York: Knopf, 1977.

Keynes, John Maynard. *The General Theory of Employment, Interest, and Money*. New York: Harcourt, Brace, 1936.

———. *Activities 1940–1944: Shaping the Post-War World; The Clearing Union*. Vol. 25 of *The Collected Writings of John Maynard Keynes*, ed. Donald Moggridge. New York: Macmillan, 1980.

Kiewe, Amos, and Davis W. Houck. *A Shining City on a Hill: Ronald Reagan's Economic Rhetoric, 1951–1989*. New York: Praeger, 1991.

Kiger, Joseph C. *American Learned Societies*. Washington, D.C.: Public Affairs Press, 1963.

Kindleberger, Charles P. *Marshall Plan Days*. Winchester, Mass.: Allen and Unwin, 1987.

King, John E. *Economic Exiles*. New York: St. Martin's, 1988.

King Lord. *The Life of John Locke*. London: Colburn and Bentley, 1830.

Kingsland, Sharon E. *Modeling Nature: Episodes in the History of Population Ecology*. Chicago: University of Chicago Press, 1985.

Klausner, Samuel, and Victor Lidz, eds. *The Nationalization of the Social Sciences*. Philadelphia: University of Pennsylvania Press, 1986.

Klein, Lawrence R. *The Keynesian Revolution*. New York: Macmillan, 1947.

Kleinman, Daniel Lee. *Politics on the Endless Frontier: Postwar Research Policy in the United States*. Durham, N.C.: Duke University Press, 1995.

Knight, Frank H. *On the History and Method of Economics: Selected Essays*. Chicago: University of Chicago Press, 1963.

Kolko, Gabriel. *The Triumph of Conservatism: A Reinterpretation of American History*. Glencoe, Ill.: Free Press, 1963.

Koopmans, Tjalling C., ed. *Activity Analysis of Production and Allocation: Proceedings of a Conference*. New York: Wiley, 1951.

———. *Three Essays on the State of Economic Science*. New York: McGraw-Hill, 1957.

Krause, Elliott A. *Death of the Guilds: Professions, States, and the Advance of Capitalism, 1930 to the Present*. New Haven, Conn.: Yale University Press, 1996.

Kreps, David M. *Game Theory and Economic Modelling*. Oxford: Oxford University Press, 1990.

Kuhn, Thomas S. *The Structure of Scientific Revolutions*. Chicago: University of Chicago Press, [1962], 1966.

———. *The Essential Tension: Selected Studies in Scientific Tradition and Change*. Chicago: University of Chicago Press, 1977.

Kunz, Diane B. *Butter and Guns: America's Cold War Economic Diplomacy*. New York: Free Press, 1997.

Kutler, Stanley I. *The Wars of Watergate: The Last Crisis of Richard Nixon*. New York: Norton, 1992.

Kuttner, Robert. *Everything for Sale: The Virtues and Limits of Markets*. New York: Knopf, 1997.

Laffer, Arthur B. *The Economics of the Tax Revolt: A Reader*. New York: Harcourt, Brace, 1979.

Lagemann, Ellen Condliffe. *The Politics of Knowledge: The Carnegie Corporation, Philanthropy, and Public Policy*. Middletown, Conn.: Welseyan University Press, 1989.

Lakatos, Imre, and Alan Musgrave, eds. *Criticism and the Growth of Knowledge*. Cambridge: Cambridge University Press, 1970.

Lampman, Robert J., ed. *Economists at Wisconsin: 1892–1992*. Madison: University of Wisconsin Press, 1993.

Lanchester, Frederick W. *Aircraft in Warfare: The Dawn of the Fourth Army*. London: Constable, 1916.

Landreth, Harry. *History of Economic Thought*. Boston: Houghton Mifflin, 1976.

Larsen, Otto N. *Milestones and Millstones: Social Science at the National Science Foundation, 1945–1991*. New Brunswick, N.J.: Transaction Publishers, 1992.

Larson, Magali Sarfatti. *The Rise of Professionalism: A Social Analysis*. Berkeley and Los Angeles: University of California Press, 1977.

Lasch, Christopher. *The True and Only Heaven: Progress and Its Critics*. New York: Norton, 1991.

———. *The Revolt of the Elites and the Betrayal of Democracy*. New York: Norton, 1995.

Latour, Bruno. *The Pasteurization of France*. Cambridge: Harvard University Press, 1988.

Latour, Bruno, and Steve Woolgar. *Laboratory Life: The Construction of Scientific Facts*. Princeton, N.J.: Princeton University Press, 1988.

Lears, Jackson. *No Place of Grace: Antimodernism and the Transformation of American Culture, 1880–1920*. New York: Pantheon, 1981.

———. *Fables of Abundance: A Cultural History of Advertising in America*. New York: Basic Books, 1994.

Lebergott, Stanley. *Manpower in Economic Growth: The American Record since 1800*. New York: McGraw-Hill, 1964.

Lee, Susan. *Hands Off: Why the Government Is a Menace to Economic Health*. New York: Simon and Schuster, 1996.

Leffler, Melvyn P. *A Preponderance of Power: National Security, the Truman Administration, and the Cold War*. Stanford, Calif.: Stanford University Press, 1992.

Leontieff, Wassily. *The Structure of American Economy, 1919–1939: An Empirical Application of Equilibrium Analysis*. New York: Oxford University Press, 1951.

Leslie, Stuart W. *The Cold War and American Science: The Military-Industrial-Academic Complex at MIT and Stanford*. New York: Columbia University Press, 1993.

Levin, Richard P., and Rudolph P. Lamone. *Linear Programming for Management Decisions*. Homewood, Ill.: Richard Irwin, 1969.

Levine, David P. *Economic Studies: Contributions to the Critique of Economic Theory*. London: Routledge, 1977.

Levy, David M. *The Economic Ideas of Ordinary People: From Preference to Trade*. New York: Routledge, 1992.

Lewis, Lionel S. *Cold War on Campus: A Study of the Politics of Organizational Control*. New Brunswick, N.J.: Transaction Books, 1988.

Lilienthal, David E. *The Journals of David E. Lilienthal: The TVA Years 1939–1945*. New York: Harper and Row, 1964.

Lindblom, Charles E., and David K. Cohen. *Usable Knowledge: Social Science and Social Problem Solving*. New Haven, Conn.: Yale University Press, 1979.

Lindsey, Lawrence. *The Growth Experiment: How the New Tax Policy Is Transforming the U.S. Economy.* New York: Basic Books, 1990.

Link, Arthur S., ed. *The Papers of Woodrow Wilson.* Princeton, N.J.: Princeton University Press, 1983.

Lipsitz, George. *Class and Culture in Cold War America: A Rainbow at Midnight.* Westport, Conn.: Greenwood, 1981.

Livermore, William R. *The American Kriegspiel: A Game for Practising the Art of War upon a Topographical Map.* Boston: Houghton Mifflin, 1882.

Livingston, James. *Origins of the Federal Reserve System: Money, Class and Corporate Capitalism, 1890–1913.* Ithaca, N.Y.: Cornell University Press, 1986.

———. *Pragmatism and the Political Economy of Cultural Revolution, 1850–1940.* Chapel Hill: University of North Carolina Press, 1994.

Locke, John. *Two Treatises of Government* Ed. P. Laslett. Cambridge: Cambridge University Press, [1696] 1960.

———. *Of Civil Government Second Treatise.* London: Regnery Company, [1696] 1971.

Lomask, Milton. *A Minor Miracle: An Informal History of the National Science Foundation.* Washington, D.C.: National Science Foundation, 1975.

Lowen, Rebecca S. *Creating the Cold War University: The Transformation of Stanford.* Berkeley and Los Angeles: University of California Press, 1997.

Lucas, Robert E., Jr., and Thomas J. Sargent, eds. *Rational Expectations and Econometric Practice.* Minneapolis: University of Minnesota Press, 1981.

Luce, R. Duncan, and Howard Raiffa. *Games and Decisions.* New York: Wiley, 1958.

Lustig, Jeffrey. *Corporate Liberalism.* Berkeley and Los Angeles: University of California Press, 1982.

Lynch, Michael. *Scientific Practice and Ordinary Action: Ethnomethodology and Social Studies of Science.* Cambridge: Cambridge University Press, 1993.

Lynd, Robert S. *Knowledge for What? The Place of Social Science in American Culture.* New York: Grove Press, 1939.

Lynd, Robert S., and Helen Lynd. *Middletown: A Study in American Culture.* New York: Harcourt, Brace, 1956.

Lyons, Gene M. *The Uneasy Partnership: Social Science and the Federal Government in the Twentieth Century.* New York: Russell Sage Foundation, 1969.

Lyons, Gene M., and Louis Morton. *Schools for Strategy: Education and Research in National Security Affairs.* New York: Praeger, 1965.

MacLeod, Roy, ed. *Government and Expertise: Specialists, Administrators, and Professionals, 1860–1919.* New York: Cambridge University Press, 1988.

Maier, Charles, ed. *The Changing Boundaries of the Political: Essays on the Evolving Balance between the State and Society, Public and Private in Europe.* New York: Cambridge University Press, 1987.

Malatesta, Maria, ed. *Society and the Professions in Italy, 1860–1914.* Cambridge: Cambridge University Press, 1995.

Malcolm, Ian, and David Little. *A Critique of Welfare Economics.* Oxford: Oxford University Press, 1950.

Maloney, John. *Marshall, Orthodoxy, and the Professionalization of Economics.* New York: Cambridge University Press, 1985.

Malthus, Thomas R. *An Essay on the Principle of Population.* New York: Modern Library, [1798] 1960.

———. *Principles of Political Economy Considered with a View to their Practical Application.* London: J. Murray, 1820.

Mannheim, Karl. *Ideology and Utopia: An Introduction to the Sociology of Knowledge.* Trans. Louis Wirth and Edward Shils. New York: Harcourt Brace Jovanovich, [1929] 1936.

Marchand, Roland. *Advertising and the American Dream: Making Way for Modernity, 1920–1940.* Berkeley and Los Angeles: University of California Press, 1985.

Marglin, Stephen A., and Juliet B. Schor, eds. *The Golden Age of Capitalism.* Oxford: Clarendon Press, 1990.

Marshall, Alfred. *Principles of Economics.* London: Macmillan, [1890] 1961.

Marx, Karl. *Grundrisse: Foundations of the Critique of Political Economy.* Trans. M. Nicolaus. New York: Vintage, [written 1857–58, first published in German 1941] 1973.

―――. *Capital.* Trans. E. Aveling and S. Moore. Ed. F. Engels. New York: International Publishers, [written 1863–68, first published in English 1887] 1967.

Marx, Karl, and Fredrick Engels. *The Communist Manifesto.* New York: Pathfinder Press, [1848] 1970.

Matusow, Allen. *The Unraveling of America: A History of Liberalism in the 1960s.* New York: Harper and Row, 1984.

May, Lary, ed. *Recasting America: Culture and Politics in the Age of the Cold War.* Chicago: University of Chicago Press, 1989.

Mayer, Martin. *The Greatest-Ever Bank Robbery: The Collapse of the Savings and Loan Industry.* New York: Collier, 1990.

McClelland, Charles E. *The German Experience of Professionalization: Modern Learned Professions and Their Organizations from the Early Nineteenth Century to the Hitler Era.* New York: Cambridge University Press, 1991.

McCloskey, Dierdre M. *The Rhetoric of Economics.* Madison: University of Wisconsin Press, 1985.

―――. *If You're So Smart: The Narrative of Economic Expertise.* Chicago: University of Chicago Press, 1990.

―――. *Knowledge and Persuasion in Economics.* Cambridge: Cambridge University Press, 1994.

McMaster, H. R. *Dereliction of Duty: Lyndon Johnson, Robert McNamara, and the Joint Chiefs of Staff, and the Lies That Led to Vietnam.* New York: HarperCollins, 1997.

Mee, Charles L., Jr. *The Marshall Plan: The Launching of the Pax Americana.* New York: Simon and Schuster, 1984.

Meek, Ronald L. *The Economics of Physiocracy.* Cambridge: Harvard University Press, 1963.

―――. *Economics and Ideology and Other Essays.* London: Chapman and Hall, 1967.

―――. *Studies in the Labour Theory of Value.* London: Lawrence and Wishart, 1973.

Mencken, Henry L. *Notes on Democracy.* New York: Knopf, 1926.

―――. *Heathen Days, 1890–1936.* New York: Knopf, 1943.

Menger, Carl. *Principles of Economics.* Trans. and ed. J. Dingwall and B .F. Hoselitz. New York: Free Press, [1871] 1950.

Merton, Robert K. *The Sociology of Science: Theoretical and Empirical Investigations.* Chicago: University of Chicago Press, 1973.

Milgrom, Paul. *Auction Theory for Privatization.* New York: Cambridge University Press, 1996.

Mill, John Stuart. *Principles of Political Economy.* Ed. W. J. Ashley. London: Longmans Green, [1848] 1909.

Miller, James. *"Democracy Is in the Streets": From Port Huron to the Siege of Chicago.* New York: Simon and Schuster, 1987.

Mills, C. Wright. *White Collar: The American Middle Classes*. New York: Oxford University Press, 1951.

Milward, Alan S. *The Reconstruction of Western Europe, 1945–1951*. London: Methuen, 1984.

Minsky, Hyman P. *Stabilizing an Unstable Economy*. New Haven, Conn.: Yale University Press, 1986.

Mirowski, Philip. *More Heat Than Light: Economics as Social Physics, Physics as Nature's Economics*. New York: Cambridge University Press, 1991.

———. *Natural Images in Economic Thought*. New York: Cambridge University Press, 1994.

Mitchell, Broadus. *A Preface to Economics*. New York: Henry Holt, 1932.

———. *Depression Decade: From New Era through New Deal, 1929–1941*. New York: Rinehart, 1955.

Mitchell, Lucy Sprague. *Two Lives: The Story of Wesley Clair Mitchell and Myself*. New York: Simon and Schuster, 1953.

Mitchell, Wesley Clair. *Business Cycles*. Berkeley and Los Angeles: University of California Press, 1913.

Moggridge, Donald E. *Keynes*. New York: Fontana/Collins, 1976.

Molz, Redmond Kathleen. *National Planning for Library Service: 1935–1975*. Chicago: American Library Association, 1984.

Montgomery, David. *Workers' Control in America*. New York: Cambridge University Press, 1979.

Moore, Geoffrey H. *Statistical Indications of Cyclical Revivals and Recessions*. NBER Occasional Paper 31. New York: National Bureau of Economic Research, 1950.

Morantz-Sanchez, Regina. *Sympathy and Science: Women Physicians in American Medicine*. New York: Oxford University Press, 1985.

Morgan, Mary S. *The History of Econometric Ideas*. New York: Cambridge University Press, 1990.

Morgenstern, Oskar. *The Question of National Defense*. New York: Random House, 1959.

———, ed. *Economic Activity Analysis*. New York: Wiley, 1954.

Morison, Samuel Eliot. *The Two-Ocean War*. Boston: Little Brown, 1963.

Morris, Aldon. *The Origins of the Civil Rights Movement: Black Communities Organizing for Change*. New York: Free Press, 1984.

Moss, David. *Socializing Security: Progressive-Era Economists and the Origins of American Social Policy*. Cambridge: Harvard University Press, 1996.

Moynihan, Daniel Patrick. *Miles to Go: A Personal History of Social Policy*. Cambridge: Harvard University Press, 1996.

Mukerji, Chandra. *A Fragile Power: Scientists and the State*. Princeton, N.J.: Princeton University Press, 1989.

Murray, Charles. *Losing Ground: American Social Policy, 1950–1980*. New York: Basic Books, 1984.

Myrdal, Gunnar. *The Political Element in the Development of Economic Theory*. Trans. Paul Streeten. London: Routledge and Kegan Paul, 1953.

Nasar, Sylvia, *A Beautiful Mind*. New York: Simon and Schuster, 1998.

Nash, George. *The Life of Herbert Hoover*. New York: Norton, 1983.

———. *Herbert Hoover and Stanford University*. Stanford, Calif.: Hoover Institution Press, 1988.

National Bureau of Economic Research. *Income in the United States: Its Amount and Distribution, 1909–1919*. New York: National Bureau of Economic Research, 1921.

National Bureau of Economic Research. *Distribution of Income by States in 1919*. New York: National Bureau of Economic Research, 1922.

———. *Business Cycles and Unemployment, Including an Investigation Made under the Auspices of the National Bureau of Economic Research*. New York: McGraw-Hill, 1923.

———. *Income in the Various States*. New York: National Bureau of Economic Research, 1924.

———. *Business Annal*. New York: National Bureau of Economic Research, 1926.

———. *Migration and the Business Cycle*. New York: National Bureau of Economic Research, 1926.

———. *The Behavior of Prices*. New York: National Bureau of Economic Research, 1927.

———. *Business Cycles: The Problem and Its Setting*. New York: National Bureau of Economic Research, 1927.

National Science Foundation. *Federal Funds for Research and Development, 1967–83*. Washington, D.C.: National Science Foundation, 1983.

Nearing, Scott. *The Making of a Radical: A Political Autobiography*. New York: Harper and Row, 1972.

Nelson, Donald M. *Arsenal of Democracy: The Story of American War Production*. New York: Harcourt, Brace, 1946.

Nelson, John S., Allan Megill, and Donald N. Magee, eds. *The Rhetoric of the Human Sciences*. Madison: University of Wisconsin Press, 1987.

Nelson, Julia A. *Feminism, Objectivity and Economics*. New York: Routledge, 1997.

Nelson, Richard, and Sidney Winter. *An Evolutionary Theory of Economic Change*. Cambridge: Harvard University Press, 1982.

Neumann, John von, and Oskar Morgenstern. *Theory of Games and Economic Behavior*. Princeton. N.J.: Princeton University Press, 1947.

Noble, David F. *America by Design: Science, Technology, and the Rise of Corporate Capitalism*. New York: Knopf, 1977.

Noggle, Burl. *Into the Twenties: The United States from Armistice to Normalcy*. Urbana: University of Illinois Press, 1974.

Norton, Hugh S. *The Employment Act and the Council of Economic Advisers, 1946–1976*. Columbia: University of South Carolina Press, 1977.

Nourse, Edwin G. *America's Capacity to Consume*. Washington, D.C.: Brookings Institution, 1934.

———. *America's Capacity to Produce*. Washington, D.C.: Brookings Institution, 1934.

———. *Economics in the Public Service: Administrative Aspects of the Employment Act*. New York: Harcourt Brace, 1953.

Novick, David. *Efficiency and Economy in Government through New Budgeting and Accounting Procedures*. RAND Corporation, Report R-254, February 1, 1954.

Novick, Peter. *That Noble Dream: The "Objectivity Question" and the American Historical Profession*. New York: Cambridge University Press, 1988.

Oakes, Guy. *The Imaginary War: Civil Defense and American Cold War Culture*. New York: Oxford University Press, 1994.

O'Connor, Alice. *Poverty Knowledge*. Princeton, N.J.: Princeton University Press, 2001.

Office of Aerospace Research, U.S. Air Force. *Air Force Research Objectives: 1968*. Arlington, Va.: U.S. Air Force, n.d.

———. *Air Force Research Objectives: 1969*. Ed. J. Seiden. N.p., n.d.

Office of Naval Research, Department of the Navy. *Office of Naval Research: Forty Years of Excellence in Support of Naval Science*. Ed. F. E. Saalfeld. N.p., n.d.

——— *Windows to the Origins*. N.p., n.d.

Okun, Arthur M. *The Political Economy of Prosperity.* Washington, D.C.: Brookings Institution, 1969.

———. *Equality and Efficiency: The Big Tradeoff.* Washington, D.C.: Brookings Institution, 1975.

———. *Prices and Quantities: A Macroeconomic Analysis.* Oxford: Blackwell, 1982.

Olney, Martha L. *Buy Now, Pay Later: Advertising, Credit, and Consumer Durables in the 1920s.* Chapel Hill: University of North Carolina Press, 1991.

Olson, James S. *Herbert Hoover and the Reconstruction Finance Corporation 1931–1933.* Ames: Iowa State University Press, 1977.

———. *Saving Capitalism: The Reconstruction Finance Corporation and the New Deal, 1933–1940.* Princeton, N.J.: Princeton University Press, 1988.

Organization for Economic Cooperation and Development. *Labour Force Statistics: 1960–71.* Paris: OECD, 1973.

———. *Labour Force Statistics: 1966–77.* Paris: OECD, 1979.

Ortner, Robert. *Voodoo Deficits.* Homewood, Ill.: Dow Jones-Irwin, 1990.

Pach, Chester, Jr. *Arming the Free World: The Origins of the United States Military Assistance Program, 1945–1950.* Chapel Hill: University of North Carolina Press, 1991.

Palmer, Phyllis. *Domesticity and Dirt: Housewives and Domestic Servants in the United States, 1920–1945.* Philadelphia: Temple University Press, 1989.

Pareto, Vilfredo. *Manual of Political Economy.* New York: Kelley, [1898] 1971.

Parsons, Wayne. *The Power of the Financial Press: Journalism and Economic Opinion in Britain and America.* New Brunswick, N.J.: Rutgers University Press, 1990.

Patten, Simon N. *The Premises of Political Economy.* New York: Kelley [1885], 1968.

Patterson, James T. *Grand Expectations: The United States, 1945–1974.* New York: Oxford University Press, 1996.

Pechman, Joseph. *Who Paid the Taxes, 1966–85?* Washington, D.C.: Brookings Institution, 1986.

Peck, Merton J., and Frederic M. Scherer. *The Weapons Acquisition Process: An Economic Analysis.* Boston: Harvard University Graduate School of Business, 1962.

Perelman, Michael. *The End of Economics.* New York: Routledge, 1996.

Peritz, Rudolph J. R. *Competition Policy in America, 1888–1992: History, Rhetoric, Law.* New York: Oxford University Press, 1996.

Petzinger, Thomas, Jr. *Hard Landing: The Epic Contest for Power and Profits That Plunged the Airlines into Chaos.* New York: Times Business, 1996.

Phelps, Edmund S. *Rewarding Work: How to Restore Participation and Self-Support to Free Enterprise.* Cambridge: Harvard University Press, 1997.

Phillips, Kevin P. *The Politics of Rich and Poor: Wealth and the American Electorate in the Reagan Aftermath.* New York: Random House, 1990.

Pigou, Arthur C. *The Economics of Welfare.* London: Macmillan, 1932.

———. *Theory of Unemployment.* London: Macmillan, 1933.

———. *The Economics of Stationary States.* London: Macmillan, 1935.

Piven, Francis Fox, and Richard Cloward. *The New Class War.* New York: Pantheon, 1982.

Polanyi, Karl. *The Great Transformation.* Boston: Beacon Press, 1994.

Popper, Karl. *The Logic of Scientific Discovery.* New York: Harper and Row, 1959.

———. *The Poverty of Historicism.* New York: Harper and Row, 1961.

———. *Conjectures and Refutations: The Growth of Scientific Knowledge.* New York: Basic Books, 1962.

———. *Objective Knowledge: An Evolutionary Approach.* Oxford: Clarendon Press, 1972.

Porter, Theodore M. *Trust in Numbers: The Pursuit of Objectivity in Science and Public Life*. Princeton, N.J.: Princeton University Press, 1995.

Posner, Richard A. *Economic Analysis of Law*. Boston: Little Brown, 1972.

———. *The Economics of Justice*. Cambridge: Harvard University Press, 1981.

Posner, Richard A., with William M. Landes. *The Economic Structure of Tort Law*. Cambridge: Harvard University Press, 1987.

Poundstone, William. *Prisoner's Dilemma*. New York: Doubleday, 1992.

President's Committee on Recent Economic Changes, Conference on Unemployment. *Recent Economic Changes in the United States*. New York: McGraw-Hill, 1929.

Price, Don K. *Government and Science: Their Dynamic Relation in American Democracy*. New York: New York University Press, 1954.

Pundt, Helen. *AHEA: A History of Excellence*. Washington, D.C.: American Home Economics Association, 1980.

Purcell, Edward, Jr. *The Crisis of Democratic Theory: Scientific Naturalism and the Problem of Value*. Lexington: University Press of Kentucky, 1973.

Rader, Benjamin G. *The Academic Mind and Reform: The Influence of Richard T. Ely in American Life*. Lexington: University Press of Kentucky, 1966.

Ratner, Sidney. *The Tariff in American History*. New York: Van Nostrand, 1972.

Rauch, Basil. *The History of the New Deal: 1933–1938*. New York: Creative Age Press, 1944.

Reddy, William. *The Rise of Market Culture: The Textile Trade and French Society, 1750–1900*. New York: Cambridge University Press, 1984.

Reich, Robert B. *The Next American Frontier*. New York: Penguin, 1983.

———. *Locked in the Cabinet*. New York: Knopf, 1997.

Ricci, David M. *The Transformation of American Politics: The New Washington and the Rise of Think Tanks*. New Haven, Conn.: Yale University Press, 1993.

Raymond Rich Associates. *American Foundations and Their Fields*. Vols. 2–5. New York: Twentieth Century Fund, 1931–42.

Rieder, Johnathan. *Canarsie: The Jews and Italians of Brooklyn against Liberalism*. Cambridge: Harvard University Press, 1985.

Riesman, David. *The Lonely Crowd: A Study of the Changing American Character*. New Haven, Conn.: Yale University Press, 1950.

Rima, Ingrid. *The Joan Robinson Legacy*. Armonk, N.Y.: M. E. Sharpe, 1991.

Ringer, Fritz K. *The Decline of the German Mandarins: The German Academic Community, 1890–1933*. Cambridge: Harvard University Press, 1969,

Robbins, Lionel. *An Essay on the Nature and Significance of Economic Science*. London: St. Martin's, 1969.

———. *The Economic Problem in Peace and War: Some Reflections on Objectives and Mechanism*. London: Macmillan, 1947.

Robin, Ron. *The Barbed-Wire College: Re-educating German POWs in the United States during World War II*. Princeton, N.J.: Princeton University Press, 1995.

Robinson, Joan. *The Economics of Imperfect Competition*. London: St. Martin's, [1933] 1961.

———. *The Accumulation of Capital*. London: Macmillan, [1956] 1971.

Rodgers, Daniel T. *The Work Ethic in Industrial America, 1850–1920*. Chicago: University of Chicago Press, 1974.

Roemer, John. *Analytical Marxism*. Cambridge: Cambridge University Press, 1986.

———. *Free to Lose: An Introduction to Marxist Economic Philosophy*. Cambridge: Harvard University Press, 1988.

Romasco, Albert U. *The Poverty of Abundance: Hoover, the Nation, the Depression.* New York: Oxford University Press, 1965.

————. *The Politics of Recovery: Roosevelt's New Deal.* New York: Oxford University Press, 1983.

Roosevelt, Franklin D. *The Public Papers and Addresses of Franklin D. Roosevelt.* 13 vols. New York: Macmillan, 1941.

Rosenof, Theodore. *Economics in the Long Run: New Deal Theorists and Their Legacies, 1933–1993.* Chapel Hill: University of North Carolina Press, 1997.

Ross, Dorothy. *The Origins of American Social Science.* New York: Cambridge University Press, 1991.

Ross, Edward. *Seventy Years of It: An Autobiography.* New York: Appelton-Century, 1936.

Ross, William D., ed. *The Works of Aristotle.* Trans. B. Jowett. Oxford: Clarendon Press, 1921.

Rossiter, Bernard D. *Fat Years and Lean: The American Economy since Roosevelt.* New York: Harper and Row, 1990.

Rossiter, Margaret W. *Women Scientists of America: Struggles and Strategies to 1940.* Baltimore: Johns Hopkins University Press, 1982.

Rubin, Michael R. *The Knowledge Industry in the United States, 1960–1980.* Princeton, N.J.: Princeton University Press, 1986.

Rudenstine, David. *The Day the Presses Stopped: A History of the Pentagon Papers Case.* Berkeley and Los Angeles: University of California Press, 1997.

Rufener, Louis A. *Principles of Economics.* Boston: Houghton Mifflin, 1927.

Rutkoff, Peter, and William Scott. *New School: A History of the New School for Social Research.* New York: Free Press, 1986.

Salant, Walter S. *Some Intellectual Contributions of the Truman Council of Economic Advisers to Policy-Making.* Washington, D.C.: Brookings Institution, 1973.

Sale, Kirkpatrick. *Power Shift: The Rise of the Southern Rim and Its Challenge to the Eastern Establishment.* New York: Random House, 1975.

Samuelson, Paul A. *Foundations of Modern Economics.* Cambridge: Harvard University Press, 1947.

————. *Economics: An Introductory Analysis.* New York: McGraw-Hill, 1948.

————. *Economics.* New York: McGraw-Hill, 1972.

Sandilands, Roger. *The Life and Political Economy of Lauchlin Currie: New Dealer, Presidential Adviser, and Development Economist.* Durham, N.C.: Duke University Press, 1990.

Sapolsky, Harvey M. *Science and the Navy: The History of the Office of Naval Research.* Princeton, N.J.: Princeton University Press, 1990.

Sayers, Richard S. *Financial Policy: 1939–45.* London: HMSO, 1956.

Schaffer, Ronald. *America in the Great War: The Rise of the War Welfare State.* New York: Oxford University Press, 1991.

Schaller, Michael. *The American Occupation of Japan: The Origins of the Cold War in Asia.* New York: Oxford University Press, 1985.

Schattschneider, Elmer E. *Politics, Pressures and the Tariff: A Study of Free Private Enterprise in Pressure Politics, as Shown in the 1929–1930 Revision of the Tariff.* Hamden, Conn.: Prentice-Hall, 1935.

Schelling, Thomas. *The Strategy of Conflict.* Cambridge: Harvard University Press, 1960.

Schild, Georg. *Bretton Woods and Dumbarton Oaks: American Economic and Political Postwar Planning in the Summer of 1944.* New York: St. Martin's, 1995.

Schiller, Herbert I. *Culture, Inc.: The Corporate Takeover of Public Expression*. New York: Oxford University Press, 1989.

Schlesinger, Arthur, Jr. *A Thousand Days: John F. Kennedy in the White House*. Boston: Houghton Mifflin, 1965.

Schrecker, Ellen W. *No Ivory Tower: McCarthyism and the Universities*. New York: Oxford University Press, 1986.

Schriftgeisser, Karl. *Business and Public Policy: The Role of the Committee for Economic Development, 1942–1967*. Englewood Cliffs, N.J.: Prentice-Hall, 1967.

Schumpeter, Joseph A. *Business Cycles: A Theoretical, Historical, and Statistical Analysis of the Capitalist Process*. New York: McGraw-Hill, 1939.

———. *Imperialism and Social Classes*. New York: Kelley, 1951.

———. *History of Economic Analysis*. Oxford: Oxford University Press, 1954.

———. *Economic Doctrine and Method: An Historical Sketch*. Trans. R. Aris. New York: Oxford University Press, [1912] 1967.

Schwartz, Barry. *The Costs of Living: How Market Freedom Erodes the Best Things in Life*. New York: Norton, 1994.

Schwarz, Jordan A. *The New Dealers: Power Politics in the Age of Roosevelt*. New York: Knopf, 1993.

Scitovsky, Tibor. *The Joyless Economy: An Inquiry into Human Satisfaction and Consumer Dissatisfaction*. New York: Oxford University Press, 1976.

Scitovsky, Tibor, Edward S. Shaw, and Lorie Tarshis. *Mobilizing Resources for War*. New York: McGraw-Hill, 1951.

Scott, James C. *Seeing Like a State: How Certain Schemes to Improve the Human Condition Have Failed* New Haven, Conn.: Yale University Press, 1998.

Seager, Henry R. *Introduction to Economics*. New York: Holt, 1904.

Seligman, Edwin R. A. *Principles of Economics, with Special Reference to American Conditions*. New York: Longmans, Green, 1905.

Shackle, George L. S. *The Years of High Theory: Invention and Tradition in Economic Theory*. Cambridge: Cambridge University Press, 1967.

Shapin, Steven. *A Social History of Truth: Civility and Science in Seventeenth-Century England*. Chicago: University of Chicago Press, 1992.

Shapin, Steven, and Simon Schaffer. *Leviathan and the Air-Pump: Hobbes, Boyle, and the Experimental Life*. Princeton, N.J.: Princeton University Press, 1985.

Shaw, George Bernard. *The Doctor's Dilemma: A Tragedy*. London: Constable and Company, [1906] 1920.

Sheffrin, Steven. *Rational Expectations*. New York: Cambridge University Press, 1983.

Sherry, Michael S. *Preparing for the Next War: American Plans for Post-war Defense, 1941–1945*. New Haven, Conn.: Yale University Press, 1977.

———. *The Rise of American Air Power: The Creation of Armageddon*. New Haven, Conn.: Yale University Press, 1987.

———. *In the Shadow of War: The United States since the 1930s*. New Haven, Conn.: Yale University Press, 1996.

Shubik, Martin. *Strategy and Market Structure: Competition, Oligopoly, and the Theory of Games*. New York: Wiley, 1959.

Silk, Leonard. *The Economists*. New York: Basic Books, 1976.

Silva, Edward T., and Sheila A. Slaughter. *Serving Power: The Making of the Academic Social Science Expert*. Westport, Conn.: Greenwood Press, 1984.

Simon, Herbert A. *The New Science of Management Decision*. New York: Harper, 1960.

Skidelsky, Robert. *John Maynard Keynes: A Biography*. 2 vols. New York: Macmillan, 1983, 1996.

Sklar, Martin J. *The Corporate Reconstruction of American Capitalism, 1890–1916: The Market, The Law, and Politics*. New York: Cambridge University Press, 1988.

Skocpol, Theda. *Protecting Soldiers and Mothers: The Political Origins of Social Policy in the United States*. Cambridge: Harvard University Press, 1992.

Skowronek, Stephen. *Building a New American State: The Expansion of National Administrative Capacities, 1877–1920*. New York: Cambridge University Press, 1982.

Sloan, John W. *Eisenhower and the Management of Prosperity*. Lawrence: University Press of Kansas, 1991.

Smith, Adam. *An Inquiry into the Nature and Causes of the Wealth of Nations*. New York: Random House, [1776] 1937.

Smith, Bruce L. *The RAND Corporation: Case Study of a Nonprofit Advisory Corporation*. Cambridge: Harvard University Press, 1969.

Smith, James Allen. *The Idea Brokers: Think Tanks and the Rise of the New Policy Elite*. New York: Free Press, 1991.

Smith, Mark C. *Social Science in the Crucible: The American Debate over Objectivity and Purpose, 1918–1941*. Durham, N.C.: Duke University Press, 1994.

Solow, Robert M. *Capital Theory and the Rate of Return*. New York: Rand McNally, 1965.

Spulber, Nicholas. *Managing the American Economy from Roosevelt to Reagan*. Bloomington: Indiana University Press, 1989.

Sraffa, Piero. *The Production of Commodities by Means of Commodities: Prelude to a Critique of Economic Theory*. Cambridge: Cambridge University Press, 1960.

Sraffa, Piero, and Maurice H. Dobb, eds. *The Works and Correspondence of David Ricardo*. Cambridge: Cambridge University Press, 1951.

Stanley, Timothy W. *American Defense and National Security*. Washington, D.C.: Public Affairs Press, 1956.

Starr, Paul. *The Transformation of American Medicine*. New York: Basic Books, 1982.

Steel, Ronald. *Walter Lippmann and the American Century*. Boston: Little Brown, 1980.

Stefancic, Jean, and Richard Delgado. *No Mercy: How Conservative Think Tanks and Foundations Changed America's Social Agenda*. Philadelphia: Temple University Press, 1996.

Stein, Herbert. *The Fiscal Revolution in America, 1929–1964*. Chicago: University of Chicago Press, 1969.

———. *Presidential Economics: The Making of Economic Policy from Roosevelt to Reagan and Beyond*. New York: Simon and Schuster, 1984.

———. *The Fiscal Revolution in America: Policy in Pursuit of Reality*. Washington, D.C.: AEI Press, 1996.

Steinbeck, John. *The Grapes of Wrath*. New York: Penguin, [1939] 1992.

Stevens, Robert Warren. *Vain Hopes Grim Realities*. New York: New Viewpoints/Franklin Watts, 1976.

Stewart, Irvin. *Organizing Scientific Research for War*. New York: Little Brown, 1948.

Stigler, George J. *Production and Distribution Theories: The Formative Period*. New York: Macmillan, 1946.

———. *Essays in the History of Economics*. Chicago: University of Chicago Press, 1956.

Stockfisch, Jacob A., ed. *Planning and Forecasting in the Defense Industries*. Belmont, Calif.: Wadsworth, 1962.

Stockman, David. *The Triumph of Politics: How the Reagan Revolution Failed*. New York: Harper and Row, 1986.

Stoneman, William E. *A History of the Economic Analysis of the Great Depression in America*. New York: Garland, 1979.

Storr, Richard J. *The Beginnings of Graduate Education in America*. Chicago: University of Chicago Press, 1953.

Susman, Warren. *Culture as History: The Transformation of American Society in the Twentieth Century*. New York: Pantheon, 1984.

Sweezy, Paul. *The Theory of Capitalist Development: Principles of Marxian Political Economy*. New York: Monthly Review Press, [1942] 1968.

Taussig, Frank W. *Principles of Economics*. New York: Macmillan, 1911.

Taylor, Fred M. *Principles of Economics*. Ann Arbor: University of Michigan Press, 1911.

Taylor, Henry Charles. *A Farm Economist in Washington, 1919–1925*, Ed. Dawn Danz-Hale. Madison: University of Wisconsin–Madison, Department of Agricultural Economics, 1992.

Temin, Peter. *Did Monetary Forces Cause the Great Depression?* New York: Norton, 1976.

Terborgh, George. *The New Economics*. Washington, D.C.: Machinery and Allied Products Institute, 1968.

Thackray, Arnold, et al. *Chemistry in America, 1876–1976*. Boston: Reidel Publishing/Kluwer Academic Publishers, 1985.

Thomison, Dennis. *A History of the American Library Association: 1876–1972*. Chicago: American Library Association, 1978.

Tilman, Rick. *Thorstein Veblen and His Critics, 1891–1963: Conservative, Liberal, and Radical Perspectives*. Princeton, N.J.: Princeton University Press, 1992.

Tobin, James. *National Economic Policy*. New Haven, Conn.: Yale University Press, 1966.

————. *New Dimensions of Political Economy*. Cambridge: Harvard University Press, 1966.

————. *The New Economics One Decade Older*. Princeton, N.J.: Princeton University Press, 1974.

Tompkins, Jane. *Sensational Designs: The Cultural Work of American Fiction, 1790–1860*. New York: Oxford University Press, 1985.

Trachtenberg, Marc. *History and Strategy*. Princeton, N.J.: Princeton University Press, 1991.

Tucker, Albert W., and R. Duncan Luce, eds. *Contributions to the Theory of Games*. Princeton, N.J.: Princeton University Press, 1959.

Tucker, Samuel A., ed. *National Security Management: A Modern Design for Defense Decision: A McNamara-Hitch-Enthoven Anthology*. Washington, D.C.: Industrial College of the Armed Forces, 1966.

Turner, John R. *Introduction to Economics*. New York: Scribner's Sons, 1919.

Turner, Majorie S. *Joan Robinson and the Americans*. Armonk, N.Y.: M. E. Sharpe, 1989.

Turner, Victor. *Dramas, Fields, and Metaphors: Symbolic Action in Human Society*. Ithaca, N.Y.: Cornell University Press, 1974.

United States Bureau of the Budget, War Records Section. *The United States at War: Development and Administration of the War Program by the Federal Government*. Washington, D.C.: U.S. Government Printing Office, n.d.

United States Civilian Production Administration. *Industrial Mobilization for War: History of the War Production Board and Predecessor Agencies, 1940–1945*. Washington, D.C.: U.S. Government Printing Office, 1947.

United States Council of Economic Advisers. *Economic Report of the President: 1965*. Washington, D.C.: U.S. Government Printing Office, 1965.

————. *Economic Report of the President: 1984*. Washington, D.C.: U.S. Government Printing Office, 1984.

United States Department of Commerce. *Statistical Abstract of the United States*. Washington, D.C.: U.S. Government Printing Office, 1960.

United States Department of Labor. *Economic Forces in the U.S.A.* Washington, D.C.: U.S. Government Printing Office, 1960.

United States Library of Congress. *The United States at War: Organizations and Literature*. Washington, D.C.: U.S. Government Printing Office, 1917.

Valenti, Jack. *A Very Human President*. New York: Norton, 1975.

Vatter, Harold, and John Walker. *History of the U.S. Economy since World War II*. Armonk, N.Y.: M. E. Sharpe, 1996.

Veblen, Thorstein. *The Instinct of Workmanship, and the State of the Industrial Arts*. New York: Kelley, 1914.

————. *The Higher Learning in America: A Memorandum on the Conduct of Universities by Business Men*. New York: Kelley, [1918] 1957.

————. *The Place of Science in Modern Civilization*. New York: Viking, 1919.

————. *The Engineers and the Price System*. New York: Huebsch, 1921.

Veysey, Laurence R. *The Emergence of the American University*. Chicago: University of Chicago Press, 1965.

Walker, Martin. *The Cold War: A History*. New York: Henry Holt, 1993.

Wallace, Walter L. *The Logic of Science in Sociology*. New York: Aldine Atherton, 1971.

Wallis, Roy, ed. *On the Margins of Science: The Social Construction of Rejected Knowledge*. Sociological Review Monograph 27. Keele: University of Keele, 1979.

Walras, Léon. *Elements of Pure Economics: or the Theory of Social Wealth*. Trans. W. Jaffe. Chicago: Irwin [1900] 1954.

Walters, Ronald G., ed. *Scientific Authority and Twentieth-Century America*. Baltimore: Johns Hopkins University Press, 1997.

Waring, Marilyn. *If Women Counted: A New Feminist Economics*. New York: HarperCollins, 1988.

Watts, H. D. *Industrial Geography*. Harlow, Essex: Longman, 1987.

Webber, Michael J., and David L. Rigby. *The Golden Age Illusion: Rethinking Postwar Capitalism*. New York: Guilford Press, 1996.

Weber, Max. *The Protestant Ethic and the Spirit of Capitalism*. Trans. Talcott Parsons. New York: Scribner's, [1904–5] 1958.

Weinstein, Allen. *The Decline of Socialism in America, 1912–1925*. New York: Monthly Review Press, 1967.

Weinstein, James. *The Corporate Ideal in the Liberal State, 1900–1918*. Boston: Beacon Press, 1960.

Weintraub, E. Roy. *Microfoundations: The Compatibility of Microeconomics and Macroeconomics*. Cambridge: Cambridge University Press, 1979.

————. *General Equilibrium Analysis: Studies in Appraisal*. New York: Cambridge University Press, 1985.

Weiss, Nancy. *Farewell to the Party of Lincoln: Black Politics in the Age of FDR*. Princeton, N.J.: Princeton University Press, 1983.

White, Lawrence J. *The S&L Debacle: Public Policy Lessons for Bank and Thrift Regulation*. New York: Oxford University Press, 1991.

White, Leonard. *Trends in Public Administration*. New York: McGraw-Hill, 1933.

White, Theodore H. *The Making of the President: 1960*. New York: Atheneum, 1961.

Whyte, William H. *The Organization Man*. New York: Simon and Schuster, 1956.

Wicksell, Knut. *Lectures on Political Economy*. London: Routledge, 1951–56.

Wicksteed, Philip H. *The Common Sense of Political Economy*. London: Routledge, [1933] 1957.

Wiebe, Robert. *The Search for Order, 1877–1920*. New York: Hill and Wang, 1967.

Wilkins, B. Hughel, and Charles B. Friday, eds. *The Economics of a New Frontier: An Anthology*. New York: Random House, 1963.

Williams, William Appleman. *The Tragedy of American Diplomacy*. Cleveland: World Publishing, 1959.

———. *The Contours of American History*. Chicago: World Publishing, 1961.

Williamson, Oliver. *The Economic Institutions of Capitalism: Firms, Markets, and Rational Contracting*. New York: Free Press, 1985.

Wilson, Edmund. *Patriotic Gore*. New York: Oxford University Press, 1962.

Wilson, Joan Hoff. *Herbert Hoover: Forgotten Progressive*. Boston: Little Brown, 1975.

Winkler, Allan. *Life Under a Cloud: American Anxiety about the Atom*. New York: Oxford University Press, 1993.

Winks, Robin W. *Cloak and Gown: Scholars in the Secret War, 1939–1961*. New York: William Morrow and Company, 1987.

Winters, Donald L. *Henry Cantwell Wallace as Secretary of Agriculture*. Urbana: University of Illinois Press, 1970.

Wolfle, Dael. *Renewing a Scientific Society: The American Association for the Advancement of Science from World War 2 to 1970*. Washington, D.C.: American Association for the Advancement of Science, 1989.

Wood, Robert C. *Whatever Possessed the President? Academic Experts and Presidential Policy, 1960–1988*. Amherst: University of Massachusetts Press, 1993.

Wunderlin, Clarence E., Jr. *Visions of a New Industrial Order: Social Science and Labor Theory in America's Progressive Era*. New York: Columbia University Press, 1992.

Yergin, Daniel, and Joseph Stanislaw. *The Commanding Heights: The Battle between Government and the Marketplace That Is Remaking the Modern World*. New York: Simon and Schuster, 1998.

Yonay, Yuval. *The Struggle over the Soul of Economics: Institutionalist and Neoclassical Economists in America between the Wars*. Princeton, N.J.: Princeton University Press, 1998.

Scholarly Journal Articles and Anthology Chapters

"The Committee on the Undergraduate Teaching and the Training of Economists." *American Economic Review* 40 (1950).

"Economics in General Education: Roundtable on Report of the Committee on the Teaching of Elementary Economics." *American Economic Review* 41 (1951), 697–716.

Abbott, Andrew. "The Sociology of Work and Occupations." *Annual Review of Sociology* 19 (1993), 187–209.

Alpert, Harry. "The National Science Foundation and Social Science Research." *American Sociological Review* 19 (1954), 208–11.

———. "The Social Sciences and the National Science Foundation, 1945–1955." *American Sociological Review* 22 (1955), 653–61.

———. "Congressmen, Social Scientists, and Attitudes toward Federal Support of Social Science Research." *American Sociological Review* 23 (1958), 682–86.

Alston, Richard M., J. R. Kearl, and Michael B. Vaughan. "Is There a Consensus among Economists in the 1990s?" *American Economic Review* 82 (1992), 203–20.

Altonji, Joseph G. "Intertemporal Labor Supply: Evidence from Micro Data." *Journal of Political Economy* 94 (1986), S176-S215.

Amariglio, Jack L. "The Body, Economic Discourse, and Power: An Economist's Introduction to Foucault." *History of Political Economy* 20 (1988), 583–613.

Angoff, C. "The Higher Learning Goes to War." *American Mercury* 11 (1927), 179–91.

Arrow, Kenneth J. "A Difficulty in the Concept of Social Welfare." *Journal of Political Economy* 58 (1950).

———. "Cowles in the History of Economic Thought." In *Cowles Fiftieth Anniversary: Four Essays and an Index of Publications*, 1–24. New Haven, Conn.: Cowles Foundation for Research in Economics, 1991.

Arrow, Kenneth J., and Gerard Debreu. "Existence of an Equilibrium for a Competitive Economy." *Econometrica* 20 (1954), 265–90.

Arrow, Kenneth J., and Leonid Hurwicz. "Gradient Methods for Constrained Maxima." *Operations Research* 5 (1957), 258–65.

Aslanbeigui, Nahid, and Verónica Montecinos. "Foreign Students in U.S. Doctoral Programs." *Journal of Economic Perspectives* 12 (1998), 171–82.

Ayres, Clarence. "The Co-Ordinates of Institutionalism." *American Economic Review* 41 (1951), 47–55.

Ball, Terence. "The Politics of Social Science in Postwar America." In *Recasting America: Culture and Politics in the Age of the Cold War*, ed. Lary May, 76–92. Chicago: University of Chicago Press, 1989.

Barber, William J. "Government as a Laboratory for Economic Learning in the Years of the Democratic Roosevelt." In *The State and Economic Knowledge: The American and British Experiences*, ed. Mary O. Furner and Barry Supple, 103–37. New York: Cambridge University Press, 1990.

———. "The Divergent Fates of Two Strands of 'Institutionalist' Doctrine during the New Deal Years." *History of Political Economy* 26 (1994), 569–87.

———. "Reconfigurations in American Academic Economics: A General Practitioner's Perspective." *Daedalus* 126 (1997), 87–104.

Barnes, Barry, and Donald MacKenzie. "On the Role of Interests in Scientific Change." In *On the Margins of Science: The Social Construction of Rejected Knowledge*, ed. R. Wallis, 49–66. Keele: University of Keele Press, 1979.

Baron, James N., and Michael T. Hannan. "The Impact of Economics on Contemporary Sociology." *Journal of Economic Literature* 32 (1994), 1111–46.

Beck, Nathaniel Beck. "Domestic Political Sources of American Monetary Policy: 1955–82." *Journal of Politics* 46 (1984), 786–817.

Ben-David, J. "Professions in the Class System of Present Day Societies." *Current Sociology* 12 (1963), 247–98.

Berelson, Bernard. "Behavioral Sciences.' In *International Encyclopedia of the Social Sciences*, ed. David L. Sills, 2:41–45. New York: Free Press/Macmillan, 1968.

Bernstein, Michael A. "To Win the War: Defense Research at Yale University, 1939–1950." *Yale Scientific* 49 (1975), 4–8.

———. "Problems in the Theory of Production and Exchange: An Essay in Classical and Marxian Themes." *Australian Economic Papers*, December 1980, 248–63.

———. "Explaining America's Greatest Depression: A Reconsideration of an Older Literature." *Revista di Storia Economica*, 2d ser., 2 (1985), 155–74.

———. "Economic Instability in the United States in the 1930s and the 1970s: An Essay in Historical Homology." In *The Great Depression of the 1930s and Its Relevance for the Contemporary World*, ed. Ivan Berend and Knut Borchard, 35–60. Budapest: Karl Marx University of Economics, 1986.

Bernstein, Michael A. "Economic Pessimism and Material Prosperity." In *The Humanities and the Art of Public Discussion*, 2:19–27. Washington, D.C.: Federation of State Humanities Councils, 1990.

———. "Numerable Knowledge and Its Discontents." *Reviews in American History* 18 (1990), 151–64.

———. "The Contemporary American Banking Crisis in Historical Perspective." *Journal of American History* 80 (1994), 1382–96.

———. "Understanding American Economic Decline: The Contours of the Late-Twentieth-Century Experience." In *Understanding American Economic Decline*, ed. Michael A. Bernstein and David Adler, 3–33. New York: Cambridge University Press, 1994.

———. "American Economics and the National Security State, 1941–1953." *Radical History Review* 63 (1995), 8–26.

———. "Academic Research Protocols and the Pax Americana: American Economics during the Cold War Era." In *Rethinking the Cold War: Essays on Its Dynamics, Meaning, and Morality*, ed. Allen Hunter, 257–70. Philadelphia: Temple University Press, 1998.

———. "Knowledge Production, Professional Authority, and the State: The Case of American Economics during and after World War II." In *Economic Knowledges: Producers, Consumers, Consequences*, ed. Robert Garnett, 103–23. London: Routledge, 1999.

Bhaduri, A. "On the Significance of Recent Controversies on Capital Theory: A Marxian View." *Economic Journal* 79 (1969), 532–39.

Birken, Lawrence. "From Macroeconomics to Microeconomics: The Marginalist Revolution in Socio-Cultural Perspective." *History of Political Economy* 20 (1988), 251–74.

Black, A. G. "Agricultural Policy and the Economist." *Journal of Farm Economics* 18 (1936), 311–19.

Black, R. D. Collison. "W. S. Jevons and the Foundation of Modern Economics." In *The Marginal Revolution in Economics: Interpretation and Evaluation*, ed. R. D. Collison Black, A. W. Coats, and Craufurd D. W. Goodwin, 98–112. Durham: Duke University Press, 1973.

Blaug, Mark. "Kuhn versus Lakatos, or Paradigms versus Research Programmes in the History of Economics." *History of Political Economy* 7 (1975), 399–433.

———. "Not Only an Economist—Autobiographical Reflections of a Historian of Economic Thought." *American Economist* 38 (1994), 12–27.

Blendon, Robert J., John M. Benson, Mollyann Brodie, et al. "Bridging the Gap between the Public's and Economists' Views of the Economy." *Journal of Economic Perspectives* 11 (1997), 105–18.

Blinder, Alan S. "The Anatomy of Double Digit Inflation in the 1970s." In *Inflation: Causes and Effects*, ed. Robert E. Hall. Chicago: University of Chicago Press, 1982.

———. "The Fall and Rise of Keynesian Economics." *Economic Record* 64 (1988), 278–94.

———. "What Central Bankers Could Learn From Academics—and Vice Versa." *Journal of Economic Perspectives* 11 (spring 1997), 3–19.

Bortkiewicz, L. von. "On the Correction of Marx's Fundamental Theoretical Construction in the Third Volume of *Capital*." Trans. P. M. Sweezy. In Eugen von Böhm-Bawerk, *Karl Marx and the Close of His System*, 199–221. New York: Merlin Press, 1975.

Boulding, Kenneth E. "Towards a Pure Theory of Threat Systems." *American Economic Review* 53 (1963), 424–34.

Bowen, Howard. "Graduate Education in Economics." *American Economic Review* 43 (1953), 1–23.

Brands, H. W. "The Age of Vulnerability: Eisenhower and the National Insecurity State." *American Historical Review* 94 (1989).

Braude, L. "Professional Autonomy and the Role of the Layman." *Social Forces* 39 (1961), 297–301.

Bronfenbrenner, Martin. "The 'Structure of Revolutions' in Economic Thought." *History of Political Economy* 3 (1971), 136–51.

Brown, E. Cary. "Fiscal Policy in the 'Thirties: A Reappraisal." *American Economic Review* 46 (1956), 857–79.

Brownlee, W. Elliot. "Economists and the Formation of the Modern Tax System in the United States: The World War I Crisis." In *The State and Economic Knowledge: The American and British Experiences*, ed. Mary O. Furner and Barry Supple, 401–35. New York: Cambridge University Press, 1990.

Bryson, Gladys. "The Comparable Interests of the Old Moral Philosophy and the Modern Social Sciences." *Social Forces* 11 (1932), 19–27.

———. "The Emergence of the Social Sciences from Moral Philosophy." *International Journal of Ethics* 42 (1932), 304–23.

Buck, P. "Adjusting to Military Life: The Social Sciences Go to War, 1941–1950." In *Military Enterprise and Technological Change: Perspectives on the American Experience*, ed. Merritt Roe Smith, 203–52. Cambridge: MIT Press, 1985.

Burns, Arthur F. "Wesley Mitchell and the National Bureau." In National Bureau of Economic Research, *Twenty-ninth Annual Report* (1949), 23–26, 36–44.

Cagan, Phillip. "Reflections on Rational Expectations." *Journal of Money, Credit and Banking* 12 (1980), 826–32.

Callon, Michel, and John Law. "On Interests and Their Transformation: Enrolment and Counter-Enrolment." *Social Studies of Science* 12 (1982), 615–25.

Camic, Charles. "The Making of a Method: A Historical Reinterpretation of the Early Parsons." *American Sociological Review* 52 (1987), 421–39.

Canterbery, E. Ray, and Robert Burkhardt. "What Do We Mean by Asking If Economics Is a Science?" In *Why Economics Is Not Yet a Science*, ed. Alfred Eichner, 15–40. Armonk, N.Y.: M. E. Sharpe, 1983.

Capie, Forest H., and Geoffrey E. Wood. "The Anatomy of a Wartime Inflation: Britain, 1939–1945." In *The Sinews of War: Essays on the Economic History of World War II*, ed. Geoffrey T. Mills and Hugh Rockoff, 21–42. Ames: Iowa State University Press, 1993.

Cargill, Thomas F. "Irving Fisher: Comments on Benjamin Strong and the Federal Reserve in the 1930s." *Journal of Political Economy* 100 (1992), 1273–77.

Carson, Carol S. "The History of the United States National Income and Products Accounts: The Development of an Analytical Tool." *Review of Income and Wealth* 21 (1975), 153–81.

Carver, T. N. "The Marginal Theory of Distribution." *Journal of Political Economy* 13 (1905), 257–66.

Chalk, A. F. "Relativist and Absolutist Approaches to the History of Economic Theory." *South Western Social Studies Quarterly* 48 (1967), 5–12.

Charnes, A., W. W. Cooper, and B. Mellon. "Blending Aviation Gasolines: A Study in Programming Interdependent Activities in an Integrated Oil Company." *Econometrica* 20 (1952), 135–59.

Christ, Carl F. "The History of the Cowles Commission." In *Economic Theory and Measurement: A Twenty Year Report, 1932–1952*, 3–66. Chicago: Cowles Commission for Research in Economics, 1952.

———. "The Cowles Commission's Contributions to Econometrics at Chicago, 1939–1955." *Journal of Economic Literature* 32 (1994), 30–59.

Church, Robert L. "Economists as Experts: The Rise of an Academic Profession in the United States, 1870–1920." In *The University in Society*, vol. 2, *Europe, Scotland, and the United States from the 16th to the 20th Century*, ed. Lawrence Stone, 571–609. Princeton, N.J.: Princeton University Press, 1974.

Cipolla, Carlo. "The Professions: The Long View." *Journal of European Economic History* 2 (1973), 37–51.

Clapham, J. H. "Of Empty Economic Boxes." *Economic Journal* 32 (1922), 305–14.

———. "The Economic Boxes: A Rejoinder." *Economic Journal* 32 (1922), 560–63.

Coats, A. W. "The First Two Decades of the American Economic Association." *American Economic Review* 50 (1960), 555–74.

———. "The Political Economy Club: A Neglected Episode in American Economic Thought." *American Economic Review* 51 (1961), 624–37.

———. "The American Economic Association 1904–1929." *American Economic Review* 54 (1964), 261–85.

———. "Henry Carter Adams: A Case Study in the Emergence of the Social Sciences in the United States, 1850–1900." *Journal of American Studies* 2 (1968), 177–97.

———. "Is There a 'Structure of Scientific Revolutions' in Economics?" *Kyklos* 22 (1969), 289–95.

———. "The Economic and Social Context of the Marginal Revolution of the 1870s." In *The Marginal Revolution in Economics: Interpretation and Evaluation*, ed. R. D. Collison Black, A. W. Coats, and Crauford D. W. Goodwin, 37–58. Durham, N.C.: Duke University Press, 1973.

———. "The Culture and the Economists: Some Reflections on Anglo-American Differences." *History of Political Economy* 12 (1980), 588–609.

———. "Half a Century of Methodological Controversy in Economics." In *Methodological Controversy in Economics*, ed. A. W. Coats, 1–42. Greenwich: JAI Press, 1983.

———. "The Educational Revolution and the Professionalization of American Economics." In *Breaking the Academic Mould: Economists and American Higher Learning in the Nineteenth Century*, ed. William J. Barber, 340–75. Middletown, Conn.: Wesleyan University Press, 1988.

———. "Changing Perceptions of American Graduate Education in Economics, 1953–1991." *Journal of Economic Education* 23 (1992), 341–52.

Coe, Rodney. "The Process of the Development of Established Professions." *Journal of Health and Social Behavior* 11 (1970), 59–67.

Cole, Arthur H. "Economic History in the United States: Formative Years of a Discipline." *Journal of Economic History* 28 (1968), 556–89.

Collard, David. "A. C. Pigou, 1877–1959." In *Pioneers of Modern Economics in Britain*, ed. D. P. O'Brien and J. R. Presley. New York: Macmillan, 1981.

Collins, Robert M. "The Emergence of Economic Growthmanship in the United States: Federal Policy and Economic Knowledge in the Truman Years." In *The State and Economic Knowledge: The American and British Experiences*, ed. Mary O. Furner and Barry Supple, 138–70. New York: Cambridge University Press, 1990.

————. "Growth Liberalism in the Sixties: Great Societies at Home and Grand Designs Abroad." In *The Sixties: From Memory to History*, ed. David Farber, 11–44. Chapel Hill: University of North Carolina Press, 1994.

————. "The Economic Crisis of 1968 and the Waning of the 'American Century.'" *American Historical Review* 101 (1996), 396–422.

Cook, W. R. "Whatever Happened to PPBS?" *International Review of Administrative Sciences* 52 (1986), 223–41.

Critchlow, Donald T. "Think Tanks, Antistatism, and Democracy: The Nonpartisan Ideal and Policy Research in the United States, 1913–1987." In *The State and Social Investigation in Britain and America*, ed. Michael J. Lacey and Mary O. Furner, 279–322. Cambridge: Cambridge University Press, 1993.

Cross, John. "On Professor Schelling's Strategy of Conflict." *Naval Research Logistics Quarterly* 8 (1961), 421–26.

Crotty, J. R. "On Keynes and Capital Flight." *Journal of Economic Literature* 21 (1983), 59–65.

Crotty, James. "Keynes on the Stages of Development of the Capitalist Economy: The Institutional Foundation of Keynes's Methodology." *Journal of Economic Issues* 24 (1990), 761–80.

Cuff, Robert D. "War Mobilization, Institutional Learning, and State Building in the United States." In *The State and Social Investigation in Britain and the United States*, ed. Michael J. Lacey and Mary O. Furner, 388–425. Cambridge: Cambridge University Press, 1993.

Curti, Merle. "The American Scholar in Three Wars." *Journal of the History of Ideas* 3 (1942), 241–64.

Dantzig, George B. "Maximization of a Linear Function of Variables Subject to Linear Inequalities." In *Activity Analysis of Production and Allocation: Proceedings of a Conference*, ed. Tjalling C. Koopmans. New York: Wiley, 1951.

De Santis, Vincent P. "Eisenhower Revisionism." *Review of Politics* 38 (1976), 190–207.

Debreu, Gerard. "Mathematical Economics at Cowles." In *Cowles Fiftieth Anniversary: Four Essays and an Index of Publications*, 25–48. New Haven, Conn.: Cowles Foundation for Research in Economics, 1991.

————. "The Mathematization of Economic Theory." *American Economic Review* 81 (1991), 1–7.

Debreu Gerard, and Herbert Scarf. "A Limit Theorem on the Core of an Economy." *International Economic Review* 4 (1963), 235–46.

Demsetz, Harold. "The Primacy of Economics: An Explanation of the Comparative Success of Economics in the Social Sciences." *Economic Inquiry* 35 (1997), 1–11.

Dennis, Michael A. "Accounting for Research: New Histories of Corporate Laboratories and the Social History of American Science." *Social Studies of Science* 17 (1987), 479–518.

————. "'Our First Line of Defense': Two University Laboratories in the Postwar American State." *Isis* 85 (1994), 427–55.

Denzin, N. K. "Incomplete Professionalization: The Case of Pharmacy." *Social Forces* 46 (1968), 375–81.

DeVroey, Michel. "The Transition from Classical to Neoclassical Economics: A Scientific Revolution." *Journal of Economic Issues* 9 (1975), 415–40.

DiIulio, John J., Jr. "Help Wanted: Economists, Crime and Public Policy." *Journal of Economic Perspectives* 10 (1996), 3–24.

Dimand, Robert. "The New Economics and American Economists in the 1930s Reconsidered." *Atlantic Economic Journal* 18 (1990), 42–47.

Donham, Wallace B., and Esty Foster. "The Graduate School of Business Administration, 1908–1929." In *The Development of Harvard University since the Inauguration of President Eliot, 1869–1929*, ed. Samuel Eliot Morison, 533–48. Cambridge: Harvard University Press, 1930.

Dorfman, Joseph. "The Role of the German Historical School in American Economic Thought." *American Economic Review* 45 (1955), 17–28.

Duman, D. "The Creation and Diffusion of a Professional Ideal in Nineteenth Century Britain." *Sociological Review* 27 (1979), 113–38.

Durbin, E. "Economists and the Future Functions of the State." *Political Quarterly* 14 (1943), 256–69.

Dykes, Sayre E. "The Establishment and Evolution of the Federal Reserve Board: 1913–1923." *Federal Reserve Bulletin* 75 (1989), 227–43.

Eatwell, John. "Mr. Sraffa's Standard Commodity and the Rate of Exploitation." *Quarterly Journal of Economics* 89 (1975), 543–55.

Edelstein, Michael. "What Price Cold War? Military Spending and Private Investment in the United States, 1946–1979." *Cambridge Journal of Economics* 14 (1990), 421–37.

Ehrlich, Isaac. "Crime, Punishment, and the Market for Offenses." *Journal of Economic Perspectives* 10 (1996), 43–67.

Eichengreen, Barry. "The Political Economy of the Smoot-Hawley Tariff." *Research in Economic History* 12 (1989), 1–43.

Eisenhower, Dwight D. "Farewell to the Nation." In *The Eisenhower Administration, 1953–1961: A Documentary History*, ed. R. L. Branyan and L. H. Larsen, 2:1376. New York: Random House, 1971.

Eisner, Robert. "Fiscal and Monetary Policy Reconsidered." *American Economic Review* 59 (1969), 897–905.

———. "What Went Wrong?" *Journal of Political Economy* 79 (1971), 629–41.

Ellsberg, Daniel. "The Theory of the Reluctant Duelist." *American Economic Review* 46 (1956), 909–23.

———. "The Crude Analysis of Strategic Choices." *American Economic Review* 51 (1961), 472–78.

———. "Risk, Ambiguity, and the Savage Axioms." *Quarterly Journal of Economics* 75 (1961), 643–69.

Ely, Richard T. "Past and Present of Political Economy." *Johns Hopkins University Studies in History and Political Science* 2 (1884), 143–202.

———. "The Founding and Early History of the American Economic Association." *American Economic Review* 26 (1936), 141–50.

Enke, Stephen. "An Economist Looks at Air Force Logistics." *Review of Economics and Statistics* 40 (1958), 230–39.

Enthoven, Alain C. "Economic Analysis in the Department of Defense." *American Economic Review* 53 (1963), 413–23.

Epstein, Gerald A., and Juliet B. Schor. "The Federal Reserve–Treasury Accord and the Construction of the Postwar Monetary Regime in the United States." *Social Concept* 8 (1995), 7–48.

Feldstein, Martin S. "Economic Analysis, Operational Research, and the National Health Service." *Oxford Economic Papers*, n.s., 15. no. 1 (1963), 19–31.

———. "The Council of Economic Advisers: From Stabilization to Resource Allocation." *American Economic Review* 87 (1997), 99–102.

Fellner, William. "The Economics of Eisenhower: A Symposium." *Review of Economics and Statistics* 38 (1956), 373–75.

Fetter, Frank. "The Economists and the Public." *American Economic Review* 15 (1925), 13–25.

Fielding, A., and D. Portwood. "Professions and the State." *Sociological Review* 28 (1980), 23–53.

Fine, Ben, and L. Harris. "Controversial Issues in Marxist Economic Theory." *Socialist Register* (1976).

Fischer, Stanley. "Long-Term Contracts, Rational Expectations, and the Optimal Money Supply Rule." *Journal of Political Economy* 85 (1977), 191–205.

Fisher, Donald. "The Ideology of Rockefeller Philanthropy and the Development of the Social Sciences, 1910–1940." *Sociology* 17 (1983), 206–33.

Fisher, Franklin. "Games Economists Play: A Noncooperative View." *Rand Journal of Economics* 20 (1989), 113–24.

Fisher, Irving. "Economists in Public Service." *American Economic Review* 9 (1919), 7, 18–21.

Foucault, Michel. "The Discourse on Language." In *The Archaeology of Knowledge*, trans. A. M. Sheridan Smith, 215–37. New York: Harper and Row, 1972.

Fox, K. A. "Agricultural Economists in the Econometric Revolution: Institutional Background, Literature and Leading Figures." *Oxford Economic Papers* 41 (1989), 53–70.

Frank, Marguerite, and Philip Wolfe. "An Algorithm for Quadratic Programming." *Naval Research Logistics Quarterly* (1956), 95–110.

Freeman, Richard B. "Why Do So Many Young American Men Commit Crimes and What Might We Do About It?" *Journal of Economic Perspectives* 10 (1996), 25–42.

Frey, Bruno S., Werner W. Pommerehne, Friedrich Schneider, and Gilbert Guy. "Consensus and Dissension among Economists: An Empirical Inquiry." *American Economic Review* 74 (1984), 986–94.

Friedman, Milton. "The Methodology of Positive Economics." In *Essays in Positive Economics*. Chicago: University of Chicago Press, 1953.

———. "The Role of Monetary Policy." *American Economic Review* 58 (1968), 1–22.

———. "A Theoretical Framework for Monetary Analysis." In *Milton Friedman's Monetary Framework*, ed. Robert J. Gordon. Chicago: University of Chicago Press, 1974.

Friedman, Robert Marc. "The Nobel Physics Prize in Perspective." *Nature* 292 (1981), 793–98.

———. "Text, Context, and Quicksand: Method and Understanding in Studying the Nobel Science Prizes." *Historical Studies in the Physical and Biological Sciences* 20 (1989), 63–77.

Froman, Lewis A. "Graduate Students in Economics, 1904–1940." *American Economic Review* 32 (1942), 817–26.

Galambos, Louis. "The Emerging Organizational Synthesis in Modern American History." *Business History Review* 44 (1970), 279–90.

Galton, François. "Economic Science and the British Association." *Journal of the Royal Statistical Society*, September 1877.

Gardner, Roy. "L. V. Kantorovich: The Price Implications of Optimal Planning." *Journal of Economic Literature* 28 (1990), 638–48.

Geiger, Roger L. "Science, Universities, and National Defense: 1945–70." *Osiris* 7 (1992), 26–48.

Gerstein, I. "Production, Circulation and Value: The Significance of the 'Transformation Problem' in Marx's Critique of Political Economy." *Economy and Society* 5 (1976).

Gerstle, Gary. "The Protean Character of American Liberalism." *American Historical Review* 99 (1994), 1043–73.

Gieryn, T. F. "Boundary Work and the Demarcation of Science from Non-Science." *American Sociological Review* 48 (1983), 781–95.

Gilman, S. I. "Operations Research in the Army." *Military Review* 36 (July, 1956), 54–64.

Goggin, Jacqueline. "Challenging Sexual Discrimination in the Historical Profession: Women Historians and the American Historical Association, 1890–1940." *American Historical Review* 97 (1992), 769–802.

Goode, W. J. "Encroachment, Charlatanism, and the Emerging Profession." *American Sociological Review* 25 (1960), 902–14.

Gordon, D. F. "The Role of the History of Economic Thought in the Understanding of Modern Economic Theory." *American Economic Review* 55 (1965), 119–27.

Gordon, Lincoln. "Economic Aspects of Coalition Diplomacy: The NATO Experience." *International Organization* 10 (1956), 529–43.

Gordon, R. W. "Legal Thought and Legal Practice in the Age of American Enterprise: 1870–1920." In *Professions and Professional Ideology in America*, ed. Gerald L. Geison, 4–82. Chapel Hill: University of North Carolina Press, 1983.

Griffith, Robert. "Dwight D. Eisenhower and the Corporate Commonwealth." *American Historical Review* 87 (1982), 87–122.

Grossman, D. "American Foundations and the Support of Economic Research: 1913–1929." *Minerva* 20 (1982), 59–82.

Grossman, Herschel I. "A General Equilibrium Model of Insurrections." *American Economic Review* 81 (1991), 912–21.

Grossman, Sanford. "On the Efficiency of Competitive Stock Markets Where Traders Have Diverse Information." *Journal of Finance* 31 (1976), 573–85.

Hamby, Alonzo. "The Vital Center, the Fair Deal, and the Quest for a Liberal Political Economy." *American Historical Review* 77 (1972), 653–78.

Hands, Douglas W. "Second Thought on Lakatos." *History of Political Economy* 17 (1985), 1–16.

Hansen, Alvin. "Was Fiscal Policy in the Thirties a Failure?" *Review of Economics and Statistics* 45 (1963), 320–23.

Hawley, Ellis. "Herbert Hoover, the Commerce Secretariat, and the Vision of an 'Associative State,' 1921–1928." *Journal of American History* 61 (1974), 116–40.

———. "Economic Inquiry and the State in New Era America: Antistatist Corporatism and Positive Statism in Uneasy Coexistence." In *The State and Economic Knowledge: The American and British Experiences*, ed. Mary O. Furner and Barry Supple, 287–324. New York: Cambridge University Press, 1990.

Hebert, R. F. "Marshall: A Professional Economist Guards the Purity of His Discipline." In *Critics of Henry George: A Centenary Appraisal of Their Strictures on "Progress and Poverty"*, ed. R. V. Andelson, 56–71. Cranbury, N.J.: Associated University Presses, 1979.

Hendry, David. "Econometrics: Alchemy or Science?" *Economica* 47 (1980), 387–406.

Herman, Edward S. "The Institutionalization of Bias in Economics." *Media, Culture and Society* 4 (1982), 275–91.

Hicks, John R. "Mr. Keynes and the 'Classics': A Suggested Interpretation." *Econometrica* 5 (1937), 147–59.

Higgs, Robert. "Wartime Prosperity? A Reassessment of the U.S. Economy in the 1940s." *Journal of Economic History* 52 (1992), 41–60.

Hildebrand, George, et al. "Impacts of National Security Expenditures upon the Stability of the American Economy." In *Federal Expenditure Policy for Economic Growth and Stability*, 523–41. Joint Economic Committee of the Congress, 5 November 1957. Washington, D.C.: U.S. Government Printing Office, 1957.

Himmelberg, Robert F. "The War Industries Board and the Antitrust Question." *Journal of American History* 52 (1965), 59–74.

Hirshleifer, Jack. "The Expanding Domain of Economics." *American Economic Review* 75 (1985), 53–68.

Hitch, Charles J. "Suboptimization in Operations Problems." *Journal of the Operations Research Society of America* 1 (1953), 87–89.

———. "Economics and Military Operations Research." *Review of Economics and Statistics* 40 (1958), 199–209.

———. "Plans, Programs, and Budgets in the Department of Defense." *Journal of the Operations Research Society of America* 2 (1963), 1–17.

Hitchcock, Frank L. "The Distribution of a Product from Several Sources to Numerous Localities." *Journal of Mathematics and Physics* 20 (1941), 224–30.

Hogan, Michael J. "American Marshall Planners and the Search for a European Neocapitalism." *American Historical Review* 90 (1985), 44–72.

Howey, R. S. "The Origins of Marginalism." In *The Marginal Revolution in Economics: Interpretation and Evaluation*, ed. R. D. Collison Black, A. W. Coats, and Crauford D. W. Goodwin, 15–36. Durham, N.C.: Duke University Press, 1973.

Hughes, Everett. "Professions." *Daedalus* 92 (1963), 655–68.

Hurwicz, Leonid. "The Theory of Economic Behavior." *American Economic Review* 35 (1945), 909–25.

Iannaccone, Laurence R. "Introduction to the Economics of Religion." *Journal of Economic Literature* 36 (1998), 1465–96.

Jevons, W. S. "A General Mathematical Theory on Political Economy." *Report of the British Academy for the Advancement of Science* (1863).

Jewett, F. B. "The Genesis of the National Research Council and Millikan's World War I Work." *Review of Modern Physics* 20 (1948), 1–6.

Johansen, L. "L.V. Kantorovich's Contribution to Economics." *Scandanavian Journal of Economics* 18 (1976), 61–80.

Johnson, Harry G. "The Keynesian Revolution and the Monetarist Counter-Revolution." *American Economic Review* 61 (1971), 1–14.

Kantorovich, L. V. "On the Translocation of Masses." *Management Science* 5 (1958), 1–4.

———. "Mathematical Methods of Organizing and Planning Production." *Management Science* 6 (1960), 363–422.

Karl, Barry D., and Stanley N. Katz. "The American Private Philanthropic Foundation and the Public Sphere, 1890–1930." *Minerva* 19 (1981), 236–70.

Katznelson, Ira, and Bruce Pietrykowski. "Rebuilding the American State: Evidence from the 1940s." *Studies in American Political Development* 5 (1991), 301–39.

Kellogg, V. "The National Research Council." *International Conciliation* 154 (1920), 423–30.

Kendry, A. "Paul Samuelson and the Scientific Awakening of Economics." In *Twelve Contemporary Economists*, ed. J. R. Shackleton and G. Locksley. London: Macmillan, 1981.

Kennan, George. "The Sources of Soviet Conduct." *Foreign Affairs* 25 (1947), 566–82.

Kevles, D. J. "The National Science Foundation and the Debate over Postwar Research Policy, 1942–1945: A Political Interpretation of *Science—The Endless Frontier*." *Isis* 68 (1977), 5–26.

Keynes, John Maynard. "Economic Possibilities for Our Grandchildren." In *Essays in Persuasion*, 373. New York: Harcourt, Brace, 1932.

————. "National Self-Sufficiency." *Yale Review* 22 (1933), 755–69.

Klein, Lawrence R. "Econometrics at Cowles, 1944–47." *Banco Nazionale del Lavoro Quarterly Review* 177 (1991), 107–17.

Klein, Philip A. "The Neglected Institutionalism of Wesley Clair Mitchell: The Theoretical Basis for Business Cycle Indicators." *Journal of Economic Issues* 17 (1983), 867–99.

Knight, Frank H. "The Limitations of Scientific Method in Economics." In *The Trend of Economics*, ed. Rexford G. Tugwell, 229–67. New York: Crofts, [1924] 1934.

————. "Economic Psychology and the Value Problem." In *The Ethics of Competition* (New York: Harper, [1925] 1935), 76–104.

————. "The Nature of Economic Science in Some Recent Discussion." *American Economic Review* 24 (1934), 225–38.

Koopmans, Tjalling C. "Measurement without Theory." *Review of Economics and Statistics* 29 (1947), 161–72.

————. "Economic Growth at a Maximal Rate." *Quarterly Journal of Economics* 78 (1964), 355–94.

Kreps, David M. "Economics: The Current Position." *Daedalus* 126 (1997), 59–86.

Kuznets, Simon. "The Contribution of Wesley C. Mitchell." In C. E. Ayres, Neil W. Chamberlain, Joseph Dorfman, Robert A. Gordon, and Simon Kuznets, *Institutional Economics: Veblen, Commons, and Mitchell Reconsidered*, 95–122. Berkeley and Los Angeles: University of California Press, 1963.

Larson, Deborah Welch. "Deterrence Theory and the Cold War." *Radical History Review* 63 (1995), 86–109.

Leamer, Edward. "Let's Take the Con Out of Econometrics." *American Economic Review* 73 (1983), 31–43.

Leonard, Robert J. "War as a 'Simple Economic Problem': The Rise of an Economics of Defense." In *Economics and National Security: A History of Their Interaction*, ed. Craufurd D. Goodwin, 261–83. Durham, N.C.: Duke University Press, 1991.

————. "Creating a Context for Game Theory." *History of Political Economy* 24 (1992), 29–76.

————. "From Parlor Games to Social Science: Von Neumann, Morgenstern, and the Creation of Game Theory: 1928–1944." *Journal of Economic Literature* 33 (1995), 730–61.

Leuchtenberg, William. "The New Deal as Analogue of War." In *The FDR Years: On Roosevelt and His Legacy*, 35–75. New York: Columbia University Press, 1995.

Levinson, Harold C. "Experiences in Commercial Operations Research." *Journal of the Operations Research Society of America* 2 (1953), 220–39.

Lifschultz, Lawrence. "Could Karl Marx Teach Economics in the United States?" *Ramparts*, 12 April 1974, 27–30, 52–59.

————. "Could Karl Marx Teach Economics in the United States?" In *How Harvard Rules: Reason in the Service of Empire*, ed. John Trumpbour, 279–86. Boston: South End Press, 1989.

Lipsey, Richard G. "The Relation between Unemployment and the Rate of Change of Money Wage Rates in the United Kingdom, 1862–1975: A Further Analysis." *Economica*, n.s., 27 (1960).

Livingston, J. Sterling. "Decision Making in Weapons Development." *Harvard Business Review* 36 (1958), 127–36.

Lucas, Robert E., Jr. "Some International Evidence on Output-Inflation Trade-Offs." *American Economic Review* 63 (1973), 326–34.

————. "An Equilibrium Model of the Business Cycle." *Journal of Political Economy* 83 (1975), 1113–44.

————. "Econometric Policy Evaluation: A Critique." *Journal of Monetary Economics* 1 (1976), 19–46.

————. "Understanding Business Cycles." In *Stabilization of the Domestic and International Economy*, ed. Karl Brunner and Allan H. Meltzer, 7–29. New York: North-Holland, 1977.

————. "Methods and Problems in Business Cycle Theory." In *Studies in Business Cycle Theory*, 271–96. Cambridge: MIT Press, 1980.

Machlup, Fritz. "Marginal Analysis and Empirical Research." *American Economic Review* 36 (1946), 519–54.

Maddison, Angus. "Economic Stagnation since 1973, Its Nature and Causes: A Six Country Survey." *De Economist* 131 (1983), 585–608.

Maddock, Rodney. "Rational Expectations Macrotheory: A Lakatosian Case Study in Program Adjustment." *History of Political Economy* 16 (1984), 291–310.

Maddox, Robert Franklin. "The Politics of World War II Science: Senator Harley M. Kilgore and the Legislative Origins of the National Science Foundation." *West Virginia History* 41 (1979), 20–39.

Maier, Charles S. "The Politics of Productivity: Foundations of American International Economic Policy after World War II." *International Organization* 31 (1977), 607–33.

Mankiw, Gergory. "Real Business Cycles: A New Keynesian Perspective." *Journal of Economic Perspectives* 3 (1989), 79–90.

Marshall, Alfred. "Mechanical and Biological Analogies in Economics." *Economic Journal* (1898).

————. "The Old Generation of Economists and the New." In *Memorials of Alfred Marshall*, ed. A. C. Pigou, 297. London: Kelley, [1925] 1956.

Martin, L. W. "The Market for Strategic Ideas in Britain." *American Political Science Review* 56 (1962), 23–41.

Mason, Edward S. " The Harvard Department of Economics from the Beginnings to World War II." *Quarterly Journal of Economics* 97 (1982), 383–433.

McCallum, Bennet. "The Current State of the Policy Ineffectiveness Debate." *American Economic Review* 69 (1979), 240–45.

————. "New Classical Macroeconomics: A Sympathetic Account." *Scandinavian Journal of Economics* 91 (1989), 223–52.

McCloskey, Dierdre M. "The Rhetoric of Economics." *Journal of Economic Literature* 21 (1983), 434–61.

————. "The Literary Character of Economics." *Daedalus* (1984), 97–119.

————. "The Loss Function Has Been Mislaid: The Rhetoric of Significance Tests." *American Economic Review* 75 (1985), 201–5.

————. "The Standard Error of Regressions." *Journal of Economic Literature* 34 (1996), 97–114.

McCracken, Paul W. "Economic Policy in the Nixon Years." *Political Science Quarterly* 26 (1996), 165–77.

McDean, Harry C. "Professionalism, Policy, and Farm Economists in the Early Bureau of Agricultural Economics." *Agricultural History* 57 (1983), 64–82.

Meek, Ronald L. "Marginalism and Marxism." In *The Marginal Revolution in Economics: Interpretation and Evaluation*, ed. R. D. Collison Black, A. W. Coats, and Crauford D. W. Goodwin, 233–45. Durham, N.C.: Duke University Press, 1973.

Menard, Claude. "The Lausanne Tradition: Walras and Pareto." In *Neoclassical Economic Theory, 1870 to 1930*, ed. Klaus Hennings and Warren J. Samuels, 95–137 Boston: Kluwer Academic Publishers, 1990.

Mendershausen, Horst. "Economic Problems in Air Force Logistics." *American Economic Review* 48 (1958), 632–48.

Metcalf, Evan. "Secretary Hoover and the Emergence of Macroeconomic Management." *Business History Review* 59 (1975), 60–80.

Metzger, W. P. "The Academic Profession in the United States." In *The Academic Profession: National, Disciplinary, and Institutional Settings*, ed. B. R. Clark, 123–208. Berkeley and Los Angeles: University of California Press, 1987.

Miller, Gary J. "The Impact of Economics on Contemporary Political Science." *Journal of Economic Literature* 35 (1997), 1173–1204.

Mirabeau, Marquis de. "The *Tableau Economique* and Its Explanation" [1763]. In *Precursors of Adam Smith*, ed. Ronald L. Meek. London: Dent, 1973.

Mirabeau, Marquis de, and François Quesnay. "Rural Philosophy [1763]." In *Precursors of Adam Smith*, ed. Ronald L. Meek, 104. London: Dent, 1973.

Mirowski, Philip. "The Measurement without Theory Controversy: Defeating Rival Research Programs by Accusing Them of Naive Empiricism." *Economies et Sociétés: Serie Oeconomia* 23 (1989), 109–31.

———. "Problems in the Paternity of Econometrics: Henry Ludwell Moore." *History of Political Economy* 22 (1990), 587–609.

———. "When Games Grow Deadly Serious: The Military Influence on the Evolution of Game Theory." In *Economics and National Security: A History of Their Interaction*, ed. Craufurd D. Goodwin, 227–55. Durham, N.C.: Duke University Press, 1991.

———. "What Were von Neumann and Morgenstern Trying to Accomplish?" *History of Political Economy* 24 (1992), 113–47.

Mitchell, Wesley C. "The Rationality of Economic Activity I." *Journal of Political Economy* 18 (1910), 97–113.

———. "The Rationality of Economic Activity II." *Journal of Political Economy* 18 (1910), 197–216.

———. "The Prospects of Economics." In *The Trend of Economics*, ed. Rexford G. Tugwell, 3–34. New York: Crofts, [1924] 1932.

Morgan, Mary. "The Case of John Bates Clark." *History of Political Economy* 24 (1994), 229–53.

Morgenstern, Oskar. "Economics and the Theory of Games." *Kyklos* 3 (1949), 294–308.

Musto, David F. "Continuity across Generations: The Adams Family Myth." In *New Directions in Psychohistory: The Adelphi Papers in Honor of Erik H. Erikson*, ed. M. Albin, R. Devlin, and G. A. Heeger, 117–29. Lexington, Mass.: D. C. Heath, 1980.

Muth, R. F. "The Demand for Non-Farm Housing." In *The Demand for Durable Goods*, ed. A. C. Harberger, 29–96. Chicago: University of Chicago Press, 1960.

———. "Rational Expectations and the Theory of Price Movements." *Econometrica* 29 (1961), 315–35.

Najita, Tetsuo. "Introduction: A Synchronous Approach to the Study of Conflict in Modern Japanese History." In *Conflict in Modern Japanese History: The Neglected Tradition*, ed. Tetsuo Najita and J. Victor Koschmann, 3–21. Princeton, N.J.: Princeton University Press, 1982.

Nelson, K. "The 'Warfare State': The History of a Concept." *Pacific Historical Review* 40 (1971), 127–43.

Nelson, R. H. "The Economic Profession and Public Policy." *Journal of Economic Literature* 25 (1987), 49–91.

Nichols, Roy F. "War and Research in Social Science." *American Philosophical Society Proceedings* 87 (1944), 361–64.

Ohanian, Lee E. "The Macroeconomic Effects of War Finance in the United States: World War II and the Korean War." *American Economic Review* 87 (1997), 23–40.

Okun, Arthur M. "Potential GNP: Its Measurement and Significance." In *The Political Economy of Prosperity*, 132–45. Washington, D.C.: Brookings Institution, 1970.

———. "Fiscal-Monetary Activism: Some Analytical Issues." *Brookings Papers on Economic Activity* (1972:1), 123–72.

———. "The Fiscal Fiasco of the Vietnam Period." In *The Battle against Unemployment*, 150–63. New York: Norton, 1972.

Parker, William. "Slavery and Agricultural Development: An Hypothesis and Some Evidence." *Agricultural History* 44 (1970), 115–25.

Parrish, John B. "The Rise of Economics as an Academic Discipline: The Formative Years to 1900." *Southern Economic Journal* 34 (1967), 1–15.

Parsons, Talcott. "Some Reflections on 'The Nature and Significance of Economics.'" *Quarterly Journal of Economics* 48 (1934), 511–45.

———. "The Present Position and Prospects of Systematic Theory in Sociology." In *Essays in Sociological Theory*, 212–37. New York: Free Press, [1945] 1954.

Pasinetti, Luigi. "Switches of Technique and the 'Rate of Return' in Capital Theory." *Economic Journal* 79 (1969), 508–31.

Patinkin, Don. "Keynes and Econometrics: On the Interaction between the Macroeconomic Revolutions of the Interwar Period." *Econometrica* 44 (1976), 1091–1123.

Perlman, Mark. "Political Purpose and the National Accounts." In *The Politics of Numbers*, ed. William Alonso and Paul Starr, 133–51. New York: Russell Sage Foundation, 1987.

Phillips, A. William. "The Relation between Unemployment and the Rate of Change of Money Wage Rates in the United Kingdom, 1861–1957." *Economica*, n.s., 25 (1958), 283–99.

Pigou, Arthur C. "Empty Economic Boxes: A Reply." *Economic Journal* 32 (1922), 458–65.

Porter, Roger B. "Presidents and Economists: The Council of Economic Advisers." *American Economic Review* 87 (1997), 103–6.

Portwood, D., and A. Fielding. "Privilege and the Professions." *Sociological Review* 29 (1981), 749–73.

Potter, Zenas L. "The Central Bureau of Planning and Statistics." *Quarterly Publications of the American Statistical Association* 16 (1919), 275–85.

Pugh, George E. "Operations Research for the Secretary of Defense and the Joint Chiefs of Staff." *Journal of the Operations Research Society of America* 8 (1960), 839–40.

Radner, Roy. "Hierarchy: The Economics of Managing." *Journal of Economic Literature* 30 (1992), 1382–1415.

Ramsey, F. P. "A Mathematical Theory of Saving." *Economic Journal* 38 (1928), 543–59.

Rapoport, A. "Game Theory in Biology." *Evolutionary Theory* 4 (1980), 249–63.

Rappaport, Armin. "The United States and European Integration: The First Phase." *Diplomatic History* 5 (1981), 121–49.

Reeder, Charles B. "Business Economists and National Economic Policy." *Business Economics* 3 (1967), 7–10.

Ricardo, David. "Notes on Malthus's Principles of Political Economy." In *The Works and Correspondence of David Ricardo*, ed. Piero Sraffa and M. H. Dobb, vol. 2. Cambridge: Cambridge University Press, 1951.

Rima, Ingrid. "Neoclassicism and Dissent: 1890–1930." In *Modern Economic Thought*, ed. Sidney Weintraub, 7–21. Philadelphia: University of Pennsylvania Press, 1977.

Ringer, Fritz K. "The German Academic Community." In *The Organization of Knowledge in Modern America, 1860–1920*, ed. A. Oleson and J. Voss, 409–29. Baltimore: Johns Hopkins University Press, 1979.

Robinson, Joan. "The Production Function and the Theory of Capital." *Review of Economic Studies* 21 (1953–54), 81–106.

———. "Consumer Sovereignty in a Planned Economy." In *Collected Economic Papers*, 3: 70–81. Oxford: Blackwell, 1975.

Rodgers, Daniel T. "In Search of Progressivism." *Reviews in American History* 10 (1982), 113–32.

Ross, Dorothy. "The Development of the Social Sciences." In *The Organization of Knowledge in Modern America, 1860–1920*, ed. A. Oleson and J. Voss, 107–38. Baltimore: Johns Hopkins University Press, 1979.

———. "The Liberal Tradition Revisited and the Republican Tradition Addressed." In *New Directions in American Intellectual History*, ed. John Higham and Paul K. Conklin, 120. Baltimore: Johns Hopkins University Press, 1979.

Rudwick, Martin J. S. "A Year in the Life of Adam Sedgwick and Company, Geologists." *Archives of Natural History* 15 (1988), 243–68.

Salant, Walter S. "Some Intellectual Contributions of the Truman Council of Economic Advisers to Policy-Making." *History of Political Economy* 5 (1973), 36–49.

Samuels, Warren. "The Firing of E. A. Ross from Stanford." *Journal of Economic Education* 22 (1991), 183–90.

Samuelson, Paul A. "Interaction between the Multiplier Analysis and the Principle of Acceleration." *Review of Economics and Statistics* 21 (1939), 75–78.

———. "Consumption Theory in Terms of Revealed Preference." *Economica* 15 (1948), 243–53.

———. "An Exact Consumption-Loan Model of Interest with or without the Social Contrivance of Money." *Journal of Political Economy* 66 (1958), 467–82.

———. "Parable and Realism in Capital Theory: The Surrogate Production Function." *Review of Economic Studies* 29 (1962), 193–206.

———. "A Summing Up." *Quarterly Journal of Economics* 80 (1966), 568–83.

———. "Irving Fisher and the Theory of Capital." In William Fellner et al., *Ten Economic Studies in the Tradition of Irving Fisher*, 17–37. New York: Wiley, 1967.

Samuelson, Paul A., and Robert A. Solow. "Analytical Aspects of Anti-Inflation Policy." *American Economic Review* 50 (1960), 177–94.

Sargent, J. E. "Are American Economists Better?" *Oxford Economic Papers*, n.s., 15 (1963), 1–7.

Sargent, Thomas, and Neil Wallace. "Rational Expectations, the Optimal Monetary Instrument and the Optimal Money Supply Rule." *Journal of Political Economy* 83 (1975), 241–55.

Saunders, R. M. "Military Force in the Foreign Policy of the Eisenhower Presidency." *Political Science Quarterly* 100 (1985).

Scarf, Herbert E. "The 1975 Nobel Prize in Economics: Resource Allocation." *Science* 190 (1975), 649, 710–12.

Schelling, Thomas C. "Bargaining, Communication, and Limited War." *Journal of Conflict Resolution* 1 (March 1957), 19–36.

———. "Anatol Rapoport's *Strategy and Conscience* (New York: Schocken, 1964)." *American Economic Review* 54 (1964), 1082–88.

———. "PPBS and Foreign Affairs." Memorandum prepared at the request of the Subcommittee on National Security and International Operations, Committee on Government Operations, United States Senate (90th Congress: 1st Session, 1968).

Schick, Allen. "The Road to PPBS: The Stages of Budget Reform." *Public Administration Review* 26 (1966), 243–58.

Schlesinger, Arthur, Jr. "The Ike Age Revisited." *Reviews in American History* 11 (1983), 1–11.

Schorske, Carl E. "The New Rigorism in the Human Sciences, 1940–1960." *Daedalus* 126 (1997), 289–309.

Schulman, Bruce. "Slouching toward the Supply Side: Jimmy Carter and the New American Political Economy." In *The Carter Presidency: Policy Choices in the Post New Deal Era*, ed. Gary Fink and Hugh Graham. Lawrence: University Press of Kansas, 1998.

Schultze, Charles L. "The CEA: An Inside Voice for Mainstream Economics." *Journal of Economic Perspectives* 10 (1996), 39.

Scott, Joan Wallach. "American Women Historians, 1884–1984." In *Gender and the Politics of History*, 178–98. New York: Columbia University Press, 1988.

Seligman, Edwin R. A. "The Early Teaching of Economics in the United States." In *Economic Essays in Honor of J.B. Clark*, ed. J. H. Hollander. New York: Macmillan, 1927.

Seton, Francis. "The Transformation Problem." *Review of Economic Studies* 24 (1963), 149–60.

Shapin, Steven. "Pump and Circumstance: Robert Boyle's Literary Technology." *Social Studies of Science* 14 (1984), 481–520.

Shapiro, Nina. "Keynes and Equilibrium Economics." *Australian Economic Papers* 31 (1978), 207–23.

Shils, E. "The Order of Learning in the United States: The Ascendency of the University." In *The Organization of Knowledge in Modern America, 1860–1920*, ed. A. Oleson and J. Voss, 19–47. Baltimore: Johns Hopkins University Press, 1979.

Shubik, Martin. "Game Theory as an Approach to the Theory of the Firm." *American Economic Review* 50 (1960), 560–64.

Simon, Herbert A. "Theories of Decision-Making in Economics and Behavioral Science." *American Economic Review* 49 (1959), 253–83.

Skocpol, Theda, and Kenneth Finegold. "State Capacity and Economic Intervention in the Early New Deal." *Political Science Quarterly* 97 (1982), 255–78.

Slotten, Hugh R. "Human Chemistry or Scientific Barbarism? American Responses to World War I Poison Gas, 1915–1930." *Journal of American History* 77 (1990), 476–98.

Social Science Research Council. "Research Support and Intellectual Advance in the Social Sciences." *Items* 37 (1983), 35–37.

Solovey, Mark, and Daniel Lee Kleinman. "Hot Science/Cold War: The National Science Foundation after World War II." *Radical History Review* 63 (1995), 110–39.

Solow, Robert M. "A Contribution to the Theory of Economic Growth." *Quarterly Journal of Economics* 70 (1956), 65–94.

———. "Science and Ideology in Economics." *The Public Interest* 21 (1970), 94–107.

———. "How Did Economics Get That Way and What Way Did It Get?" *Daedalus* 126 (1997), 39–58.

Souter, Ralph W. " 'The Nature and Significance of Economic Science' in Recent Discussion." *Quarterly Journal of Economics* 47 (1933), 377–413.

Speier, Hans, and Herbert Goldhamer. "Some Observations on Political Gaming." *World Politics* 12 (1959), 71–83.

Spengler, Joseph J. "Exogenous and Endogenous Influences in the Formation of Post-1870 Economic Thought." In *Events, Ideology, and Economic Theory*, ed. Robert V. Eagly, 159–205. Detroit: Wayne State University Press, 1968.

Stein, Herbert. "A Successful Accident: Recollections and Speculations about the CEA." *Journal of Economic Perspectives* 10 (1996), 3–20.

Steindl, Josef. "Reflections on the Present State of Economics." *Banca Nazionale del Lavoro Quarterly Review* 148 (1984), 3–14.

Steinhardt, J. "The Role of Operations Research in the Navy." *U.S. Naval Institute Proceedings* (May 1946).

Sterling, L. J. "Decision Making in Weapons Development." *Harvard Business Review* 38 (1958), 127–36.

Steuart, Sir James. "An Inquiry into the Principles of Political Oëconomy. [1767]" In *Precursors of Adam Smith*, ed. Ronald L. Meek, 154, 167–68. London: Dent, 1973.

Stigler, George J. "Does Economics Have a Useful Past?" *History of Political Economy* 1 (1969), 217–30.

———. "The Adoption of the Marginal Utility Theory." In *The Marginal Revolution in Economics: Interpretation and Evaluation*, ed. R. D. Collison Black, A. W. Coats, and Crauford D. W. Goodwin, 305–20. Durham, N.C.: Duke University Press, 1973.

Stiglitz, Joseph. "Looking Out for the National Interest: The Principles of the Council of Economic Advisers." *American Economic Review* 87 (1997), 109–13.

Stone, N. I. "The Beginnings of the National Bureau of Economic Research." In *The National Bureau's First Quarter Century*, ed. Wesley Mitchell. New York: National Bureau of Economic Research, 1945.

Stone, Richard. "The Theory of Games." *Economic Journal* 58 (1948), 185–201.

Summers, Lawrence. "Some Skeptical Observations on Real Business Cycles." *Federal Reserve Bank of Minneapolis Review* 10 (1986), 23–27.

Sweezy, Alan R. "The Keynesians and Government Policy: 1933–39." *American Economic Review* 62 (1972), 116–24.

Sweezy, Paul. "Demand under Conditions of Oligopoly." *Journal of Political Economy* 47 (1939).

Taussig, Frank W. "The Present Position of the Doctrine of Free Trade." *Publications of the American Economic Association* 6 (1905), 56–58.

———. "Economics, 1871–1929." In *The Development of Harvard University: Since the Inaguration of President Eliot, 1869–1929*, ed. Samuel Elliot Morrison, 187–201. Cambridge: Harvard University Press.

Taylor, John B. "Changes in American Economic Policy in the 1980s: Watershed or Pendulum Swing?" *Journal of Economic Literature* 33 (1995), 777–84.

Taylor, O. H. "Economics and the Idea of Natural Laws." In *Economics and Liberalism: Collected Papers*, 37–69. Cambridge: Harvard University Press, [1929] 1955.

———. "Economic Theory and Certain Non-Economic Elements in Social Life." In *Explorations in Economics: Notes and Essays in Honor of F. W. Taussig*, 380–90. New York: Kelley, [1936] 1967.

Tenny, Lloyd S. "The Bureau of Agricultural Economics in the Early Years." *Journal of Farm Economics* 29 (1947), 1017–26.

Tintner, Gerhard. "The Theory of Choice under Subjective Risk and Uncertainty." *Econometrica* 9 (1941), 298–304.

Tobin, James. "Growth through Taxation." *The New Republic*, 25 July 1960. Reprinted in *National Economic Policy*, 78–88. New Haven, Conn.: Yale University Press, 1966.

———. "The Future of the Fed." *Challenge*, January 1961. Reprinted in *National Economic Policy*, 134–43.

———. "Academic Economics in Washington." *Ventures* 2 (winter 1963), 24–27. Reprinted in *National Economic Policy*, chap. 18.

———. "Economic Progress and the International Monetary System." *Papers and Proceedings, Annual Meeting of the Academy of Political Science*, May 1963. Reprinted in *National Economic Policy*, 161–75.

———. "Inflation and Unemployment." *American Economic Review* 62 (1972), 1–18.

———. "The Wage-Price Mechanism: Overview of the Conference." In *The Econometrics of Price Determination*, ed. Otto Eckstein. Washington, D.C.: Board of Governors of the Federal Reserve System, 1972.

———. "How Dead Is Keynes?" *Economic Inquiry* 15 (1977).

Trachtenberg, Marc. "Keynes Triumphant: A Study in the Social History of Economic Ideas." *Knowledge and Society: Studies in the Sociology of Culture Past and Present* 4 (1983), 17–86.

Trumpbour, John. "Harvard, the Cold War, and the National Security State." In *How Harvard Rules: Reason in the Service of Empire*, ed. John Trumpbour, 51–128. Boston: South End Press, 1989.

Turgot, A.R.J. "Reflections on the Formation and the Distribution of Wealth." In *Turgot on Progress, Sociology and Economics*, ed. and trans. Ronald L. Meek, 128. Cambridge: Cambridge University Press, 1973.

Ulam, S. "John von Neumann, 1903–1957." *Bulletin of the American Mathematical Society* 64 (1958), 1–49.

United States National Security Council. "United States Objectives and Programs for National Security." National Security Council Memorandum (NSC) 68, 14 April 1950. Reprinted in United States Department of State, *Foreign Relations of the United States*, 1:237–90. Washington, D.C.: State Department Publications, 1953.

Usher, Abbott Payson. "The Liberal Theory of Constructive Statecraft." *American Economic Review* 24 (1934), 1–10.

Varaiya, P., and M. Wiseman. "Investment and Employment in Manufacturing in U.S. Metropolitan Areas." *Regional Science and Urban Economics* 11 (1981), 431–69.

Vatter, Harold. "The Material Status of the U.S. Civilian Consumer in World War II: The Question of Guns or Butter." In *The Sinews of War: Essays on the Economic History of World War II*, ed. Geoffrey T. Mills and Hugh Rockoff, 219–42. Ames: Iowa State University Press, 1993.

Veblen, Thorstein Veblen. "Why Is Economics Not an Evolutionary Science?" In *The Place of Science in Modern Civilization*, 56–81. New York: Viking, [1898] 1919.

———. "The Preconceptions of Economic Science." In *The Place of Science in Modern Civilization*, 82–179.

———. "The Limitations of Marginal Utility." In *The Place of Science in Modern Civilization*, 231–51.

Verba, Sidney. "Simulation, Reality, and Theory in International Relations." *World Politics* 16 (April, 1964).

Wallich, Henry C. "The American Council of Economic Advisers and the German *Sachverstaendigenrat*: A Study in the Economics of Advice." *Quarterly Journal of Economics* 82 (1968), 349–79.

Waring, Stephen P. "Cold Calculus: The Cold War and Operations Research." *Radical History Review* 63 (1995), 28–51.

Weintraub, E. Roy. "On the Existence of a Competitive Equilibrium: 1930–1954." *Journal of Economic Literature* 21 (1983), 1–39.

Werin, L., and K. G. Jungenfelt. "Tjalling Koopmans' Contributions to Economics." In *Contemporary Economists in Perspective*, ed. H. W. Spiegel and Warren J. Samuels. Greenwich, Conn.: JAI Press, 1984.

Wicksteed, Philip H. "Political Economy in Light of Marginal Theory." *Economic Journal* 24 (1914).

Wildavsky, Aaron. "The Practical Consequences of the Theoretical Study of Defense Policy." *Public Administration Review* 25 (1965), 90–103.

———. "The Political Economy of Efficiency." *Public Administration Review* 26 (1966), 298–302.

———. "Rescuing Policy Analysis from PPBS." Subcommittee on National Security and International Operations, Committee on Government Operations, United States Senate, *Planning-Programming Budgeting: Rescuing Policy Analysis from PPBS.* 91st Cong., 1st sess., 1969. [Reprinted from *Public Administration Review* 29 (1969), 6n.10.]

Wilensky, Harold. "The Professionalization of Everyone?" *American Journal of Sociology* 70 (1964), 137–58.

Williamson, Jeffrey. "On the System in Bretton Woods." *American Economic Review* 75 (1985), 74–79.

Wilson, Woodrow. "Princeton in the Nation's Service." *Forum* 22 (1896), 450–66.

Wohlstetter, Albert. "The Delicate Balance of Terror." *Foreign Affairs* 39 (1959), 211–34.

Wolff, Robert P. "Maximization of Expected Utility as a Criterion of Rationality in Military Strategy and Foreign Policy." *Social Theory and Practice* 1 (1970), 99–111.

Woolgar, Steve. "Interests and Explanation in the Social Study of Science." *Social Studies of Science* 11 (1981), 365–94.

Wright, Gavin. "The Political Economy of New Deal Spending: An Econometric Analysis." *Review of Economics and Statistics* 56 (1974), 262–81.

Yonay, Yuval. "When Black Boxes Clash: Competing Ideas of What Science Is in Economics, 1924–39." *Social Studies of Science* 24 (1994), 39–80.

Contemporary Articles, Essays, Letters, and Speeches

"Also . . . ." *Los Angeles Times*, 29 October 1997, D3.

"Clinton Is Economical with the Economists." *International Herald Tribune*, 21 December 1992, 7.

"Court Blocks Rule on Local Phone Rivalry." *Los Angeles Times*, 16 October 1996, D1, D6.

"Employment Act of 1946." 79th Cong., 2d sess., 20 February 1946, Section 2.

"Employment Act of 1946." Public Law 304, 79th Cong., 2d sess., 2.

"Encounter." *Newsweek*, 3 August 1959, 15–19.

"FCC May Loosen Ownership Rules." *Los Angeles Times*, 8 November 1996, D4.

"FCC to Auction Wireless Licenses." *Los Angeles Times*, 12 March 1997, D3.

"Greenspan Rejects Calls to Reform Fed." *Los Angeles Times*, 14 October 1993, D1 and D5.

"Inmate Abuse Is Said Worse Than Reported." *Los Angeles Times*, 28 August 1997, A18.

"Inmate-Abuse Suit Filed by Missouri." *Los Angeles Times*, 26 August 1997, A15.

"Justice Dept. Reviews Claims of Airlines' Price Squeeze." *Los Angeles Times*, 12 February 1997, D1, D3.

"Lott Urges Expert Study of Inflation Adjustment." *Los Angeles Times*, 25 February 1997, A10.

"Merger of Baby Bells Clears Hurdle." *Los Angeles Times*, 25 April 1997, D10.

"Question: Is a Tax Cut What the Country Needs?" *Newsweek*, 16 July 1962.

"The Quack." *Omaha Evening World Herald*, 20 January 1950.

"Two Worlds: A Day-Long Debate." *New York Times*, 25 July 1959, 1, 3.

Ames, Edward. Letter to the Editor. *New York Times*, 26 May 1950.

Anderson, Richard B. "When Government Joins the Market Frenzy, We All Are at Risk." *Los Angeles Times*, 27 January 1997, B5.

Bernstein, Leonard. "San Diego Takes Step Toward Increasing Cable TV Competition." *Los Angeles Times*, 31 January 1991, B1, B5.

Bradsher, Keith. "A Split over Fed's Role." *New York Times*, 29 August 1994, D1 and D4.

Brooks, Nancy. "PacBell Hikes Coin-Call Rate." *Los Angeles Times*, 18 October 1997, D1, D3.

Cassidy, John. "The Decline of Economics." *The New Yorker*, 2 December 1996, 50–60.

Chen, Edwin. "White House Pushes Deregulation." *Los Angeles Times*, 31 January 1992, D4.

Clifford, Frank. "Approval of Smog Credits Is Suspended." *Los Angeles Times*, 28 August 1997, A26.

Colander, David. "Economists Don't Teach Students What They Need to Know." *Chronicle of Higher Education*, 13 November 1991, A52.

Cone, Marla. "Civil Rights Suit Attacks Trade in Pollution Credits." *Los Angeles Times*, 23 July 1997, A1, A19.

Coy, Peter. "Let's Not Take Feel-Good Economics Too Far." *Business Week*, 20 October 1997.

Dimmock, John O., to Michael A. Bernstein, 18 August 1988. In author's possession.

Douglass, Elizabeth. "Cox Customers Complain about Rate Hike." *San Diego Union-Tribune*, 18 November 1997, B1, B3.

Editorial. *New York Daily News*, 19 October 1949.

Egan, Timothy. "Oregon Lists Illnesses by Priority to See Who Gets Medicaid Care." *New York Times*, 3 May 1990, A1, A10.

Enthoven, Alain C., and Sara J. Singer. "Perspective on Medicare: 2010 Will Be Too Late to Reform." *Los Angeles Times*, 12 March 1997, B9.

Essoyan, Susan. "A Word of Caution on Pitfalls of Privatization." *Los Angeles Times*, 15 May 1997, A5.

Feldstein, Martin S., and Kathleen Feldstein. "Fed's Record Justifies Its Independence." *Los Angeles Times*, 8 November 1996, B9.

Galbraith, James K. "Fixing the Fed." *The Nation*, 2 June 1997, 5.

Ginsburg, Carl. "The Patient as Profit Center: Hospital Inc. Comes to Town." *The Nation*, 18 November 1996, 18–22.

Gordon, David M. "With Tyson's Appointment to Economic Chair, a Harvest of Sour Grapes." *Los Angeles Times*, 24 January 1993, D2.

Granelli, James S. "Judge Throws Out Keating Conviction in S&L Fraud Case." *Los Angeles Times*, 3 December 1996, A1, A30.

Harris, Lewis. "Poll Shows Public Doesn't Follow Economic Data." *Los Angeles Times*, 23 May 1995, D2.

Hein, W. Davis, to Michael A. Bernstein, 16 August 1988. In author's possession.

Henwood, Doug. "Toxic Banking." *The Nation*, 2 March 1992, 257.

Hook, Janet. "White House, in Shift, Endorses IRS Reform Bill." *Los Angeles Times*, 22 October 1997, A1, A6.

Hook, Janet, and Ralph Vartabedian. "House Gives Resounding OK to IRS Overhaul." *Los Angeles Times*, 6 November 1997, A1, A19.

Kaplan, Karen, and Thomas S. Mulligan. "Telephone Giants AT&T, SBC Discuss $50-Billion Merger." *Los Angeles Times*, 28 May 1997, A1, A18.

Kraul, Chris. "This Commodity's Smokin': Companies Trade Smog Credits on Online Exchange." *Los Angeles Times*, 30 April 1997, D2.

———. "PUC Opens State to Competition for Energy Customers." *Los Angeles Times*, 7 May 1997, A1, A22.

———. "The State's New Power Brokers." *Los Angeles Times*, 15 August 1997, A1, A21.

Kuttner, Robert. "Greenspan's Quarry Is Imaginary." *Los Angeles Times*, 30 March 1997, M5.

———. "Medical Firms Take a Scalpel to the FDA." *Los Angeles Times*, 31 August 1997, M5.

LaValle, Philip J. "City Suffers Costly Slash in Credit Ratings." *San Diego Union Tribune*, 6 December 1996, A1, A27.

Lesher, Dave. "Privatization Emerges as New Welfare Option." *Los Angeles Times*, 27 January 1997, A1, A16.

Lieberman, Trudy. "Social Insecurity: The Campaign to Take the System Private." *The Nation*, 27 January 1997, 11–17.

McChesney, Robert W. "Digital Highway Robbery." *The Nation*, 21 April 1997, 22–24.

Moffat, Susan. "Right Call? 10 Years Later, AT&T Split Favors Business." *Los Angeles Times*, 7 January 1992, D1, D7.

Montalbano, William D. "Bank of England Gets Rate-Setting Powers." *Los Angeles Times*, 7 May 1997, D1 and D4.

New York Times, 8 March 1997, 11, 52.

Olmos, David R. "Ruling Expands Medicare Patients' Rights." *Los Angeles Times*, 12 March 1997, D3.

———. "Survey Finds Wide Distrust of HMO Care." *Los Angeles Times*, 6 November 1997, A1, A18.

Parry, Robert. "Who Buys the Right?" *The Nation*, 18 November 1996, 5–6.

Passell, Peter. "The Tax-Rise Issue: Bush Rationale vs. Economists." *New York Times*, 10 May 1990, A14.

———. "More Advisers, Less Council?" *New York Times*, 17 December 1992, C2.

Peltz, James F. "Airline Mergers '90s-Style Might Stand a Better Chance This Time." *Los Angeles Times*, 5 December 1996, D1, D9.

Peterson, Jonathan. "'Clintonomics' to Guide Economy." *Los Angeles Times*, 6 November 1992, A28–A29.

———. "West Coast Economists Forge Axis with D.C." *Los Angeles Times*, 21 August 1994, D1 and D3.

Peterson, Jonathan, and Janet Hook. "Clinton Comes to Defense of Medicare Means Testing." *Los Angeles Times*, 23 July 1997, A16.

Phillips, Kevin. "(E)Con Artists." *Los Angeles Times*, 15 December 1996, M1.

Pine, Art. "Fed Hikes Interest Rates Moderately to Deter Inflation." *Los Angeles Times*, 26 March 1997, A1, A27.

―――. "It's Confirmed: Fed's Crystal Ball Is the Clearest of All." *Los Angeles Times*, 10 April 1997, A5.

―――. "Fed Putting a Crimp on Economy, Critics Say." *Los Angeles Times*, 11 August 1997, A1 and A12.

Risen, James. "Economists Watch in Quiet Fury." *Los Angeles Times*, 8 January 1993, A1 and A20.

――― "Clinton Kills Controversial Quayle Panel." *Los Angeles Times*, 23 January 1993, A14.

―――. "Panel Votes to Cut President's Economic Aides." *Los Angeles Times*, 7 December 1995, A17.

Risen, James, and Douglas Jehl. "Bush to Call for Freeze on New Regulations." *Los Angeles Times*, 21 January 1992, A1, A14.

Rosenblatt, Robert A. "U.S. Seeks Bank Levy to Aid FDIC." *Los Angeles Times*, 18 December 1990, A1, A28.

―――. "Congress OKs Rescue Plan for S&L Fund." *Los Angeles Times*, 1 October 1996, D2, D19.

―――. "Financial Laws May Face Major Overhaul." *Los Angeles Times*, 22 May 1997, D1, D13.

―――. "U.S. Jobless Rate Drops to 24-Year Low of 4.7%." *Los Angeles Times*, 8 November 1997, A1, A14.

Rossiter, Bernard D. "The Myth of an Independent Fed." *The Nation*, 31 December 1990, 837–38.

Rubin, Alissa J. "Panel to Propose 'Bill of Rights' for Health Care." *Los Angeles Times*, 19 November 1997, A1, A18.

Samuelson, Paul A. "A Warning to the Washington Expert." *New Republic*, 11 September 1945, 298.

Schwartz, Harry. "Soviet Economist Veers from Marx." *New York Times*, 6 November 1958, 6:1.

Shenk, David. "Money + Science = Ethics Problems on Campus." *The Nation* 268 (1999), 11–18.

Sherrill, Robert. "The Inflation of Alan Greenspan: The Real Story behind Clinton's Fateful Choice." *The Nation*, 11 March 1996, 11–15.

Shiver, Jube, Jr. "Justice Dept. Approves Merger of PacTel, SBC Communications." *Los Angeles Times*, 6 November 1996, D1, D9.

―――. "New Rules Will Let Pay Phone Rates Climb." *Los Angeles Times*, 9 November 1996, A1, A19.

―――. "Was Telecommunications Reform Just Another Act?" *Los Angeles Times*, 3 February 1997, D1, D6.

―――. "Deregulation of Phones Stirs Hornet's Nest." *Los Angeles Times*, 28 April 1997, D1, D4.

―――. "U.S. Probes Alleged Fixing of Bids for FCC Licenses." *Los Angeles Times*, 1 May 1997, D1, D5.

―――. "AT&T Rate Cut Clears Way for FCC Reforms." *Los Angeles Times*, 5 May 1997, D1, D2.

―――. "New Federal Rules Expected to Result in Pay Phone Hikes." *Los Angeles Times*, 7 October 1997, D1, D22.

Shiver, Jube, Jr. "MCI, WorldCom Agree to Record $37-Billion Merger." *Los Angeles Times*, 11 November 1997, A1, A15.

Shrage, Michael. "U.S. Should Privatize Economic Statistics." *Los Angeles Times*, 27 July 1997, D4.

Silverstein, Ken. "Privatizing War: How Affairs of State Are Outsourced to Corporations beyond Public Control." *The Nation*, 28 July/4 August 1997, 11–17.

Uchitelle, Louis. "An Appointment That Draws No Fire." *New York Times*, 7 January 1997, D3.

Unpublished Manuscripts

Barber, William. "The Divergent Fates of Two Strands of 'Institutionalist' Doctrine during the New Deal Years." Unpublished manuscript, Department of Economics, Wesleyan University, n.d.

Bernard, Paul R. "The Making of the Marginal Mind: Academic Economic Thought in the United States, 1860–1910." Ph.D. diss., University of Michigan, 1990.

Borden, William S. "Keynesianism and Military Spending: 1950–1969." Unpublished manuscript, Mathematica Policy Research, Inc., October 1991.

Church, Robert L. "The Development of the Social Sciences as Academic Disciplines at Harvard University, 1869–1900." Ph.D. diss., Harvard University, 1965.

Dennis, Michael Aaron. "A Change of State: The Political Cultures of Technical Practice at the MIT Instrumentation Laboratory and the Johns Hopkins University Applied Physics Laboratory, 1930–1945." Ph.D. diss., Johns Hopkins University, 1990.

Edelstein, Michael. "The Financing of America's 20th Century Wars." In *Cambridge Economic History of the United States*, vol. 3, ed. Stanley Engerman and Robert Gallman. New York: Cambridge University Press, forthcoming.

———. "The Size of U.S. Armed Forces during WWII." Unpublished manuscript, Department of Economics, Queens College, City University of New York, 1997.

Fritschner, Linda Marie. "The Rise and Fall of Home Economics." Ph.D. diss., University of California–Davis, 1973.

Garegnani, Pierangelo. "A Problem in the Theory of Distribution from Ricardo to Wicksell." Ph.D. diss., University of Cambridge, 1959.

Lears, Jackson. "The Ad Man and the Grand Inquisition: Intimacy, Publicity, and the Administrative State in America, 1880–1940." Paper presented at the Davis Center for Historical Studies, Princeton University, 30 March 1990.

McCune, Robert P. "Origins and Development of the National Science Foundation and Its Division of Social Sciences, 1945–1961." Ph.D. diss., Ball State University, 1971.

Myles, Jack C. "German Historicism and American Economics: A Study of the Influence of the German Historical School on American Economic Thought." Ph.D. diss., Princeton University, 1956.

Paredes, Maribel Castaneda. "Transforming the Airwaves into Property: The Rôle of Spectrum Management in the Development of Digital Television." Unpublished manuscript, Department of Communication, University of California–San Diego, 1997.

Rhees, David J. "The Chemists' Crusade: The Rise of an Industrial Science in Modern America, 1907–1922." Ph.D. diss., University of Pennsylvania, 1987.

Riddell, Thomas. "A Political Economy of the American War in Indo-China: Its Costs and Consequences." Ph.D. diss., American University, 1975.

Soffer, Jonathan. "The Moral Economy of Military Keynesianism." Paper presented at the annual meeting of the American Historical Association, January 1997, New York.

Solovey, Mark. "The Politics of Intellectual Identity and American Social Science, 1945–1970." Ph.D. diss., University of Wisconsin–Madison, 1996.

Vande Creek, Drew E. "The Construction of Economic Expertise in Philadelphia, 1890–1940." Ph.D. diss., University of Virginia, 1995.

Vargas, Joâo. "Blacks in the City of Angels' Dust." Ph.D. diss., University of California, San Diego, 1999.

Acknowledgments

THE OBLIGATIONS incurred during the many years I worked on this book are vast; it is a most pleasant duty to note them here. I am particularly indebted to several archivists and librarians who generously assisted me in my research: Dwight Miller, Shirley Sondergard, and Thomas Walsh at the Herbert Hoover Presidential Library; Paul McLaughlin, Mark Renovitch, and Nancy Snedeker at the Franklin Delano Roosevelt Library; Dennis Bilger, Raymond Geselbracht, Philip Lagerquist, and Elizabeth Safly at the Harry S. Truman Library; Dwight Strandberg and his staff at the Dwight D. Eisenhower Library; Susan Darntamont, June Payne, and Maura Porter at the John Fitzgerald Kennedy Library; Linda Hanson and Robert Tissing at the Lyndon Baines Johnson Library; Karlee Gifford at the Library of the Cowles Foundation for Research in Economics; the staff of the Manuscripts and Archives section of the Sterling Memorial Library at Yale University; R. Russell Maylone and his staff at the Northwestern University Library Special Collections; and John Hay and his staff of the Manuscript Division at the Library of Congress. James Galbraith, John McCole, and James Oakes and Deborah Bohr extended gracious hospitality to me during certain very important research field trips, which would have been neither possible nor successful without their generosity.

Financial support for the project was provided by the American Council of Learned Societies, the Herbert Hoover Presidential Library Association, the National Endowment for the Humanities, the National Humanities Center, the Andrew W. Mellon Foundation, and, at the University of California, San Diego, the Division of Arts and Humanities and the Academic Senate Committee on Research.

Various portions of the manuscript were presented before several professional audiences whose criticisms, suggestions, and encouragement played no small part in the book's realization. The venues included the economics departments at UCLA, UC-Riverside, the University of Massachusetts at Amherst, the New School for Social Research, Western Michigan University, and Yale University; the history departments at the University of Chicago, the Ohio State University, and the Washington University of St. Louis; the Washington D.C. Area Economic History Seminar; the Davis Center for Historical Studies at Princeton University; the Department of History Faculty Research Seminar and the Science Studies Program Colloquium at the University of California, San Diego; special conferences at the Université de Marne-La-Vallé (La Varenne, France), the University of Minnesota, and the University of Wisconsin at Madison; and annual meetings of the All-University of California Intercampus Group in Economic History, the American Historical Association, the Economic History Association, the European Social Science History Association, the Los Alamos International History Conference, the Policy History Conference, the History of

Political Economy Conference, the History of Science Society, the Organization of American Historians, the Social Science History Association, and the Southern Economic Association.

Many colleagues and friends read excerpts, working papers, and drafts of certain chapters; answered queries; provided compelling comments; and warned me off egregious errors. They were Susan Aaronson, Guy Alchon, Marcellus Andrews, Richard Attiyeh, Mansel Blackford, Amy Bridges, Alan Brinkley, Steven Cassedy, A. W. Coats, William Darrity, Susan Davis, Neil De Marchi, Michael Dennis, John Dower, Paul Drake, Robert Edelman, Michael Edelstein, Joseph Esherick, Robert Marc Friedman, Mary Furner, Daniel Fusfeld, James Galbraith, Robert Garnett, Gerald Geison, the late Eric Goldman, Mark Granovetter, Steven Hahn, Ellis Hawley, Robert Heilbroner, Carol Heim, Mark Hineline, Albert Hirschman, Michael Hogan, Allen Hunter, Aiko Ikeo, Sanford Jacoby, Stanley Katz, Alexander Keyssar, Rachel Klein, Jane Knodell, George Lipsitz, James Livingston, David Lloyd, Robert Locke, Lisa Lowe, David Luft, John Marino, Julie Matthaei, Arno Mayer, Timothy McDaniel, Perry Mehrling, Michael Meranze, Philip Mirowski, Allan Mitchell, Wendy Moffat, Michael Monteón, Mary Morgan, Alden Mosshammer, Chandra Mukerji, Jonathan Ocko, Alice O'Connor, Martha Olney, Naomi Oreskes, Dorinda Outram, Michael Parrish, Mark Perlman, Paul Pickowicz, Samuel Popkin, Robert Prasch, James Rauch, David Ringrose, Harriet Ritvo, Philip Roeder, Akos Rona-Tas, Dorothy Ross, Walt Rostow, Martin Rudwick, Harry Scheiber, the late Herbert Schiller, Andrew Scull, Ellen Seiter, Michael Sherry, Joel Sobel, Peter Solar, Paul Starr, David Stebenne, Tracy Strong, Barry Supple, Ross Thomson, Robert Tignor, Marc Trachtenberg, E. Roy Weintraub, Robert Westman, Yuval Yonay, Herbert York, and Charles Zappia. I would especially like to thank George Dantzig, Daniel Ellsberg, and Herbert Scarf for taking the time to share their personal recollections and insights with me.

Brandon Behlendorf, Jennifer Lu, Lori Matter, and Meri Stratton provided exemplary research assistance, but most extraordinary in this regard was Abraham Shragge III. Elton Hinshaw, Wilma St. John, and Mary Winer of the American Economic Association were particularly helpful with respect to the tracking and use of some photographs; Ellen Seiter generously assisted with their production, for which I am very grateful.

When I first began work with Princeton University Press, I was most ably assisted by Jack Repcheck. After his departure from Princeton, I had the additional great fortune to find Peter Dougherty as my editor. Peter and his colleagues have offered all the guidance and support for which an author could ever hope. Final preparation of the manuscript for publication was undertaken by two remarkable professionals—Charles Allen and Susan Ecklund.

Daniel Schiller read virtually every word of the manuscript in draft, marshaling in the process a sustained and breathtaking array of criticisms and suggestions. More than this, he was unstinting in his comradeship and good cheer, all of which kept my spirits up at crucial moments. Eric Van Young, a dear colleague and friend, also took a very special interest in this book and its author; his wisdom and decency saw me through.

Working on this book was sometimes a lonely and often an obsessive exercise. My daughters, Eleanor and Claire, learned this fact in some very hard ways. Thanking them for their understanding and forbearance seems hardly enough. I only hope that someday they will forgive me.

—M.A.B.

Index

AAAS (American Association for the Advancement of Science), 25

Abramowitz, Moses, 80

academic freedom debate, 31–34, 202n.8, 210n.64

Ackley, Gardner, 137, 150

activity analysis research, 94

Adams, Henry Carter, 22–23, 24, 33, 53

Addams, Jane, 24

Ad Hoc Committee on Graduate Training in Economics, 120

Adler, Felix, 24

advocacy role debate, 16

AEA (American Economic Association): academic freedom debate and, 31–34, 202n.8, 210n.64; annual meetings held by, 24–25; classification survey (1924) taken by, 58–59; commitment to historical research by, 16; debates stimulated by founding of, 15; economic expertise concerns by, 85–87; focus on national security state needs by, 104; international wartime alliance (W.W. I) by, 35–38; invited to work with Hoover's Commerce Department, 55; involvement with government work by, 34–38; membership/evolving focus of early, 16–20, 32; objectivity debate within, 31–34, 201n.4, 202n.7; partisanship accusations against, 31; petition to Hoover by, 1, 195n.2; postwar reconstruction contributions by, 87–88; post–W.W. I conference with AStA, 40; professional journal developed by, 20–24; regarding public policy role, 52; student curricula concerns of, 84–85, 120–21; on women members/household management study, 26–27; W.W. II interaction between government and, 84–86

AEA annual meetings: "national preparedness" focus of 1916, 53; organization of, 24–25; "War and Reconstruction" (1918), 37

AEA Executive Committee, 120, 121

AEA Executive Council: agenda for "emergency" matters by, 83–84; American Economic Review discussions by, 24; on Great Depression era government work, 75; national needs discussion (1940) by, 82–83; regarding needs of women members, 26

AER (American Economic Review): academic freedom issues and, 33–34; assessment of "polemical" articles by, 27–29, 206n.41; book review function of, 29–31; critics of, 31; establishing publication standards for, 22–24; free post–W.W. II distribution of, 87; influence of cold war on, 106; origins of, 21–22; policy excluding current economic events from, 24; read by German POWs, 232n.37; student curricula discussed in, 84

aggregate productivity politics (1960s), 118–19

Agricultural Adjustment Administration, 113

agricultural economics: government interventionist strategies and, 212n.7; New Deal use of, 226n.9; student curricula training on, 231n.32; trade interests and, 59–60, 208n.54

AHEA (American Home Economics Association), 26, 205n.35

Airline Deregulation Act (1978), 174

Air Quality Management District (Los Angeles), 179

American Association for Labor Legislation, 43

American Bankers Association, 55

American Chemical Society, 20

American economic practitioners: AEA annual meeting facilitating intergenerational reproduction of, 25–26; cold war monitoring role by, 105–8; cooperation between Soviet and, 185–88; current state of, 192–94; impact of AER publication policy on, 29; impact of cold war research on prestige of, 103–5; impact on political affairs by, 3–4; mutual aggrandizement between government and, 54–55; New Deal involvement of, 76; PPBS, 98–99; professional fulfillment project of, 15–16; Republican Party facilitation of using, 52, 53; student curricula concerns by, 84–85. See also economic professional expertise

American economics: agricultural, 59–60, 208n.54, 212n.7, 226n.9, 231n.32; changing analytical framework of 1970s, 157–68; cold war military application of, 93–100; current state of, 192–94; debate over public policy role by, 15–16; economic statistic privatization and, 181–82, 183; emergence as academic discipline, 3–4; emergence of "feminist," 286n.74; impact of cold war

American economics (*cont.*)
anticommunism on, 105–8; impact of Great Depression on, 75–77; impact of prosperity (1950s/1960s) on, 117–19; institutional school of, 44–46, 44–48, 215n.21, 216n.24; international context of 1960s, 132–33; interwar challenges for, 40–48; market-driven solutions adopted by, 179–80; Marxist, 123–25, 126, 260n.20; New Left, 123–25, 126, 261n.28, 262n.32; performance during Great Depression by, 64; relations between government and early, 4, 34–38; shaped by W.W. II interactions, 88–90; shaped by W.W. I work, 34–38, 39, 48–52; shaping of authoritative community of, 38–39; study of household management excluded by, 26–27; subfield classifications of, 83; supply-side, 147, 161, 163–67, 165, 282n.44. *See also* economic research; neoclassical theorists; New Economics
American economy: "dollar drain" (1960s) on, 267n.56; during Great Depression, 60–64, 72–78, 79; impact of supply-side economics on, 167; impact of Vietnam War on, 149–54, 188; during interwar period, 40–52, 59–60, 78–79; during Johnson administration, 149–56; macroeconomic management of postwar, 118; New Frontier proposed policies for 1960s, 131–39; political culture (late 20th century) and, 162–63; post–W.W. II prosperity of, 91–92; professional economics and 1950s/1960s prosperity of, 117–19; recession during Carter administration, 189; rising living standards of post–W.W. II, 266n.48; rising oil prices and, 154–55, 158; three recessions during 1950s, 130–31; during W.W. I, 50–51. *See also* inflation; United States
American Federation of Labor, 55
American Historical Association, 17, 20, 31
American Library Association, 87
American Medical Association, 20
American political culture: balance between Progressivism/populism in, 41; liberalism of, 171–72; McCarthyism, 105–8, 120, 121, 127; Progressive Era, 1; Progressivism, 2–4, 12–13; reaction/resentment of late 20th century, 162–63. *See also* government; United States
American Political Science Association, 21, 37
American Sociological Association, 21, 37
American universities: cold war research funding to, 244n.35; concerns on economic student curricula in, 84–85; fiscal dependence on outside research funding by, 102, 103; left-wing graduate programs in current, 261n.28; Marxism excluded from student cur-
ricula, 122–23, 260n.20; postwar efforts to standardize economic curricula in, 119–26, 260n.22
Annals of the American Academy of Political and Social Science, 21
Antitrust Division of the Department of Justice, 174
APSA (American Political Science Association), 32
Arrow, Kenneth, 97
Arthur, Chester, 48
ASA (American Sociological Association), 32
AStA (American Statistical Association), 35, 40, 55
AT&T (American Telephone and Telegraph Corporation), 174, 177
AT&T antitrust decision, 178

Babson, Roger, 61
Baker, Newton, 51
balanced budget amendment: economists' opposition to, 171; National Governors Association endorsement of, 170
Bancroft, George, 19
banking industry: deregulation of, 174–76, 283n.60; Regulation Q rule over, 175
Baran, Paul, 80
Bardin, James, 28
Barnett, George, 36
Bell, James Washington, 104, 106, 121
Bemis, Edward, 32
Bennett, John, 29
Bergson, Abram, 80
Berle, Adolph, 76
Berlin blockade crisis, 111, 135, 139
Berlin Wall, 269n.66
Bernal, John Desmond, 1
Bernhard, Carl Gustav, 185
Berridge, William, 56
Board (later Office) of Economic Warfare, 80
Board of Governors, Federal Reserve System: attuned to banking industry, 136; membership and appointments to, 270n.69; monetarist policy formula used by, 189; patronage appointments to, 49. *See also* Federal Reserve System (Fed)
Boston Chamber of Commerce, 43
Bretton Woods agreement (1944), 92, 118, 132, 158, 234n.3
Britt, Steuart Henderson, 84
Brookings Institution, 42, 48
Brookings, Robert S., 42
Brown, Rev. Edwin, 61

Bureau of Business Research (Harvard University), 58
Burke, Edmund, 185, 188
Burns, Arthur, 105, 107, 116, 126–27, 129, 130, 143p, 263 nn.35 and 36
Bush, George, 167, 174
Business Cycle Committee, 57
business cycles: Conference on Unemployment report on, 56–57; NBER work on, 43, 46–47, 56, 57, 78; stabilization policy techniques and, 118; statistical reporting of, 55
Business Cycles and Unemployment (NBER), 56
Business Week magazine, 173

Calhoun, A. W., 30
California Proposition 13 (1978), 163, 281n.38
Campbell, Robert, 186
Cannan, Edwin, 53
Capital (Marx), 193
Carnegie Corporation, 42, 56
Carnegie Foundation, 58
Carr-Saunders, A. P., 10
Carter administration, 165, 174, 175, 189
Carter, Jimmy, 163, 189
Carver, Thomas N., 17, 24, 28, 33, 35, 52
CEA (Council of Economic Advisers): continued science vs. political struggle in, 116–17; emergency economic stabilization discussions by, 104–5; evolution during Eisenhower administration of, 126–30; growing political partisanship (1960s) of, 128–29; impact of 1952 election on, 116; Kennedy administration and, 131–39, 266n.53, 270n.72; Nourse-Keyserling struggle within, 109–14, 126, 128, 251n.58, 253n.64; optimism of 1965 report by, 118; origins and developing focus of, 108–11; public policy contributions of, 92–93; recruitment practices and female members of, 271n.74; security checks required by, 107, 247n.45; struggles between Federal Reserve System and, 133, 136, 137, 188–90, 268n.59, 271n.75; support of anti-inflation tax increase (1967) by, 150; unemployment plan (1961) by, 133–34
Central Bureau of Planning and Statistics, 40
Chamber of Commerce (U.S.), 56
Chamberlain, Neville, 79
Churchman, C. West, 186
CIA (Central Intelligence Agency), 104
Civil Aeronautics Administration, 174, 177
civil rights movement, 139, 248n.46
Civil Service Commission, 36
Clark, John, 110

Clark, John Bates, 36
Clark, John Maurice, 76, 85
classical monetary theory, 159–60
Classification Act (1923), 58–59, 82
Clinton administration, 190
Clinton, William, 167, 174, 190
cold war: civil rights movement and, 248n.46; economic statecraft during, 185, 187, 194; government use of social scientists during, 98; impact on American economists of, 105–8; Keynesianism foundations in, 108; military application of economic research during, 93–105; military-industrial research projects during, 244n.34; research funding of universities during, 244n.35; U.S. national security and, 93–94
Combined Production and Resources Board, 80
Combined Shipping Adjustment Board, 81, 82, 95
Commission of Inquiry on Public Service Personnel, 75
Committee on Graduate Training in Economics, 85
Committee on Undergraduate Teaching (AEA), 85
Commons, John R., 36, 44, 51, 56
Commonwealth Fund, 42, 56
communism expertise principle of science, 9
competition: deregulated markets stifling, 180–81; monopolistic and oligopolistic, 237n.13; tariffs protecting agricultural, 59
Conference on Unemployment, 56–57
Consensus Report (AEA), 86
consumption, post–W.W. II U.S., 91–92
Coolidge, Calvin, 52, 60
Council on Competitiveness, 174
Council on the Defense Mobilization Board, 105
Council of Economic Advisers. *See* CEA (Council of Economic Advisers)
Council on Foreign Relations, 43
Cowles Commission for Research in Economics, 95
Cowles Conference (Chicago, 1949), 95, 98
Cowles Foundation for Research in Economics, 82
Cunningham, Theodora B., 26
Currie, Lauchlin, 76

Davenport, H. J., 18
Davis, Joseph, 59
Dawes Commission, 59
Debreu, Gerard, 97
Defense Plant Corporation, 80

"Defense Policy Seminars" (RAND Corporation), 99
defense production conversion (W.W. II), 80–82
deficit spending: impact of Kennedy tax cut on, 148; New Economics on budget, 112; New Frontier on economic growth and, 133–34; proposed balanced budget amendment and, 170, 171; during Reagan administration, 166–67. *See also* national debt
Deibler, Frederick, 73
Democratic Party: civil rights movement and, 139; "flip-flop" of, 256n.3; Johnson's agenda to ensure status of, 148; power struggle (early 1950s) in, 115; Reagan tax cut and, 169
Depository Institutions Deregulation and Monetary Control Act (Diddymac) [1980], 175
deregulation: banking and brokerage, 174–76, 283n.60; bipartisan origins of, 174; of economic statistics, 181–82, 183; major sector outcomes of, 284n.63; market competition stifled by, 180–81; S&Ls, 176–77; as social reform instrument, 180; of telecommunications sector, 177–78, 286n.71. *See also* privatization
Despres, Emile, 80
Dewey, Davis R., 18, 19, 23, 24, 26, 27, 29, 31, 33, 65p, 89
Dillon, Douglas, 133, 135, 136
direct costs, 81
disinterestedness principle of science, 9
Division of Planning and Statistics (U.S. Shipping Board), 44
"Dixiecrat" rebellion (1948), 115
DOA (U.S. Department of Agriculture), 34
DOD (U.S. Department of Defense), 96, 97
Douglas, Paul H., 30, 61, 87
Duesenberry, James S., 152
Dunayevskaya, Raya, 106

economic professional expertise: AEA concerns with, 85–87; calls for privatization of, 181–82; cold war focus of, 107–8; Commerce Department use of, 56–58; contributions of historical scholarship to, 11–14; four central principles of, 9; functionalist approach to, 10; government W.W. I use of, 34–38, 39, 48–52; during Great Depression, 62–64, 73–74; as historical problem, 7, 13–14; internalist/externalist learning and, 9–10; national security state and, 99–100; Progressivism in context of, 12–13; public policy advising (1950) development and, 126–30; understanding origins of, 8–9, 38–39; during W.W. II, 84–86, 228n.16. *See also* American economic practitioners; expert knowledge

Economic Recovery Tax Act (1981), 164
Economic Report of the President (CEA), 108
economic research: activity analysis, 94; AEA commitment to historical, 16; on business cycles/unemployment, 56, 57, 78; cold war military support/application of, 93–105; Commerce Department agenda on, 56–58, 60; fiscal dependence of universities on outside, 102, 103; game theory used in, 96–97, 98, 103, 236n.11, 237n.12; Hoover's promotion of, 60; institutional survey research legacy to, 216n.24; linear programming/operations research used in, 94, 95–96, 103, 239n.19, 240n.20; privately funded policy-oriented, 42–48; privileged position/funding advantages of, 102; theory used in national security, 94–95
"The Economic Significance of Degeneracy among the Negroes" (Bardin), 28
economic statistics: Commerce Department unemployment (1930), 61–62; information revolution and availability of, 191–92; NBER unemployment, 62; privatization of, 181–82, 183
economic student curricula: AEA concerns with quality of, 84–85, 120–21; on agricultural economics, 231n.32; current programs with left-wing, 261n.28; efforts to exclude Marxism from, 122–23, 260n.20; New Left vs. neoclassical, 123–25; post–W.W. II efforts to standardize, 119–26, 260n.22
economic subfield classifications, 83
economic theory: authority/legitimacy of cold war, 96; game theory used in, 96–97, 98, 103, 236n.11, 237n.12; institutional, 44–48, 215n.21, 216n.24; national security research using, 94–95; new classical, 159–61, 169; PPBS adherence to neoclassical, 99; rational expectations, 160, 180, 279n.31. *See also* Keynesianism; neoclassical theorists
"Economists' Statement Opposing the Balanced Budget Amendment" (1997), 171
economy. *See* American economy
Edgeworth, Francis, 24
Eisenhower administration: American economics and prosperity of, 117–19; Democratic Party power struggle during, 115; evolution of public policy advising during, 126–30; three recessions during, 130–31
Eisenhower, Dwight, 7, 115, 126, 257n.5
Ely, Richard T., 15, 22, 32, 38
Emergency Banking Act (1933), 63
Employment Act (1946), 108, 112, 114, 116, 128, 129, 249n.49
evolution of learning notions, 9–10

expert knowledge: competing belief systems in, 10; historical scholarship understanding of, 11–12; on internalist/externalist learning and, 9–10; principles of, 9; Progressivism in context of, 12–13. *See also* economic professional expertise
Ezekiel, Mordecai, 76

Fair Deal (Truman administration), 119
Farnam, Henry, 30
FCC (Federal Communication Commission), 177–78
FDA (Food and Drug Administration, 178
FDIC (Federal Deposit Insurance Corporation), 175
Federal Home Loan Bank Board, 176
Federal Reserve System (Fed): as arbiter of public policy, 188–91, 289n.15; business cycle report promoted by, 56; concerns with Kennedy administration by, 134, 135; independent of, 136; inflation strategies by, 189–90, 275n.7; limited economists role in, 49; monetary stringency (1970s) of, 163; structure/organization of, 270n.69; struggles between CEA and, 133, 136, 137, 188–90, 268n.59, 271n.75. *See also* Board of Governors
Federated Farm Bureau, 55
"feel-good economics," 173
"feminist economics," 286n.74
Fetter, Frank, 21–22, 25, 28, 29, 30, 33
"fiscalism in reverse" measures, 159
Fisher, Irving: accomplishments/contributions of, 200n.1; correspondence between Hoover and, 222n.60; correspondence between Roosevelt and, 226n.10; Hoover's confidence in, 62; on need to increase economists' influence, 15, 20, 21, 38; promoting AEA economic research, 37; relationship between FDR and, 77; social scientific learning promoted by, 90; Tariff Commission appointment of, 50
Fisher, Willard, 33
Flanders, Ralph, 111
Flemming, Arthur, 104, 105
Food Research Institute (Stanford University), 60
Ford administration, 174
Ford, Gerald, 190
Foreign and Domestic Commerce Bureau (Dept. of Commerce), 54
Foreign Economic Administration, 80
Free Speech Movement, 262n.33
Friedman, Milton, 128, 138, 159
FSLIC (Federal Savings and Loan Insurance Corporation), 175

Full Employment and Stabilization Act (1946), 90. *See also* unemployment
functionalist approach to professionalism, 10

Galbraith, John Kenneth, 76, 124
game theory, 96–97, 98, 103, 236n.11, 237n.12
Garn-St. Germain Bill (1982), 176
Gay, Edwin, 42, 43–44, 56, 66p
Gayer, Arthur, 76
General Theory (Keynes), 78
General Theory of Employment, Interest, and Money, The (Keynes), 8, 159
German National Socialism, 124
Germany: AEA rebuilding of guild in postwar, 87; W.W. II invasion by, 83, 187
GI Bill (Servicemens' Readjustment Act of 1944), 92
Gideonse, Harry, 86
Gilbert, Richard, 76
Glass, Carter, 49
Glass-Steagall Act (1933), 176
gold standard: economists' petition to FDR on, 73, 224n.2; Hoover's refusal to change, 63
Gonzalez, Henry B., 190
Gordon, Kermit, 131, 132, 134
Gordon, Robert A., 107
government: American economics/W.W. I and, 34–38, 48; cold war economic research funding by, 98, 105; defense production conversion issues for, 80–82; "demonstration effect" of economists' work for, 79; dismantling of Keynesian apparatus in, 173–74; economic community shaped by relation with, 4; economics and national security focus of, 93–100; mutual aggrandization between economists and, 54–55; reorganization of civil service, 58–59; under utilized economic expertise by, 48–49; W.W. II interaction between AEA and, 84–86. *See also* American political culture; public policy; United States Department of Commerce
Graham, Frank, 86
Gray, John, 25, 35
Great Depression: economic devastation during, 73; economic expertise used during, 62–64, 73–74; events prior to, 221n.59; FDR as public hero of, 63, 64; Hoover's responses to, 60–64; impact on economic profession by, 75–77; Keynes' fiscal spending advocated during, 78; unemployment reporting during, 61–62; W.W. II contribution to ending, 74–75, 79
Great Society programs, 151, 153–54, 163
Great War. See World War I
Greenspan, Alan, 190

Hadley, Arthur, 49
Hamilton, Alexander, 52
Hamilton, Walton, 37
Hansen, Alvin, 76
Harding, Warren, 52, 54
Harriman, Averell, 115
Harrington, Michael, 138
Hart, Albert Gaylord, 76
Hart, Thomas C., 100
Harvard University Business School, 43, 56
Hawley, Willis, 1
Hawtrey, Ralph G., 30
Heisenberg, Werner, 160
Heller, Walter, 131, 132, 133, 136, 139, 144p,
    148, 168
Hicks, John R., 78
historical scholarship: AEA commitment to pro-
    moting, 16; contributions to professional ex-
    pertise by, 11–14; on institutional school of
    economics, 215n.21; on military application
    of economics, 240n.20; professional expertise
    difficulties for, 7, 13–14; understanding of ex-
    pert knowledge in, 11–12
Hitch, Charles, 72p, 98
Hitler, Adolph, 79, 87
HMO (health maintenance organization), 178
Hoadley, Horace, 19
Ho Chi Minh, 111
Hollander, Jacob, 23
Holmes, Clyde, 83
Homan, Paul T., 106
Hoover, Calvin Bryce, 80
Hoover, Herbert: accomplishments of, 69p; on
    availability of economic information, 183;
    correspondence between Fisher and, 222n.60;
    Department of Commerce transformed by,
    54–57, 77; economic research promoted by,
    60; economics professional respected by, 52;
    economists' petition to, 1, 195n.2; education/
    professional background of, 53–54; expertise
    to Dawes Commission promoted by, 59; his-
    toric judgment on, 219n.41; McNary-Haugen
    Act opposition by, 59, 60; NBER engaged for
    research by, 43; responses to Great Depres-
    sion by, 60–64; Smoot-Hawley tariff signed
    by, 2; unemployment research promoted by,
    55–56, 222n.60; on W.W. I transportation
    problems, 51
Hotchkiss, Willard, 29
Houston, David F., 34, 35
Hughes, Charles Evans, 58
Hunt, Edward Eyre, 56–57
Hurley, Edward N., 50

IE (Institute of Economics), 42, 109
IGR (Institute for Government Research), 42
immigration restriction, 52–53
incommensurability theorem, 216n.22
Industrial Codes of the National Recovery Ad-
    ministration, 76
inflation: call for private research on, 182; Car-
    ter administration, 165; CEA support of tax
    increase combating, 150; Fed's strategies for
    reducing, 189–90, 275n.7; "fiscalism in re-
    verse" measures combating, 159; impact of
    rising oil prices (1973) on, 154–55, 172; mis-
    ery index of, 158; Vietnam War and, 149–54;
    during W.W. I, 50–51. See also American
    economy
Institute of Economics (later Brookings Institu-
    tion), 42, 109
Institute for Government Research, 54
institutional school of economics: compared to
    neoclassical, 47–48; described, 44–46; schol-
    arship on, 215n.21; survey research legacy
    of, 216n.24
interest rates: just prior to deregulation, 175;
    "pump priming" through flexible, 133
International Bank for Reconstruction and De-
    velopment (World Bank), 92
International Economic Conference (1927), 59
interwar period: American economics chal-
    lenges during, 40–48; government increased
    use of expertise during, 48–52; Hoover's
    "waste elimination" initiatives during,
    220n.51; national accounts system developed
    during, 78–79; trade protectionism during,
    59–60. See also Great Depression
investment (post–W.W. II), 91

Jackson, Andrew, 131
Jacoby, Neil, 116, 129, 130, 150
JEC (Joint Economic Committee), 110
Jeffords, James, 178
Johnson administration: Great Society programs
    of, 151, 153–54, 163; national security
    agenda inherited by, 139–40; New Econom-
    ics response to inflation during, 149–56; Viet-
    nam deployment of troops by, 149–50; War
    on Poverty program of, 139, 148, 171
Johnson, Lyndon, 118, 119, 139, 151
Joint Committee, 32–33
Journal of Political Economy, 21

Kantorovich, Leonid V., 185–87, 194
Kaysen, Carl, 80
Kefauver, Estes, 115

Kennedy administration: CEA activism during, 131–39, 266n.54, 270n.72; national security agenda inherited by, 139–40; New Economics used by, 131–39, 149; New Frontier initiative of, 131, 133, 136, 162, 163; struggle between Fed independence and, 136–37; tax cut during, 137–38, 139, 149
Kennedy, John F., 98, 128, 130–31, 132, 134, 137
Kerr, Clark, 102
Keynesianism: anti-Keynesian rhetoric against, 172–73, 277n.17, 282n.44; centralized economic intervention using, 109; cold war foundations of, 108; Congress revolt against "New Deal liberalism" and, 154; contributions to economic thought by, 118; diminished confidence in, 158–61, 170; dismantling government apparatus using, 173–74; macroeconomic framework using, 78; neoclassical critique by, 233n.41; new classical economics challenge to, 159–61; optimism and collapse of, 8–9; Reaganomics and, 167–68; W.W. II relevance of, 85
Keynesian Revolution, The (Klein), 106
Keynes, John Maynard: attacks on neoclassical doctrine by, 74, 132; contributions of, 274n.1; on economic professional expertise, 8, 148; The General Theory of Employment, Interest, and Money by, 8, 159; "general theory" of, 8, 159, 165; Keynesian revolution by, 108; partisanship of, 192; on saving levels and investment, 169
Keyserling, Leon: attacks against, 254n.69; manifesto on direct federal spending by, 134; struggle between Nourse and, 110, 112–14, 116, 117, 126, 251n.58; support given to, 255n.70
Khrushchev, Nikita, 107
Kilgore, Harley M., 100
Kindleberger, Charles, 80
Kinley, David, 31
Kinley, Davis, 23
"Kitchen Debate" (Khrushchev-Nixon), 107, 248n.47
Klein, Julius, 54
Klein, Lawrence R., 106
Knight, Frank, 47
Koopmans, Tjalling C., 47, 71p, 81, 82, 91, 95, 185–87, 188, 194, 234n.1
Korean War, 92, 104, 111, 120
Koren, John, 35
Kuhn, Thomas, 9, 10
Kuznets, Simon, 70p, 78, 79, 82

Laffer, Arthur, 147p, 165
Laffer curve, 165–66
laissez-nous-faire, 173
Lamont, Robert P., 78
Leontief, Wassily, 80
LeRossignol, James, 36
linear programming/operations research, 94, 95–96, 103, 239n.19, 240n.20
Lowell, A. Lawrence, 54
Lubin, Isador, 76
Lusitania sinking (W.W. I), 36

McAdoo, William Gibbs, 48, 49, 50, 51, 54
McCarthyism, 105–8, 120, 121, 127
McGovern, George, 189
McNamara, Robert, 98
McNary-Haugen bill, 59–60
macroeconomic management: deteriorated growth rates of 1970s, 158; Kennedy administration commitment to, 132; Keynesianism framework for, 78; new classical, 159–60; of post–W.W. II, 118
Management Science, 186–87
Mankiw, N. Gregory, 172
manufacturing employment, 157
market-driven solutions, 179–80
Marshall, Alfred, 192
Marshall Plan, 92, 245n.36
Martin, William McChesney, 133, 135, 136, 137, 189
Marxism: An Autopsy, 87
Marxist economists, 123–25, 126, 260n.20
Marx, Karl, 123, 192
Mason, Edward S., 80
Massachusetts Citizens' Committee, 43
Means, Gardiner C., 30, 76
"measurable motives" approach, 46
medical care privatization, 178–79
Medicare, 178–79
Meech, Stuart Putnam, 63
Meeker, Royal, 25
Merton, Robert, 9
middle class progressivism, 13
military application: during cold war, 93–100; scholarship on, 240n.20; during W.W. II, 84–86, 228n.16
Miller, Adolph C., 56
Mill, John Stuart, 192
Mills, Wilbur, 154
misery index, 158
Mitchell, Wesley: accomplishments of, 67p; business cycle research role by, 56, 57; Department of Commerce work by, 54, 55; institutionalism promoted by, 44, 45, 46, 47;

Mitchell, Wesley (*cont.*)
   NBER founded by, 42, 43; reputation of, 78;
     on revival of economic vitality, 37
Monetary and Financial Conference of UN
   (1944), 92
Morgenstern, Oskar, 96, 97
Morgenthau, Henry, 76
Morse, Chandler, 80

NAFTA (North American Free Trade
   Agreement), 287n.77
NAIRU (non-accelerating inflation-rate of un-
   employment), 157
Nathan, Robert R., 76, 79, 82
national debt: attacks against, 170–71; World
   War II, 171, 252n.63. *See also* deficit spend-
   ing
National Governors Association, 170
National One Cent Letter Postage Association,
   32
National Recovery Administration, 77
National Resources Planning Board, 83
National Retail Farm Implement Dealers, 112
National Roster of Scientific and Specialized
   Personnel, 83, 84
National Security Act (1947), 252n.61
national security state: American economics mo-
   bilization and, 105–8; cold war and emerg-
   ing, 93–94; game theory used for, 96–97, 98;
   Kennedy/Johnson administrations and, 139–
   40; professionalization of economics and,
   99–100, 103–5; theoretical economic research on behalf of, 94–105; during Truman
   administration, 111–14. *See also* United
   States
Nation (publication), 31
NATO (North Atlantic Treaty Organization),
   104, 187
NBER (National Bureau of Economic Research): accomplishments of, 44, 54, 55; origins of, 42; unemployment/business cycle research by, 43, 46–47, 56, 57, 78;
   unemployment data retained through, 62
Nearing, Scott, 33, 38, 207n.52
NEC (National Economic Council), 190
neoclassical theorists: on applicability to wartime economy, 233n.44; "Cambridge criticisms" of, 125; classical origins of, 201n.5;
   compared to institutional approach, 47–48;
   deployment of, 193; described, 46–47;
   Keynes' critique, 233n.41; New Left attacks
   against, 123–26; PPBS use of, 99; on rational
   choice problems, 81–82; W.W. II application
   of price theory by, 81

new classical economics: emergence of, 159–
   61; supply side economics manifestation of,
   161; tax cut "Holy Grail" of, 169
New Deal (1930s): agricultural economics used
   in, 226n.9; American Jewry linked to,
   264n.39; CEA Trojan horse symbolism of,
   112; circumstances animating, 74; disagreement within recovery policies of, 75–76;
   economists involved in, 76; Great Depression
   proliferation of programs, 75; notion of two,
   226n.8; politicized nature of spending policy
   of, 223n.66; public perception vs. reality of,
   64, 77
New Economics: American military expansion
   focus of, 108–9; benefits/costs of policy
   focus of, 117; born of cold war, 108; on budget deficits, 112; classical monetary theory
   counterpart to, 159–61; declining influence
   of, 159–62, 167–68; distributive issues side-
   stepped by, 257n.9; influence on Kennedy by,
   135; Kennedy administration use of, 131–39,
   149; response to Johnson administration inflation by, 149–56; statecraft establishment
   of, 125–26; War on Poverty and, 139, 148
New Federalism (Nixon administration), 119
"New Freedom" platform (Wilson administra-
   tion), 52
New Frontier (Kennedy administration), 131,
   133, 136, 162, 163
New Left economics, 123–25, 126, 261n.28,
   262n.32
New School for Social Research, 44
New York Evening Post, 43
New York Times, 1, 185
Nixon, Richard, 107, 119, 129, 131, 153, 163,
   168, 188
Noble Memorial Prize, 185, 187, 188, 234n.1
Non-Aggression Pact between Germany and the
   Soviet Union (1939), 121
Nourse, Edwin G., 109–11, 112, 116, 117, 126,
   141p, 152, 251n.58
Noyes, Charles, 86
NRSSP (National Roster of Scientific and Spe-
   cialized Personnel), 120
NSC 68 (National Security Council Memoran-
   dum No. 68), 111
NSF (National Science Foundation), 100, 101,
   243n.30

objectivity role debate (AEA), 16
OECD (Organization for Cooperation and Development), 281n.42, 283n.56
OEO (Office of Economic Opportunity), 153
"off-budget financing," 62

Office for Coordination of National Defense Purchases, 80
Office of Defense Mobilization, 104
Office of Defense Transportation, 80
Office of Merchant Ship Control, 80
Office of Naval Research, 97, 239n.17
Office of Price Administration, 80
Office of Thrift Supervision, 176
Oikonomika (household management), 26
oil market: American economy weakened by 1970s, 157–58; increased prices (1970s) of OPEC, 154–55, 158
Okun, Arthur M., 115, 117, 134, 146p, 153, 168, 256n.1, 268n.64
"Okun's law," 134
OPEC price increases (1970s), 154–55, 158, 172
Open Market Committee (Fed), 189
opportunity costs, 81
organized skepticism principle, 9
OSRD (Office of Scientific Research and Development), 100
OSS (Office of Strategic Services), 80
Owen-Glass Bill, 49

Parry, C. E., 25
Parsons, Talcott, 9
Patten, Simon N., 17
Pax Americana (1950s), 87
Pearl Harbor attack, 80
People's Republic of China, 93, 102, 104
Perrin, John, 36, 39
Personnel Classification Board (U.S. Civil Service Commission), 59
Persons, Warren, 55
Petroleum Administration for War, 80
Phelps, Edward, 104, 105
Phillips, A. William, 155–56
Phillips curve, 156, 157, 158
Pigou, Arthur C., 40, 41
Plehn, Carl, 22
Polanyi, Karl, 123
policy ineffectiveness proposition, 160
Political Science Association, 17
Political Science Quarterly, 21
populism, balance between Progressivism and, 41
positivist approach, 8, 9
post–W.W. II era: AEA on reentry to civilian life during, 120; economic reconstruction of, 87–88; ending prosperity (1970) of, 157–59; evolution of professional policy advising during, 126–30; standardization of economic cur-

ricula efforts during, 119–26. *See also* national security state
Powell, Raymond, 186
PPBS (Planning-Programming-Budgeting System), 98–99, 154
President's Conference on Unemployment, 56
Price Section of the War Industries Board, 44
Principles of Political Economy (Mill), 193
Principles of Political Economy and Taxation (Ricardo), 193
Pritchett, Henry, 56
privatization: conceptual/historical assessment of, 211n.4; of economic statistics, 181–82, 183; of medical care delivery, 178–79; opportunity costs of, 180; productivity losses due to, 181; proponents of, 174. *See also* deregulation
professional expertise. *See* economic professional expertise
professional organizations journals, 21–22
Program for Economic Recovery (1981), 164, 166, 281n.40
Progressive Era: emergence of economics as academic discipline during, 3–4; history of middle class and, 13; professional authority/expert knowledge context of, 12–13; vast literature on, 195n.6, 199n.14; volatile political climate during, 2
Project RAND, 97–98
Proxmire, William, 138, 168
Public Ownership (Thompson), 30
public policy: AEA regarding role in, 52; benefits/costs of New Economics focus on, 117; CEA contributions to, 92–93; debate over role of economics in, 16–17; economists on rise and fall of regimes of, 8; economists' support of immigration restriction, 52–53; Eisenhower's concerns over future of, 7; evolution of professional advising (1950s) of, 126–30; market-based practice and, 178–80; positivist approach to, 8; private research on economics and, 42–48; privatization of economic statistics as, 181–82, 183; resurgence of Fed as arbiter of, 188–91; supporting aggregate productivity (1960s), 118–19; "Troika" and "Quadriad" formulation of, 137, 272n.76. *See also* government; United States
Putnam, Bertha Haven, 31

"Quadriad" policy formulation, 137, 272n.76
Quarterly Journal of Economics, 21
Quayle, Dan, 174
Quesnay, François, 192

RAND Corporation, 95, 97–98, 99, 105
rational choice problems, 81–82
rational expectations theory, 160, 180, 279n.31
Reagan administration: deficit spending of, 166–67; deregulation during, 174, 175–76; federal program cuts (Reaganomics) by, 164–65, 167–68; Program for Economic Recovery (1981) of, 164, 166, 281n.40; supply-side economics of, 163–64; tax cut by, 164–66, 169–70
Reaganomics, 164–65, 167–68
Reagan, Ronald, 163, 165, 176, 189, 190
Recent Economic Changes (Commerce Department), 60
Reconstruction Finance Corporation, 61, 62
Regulation Q rule, 175
Reich, Robert, 190
Reinhardt, Uwe, 178
"Report of the Business Cycle Committee," 56
"Report on Wartime Changes in Economics Curriculum" (AEA), 85
Republican Party: agenda following 1952 election by, 115–16; CEA involvement with, 128–29; facilitating increased use of economists, 52, 53; "flip-flop" of, 256n.3; Reagan tax cut and, 169
Research and Analysis Branch (OSS), 80
Research Committee on Social Trends, 44
Revenue Act (1964), 136
Review of Economics and Statistics, 47
Ricardo, David, 192
Robinson, Henry M., 59
Robinson, Joan, 125
Rockefeller Foundation, 85, 101, 120
Roosa, Robert, 133, 135
Roosevelt administration, 76–77. See also New Deal (1930s)
Roosevelt, Franklin Delano, 63, 64, 73, 76–77, 131, 224n.2
Ross case (1900), 32, 33, 207n.50
Ross, Edward, 32
Rubin, Robert, 190
Ruml, Beardsley, 76
Russell, Richard, 115
Russell Sage Foundation, 101

S&Ls (savings and loans): "Diddymac" deregulating, 175; risky investment schemes/bailout of, 176–77
Salant, Walter, 76
Samuelson, Paul A., 73, 118, 224n.1, 258n.10
Saulnier, Raymond, 105, 107, 129
Schumpeter, Joseph, 123
scientific knowledge principles, 9

Seligman, Edwin, 20, 24, 33, 49
Servicemen's Readjustment Act (1944) [GI Bill], 92
Shaw, Arch, 63
Shaw, George Bernard, 7
Slichter, Sumner, 83
Smith, Adam, 192
Smith, J. Russell, 73, 89
Smoot-Hawley Act (1929), 1, 50, 60, 73, 195 nn. 2 and 3
Smoot, Reed, 1
social reform market practice, 178–80
social science research, 101–2. See also economic research
Social Science Research Council (SSRC), 43, 101, 109, 243 nn.31 and 32
sociology of science: contributions of historical scholarship to, 11–14; on internalist/externalist learning, 9–10; on scientific knowledge expertise, 9
Sorensen, Theodore, 138
Soviet Communism, 124
Soviet Union: cooperation between economists of west and, 185–88; devolution of, 188; economic five-year plans of, 124; superpower competition of U.S. and, 93, 102, 104, 111
Spengler, Joseph, 121
Sprague, O.M.W., 51
Sputnik (1957), 102, 244n.34
stabilization policy techniques (1960s), 118
stagflation, 158, 163
Stalin, A Critical Survey of Bolshevism, 87
Stalin's five-year plans, 124
Stanford's Food Research Institute, 60
State Capitalism and Marxism (Dunayevskaya), 106
Stevenson, Adlai, 115
Strong, Benjamin, 51, 189
"Study of Business Cycles" (Commerce Department), 56
supply-side economics: described, 147, 165; economic impact on, 167; Keynesianism condemned by, 282n.44; new classical, 161; Reagan administration use of, 163–64
Survey of Current Business (Commerce Department), 43, 55
Sweezy, Alan, 76
Sweezy, Paul, 80

Taft, Robert, 112, 113, 115, 142p
Tarbell, Ida, 50
tariffs: agricultural interests promoting, 59; McNary-Haugen bill, 59–60; Smoot-Hawley

Act (1929) on, 1, 50, 60, 73, 195 nn.2 and 3;
W.W. I depressed receipts from, 50
Taussig, Frank, 30, 36, 50, 55
tax cuts: CEA push for, 133–34, 135–36;
Reagan administration, 164–66, 169–70; unemployment and Kennedy 1964, 137–38,
139, 149
taxpayer's revolt movement (1978), 163
tax rates: CEA support of anti-inflation increase
of, 150; Laffer curve on, 165–66; New Frontier economists policies on, 133–34; supply-
side theory on, 164; transfer payment
through, 153; W.W. I impact on raised, 50,
51–52
Taylor, Alonzo, 59–60
Taylor, Horace, 30
telecommunications deregulation, 177–78,
286n.71
Thompson, Carl D., 30
Tobin, James, 131, 132, 134, 136, 138, 145p,
151, 171
"Training of Economists" (AEA), 85
"Troika" policy formulation, 137
Truman administration: Fair Deal of, 119; na-
tional security matters during, 111–14
Truman Doctrine, 112, 250n.51, 252n.60
Truman, Harry, 110, 112, 113, 115, 132
Tugwell, Rexford G., 113
Twentieth (Soviet) Communist Party Congress
(1956), 121
Tyson, Laura, 190

"uncertainty principle," 160
unemployment: CEA plan (1961) to lower,
133–34; changes in U.S. manufacturing, 157;
Hoover's investigation on, 55–56, 222n.60;
impact of tax cut (1964) on, 137–38; misery
index of, 158; Phillips curve on, 156, 157,
158; Phillips study of Great Britain, 155–56;
Reaganomics on, 164–65; reporting Great Depression, 61–62; as social problem, 278n.24;
supply-side economics solutions to, 147;
W.W. II impact on lowering, 74
UNESCO (United Nations Educational, Scientific, and Cultural Organization), 121
United States: cold war McCarthyism of, 105–
8, 120, 121, 127; cold war and national security of, 93–105; during Great Depression
years, 60–79; national debt of, 170–71; post–
W.W. II economic prosperity of, 91–92; post–
W.W. II living standards in the, 266n.48; response to Russian scientific development by,
102; superpower competition of Soviet and,
93, 102, 104, 111; during World War I, 34–

38, 39, 48–52; during World War II, 74–75,
79–87, 89–90. See also American economy;
American political culture; public policy
United States Civil Service Commission, 36
United States Department of Agriculture, 42
United States Department of Commerce: eco-
nomic research agenda of, 56–58, 60; Survey
of Current Business by, 43, 55; transformed
by Hoover, 54–57, 77; unemployment data
(1930) estimated by, 61–62
United States Department of Defense (DOD),
96, 97
United States Department of State, 35
United States Shipping Board, 44
United States War Production Board, 79
universalism principle of science, 9
universities. See American universities
UN Monetary and Financial Conference (1944),
92
URPE (Union for Radical Political Economics),
123
U.S. Department of Defense (DOA), 34
U.S. Department of Defense (DOD), 96, 97
U.S. Information Agency, 88

Veblen, Thorstein, 44, 45, 46, 68p, 123,
215n.17
Veterans Administration, 120
Vietnam, 111
Vietnam War: impact on American economy by,
149–54, 188; Pentagon Papers scandal dur-
ing, 241n.26; protests against, 123, 124
Viner, Jacob, 76
Voice of America, 88
Volcker, Paul, 189
von Neumann, John, 96, 97
"voodoo economics," 166, 281n.42

"Wage Disputes and Profiteering" (Bennett), 29
Walras, León, 192
Ward, Harry F., 61
War Labor Board, 84
War Manpower Commission, 80, 84
War on Poverty (1960s), 139, 148, 171
War Production Board, 80
"War and Reconstruction" (AEA meeting,
1918), 37
War Resources Board, 80
Watergate scandal (1972), 163
Wealth of Nations, The (Smith), 193
Weapons Systems Evaluation Group, 96
Wharton School (University of Pennsylvania),
56
Wilcox, Clair, 2

Williams, William Appleman, 173
Wilson, P. A., 10
Wilson, Woodrow, 36, 48, 49, 51, 131, 217n.27
Wohlstetter, Albert, 97
women: AEA on acceptance of, 26–27; CEA recruitment practices and, 271n.74; "feminist economics" and, 286n.74
Women's Educational and Industrial Union, 43
World Bank, 92
World War I: American economics shaped by, 34–38, 39, 48–52; depressed tariff receipts during, 50; impact on taxes by, 50, 51–52; inflation during, 50–51; lost prospects for economists of, 40
World War II: AEA initiatives facilitating reentry of civilians after, 120; AEA national needs discussion (1940) prior to, 82–83; AEA and reconstruction following, 87–88; American

economics shaped by, 88–90; contribution to ending Great Depression by, 74–75, 79; defense production conversion issues during, 80–82; economic expertise during, 84–86, 228n.16; German invasion starting, 83, 187; national debt following, 171, 252n.63
Wright, David, 106

Yale Review, 21
Yntema, Theodore O., 109
Young, Allyn: AEA membership promoted by, 17, 18, 20; on AEA public policy role, 33; Civil Service Commission work by, 36; intergenerational profession promoted by, 25–26; on lack of influence by economists, 38–39, 53; regarding DOA failures, 34–35; unemployment investigation role by, 56
Young, Owen, 57

About the Author

Michael A. Bernstein is Professor of History
and Associated Faculty Member in Economics
at the University of California, San Diego. A
former Fulbright Scholar at Christ's College,
Cambridge, and Mellon Fellow at the National
Humanities Center, he is the author of *The
Great Depression: Delayed Recovery and
Economic Change in America, 1929–1939*
(Cambridge, 1987) and co-editor of *Understanding American Economic Decline* (Cambridge, 1994).